SOCIAL WORK

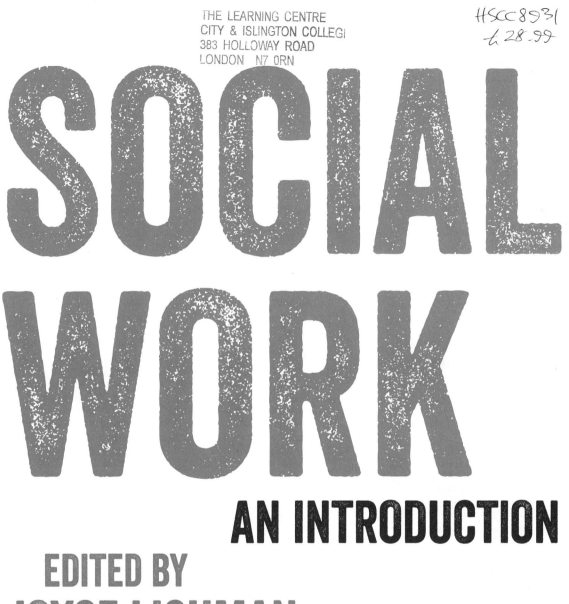

SOCIAL WORK

AN INTRODUCTION

EDITED BY
JOYCE LISHMAN
CHRIS YUILL
JILLIAN BRANNAN
ALASTAIR GIBSON

Los Angeles | London | New Delhi
Singapore | Washington DC

Los Angeles | London | New Delhi
Singapore | Washington DC

SAGE Publications Ltd
1 Oliver's Yard
55 City Road
London EC1Y 1SP

SAGE Publications Inc.
2455 Teller Road
Thousand Oaks, California 91320

SAGE Publications India Pvt Ltd
B 1/I 1 Mohan Cooperative Industrial Area
Mathura Road
New Delhi 110 044

SAGE Publications Asia-Pacific Pte Ltd
3 Church Street
#10-04 Samsung Hub
Singapore 049483

Editor: Kate Wharton
Editorial assistant: Laura Walmsley
Production editor: Katie Forsythe
Copyeditor: Elaine Leek
Proofreader: Christine Bitten
Indexer: Silvia Benvenuto
Marketing manager: Tamara Navaratnam
Cover design: Jennifer Crisp
Typeset by: C&M Digitals (P) Ltd, Chennai, India
Printed and bound in Great Britain by Ashford
Colour Press Ltd

Introduction and editorial arrangement © Joyce Lishman, Chris Yuill, Jillian Brannan and Alastair Gibson 2014

Chapter 1 © Julian Bell
Chapter 2 © Heather Munro
Chapters 3 and 28 © Mike Maas-Lowit
Chapter 4 © Megan Todd and Chris Yuill
Chapter 5 © Chris Yuill
Chapter 6 © Carmen-Maria Fyfe
Chapter 7 © Stewart Brodie and Clare Swan
Chapter 8 © Sheila Slesser and Jenny Blair
Chapter 9 © Iain Turnbull and Joyce Lishman
Chapter 10 © Angela Duvollet
Chapter 11 © Jillian Brannan
Chapter 12 © Janine Bolger and Patrick Walker
Chapter 13 © Kirstin Parkes and Mike Shepherd
Chapter 14 © Ruth Taylor and Jillian Brannan
Chapter 15 © Jillian Brannan, Denise Cromar, Simon Gardner, Margaret Junner, Steve Morrison and William Rae
Chapter 16 © Tuck-Chee Phung
Chapter 17 © Angela Duvollet
Chapter 18 © George Allan
Chapter 19 © Dave Humphrey
Chapter 20 © Jeremy Millar
Chapter 21 © Neil Gibson
Chapter 22 © Neil Gibson and Inga Heyman
Chapter 23 © Anne Shirran
Chapter 24 © Jim Dressel and Jillian Brannan
Chapter 25 © Fiona Feilberg
Chapter 26 © Sharon Munro and Patrick Walker
Chapter 27 © Claire Marsden
Chapter 29 © Isobel Townsend
Chapter 30 © Fiona Feilberg
Chapter 31 © Sheila Slesser
Chapter 32 © Iain Fisk
Chapter 33 © Joyce Lishman

First published 2014

Library of Congress Control Number: 2013948362

British Library Cataloguing in Publication data

A catalogue record for this book is available from the British Library

ISBN 978-1-4462-0888-5
ISBN 978-1-4462-0889-2 (pbk)

CONTENTS

LIST OF FIGURES

LIST OF TABLES

ABOUT THE EDITORS

Joyce Lishman was Head of the School of Applied Social Studies at the Robert Gordon University, Aberdeen, and is now Emeritus Professor. She has been heavily involved in the development of social work education in Scotland and has published on social work practice, practice learning, research, evidence-based practice and evaluation.

Chris Yuill is a sociologist at Robert Gordon University, Aberdeen, whose work focuses on the sociology of health and the sociology of urban experiences. In addition to a variety of journal publications and research reports he has written and co-edited a number of textbooks for Sage, one of his most recent being *Sociology for Social Work* co-edited with Alastair Gibson. Other texts include *The Sociology of Health: An Introduction* with Anne-Marie Barry, which is now in its third edition and has also been translated into Chinese. Chris has also served two terms on the executive of the British Sociological Association.

Jillian Brannan began her social work career in 1993 in Edinburgh, working in the field of community care. Areas of particular interest included social work with older people and people with mental health problems. After moving to Aberdeen in 2002 Jillian worked for Aberdeenshire Council in a variety of roles, including social worker in a community dementia team and team manager of a care management team for older people. In 2008 Jillian took up post as a social work lecturer at Robert Gordon University, where she worked for four years. Latterly Jillian has been working for Aberdeenshire Council firstly as a commissioning manager and then workforce development team manager.

Alastair Gibson worked in various social work settings before moving to Robert Gordon University. He was Senior Lecturer in Social Work until he retired in 2009. Alastair led the BA (Hons) in Social Work by Distance Learning and taught Human Growth and Behaviour and Interprofessional Practice. Since his retirement he has been working as an Independent Practice Teacher, External Examiner and day carer to his grandson.

ABOUT THE AUTHORS

George Allan qualified as a social worker at Aberdeen University in 1976. Although he has also worked in the single homeless and criminal justice fields, he has specialised latterly in working with people with substance problems. He retired in 2013 from a lecturer post at Robert Gordon University where he designed and taught substance problems modules to social work students. He has contributed chapters to various texts and has recently completed a book on working with people with drug and alcohol problems.

Until retirement from full-time employment, **Julian Bell** was a Senior Lecturer in the School of Applied Social Studies at RGU, teaching both sociology and applied ethics. In recent years, he has continued – as a part-time lecturer – to teach professional ethics to social work students. This continuing involvement in professional education reflects a long-standing interest in social service provision – an interest also evident in his previous involvement (as volunteer or management committee member) in voluntary sector organisations concerned with drug problems or providing services for children and families. Julian is currently a member of Grampian Regional Equality Council.

Jenny Blair is an eLearning Advisor within the School of Applied Social Studies at Robert Gordon University, where she has worked since 1999. Jenny has specific expertise in online communication. Jenny works primarily in advising academics on the best way to incorporate eLearning into teaching and social work/social science practice. She also carries out training in the use of virtual environments and various software packages. Jenny has previously worked on development of an online educational community, the Virtual Learning Space and as an eLearning Advisor on the Stòr Cùram Project providing support and training to academics from across Scotland in the use of eLearning within social work education.

After qualifying as a social worker **Janine Bolger** ran a weekend programme for young women in the Bronx, New York. On returning to the UK she spent time working in Child Protection in Moss Side, Manchester before spending nine years as Assistant Principal of a residential special school in the Highlands. Janine took up a lecturing post at Robert Gordon University in 2001. Her work was mainly focussed around planning, writing materials and teaching on the BA(Hons) Social Work (Residential Child Care) by distance learning, becoming Course Leader in 2010. In February 2013 Janine became Head of Social Work, Associate Head of the School of Applied Social Studies.

Stewart Brodie started in social work in 1976 and completed 16 years in different child and family care social work settings including residential care, local authority area teams and child and family psychiatry. He moved to Dundee University in 1992 and then to Robert Gordon University in 1995. Stewart has completed post qualifying training including an MPhil in Child Care and Protection and Advanced Family

Therapy training. His main interests lie in the area of Child Care and Protection and Human Development. He is a Form F Assessor and completes several Fostering and Permanence Assessments each year.

Denise Cromar was born with cerebral palsy and has been in a wheelchair all of her life. In 2005, she gained a BA in Applied Social Sciences from Robert Gordon University. Denise has been a service user of many care organisations and services and has been involved in various types of volunteering in the social care and social work field.

Jim Dressel has worked as a manager with three organisations supporting adults with learning difficulties in the community. Since 2006 he has been a Social Work Practice Teacher at Robert Gordon University. He has supported final placement students in residential and fieldwork placements within local authority and voluntary organisations. The agencies he has worked with have focussed on children and families including youth justice and children with disabilities. He has maintained his practice skills as a counsellor with Aberdeen Counselling and Information Service. He has a particular interest in Transactional Analysis as a theory of communication and personality development.

After qualifying as a social worker at Robert Gordon University **Angela Duvollet** worked as a Manager in the mental health field. During this time she was also a lecturer and SVQ Assessor at a local college. Since 2002 she has been employed at RGU initially as a Practice Teacher and placement co-ordinator and latterly as a full-time lecturer in social work for the distance learning team, undergraduate and postgraduate courses. Angela has undertaken post-qualification training and has achieved Post Graduate in Higher Education Learning and Teaching and a Post Graduate Certificate in Research Methods.

Fiona Feilberg is Head of Continuing Professional Development (CPD) and of Interprofessional Education (IPE) within the School of Applied Social Studies at Robert Gordon University. She has worked at Robert Gordon University since 1997 having had a varied professional history including working in a residential therapeutic community with young people, working with adults with addictions, managing a day centre for adults with a range of disabilities and undertaking a range of training and consultancy for teams, agencies and organisations. Fiona is joint-qualified in social work and in counselling and psychotherapy and draws on both in her teaching, consultancy and writing. Fiona has a particular interest in the psychodynamic approach to understanding individuals and to understanding and working within organisations.

Iain Fisk has been a lecturer in social work at Robert Gordon University since 2010. Previous to this he worked in local authority social work for 25 years at different levels and across several adult care user groups, including mental health, substance misuse and older people. He has a particular interest in issues around the use of compulsion for people lacking capacity or requiring treatment for mental disorder and is currently in the closing stages of a doctorate looking at the Scottish legal framework in this regard. Iain has also been a general member of the Mental Health Tribunal for Scotland since its inception in 2005.

Carmen-Maria Fyfe is a Social Psychology lecturer and part of the Social Science team at Robert Gordon University. She is actively involved in lecturing Social Sciences and Social Work students and postgraduates. Carmen's research interests range from the development of social and national identities in children to attitudes, implicit and explicit, their development and impact on group favouritism, stereotyping and prejudice. Recent research has looked at Cognitive Behavioural Therapy (CBT) as a therapy to change race and hate crime offenders' attitudes and actions towards others.

Simon Gardner has played a big part in the development of the inclusion movement and has been involved in a number of campaigns. Simon was a member of the Sutton Merton community health council and worked with the King's Fund evaluating services for people with learning disabilities in Hillingdon. Simon moved to Scotland in 2011 and is an active member of the service user panel at Robert Gordon University.

Neil Gibson studied on the PG Social Work course at Robert Gordon University in 2003. Upon qualifying, Neil went to work in the social work team based at Aberdeen Royal Infirmary. After 2 years he went to work for the Criminal Justice Addictions Team, then moved into a senior practitioner position within Aberdeenshire's Adult Protection Team, before taking up a senior position at Aberdeen City Council within their Adult Protection Unit. Neil joined the teaching team at RGU in 2011.

Inga Heyman is a lecturer in Mental Health Nursing at Robert Gordon University, Aberdeen. Inga trained as an adult and mental health nurse practising in Australia for 18 years, specialising in problematic substance use in pregnancy and parenting. On return to the UK Inga continued to work within problematic substance use services with a focus on cocaine and alcohol use in the energy sector before joining Police Scotland in Grampian as Adult Protection Co-ordinator. Inga is a member of the Aberdeen Centre for Trauma Research with interests in police and health service interactions in relation to those attempting suicide.

Dave Humphrey is a lecturer at the Robert Gordon University where he works with the Centre for Excellence for Looked After Children in Scotland (CELCIS). Prior to joining RGU in 2009, Dave worked for several years as a children and families social worker, a specialist child protection social worker and as a multi-agency training officer for an area child protection committee. His current teaching interests are primarily in the field of child care and protection.

Margaret Junner had worked as a project leader in Records Management before becoming a full time carer. Margaret believes ardently in the importance of professionals working alongside carers, although her experience has been that professionals take this on board to different degrees! During her time as a carer, Margaret has undertaken courses in counselling, including a COSCA course. She has found these courses valuable and this has helped Margaret to re-evaluate her role within her family. Margaret is a keen plant and vegetable gardener, finding this a useful pursuit for de-stressing.

Michael Maas-Lowit started his career in social work in the early 1970s, doing voluntary work and work in residential child care. He qualified with a postgraduate certificate in social work from Aberdeen University and worked in psychiatric hospitals in England and Scotland, moving into social work education in the early 1990s. He has had a long-term interest in developing specialist education for mental health social workers and has advised the Scottish Government on implementation of aspects of mental health law. He has co-written and edited several books. Currently, he is course leader for a busy social work course at RGU.

Claire Marsden qualified as a social worker in 2005, after which she worked with individuals with drug and alcohol problems, those affected by someone else's substance problem, and children affected by parental substance misuse in community and residential settings. She has undertaken therapeutic and harm reduction work with women in the sex industry, and research for the Scottish Government into service access barriers for individuals from ethnic minority communities with substance problems. Claire joined Robert Gordon University in 2010 as a lecturer in Social Work and is currently undertaking a PhD investigating effective interventions for children affected by parental substance misuse in Scotland.

Jeremy Millar is a white middle class man whose experience of the punk era and fighting the destructive policies of the Thatcher years informed his practice across a range of residential care settings up until 2002 when he moved into teaching. The importance of being in relationship, empowering the voice of the 'other' and using the 'love' word are some of the key ingredients for positive group care. He has an Open University degree, a Diploma in Social Work and a MSc in Advanced Residential Child Care. Social work is a political activity!

Steve Morrison was born in Aberdeen. He studied English and Philosophy at the University of Strathclyde in Glasgow. After spending many years as a drone in the Civil Service Steve decided to change sides and become a Welfare Rights Officer for Aberdeen City Council. He has been a patients' Advocacy Worker at Royal Cornhill Hospital for Advocacy Service Aberdeen since 2008. Steve works mostly with people detained under the Mental Health (Care and Treatment) (Scotland) Act 2003. Outside of work, Steve enjoys music, reading and running.

Heather Munro graduated from Glasgow University in 2006 with an LLB (Hons) in Law with German Language. She was awarded the Diploma in Legal Practice in 2007 and obtained an LLM from the University of Auckland in 2008. She completed her legal traineeship with a commercial firm in Edinburgh, and after qualifying she spent two years as a solicitor practising in public law before joining Robert Gordon University as a Lecturer in Law in 2013.

Sharon Munro qualified as a social worker in 1982 and joined the CELCIS team in Robert Gordon University in 2009. She has worked in both the statutory and voluntary sectors in a variety of roles spanning from basic grade practitioner to senior manager. The emphasis of her work has been either residential child care or working in services that support those who are at risk of or have a history of being accommodated and carry the ensuing vulnerabilities.

Kirstin Parkes qualified as a social worker in Scotland in 2000. Subsequent to qualification she worked in Criminal Justice Social Work fieldwork and management, and as a Multi-Agency Public Protection (MAPPA) Co-ordinator, as well as completing her social work practice-teaching qualification. Following this she held an Adult Protection Co-ordinator post. In 2010, Kirstin became a lecturer at Robert Gordon University, teaching a range of subjects including Criminal Justice Social Work and Social Policy.

Kirstin's research interests relate to risk, professional judgement and uncertainty, in particular exploring social work practitioner's constructions of risk and risk assessment in work with sex offenders.

Tuck-Chee Phung was born in Malaysia and has lived in Scotland for 35 years. He studied Fine Arts and History of Art in Malaysia, Scotland and the USA. Since qualifying as a social worker in 1989, Tuck-Chee has worked in the field of disability and been involved in training and staff development for the Grampian Social Work Department. Currently he tutors and lectures on the BA (Hons) Social Work course at Robert Gordon University. His areas of interest include cross-cultural social work, therapeutic practice and counselling. He returned recently to art after 27 years, using painting as a medium to explore personal narratives and cultural identities.

William Rae was born in Aberdeen in 1987. In his early years he lived with his mother, but as a result of family breakdown he was moved into care. William was a looked after child until the age of 16. As an adult William has lived in a variety of supported accommodation settings. At times William has experienced mental health problems and spent a period of time in psychiatric hospital. William is an active member of his community and has helped young people complete their Duke of Edinburgh award. At present he is vice-chair of a local Community Council.

Mike Shepherd is lecturer in Social Work at Robert Gordon University. Previous to joining RGU in 2007, Mike held various positions within the North East of Scotland Voluntary Sector before working in Criminal Justice Social Work at Aberdeen City Council. His main subject areas of interest include social work methods; social work in society; criminal justice social work; crime, criminology and the justice system; and law and policy.

Anne Shirran was formerly a lecturer in Social Work at Robert Gordon University until taking up her current post as a Practice Teacher in Children's Services with Aberdeen City Council. Since qualifying as a social worker, Anne has worked in criminal justice, both as a field officer and as a prison-based social worker, and latterly as team manager at HMP Peterhead. Anne was seconded as a Practice Learning Facilitator within Children's Services in Aberdeenshire between 2003 and 2005 as part of the Learning for Ethical and Effective Practice project commissioned by the Scottish Social Services Council.

Sheila Slesser qualified as a social worker in 1986 and began her career working within a social work court team. In 1987 Sheila moved to join a voluntary organisation in Aberdeen working with Deaf and Hearing Impaired People and remained there for over 16 years as a basic grade Social Worker, then as Senior Social Worker working within both a statutory and non-statutory framework. Sheila joined RGU in March 2004 and divides her role between course leading the Practice Learning Qualification (PLQ), lecturing and tutoring on the undergraduate BA (Hons) Social Work course.

Clare Swan qualified as a social worker in 1994 and subsequently worked in a variety of social work settings within Aberdeen City. Her practice background included social work training, duty and work in the mental health field, where she also undertook statutory duties as a mental health officer. Clare joined the staff team at Robert

Gordon University in 2004 and is currently senior lecturer and course leader for the MSc Social Work programme, as well as having overall responsibility for Practice Learning.

Ruth Taylor is a Professor in Nursing and the Deputy Dean in the Faculty of Health, Social Care and Education at Anglia Ruskin University. As a clinician Ruth worked as an oncology nurse and as a practice nurse – roles in which she worked closely and collaboratively with a range of professions. As a nurse educator she has expertise in clinical leadership, research, professional practice and interprofessional working. She played a key role in the development and implementation of interprofessional education in a previous organisation, and is passionate about the way in which students are educated for interprofessional practice.

Megan Todd is a lecturer in social science at the University of Central Lancashire. Prior to this she lectured in sociology at Robert Gordon University, having completed an ESRC-funded PhD on community responses to lesbian domestic violence at Newcastle University. Research projects she has worked on include a British Academy project investigating educational capital and same-sex parenting and an ESRC-funded project researching into LGBT equality initiatives in local government. Research areas include sexuality, gender and violence. Megan has recently had chapters on intimacies and sexuality and health published in edited collections and has a textbook on sexualities forthcoming with Sage.

Initially working in residential care with young people and as a community worker in the North East of England, **Isobel Townsend** qualified in 1991. She worked as a probation officer for Teesside Probation Service in a variety of settings – community supervision, through-care, group work, prison-based probation and courts for nine years. Promoted to Senior Probation Officer, Isobel managed a busy Community Reintegration Team and subsequently jointly managed the Police and Probation Public Protection Team. From September 2006, Isobel worked as the Service Manager for Angus Council Criminal Justice Social Work Service. Isobel joined Robert Gordon University in 2009 as a lecturer in Social Work.

Iain Turnbull is lecturer in Social Work at the Robert Gordon University. He has worked in both statutory and voluntary sectors in a range of operational and strategic roles. These include lead officer for a drug and alcohol partnership, managing court services in criminal justice social work, working with people with acquired brain injury and supporting carers. His interests include social policy and interdisciplinary practice.

Patrick Walker is a senior lecturer and course leader at the School of Applied Social Studies and the Centre for Excellence for Looked After Children in Scotland (CELCIS), Robert Gordon University, Aberdeen. Before joining Robert Gordon University Patrick gained extensive main grade and managerial practice experience working both in children and families field work and also in young people's residential and secure services. Patrick's current teaching specialises in Child Care/Child Protection along with Social Policy. His research interests centre on interdisciplinary practice and education and he is a member of the Interprofessional Research Team at RGU and Aberdeen University.

PREFACE

Social work is an interesting and varied profession with a rich and diverse history. The delivery of social work services in local, national and international contexts is dependent on a range of interconnecting factors that shape and define how social work activity takes place. At times social work focuses on supporting individuals and families; at other times it focuses on developing communities. Very often the focus is on the interaction between individuals and families and the communities they are part of. Social work is always about relationships but it is almost always about politics as well. Recognising that we are all affected by forces within and outside our immediate control is central to understanding what social work aims to do and what it is able to achieve.

To work effectively in the complex arena of social work activity, practitioners require significant skill, knowledge and expertise. Gaining, developing and honing relevant skills and understanding represents the core building blocks upon which social work education is founded. The overarching aim of this text, therefore, is to contribute to the process of assisting social work practitioners to develop.

Our objectives in writing this book were fourfold:

To build knowledge – Social work is underpinned by a broad knowledge base drawing on learning from a range of disciplines. In order to strengthen their effectiveness practitioners need to acquire a deeper understanding of service users' underlying issues and the context within which people live.

To develop skills – Many (arguably all) students embarking on social work education and training will identify a range of personal attributes that are beneficial when working with users of social work services. We are thinking here of attributes such as being a good listener, treating others with respect, patience and self-awareness. Where such attributes are recognisable then this is a strength; however, having certain attributes is not the same as developing skills to use those attributes successfully. Being a social worker is a skilled undertaking and understanding how to use and refine skills to their best effect is essential.

To support the acquisition of tools for practice – It would be erroneous to see social work activity as mechanistic or formulaic. Whilst in some disciplines it may be possible to apply a logic consisting of 'if X happens, do Y and you will get Z outcome' – such a logic does not particularly apply in social work. That is not to say social work is not evidence-based or that social work is not founded upon tried and tested approaches that offer ways of engaging with service users – it very clearly is!

Developing a range of tools to support ways of engaging and intervening with individuals, families and communities is important and, crucially, being able to use those tools flexibly is a necessary part of developing as a social work practitioner. Every developing (and indeed experienced) practitioner requires a 'tool kit' to draw upon providing options to consider when engaging in processes of 'helping'.

To facilitate critical thinking around applying learning to practice – Finally we wanted to provide some demonstration within the text of how knowledge, skills and approaches are applied in social work practice. Understanding the key issues in work with different groups of service users and how work might be approached should act as a critical sounding board for addressing practice issues. We do not seek to be prescriptive here but to be illustrative, with the purpose of encouraging critical engagement.

Joyce Lishman, Chris Yuill, Jillian Brannan and Alastair Gibson

ACKNOWLEDGEMENTS

Joyce – My continuing gratitude for the support of Roly, Tamsin and Ben.

Chris – I would like to thank Ruth, Sophie and Jo for their invaluable support and letting me type away at night! Special thanks must also go to Emma Milman at Sage, who has been invaluable in completing a number of projects upon which I have worked.

Jillian – I would like to thank: the many service users, carers, colleagues, students, practitioners and academics who have contributed to my understanding of social work over the past 20 years – the learning never stops; Steve Smith at Robert Gordon University for his helpful review of the solution-focused approach (Chapter 24); my co-editors for their advice, support and periodic re-energising of this project; Emma Milman and Kate Wharton at Sage for all their support and assistance; my family and in particular Michael, for too many things to mention.

Alastair – Thanks to everyone who has helped me and especially to all the current and former students who have been an inspiration to me.

GUIDED TOUR OF THE BOOK

Social Work: An Introduction is structured over four parts – Part One: Knowledge Base; Part Two: Assessment; Part Three: Models of Intervention and Part Four: Interventions in Practice. Across the entire book each chapter contains similar learning features to enable you to navigate the text, critically engage with the material presented and reflect on what you have learned. Within each chapter you will find:

Key themes: A summary of the main issues and content discussed in the chapter.

Introduction: To set the scene and place the chapter in context.

Case studies: Cases and practice vignettes to help illustrate particular key points and issues, as well as demonstrate how theory translates to practice.

Exercises: Activities and exercises to help you test your understanding.

Critical thinking boxes: To enable you to pause for thought and consider the implications of particular points.

Conclusion: To summarise the key points made in the chapter.

Reflective questions: To encourage you to review what you have learned and engage with the core content of the chapter.

Recommended reading: Suggested further reading to help you develop your understanding.

Companion website icon: To direct you to further useful information and content.

At the end of the book you will also find a **Glossary** to help you get to grips with those terms that may not be so familiar. Words emboldened in the text can be found in the glossary.

COMPANION WEBSITE

As a purchaser of *Social Work: An Introduction* you can access a Companion Website featuring additional chapter-by-chapter resources. The Companion Website is designed to enhance the learning and understanding students will gain through reading and engaging with this book. The website features include: journal articles, podcasts, links to online resources, annotated case studies, activities and exercises.

 Prompts for you to refer to these extra resources are indicated in the text by the website icon. When you see this icon, visit www.sagepub.co.uk/SocialWork to view the relevant material.

INTRODUCTION

Social work and social work education are continually evolving. Research findings enhance knowledge and understanding, in turn influencing and shaping practice; new societal challenges demand new service solutions; law and policy changes create shifting contexts within which practice takes place, and practitioners continuously seek innovative ways of supporting service users, carers and communities to enhance quality of life and achieve outcomes. Social work is not static and quite rightly so – the profession needs to be responsive, dynamic and forward thinking; it needs to be clear about what it is, what it does and what difference it can make. To achieve these goals social work requires well-informed, competent and confident practitioners who have a strong ethical and value base and a range of appropriate skills. *Social Work: An Introduction* aims to contribute towards supporting the development of such practitioners.

This is a broad-based text designed around the links between knowledge, theories of assessment, approaches to intervention and practice. It is a text that aims to equip students of social work with the necessary foundations for understanding different concepts and themes and being able to use their learning flexibly. The text is a comprehensive overview of social work theory and practice, which will act as a springboard for further learning. It is not a manual for social work – we do not believe that such a text could exist – but should be seen as a guidebook offering information and insights that will support learning around different subjects studied over the course of a social work programme.

Part One focuses on the Knowledge Base, setting out the core underpinning knowledge required for social work practice. Chapter 1 introduces discussion of values and ethics, exploring different philosophical stances, different types of values and the ethical dilemmas encountered in social work practice. Chapter 2 provides a discussion of the law that represents much of the framework within which social work practice takes place. The societal influence of the law is pervasive and thus it follows that social workers need an in-depth understanding of legal issues. Chapter 3 addresses politics and social policy, arguing that these underpin everything we do and thus impact significantly on social work practice. Chapters 4 and 5 are closely related, addressing core concepts in sociology and social inequality. It is argued that understanding societal structures and the lived experiences of service users, especially those experiencing poverty, is fundamental to developing as a well-informed social work practitioner. Chapter 6 focuses on the learning social workers can gain from an understanding of psychology and the five psychological approaches. Chapter 7 builds on the insights offered by the preceding chapters to address core areas of human growth and development. The chapter explores the importance of early childhood experiences, interactions in families and coping with loss and change. Chapter 8 addresses the importance of communication skills and the role of information and communication technology. The chapter explores in detail the complexity of communication in its many forms. Chapter 9 introduces the subject of research, highlighting different forms of research and the importance of the research and evidence base to social work practice. Finally in Part One, Chapter 10 addresses reflective practice, noting the role of structured models of reflection and the learning that can be gained from any situation, both positive and negative.

Part Two focuses on assessment and seeks to explore in detail the range of factors that influence and impact upon this core area of social work activity. Chapter 11 considers the complexity of social work assessment exploring the role of power in the social work exchange. The chapter proceeds to consider skills and knowledge necessary for effective assessment and the ability of social work practitioners to manage situations of uncertainty. Chapter 12 addresses the principles underpinning good assessment practice and outlines different models of assessment. The chapter emphasises the importance of assessment as a process and not a one-off task. Chapter 13 hones in on risk assessment and the management of risk in social work. Risk is such a central concept to much social work practice that this chapter has particular significance, not least because of the assertion that risk can be both positive and negative and both these aspects need to be embraced in the process of assessment. Chapter 14 addresses interprofessional practice and the role of social work alongside a range of other professions. The chapter outlines why interprofessional working is seen as the way forward and the challenges that might present, before considering what is distinctive about the social work profession. Chapter 15 is a particularly important inclusion in this book. We felt very strongly that a social work text would not be complete without the perspective of social work service users. To this end you will find in Chapter 15 the narratives of three service users and one carer. We would urge all readers of this book to pay particular attention to what these authors have to say – this book is enhanced by these contributions and we are very grateful to Denise, Simon, Margaret and William for sharing their perspectives.

Part Three contains 10 chapters that deal with different approaches to social work intervention. When working with individuals, families or communities the choice of approach is dependent on a variety of factors; however, the assessment of the situation should be a central determinant of the approach used. Only by developing an extensive repertoire of skills and knowledge regarding the use of different approaches can social work practitioners develop confidence that the way in which they are supporting and assisting users of services is appropriate and effective. A social worker needs a comprehensive tool kit to practise and to be able to respond flexibly, creatively and appropriately. The purpose of this part of the book is to provide a broad understanding of the development of an approach, its central tenets, tools and structures which underpin its use and research evidence which supports its effectiveness. We have included chapters on relationship-based work (Chapter 16); crisis intervention (Chapter 17); cognitive behavioural work (Chapter 18); task-centred work (Chapter 19); working in the life space (Chapter 20); person-centred practice (Chapter 21); narrative therapy (Chapter 22); motivational interviewing (Chapter 23); solution-focused approach (Chapter 24) and counselling (Chapter 25).

Part Four turns to focus more specifically on social work practice and key issues in working with different service user groups. We have included work with children and families (Chapter 26); individuals with substance problems (Chapter 27); people with mental health problems (Chapter 28); learning disabilities (Chapter 30) and disability and sensory impairment (Chapter 31); and older people (Chapter 32). The aim here is to give a broad indication of key concepts and to introduce possible ways of working with service users. There are some important caveats to Part Four which are necessary to highlight. Firstly, these chapters provide a flavour of some of the issues to be aware of when working with different groups; the chapters do not provide a comprehensive overview of practice in a particular field. The chapters need to be seen in an introductory context, as anything more than this has not been possible within the scope of this book. Secondly, when methods of intervention are applied to work with specific groups this should not be interpreted as all service users in this group can be supported by using this method of intervention. Our purpose in these chapters is to flesh out the approaches discussed in Part Three but we cannot overemphasise that this should not be seen as prescriptive or formulaic. Lastly, we have included a chapter on criminal justice social work (Chapter 29) which has a clearly Scottish context. Criminal justice social work in Scotland is distinctive from the social work practice undertaken with offenders elsewhere in the UK. We felt that this inclusion of this group was important, despite the more parochial nature of the chapter, and hope that it can offer insights for students in other parts of the United Kingdom.

Finally in Part Four we address the subject of evaluation, focusing on what evaluation means, how it can be undertaken and the importance of evaluation to practice, service delivery and policy development.

Our hope is that this book will develop interest in and spark debate about social work. As noted earlier it is a broad volume and one that we hope can contribute to the development of knowledgeable and skilled practitioners who demonstrate a real commitment to enhancing the lives and achieving the preferred outcomes of service users and carers.

Joyce Lishman
Chris Yuill
Jillian Brannan
Alastair Gibson

PART ONE

KNOWLEDGE BASE

1 VALUES AND ETHICS

Julian Bell

Key Themes

- Values permeate our lives and often underpin ethical principles, rules and virtues.
- Knowledge of ethical theory contributes to an understanding of social work values.
- There are two main strands of social work values: 'traditional' and 'emancipatory'.
- Ethical codes are an important component of professional accountability.
- 'Social justice' and 'valuing diversity' are core social work objectives, and ethical dilemmas present a particular challenge.

INTRODUCTION

Social workers are involved in many aspects of people's lives – including problematic family relationships, financial difficulties, homelessness, ill-health, drug-dependence and crime. Given this wide-ranging and sometimes intense involvement, social workers can do much good, but there is also the risk of causing harm. So, social workers must always be sensitive to the **ethical** dimension of their practice.

This chapter focuses on this ethical dimension. First, there is an analysis of key ethical concepts. Then, two ethical theories are outlined and their relevance to social work is considered. Next, different strands of social work values are examined and ideas concerning social justice and valuing human diversity are explored. Attention then turns to accountability, ethical codes and the difficulties posed by ethical dilemmas.

VALUES AND RELATED ETHICAL CONCEPTS

What makes your life worthwhile? Friends? Music and art? Creating a fairer society? If so, these may be *particular* values of yours: friendship, beauty and social justice. Explaining the *general* nature of 'values' is more challenging (Clark, 2000); but, basically, 'values' are those elements of life that one believes should be cherished, preserved, promoted or respected. So, if you value friendship, you cherish your friendships because of the joy they bring.

Values, then, are not mere personal 'likes': we believe that others consider, or *should* consider, them important too. This indicates that values typically derive from social group membership. Indeed, culturally embedded values – ethical, political, legal, spiritual and aesthetic – pervade our lives and yet may be taken for granted. Consequently, we do not always appreciate how deeply values permeate our actions, thoughts and feelings. Language, for instance, embodies values – derogatory terms, such as 'scroungers', being clearly value-laden.

Our main concern in this chapter relates specifically to *ethical* values, which determine what we ought to do. How do ethical values relate to other concepts? First, a distinction may be drawn between 'values' and 'principles'. We value 'human dignity', *and* the principle relating to this value is 'don't behave in a way that undermines human dignity'. So, an ethical principle usually determines moral behaviour, and there may be a corresponding moral right, for example entitlement to privacy, of which we are aware.

However, the general nature of values, principles and rights leaves them open to differing interpretation, and, therefore, more specific rules of conduct may be needed to provide detailed guidance. A rule such as 'don't open someone else's correspondence without permission' may help ensure protection of the more general right to privacy.

Morality is not, though, just about behaviour, it is also concerned with 'character', the sort of person one should be. Individuals may possess 'virtues' (desirable traits) and/or 'vices' (undesirable traits). Any such virtues can be linked to values, for example if we value 'truth' we will regard 'honesty' as a virtue.

Table 1.1 Examples of values, virtues, principles and rules

Values	**Virtues**
(Things we cherish)	*(Valued character traits)*
Truth	Honesty
Liberty	Autonomy/Independence
Ethical principles	**Ethical rules**
(fundamental moral requirements)	*(more specific moral requirements)*
• Don't deceive other people	• Don't falsify qualifications in job applications
• Restrict people's liberty only if necessary to prevent harm	• Ensure care home residents can move freely, unimpeded by unwarranted obstructions

ETHICAL THEORY

At this point, let us think about two types of theory.

(a) Consequentialist Theories

Consequentialist theories claim that promotion of some general value, for example human well-being, is the basis of morality. The morally right action is the one that produces the best overall outcome, with equal weight being assigned to the interests of everyone affected. Hence, 'classical utilitarianism', 'regards an action as right if it produces more happiness for all affected by it than any alternative action ...' (Singer, 2011: 3). Here, happiness is seen as pleasure and the absence or minimisation of pain. So, 'more happiness' really means 'more net happiness', i.e., the greatest amount of happiness remaining once any pain caused has been subtracted.

However, an action might produce the best overall outcome with regard to human welfare and yet seem clearly *immoral*.

Case Study

You are working with a family with three preschool children. They are in extreme financial difficulty, maintaining a basic diet is difficult, clothing the family is a problem and the whole situation is detrimental to both adults and children. You find out that father is earning money, but not declaring it, and receiving benefits. The earned money is helping maintain a precarious balance. Do you report this illegal action or do you take the view that it is helping promote some degree of well-being?

Is morality solely about producing good *consequences*? Aren't certain kinds of action, for example being loyal to friends, simply right in themselves? This brings us to deontology.

(b) Deontological Theories

Deontological theories typically claim that some *intrinsic* feature of an action makes it morally right or wrong. So, certain types of action may be morally required regardless of their consequences. How, though, do we know what is intrinsically right, what ethical principles to adopt?

'Divine-command theory' maintains that God has specified these principles, for example the Ten Commandments. 'Intuitionism' claims it is self-evident that we have 'prima facie duties', such as keeping promises and not harming others (Ross, 1930).

Another view, though, is that reason reveals our duties. According to Kant, there is 'a categorical imperative': one acts morally only if one can rationally will that the principle one is adopting be acted upon by everyone in a similar situation (Kant, [1785]1997). Kant believes that by applying this universalisability requirement, it can be shown that we have certain absolute moral duties. For example, he asserts that it is never morally permissible to intentionally deceive, that even lying from benevolent motives – to prevent harm – is unacceptable. There is disagreement, however, about which duties *can* be derived from the 'categorical imperative', but to Kant, telling the truth is a moral absolute.

Many consider this absolutist position untenable. They also question whether Kant provides a plausible account of how conflicts between moral duties should be resolved. (Should telling the truth *always* take priority over prevention of harm?) Nevertheless, Kant's principle of 'respect for persons' is very important: persons must be treated as 'ends-in-themselves'; one must never treat another person 'solely as a means' to attaining one's own goals (Kant, [1785] 1997: 38). So, 'respect for persons' would appear to be an absolute moral obligation.

(c) Other Theoretical Perspectives

Adherence to principles is regarded by many as crucial to moral conduct. Some, though, question this. 'Virtue theorists' believe that living a good life requires certain moral traits, acquisition of life experience and mature judgement. Moreover, many feminists claim that theories focusing exclusively on principles and rights constitute a male-centred 'ethics of justice'. In contrast, they advocate an 'ethic of care' which highlights: compassionate caring; maintaining intimate relationships; attention to particular circumstances (rather than application of general principles); plus compromise (rather than appeal to rights) as a means of resolving conflicts. So we will return to some of these issues in considering social work values.

SOCIAL WORK VALUES: 'TRADITIONAL' AND 'MODERN'

Discussions of social work values have become increasingly complex (Gray and Webb, 2010), but we will focus here on the key distinction between 'traditional' and 'modern' values – the latter also being described as 'radical', 'anti-discriminatory', 'anti-oppressive' and 'emancipatory'.

(a) Traditional Social Work Values

The 'traditional values' were formulated as social work developed (Barnard, 2008; Payne, 2005b). They reflect Western, liberal values; being 'an ethic of personal service rooted in recognition of the value, uniqueness and intrinsic worth of every individual who must be respected' (Whittington and Whittington, 2007: 89). Hence, our analysis will begin with the principle of respect for persons. Also, particular reference will be made to Biestek's influential account of these traditional values.

Despite its fundamental status, interpretation of respect for persons is controversial. First, should *all* human beings be regarded as persons? On one view, 'persons' are beings possessing a capacity for practical rationality and self-determination. Hence, those lacking these characteristics may not qualify as persons: infants being classified as 'potential persons' and individuals with dementia as 'lapsed persons' (Downie and Telfer, 1980). Many, though, favour a more inclusive definition of 'personhood' which embraces a wider range of characteristics, including abilities to communicate, experience emotions and express affection. Moreover, possessing just *some* of these *typical* features may be considered sufficient to be counted as a person.

Let us assume, therefore, that *all* humans are persons. What, then, constitutes 'respect'? Sometimes, 'respect' means 'admire' or 'hold in high esteem': an individual *merits* this kind of 'respect' because she possesses a valued characteristic, such as honesty, to a high degree. But respect for persons is rather different, as this form of 'respect' must be shown to *all* persons, no matter their individual characteristics. It is a universal form of respect that applies to both the caring, responsible citizen *and* the sadistic, violent offender. Generally 'respect for persons' requires one to see the world from the other person's point of view; take account of her beliefs; consider her needs; and assist her, where appropriate, to achieve her aims. It means not exploiting the individual, not using her solely for one's own purposes.

Next, individualisation requires the individual be treated 'not just as a human being but as this human being' (Biestek, 1961: 25). The person's unique qualities must be recognised. Moreover, in order to provide an 'individualised' service, the social worker must be considerate, listen to the individual's own story, enter into her feelings and move at her pace. This links to two other principles: allowing 'purposeful expression of feelings' means the service user may share experiences freely; while the social worker's 'controlled emotional involvement' requires sensitivity to the person's feelings and an appropriate response to them.

In addition, acceptance means the individual being valued as a person and dealt with as he is, with both strengths and weaknesses. The social worker 'while seeing the client's negatives realistically, maintains an equally real respect for him' (Biestek, 1957: 70–1). Closely linked, the non-judgemental attitude suggests that 'assigning guilt or innocence, or degree of client responsibility for causation of the problems …' should be excluded from social work (Biestek, 1961: 90). Assessment should focus on need, not 'deservingness'. Aid, not punishment, should be the objective of social work. So, social workers should realise that judgements of the person, for example 'she is a life-long spendthrift', are irrelevant, merciless and hazardous. Even so, moral judgments of the service user's attitudes and actions *are* permissible.

Next, the principle of self-determination supports the right of service users 'to freedom in making their own choices and decisions' (Biestek, 1957: 103). This requires activating potential for self-direction and providing guidance about resources. Nevertheless, self-determination must sometimes be curtailed to protect vulnerable others, for example where children are at serious risk, parents' rights may be removed. Secondly, limits may be placed on self-determination because of deficiencies in the individual's own 'capacity for positive and constructive decision-making' (Biestek, 1961: 103). Some may lack the ability to assess risks, so the social worker may need to be directive and act paternalistically to prevent the service user making choices that would harm him. For Biestek, then, self-determination is the capacity to make rational, informed and morally grounded decisions.

The principle of confidentiality requires responsible care of information relating to service users (Prince, 2000). However, a number of people within the social work agency –or who form part of a multiprofessional, integrated service – may require access, on a 'need-to-know' basis, to this information. Thus there is 'a circle of confidentiality' encompassing those with whom the service user's personal information may be shared without there being any breach of confidentiality (Brown et al., 1992). The service user should, though, know who is included in this circle. Also, grounds for *exceptional disclosure* – revealing confidential information to a third party *without* the service user's permission – require explanation. Confidentiality, then, relates specifically to information, but should be recognised as part of a wider right to privacy that has both physical/spatial and informational aspects.

These, then, are some traditional social work values. In emphasising rights of the individual, they mirror values widely held in British society. So, why have they been criticised and are these criticisms warranted?

One example of traditional values is that they are said to be so 'generalised' that they fail to provide adequate practical guidance (Hugman and Smith, 1995: 10). However, values and principles are inevitably broad and open to interpretation. They may not often indicate precisely what is to be done in particular circumstances, but they identify crucial ethical considerations and can be supplemented by specific rules. Secondly, it is said that these principles often conflict with one another, for example respecting service user self-determination *and* guaranteeing other people's safety may clash. However, advocates of traditional values *do* recognise these conflicts between principles and the resulting need to weigh up competing ethical considerations; for example, Biestek stresses that the social worker's duty to respect the service user's rights is 'accompanied by the duty to respect the rights of others' (1961: 109–10).

It is more difficult, though, to counter a third criticism, i.e., that traditional values focus almost exclusively on the relationship between the social worker and service user. Furthermore, advocates of traditional values often assume social workers should simply help service users to adjust to the *existing* social environment and they fail to analyse fully the social injustices affecting people's lives. In short, this criticism – that insufficient consideration is given to ethical issues concerning social inequality and injustice – seems more telling. Indeed, the two sets of values seem to differ most sharply in their views of society and individual identity.

(b) Modern, Emancipatory Social Work Values

The development of 'modern social work values' can be traced to the 1970s and reflects ongoing changes in Western societies. Beliefs advanced by various social movements – feminism, anti-racism, 'gay liberation', the disability rights movement, etc. – have had a notable influence. Service users' problems are seen as originating from social inequalities and disadvantages, rather than arising primarily from purely 'individual' characteristics. Social factors – **gender**, age, **ethnicity**, social **class**, etc. – are regarded as central to individual identity and life chances.

Exercise

You should think about how social workers work with people who have committed violent or sexual offences; for example, some of those people you will have read about or seen on television news programmes. To what extent can they apply traditional values to their work and how might emancipatory values be applied?

In particular, discrimination is highlighted as a factor contributing significantly to people's problems, 'discrimination' being unfair and 'unequal treatment of an individual or group of persons on the basis of features such as race, age, sexual orientation, gender, religion or disability' (Gaine, 2010: 123). However, such discrimination forms part of a broader experience of systematic oppression, i.e., 'Inhuman or degrading treatment of individuals or groups; hardship or injustice brought about by the dominance of one group over another; the negative and demeaning use of power' (Thompson and Thompson, 2008: 198).

On this view, certain groups dominate, often disregard the rights of other groups and deny members of these groups full citizenship. These other groups, such as women and people with disabilities, are relatively powerless. Their members are subordinated, often denied a voice and consequently may have lower self-esteem. Service users' problems are, in part, the consequence of oppressive forces, and social work interventions need to tackle this oppression through anti-discriminatory *and* anti-oppressive practice and an understanding and application of relevant legislation.

These modern values are 'emancipatory' in that their objective is to free people from oppression, and a key objective is empowerment.

Obviously, an individual might be empowered *within* a group: for example a teenager's views being accorded more respect within a family or an individual gaining increased choice with regard to services offered. These are examples of 'self-empowerment', but arguably full 'empowerment' requires action at the group and community level, not just in relation to particular individuals. Certainly a radical approach involves 'mainstreaming the concerns of marginalised or dispossessed groups' (Dominelli, 2002: 117). It requires 'collective empowerment', support for groups to realise their own power and take action for themselves. This might, for instance, mean enabling groups of people with learning disabilities to speak out about abuse; influence social policies affecting their lives and gain enhanced opportunities for independent-living arrangements for group members.

Clearly, empowerment is linked to advocacy, participation and partnership. Participation in policy formation and decision-making concerning service provision increases the influence of previously disempowered people. More generally, working in partnership is important – professionals and service users working collaboratively to identify problems and decide how to tackle them. This implies that social work is a shared process, 'a collective endeavour with people, rather than something we do *to* them or *for* them' (Thompson and Thompson, 2008: 1999).

Nevertheless, advocacy may be needed to ensure people's views are considered. *Advocacy* means representing people's interests by ensuring their voice is heard. It involves an individual, a group or their representative 'pressing their case with influential others, about situations which either affect them directly or ... trying to prevent proposed changes which will leave them worse off' (Brandon, 1995: 1). Here there is a timely reminder that policy changes – particularly in an economic recession – are likely to impact most severely on vulnerable people who may be especially reliant on publicly-funded services.

SOCIAL JUSTICE, EQUALITY AND DIVERSITY

Emancipatory values, then, are 'anti-oppressive'. As the International Federation of Social Workers proclaims, social workers have a responsibility to 'challenge social conditions that contribute to social exclusion, stigmatisation or subjugation, and to work towards an inclusive society' (IFSW, 2004: Principle 4.2.5). This brings social justice – along with equality, human rights and diversity – very much into the picture (Clifford and Burke, 2009: 124–5). But what is social justice?

Justice has two aspects. First, legal/criminal justice is concerned primarily with punishment and its justification, and there are issues here for social work consideration. Is, for example, harsh sentencing as a deterrence to others a morally legitimate objective of punishment? Should social workers favour rehabilitative, reparative and community-based punishments?

Secondly, there is social justice – the core of the broader ethical aspirations of social work (Clark, 2000). One view of social justice relates it to the distribution of benefits and burdens throughout society. Such 'burdens' include taxes, while 'benefits' relate to 'wages, profits, housing, medical care, welfare benefits and so forth' (Heywood, 2004: 294). Social justice is, therefore, distributive and concerned with 'who *should* get what'. Some argue this should be decided on the basis of merit; others identify need as the relevant criterion. Social justice with regards to needs may *sometimes* requires equality of outcome, for example nutritional needs being met by ensuring everyone has a diet containing required nutrients. Obviously, though, this would not mean providing the same diet for everyone: some will have special dietary requirements, so resources may have to be distributed *unequally* to ensure equality of outcome.

While huge pay gaps seem highly questionable, most people regard *some* income differences relating to types of work as fair in view of the significant differences in required expertise, effort, etc. For example, doctors being paid somewhat more than road-sweepers seems acceptable. However, fairness in terms of equality of opportunity may be crucial here: 'a level playing field' – with everyone having an equal chance to gain qualifications and compete in the job market – may be considered essential. This requires *fair procedures* for selecting people for educational places, appointment to posts, etc. But such procedures will not be enough to secure equal opportunity if the playing field remains significantly uneven in other ways. Basically, while some have a far 'better start' in life (in terms of education, family support, etc.) than others, social disadvantage makes such equality of opportunity a distant prospect.

In addition, equality of access to services, as a means of ensuring justice in the distribution of social work and other resources, is vital. Hence, an understanding of the factors that impede access to services is needed. Such barriers range from the stigma attached to certain services to the location of social work offices, and taking measures to remove them is one important way social workers can promote social justice. Indeed, as the British Association of Social Workers 'Code of Ethics for Social Work' emphasises, social workers 'should ensure that resources at their disposal are distributed fairly, according to need' (BASW, 2012: 9). But, if social work is to be guided by a needs-based conception of social justice, the concept of 'basic human needs' requires some critical consideration.

Meeting basic human needs involves providing services for psychological and social, as well as material, needs. But should *all* of them be classified as '*basic* human needs'? If so, should they all be met as a matter of social justice – rather than, say, as an expression of collective charity? What if needs appear to be 'self-inflicted'? Finally, what procedures are required to ensure fair assessment of needs by social workers?

Furthermore, in allocating scarce social work resources, should *factors other than social justice* be considered? Some refer to a duty of realism (Beckett and Maynard, 2012) or suggest that utilitarian considerations require us to maximise the effectiveness of our use of scarce resources. This might imply directing resources to where they produce the greatest benefit, i.e., the maximum effect, rather than always giving priority to those with the greatest needs.

Exercise

How would you respond to a service user who insisted that a computer is now a basic need as so many claims now have to be made online?

So far we have outlined 'a distributive model' of social justice that focuses particularly on allocation of resources. Nevertheless, the concept of oppression strongly suggests that injustice does not arise solely from unfair allocation of benefits and burdens. It also stems from powerlessness; exclusion from decision-making; experience of violence and harassment; and being stigmatised and treated as of lesser worth. Many believe social work can address the full range of these matters best by adopting a human-rights conception of social justice. Certainly, human rights as outlined in the 1948 Declaration of Human Rights include important social and economic rights (relating to education, employment, standard of living, etc.) as well as political and civil rights (relating to liberty, political participation, etc.).

In addition, we must consider the idea of 'human diversity', human differences 'with social significance, diversity that makes real differences to people's lives' (Gaine and Gaylard, 2010: 2). Differences are of concern when they lead to unfair discrimination, for example being treated unfavourably at a job interview on the basis of a 'protected characteristic' – such as race, age, religion or sexual orientation – not relevant to the post. Concern with diversity also means adopting a positive attitude to most human differences relating to beliefs and behaviour. So it is not a matter of just 'putting up with', or refraining from interfering in, other people's lives. Rather valuing diversity means celebrating human diversity: welcoming, respecting and supporting the cultural differences between social groups.

This, though, raises the issue of 'multiculturalism', broadly viewed as the positive endorsement of communal diversity with respect to racial, ethnic, religious, linguistic and other differences (Heywood, 2004). This may require recognition of multicultural or minority group rights to engage in certain practices, for example maintaining faith schools, undertaking rituals concerning food preparation, language preservation or wearing symbols of religious commitment. Optimistically, Heywood suggests that 'multiculturalism brings the benefits of diversity: a vibrancy and richness that stems from cultural interplay and encourages tolerance and respect for other cultures …' (Heywood, 2004: 215).

There are, though, criticisms of multiculturalism. Some argue that to have a stable, well-ordered society, we must see ourselves as citizens, sharing common values, having an allegiance to the one state and a feeling of membership in the wider society (not just our own cultural group). The claim is that by encouraging cultural diversity we encourage dual-allegiances and political divisions, leading to social segregation, and generating inter-group conflict. Furthermore, multiculturalism is said to remove incentives for 'assimilation' into the 'host culture'.

There are other issues too. Some cultural groups may promote beliefs relating to family, gender roles or sexual orientation that deny opportunities and freedom to some of their members. In such cases, should social workers maintain their commitment to emancipatory goals of self-empowerment and equality *or* accept that strongly held beliefs of minority groups must be respected and left unchallenged?

Critical Thinking

Consider your own values and beliefs. How easy do you find it to tolerate or accept those people who hold opposing views or behave differently? How realistic is it to work towards social justice and freedom from oppression?

Obviously there are difficult issues relating to the application of emancipatory values. These objectives seem to require social workers to take on a 'political' role in pressing for social justice, but should politics be kept separate from professional practice? Social work has always displayed *some* concern with social reform and, given the 'social' element in 'social work', a refusal to engage with issues concerning social justice and oppression would simply be an abdication of professional responsibility. This brings us to the important topic of professional accountability.

ETHICAL CODES AND ACCOUNTABILITY

What is 'professional accountability'? The issue raised above indicates that the social work profession *as a whole* may be held accountable for its acts or omissions. Such collective accountability as a profession is of considerable importance, but the focus here will be on the accountability of the individual social worker.

Accountability relates to *all* the actions and decisions of professionals, but being *called upon* to account for one's actions is typically associated with problematic conduct and the apportioning of blame (Banks, 2004). To whom, though, is the individual social worker accountable? Accountability to the service user may be of prime importance, but the social worker has multiple and sometimes conflicting accountabilities (Kline and Preston-Shoot, 2012) – to regulatory bodies, employers, members of the public, etc. – which reflect the diverse character of social work. All these forms of accountability are important, but the professional accountability associated with codes of ethics or practice has now assumed particular significance.

Broadly, a professional code of ethics or practice is: 'a written document produced by a professional association, occupational regulatory body or other professional body with the stated aim of guiding the practitioners who are members, protecting service users and safeguarding the reputation of the profession' (Banks, 2004: 108). Social work in the

UK is now governed by a 'Code of Practice', relating to both social workers and other social service workers, introduced by the various 'Councils' set up in England and Wales, Northern Ireland and Scotland to regulate social services. (Another, complementary, code sets out the responsibilities of employers in the regulation of social service workers.)

For links to the Scottish Social Services Council (SSSC) the Health and Care Professions Council (HCPC) and other professional and regulatory bodies visit the Companion Website (www.sagepub.co.uk/SocialWork).

Basically, the 'Code of Practice' specifies standards of professional conduct and practice, requiring social service workers to:

- Protect the rights and promote the interests of service users and carers.
- Strive to establish and maintain the trust and confidence of service users and carers.
- Promote the independence of service users while protecting them as far as possible from danger or harm.
- Respect the rights of service users whilst seeking to ensure that their behaviour does not harm themselves or other people.
- Uphold public trust and confidence in social services.
- Be accountable for the quality of their work and take responsibility for maintaining and improving their knowledge and skills. (SSSC, 2009; GSCC, 2010)

With regard to each general requirement, the code specifies particular obligations, though these too are often fairly broad in character. For example, the social service worker must be 'honest and trustworthy' (2.1) and must not 'abuse, neglect or harm service users, cares or colleagues' (5.1).

Professional misconduct is conduct that falls short of the standard expected of someone registered with the Council, having particular regard to the requirements stipulated by the Code. Where a social service worker is found guilty of misconduct, the sanction imposed may range from admonishment to removal from the register. In short, this is the code that has statutory force.

There is, though, also The Code of Ethics for Social Work adopted by the British Association of Social Workers. BASW is a membership organisation representing the interests of social workers and its code has a longer history – being first produced in 1975, and then revised in 1986, 1996, 2002 and 2012.

The BASW Code of 2012 is more detailed than the Code of Practice and it states that its values are based on respect for the equality, worth and dignity of all people. Three central 'values and ethical principles' are identified:

- Human rights
- Social justice
- Professional integrity

In addition, the BASW Code highlights the need to treat people with compassion, empathy and care. It also enumerates 17 more detailed 'ethical practice principles'. These principles relate to such matters as: empowering people; challenging the abuse of human rights; acting with the informed consent of service users; maintaining confidentiality; assessing and managing risk; striving for objectivity and self-awareness in practice; and taking responsibility for continuing professional development.

A full analysis of the two codes cannot be attempted here, but some important matters need to be considered.

- The 'Code of Practice' is the basis of regulation of the profession, specifying relevant standards with regard to both guiding and disciplining members of the profession. So, does the BASW 'Code of Ethics' now serve any useful purpose?
- Is the ethical content of the codes significantly different? How strongly do 'traditional' and 'emancipatory' values feature? In addition, do both codes also incorporate a *'governance stream of values'*, reflecting government policies in recent times, and including 'probity, efficiency, partnership, the importance of managing risk, the right to high quality, effective services, involvement of service users and accountability to stakeholders, who include taxpayers, government and service users' (Whittington and Whittington, 2007: 90).
- Do the codes assist social workers to resolve particular ethical problems and dilemmas they may face?

ETHICAL DILEMMAS

The last question, concerning the usefulness of ethical codes, highlights the challenges for social workers in making ethically sound decisions in real-life situations. Such decision-making often has to take account of the welfare and rights of many people, establishing which is most important. Sometimes it is clear which carries most weight: where there is reason to believe that parents are seriously harming their child, the child's right to protection will be considered of greater importance than parental rights to privacy and self-determination.

However, when ethical considerations *appear* to be evenly balanced, an ethical dilemma may arise. Such a dilemma occurs when there are two (or more) possible courses of action, both (or all) of which have undesirable features. It requires 'a choice in which any alternative results in an undesirable action' (Rhodes, 1986: xii). Typically, too, it involves 'a conflict of ethical values, and it is not clear which choice will be the right one' (Banks, 2012: 2012), i.e., it is not clear which of the competing values/ethical principles should be accorded priority in the circumstances.

Case Study

You are a hospital-based social worker, and a patient with a life-threatening illness wishes to discharge herself. The doctor argues that more treatment will extend her life, the patient argues that she does not want to continue the suffering and indignity of the treatment. The doctor wants your support in persuading the patient to stay: the patient wants your support to return home. What might your response be?

It is worth noting that usually the alternative courses of action have both undesirable *and* desirable features, negative *and* positive aspects. Resolution of dilemmas typically involves weighing up very carefully the interests and rights of all those involved. Furthermore, decision-making may be made even more challenging because of uncertainty concerning the probable outcomes of the alternative courses of action. Some have argued that certain social work principles should *always* take priority over others (Reamer, 1995). It seems doubtful, though, whether it is possible to produce an overall ranking of ethical principles that will be generally accepted by social workers as being applicable to social work in all contexts.

Perhaps the best that can be done is to identify all the relevant ethical principles and consider the interests and rights of all involved. Consultation with colleagues to try to reach a reflective and considered assessment will be especially important. It allows a sharing of experience and professional wisdom, as well as testing one's own perceptions and provisional judgements against those of others.

To further develop your understanding of ethical issues in decision-making see the articles by Houston (2003) and Clark (2012) on the Companion Website (www.sagepub.co.uk/SocialWork).

CONCLUSION

This chapter has explored the nature of ethics by considering some key ethical concepts and theories. It also examined different strands of social work values; analysed concepts of social justice and human diversity; highlighted the increasing importance of ethical codes in professional accountability; and discussed the challenges posed by ethical dilemmas. It is hoped, therefore, that this has enhanced your appreciation of the ethical dimension of social work practice. No doubt, though, the discussion will sometimes have proved challenging. But remember that – in the wise words of Professor Eric Matthews – *'Ethics is hard'!* So, this chapter will have served its purpose if it has made things a little easier by increasing your understanding of social work values and sensitivity to ethical considerations. If successful in these respects, it should also help you to grapple in future with the many real-life ethical issues that arise in day-to-day practice as a social worker.

Reflective Questions

1 Social work has operated on two main approaches to values and ethics: traditional and emancipatory. First, define what each of them means and then, second, reflect on how they differ from each other in terms of how they may influence social work practice generally.

2 Elsewhere in this book the importance of how you understand yourself in relation to practice and to service users is highlighted. An important element of the use of self is being aware of your own ethical values. What would you say your ethical values are? Try to outline what they are and reflect on how they may have influenced you in choosing social work as a career.

3 Following on from the above question, how do you think your personal ethical values will influence your practice? Do you think your ethical values are closest to the traditional or emancipatory approaches?

Now look at the case study on the Companion Website (www.sagepub.co.uk/SocialWork) where Geraldine, an adult services social worker, tries to balance the needs and rights of Jane and William.

RECOMMENDED READING

These three books all provide useful introductions to social work ethics:

Banks, S. (2012) *Ethics and Values in Social Work*, 4th edn. Basingstoke: Palgrave Macmillan.

Beckett, C. and Maynard, A. (2012) *Values and Ethics in Social Work*, 2nd edn. London: Sage.

Parrott, L. (2010) *Values and Ethics in Social Work Practice*. Exeter: Learning Matters.

2 LAW

Heather Munro

Key Themes

- The UK does not have a codified **constitution**, thus there is no one formal document defining the institutions and powers of the state and its relationship with the citizen.
- The constitution has evolved over centuries, is underpinned by legal **doctrines** or principles, and the independence of the Judiciary is deemed to be crucial in the administration of justice.
- The rule of law is a fundamental concept, and it concerns equality, access to justice, and the protection of the rights of the individual.
- Social workers must be aware that the law evolves and changes, reflecting societal changes, political and cultural forces, which impacts directly on practice.
- Public, private and criminal law are all relevant to social work.

INTRODUCTION

> In the state of nature ... all men are born equal, but they cannot continue in this equality. Society makes them lose it, and they recover it only by the protection of the law.
>
> Charles de Montesquieu, French lawyer and philosopher (1689–1755)

The law provides a structure in which society operates and is constantly evolving to reflect societal change. It defines relationships between individuals (through private law) and between individuals and the state (through public law). It imposes sanctions on individuals who commit a crime (through criminal law). It enables those whose rights have been infringed to enforce their rights or to obtain compensation through the courts or tribunals, and it regulates those procedures. It guarantees certain procedural rights such as the right to a fair hearing in front of an independent and impartial decision-maker.

The law provides a framework for social work practice. It sets out the powers and duties of the local authority in providing social work services and establishes the rights of service users. It sets out procedural rules which social workers must follow and establishes principles of practice to ensure that social workers properly discharge their professional duties. Social work and the law are underpinned by shared values including justice, equality and respect for the rights of the individual.

In day-to-day practice, social workers require a sound working knowledge of the law pertaining to their area of service. Much of the relevant law, for example the law concerning the powers and duties of the local authority in providing services, concerns public law. However private law is also highly relevant: for example the law of negligence, family law, housing actions and debt recovery actions concern matters of private law.

This introductory chapter to the law provides an overview of the legal context within which social workers practise. It begins with the state and its core institutions and then examines the constitution and the principles governing the relationship between citizen and state. It then considers the main sources of law in the UK and sets out the court and tribunals system. It examines a number of important legal instruments in detail including the Human Rights Act 1998 which is highly relevant to social work. It provides an introduction to judicial review, the procedure by which individuals can seek to challenge the legality of decisions by public bodies.

THE STATE

When we refer to the state we mean the United Kingdom of Great Britain and Northern Ireland. Its core institutions are the *legislature*, the *executive* and the *judiciary*.

The Parliament at Westminster is the legislature, with responsibility for law-making. Its other functions are to scrutinise the work of the executive by questioning government ministers in the House of Commons and by appointing select committees to investigate particular topics, to authorise government taxation and redress grievances.[1]

The doctrine of Parliamentary Supremacy is a constitutional principle which limits the power of the executive and judicial branches of the state. It means that law made by the UK Parliament is inviolable. The courts cannot override or ignore a UK Act of Parliament[2] irrespective of its content.

The Welsh Assembly, the Northern Ireland Assembly and the Scottish Parliament were created in 1998 by separate Acts of Parliament.[3] These are devolved legislatures which have the power to legislate on prescribed matters such as education, health, local authorities, family law, policing and criminal law.[4] They may not legislate on matters retained by Westminster, which include the Crown, foreign affairs, defence, the benefits system and immigration.[5]

---

1   HC Select Committee on Procedure HC 588-1 (1977–1978), p. viii.
2   The constitutional lawyer Albert Venn Dicey stated that the principle 'means ... that Parliament thus defined has, under the English constitution, the right to make or unmake any law whatever; and, further, that no person or body is recognised by the law of England as having a right to override or set aside the legislation of Parliament' (Dicey, 1885).
3   The Scotland Act 1998, the Northern Ireland Act 1998 and the Government of Wales Act 1998.
4   Schedule 4 Scotland Act 1998.
5   Schedule 5 Scotland Act 1998.

For links to the UK Parliament, Scottish Parliament and the Welsh and Northern Ireland Assemblies see the Companion Website (www.sagepub.co.uk/SocialWork).

The Crown and the government form the executive, which undertakes policy-making, drafting legislation, the administration of the state and law enforcement. It is supported by the civil service, who are employees of the Crown. There are devolved administrations in Scotland, Wales and Northern Ireland, whose ministers are selected from the members of the devolved Parliaments.

The judiciary is responsible for administering justice in accordance with the law laid down by Parliament and the common law.

The Constitution

The UK does not have a codified constitution[6] which means that there is no one formal document defining the institutions and powers of the state and its relationship with the citizen. The UK constitution has evolved from a range of sources, including statute law, common law, principles, conventions and authoritative writings.[7]

Significant historical statutes include the Act of Union 1707, the Magna Carta 1297 and the Bill of Rights 1688, sections of which remain in force today.[8] More recently the Human Rights Act 1998 which provides for the protection of individual rights against state infringement has been highly influential in the development of the relationship between citizen and state. The constitution has been shaped externally by the UK's membership of the European Union, and internally by devolution.

The separation of powers is a fundamental principle which underlies the relationship between government, Parliament and the courts. It provides that each of the branches of the state should remain separate to, and independent from, the others. The principle is intended to prevent the concentration of power in one branch and thus the potential for abuse, and provides a means for each branch to operate as a check on the actions of the others.

The separation of powers doctrine is fundamental to protecting the independence of the judiciary.[9] Judges have a long history of independence from the government, reinforced by the Act of Settlement in 1701 which provided that judges cannot be removed from office during periods of good behaviour. The principal of judicial independence has more recently been preserved in statute in the Constitutional Reform Act 2005 (s.3(1)).

---

6   The constitution concerns 'the structures of state institutions, their relationship to each other, and the relationship of citizens and the state' (Beatson, 2010).

7   Jowell and Oliver (2011: 3) state that 'It is not accurate to say that the British constitution is unwritten. It is not codified, with all the rules and principles set out in one document, but a great deal of its content is based on written sources …'.

8   For example, the Bill of Rights 1688 curtailed the power of the King by declaring a number of limitations on his power, including that the King cannot suspend laws made by Parliament, or keep a standing army in peacetime without Parliament's consent.

9   'Under our constitution the separation of powers protecting judicial independence is now total and effectively so' (Steyn, 2006).

The rule of law is another fundamental constitutional principle.[10] There is no single definition of the rule of law, although there are many meanings attributed to it, the influential writings from 1885 of the constitutional lawyer Albert Venn Dicey being a starting point for an analysis of the doctrine.[11] Essentially, the rule of law requires that all citizens enjoy equality before the law,[12] that no one is above the law, that the law should be applied consistently and prospectively, and that everyone should have the right to access to justice[13] and a fair trial through the ordinary courts.

The expansion of the state and its institutions has led to the emergence of a number of theories about the rule of law and the principles it should uphold in our modern democracy. It has long been associated with the protection of individual rights against the abuse of executive power (Craig, 1997). The rule of law has become enshrined as a 'constitutional principle' under the Constitutional Reform Act 2005 (s.1) and is incorporated into international treaties.[14] The importance of the doctrine, which is described by the Council of the International Bar Association as 'the foundation of a civilised society', cannot be overstated.[15]

It is conceived by many to be the role of the courts to uphold and ensure observance of the rule of law, and it is referred to frequently in judicial decision-making. Lord Steyn has thus declared that the Courts are 'the guardian of the Rule of Law in a constitutional democracy' (Steyn, 2009).

Constitutional Conventions

Constitutional conventions consist of customs that are not legally binding but are observed by the government, the courts and the Crown. For example, it is convention that any Bill passed in Parliament will automatically be given the Royal Assent and that the monarch will abstain from involvement in political matters.[16] Conventions may eventually become codified in legislation, such as the Fixed Term Parliaments Act 2011 which codified a pre-existing convention on the calling of a General Election.

The European Union

The UK's membership of the European Union (EU) has had a significant impact on the constitution. The EU is an economic and political union of 28 member states. Its

---

10   Described as a 'central principle of constitutional governance' (Craig, 1997).
11   Dicey was 'effectively responsible for ensuring that no discussion of modern democratic government can properly omit reference to it' (Bingham, 2002).
12   *A and Others v Secretary of State for the Home Department X and Another v Secretary of State for the Home Department* [2004] UKHL 56.
13   *Chester* v *Bateson* [1920] 1 KB 829.
14   For example see the preamble to the Treaty of London establishing the Council of Europe.
15   Resolution of the International Bar Association on the Rule of Law 2005, accessed at www. ibanet.org.
16   *HRH Prince of Wales* v *Associated Newspapers Ltd* [2006] EWHC 522 (Ch).

origins are in the six-member European Coal and Steel Community (ECSC)[17] which formed in 1951.

The formation of the ECSC was intended to strengthen the ties between the member states as well as ensuring economic progress through a 'common market' with 'common objectives' and 'common institutions'.[18] It established the European Council and the European Court of Justice to ensure the observance of the laws contained in the ECSC Treaty.[19] Reforms led to the establishment of the European Economic Community (EEC) in 1987 under the Single European Act.

The European Union was created from the European Community in November 1993 by the Treaty of Maastricht.[20] As well as an economic union, the EU treaty set out common political and social aims for its members.[21]

The UK joined the EEC when Parliament enacted the European Communities Act 1972. The Act incorporates the supra-national law of the EU directly into UK domestic law by providing that the contents of the Treaties are directly enforceable in the UK.[22] The Act also requires UK Courts to determine issues or disputes involving the Treaties in accordance with the principles laid down by the European Court of Justice (ECJ).[23]

The ECJ should not be confused with the European Court of Human Rights, which determines legal claims under the European Convention on Human Rights. Although it is a condition of membership of the EU that states ratify the ECHR, the EU and its institutions are entirely separate from the Council of Europe and the European Court of Human Rights.

SOURCES OF LAW

In England, Wales and Northern Ireland the legal system is based on English common law. In Scotland the legal system has been influenced by a mixture of Roman civil law, the common law (MacQueen, 2012: 1.16), and Institutional Writers, who in the seventeenth and eighteenth centuries expounded principles that are still relied on and applied today.[24].

This chapter focuses on the two main sources of law, the common law and legislation, and looks at guidance and standards as non-formal sources of law.

The Common Law

The common law is 'judge-made law', consisting of principles and customs that have been created and developed by the courts. The tradition of law in the UK assumes that

---

17   Under the ECSC Treaty.
18   Title 1 Article 1 ECSC Treaty.
19   Article 33 ECSC Treaty.
20   Which incorporated the previous treaties establishing and amending the ECSC and EEC.
21   Article 1 Treaty of Maastricht.
22   S.2(1) European Communities (EC) Act 1972.
23   S.3 EC Act 1972.
24   See *Connelly* v *Simpson* (1993) S.C. 39.

unless something is forbidden an individual is free to do it. This 'spirit of liberty' is considered to be the 'dominant theme' of the common law (Steyn, 2006).

The doctrine of *stare decisis* (or judicial precedent) is a fundamental principle of the common law. It provides that decisions of the superior courts establish 'legal precedents' which are binding on lower courts. One example is found in the famous case of *Donoghue* v *Stevenson*[25] in which the House of Lords set out common law principles on the existence of a duty of care which have become the foundations for the modern law of negligence.[26]

A decision of the highest UK Court, the Supreme Court, must be followed by the Court of Session in Scotland or the Court of Appeal in England and Wales. Apart from decisions of the Supreme Court in civil (not criminal) cases, Scottish courts are not generally required to follow the decisions of English courts, although judgments may be cited as being of persuasive value.

Enacted Law

Enacted law or statute consists of primary legislation such as Acts of Parliament and secondary (or subordinate or delegated) legislation such as Statutory Instruments, Regulations and Bye-orders.

When legislation is brought into force it overrides any pre-existing common law on a matter. For example, the common law duty of care owed to visitors by the occupier of premises has been codified in the Occupiers Liability Acts. A tenant seeking damages for injuries from slipping on a damaged step due to the alleged negligence of a landlord might seek to rely on the relevant section of the statute for a remedy rather than the common law.

In accordance with the doctrine of implied repeal, where there is conflict between two Acts, the court must give effect to the later Act.

When the courts apply legislation 'the overriding aim of the court must always be to give effect to the intention of Parliament ...'.[27] In the case of *AB and Others* v *Ministry of Defence*[28] servicemen and their families raised a group action claiming that the Ministry of Defence breached its duty by exposing them to damaging radiation during experimental thermonuclear testing in the 1950s. The question for initial determination was whether the claims were time-barred under the Limitation Act 1980. The claims were time-barred if the claimants had the requisite knowledge of their injuries outside the statutory time limit for bringing a claim. The decision depended upon the Supreme Court's interpretation of the word 'knowledge'. Their interpretation of the statute led the majority of the court to hold that the claimants had the requisite 'knowledge', resulting in the claims being deemed time-barred.

---

25   1932 AC 362.
26   *Donoghue* v *Stevenson* concerned the liability of a drinks manufacturer for a defect in a bottle of ginger ale consumed by a customer in a café (the defect being a decomposed snail in the contents).
27   *R* v *Environment Secretary, ex p Spath Holme Ltd* [2001] 2AC 349, per Lord Bingham at 388.
28   [2012] UKSC 9.

The court may refer to Hansard (the official record of debates in Parliament) for assistance in interpreting the intention of Parliament if the meaning of a statute is unclear.

The Passage of a Bill through Parliament

Primary legislation is created through a Parliamentary process which begins with the introduction of a Bill in Parliament. A Bill may be introduced by the government (known as a public Bill) or by an individual MP (known as a private member's Bill). A Bill might be drafted to reflect a government policy or manifesto commitment; it could be introduced in reaction to an event; or it could be intended to codify the common law.

Before they are introduced Bills are normally published for consultation. To become an Act the Bill needs to pass through a number of stages of scrutiny, debate and amendment involving Parliamentary committees and both the House of Commons and the House of Lords. The Bill cannot be passed until agreement on the final version is reached by both Houses, then it must receive the Royal Assent to become an Act of Parliament. Acts are often accompanied by explanatory notes that provide background information on the legislation and clarification of individual provisions.

An Act is not law until it has come into force, which may be immediately upon receiving the Royal Assent or at a future specified date.

The Scottish Parliament

The Scotland Act 1998 provides for the establishment of the Scottish Parliament with law-making powers.[29] The Parliament has a single chamber. A Bill must pass through three stages within the Parliament before the Presiding Officer submits it for the Royal Assent, then it becomes an Act of the Scottish Parliament (ASP).

A 'Devolution Issue' may be raised to challenge the legislative competency of an Act of the Scottish Parliament on the basis that it relates to a reserved matter or is in breach of the European Convention on Human Rights.[30] One such (unsuccessful) challenge was made by a tenant of a local authority who argued that s.36 of the Housing (Scotland) Act 2001, which provided for her eviction from her property, was incompatible with her right to a private and family life under Article 8 of the European Convention on Human Rights.[31]

Secondary Legislation

An Act may provide for the creation of secondary legislation, where detailed provisions are required in order to enforce the Act or parts of the Act, and which are at a level too

---

29   S.1(1) of the Scotland Act 1998.
30   Under Schedule 6 of the Scotland Act 1998 a devolution issue may also be raised to determine whether a member of the Scottish Executive has acted within their devolved powers.
31   *South Lanarkshire Council* v *McKenna* 2013 S.L.T. 22.

great to be included in the Act itself. Secondary legislation may also update or amend primary legislation without the need to amend the Act itself.

Most secondary legislation is enacted as Statutory Instruments (in Scotland, Scottish Statutory Instrument). It also comprises Regulations, Rules, Orders and Bye-Orders. Secondary legislation has the force of law, but is secondary to Acts. If there is a difference between the two, the primary Act takes precedence.

The Distinction between a Power and a Duty in Statutes

There is a distinction between a power and a duty in statutes. In general, the words 'must' and 'shall' denote duties that are binding on the relevant individual, court or decision-maker to whom it refers. For example s.17(1) of the Children Act 1989 (Provision of services for children in need, their families and others) provides that:

> It shall be the general duty of every local authority (in addition to the other duties imposed on them by this Part)
>
> (a) to safeguard and promote the welfare of children within their area who are in need; and
> (b) so far as is consistent with that duty, to promote the upbringing of such children by their families,
>
> by providing a range and level of services appropriate to those children's needs.

The word 'may' indicates a power: for example, s.17(3) of the Children Act 1989 provides that:

> Any service provided by an authority in the exercise of functions conferred on them by this section may be provided for the family of a particular child in need or for any member of his family, if it is provided with a view to safeguarding or promoting the child's welfare.

Guidance and Standards

Guidance, standards and circulars are important frameworks within which the local authority carries out its functions. Their purpose is to inform decision-making and to promote best practice. They may set expected standards and require practitioners to uphold certain principles in practice and are an aid to interpreting and applying the law. At a national level they may promote a unified approach to service provision across the different local authorities.

Guidance may be issued by the Secretary of State in accordance with powers conferred by statute, or it may be non-statutory in source. In promoting the adoption of a particular approach, guidance is regarded as 'a mechanism by which central Government can exert control and influence on local authorities' (Bailey and Elliott, 2009).

While guidance is not a formal source of law, case law has established that a local authority may not depart from it unless they can demonstrate that they have taken it into account and, in deciding to depart from it, have given clear reasons for doing so.[32]

---

32 *R. (Khatun)* v *Newham L.B.C.* [2004] EWCA Civ 55.

The Guidance on the Adoption and Children Act 2002 issued under section 7 of the Local Authority Social Services Act 1970 states that it does not have the full force of statute, but should be complied with unless local circumstances indicate exceptional reasons that justify a variation. An alleged failure to follow guidance may result in legal action being taken against the local authority[33] and may ultimately result in a finding that the local authority has acted unlawfully.[34]

IMPORTANT LEGAL INSTRUMENTS

The European Convention on Human Rights and the Human Rights Act

The origins of the European Convention on Human Rights lie in the aftermath of the Second World War and the establishment of the Council of Europe by 10 European States[35] united by the 'pursuit of peace based upon justice and international cooperation'.[36] The European Convention on Human Rights (ECHR) is described as the Council of Europe's 'crowning achievement'.[37]

The ECHR is an international treaty designed to 'create a binding international code of human rights, with safeguards against abuses of power and effective remedies for victims of violations by contracting states' (Lester, 2009). The Convention was ratified in 1951 and came into force in 1953. The original 12 signatories to the ECHR has increased to 47 states parties.

Part I of the Convention sets out fundamental rights and freedoms in 18 Articles and 13 protocols.[38] Some of the rights it contains are absolute and inviolable rights, such as the right not to suffer torture or inhuman or degrading treatment under Article 3. Other rights are limited rights, such as the right to liberty under Article 5, which right a person may only be deprived of through lawful means such as their lawful arrest and detention. Other rights are qualified rights, such as the right to a private and family life under Article 8, which means that a public authority may interfere with that right, but only if the interference is lawful and if it is 'necessary in a democratic society'.

Part II of the Convention establishes the European Court of Human Rights to ensure observance of the Articles by the Contracting States.

---

33   See for example *R (Munjaz) v Mersey Care NHS Trust* [2005] UKHL 58.
34   The implementation of the local authority guidance in applying for Emergency Protection Orders (EPO) was considered in detail in X Emergency Protection Orders Re: [2006] EWHC 510 (Fam).
35   Belgium, Denmark, France, Ireland, Italy, Luxembourg, the Netherlands, Norway, Sweden and the UK.
36   Preamble to the Treaty of London.
37   www.echr.coe.int/NR/rdonlyres/7EE16B23-65FD-4342-9124-ECD431425A60/0/DG2ENHRFILES012005.pdf.
38   The full text of the ECHR can be read here: www.echr.coe.int/NR/rdonlyres/D5CC24A7-DC13-4318-B457-5C9014916D7A/0/Convention_ENG.pdf.

As an international treaty, the ECHR is not directly enforceable in UK domestic courts. Prior to the enactment of the Human Rights Act 1998[39] (HRA 1998), individuals whose rights were breached had to rely on the common law to protect their rights[40] or make an application directly to the European Court of Human Rights, which was expensive and time-consuming. The HRA 1998 was enacted in order to 'bring rights home'[41] by embedding the law of the ECHR in UK domestic law.

Section 6(1) of the HRA 1998 makes it unlawful for a public authority to act in a way that is incompatible with a Convention Right.[42] The definition of a public authority includes courts and tribunals, local authorities, the police and government departments, state schools, the immigration service and armed forces, and bodies whose functions are those of a public nature.[43]

Only the 'victim' of an unlawful act may raise proceedings against a public authority.[44] The court may award that person damages if it is found that the public authority has acted contrary to section 6(1).[45] When determining a breach of the ECHR, the court must take into account the case law of the European Court of Human Rights at Strasbourg.[46]

Human Rights claims have been raised in a wide range of areas of state involvement: criminal law, anti-terrorism legislation, housing law, mental health law, immigration law and family law.

In *Z* v *UK*[47] it was held that the failure of a local authority to protect children from sustained neglect and abuse by their parents was a breach of the children's right not to suffer torture or inhuman or degrading treatment under Article 3 ECHR.

In *R. (on the application of KB)* v *South London and South West Region Mental Health Review Tribunal (Damages)*[48] it was held that the failure to arrange a speedy hearing to determine the lawfulness of detaining a person under the Mental Health Act was a breach of their rights under Article 5(4) ECHR.

In *Hounslow LBC* v *Powell*[49] it was held that where the local authority seeks to evict a tenant and recover possession of their home, the court must consider the proportionality of the decision in terms of their right to a private and family life under Article 8 EHCR.

---

39 On 1 October 2000.
40 See *R* v *Secretary of State for the Home Department, Ex parte Brind* [1991] 1 A.C. 696, per Lord Bridge at 748: although the ECHR was not applicable in the domestic courts, he does 'not accept that this conclusion means that the courts are powerless to prevent the exercise by the executive of administrative discretions, even when conferred, as in the instant case, in terms which are on their face unlimited, in a way which infringes fundamental human rights'.
41 See the Government White Paper on the Human Rights Bill. Cm 3782 TSO (010137822X).
42 The HRA 1998 does not implement all of the Rights under the Convention, for example it excludes the Right to an Effective Remedy under Article 13.
43 www.publications.Parliament.uk/pa/jt200607/jtselect/jtrights/77/77.pdf.
44 S.7 HRA 1998.
45 S.8 HRA 1998.
46 S.2 HRA 1998.
47 [2002] 34 EHRR 3.
48 [2003] EWHC 193 (Admin).
49 [2011] UKSC 8.

In *Anderson* v *SSHD*[50] the House of Lords held that the practice of the Home Secretary setting the tariff on the minimum period of time which a mandatory life sentence prisoner must serve was contrary to the right to a fair trial under Article 6 ECHR because the Home Secretary was a member of the Executive and therefore was not an independent or impartial adjudicator.

The HRA 1998 does not prevent the UK Parliament from enacting legislation that is incompatible with the ECHR as this would be contrary to the principle that Parliament has unrestricted law-making powers. For example, a number of cases have challenged the UK's blanket ban on prisoners' right to vote under the Representation of the People Act 1983. The European Court in Strasbourg has held in repeated judgments[51] that the law is in breach of prisoners' Convention Rights.[52] This has not affected the validity of the legislation which still stands; however the Government has indicated that it will consider modifying the existing law so as to give effect to the judgments.[53]

The devolved Scottish Parliament is prohibited from legislating incompatibly with the ECHR[54] and the courts have the power to strike down any such incompatible legislation.

In relation to the courts, the HRA 1998 provides that *as far as possible* legislation must be read and given effect to in a way that is compatible with the Convention rights.[55] The courts cannot overturn or override primary legislation[56] that they hold to be incompatible with the ECHR. If primary legislation cannot be interpreted or applied in a way that makes it compatible, the superior courts[57] have the power to make a *declaration of incompatibility*. This does not affect the Act's validity, but it may prompt the government to amend the relevant Act to make it ECHR compatible, or repeal it.

In *Baiai* v *SSHD*,[58] it was held that the requirement for migrants to obtain prior approval from the Home Office before being permitted to marry was incompatible with the rights to a family life under Article 8, the right to marry under Article 12 and the provision on non-discrimination under Article 14 ECHR. This prompted a subsequent change to the immigration rules.

In *Williamson* v *Secretary of State for Education and Employment*[59] a number of parents and teachers of independent private schools challenged the mandatory ban

---

50   [2002] UKHL 46.
51   See *Greens* v *UK* (60041/08) (2011) 53 E.H.R.R. 21.
52   To free elections under Protocol 1, Article 3 ECHR.
53   www.parliament.uk/documents/joint-committees/human-rights/Letter_from_Mr_Grayling_on_Prisoner_Voting.pdf.
54   S.57 Scotland Act 1998.
55   S.3 HRA 1998.
56   The superior courts have the power to quash (strike down) subordinate legislation which is incompatible with the ECHR.
57   The Supreme Court and Judicial Committee of the Privy Council, the High Court or Court of Appeal and Court of Protection in England and Wales and the High Court of Justiciary or Court of Session in Scotland.
58   *R (Baiai)* v *SSHD* [2007] EWCA Civ 478.
59   [2005] UKHL 15.

on corporal punishment introduced in the Education Act 1996 as being contrary to their freedom to manifest their religion or belief under Article 9, their right to education in conformity with their religious convictions under Article 2, Protocol 1 and Article 8. Their challenge failed. The court held that the statutory ban was a proportionate means of pursuing a legitimate aim of protecting children from the deliberate infliction of physical violence, and thus there was no incompatibility with the ECHR.

In Northern Ireland the adoption law which prevented one member of an unmarried couple from adopting the child of their partner was successfully challenged as a breach of Articles 8 and 14 ECHR.[60]

The UN Convention on the Rights of the Child

The UN Convention on the Rights of the Child (UNCRC) is an international treaty providing children with specific rights and protections. It has been ratified by 192 states, the only two exceptions being the United States and Somalia. The United Kingdom ratified the treaty in 1991.

The UNCRC determines children's civil rights, social and welfare rights, and rights to family life. It provides for protection of children from exploitation or exposure to armed conflict, and provides procedural protection for children who are involved in the justice system or exposed to armed conflict.

As an international treaty the UNCRC is not part of UK domestic law. The current UK government has indicated its commitment to implementation of the UNCRC through the introduction of new law and policy-making.[61] The devolved administrations in Scotland, Wales and Northern Ireland each hold responsibility for implementing the UNCRC within their devolved competencies.

Despite its non-binding nature, the UNCRC's principles have had a strong influence on domestic law and policy. The principle that the best interests of the child is a primary consideration under Article 3 UNCRC[62] is reflected in the Children Act 1989 and the Children (S) Act 1995. In *ZH Tanzania*,[63] after reflecting on the position under the law, including the UNCRC, the Supreme Court held that the principle must constitute a *primary consideration* in assessing human rights claims under Article 8 ECHR.[64] In terms of policy-making, local authorities individually recognise the importance of the UNCRC in informing their practice.[65]

---

60   Re: G (Adoption: Unmarried Couple) [2008] UKHL 38.
61   www.education.gov.uk/childrenandyoungpeople/healthandwellbeing/b0074766/uncrc.
62   'In all actions concerning children, whether undertaken by public or private social welfare institutions, courts of law, administrative authorities or legislative bodies, the best interests of the child shall be a primary consideration'.
63   [2011] UKSC 4.
64   The right to a private and family life.
65   www.sccyp.org.uk/uploaded_docs/strategic%20plan%20consultation/dundee%20city%20 council%20social%20work%20department.pdf.

Equality Act 2010

The Equality Act 2010 (EA 2010) came into force on 1 October 2010 replacing the previous framework of separate Acts, secondary legislation and codes of practice which previously constituted discrimination law.[66] The Act is designed to strengthen the law and extend the protections it confers, including a new equality duty on public bodies.

In general, the EA makes it unlawful to discriminate, victimise or harass someone because of what is termed as a 'protected characteristic'. There are nine protected characteristics in the Act: age, disability, gender reassignment, marriage and civil partnerships, pregnancy and maternity, race, religion, sex or sexual orientation.[67] The law provides protection from unlawful discrimination in relation to services and public functions, premises, work, education and associations.[68] Part 9 of the Act sets out when a claim may be brought in a court or tribunal, the time limits and the remedies that may be granted.

The Equality and Human Rights Commission (EHRC) was created to assist with the implementation and enforcement of the EA 2010.[69] The EHRC covers England, Scotland and Wales (in Scotland and Wales, separate statutory bodies have been established). It has overarching aims of promoting the development of society in which there is respect for and protection of each individual's human rights, in which no one is limited from achieving his or her potential due to prejudice or discrimination, and in which there is respect for the dignity and worth of each person in society.[70] The EHRC has powers of investigation and enforcement[71] and a remit to produce codes of practice and training.[72]

On the Companion Website (www.sagepub.co.uk/SocialWork) you will find a link to the Equality and Human Rights Commission, as well as an activity to develop your understanding of the public sector equality duty. In addition, it is suggested you read the article by Braye et al. (2013) examining how social workers use the law to promote social justice and human rights.

Data Protection Act 1998 and Freedom of Information Acts

Information-sharing is considered essential in social work practice to ensure effective working and early intervention to protect children and vulnerable adults and to facilitate the delivery of better services to service-users. There is a strong emphasis in the relevant codes of practice and guidance on facilitating the sharing of information and encouraging joint-working between social workers, the police, education bodies and the third sector.[73]

It is against this background that social workers must act within the framework of the law.

---

66 Anti-discrimination law formerly comprised nine pieces of primary legislation, 100 Statutory Instruments and 2,500 codes of practice.

67 Chapter 1, Part 2 of EA 2010.

68 Parts 3–6 of EA 2010, respectively.

69 Created under the Equality Act 2006.

70 S.3 EA 2006.

71 S.20 EA 2006.

72 S.14 EA 2006.

73 See, for example, the UK government publication *Information Sharing: Guidance for Practitioners and Managers* (HM Government, 2008) and in Scotland, *Getting our Priorities Right: Good Practice Guidance for Working with Children and Families Affected by Substance Misuse* (Scottish Executive, 2006b).

There are a number of sources of law that govern the sharing of information, confidentiality and the protection of personal information. These include the common law, the HRA 1998, European law, the Data Protection Act 1998 and the Freedom of Information Act 2002. This chapter briefly introduces the latter two Acts.

The Data Protection Act 1998 (DPA 1998) governs the handling of personal information by persons or organisations. The Act provides that a 'data controller', i.e., the person or organisation handling personal information about individuals, must comply with a number of data protection principles.[74] The principles include that information must be handled fairly and lawfully, that it shall only be obtained for one or more lawful purposes and that it must not be kept for longer than is necessary for that purpose or those purposes.[75] The Act provides individuals with certain rights to access personal data which is held by the data controller, to be informed of the purposes for holding their data and to whom it is being released.[76] The UK Information Commissioner is responsible for data protection throughout the UK.[77]

The Freedom of Information Acts of 2000 and 2002 provide individuals with certain rights to access information held by public authorities. Subject to exceptions, a local authority must comply with a request to provide an individual with the information they hold about them and within a certain time limit.[78]

JUDICIAL REVIEW

Judicial review is the process by which the legality of the decisions and actions of the executive are subject to scrutiny. A petition for judicial review may be brought by a private individual (a petitioner) against a public body to challenge the lawfulness of its decision-making. Judicial review cases cover a wide range of administrative action, including planning decisions, criminal law and procedure, and mental health law, and they are particularly prevalent in immigration and asylum law.[79] The number of applications for judicial review has increased from less than 700 in 1970, to over 11,000 in 2011.[80]

There are a number of grounds upon which judicial review may be brought[81] which have evolved through judicial precedent. The grounds act as an important control on the exercise of executive power. A decision could be challenged on the ground it is illegal or '*ultra vires*' on the basis that the decision-maker did not have sufficient legal powers to make the decision. One local authority was held to have failed to have acted

---

74 S.4(4) DPA 1998.
75 Part 1, Schedule 1 DPA 1998.
76 S.7 DPA 1998.
77 www.informationcommissioner.gov.uk.
78 S.1 and s.11 Freedom of Information Act 2000.
79 Ministry of Justice Judicial and Court Statistics. Retrieved from www.justice.gov.uk/downloads/statistics/courts-and-sentencing/jcs-2011/judicial-court-stats-2011.pdf.
80 www.guardian.co.uk/news/datablog/2012/nov/19/judicial-review-statistics.
81 Identified in *CCSU* v *Minister for the Civil Service* [1985] A.C. 374

in accordance with its statutory powers when it banned deer hunting with hounds, any moral arguments invoked to establish the ban deemed irrelevant to the lawfulness of the decision.[82]

A decision is irrational (known as *Wednesbury unreasonable* after the famous case of that name in which it was created)[83] if it is so unreasonable that no reasonable authority could ever have come to it. In *Kelly* v *Monklands DC*[84] the decision of a local authority that a teenager was not 'vulnerable' in terms of the Housing (Homeless Persons) Act 1977, and their refusing her application for accommodation, was held to be Wednesbury unreasonable.

Procedural impropriety is invoked as a ground of review where a public authority showed bias in making a decision, did not act consistently in its decision-making or did not allow a person to have a fair hearing.[85] Procedural impropriety also occurs if a decision-maker has unlawfully fettered his discretion by rigidly applying a particular policy affecting an individual without taking into account his or her particular circumstances.

Since the introduction of the HRA 1998, judicial review may be used to challenge decisions of the local authority as being in breach of the ECHR.

Only the superior courts of the UK are entitled to undertake judicial review. The court can only review the legality of a decision and cannot simply substitute its own decision for that of the decision-maker because it considers the decision to be a 'bad' decision. Judicial review is not concerned with the morality or 'merits of the decision in question' (Goodwin, 2012). This means that if the court determines that a decision was within the legal powers of the decision-maker, the question of whether the decision may or may not be a 'good' decision is irrelevant.

If an application for judicial review is successful, the court may grant one of a number of remedies. These include a declaration clarifying the legal rights and duties of the parties, an order to prevent a decision-maker from acting unlawfully, or quashing the decision (making it invalid). If a decision is quashed it is open to the authority to re-make the decision in a way that is lawful.

INTRODUCTION TO CIVIL AND CRIMINAL LAW

Civil Law

Civil law concerns the private rights of individuals and regulates the relationships between them. For example, it covers the law on contract, civil wrongs (tort or delict in Scots law), family law and housing law. A person who raises a civil action in England and Wales is called the 'claimant' (or 'plaintiff') and in Scotland is called the 'pursuer'.

---

82   *R* v *Somerset CC ex p. Fewings* [1995] 3 All ER 20.
83   *Associated Provincial Picture Houses Ltd.* v *Wednesbury Corporation* [1948] 1 K.B. 223.
84   1985 S.C. 333.
85   *R.* v *Norfolk CC Ex p. M* [1989] QB 619.

The person against whom the case is brought is known as the 'defendant' in England and Wales and the 'defender' in Scotland.

In civil cases the claimant or pursuer lodges a claim in writing with the appropriate court specifying on what basis they are raising an action against the defendant or defender. The defendant or defender must answer the claim to state whether they intend to defend the action. If the matter proceeds to court, evidence is led about the facts of the case by each of the parties who have the opportunity to challenge each other's evidence. The judge will deliver a judgment after hearing the relevant evidence of the parties and witnesses and assessing any documentary evidence.

If the claimant is successful, the court may grant one or more of a range of remedies or orders. The judge may order the defendant to pay money owed or compensation to the claimant, or may require them to fulfil an obligation under a contract. The judge may order the repayment of a debt, grant a divorce, or issue an eviction order. Orders may prohibit an individual from acting in a particular way such as approaching the claimant (e.g. an injunction or interdict) or they may prevent the disclosure of information.

Criminal Law

Criminal law concerns bringing offenders to justice. It is the state which is responsible for prosecuting and punishing individuals who have committed a crime. In England and Wales the Crown Prosecution Service (CPS) headed by the Director of Public Prosecutions is the principal public service responsible for bringing prosecutions. In Scotland the Crown Office and Procurator Fiscal Service (COPFS) under the authority of the Lord Advocate is the sole prosecution service and in Northern Ireland prosecutions are brought by the Public Prosecution Service (PPS) headed by the Director of Public Prosecutions for Northern Ireland.

The police are responsible for investigating alleged crimes and have powers to detain and question suspects.[86] The state prosecutor will assess the results of their investigations and in serious cases they may decide who to charge and what the charge should be. Before proceeding, the state prosecutor has to decide that there is sufficient evidence to justify a prosecution and that it is in the public interest. They must act in accordance with a code of practice in carrying out their duties and act fairly, independently and objectively.[87]

If a suspect is charged with an offence he or she becomes known as the 'defendant' in England and Wales and the 'accused' in Scotland. They will be required to attend court and at their first hearing may be granted bail or remanded in custody until their trial is scheduled.[88] Less serious criminal cases may be decided by a judge sitting alone, whereas more serious cases are decided by a jury of lay persons under the direction of a judge who will decide on the appropriate sentence if the person is found guilty.

---

86   See, for example, s.14 Criminal Procedure (S) Act 1995.
87   See for example the Code for Crown Prosecutors at: www.cps.gov.uk/publications/docs/code2013english_v2.pdf.
88   S.4 Bail Act 1976.

There are situations where elements of both criminal law and civil law may apply. An example of this would be a road traffic accident involving two cars, where one of the drivers is tried for dangerous driving in the criminal courts and is sued in the civil courts by the other driver for compensation for injuries sustained in the crash.

The 'standard of proof' refers to the burden that must be discharged in order to find a person guilty of a crime in a criminal case and to make a finding in relation to a respondent or defender in a civil case. The common law recognises two standards of proof. In criminal cases (and in areas of dispute such as contempt of court or disciplinary proceedings against members of a profession[89]) the standard of proof is '*beyond reasonable doubt*'.[90] In civil cases the standard of proof is '*on the balance of probabilities*'[91], which means establishing, on the evidence, that the occurrence of the event was more likely than not.[92] The criminal standard has exceptionally been applied to certain civil proceedings.[93]

In a child protection case a social worker may seek measures to protect the child through the civil courts where the lesser standard, 'on the balance of probability', applies, while the police may be investigating whether a crime has been committed, seeking evidence that would be required to meet the higher standard of proof in criminal proceedings of 'beyond reasonable doubt'.

See the article on the Companion Website (www.sagepub.co.uk/SocialWork) by Braye and Preston-Shoot (2006) who undertook research around the extent to which social workers used the law in their case work.

THE COURTS

The UK does not have a unified court system. There are separate court systems for England and Wales, Scotland and Northern Ireland.

The Criminal Courts in England and Wales

In England and Wales criminal cases begin in a magistrates' court. A magistrates' court has jurisdiction to try any summary offences[94] that are of a more minor nature, such as driving offences or being drunk and disorderly. Cases are not decided by a jury but by a district judge or three magistrates (known as Justices of the Peace). Magistrates are not legally qualified, but are lay persons who have received training for their role. The maximum sentencing powers of a magistrates' court are six months in prison[95] (12 months in some cases) or a fine of up to £5,000[96] or community service.

Appeals from a magistrates' court and more serious offences such as rape and murder are committed (referred) to the Crown Court.[97] The Crown Court has exclusive jurisdiction

---

89   Re D (Secretary of State for Northern Ireland intervening) [2008] UKHL 33.
90   *M Kenzie* v *HMA* (1959) JC 32.
91   *Lamb* v *Lord Advocate and others* (1976) SC 110.
92   Re D (Secretary of State for Northern Ireland intervening) [2008] UKHL 33.
93   *R(N)* v *Mental Health Review Tribunal (Northern Region) and others* [2005] EWCA Civ 1605.
94   S.2 Magistrates' Courts Act 1980.
95   S.78 Powers of Criminal Courts (Sentencing) Act 2000.
96   S.131 Powers of Criminal Courts (Sentencing) Act 2000.
97   Established by the Courts Act 1971.

to try indictable offences.[98] Cases in the Crown Court are decided by a jury of 12 and sentencing is carried out by a judge. The sentencing powers of the criminal courts are contained in the Powers of Criminal Courts (Sentencing Act) 2000. Some offences are known as either-way offences which means that they can be tried summarily in a magistrates' court or by indictment in the Crown Court.

Appeals from the Crown Court are sent to the Court of Appeal Criminal Division. From there the highest appeal court is the Supreme Court.

The Criminal Courts in Scotland

Summary trials for less serious offences are conducted in either a Justice of the Peace Court (JP court) or a Sheriff Court. JP courts were established to replace district courts following legal reforms.[99] A Justice of the Peace (JP) is not legally qualified and is assisted in court by a legally qualified clerk.[100] The maximum penalties JPs may impose are 60 days' imprisonment and/or a fine up to £2,500.[101] In summary cases in a Sheriff Court the maximum penalties a sheriff can impose are 12 months' imprisonment and/or a fine of up to £10,000.

Solemn cases are reserved for more serious crimes and are heard in either a Sheriff Court or the High Court with a judge and a jury of 15. In solemn cases in a Sheriff Court the maximum penalties a sheriff can impose are 5 years' imprisonment and/or an unlimited fine. If the sheriff thinks that a longer sentence is warranted in view of the nature of the offence the case may be remitted to the High Court for sentencing.

The High Court is presided over by the Lord Justice General and the Lord Justice Clerk. The High Court sits as both a trial court and as the appeal court for all criminal appeals. As a trial court the High Court sits at Edinburgh, Glasgow and Aberdeen, and travels on circuit around Scotland. The High Court hears only solemn cases and has unlimited sentencing powers. As an appeal court the High Court sits only in Edinburgh and three or more judges may sit on a case.

Children and Young Persons and the Criminal Law

The age of criminal responsibility in England, Wales and Northern Ireland is 10 years.[102] Young persons in England and Wales aged between 10 and 17 years old are tried in a youth court, which is a specific type of magistrates' court.[103] The proceedings

---

98 S.46 Senior Courts Act 1981.
99 Under the Criminal Proceedings etc. (Reform) Scotland Act 2007.
100 In Glasgow only, a stipendiary magistrate (a professional judge with at least 5 years' legal experience as an advocate/solicitor) may sit in the JP court.
101 If a stipendiary magistrate is sitting, s/he has the same sentencing powers as the sheriff sitting in a summary case.
102 S.50 Children and Young Persons Act 1933 (CYPA 1933).
103 S.45 CYPA 1933.

are designed to be less formal and there are restrictions on the reporting of the proceedings.[104] The most serious offences involving a young person may be committed to the Crown Court.

The age of criminal responsibility in Scotland is 12 years. It was increased from the age of 8 years in August 2010,[105] bringing Scotland into line with other countries in Europe. Most young persons aged 12 to 16 years who are charged with a criminal offence will be dealt with through the children's hearing system, which is an entirely separate system to the courts. Young persons over age 16 years may be dealt with in the criminal courts.

The Civil Courts in England and Wales

The majority of civil cases in England and Wales are heard in the County Court. County Courts were established in each district in England and Wales[106] with a general jurisdiction to hear actions based on contract and tort (civil wrongs)[107] and claims for the repayment of debts, cases relating to wills and trusts, and actions for the recovery of land.[108] Cases are decided by a circuit or district judge. Decisions may be appealed from the County Court to the Court of Appeal.[109]

Cases involving a high degree of complexity or large sums of money are heard in the High Court.[110] The High Court is housed together with the Court of Appeal in the Royal Courts of Justice in London. These two courts together with the Crown Court are the Senior Courts of England and Wales.[111]

The High Court comprises three distinct divisions.[112] The Queen's Bench Division (QBD) headed by a President decides personal injury cases, contractual disputes and debt recovery actions. It also houses the Admiralty Court and the Commercial Court. The Administrative Court is a separate division of the QBD which has jurisdiction to determine applications for judicial review, statutory appeals and actions including habeas corpus.

The Chancery Division headed by a Chancellor decides cases on business law, competition, insolvency and patent law. Within the Chancery Division are the highly specialised Chancery Chamber, Bankruptcy and Company Court and Patents Court.

The Family Division headed by a President hears family law cases, matrimonial and domestic violence cases and inheritance disputes.

---

104 S.49 CYPA 1933.
105 Under the Criminal Justice and Licensing (Scotland) Act 2010.
106 S.1 County Courts Act 1984 (CCA 1984).
107 S.15 CCA 1984.
108 S.21 CCA 1984.
109 S.77 CCA 1984.
110 Under s.4A of the High Court and County Courts Jurisdiction Order 1991/724 as amended, proceedings that include a claim for damages in respect of personal injuries may only be commenced in the High Court if the value of the claim is £50,000 or more.
111 S.1 Senior Courts Act 1981 (SCA 1981).
112 S.5(1) SCA 1981.

The Court of Appeal comprises a civil and a criminal division.[113] Appeals in civil matters from the High Court may be heard and determined by the Court of Appeal. Appeals from the Court of Appeal go to the Supreme Court, which is the highest court in the UK.

The Civil Courts in Scotland

The Sheriff Court determines civil cases as well as having a criminal jurisdiction. Scotland has 49 Sheriff Courts across six sheriffdoms.[114] There is one Sheriff Principal in charge of each sheriffdom. One sheriff sits to hear a civil case without a jury.

The procedures in the Sheriff Court are divided into small claims procedures for claims up to £3,000,[115] summary cause procedure for claims up to £5,000[116] and ordinary cause for claims valued at over £5,000. Family law cases, debt recovery and housing actions normally proceed by ordinary cause. A party who disagrees with the decision of the sheriff may appeal to the Sheriff Principal or there may be recourse to appeal to the Court of Session.[117]

Civil cases that are high value and complex actions are heard in the Court of Session. The Court of Session sits in Edinburgh and is headed by the Lord President. The court comprises an Outer House, which is a court of first instance, and an Inner House, which hears appeals from the Sheriff Court and the Outer House.[118] In the Outer House a case is decided by one Lord Ordinary, whereas three or more judges decide cases in the Inner House.

The Supreme Court

The Supreme Court was established by the Constitutional Reform Act 2005,[119] replacing the House of Lords Appellate Committee (commonly known as the House of Lords) as the final court of appeal in the UK.

The Supreme Court comprises 12 judges called Justices of the Supreme Court.[120] They are appointed by the Queen on the recommendation of the Prime Minister[121] following notification by a selection committee.[122] The Justices may only be removed from office on address of both Houses of Parliament[123] and subject to a compulsory retirement age of 70.[124]

---

113 S.3 SCA 1981.
114 The government has now approved the closure of 10 of the 49 Sheriff Courts in Scotland.
115 Small Claims (S) Order 1988.
116 S.35 Sheriff Courts (Scotland) Act 1971.
117 S.28 Sheriff Courts (Scotland) Act 1907.
118 S.2 Court of Session Act 1988.
119 S.23 (1) Constitutional Reform Act 2005 (CRA 2005).
120 S.23 (2) CRA 2005.
121 S.26 CRA 2005.
122 Schedule 9 CRA 2005.
123 S.33 CRA 2005.
124 S.26 Judicial Pensions and Retirement Act 1993.

Until 2009 when the Act came into force cases brought to the House of Lords were heard in a Committee Room in Westminster and decided by judges called Lords of Appeal in Ordinary. The court is now housed in its own building on Parliament Square in London. Although the House of Lords sitting as a court was uninfluenced by Parliament or the government, the reforms under the 2005 Act were constitutionally significant in formalising the independence of the judiciary from the executive.

As well as reforming the court, the 2005 Act redefined the role of the Lord Chancellor, who held constitutionally overlapping positions as head of the judiciary, member of the cabinet and Speaker of the House of Lords in Parliament. The Act designates the Lord Chief Justice as the head of the judiciary of England and Wales and President of the Court of England and Wales.[125]

The Supreme Court is the highest court in the UK for civil matters. It is also the highest court for England, Wales and Northern Ireland in relation to criminal matters.[126] In Scotland the High Court of Justiciary sitting as an appeal court is the highest criminal appeal court and its decisions are final.[127]

The Supreme Court decides devolution issues raised under the Scotland Act 1998 in relation to both civil and criminal matters. An example of a devolution issue in a criminal case is *Cadder* v *HMA*[128] in which the accused's conviction for assault relied in part on evidence given during interview by police without a solicitor. He lodged a devolution issue arguing that this amounted to a breach of his right to a fair trial under Article 6 ECHR. The Supreme Court applied recent case law of the European Court of Human Rights, which held that a person must have the right to legal advice before being questioned. The ruling in *Cadder* led to the enactment of the Criminal Procedure (Legal Assistance, Detention and Appeals) (Scotland) Act 2010, which provides suspects with a right of access to a solicitor during detention and questioning.[129]

The Judicial Committee of the Privy Council is the highest criminal and civil court of appeal for Commonwealth countries. It rarely hears appeals from UK courts.

EVIDENCE

The purpose of evidence in criminal and civil cases is to enable a court to reach a decision about the facts of a case. Evidence can be anything that persuades a court of the truth or probability of a fact, including oral testimonies by witnesses, expert witnesses and physical and documentary evidence. The legal representatives who act on behalf of a party will try to obtain the best evidence they can from the witnesses (Welsh, 2006: 16.43).

---

125 S.7(1) CRA 2005.
126 S.40(1)-(3) CRA 2005.
127 s.124 Criminal Procedure (Scotland) Act 1995.
128 [2010] UKSC 43.
129 Under the Scotland Act 2012 devolution issues raised in relation to Scots criminal law are to be replaced with 'compatibility issues'.

Having heard the evidence, the court will assess its reliability and credibility and determine what weight to place on it. A case will be decided once the judge has made relevant findings in fact and law.

It is a 'fundamental tenet' of the criminal law that a person is presumed innocent of a crime until proven guilty.[130] The onus of proving a person's guilt is on the prosecution and the accused is under no obligation to assist the Crown to prove its case (Sheils, 1996: 24-02.2). If the facts of the case have been proven this may raise a presumption of guilt, and if the accused is unable to provide a satisfactory explanation of the circumstances a jury or judge may find the person guilty.[131] In a few specific cases the common law and the ECHR[132] have permitted reverse burdens of proof with the onus on the accused to prove that he or she is not guilty.[133]

In Scots criminal law it is a basic requirement that there must be evidence from at least two independent sources in order to establish a person's guilt. The source of this principle is historical and is said to derive from canon (church) law and continental Europe. This rule of corroboration is not generally applicable in the criminal law of England and Wales, which has developed through the common law.[134] This requires that there is *sufficient evidence* to provide a *realistic prospect* of conviction (Richardson, 2013).

There are complex rules in civil and criminal law on the use of evidence and on the giving of evidence by expert witnesses such as social workers, which are beyond the scope of this chapter. In social work practice with children and vulnerable adults it should be noted that there are a range of special measures available to assist vulnerable witnesses in giving evidence.

There is no minimum age for a child witness,[135] although a child will not be required to give evidence if it appears to the court that he or she is unable to understand questions or to give answers that can be understood.[136]

Special measures are provided in the Youth Justice and Criminal Evidence Act 1999 to assist certain witnesses. These include screening the witness from the accused when giving evidence in court,[137] allowing the witness to give evidence by live video link,[138] and the removal of wigs and gowns by the judge and legal representatives in the courtroom.[139] The measures are intended to minimise potential distress to the witness and to ensure the witness has the opportunity of giving coherent and accurate evidence.

---

130 *M Kenzie* v *HMA* (1959) J.C. 32.

131 *HMA* v *Hardy* (1938) J.C. 144.

132 *Salabiaku* v *France* (1988) 13 EHRR 379, 388, para 28.

133 Attorney General's Reference (No. 1 of 2004), Re [2004] EWCA Crim 1025.

134 The Carloway Review into the future of Scottish Criminal Justice recommended that the requirement of corroboration should be abolished, noting it is an 'archaic rule that has no place in a modern legal system' (Carloway, 2011: 7.2.55).

135 S.53 Youth Justice and Criminal Evidence Act 1999 (YJCE 1999).

136 S.53(3) YJCE 1999.

137 S.23 YJCE 1999.

138 S.24 YJCE 1999.

139 S.26 YJCE 1999.

Witnesses who may be eligible for special measures include children under the age of 18 and persons suffering from physical or mental impairments if the court is satisfied that their age or impairment would diminish the quality of the evidence they were able to give.[140]

An adult witness may be eligible for special measures if the court considers that the quality of their evidence would be diminished through fear or distress, taking into account factors including their age, their social, cultural and ethnic background, religious and political views, any behaviour of the accused or their family toward them, and their employment.[141] The defendant is prohibited from cross-examining a witness in relation to certain sexual and other offences.[142]

A party to the proceedings who wishes to use special measures must apply to the court for a Special Measures Direction using a particular form and within a specific time limit, or the court may raise the issue.[143] If a witness is eligible for special measures the court must decide which special measures would be likely to assist that witness in giving evidence. In making a direction, the court must take into account factors including the views of the witness.[144]

Similar provisions were introduced in Scotland by the Vulnerable Witnesses (Scotland) Act 2004 which apply to children under the age of 16. The use of special measures is also available in civil cases, including Children's Hearings.

Tribunals

Tribunals are a specialist form of court. They were originally established by the Government to enable citizens to appeal against administrative decisions (Leggatt, 2000: 1.1). Tribunals have since been afforded legal recognition as part of the judiciary and are independent of the executive.[145]

There are many different types of tribunal which cover immigration and asylum, social security, mental health, special educational needs, and tax and social care. Employment Tribunals adjudicate on disputes between employee and employer, and the Land Tribunal determines disputes over land.

The key features of tribunals are that they are less formal, less expensive and less time-consuming than courts. The judges who preside over tribunals are independent and have specialist expertise in their particular field. Tribunals process a large number of cases and are designed to 'combine fairness and accessibility'[146] to enable effective access to justice.

---

140 S.16 YJCE 1999.
141 S.17 YJCE 1999.
142 S.34 and s.35 YJCE 1999.
143 S.19(1)(b) YJCE 1999.
144 S.19(3)(a) YJCE 1999.
145 S.1 Tribunals, Courts and Enforcement Act 2007 (TCE 2007).
146 Transforming Public Services: Complaints, Redress and Tribunals, July 2004, CM6423 http://webarchive.nationalarchives.gov.uk/+/http:/www.dca.gov.uk/pubs/adminjust/transformfull.pdf.

Appeals against decisions of government bodies are heard in the relevant First-Tier Tribunal,[147] which hears issues of fact and law and determines whether to allow or refuse the appeal. There is a right of appeal to the Upper Tribunal on a point of law against the decision of the First-Tier Tribunal.[148] There may be a further right to appeal to the Court of Appeal (Court of Session in Scotland).[149]

Tribunals should not be confused with Tribunals of Inquiry which are set up to investigate matters of public concern, such as the Victoria Climbié Inquiry.[150]

LEGAL PERSONNEL

Solicitors, barristers/advocates and judges are all members of the legal profession. Solicitors generally advise and assist clients in criminal and civil matters and represent clients in court. They are regulated by the Law Society of England and Wales, the Law Society of Northern Ireland and the Law Society of Scotland, and they must hold practising certificates issued by these professional bodies.

Barristers (known as advocates in Scotland) are specialist lawyers who primarily undertake advocacy in the courts and advisory work. Barristers and advocates have rights of audience (the right to appear) in the superior courts of the UK. They do not normally take instructions directly from a client but are instructed by a solicitor on behalf of a client. They are regulated by the Bar Council in England and Wales and by the Faculty of Advocates in Scotland. It is now possible for solicitors to qualify to appear in the higher courts. Highly skilled and experienced barristers or advocates may be awarded Queen's Counsel (QC), known as 'taking silk'.

Judges hold positions of power in society. In carrying out their duties they are bound to uphold high standards of conduct and maintain the principle of judicial independence. In England and Wales judges are appointed by Royal Warrant upon the recommendation of the Judicial Appointments Committee. In Scotland full-time judges are appointed by the Queen upon recommendation of the First Minister. They must swear the judicial oath or affirmation upon being appointed.

LEGAL AID

Legal aid is available from the government to assist eligible individuals to obtain legal advice who otherwise could not afford it.

Criminal legal aid covers criminal proceedings in court, appeals and other criminal matters.[151] It may be provided for individuals detained in custody for police questioning.

---

147 S.3 TCE 2007.

148 S.11 TCE 2007.

149 S.13 TCE 2007.

150 See The Victoria Climbié Inquiry Report. House of Commons Health Committee, Sixth Report of Session 2002–2003. www.publications.parliament.uk/pa/cm200203/cmselect/cmhealth/570/570.pdf (accessed 9 February 2012).

151 S.13 Legal Aid, Sentencing and Punishment of Offenders Act 2012 (LASPO 2012).

The availability of criminal legal aid is determined by the individual's financial resources and whether it is in the interests of justice.

Civil legal aid covers advice, assistance and representation in court[152] in a range of matters including the care and protection of children, vulnerable adults, mental health, welfare benefits, family homes and domestic violence, immigration, homelessness and anti-social behaviour.[153] The provision of civil legal aid to an individual is determined by certain eligibility criteria, including their financial resources, by factors such as the nature and seriousness of the particular matter, the importance to the individual of the matter, and the prospects of success.[154] Depending on a person's means, they may be required to contribute to their legal fees. There is a similar scheme in Scotland and the law has recently been amended to create a scheme for legal aid and assistance for legal representation to be provided in relation to children's hearings.[155]

Watch vodcasts 2.1 and 2.2 on the Companion Website (www.sagepub.co.uk/Social-Work) to see two social work students discuss their experience of studying law, and why they think an understanding of law assists in developing the skills required to be an effective social worker.

Reflective Questions

1 How important do you think it is for people in the UK to have recourse to the European Court of Human Rights? What do you think are the key advantages? Are there any disadvantages as far as you can determine? If so, for whom?
2 When you have been practising as a social worker – for example, on a practice placement – how conscious have you been of the law shaping the work taking place? Do you think the use of the law is more 'obvious' in certain settings? If so, why do you think that is the case?
3 How do the Data Protection Act and Freedom of Information Act impact on the social work task of recording? What are the key things you need to consider in terms of the wider issue of confidentiality?

RECOMMENDED READING

Guthrie, T. (2011) *Social Work Law in Scotland*. Haywards Heath: Bloomsbury Professional.

Johns, R. (2011) *Using the Law in Social Work*, 5th edn. Exeter: Learning Matters.

Laird, S. (2010) *Practical Social Work Law: Analysing Court Cases and Inquiries*. Harlow: Pearson.

White, C. (2004) *Northern Ireland Social Work Law*. London: Tottel. [Second edition forthcoming December 2014, Bloomsbury Professional.]

---

152 S.8 LASPO 2012.
153 Part 1, Schedule 1 LASPO 2012.
154 S.11 LASPO 2012.
155 Children's Hearings (S) Act 2011.

POLITICS AND
3 SOCIAL POLICY

Mike Maas-Lowit

Key Themes

- All citizens in a democracy are involved in politics, and you, the reader, are a citizen and a student of social work.
- Social work is a political activity. To be involved in social work is to be inescapably involved in politics.
- Politics, policy and law are tightly bound together and are major influences on what social workers do and how they do it.
- Political ideology shapes the law and policy that any given government produces.
- Understanding politics and policy gives students a framework for understanding the relationship between social policy, agency policy and practice.

INTRODUCTION

Assuming the voting habits of social work students typify those of the average citizen of the UK, and assuming that voting habits are an indicator of interest in politics, only around two-thirds of the readers of this chapter will be interested in what follows (Fisher, 2006). Pondering why so relatively few people bother to vote may lead us to conclude that some people reading this may have thought that politics has little or no relevance to their lives. On this assumption that some readers will not see what politics has to do with them, this chapter will treat you both as students of social work and as citizens in a democracy, in order to demonstrate that we are all deeply and inescapably involved in politics and that it influences and shapes us, as we shape it. Such is the inescapable hold that politics has on us that this is true, whether or not we take an active or even a passive interest in it. The chapter will highlight two strands arising from this: firstly, people who use social work services are no less citizens in a democracy than anyone else and therefore they are also recipients and shapers of politics. The chapter will examine an assumption that many people who use social work have been failed by politics. This will lead to the second theme: that social work is an activity that is highly charged with politics. It is also strongly shaped by politics. Indeed, social work would not exist at all but for the politics that has given it life.

Exercise

Do you know who your local councillor is, or your MSP, or AM, or MLA, or your MP? You do? Very good. You don't? Find out.

Two of the main ways in which social work is shaped by politics are the relationships between social work practice and law and the relationship between it and social policy. As law is the subject of another chapter, it will be glossed over here, whereas policy will be discussed latterly. An assumption of the chapter is that some readers will not know what policy is. Therefore it will be explained and contextualised in the discussion of how social work is shaped by policy and how it uses policy.

WHAT IS POLITICS?

We must begin our discussion by asking this question, but unfortunately, there is no easy answer. Leftwich (2004) suggests that there is little agreement in any given political system as to what politics actually is, let alone agreement between political systems or countries. However, Weale holds that politics is 'collective choice': a sort of trading ground in which individuals and groups with shared interests try to get that which is to their maximum benefit at minimum cost (Weale, 2004). This may mean something to you if you are already interested in politics, but it may need some contextualisation for the reader who is not.

Firstly, what is being traded? As will be discussed below, it is political power that is being traded. This collective power can be used to influence and change the world in ways that the participants think will be of worth. For example, if you and your political friends want a world in which we cause less damage to the environment by burning carbon fuels, and I and my friends want better housing for poorer families, I might trade with you, such that I lend you my support, if you will lend me yours.

This 'trading' involves compromise and sometimes involves people in the support of ideas which they do not believe in, in order to get support for their own ideas. One can see from study of organisations such as the militant sectarian organisations in Scotland and Northern Ireland, how refusal to negotiate leads to extremism and isolation in the world of politics.

Abraham Maslow (1943) proposed a hierarchy of motivation which is likely to be familiar to many students as the hierarchy of need. In it, he speaks to the universality of human need, which he ranges on a hierarchy from physiological needs for food, water and air, through needs to be loved and to feeling a sense of belonging, to higher needs to maximise our potential as human beings. We all have to find ways to have the complex range of our needs met and we do this on an uneven playing-field where some have more resources such as personal safety, money and education than others. Much of what enables some people to meet their needs more easily than others boils down to power. At least two of the resources mentioned above (education and money) are major sources of power. Politics is about the use of forms of power that enable people to negotiate in order to obtain their needs. There is a notion in this of collective strength which may combat lack of access to other sources of power. Consider one woman who lacks money and education, but who wants a fairer chance at employment opportunities in competition with men, who constitute the more powerful group in the arena of job opportunities. This single woman has little power to negotiate her needs. Two million such women have a vastly amplified negotiating power when they organise themselves to give voice to their cause.

Case Study

In 2012/13 protests by customers and consumers against companies such as Starbucks and Google forced some changes in taxation practices of these companies.

Some politics happens at a low level: for example, community councils are legally constituted collectives that represent the citizens of a given area to their local (town or county) council. Under differing legislation, they exist in Scotland, England and Wales. They exist to provide an interface between the residents of a locality and its local government. They deal with issues such as concern caused by vandalism or litter and local views on policing, schools and town planning. Their power lies in the members being able to bring a consensus view to those in power in the local government. The objective of community councils is to give local residents a collective voice in the political process of how the needs of the community are met.

Other politics happens on a larger scale. For example, at the time of writing this (the middle of June 2012), the UK government is using its leverage with those members of the European Union who use the Euro as currency to try to stabilise what is called *the Euro zone* in the light of countries in extreme financial crisis. The UK government is doing this in its own interest. The *interest* of the UK, in this context, refers to the needs of its economy and its own citizens.

Thinking about it in this way, we begin to see that, given the breadth of our needs, from those for clean water, food and personal safety to those for finding a sense of achievement and purpose through work, politics has a place in every aspect of our lives. Politics plays a part in our clean drinking water supplies and our sewage disposal and our street lighting and our policing to keep the streets safe and our education and our ownership/rental/mortgaging of our home and our transport systems which bring our food to the shops and by which we get to work or study and our legal relations, governing things as diverse as marriage and arrangements for childcare, work and pensions and health and safety. We would not want to exaggerate the case to say that politics is everything in the world, but it is difficult to think of anything with which politics does not have a relationship.

As this chapter argues, almost everything in life has a political dimension, it is difficult to discuss politics without becoming caught in a mire of complexity – that everything is political and that the politics of everything interconnects all things. If this level of complexity is accessed by discussing politics in the widest sense, we have to set parameters around the subject. Some sources define and discuss politics very narrowly, in terms of the formal politics as played out in the UK Houses of Parliament and in the devolved Scottish Parliament and the Welsh and Northern Irish Assemblies. While this is undoubtedly an important and unavoidable aspect of politics, for our purposes it misses several points:

- that we the citizens are both the end recipients of political decisions and the people who interact with those decisions, shaping and changing the politics which we receive;
- that we, readers and author of this chapter, are particularly interested in how those who receive social work services are recipients of politics and how we enter into an interactive dynamic with it;
- that social work itself is shaped by, and in turn shapes politics;
- that, to some extent, individual social work practitioners are agents of the state and, by extension, are shaped in their work by the political decisions made by their political leaders; and
- that individual practitioners have opportunity to engage in the politics that shapes them and that they can effect political change so that they are not just passive actors in the highly politicised activity of social work.

Therefore, while we will be selective in where we turn our gaze in this chapter, our focus on politics will be in the broadest sense, from top level to bottom.

We are all involved in politics and it is involved with us, whether we realise it or not.

At the outset of this chapter the claim was made that everyone of us is caught up in politics, whether he or she realises it or not. If this is true, it must mean that our actions have political consequences, whether we realise or intend them to or not. There are around 47 million people registered to vote in UK elections (Office of National Statistics, 2012a). Therefore everyone has an approximate potential 1/47,000,000th share of the say in who should get into power. If we choose not to use it, we give that share of power away to the remaining 46,999,999 people, all of whom have a little bit more power.

POLITICS AND IDEOLOGY

Before advancing the themes of this text in relation to how politics interacts with service users and with social work itself, we need to consider a couple of issues in relation to ideology: we need to identify what ideology means in respect of politics and then we need to look briefly at the ideology of welfare and its recent history. In this way we can understand the political strands from which social work itself has emerged. In this way we may even begin to identify the direction in which that ever-changing activity called social work appears to be heading, as those charged with decision-making powers in politics shape its future.

Ideology assumes that no purposeful action is possible unless it has an idea, a vision or some broader-based intention behind it. In terms of political ideology, think back to our original definition of politics as collective choice (Weale, 2004). The word *collective* is an important one in politics. One of the essential ingredients that makes things political is that they are arrived at collectively. Therefore, if ideology is the set of ideas or the underpinning philosophy behind a course of action, political ideology is a set of ideas that binds a group of people together in common goals. As Schwartzmantel says: 'One cannot understand political activity without understanding the ideas and visions that have moved people to political action' (2008: 3–4). More importantly for social work, one cannot understand the influences of politics upon social work without understanding the ideologies of the dominant political forces of the time.

Some ideologies come in easily identified packages. This was the case with the traditional ideologies of the left and right of politics. On the assumption that not all readers will understand what is meant by left and right in this context, it is important to attempt to say a little on this complicated subject: it speaks to a notion that political ideologies can be mapped on a continuum from left to right, with the opposing ends representing extremes, perhaps most strongly characterised in history by radical socialism such as gave momentum to the communist revolutions of the twentieth century on the left, and the fascism of Hitler and Mussolini on the right.

While many would identify the extreme politics of the British National Party (BNP) with its ideas about immigration watering down the purity of the indigenous white population, as being extremely right wing, the extremes of this continuum are marginalised in modern British politics, with an increasing tendency towards the centre of the spectrum. Most simply understood, in the UK the traditional left of politics was characterised by old Labour (left wing/socialist principles) and the old Conservative party was motivated by a right-wing ideology. If, as yet, this is unclear to you, keep reading and an explanation will emerge.

The notion of a mass working class which is oppressed by a society of factory owners has less relevance today than it had for the left wing of politics 100 years ago. Similarly, the idea of a wealthy upper class, which has the education and resources to manage the country's wealth and holds a tradition that gives them a responsibility to do so, may seem of less relevance now than it did for the traditional right. (However, criticism that the Conservative party of David Cameron is characterised by 'posh boys' [*The Guardian*, 2012] may yet invalidate this statement.) It is not that power and wealth have ceased to exist or that the oppression that causes poverty is a thing of the past which is making these ideologies obsolete. It is simply that society has become more fragmented in recent decades and this causes many commentators, such as Schwartzmantel (2008) and Brown (2010), to suggest that the old left and right have at best become blurred. These ideologies became more blurred in the post-Thatcher years of New Labour, as Tony Blair's speech to the 2001 Labour Party Conference indicated:

> Our values are the right ones for this age: the power of community, solidarity, the collective ability to further the individual's interests. People ask me if I think ideology is dead. My answer is: In the sense of rigid forms of economic and social theory, yes.

The twentieth century killed those ideologies and their passing causes little regret. But, in the sense of a governing idea in politics, based on values, no. The governing idea of modern social democracy is community. Founded on the principles of social justice. That people should rise according to merit not birth; that the test of any decent society is not the contentment of the wealthy and strong, but the commitment to the poor and weak.

POLITICS AND THE IDEOLOGIES OF WELFARE

Brown (2010) indicates the central importance of ideology for social work, in his discussion of welfare capitalism, the left wing tradition out of which the Welfare State was created after the Second World War. Social work as we know it emerged from this political movement which harnessed the wealth-generating potential of industrial capitalism and turned it away from individual profit for the wealthy and towards a collective benefit that could fund a National Health Service, state provision of education for all and a framework of financial support for those who need it, through state pensions and welfare benefits.

Brown goes on to examine the influence of Hayek (1960) upon the politics of Margaret Thatcher in the 1980s. The notion was that mass provision of state-owned welfare is limiting to individual choice and freedom, much as choice would be limited were the government to allow for the production of only one sort of shoe for people to wear. Instead of competition driving the production of a diverse range of footwear from the most fashionable to the most practical, everybody would have to wear one style of shoe, which might broadly meet everyone's needs but would not allow for diversity, taste, preference and the specific needs of the individual. Thatcher would argue that the state was imposing such a restriction upon the public, not in terms of footwear, but in terms of needs for health care, education etc. A lingering side-effect of this situation can be seen in the current preoccupation with what Norman Tebbit (2010) ungraciously referred to as 'the welfare junky'. The term speaks to the idea that state welfare erodes individual freedom to the extent of making people dependent upon a self-limiting expectation that the state will give them a living without having to work or take any responsibility.

Exercise

To examine the various perspectives, you should compare the coverage of a variety of newspapers on current issues. *The Guardian* has traditionally represented left-of-centre views, *TheIndependent* may attempt to be balanced and the *DailyMail* may represent right-of-centre views.

Therefore, Thatcher sought to reduce state welfare provision by encouraging a private economy of welfare – private health care, expanded private education, private ownership of what were once council houses and so on.

Into this erosion of the welfare state, Blair (1998) introduced what he called 'the Third Way' in the 1990s. This was an attempt to preserve some aspects of state welfare, less as a never-ending sticking plaster upon the wounds of poverty and disadvantage and more as a focus upon tackling their root causes. The idea was that, by the Third Way, people would become less dependent upon welfare, as they became included within the mainstream of society and economic productivity. *Social inclusion* is at the heart of the Third Way.

This brings us up to the present moment in politics, in which David Cameron's 'Big Society' is a step beyond social inclusion to a sort of world in which people participate rather than become included. The success is yet to be seen of ventures such as 'welfare to work' (which aspire to get people away from welfare dependency) and NHS reforms (which seek to devolve big healthcare budgets from managers to doctors). However, in all of the ideological rhetoric of the moment, there is a sense that a model of social work which is too preoccupied with pure welfare provision is a social work that is out of step with the times. Below, we will discuss the shrinking of social work services and the social care sector. Some of this is done under the mantle of economic necessity – if there is no more money in the pot to pay for welfare, we have to reduce services. What is less clear is whether or not this is an opportunity for the politics of Cameron to steer the country towards ideological goals of shrinking welfare and maximising private enterprise.

Now you have read about ideology and politics you should undertake an activity on the Companion Website (www.sagepub.co.uk/SocialWork) which asks you to research core political values and beliefs.

POLITICS AND THE PEOPLE WHO USE SOCIAL WORK

Elsewhere in this book and in your broader studies, you may be aware of a central preoccupation of social work in relation to the oppression and discrimination of the people who use social work services; see, for example, Thompson (2003b, 2005). If politics is about the collective negotiation between groups who share a need, an interest or vision about how the world should be, and ideology is the underpinning set of beliefs about that world, could it be that the disparate and vulnerable collection of people who use social work lack the attributes that allow them to motivate, organise and marshal themselves to political action?

Evidence for this generalisation would be that those who collectively organise their case on the political stage do not usually remain oppressed and disadvantaged.

Case Study

The position of women, who have slowly moved from not even having the vote in 1918, through the Suffragette movement, to feminism, is still far from perfect in its equality with men, but it is vastly improved from the level of oppression they faced a hundred years ago. The improvements have been made by collective political action, which continues in the 2013 debate on attitudes to women expressed in social media.

It might be argued that the improvement of women's lot is not equally distributed across the group of all women in the UK. It might be further argued that those women who remain relatively oppressed and disadvantaged are those women who are more likely to have to fall back upon the support of social work. It may therefore be the case that the experience of oppression is one that fragments and disorganises people in modern society, such that they are less likely to be able to achieve the sort of unity necessary for political success.

If this is the case, could it be that one defining characteristic of social work is that it deals with the casualties of politics or with those whom politics has failed? Put in this way, need you ask any further what politics has to do with social work? The only question that remains is: To what extent can social work become a tool in redressing the failure of politics? Adams et al. suggest:

> critical theory proposes that when we say social work is concerned with action, acting within the interpersonal situations is always part of a wider action concerned with broader social forms. Such action is always political in the sense that interpersonal action always has an impact on the interaction of wider groups in society. (Adams et al., 2002: 9–10)

This suggests that your practice is always political.

To illustrate how politics and policy are relevant right across the life-course of service users see the journal articles by Spratt (2011) and Foster (2011) which are available on the Companion Website (www.sagepub.co.uk/SocialWork).

A BRIEF WORD ABOUT THE STRUCTURES OF POLITICS IN THE UK

The situation in the UK in relation to the formal structures of government is very complicated. It is less of a thing specifically designed for its purpose as it is a thing that has grown and developed over the past 800 years. We will undertake the minimum necessary explanation of its institutions here before directing you to a basic reader in the Recommended Reading section of this chapter (Jones and Norton, 2010).

There is a central government for the UK, located in the Palace of Westminster in London. It is headed by the prime minister and the ministers of government, representing the majority party/parties in power. At time of writing, since no one party won an overall majority of seats in Parliament at the last general election (in 2010), the government is a coalition of the Conservative party (which has the largest number of seats) and its Liberal Democrat partner. The Westminster government manages a core set of powers for all of the UK. Examples of these are:

- Defence
- Pensions and welfare benefits
- Border control
- Regulation of drugs
- Relationships with other countries.

Westminster also makes key decisions for all of England in relation to many other matters such as:

- Health
- Education
- Housing
- Transport
- Environment
- Justice

The other three countries within the UK have different relationships with the Westminster government, as follows:

- Scotland, which has the greatest amount of power devolved to it, has a separate Parliament in Edinburgh. It has specific law-making powers in relation to matters amongst which those listed above (health to justice) are examples. Scotland is also in the process of making a law to give itself limited tax-raising powers.
- Northern Ireland and Wales have separate Assemblies. Both manage the same range of powers but the Northern Irish Assembly can make only what is called *secondary legislation*. In other words, it can pass laws, but only with permission from Westminster. These laws are usually called *orders*.
- The Welsh Assembly has no law-making powers at the moment but is seeking to change this. Therefore, while the Welsh Assembly can make decisions about how it manages matters like health and education, it is dependent upon the same laws as England to do so.

It is worth taking note that some of the powers devolved to these three countries are those most important to social work. Therefore social work in the four countries of the UK has very different sets of laws and very different characteristics.

There is yet another tier of government in the UK. This is local government. Since it differs greatly depending on where you live, we will say only the most general things about it. Local government is of key importance because it manages the local services in any given town, county, city or borough. These services range from bin collection and street lighting to local social services/social work services (Northern Ireland excepted, where social work is linked with health into five Health and Social Care Trusts) and education. Most of what we call statutory social work is run by local government.

One last consideration before we depart from the structures of politics in the UK: at the outset we might well have warned you that the most difficult thing in writing about politics is that, just when you have neatly described how it is, it all changes. A new event in the world or a budget or a law can radically alter the landscape so as to make all this obsolete. In this case, particularly in England, local government is being forced to contemplate major changes to what it does and how it does it. These changes are being imposed by financial restrictions from reduced funds from Westminster, in the Coalition government's response to the financial situation in the UK. Many councils are thinking about drastically axing their services, social work amongst them. Barnet

Council has been dubbed 'Easy Council' (Public Service.co.uk, 2009) for its approach, which could be likened to easyJet's famous no-frills approach to air transport. The idea is that the council becomes little more than a broker and that it farms out all its services to private companies, presumably to the cheapest bidder.

HOW DOES POLITICS SHAPE SOCIAL WORK?

In large part we have answered the above question in the previous discussion about 'Easy Council'. It is the sweep of politics, from central to local government, which is changing the face of social work across the land. Not every local government will adopt the Easy Council approach to its service. Some will make attempts to resist change, but when central government tightens the purse-strings, there is little option than to find a solution through change.

This change does not just involve the structure of social work services and the relationship between who runs them and government. It devolves down to what social workers actually do and how they do it. Margaret Thatcher famously said 'Economics are the method; the object is to change the heart and soul' (*Sunday Times*, 1981). It is perhaps an exaggerated claim, but it speaks to the way that, like it or not, politics gets inside us, inside our personal and professional beings, and alters our thinking and behaviour.

For example, to revert to Thatcher's heyday, in 1984 Strathclyde Council used its legal powers of disbursing money and assistance under section 12 of the Social Work (Scotland) Act 1968 to provide cash for the families of striking miners until this was seen as a political means of prolonging a strike that was effectively a duel to the death between the miners and the Thatcher government (Brodie et al., 2008). Social work was the instrument of this power to hand out cash. Today such a thing would be unthinkable, when many local government social work services are moving in the opposite direction, changing the criteria upon which assessment of need is made, so as to take services away from people who were, until recently, deemed in need of them. One day you are a social worker with a cheque book, writing cheques to miners' families, and the next you are a social worker explaining to someone with mental health problems why they no longer are thought to be in need of support.

Critical Thinking

Reflect on your attitudes, the attitudes of your family and those of people you know. What do you and they feel about what is happening in their lives and in their area? Do they have strong views? To what extent are people questioning what is happening and taking any form of action? What has influenced their action or non-action?

WHAT IS POLICY?

Our final word in relation to politics is given to describing policy as the link between politics and practice. Policy is the means by which politicians turn their ideas into action. For example, at the time of writing, the Coalition government was attempting to change the way that the NHS is funded and managed. This would have remained an idea for empty discussion had they been unable to turn it into a plan of action. The Coalition government did implement this measure in 2013. Therefore, policy has two related meanings: it is the plans that governments make and it is the set of directives that governments pass on to the relevant agencies in order to make things work.

We might say that policy is at the opposite end of the range of activity of governments from ideology: if ideology is the philosophy that informs the nature of the changes a government hopes to affect upon the world, policy is the negotiated set of plans for action to affect change. From this, there are two things to observe.

Firstly, many things go into the process of policy-making which will water down the ideological principles of the government. There is no use in trying to make an ideal policy if it is not going to work. Therefore, policy will be limited by a realistic idea of what is achievable in the vastly complicated process of turning ideas into action in a fast-moving and all-together unpredictable world.

Secondly, the range of things government has to act upon is vast. We have already discussed the range, from bin-collection and waste disposal to policing no-fly zones in unstable foreign countries; from improving the survival of cancer patients to planning for the future of our energy needs in the next 50 years, in the face of climate change and shrinking oil supply. Parliament, which debates issues, the people in power and the civil service they employ to turn policy into action will always lack the specific and detailed technical knowledge on this range. Therefore policy will always need to be informed by expert advisers and by lobby groups who criticise what the government is doing or how it is doing it.

This brings us home to the specific slice of policy that is to do with social work. We really should say 'the specific *slices* of policy that are to do with social work', since it is not just direct policies – such as the changes to social work training, education and organisation in England following the Laming report into the death of Peter Connelly (Baby P) – which affect social work (Lord Laming, 2009). The proposed policy to make changes to the NHS in England and Wales will have implications for social work, as will the policies that will pass on reductions in funding of public services to local government.

If, as we concluded in the foregoing section on *politics and the people who use social work*, all social work activity has a political edge to it, the involvement of social work in politics goes deeper still. Policy is the way in which politicians shape what social workers do and think.

CONCLUSION

In this chapter we have ranged widely over the subject of politics. We have defined it as collective action that seeks to meet the shared needs of a group of individuals through negotiation with others. We have refined this definition by placing it within the formal political structures of UK government, devolved governments in Wales, Scotland and Northern Ireland and in local government across the UK. We have examined how politicians and those who are actively politically involved use ideology as their guiding philosophy. We have seen how those in power use policy to try to achieve their aims.

Specifically, in relation to social work, we have suggested that it is a deeply and inescapably political activity, in that it serves the casualties of politics, those whom politics has failed, and in that social work is invariably shaped by the political desires of those in power through policy.

We have left you with the unanswered question of what you intend to do in relation to your awareness of the fact that you are entering into a profession so deeply political.

Watch vodcast 3.1 on the Companion Website (www.sagepub.co.uk/SocialWork) to see a social work student discuss his experiences of studying social policy and politics, and why he thinks an understanding of politics and its influence on social policy assists in developing the skills required to be an effective social worker.

Reflective Questions

1   A key point of this chapter is to highlight how all aspects of life, whether we realise it or not, are affected and shaped by politics and the ideologies of political parties. In what ways do you think that social work is itself political and how do you think that social work practice is shaped by politics?

2   As with politics, social policy exerts a powerful force in our daily lives. Reflect on your own life and attempt to identify ways in which social policy has made a negative or positive difference to your life. Remember that social policy covers a wide range of services and institutions: health, education, welfare, housing and so on.

3   The various nations or regions of the United Kingdom are becoming increasingly devolved, with separate powers and law-making capacities existing in each of the devolved governments or assemblies. Outline the differences between two of the main regions, Scotland, England and Wales and Northern Ireland. In what ways are they different and in what ways are they similar? Are there any useful lessons or examples of better practice that can be identified on doing such a cross-border comparison?

RECOMMENDED READING

Alcock, P. (2008) *Social Policy in Britain*. Basingstoke: Palgrave Macmillan.

Cunningham, J. and Cunningham, S. (2012) *Social Policy and Social Work: An Introduction*. London: Sage.

Jones, B. and Norton, P. (2010) *Politics UK*. London: Longman.

We also advise you that there is no substitute for regular reading of a quality newspaper such as *The Guardian* or *The Independent*. We say this because, if you wish to understand the ever-changing face of politics, the only way is by observing it in practice. By the time you read the words written in this chapter, politics will have moved on from what it was at that time. Only by reading about politics in action will you be able to track that difference.

You can also access some useful social policy and organisational links by visiting the Companion Website (www.sagepub.co.uk/SocialWork).

4 SOCIOLOGY

Megan Todd and Chris Yuill

Key Themes

- The important contribution that sociology can make to effective social work practice.
- The benefits of the sociological imagination.
- To understand people we need to understand their social context.
- The influence that social structure can exert in shaping and conditioning service user's lives.
- How social theory can assist in understanding society.

INTRODUCTION

Sociology offers important knowledge and understanding in relation to the practice of social work. As a social science it can assist in making sense and understanding a complex and changing world, which, while creating improvements in the day-to-day lives of people, also leaves many other people vulnerable or marginalised. Sociology does so by providing insights into the various social structures, such as class, gender and ethnicity, which, in a variety of often subtle and unseen ways, condition and influence the lives of people in society and form the deeper contexts of service users' lives. What becomes evident from sociological research is just how much of people's actions or choices are, in many respects, beyond their control and are instead framed by various social norms and values.

Using sociological theory and critical thinking, social workers can explore and understand social processes such as inequality, racism and sexism which help to shape the lives and life chances of service users. Having awareness of such processes is useful, if not essential, as it provides a wider perspective of the issues that surround a service user rather than simply taking an individual approach.

This chapter begins by defining what sociology is and the importance of the role that social structure plays in influencing people's lives. It explores the three main social structures of ethnicity, class and gender in greater depth, before providing a summary of the main sociological theories. The chapter ends with a brief discussion of the practical applications of sociology to social work.

WHAT IS SOCIOLOGY?

It can be difficult to outline a simple all-encompassing definition of sociology. Giddens (1989) provides a useful starting point, suggesting that sociology is the 'study of human social life, groups and societies'. How people's lives are crucially enmeshed and influenced by the society in which they live forms the bedrock of sociological thinking. In trying to understand why people do what they do a sociologist would primarily refer to the social context in which that person exists, not individual psychology, and how that social context helps and hinders the choices that individuals can make in their life.

In effect sociology asks us to think differently about ourselves, requiring us to reflect on our and others' relationships with the society in which we live. A useful technique termed the sociological imagination can assist us in thinking more sociologically about society, and this is considered next.

The Sociological Imagination

Developing a sociological imagination is one of the most useful ways that sociology can assist social workers in deepening and making their practice more effective. The sociological imagination invites us to think differently about the society in which we live by encouraging us to adopt a perspective that delves beneath the surface of everyday layers of life in order to try to capture and explore what processes create, maintain and shape our lives. At one level the sociological imagination encourages objective as opposed to subjective thinking, where we put aside our own thoughts and experiences and look at society from a more neutral perspective.

One aspect of life that the sociological imagination is particularly useful in highlighting is the relationship between what the concept's originator Charles Wright Mills (1959) termed 'private troubles' and 'public issues'. Here the relationships between seemingly separate domains become visible and connected. The predicament of an individual is no longer just their bad luck or exceptional circumstance but becomes explicable in context and as part of a wider trend in society.

Case Study

Someone may become unemployed, which is a private trouble as the individual's financial situation becomes difficult and problems associated with unemployment arise. That individual's experience of unemployment is, however, not unique but actually part of a wider trend in society and the economy, where many people are losing their jobs.

The relevance for social work is that the sociological imagination allows for the deeper and wider aspects of service users' lives to be brought to the fore allowing for greater depth of understanding as to why someone has become a service user and in assessing the challenges that they may face in bringing about meaningful change in their life.

> ## Exercise
>
> The sociological imagination is a method of thinking about the world in a different way, to see commonplace occurrences and ways of being in a different and more analytical light. Identify some commonly held assumptions about society (this could be crime, immigration, or poverty, for example) and try to think about them in a different way. The main point to think about is how much of what you have chosen to think about is explicable by reference to the choices made by an individual and how much can be explained by looking at the wider social context in which people exist.

THE INFLUENCE AND POWER OF SOCIAL STRUCTURE

The focus now turns to the three main structures that exist in society: class, gender and ethnicity. When the concept of structure is used in sociology it is not referring to a physical structure, such as a table or a building, but rather a particular arrangement of social practices and power relations that exist between people that can exert considerable influence over their lives. These particular structures often operate without people being aware of their existence as they are experienced as being part of the normal texture of everyday life; for example, marriage replicates the social structure of gender reactions.

So how do social structures influence people? Firstly, care needs to be taken here not to lapse into what is termed 'determinism'. A major mistake to make is to think that social structures exert a monolithic power that cannot be resisted or modified, and that people are just mindless robots who willingly do the bidding of society to some pre-designed plan. That particular approach to understanding structure can be referred to as determinism or deterministic and it is one that should be avoided. The effects that social structures exercise on people are much more complex and in many respects far more subtle.

> ## Exercise
>
> The following sections deal with different forms of inequality in society: class, gender and ethnicity. After you have read each one try to identify and discuss examples, whether from your own life, in the media or from the experiences of people with whom you have worked, where those inequalities have made a negative impact on the lives of people in wider society.

Thompson's (1997) Personal, Cultural and Structural (PCS) model of **discrimination** and **prejudice** provides two useful insights. First, it can inform us how the lives of

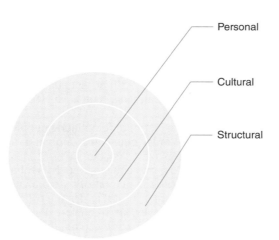

Personal

Cultural

Structural

Figure 4.1 Thompson's PCS model

people are influenced and conditioned by social structures and secondly how sociology can contribute to effective social work practice.

Thompson's three-part model identifies how discrimination comes into being and operates in society. It is important to note that this is an *interactive model*, with each element of the model influencing and shaping the next and *not* three separate disconnected units. The main message that Thompson conveys in his PCS model is best summarised by borrowing an observation made by Labriola ([1918] 2005: 55), that 'Ideas do not fall from heaven and nothing comes to us in a dream'. What is meant here is that the ideas people hold are not their sole unique or personal invention, and that those ideas have their basis in origin somewhere *external* to the individual. For Thompson, the prejudicial ideas of people are the individual expressions of long-standing ideas that have developed over time with their origins in specific historical events. These ideas have become embedded within social structures that allow for the cultural transmission and persistence of that prejudicial idea.

Case Study

So why does racism exist in society and why are some people racist? For a start, racism is not a phenomenon that is solely located in people's minds as an idea that some people for some reason hold. Rather it is an idea that already exists in society and popular culture (the structural and cultural levels of the PCS model) that people adopt and begin to incorporate into their daily lives and self-identity. Racism is a pre-existing set of beliefs but how does racism became part of a social structure?

A social–historical perspective is both useful and necessary here. It may seem reasonable to assume that people have always been racist and that racism is a

(Continued)

(Continued)

'natural' aspect of being human. By taking a historical perspective, that particular reason can be dismissed. As Bauman (1989) notes, humans have always been to some extent **heterophobic**, which means that they have always been wary or afraid of strangers.

Using skin colour as a means not just of differentiating people but also of placing them in some form of hierarchical order emerges at a point in time when European countries were beginning to develop overseas colonial territories, the prime purpose being the founding of plantations to grow cash crops such as tobacco and sugar. The main sources of labour used to work the plantations were black slaves captured in Africa. The slaving system was extremely brutal and some estimates put the number of black Africans who died during slavery at 14 million. While the barbarity of the slavery-plantation system was abhorred by some, plantation owners and merchants who benefited from the plantations began to develop ideas and theories that justified the exploitation of black slaves. The ideas and theories that they developed claimed that slavery was justifiable on the grounds that black people were culturally inferior, of lower intelligence and only suited to certain forms of punishing hard labour (Blackburn, 2010). In turn these flawed and unscientific ideas and theories become part of everyday life and everyday culture.

It is also important to note that just because a prejudice is present on a structural level (such as the example of racism discussed above) it does not automatically follow that every part of the culture is imbued with racism or every person racist. Following such a direct mapping and rigid chain of events means denying people's agency and ability to think things through for themselves. Rather what we should understand here is that the structural conditions outline the terrain.

Class

An understanding of class is vital for effective social work practice, as the way that class shapes service users' lives is one of the central reasons to why people become users of social work services. The various chances we have in life are very much shaped by the class into which we are born and in which we live our lives as adults. Sometimes the effect that class exerts on people's lives is positive and other times it is negative.

Education provides an example of how class can mould and direct people's lives. The various class facts and figures presented in Figure 4.2 provide examples of how class can influence our lives. The first graph presents information that displays the school background of the people in some of the most powerful professions and positions in the United Kingdom. What is notable here is that the percentage of people who are from independent fee-paying schools represented in each profession is very high, particularly judges and those in the legal professions. There are other professions, such as medical professionals and journalists, where it appears to be more equal. Where the power of class becomes evident is that the independent school sector comprises only 6% of the whole British education system. What the data represented in the graph mean is that if someone can attend an independent fee-paying school then they have a disproportionate chance of accessing some of the top echelons of British society.

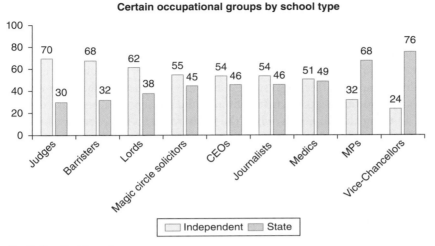

Certain occupational groups by school type

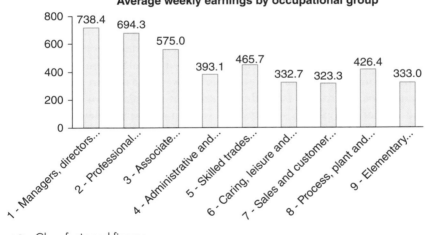

Source: The Sutton Trust (2009)

Average weekly earnings by occupational group

Figure 4.2   Class facts and figures

Source: Annual Survey of Hours and Earnings (ONS, 2012b)

To explain how class is defined in contemporary society, sociology draws on Bourdieu's cultural capital theory (Bourdieu, 1984). Central to the cultural capital theory is the idea that, as society is now defined by consumerism, it is consumption patterns that now allow access to social groups. Using this approach, access or denial to cultural capital is defined through the traditional structures of social class inequalities. However, some cultural capitals are more equal than others. Much in British society is arguably controlled by middle-class cultural-capital, which dominates other social class cultural-capitals. It is a process whereby middle-class children learn their class capital through interaction with their parents, peers and the education system. This capital is transformed into what might be termed symbolic capital, which is traded within society. As Lawler (2008: 129) suggests, 'it is only when cultural capital is sufficiently legitimated [that] it can be converted into symbolic capital'. These individuals, it is argued, have the power of middle class membership, with the ability to include or exclude other class cultural-capitals. This suggests that because of structural factors within society, social class identities are constructed through the concept of a person's cultural background. In using this approach, when the study refers to the concept of middle-class and working-class individuals it is not just referring to their employment roles but to their cultural background.

Gender

As with so many other areas of study, there is no one definitive explanation of gender. A useful definition of gender to get us started is, however, offered by Wharton, who suggests that gender is 'a system of social practices', one that 'creates and maintains gender distinctions and it organises relations of inequality on the basis of these distinctions' (Wharton, 2005: 7). Viewing gender in this way moves away from understanding it as biologically driven and acknowledges that gender creates both differences and inequalities. Such an understanding also conceptualises gender as a process rather than fixed or static, in other words gender is something that we 'do'. We can also begin to understand the ways in which gender is not simply experienced at the individual level and occurs at all levels of our social structure. For instance (see Figure 4.3), women still generally receive lower wages than men and have less access to top positions. There are also different expectations placed on the domestic roles men and women will play in society, with women on average devoting more time to household chores than men.

Feminists use the concept of 'patriarchy', which refers to the social system whereby men as a group have power over women as a group, to explain women's subordinate position in society. Walby (1990) argued that patriarchy operates at six levels: paid work, the private sphere, culture, sexuality, violence and the state. For example, many feminists have pointed to the fact that heterosexual women, as a group, are more likely than men to be abused by a current or ex-partner. While the situation for women has shifted significantly, many women now have access to better education and employment. Walby (1997) argues, however, that this does not mean that patriarchy has disappeared; it has simply changed in form.

Although many people now believe that men and women are equal, a closer investigation indicates that many societies are still organised in such a way as to benefit men, perhaps at the expense of women. For example, the global economic crisis which began in 2008 has resulted in a disproportionate burden on women. Cuts in the public sector, where women account for almost two-thirds of the workforce, have had a disproportionate affect on women (Sands, 2012).

Some gender facts and figures are given in Figure 4.3.

For a discussion of issues around workplace gender inequality see the article by Williams (2013) on the Companion Website (www.sagepub.co.uk/SocialWork).

Occupations by gender

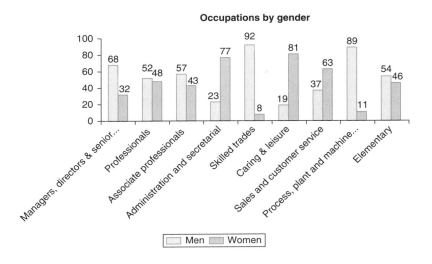

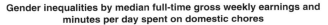

Gender inequalities by median full-time gross weekly earnings and minutes per day spent on domestic chores

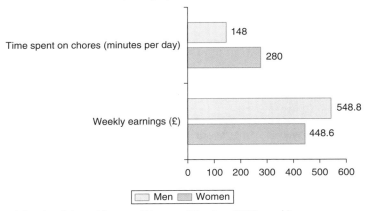

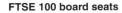

Sources: Kan et al. (2011) and *Annual Survey of Hours and Earnings* (ONS, 2012b)

FTSE 100 board seats

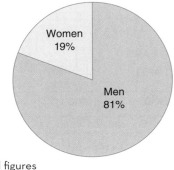

Figure 4.3   Gender facts and figures

Source: Professional Boards Forum BoardWatch (2012)

Ethnicity

The United Kingdom as a whole is becoming increasingly multicultural. The ethnicity facts and figures in Figure 4.4a–d indicate that England now has an ethnic population of nearly 20%. As Vertovec (2007) notes, we should understand the current levels of ethnic population as being an example of 'super-diversity', a concept that refers to the rich and complex dynamic set of relationships between all ethnic groups. One point on this note of complexity is that nearly a third of the ethnic minority population comprises of people who are white (mainly of a Eastern European origin).

Racism is one of the processes that influences and conditions the lives of people from ethnic minority groups. In the earlier section on Thompson's PCS theory we explored how racism is not a natural part of people's lives. People are perhaps heterophobic in that they display a fear or dislike of that which is different from themselves, but the concept of people disliking other fellow humans on the grounds of racial difference is socially constructed and of relatively recently historical origin. Just because we can explain that there is nothing

(a)

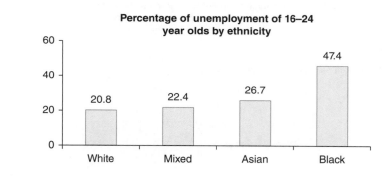

Source: Labour Force Survey (ONS, 2012c)

(b)

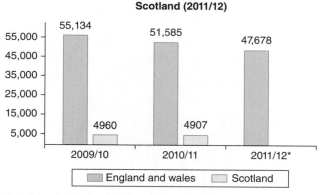

*2011/12 statistics not available for Scotland at time of press.

Sources: Scottish Government's Statistical Bulletin, Crime and Justice Series (Scottish Government, 2012)

Fig 4.4 cont.

(c)

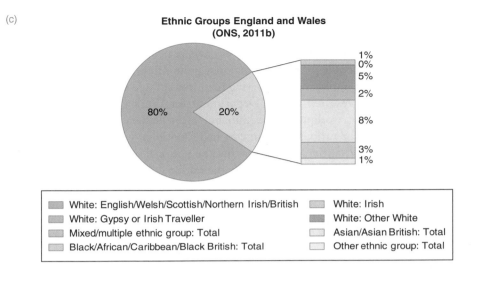

**Ethnic Groups England and Wales
(ONS, 2011b)**

(d)

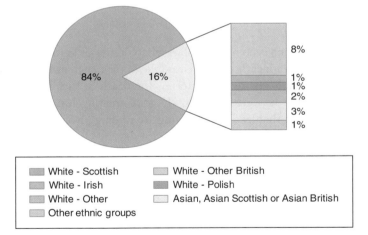

**Ethnic Composition of Scotland, 2011
(National Records for Scotland, 2013)**

Figure 4.4   Ethnicity facts and figures

natural about racism and that it is a social construction does not, however, remove the fact that for many people from ethnic-minority groups racism exerts a very real and present challenge. Racism exists in many different forms:

Prejudice – People can hold negative or false ideas about people with different ethnic identities, often lapsing into false stereotypes or negative caricatures. This form of racism is most likely to be experienced on a one-to-one basis, for example name-calling on the street or in violent behaviour. The graph in Figure 4.4 illustrates that while the number of racist incidents is declining in recent years, the rate is still quite high.

Discrimination – Following on from prejudice, discrimination refers to when people are prevented from accessing resources or opportunities because of their ethnic identity. An obvious example can be found in employment, where people from ethnic minorities may find it harder than people from ethnic majority groups in finding employment. Figure 4.4 indicates high unemployment for young men from ethnic minority backgrounds, and recent government research by the Department for Work and Pensions (Wood, 2010) found evidence of workplace discrimination. Researchers there sent out three identical CVs to apply for various jobs but one had a notional white name, one Asian and the third African. What they found was that the notional white candidate received a positive response after nine applications while the notional Asian or African candidate had to send off 16 applications before receiving a positive response.

Institutional racism – The public inquiry into the police handling of the murder of black student Stephen Lawrence in 1997 identified serious shortcomings in the workings of the Metropolitan Police. Sir William Macpherson, the chair of the inquiry, found that the police were guilty of institutional racism, which he defined as follows:

> The collective failure of an organisation to provide an appropriate and professional service to people because of their colour, culture, or ethnic origin. It can be seen or detected in processes, attitudes and behaviour which amount to discrimination through unwitting prejudice, ignorance, thoughtlessness and racist stereotyping which disadvantage minority ethnic people.

It is not only organisations such as the police where issues of institutional racism have been raised. There is also concern that other public bodies, such as the National Health Service, potentially exhibit institutional racism. The death of psychiatric patient David 'Rocky' Bennett in 1998 was attributed to the staff treating him in a degrading and overly aggressive manner that lead to him dying after being physically restrained by five member of the nursing staff for 25 minutes.

Having now read about issues in relation to class, gender and ethnicity read the article on the Companion Website (www.sagepub.co.uk/SocialWork) by Walby et al. (2012) discussing intersectionality and the challenges of addressing multiple inequalities.

SOCIAL THEORY

An important aspect of sociology is the use of social theory. Care needs to be taken not to confuse the way in which sociologists use the concept of theory. In everyday life, theory or being theoretical is often used to denote an idea that is more speculative than real or an idea that will never actually be real. In sociology the concept of theory refers to bodies of ideas that help make sense of the mass of data, statistics and research that exists. We have already encountered examples of the use of social theory in this chapter. In the section on gender, for instance, we discussed how one could explain the various inequalities that exist between men and women by using the feminist theory of patriarchy. Feminism is just one of the many families of theories that sociologists regularly deploy in their work. The other main theories are summarized and outlined below.

Karl Marx

Marx, perhaps the most famous of the founding figures of sociology, was not a sociologist in any formal sense, but his work has made a considerable contribution to sociology. In particular, he wanted to understand why it was that capitalism organised society into two antagonistic classes: the owners (the bourgeoisie) of the means of production – such as factories – used, or exploited, the labour of the workers (the proletariat) in order to make a profit. These owners of capital became the new ruling class, who paid workers a wage in return for their labour, but one small enough to enable the bourgeoisie to make a profit. The two classes were seen as 'two great warring and hostile camps' (Marx and Engels, 1848: 49), thus society operates mainly through class conflict. The new elite were a minority, and part of Marx's work was an attempt to understand why such a small minority were able to exploit the majority. In part, he argued, this was due to discursive tactics that make this division seem a natural state. Periods of social stability and peace benefit the rich and powerful. The success of capitalism, he argued, would also be its downfall. As capitalists maximise profit – by reducing wages for example – workers would increasingly feel a sense of degradation and alienation. Alongside periods of economic growth and prosperity would come moments of socioeconomic crises. Only once the workers have experienced solidarity and collective action will they achieve a class consciousness. He believed that the proletariat would become political agents in order to preserve their human dignity. As a result of living, working and socialising together, their dissatisfaction manifests as a unified working-class consciousness, whereby they identify the capitalist system as the source of their discontent, which would perhaps result in attacks on the means of production, the formation of unions and political parties. Thus, social change occurs as a result of class conflict. According to Marx's critical structuralist approach, societies, social bodies and institutions, and social relations within them, are fundamentally a product of the economic system. Marx also had the foresight to predict that the nature of the social class system would shift as capitalism progressed. Many have argued that much of Marx's arguments still have much relevance for today. For example, his predictions about globalisation, insatiable capitalism and the instability of international finance have, arguably, proved to be true (Eagleton, 2011).

Émile Durkheim

Durkheim is considered to be one of the most influential of sociology's forebears. He hoped that sociology would prove to be a vehicle for a reformed liberal France and saw society based on a variety of social institutions, the most basic of which is the family. Social institutions are, in simple terms, a group of people organised for a specific purpose. As society develops and becomes more complicated, so does the complexity of its social institutions. Durkheim argued that societal institutions were organised around economics, politics, worship, culture and community, and that they operate in a way comparable to a biological organism, each one working for the benefit of the whole of society, just as various organs in the body rely on one another. This particular way of viewing society and its institutions has led Durkheim's work, and that of his followers, to be called functionalism. For functionalists, unequal possession of power within society is necessary and only those in power are able to make the necessary decisions. Social change occurs when it is functionally necessary, thus is seen as evolutionary, rather than revolutionary. Order is the normal state of affairs, according to this viewpoint, disorder being an abnormal state. The basis of order is a collective moral conscience, those values common to the average members of society. Various institutions, therefore, have the important task of teaching social values effectively. The individual is formed through the influence of those social institutions. Durkheim argued, however, that as societies transform from mechanical to organic solidarity, the norms of society can become confused or lost. In other words, as society changes rapidly, and economic growth may advance more quickly than moral regulations, a sense of 'anomie' develops, a psychological sense of disorder and meaninglessness.

Symbolic Interactionism

Symbolic interactionists believe that within the social forces that frame our lives we can choose how to interpret those forces and how to react to them. Humans, in other words, have more agency than the grand theorists gave credit. Social interactionists argue that we live in a symbolic world, in which various symbols and gestures have context-specific shared meanings. For example, a soldier shooting someone dead during wartime, we are told, is an act of heroism and bravery, whereas the same act committed on civilian streets is viewed as a crime. The ability to interpret symbols and apply meanings to them is the basis of all interaction. The meanings of symbols are also subject to change over time: for example, the clothing label Burberry, once seen as the preserve of the middle classes, more recently became a symbol that has been linked to 'chav' or casual culture.

The idea of self is of central importance to this theoretical approach. It is argued that humans, unlike other animals, have a self that they have the capacity to reflect on, and be aware of how they present to others. Mead (1934) argued that we have an 'I' and a 'Me', the 'I' being the part from which raw, basic impulses have their origin and the 'Me' being the part that is more refined and developed and receives and interprets data from the outside world. Mead suggested that there is a constant dialogue between the two selves, which results in the ever-changing 'social self'.

Such a theoretical approach also points to the ways in which our identity and position in society is incredibly fragile, as our actions can be defined in certain ways at certain times. This approach, therefore, has many applications for social workers who work with people who may have certain labels attached to them, such as delinquent or mentally ill.

Feminism

Feminist theory grew out of the women's movements of the 1960s and 1970s. The women's movements of Europe and America at the time, though very distinct in many ways, sought to effect social change. The intention was to end women's subordination in patriarchal and capitalist societies. Gradually, these political goals became entrenched in academic life and many universities began to teach Women's Studies (Women's Studies gradually became replaced by Gender Studies). Feminism was, therefore, political in nature, being committed to social and material change.

Many scholars distinguish between first wave feminism (1830–1920), which was primarily concerned with issues such as women's suffrage and the extension of civil rights to women, and second wave feminism (post-1960). Whilst sharing many of first wave feminism's goals, and agreeing with the tenet that women's oppression is tied to their sexuality, second wave feminism's starting point is often argued to be around the issue of the private sphere, and of reproductive rights in particular. For example, it is argued that the notion of 'biological fate' still lies behind many women's entry into low-paid, part-time work. Connections were made between the continued gaps in rights and opportunities of women experienced in the public sphere to the roles they played in the private realm. A focus on the private sphere brought with it many new areas for research and activism, including sexuality, domestic labour and domestic violence

Introductions to feminist theory very often categorize feminist as belonging to one of three main camps: liberal, Marxist/socialist or radical feminism. This division is, to some extent, arbitrary, and does not fully reflect the diversity of feminism. Nevertheless, these labels are a useful starting point. One of the earliest published liberal feminists was Mary Wollstonecraft, who wrote during the eighteenth century. In very simple terms, liberal feminists believe that women's subordination is rooted in a variety of social and legal constraints that block women's entry into the public sphere, and their goal is to redress this imbalance by reforming existing society. Marxist/socialist feminists (such as Juliet Mitchell) argue that women's oppression is in part due to patriarchy but, perhaps more importantly (especially for Marxist feminists), is a feature of capitalism, whereby women's material subordination benefits capital. Radical feminists (e.g. Adrienne Rich) view patriarchy, 'a system of social structures and practices in which men dominate, oppress, and exploit women' (Walby, 1989: 214), as the main source of women's subjugation. One criticism of feminist theory was that it did not reflect the experience of all women: for example, that it ignored black women's lives. To redress this imbalance, other branches of feminism, such as black feminism, postmodern feminism and psychoanalytic feminism, developed.

The main theoretical concern with the state of feminist theory is that the 'cultural turn' (see below), alongside a decline in Women's Studies in academic establishments, has potentially weakened its ability to make political connections.

Postmodernism

Influenced by wider political shifts and social action, many academic subjects, including sociology, began to question traditional theoretical approaches. By the mid-1980s postmodernism had become an established, and contested, movement within academia. At its heart is the premise that there is no one truth. In this sense, postmodernism is a clear move away from modernism. Modernism is frequently described as an era when there was a belief in big, overarching theories of social life, a time when it was felt that there were certain universal truths about how societies worked. The foundations of modernism are often said to have been forged from Enlightenment thinking. Because many of these broad theories, or what became known as 'grand or meta- narratives', were written by middle-class, white men, it was felt that many voices had been silenced. As a result, there was a turn away from these theories, though many have argued that this rejection was premature (Callinicos, 1989). Instead, there was a move towards an acknowledgement of multiple truths, diversity and fragmentation. The postmodern becomes a state of mind, a self-reflexive consciousness of the fragility and plurality of life.

An undeniable benefit of postmodernism in sociology has been the inclusion of black, gay and other minority voices within academia. It has, however, been criticised for being obscurantist, ignoring material inequalities and thus bearing little relevance to the lived experienced; a case of style over substance.

SOCIOLOGY AND ITS SOCIAL APPLICATIONS

As an academic discipline, sociology has an established theoretical tradition, and a methodological rigour when conducting social research. An understanding of sociological theory is important as it summarises and explains what sociology can reveal to those interested in society. More particularly, it is strongly related to the relationships and interaction between human beings, and thus has a special relevance for those professionals involved in different aspects of social work – whether through influence on social developments or to help improve the lives of those who are experiencing social problems. Sociology is especially applicable to a wide range of social aspects including: gender, class, sexual orientation and ethnicity issues; marriage, family and child-rearing problems – such as domestic violence and abuse; the experiences of various minority groups; social exclusion and/or inequality issues; ill-health problems; crime; and schools and education.

For these – and various other – reasons, sociology is very useful to social workers, as making sense of society can help people better understand their own life and the lives of others; it also makes us more effective agents for social amelioration and change.

CONCLUSION

Whilst the radical social, economic and political transformation of the nineteenth century seems, in many ways, far removed, we are nevertheless living in a time of great social upheaval, upheaval that is born of the nineteenth-century revolutions. Sociology, therefore, remains a powerful tool to help us think and act critically in order to understand and negotiate the world into which we were born. We become better placed to appreciate the relationship between individuals and the wider social world. By employing a sociological imagination, it becomes possible to reflect on the wider structural factors that have impacted on service users. Sociology, in other words, allows us to consider the wider political, social and economic context, and the role this plays in the persistence of social inequalities. Thinking critically in this way also, crucially, allows for the potential of change.

 Visit the Companion Website (www.sagepub.co.uk) to think about the case of Lottie and consider how an understanding of sociology can inform your assessment. Also watch vodcast 4.1 to see a social work student discuss her experiences of studying sociology and why she thinks a knowledge of sociology assists in developing the skills required to be an effective social worker.

Reflective Questions

1 Sociology and social work do share many of the same concerns with the social and with society. So, firstly define what sociology is and what it seeks to do as a social science. Secondly, discuss how a knowledge of sociology may contribute to social work theory and practice.

2 The chapter discusses Thompson's PCS model of discrimination, making the point that sociology can at least assist in understanding the structural elements of discrimination and oppression. These deeper structural elements of discrimination and oppression are often hard to detect as they are not readily visible on the 'surface' of everyday life, and the various tools and techniques that sociology offers provide useful tools in making them visible. Try to think of another example, other than the racism example we used here, of oppression and discrimination, and discuss how social structures produce and reproduce that oppression and discrimination.

3 Sociology makes extensive use of theory in trying to make sense of the complexities of society. Reflect on the theories we have summarised above and note down the main points that each one makes about the inner workings of society. Which one or ones do you find the most convincing? Provide some reasons for your answer.

Critical Thinking

Sociology maintains that a great deal of what we are and what we do is a result of the societies in which we live. If that is the case that society is quite powerful in affecting and shaping people's lives, what are the implications for social work? Does it mean that regardless of what a social worker does for a client they will be unable to effect real change in the circumstances of that person's life?

RECOMMENDED READING

Giddens, A. and Sutton, P. (2013) *Sociology*, 7th edn. Cambridge: Polity Press.

Simpson, G. and Price, V. (2007) *Transforming Society? Social Work and Sociology*. Bristol: The Policy Press.

Yuill, C. and Gibson, A. (eds) (2010) *Sociology for Social Work*. London: Sage.

5 MATERIAL CIRCUMSTANCES, POVERTY AND INCOME INEQUALITY

Chris Yuill

Key Themes

- The constraints placed on service users by material conditions and income inequality.
- Definitions and debates concerning poverty.
- The lived experience of poverty.
- The effects of income inequality.
- The need to consider alternative approaches to practice.

INTRODUCTION

Social work often takes place as an activity that operates on an individual face-to-face basis, with the service user and the social worker meeting together in order to discuss the service user's situation. The logic of this situation of two individuals in a room may potentially lead to an assessment where the emotional and psychological aspects of the service user's life are viewed as more important than the physical, economic and social context of the service user. While the various techniques, for example **cognitive behavioural therapy** and solution-focused social work, that you will read later in this book are highly useful and essential for effective social work practice, they need to be practised with a clear understanding of a wider context. For many service users the problems they encounter and deal with in their daily lives are not entirely caused by problems within themselves that can be assessed psychologically or by their anti-social attitudes, but by the material and unequal circumstances in which they live. Without an appreciation of just how constraining and damaging the social situation of service users can be, we may restrict and limit what social work can achieve.

To expand on the points raised above, this chapter opens by discussing what the concept 'material' means, before moving on to exploring how material conditions, poverty and social inequality shape both the society in which we live and adversely affect the lives of service users. In doing so we touch upon some of the debate and issues surrounding poverty as well as Wilkinson and Pickett's (2010) work on inequality. The chapter then finishes with a discussion of the deeper implications for social work, the main contention being that to effect meaningful change in the lives of service users may require a different approach from the instrumental and managerialist direction of contemporary social work.

WHAT IS MEANT BY MATERIAL?

The use of the terms 'material', 'materialism' and 'materialist' in the following discussions derive from philosophical concepts that are not to be confused with the commonly used expression 'materialistic', which refers to the pursuit of wealth and possession. Being materialistic is often negatively associated with how people behave in consumer societies where the need to have certain consumer products, such as the correct shoes or cars, outweighs other concerns in life such as developing meaningful bonds with other people or putting the needs of others before your own needs. Material in this context refers on one level to the immediate physical circumstances of someone's life: what sort of house or accommodation they live in, what the area is like in which they are housed, how much money they have, or can they access the natural and social resources that enable them to lead a happy and healthy life. It can also refer to the deeper levels of social existence, to the various social structures (as discussed in Chapter 4 on sociology) of which society is comprised and which operate in ways that can be hard to detect or sometimes comprehend.

Materialist perspectives are often contrasted to 'idealist' perspectives. Again, do not confuse idealist with the more commonly used expression and adjective 'idealistic', which connotes fanciful aspirations that are perhaps hard to realise in everyday life. Idealist and idealism in philosophy refer to a perspective that understands that the world and people's existence are created by their thoughts and ideas, and that by thinking in a different way reality can consequently be changed. Many of the approaches that are commonly used by social workers could be classified as idealist in this sense. For example, the various intervention strategies that rely on altering service users' thought processes (cognitive behavioural therapy or motivational interviewing) seek to alter and change the situation of service users by assisting them to think differently. Such an approach is valuable in certain contexts but for some service users thinking in a different way will have very little impact on their circumstances as the causes of their problems lie not in their thinking but in the situation in which they live. Poverty provides a useful example here and is discussed in greater depth later in this chapter. What a different

Table 5.1   Summary of materialist and idealist perspectives

	Materialist perspectives	Idealist perspectives
Main focus:	A reordering and transformation of the physical, economic and social contexts in which people live	Ideas and perceptions
Change can be brought about by:	A reordering of the conditions in which someone lives	By thinking differently

world it would be if someone is living in poverty, and then by thinking that they are not poor they no longer become poor.

It is important to have sight of what materialism and idealism mean, as the various social work interventions that are commonly adopted throughout the United Kingdom by social workers can be described as belonging to one of the two perspectives: an issue that will be returned to throughout this chapter. Table 5.1 summarises the two perspectives.

Exercise

Once you have read through more of this book, return to the point just made above. How many of the interventions that social workers adopt in their daily practice are aimed at altering how people think and how many are aimed at changing the material circumstances in which they live?

SOCIAL WORK, MATERIAL CIRCUMSTANCES AND POVERTY

An appreciation of the effects of the material conditions on service users' lives has long been present to some extent within social work. In their classic work *The Client Speaks: Working Class Impressions of Casework*, Mayer and Timms (1970) brought to the fore that for many of the service users (or 'clients' in the language of the time) it was not their emotions and feelings that needed attention, to be changed and altered, but rather the material conditions and the context in which they lived. What the research noted, however, was that for a great many of the service users all the help they received focused on the emotional element of their problems rather than the material or contextual conditions that played a powerful role in creating their problems in the first place. As the authors reflected on the service users with whom they worked:

> To offer clients, such as those studied, psychological help – without satisfying, and preferably at the start, their material needs – in our view utterly fails to come to grips with their problems. The persons we interviewed were desperately trying to

survive. They were consumed with worry over debts, the possibility of an eviction, the cutting-off of their electricity, and it is absurd to expect that the urgency of their needs could be met by a non-material approach ... (Mayer and Timms, 1970: 140)

The awareness of material circumstances in the lives of service users as outlined in the passage above, as well as many of the other insights, have not always been at the forefront of social work, as Ferguson and Woodward (2009) have recently argued, an issue discussed later in the final section of this chapter. One useful place to begin a deeper appreciation of the role material considerations play in service users' lives is to consider poverty and inequality. The reason for this is that poverty provides the clearest example of how material conditions shape and affect the lives of millions of people in the UK, which leads to many of the people who live in poverty coming into contact with social work services.

Poverty can be defined in two ways. There is absolute poverty, which relates to a minimum level of food, shelter and clothing that can sustain human life. This can also be measured using various indicators, such as that employed by the United Nations who define absolute poverty as living on less than one US dollar per day. There is also relative poverty that relates to what is deemed to be an appropriate and acceptable minimum standard of living in a given society. So, while someone who is living in relative poverty may have somewhere to live, have food to eat and clothes to wear, these are of a standard that lags far behind what most people would think of as being reasonable or normal. Living in such circumstances can also mean that people cannot also afford culturally to participate in the society in which they live. A European Union document defines relative poverty thus:

> People are said to be living in poverty if their income and resources are so inadequate as to preclude them from having a standard of living considered acceptable in the society in which they live. Because of their poverty they may experience multiple disadvantage through unemployment, low income, poor housing, inadequate health care and barriers to lifelong learning, culture, sport and recreation. They are often excluded and marginalised from participating in activities (economic, social and cultural) that are the norm for other people and their access to fundamental rights may be restricted.

In the United Kingdom the percentage of all individuals living below or on the 60% (AHC) relative poverty measure has been stable since the middle 1990s at somewhere between 22% and 25% of all individuals (Figure 5.1). While the percentage of children living below or on the same measure has decreased from 33% to 29%, this means that nearly one in five children in the UK are living on or near the poverty line (see Figure 5.2). The general downward trend evident in childhood poverty is however expected to reverse due to the various changes and reforms being implemented in response to the prevailing poor economic outlook following the recession of the early 2010s (Brewer et al., 2012).

What can be gathered from the discussion above on defining the term 'relative' is that the effects that poverty can exert on people's lives are quite wide ranging, encompassing a number of negative outcomes in health, in education and in wider social participation. One of the immediate effects of relative poverty is to limit the choices that can be made. For example, food does not become a choice about whether you want to eat in or grab a

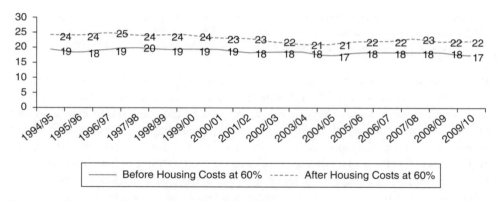

Figure 5.1   Trends in relative poverty, all individuals

Source: DWP (2012b)

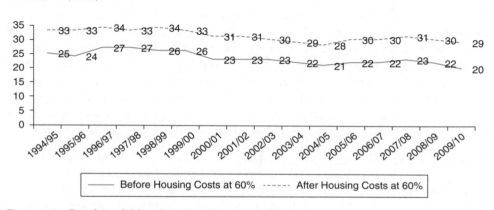

Figure 5.2   Trends in children living in relative poverty

Source: DWP (2012b)

take-a-way, or whether tonight's meal is one that is Italian or Thai themed, but instead becomes what is the cheapest. Often, for people living in poverty, food becomes an elastic element of their weekly shopping that can be contracted or expanded depending on what other expenditures are required. If an energy bill, for instance, is due, then that can mean cutting back on the food budget to free up money to pay that bill.

Other challenges and problems related to living in poverty, include:

- Poor health: people who are living in **deprivation** are considerably more likely to experience higher levels of ill-health and die younger than people who are not living in deprivation. In Scotland, for example, people living in the 15% most deprived areas can expect on average to live till just over 68 years and have 57.5 years of healthy life expectancy, which is considerably less than the national average, which would be 75 years and 68 years respectively (Scottish Government, 2011a)
- Making tough decisions: Living in poverty or on a low income requires people to make very difficult decisions about what they spend their money on. Parents living in

poverty, for example, may decide to restrict the food they eat themselves in order to create a surplus in order to afford to buy their children a pair of trainers so that they can keep up with their friends at school (Women's Budget Group, 2005).

- Stigma: People living in poverty or in areas of deprivation are frequently depicted in very negative stereotypes which often centre around false images of the poor being voluntarily unemployed, feckless and living a luxurious lifestyle on state benefits. They may sometimes be used as a source of entertainment on daytime television shows (McKendrick et al., 2008). The issue of popular perception of poverty, and the use and misuses of the benefit's system is covered in more detail next.

An activity on the Companion Website (www.sagepub.co.uk/SocialWork) invites you to look at the Black Report and to consider in more detail the issue of health inequalities.

It is important to contextualise claims made and popular perceptions of large-scale fraud and abuse of benefits. Such a perspective was revealed in the British Social Attitudes (2011) survey, with many respondents reporting negative images of benefit claimants, describing them as scroungers and unwilling to work. One popular common misperception is that levels of fraud are widespread and that many people who rely on social security dishonestly abuse the various benefits that are available. The government department that oversees the provision of benefits, the Department for Work and Pensions, in their official figures estimate that £1.2bn or 0.7% of all benefit expenditure is lost to fraud (DWP, 2012a). The figure of benefit fraud could be contrasted with the amount of money that is not paid because of tax evasion either by wealthy individuals with the financial resources and access to accountancy expertise or by large corporations. The figure there is considerably higher. Some estimates place the amount lost to tax evasion and tax avoidance as being close to £9bn (HM Revenue & Customs, 2012) while others put it much higher.

The article by Garrett (2002) on the Companion Website (www.sagepub.co.uk/SocialWork) argues that social workers should refocus on poverty and hardship in their work with service users. Read this article now to extend your understanding.

Case Study

Both Tanya and Steve are in employment, but the work is highly precarious. Both are employed on zero-hour contracts in a local retail superstore. The zero-hour contract means that they do not know how often they are going to work in a particular week and they have to wait until they are contacted by their employer to be informed what hours they are working that week. As a result, budgeting is a real problem and, with no regular income, household expenditure is stripped down to the barest minimum. Even in good weeks it can be difficult to make ends meet. Steve often waits to the end of the day to shop in the local discount supermarket, hoping that he can save money by buying the reduced goods on their sell-by date. Both Tanya and he prioritise food for their daughter over food for themselves. It has been two years since they last had a family holiday together, and that was to stay for a few days with a relative who lives in Wales.

(Continued)

(Continued)

They would both love to be in full-time employment that allows them to have a regular income and to lead a more stable life, but there are few job opportunities open to them. They could move if work becomes available elsewhere but their daughter is in the first year of primary school and they do not want to disrupt her education. They do not also want to move away from the informal support network provided by Tanya's immediate family, who live in the local area.

As their income is low they are entitled to benefits, the main benefit being their housing benefit. On the surface, that benefit appears quite generous, coming to £17,000 a year. However, all of it goes straight to their landlord who rents out several properties in the area. He seems to prefer letting to people who are in receipt of benefits as he can keep putting the rent up regardless, as it will be covered by the housing benefit.

In the last year Steve has become increasingly despondent and depressed, because no matter how much he keeps trying to find regular work, applying for as many jobs as he can, he keeps getting knocked back by prospective employers. One problem in applying for jobs is that everything is now done online. Steve and Tanya cannot afford the Internet, and he has to make his way across town to one of the few remaining public libraries and wait until he can access a computer there.

He is beginning to think that he is letting himself and his family down. Tanya too feels worried and anxious about the future, as she cannot see it improving and changing in any substantial way.

The amount of money available on benefits is very low, both in relation to average wages and in relation to estimates of the minimum level of income necessary to enjoy a basic standard of living. The first point is illustrated in Figures 5.3 and 5.4. What we can see here is how benefits have not kept pace with the average wage in the UK and that the replacement value of benefits (the percentage of the average wage that benefits replace) has been steadily declining over the past 20 or so years. That second point is highlighted in Figures 5.3 and 5.4. Hirsch et al. (2009) have identified what a reasonable minimum income would be for various groups of people living in Britain. The various amounts deemed to be a minimum income were derived by using focus groups and interviewing ordinary members of the public in order to establish what a reasonable comfortable standard of living would be, but one that was still relatively basic.

That minimum income would allow someone to fully participate in many of the cultural norms of British life but the minimum income proposed is in no way overly generous. Tobacco, for instance, is not included but some allowance for attending social and leisure activities is included. What Figure 5.5 denotes is that for many types of claimants (for example, lone parents, single people or a couple with children) the benefits available fall short of that minimum income. So, for a lone parent, the benefits available are 67% of what the Joseph Rowntree Foundation would deem to be the minimum income for people in that group.

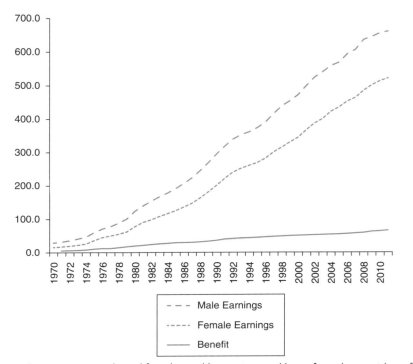

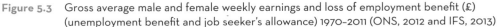

Figure 5.3 Gross average male and female weekly earnings and loss of employment benefit (£) (unemployment benefit and job seeker's allowance) 1970–2011 (ONS, 2012 and IFS, 2013)

Notes: For both male and female earnings the highest level of income was selected if changes in gathering data generated more than one result in a year.
Loss of Employment Benefit refers to Unemployment Benefit (1970–1995) and Job Seeker's Allowance (1996–2011). For Loss of Employment Benefit the highest level of benefit was selected if changes in gathering data generated more than one result in a year.
Job Seekers' Allowance refers to the 25 plus age-group level.

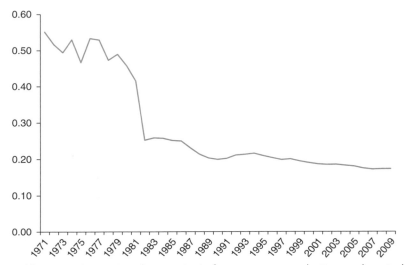

Figure 5.4 Net unemployment replacement rate for an average production worker, single person (Van Vilet and Caminada, 2012)

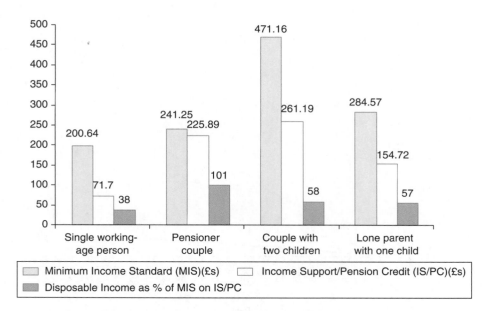

Figure 5.5   Disposal income on Income Support or Pension Credit as a percentage of Minimum Income Standard (adapted from Joseph Rowntree foundation, 2013)

In terms of a minimum income, the Joseph Rowntree Foundation (2013: 15) in their research has identified that for a single working-age person in 2013, for example, a weekly wage of £200.64 (excluding rent) is the minimum required to live a reasonable life in the United Kingdom today. That amount would cover expenditure on the following:

Food   £50.11
Social and cultural participation   £47.81
Alcohol   £5.26
Travel costs   £22.86
Other costs*   £74.60

Total   **£200.64**

*(council tax, water, household goods & services, heating etc.)

Exercise

What do you think of the minimum income laid out above? Does it seem too generous, a bit tight or just about right? What about your own income and expenditure? How does it map onto the above amounts?

In terms of the perception that people in receipt of benefits are work shy and deliberately not choosing to work, that too is questionable. Again, using the DWP official statistics is useful here, and these indicate that for every job that becomes available

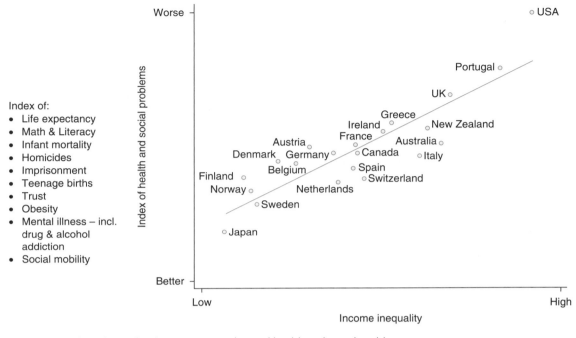

Figure 5.6 The relationship between inequality and health and social problems (Wilkinson and Pickett, 2010)

By kind permission of The Equality Trust

there are five applicants. That means that for every successful job-seeker there are four unsuccessful applicants, which in turn means that there are fewer jobs going around than people available to work and therefore not everyone can get a job.

INEQUALITY

The recent work of Wilkinson and Pickett (2012) has brought attention to the corrosive and damaging effects that inequality can exert both on individuals and on society as a whole. They contend that the more unequal a society is, measured by the size of the income gap between the richest and poorest, the worse certain social problems will be. Figure 5.6 illustrates this relationship between inequality and specific social problems. What is evident here is that highly unequal countries such as the United Kingdom and the United States experience higher levels of the problems that are listed on the left-hand side of the graph, while the more equal countries such as Japan and the Nordic countries of Sweden and Norway, for example, experience fewer of those problems.

Differences in life expectancy provide another useful example of the same trend as laid out in Figure 5.7, where the more equal nations mentioned above have longer life expectancies than the less equal nations.

Recent work by Marmot (2010) has further identified the deep and damaging effects that inequality has on health. In England and Wales if everyone enjoyed the same life

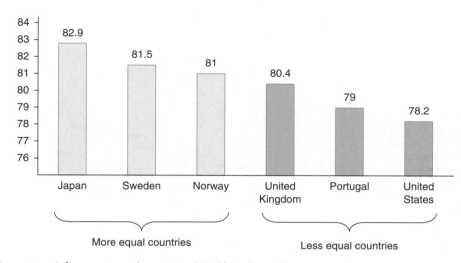

Figure 5.7   Life expectancy by country (World Bank, 2012)

span as the most advantaged in society then there would be 1.3–2.5 million extra years of life and 2.8 million years free of limiting illness in the overall population. Economically health inequalities also create problems. Marmot has argued health inequalities lead to a loss in productivity of between £13bn and £33bn per year and a further loss in tax and increased welfare costs totalling £20bn to £32bn per year. Overall, if everyone in England and Wales shared the same levels of health there would be significant benefits both in terms of general well-being and boosting national finances and productivity.

The reasons why inequality appears to be significant in creating negative social outcomes can be found in how inequality shapes and distorts people's lives. Unequal societies typically exhibit certain features such as high individualism, an emphasis on status displays, competitiveness and social fragmentation, creating a context where people do not trust or support each other, where personal value is mediated through the display and pursuit of consumer goods, where there is over-reverence for those deemed to be successful but a hostility towards those who are regarded as failures. Jones (2010) has argued there is an increasingly hostile perception, not just of the poor, but of people who in the past would have constituted the working class, that is people employed in a variety of non-professional occupations, and who have experienced a reduction in their social status, perceived as being worthy of contempt and written off as 'chavs'.

Case Study

Referring back to Steve and Tanya again; both of them feel that they can just about manage to cope with the physical challenges of living on a very low income and benefits, but it is the psychological pressures that are the hardest to deal with. Last night Tanya was sitting on the bus coming home from a late evening shift at work. A group of younger people from a more affluent part of town were also on the bus. For them travelling by public transport was treated as a bit of a laugh, something that only poor people do. She became aware that they were sniggering at her. It was her jacket that they were finding amusing. It was old and the sleeve was patched, but what the younger people were saying was that she was a 'total state' and obviously didn't care about her appearance.

Wilkinson and Pickett's work provides a deeper understanding of certain social problems in society, that these social problems emerge out of trends in wider society, in particular government policy that has overseen a redistribution of wealth and income upwards in society, thus creating increased social inequality that tears at the social fabric. There is therefore nothing inevitable about inequality. In the United Kingdom it has increased because of decisions made by various governments and could therefore be reversed by governments focusing on creating a more equal society.

Visit the Companion Website (www.sagepub.co.uk/SocialWork) for a weblink to the Equality Trust and to read an article by Chase and Walker (2013) who explored the emotion of shame and the experience of poverty.

PAST TRADITIONS AND FUTURE AGENDAS FOR SOCIAL WORK?

By discussing and exploring the material issues and the effects of inequality, certain very profound questions are posed for social workers. The main question being that, if you accept the importance of material conditions in conditioning and shaping the lives, the opportunities and circumstances of service users, then where should social work intervention be focused? The current direction that social work is taking in Britain today is one of increasing 'instrumentalism' and 'managerialism', which places an emphasis on meeting outcomes and following set procedures to reach certain targets. Whilst at one level such an approach may be useful in that it offers a structured outline in which social workers can operate, it does contain some potential problems. One criticism is that, by being more instrumental, we begin to individualise the problems presented by service users. What that means is that the problems being expressed by a service user, the actual issues that have led an individual to come into contact with social work services, are the sole responsibility of the service user; that the service users, in effect, are to 'blame' for the situation in which they find themselves. The solutions that follow for the service users are therefore focused on them, isolating them and promoting continuing dependency.

CONCLUSION

The main lesson to draw from the points being made throughout this chapter is that it is the structures of society that cause problems rather than 'bad' people that cause society problems. Therefore a different orientation to intervention is required, one that perhaps looks outwards beyond the individual service user and attempts to address the material circumstances and inequalities that frame a service user's life. In contemporary social work there are, however, very few such intervention perspectives that offer that approach. Such a perspective is arguably needed given that the UK economy is predicted not to grow as fast as it has in previous decades (OECD, 2012). The result of this economic slowdown will, according to the Institute of Fiscal Studies (IFS, 2012), be an increase in the number of people, both adults and children, who will face difficult and trying circumstances often beyond their control. For people who become service users as a result of these challenging economic conditions the solutions to their needs are more likely to be found in supporting the material circumstances of their lives, rather than by affecting change to their attitudes and behaviours.

Critical Thinking

Given that various respected organisations such as OECD and the IFS predict that for many people the effects of the current recession will last beyond any recovery, what challenges does this present to social work? What could social workers do in order to improve the lives of service users?

Reflective Questions

1   The purpose of this chapter is to highlight the effects that both material circumstances and wider social inequality can exert on the lives of service users. First of all, define what is meant by material circumstances and social inequality. Then, secondly, discuss why having knowledge of these social processes may improve social work practice.

2   One key point raised in the above discussion is that poverty exerts powerful constraints on the choices that individuals and families can make. What are the implications of that for service users in terms of (a) why they may have initially come into contact with social work services, and (b) how they can affect any real meaningful change in their lives so they can exit social work services?

3   This question looks ahead to the other chapters in this book that deal with a variety of social work intervention techniques and strategies. When you are reading them and thinking about them, reflect on how the effectiveness of those techniques may be affected and influenced by material circumstances and wider social inequalities. For example, can interventions such as cognitive behavioural therapy work when people are living in deprived circumstances that are not of their choosing?

RECOMMENDED READING

Dorling, D. (2011) *Injustice: Why Social Inequality Persists*. Bristol: The Policy Press.

Fergusson, I. and Woodward, R. (2009) *Radical Social Work in Practice: Making a Difference (Social Work in Practice)*. Bristol: The Policy Press.

Wilkinson, R. and Pickett, K. (2010) *The Spirit Level: Why Equality Is Better for Everyone*. Harmondsworth: Penguin.

6 PSYCHOLOGICAL APPROACHES: THEIR APPLICATION AND RELEVANCE TO SOCIAL WORK

Carmen-Maria Fyfe

Key Themes

- Psychology literally means 'study of the mind'.
- Psychologists provide detailed theories and structured tools to help understand people's attitudes, behaviour and mental processes.
- Psychology provides one of the social work tools for making assessments of people and their problems.
- Psychology attempts to understand individual differences and development throughout the life span and to provide a more holistic picture of service users' problems.
- Knowledge of psychology assists social workers to use a range of interpersonal skills when working with service users whatever the presenting problem.

INTRODUCTION

Psychology is a relatively young science compared to other sciences, its origins dating from the end of the nineteenth century. The role of psychology in social work and social care is aptly paraphrased by Bernstein (2008: 3):

Psychology is the science that seeks to understand behaviour and mental processes and apply that understanding to the service of human welfare.

Over the years the discipline of psychology has developed five major approaches, with varying schools of thought stemming from these. Each approach aims to understand human mental functions by looking at the physiological and neurological processes involved in the behaviour and attitudes of individuals and their reactions in social groups. Psychologists today use a combination of theoretical concepts, employing empirical and deductive methods from social and natural sciences, to explore conscious and unconscious concepts, such as: attention, behaviour, brain functioning, cognition, emotion, motivation, perception and personality.

This chapter intends to provide an introduction to the understanding of psychology and how psychological approaches and applications can enhance a social worker's 'tool box' when working with service users.

THE FIVE APPROACHES

The five main approaches in psychology are:

- The *behaviourist* approach, which is concerned only with observable behaviour.
- The *biological* approach, which takes the view that behaviour is a direct result of genetics and physiology.
- The *cognitive* approach, focusing on how information is taken in and made sense of through our internal mental processes.
- The *psychoanalytic* approach, based on the assumption that all human behaviour is determined by our unconscious mind.
- The *humanistic* approach, which emphasises the uniqueness of the individual and stresses the importance of personal motivation.

The following sections of the chapter offer an understanding of the five psychological approaches and their applications in supporting social work practice. It is from a greater understanding of the input and interactions between our psychological processes (thoughts, feelings, behaviours etc.), the life sciences (human biology and physiology) and sociology (social and cultural environment) that we endeavour to provide improved social and health care.

THE BEHAVIOURIST APPROACH

The behaviourist approach places a significant emphasis on the role of the environment and is based on the fundamental principle that human behaviour is shaped through learning and experience. Behaviourism focuses on the systematic study of observable behaviour.

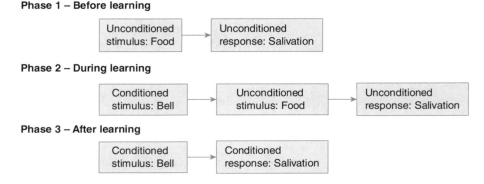

Phase 1 – Before learning

Unconditioned stimulus: Food → Unconditioned response: Salivation

Phase 2 – During learning

Conditioned stimulus: Bell → Unconditioned stimulus: Food → Unconditioned response: Salivation

Phase 3 – After learning

Conditioned stimulus: Bell → Conditioned response: Salivation

Figure 6.1   Classical conditioning (extracted from Pavlov, 1927)

There are two models of learning within the approach – classical conditioning and operant conditioning.

Classical Conditioning

Learning by association was first proposed by Russian physiologist Ivan Pavlov (1927). While studying the digestive system of dogs, Pavlov experimented with ringing a bell prior to the presentation of food. He noticed that the dogs started to salivate in response to the bell, even when no food was presented, and recognised that the bell became the stimulus for salivation to occur. This procedure became known as classical conditioning (see Figure 6.1). In classical conditioning a reflex is always a naturally occurring action; in the case of Pavlov's experiment the reflex was salivation. It should be noted that it is highly unlikely that all our actions are conditioned using a physiological reflex.

Operant Conditioning

Burrhus Skinner, an American psychologist, was responsible for demonstrating operant conditioning. The key feature of operant conditioning is that every action has a consequence and that these consequences impact on future actions. Skinner carried out experiments with rats using a box containing a bar which, once pressed, would release pellets of food. When a rat was put into the box and discovered that pressing the bar released food, it would become attracted to that part of the box and return to repeat the process. The pellet of food acts as a reinforcer, increasing the probability of the behaviour being repeated.

Applying Skinner's principles to humans and thinking about today's society, we see how a range of different things can act as reinforcers for different groups, for example sweets, praise or money. These reinforcers are known as conditioned reinforcers. Skinner recognised that in addition to positive reinforcers there are also negative reinforcers, which are typically unpleasant.

> ### Case Study
>
> In group care settings for young people, conditioning may be a feature of social work practice. Behaviour may be modified by the use of rewards to reinforce acceptable behaviour and withdrawal of enjoyable activities to punish, or negatively reinforce.

Social Learning

Social learning theorists argue that learning processes are not just developed from classical and operant conditioning. Such theorists recognise that we are also influenced by other forms of learning such as observation and modelling of others within social groups. For example, Bandura and other social learning theorists, argue that a child is not born predisposed to be aggressive, but that aggressive responses are a result of observational learning.

In a series of studies Bandura and Walters (1963) observed children displaying verbally and physically aggressive behaviour to an inflated 'Bobo doll'. The experiments were carried out with different consequences to the displayed behaviour: reward, no consequences, punishment. These observations allowed Bandura and Walters (1963) to develop social learning theory, in which they suggested all behaviour and aggression is learned. Bandura also clearly distinguished between learning and application of behaviour. Whether the observation has been of parent, peers, television or something else, the likelihood of behaviour being imitated is dependent upon the perceived consequences.

Although Bandura's experiments have been criticised, for example due to the fact that the aggression was towards a doll and not a real person, similar patterns of behaviour have been found in other studies. In Liebert and Baron's (1972) experiment, children were witnessed copying violent behaviour to other children after viewing violence on television clips. Similarly, Munroe and Munroe (1975) in a cross-cultural study of children found high levels of childhood aggression in societies where families punished their children's aggressive behaviour. Social learning theory, therefore, can provide us with an understanding of aggressive behaviours.

Øverlien (2010) undertook a review of the literature on children exposed to domestic violence. Read the article on the Companion Website (www.sagepub.co.uk/SocialWork) and think about the findings.

THE BIOLOGICAL APPROACH

In seeking to comprehend human behaviour and actions biological psychologists, working with geneticists and physiologists, focus their research on understanding what is happening within the brain. They focus primarily on the mechanics of brain functioning and are not necessarily concerned with the wider explanations.

The biological psychology perspective has three main aspects of investigation: comparative, biological and genetics:

Comparative – studying and observing animals such as rats and monkeys. These comparisons have provided significant insight into human social behaviour.

Biological – by researching the physiological make-up of the human body, its structures and functions, the bio-psychologists have expanded our understanding of the effects of specific chemicals the body produces and how hormones affect our well-being.

Genetics – studying genetic inheritance in animals and the surrounding mechanisms has allowed researchers to see the role of inheritance in the human nervous system.

Biological psychologists have assisted in the research of people suffering from cognitive disorders, such as autism and Alzheimer's disease, which has developed understanding of the nervous system. In the **nature–nurture debate**, it is heavily in favour of nature.

THE COGNITIVE APPROACH

Cognitive psychology grew from a realisation that the behaviourist stimulus–response approach developed by Skinner was relatively limited. Human behaviour was perceived to be far more complex, resulting in a need to study the mental processes that are occurring – literally a need to explore what is going on 'inside the head'. The assumption of cognitive psychologists is that through an understanding of internal mental processes we will understand behaviour. As humans we do not simply react in response to situations in our environment, simultaneously there are thought processes and conscious decisions being taken.

The cognitive approach has led to the development of a greater understanding of the human mind, proposing various models and theories on how the human mind functions. The five areas of perception, attention, thinking, language and memory will be briefly explored within this section of the chapter.

On the Companion Website (www.sagepub.co.uk/SocialWork) you will find an activity focusing an Alzheimer's disease and Autistic Spectrum Disorder, conditions which affect cognition. After you have read this section visit the website to undertake the exercise.

Perception

This is the process by which we analyse and make sense of incoming sensory information, and it involves higher-level brain activity. How we respond and process these experiences is unique to the individual. In order to create a perception the brain processes information in two ways simultaneously: *bottom-up* and *top-down*. In the bottom-up process the brain analyses information individually. In top-down processing the brain uses higher order activities drawing on pre-obtained knowledge. For example, in visual perception, when reading you recognise the shape of the individual letters (bottom-up processing) and collectively derive the word. Simultaneously top-down processing using pre-obtained knowledge allows you to recognise the word-shape as a whole, interpret the sentence meaning and affect a response. Gregory's theory (1997) suggested that with higher-order top-down processing, we understand what is happening and expect what will happen next because we are drawing on past memories (learned or experienced), expectations, motivational and emotional factors.

Attention

This is the process by which we focus on sensory information so that we can respond appropriately. It is the conscious effort to concentrate on a specific stimulus to make sense of it. Psychologists have identified three important factors concerning attention:

- it improves one's mental processing abilities
- it takes effort and if prolonged can be tiring and becomes strenuous
- it can be selective; concentration on one specific stimulus limits your ability to be fully attentive to others.

Norman and Shallice (1986) proposed three different levels of attentive awareness:

- Fully automatic in which actions are controlled by schemas, with no conscious awareness.
- Semi-automatic which involves a level of control of the schemas, resolving any conflicts over decision-making.
- Deliberate control where we are fully aware of the situation and give direction to the situation.

Exercise

You are currently using these skills to make sense of this chapter. Try to link these points to what is happening to you: have you any prior knowledge, experiences or understanding that shape your perception? Are you able to concentrate fully, or are there distractions?

We have a capacity to attend to what we see and hear at the same time, for example, driving and holding a conversation, or being in one conversation and hearing something familiar to ourselves, such as our own name, across a room. However attention cannot be divided beyond a certain point, for example, driving and talking on a mobile phone (even hands-free) have been proven to cause errors of judgement (Strayer and Drews, 2007).

Thinking

Thinking is the ability that allows us to be able to problem solve, develop and create. The brain links perception, attention and memory to process information and makes a response. Piaget's theory (1926) of cognitive development suggested children adapted cognitively to their environment. This adaption consisted of two independent processes:

Table 6.1   Piaget's four stages of child development

Age (yr)	Stage	Characteristics
0–2	Sensorimotor	The infant gradually discovers the relationships between sensations and motor behaviour
2–7	Preoperational	The child learns to use speech, mental images and symbols but cannot make general logical statements
7–11	Concrete operation	The child now becomes capable of logical thought with regards to observable objects, can perform mental operations and appreciate other perspectives
11+	Formal operation	The child is able to develop scientific reasoning, is capable of solving abstract problems and dealing with hypothetical possibilities

- *Assimilation* – the way in which one incorporates and organises new material into existing schemas.
- *Accommodation* – how one alters existing schema to incorporate new information.

The following example will illustrate these processes:

> A child has learnt to recognise a dog: it has four legs, a head and a tail that waggles.
>
> On seeing a cat the child says 'dog'. The parent, however, explains it is a cat. The child *assimilates* this information and *adaption* is made.
>
> In doing so the child has learnt that there are differences between a cat and a dog. The child has *accommodated* the new information and the appropriate mental *adaption* is made.

Piaget outlined four main stages of cognitive development, giving approximate ages for each stage in which the child is able to resolve different problems successfully (see Table 6.1).

Piaget's work has influenced how we view children's development, the toys we provide, the methods of teaching in nursery and primary schools and how we understand the development of logic, concepts and language. Critics have noted his failure to consider the effect of family conditions and his minimisation of other external influences.

Vygotsky (1962) criticised Piaget's biological maturation approach and proposed that children be viewed as apprentices. He believed that social influences (environmental) were of greater influence to cognitive development; a view later upheld by Bruner (1983) in his observation of parents encouraging their children with problem-solving. Vygotsky suggested that during a child's early years, language and the ability to socially interact, especially with adults, was crucial to children's cognitive development.

In contrast to Piaget, Vygotsky's approach ignored biological development and focused instead on the individual's rate of social cognitive developmental processes.

Case Study

A child of 4 years loses his father. His mother tries to explain to him what has happened, but at this age John has no clear understanding of permanence. Mother finds it distressing to find ways of explaining a death: concepts such as going to sleep, being in Heaven and so on do not mean much to John, and he will have to make up in his own mind what they actually mean. Can you think how you might explain this to a 4-year-old?

Language

There are a range of different perspectives regarding the development of spoken language. Skinner (1957) argued that language is acquired through the principle of operant conditioning, words being a behavioural response. Bandura (1989), in his social learning theory, suggests that language is obtained through observational learning or imitation backed up by positive reinforcements from the parent. This is disputed by the nativist theorists, such as Chomsky (1965, 1972), who believed that children have an innate language acquisition device (LAD), a theory that lies within a biological approach. Chomsky believed that during development the child has a limited period in which to develop linguistically. This approach presents the child as rather mechanical, suggesting that a child acquires language automatically by observation and imitation from parents and peers.

Bruner (1983) proposed an alternative to Chomsky's LAD with his interactionist approach – the language acquisition support system (LASS). He believed that the mother–child relationship (or caregiver–child relationship) was critical in the development of social skills, an approach similar to that of Vygotsky. Bruner believed language accelerated cognitive development and the ability to think, unlike Piaget who saw language as merely a tool. Support for Bruner comes from research carried out by Sachs et al. (1981). Sachs and his research team reported on a case study of "Jim' and his younger brother, whose parents were deaf and whose only exposure to spoken language up until the age of 3 years was the television. Although 'Jim' produced speech it was poorly articulated, which suggests there must be some level of social interaction in order to develop optimally.

Memory

Memory is the process by which we retain information. It works continuously, controlling and monitoring our life, our thoughts, experiences and knowledge. Without memory one would be virtually helpless; every action would have to be learned and every experience 'new'. Three basic memory processes, acquisition, retention and retrieval, have been identified, and Atkinson and Shiffrin (1968, 1971) developed an information-processing model (Figure 6.2) that likened the brain to a highly sophisticated computer, taking in information in the form of sensory stimuli, storing it and then retrieving it to provide an output in the form of a behavioural response.

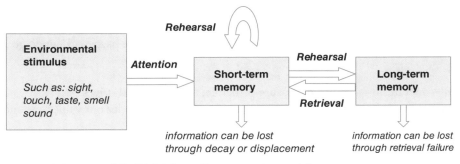

Figure 6.2 Atkinson and Shiffrin's information-processing model

Cognitive psychology, in conjunction with behaviourist, psychoanalytical and humanistic psychology, has produced integrated theories and applications, such as social cognition, cognitive development theory and cognitive neuropsychology. Elements of behaviourism and cognitive psychology were synthesised to form the basis of cognitive behavioural therapy (CBT), a form of psychotherapy modified from techniques developed by American psychologist Albert Ellis (1962) and American psychiatrist Aaron T. Beck (1963).

THE PSYCHOANALYTICAL APPROACH

The founder of the psychoanalytical approach was Sigmund Freud, probably the most famous psychologist of all time. His work has influenced not only psychology but also how Western cultures perceive morality, family life and childhood.

The psychoanalytic approach attempts to explain both the mind and behaviour in terms of our personality, by focusing on the importance of unconscious conflicts and biological instincts. Freud (1933) likened the mind to an iceberg, of which only the tip can be observed. This analogy is clarified by Freud's proposed three levels of consciousness:

- Consciousness, being our level of awareness
- Preconscious, a level of memory that we can recall easily
- Unconscious, a level that, according to Freud, contains suppressed, negative and often painful memories.

There are three basic assumptions behind the psychoanalytical approach:

1 Nothing we do is accidental.
2 The unconscious mind plays an active role in our behaviour.
3 The unconscious can override conscious will – having an underlying force or motivation.

Freudian psychology views one's personality as a pattern of thoughts, emotions and intellectual skills, which gives us our individuality. With the unconscious responsible for much of our personality and therefore behaviour, Freud argued that any negative or disturbing life experiences could explain later life psychological and/or social problems. Freud developed a theory of personality, which comprises three parts – id, superego and ego:

- Id – operates on a carefree pleasure principle; the instinctual drives
- Superego – operates our conscience or inner voice and includes our values and moral attitudes
- Ego – this is the conscious part of personality which looks at the whole individual – the external self.

The role of the ego is to balance the instincts of the id against the needs of the super-ego in line with external reality. In order to achieve this, the ego develops a number of defence mechanisms, such as:

- *Displacement* – redirection of an attitude or idea; for example you might feel angry towards your partner but you cannot express this anger to him/her, so you snap at the children instead.
- *Regression* – occurs when a person reverts to some behaviour reminiscent of an earlier stage of life; for example, cuddling a soft toy for security during an anxiety attack.
- *Denial* – when someone refuses to accept events or situations; for example, a person with alcohol problems may refuse to admit that he/she is dependent on alcohol.

Exercise

Think of when you have used these defence mechanisms. The above examples should be easy to identify with, and it is appropriate to see them as natural and normal reactions. Think of the impact that such defences may have on other people, in particular if they move to a more extreme or ongoing use.

The over-dependence on defence mechanisms in Freud's patients led him to the concept of **neuroses** such as phobias, obsessions or hysteria. In seeking to explain these situations Freud proposed his theory of psychosexual development.

Psychosexual Stages of Development

According to Freud the young child develops from being totally controlled by the id to having a balanced personality. Reaching this balance, however, is not easy and the child has to go through a number of stages in order to mature into a balanced individual. These phases of development are called the psychosexual stages of development.

- The oral stage (0–2 years) – the infant is preoccupied with the mouth; it is the source of pleasure and means of expression.

- The anal stage (2–3 years) – marks the beginning of ego development; a major issue at this stage is toilet training.
- The phallic stage (3–6 years) – sexual energy is focused on the genitals; the major conflict of this stage is the Oedipus complex.
- The latent stage (6–12 years) – the child develops their confidence and mastery of the world around them.
- The genital stage (12+ years) – the final stage of sexual development begins at adolescence and continues throughout adult life.

Fixation, becoming stuck, can occur at any of the stages and can manifest itself in adulthood. For example, Freud would view smokers or adult nail biters as being in oral stage fixation. Similarly, Freud identified types of people in anal stage fixation: (1) anal retentive personality – those who are overly possessive, stubborn, clean and tidy and (2) anal expulsive personality – those who repeatedly give things away.

Many psychologists have since developed psychoanalytical theory based on Freud's principles, and some of these can be found in Chapter 7.

THE HUMANISTIC APPROACH

The humanistic approach clearly emerged in the 1950s in America, resulting in a focus on the whole person and the person's development to fulfilment. The humanistic perspective challenged the behaviourists as being dehumanising and the psychoanalytical approach as failing to realise that humans have free will. Humanists look at individuals as unique beings with an ability to reflect on life experiences, to develop a sense of self and to differentiate self from others. In order to understand behaviour, humanistic psychology emphasises the significance of conscious awareness, the power of personal choice and holistically the sense of self in a social concept.

The pioneers of humanistic psychology were Abraham Maslow and Carl Rogers. Maslow (1954) famously proposed a hierarchy of needs, which broadly divided into five layers (see Figure 6.3), incorporating the importance of one's basic physiological needs, through to one's higher needs such as esteem through to self-actualisation. Needs at the bottom of the pyramid are required to be met in order to facilitate the meeting of needs at the higher levels:

- Physiological needs – food, drink, temperature regulation, rest, activities, sex.
- Safety and security needs – protection from potentially dangerous objects or situations, such as the elements or physical illness. The threat is both physical and psychological: for example fear of the unknown; importance of routine and familiarity.
- Love and belongingness – receiving and giving love, affection, trust and acceptance. Affiliating, being part of a group – family, friends, work.
- Esteem needs – the esteem and respect of others, self-esteem and self-respect; a sense of competence.
- Self-actualisation – realising one's full potential, becoming everything one is capable of becoming.

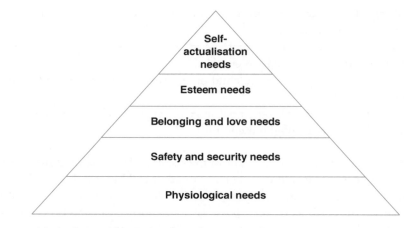

Figure 6.3   Maslow's (1954) hierarchy of needs

Maslow's hierarchy of needs provided the foundations for the future development of the humanistic approach. The first four stages show us (as human beings) as having an inbuilt drive to satisfy and maintain a physical or psychological balance. Maslow argues that human beings also have an innate desire to develop their capabilities in order to reach our fullest potential – self-actualisation.

Writing from an organisational development perspective, O'Connor and Yballe (2007) provide a critical examination of representations of Maslow's work. To read the article visit the Companion Website (www.sagepub.co.uk/SocialWork).

Carl Rogers (1959) used his experience as a clinical psychologist with a psychoanalytical background to develop a theory on personality, which centred on the concept of self and one's varying perception of self-identity.

His theory has three primary constructs:

- 'Organism', defining the holistic view of an 'individual' whole being.
- 'Phenomenal field', this takes account of all one's experiences embedded at an unconscious level.
- 'Self', the development of 'I' and 'me' through experiences and the definition of self by others.

Rogers made a significant contribution to the theory on the formation of self and used this to develop his 'client-centred' or 'person-centred' non-directive therapy. Rogers believed that therapists (and counsellors) should show:

- Genuineness – sincerity towards building up a real relationship with the client.
- Unconditional positive regard – believing in the client's ability to find causes and solutions to their own problems.
- Empathy towards the client – visualising the client's perspective of their world, values and issues.

Table 6.2 Strengths and weaknesses of different psychological perspectives

	Areas of strength	Areas of weakness
Behaviourist	Offers significant insight to the process of learning and how learning and behaviour can be manipulated with positive and negative reinforcement. Wide range of applications including treatment of phobias, substance misuse and reward-based programmes for children	Tends to simplify and mechanicalise behaviour ignoring conscious thought processes and the impact of social and interpersonal situations. Focuses on behaviour modification rather than the causes behind the behaviour
Biological	Informs better understanding of service users suffering from a range of cognitive disorders, including an understanding of the issues behind the causes. Enhances the understating of how certain conditions effect memory, for example, Alzheimer's disease or Korsakoff syndrome	Can be interpreted as overly simplistic in that it assumes human actions are all chemically driven reactions with the environment. It fails to explain adequately how the mind and the body interact, i.e. how an individual's explicit and implicit attitudes and emotions affect reactions
Cognitive	The focus on learning processes enables the practitioner to develop a deeper understanding of the issues faced by those with learning difficulties or disabilities. This understanding also develops practitioner empathy. The theoretical applications of the cognitive approach (e.g. CBT) have a significant impact on social work practice in specific fields, e.g. substance misuse or mental health	Even with its combination of scientific experiment and observational study and evaluation, the cognitive approach is largely based on hypothetical theories. There is a tendency towards ignoring biological factors and simplifying the human mind to that of a computer. In this way the approach fails to explain the complexity of human emotions
Psychoanalytical	The approach has significantly developed our understanding of the underlying causes of psychological difficulties in adult life and brought to the fore the link between early life experiences and personality development. Recognition of the interplay between the individual and the social environment. The development of play therapy has been informed by this approach	Freud's theory makes each of us victims of our past, without accounting adequately for the range of human experience. Indeed Freud's theories were based on a very limited number of patients, all of whom had psychological issues. The approach fails to meet scientific criteria with difficulties in experimental methodology, objectivity and replication
Humanistic	Understanding the psychology behind the need to empathise with clients, and tailoring one's approach, can improve the effectiveness of practitioner input. Appreciation of the hierarchy of needs and the client's position within that, will aid identification of key issues and enhance support planning. The focus on interpersonal skills and communication skills informs a counselling approach	The humanistic approach is not regarded as scientific, as it lacks objectivity and rigour. The approach leans heavily towards a positive view of human nature – striving for self-actualisation – which is perhaps unrealistic. Places an emphasis on the observer's view and thus is subjective in interpretation

By doing so, the helper allows clients to deal with what they consider important at their own pace, and thus helps them to become more comfortable with themselves as holistic beings. Rogers' approach placed a particular emphasis on the concept of 'client' rather than patient. Whilst this can be viewed as symbolic, the terminology used emphasised a degree of dignity and a shift towards the role played by the therapist as being that of a consultant.

DEVELOPING A CRITICAL UNDERSTANDING

The five approaches outlined in this chapter offer different psychological perspectives from which a social worker can understand and respond to the needs of service users. It is important to recognise that whilst each approach contributes to a social worker's knowledge base, the theories have strengths as well as weaknesses. Table 6.2 outlines some of these strengths and weaknesses and, whilst not seeking to be comprehensive, should provide some points for more critical engagement with the issues addressed in this chapter.

Critical Thinking

Analyse Table 6.2 carefully. To what extent do you agree with the positives and negatives identified? How scientific is it possible to be when considering the behaviour of an individual?

CONCLUSION

Many of the skills and areas of understanding outlined throughout this book are founded on the knowledge and integration of psychological approaches and theories. It is through the knowledge and application of psychology that social workers will be better equipped to understand the situations service users present and the potential causes underpinning the issues experienced. The differing psychological approaches each provide a piece of the jigsaw with which you can begin to understand the human mind. By doing so the interaction between the disciplines of psychology and social work should become more tangible, alongside the recognition of how both can contribute to the support of human welfare.

 Watch vodcasts 6.1 and 6.2 on the Companion Website (www.sagepub.co.uk/ SocialWork) to see two social work students discuss their experiences of studying psychology and why they think a knowledge of psychology assists in developing the skills required to be an effective social worker.

Reflective Questions

1 Consider what you have read about classical and operant conditioning. How do you think these models have been applied in social work situations? Do you

think the behaviourist approach is a useful lens through which to understand human behaviour?

2   Consider the practical steps that a social worker may be able to take in order to assist service users who have difficulties with some aspect of cognition. For example, consider social work practice with children who have ADHD; social work practice with people who have mental health problems and who hear voices or social work practice with people who have memory difficulties as a result of acquired brain injury. What challenges might a social worker be presented with and what can the practitioner do to counter these?

3   Taking into account what you have read earlier in this text about values and ethics, what parallels can you draw between social work values and the humanistic approach? How does an understanding of Maslow's theory underpin the practitioner's knowledge and skills base when working with disadvantaged individuals or groups?

RECOMMENDED READING

Banyard, P., Davies, M.N.O., Norman, C. and Winder, B. (2010) *Essential Psychology*. London: Sage.

Braisby, N. and Gellatly, A. (2012) *Cognitive Psychology*, 2nd edn. Oxford: Oxford University Press.

Gross, R. (2010) *Psychology: Science of Mind and Behaviour*, 6th edn. London: Hodder & Stoughton.

Holt, N., Bremner, A., Sutherland, E., Vliek, M., Passer, M. and Smith, R. (2009) *Psychology – The Science of Mind and Behaviour*. Maidenhead: McGraw-Hill Education.

You will find some additional links to web-based materials on the Companion Website (www.sagepub.co.uk/SocialWork).

7 HUMAN GROWTH AND DEVELOPMENT

Stewart Brodie and Clare Swan

Key Themes

- The life course and how different stages may be experienced positively or negatively.
- The significance of childhood in our emotional development.
- The development of attachment and bonds.
- The broader family environment in which attachments and relationships are made.
- The common experience of loss and change, which we all experience at different times in our lives; not just about death, but also transitions.

INTRODUCTION

The focus of this chapter is the influence on individual development of environment, social context and relationships. Apart from helping us understand others, you should also reflect on how these aspects apply to you and how this affects your role as a social worker.

PSYCHOSOCIAL THEORIES OF DEVELOPMENT: LIFE CYCLE/ LIFE CRISIS THEORY, OBJECT RELATIONS THEORY AND ATTACHMENT THEORY

These three theoretical approaches are similar in that they all place great emphasis on the importance of experiences in the early years of childhood and agree that the feelings we had in these early years can be so strong that they remain within us and affect our behaviour in adult life **unconsciously**. They differ in how they describe the processes of development, and this difference gives social workers a useful range of theoretical explanations for aspects of behaviour across the whole lifespan.

Erik Erikson's (1965) *life crisis theory* suggests we each pass through eight stages of crisis in our development, and, the greater the positive experiences, as opposed to the negative, at each stage, the more fully we are prepared for the next stage and the stronger we are emotionally. Ronald Fairbairn's (1952) *object relations theory* draws on Freudian theory but moves on to consider the importance of relationships for emotional well-being. The libido is seen as a basic drive from birth to form relationships with others, and a baby from birth has a central ego (not an id, as Freud suggested), capable of meaningful relationships with its primary caregiver. This drive provides us with the means to survive and develop, but what happens in the childhood years continues to affect us in adult life. This is similar to *attachment theory*, the basic sense of belonging that makes us feel safe and secure. Humans need attachments with others for their psychological and emotional development, and we need the protection of attachment figures to ensure survival.

In all three theories, the quality of caregiving to babies, toddlers and young children is hugely important. Quality caregiving that meets the needs of young children, allowing them to enjoy the experiences of developing movement, control and the ability to think and create, while keeping them safe, gives us the capacity to cope better with situations in later life. Care that does not meet a child's needs, or punishes children for their behaviour, may lead to behavioural or relationship problems in later life.

In the first years of life, Erikson identifies two crisis stages. The first, basic trust versus mistrust, is the stage where a baby is totally dependent on caregivers for everything and, if the carers are loving, responsive, patient and consistent, the baby builds a strong basic feeling of trust and safety in the world, i.e., with other people. It is, however, impossible to be a perfect parent who anticipates a child's needs or responds lovingly to a child's behaviour all the time, and it is actually helpful for a baby to experience some frustration, because some basic mistrust is useful to have in a world that is not always safe or reliable. However, too much unresponsive, harmful or inconsistent caregiving can result in too much basic mistrust, and a consequent inability to relate to others.

Erikson's second stage corresponds to the toddler stage of development, when the baby has progressed to a mobile young child, crawling, walking, playing and generally being into everything. The toddler is still very reliant on caregivers for affection and protection, but is also able to express his or her strong will. The crisis identified by Erikson is autonomy versus shame and doubt: the positive balance, where a toddler enjoys the experiences of childhood, produces an inner self-confidence, while a negative balance, being punished or criticised for doing those same things, produces inner feelings of self-doubt or embarrassment. Given that this is the stage where most children are 'toilet trained', any bad feelings from this may translate into shame, as well as doubt. Just as in Erikson's first stage, a child needs to experience some of the negative balance, in this case doubt or shame, because over-confidence is potentially dangerous in a personality.

In object relations theory, these baby and toddler years are seen as the first of three stages, namely, infantile dependence. The baby needs to feel loved by and to feel love for the primary carer. If the primary carer behaves in the positive way we have described above, the baby's central ego develops strongly based on real experiences. However, any responses from caregivers that are not felt as loving threaten the child's well-being. Remember, the basic drive is to form relationships, to love and be loved. So any behaviour from caregivers that might make the child feel unloved has to be got rid of: at this stage a child cannot entertain the idea that a parent/caregiver can, at the same time, be good and bad. In object relations theory the process of getting rid of bad feelings is called **splitting**, and this takes two distinct forms. Where a caregiver does love us, but cannot always respond to our needs immediately, such unmet need is split off from our conscious central ego into what Fairbairn calls the *libidinal ego*, or to describe it another way, our 'needy child'. When caregivers are very negative in their responses, for example, shouting, chastising, or physically aggressive, Fairbairn suggests the baby/toddler feels that needs are being punished and splits off these feelings into the *anti-libidinal ego*, or 'punitive child'. From this theory, it is possible to say that everyone has a 'split personality', because we are formed by an ego that is our conscious self, and both libidinal and anti-libidinal egos, which are part of us, but unconscious.

Attachment theory sees these early years in a similar way, but offers more specific guidance. For Bowlby (1969), three stages in the development of a healthy attachment relationship occur within the first year of life:

1 The newborn baby is not focused on any one person but is engaged in active attachment behaviour and needs affection and consistency of care.
2 By age 3 months the infant can focus on one or more figures.
3 By the age of 6–9 months secure base behaviour is displayed when a child shows clear preferences for certain people. If these key attachment figures are responsive to the child's needs, a secure bond is formed with caregivers that gives the infant confidence to explore the world.

Secure attachment (corresponding to Erikson's positive balances or Fairbairn's strong ego) means the caregiver is in tune with the child's needs, responds to the child's verbal and non-verbal communication, is tactile and sensitive to the needs and desires of the child but does not invade their personal space. The child forms an **internal working model** that significant people are available, are consistent in their response and can be trusted. The world is seen as a safe place and even when things go wrong, all is not lost, because there are people who can help.

Negative early experiences, corresponding to Erikson's basic mistrust, shame and doubt, and Fairbairn's libidinal and anti-libidinal egos, can, according to attachment theorists, produce insecure attachments. Ainsworth et al. (1978) identified the following types.

● *Insecure anxious ambivalent attachment* occurs where there is a pattern of attachment showing anger and resistance. Children demonstrate a desire to be close to the caregiver, then almost simultaneously an inability to be comforted. The child's preoccupation with attachment issues, about how to gain and keep the attention of an attachment figure, gives the child far less time and energy to explore the world around them and play with other children. This form of attachment behaviour tends to come from inconsistent parental response to initial attachment 'signals' from the child, sometimes sensitive, sometimes insensitive and often unavailable. The internal working model for a child is that love is not unconditional and it has to be fought for in whatever way possible.

- *Insecure detached avoidant attachment* occurs when caregivers are consistently unavailable, where they do not respond to attachment behaviour and reject the infant's attempts to gain their attention. The message that the child receives is that showing emotion is bad. With avoidant attachment patterns caregivers find it hard to respond to the child. They appear indifferent, and interaction is controlling rather than cooperative and encouraging. The result is that the child has hidden, cut off feelings and learns to be overly self-reliant. The internal working model is that the child is not loveable, and that it is not worth trying to get close to people as this will only cause hurt. The world is a lonely and isolated place.
- *Insecure disorganised attachment* occurs when caregivers may be abusive, extremely chaotic or inconsistent. This attachment behaviour may also be created when there are frequent changes of carer and no stable attachment figures. The result is that the child's behaviour may be frozen or chaotic, it is stressful to engage with others, play is difficult and there may be feelings of extreme and unbearable anxiety. The caregiver, showing little or no sensitivity to the child's needs, is rejecting, unpredictable and frightening or frightened. The child experiences the caregiver as being hostile or helpless.

Case Study

A 4-year-old child referred by his nursery because of aggressive behaviour to other children and adults may be understood in the following ways:

- He has no feeling of security in contact with others (basic mistrust), no feeling of comfort about himself (shame, doubt).
- He finds it difficult to rely on other people (anti-libidinal ego) and feels that others are rivals or opponents (anti-libidinal).
- He is attention-seeking (insecure anxious ambivalent) or he is stressed by the closeness of others (insecure disorganised).

These theoretical perspectives provide potential areas for an in-depth assessment of a child's early life experiences and how they affect current behaviour.

Moving on through childhood, Erikson sees the third life crisis as initiative versus guilt, and this stage corresponds to the child's growing cognitive ability, in particular, the ability to reason. This would relate to a child from the age of 3 or 4 to the very early years of primary school. Initiative is all about feeling good about the choices we make: where autonomy was about being able to do things, initiative is about choosing to do things. Guilt is the result of things going wrong, but often the guilt we carry around from this stage may have no rational basis. For example, a child wanted to be close to a particular parent at a time when her parents were unhappy with each other. They separated, but the reason was not explained to the child who believed for years afterwards that her strong feelings for one parent caused the other to leave. This feeling can be so deeply rooted in the unconscious that the guilt element remains through adulthood, inhibiting the formation of genuinely close relationships because of the fear of consequences.

Erikson's fourth life crisis of industry versus inferiority coincides with the primary school years. This stage involves feeling good about meeting other people's expectations or feeling bad about not being as good as others. The impact of previous stages is still important, because a child with strong positive balances from the first three stages will be better equipped to deal with the ups and downs of school and family life.

Erikson's fifth life crisis, identity versus role confusion, covers the adolescent years, and is based on the emotional struggle to prepare for mature adulthood. In this respect, he suggests that adolescents are in a continuing state of upheaval, trying to work out who they are, what they believe in, how they look, who they are attracted to and so on, and on it goes. The negative balances from the earlier stages can be revisited, as they grapple with identity issues, but, remember: many of these issues are unconsciously rooted in the personality, and the adolescent is not necessarily consciously aware of all the issues. In this way, aspects of libidinal or anti-libidinal egos may come to the fore, as may some of the insecure attachment behaviours.

Object relations theory sees these age ranges as the second stage of development, the transitional stage, which is the process of moving from total dependence on adults, through the loosening of dependence, the building of peer friendships, before arriving at the final stage of adulthood. Just as Erikson's eight life stages are based on how successfully or unsuccessfully we form relationships, object relations theory's three stages are based on the same approach. Through this transitional stage and into adulthood, we can see how the splitting of our early years' experiences impacts on our development.

Fairbairn suggests that someone with a large split-off libidinal ('needy child') or anti-libidinal ego ('punitive child') will have a weaker central ego. It is our central ego that allows us to see others as they really are, with their good points and their bad points, and the real person is called, in the jargon of object relations, the *ideal object*. If it is less strong, we are less able to see others as they really are, and if we have a dominant libidinal ego we are likely to relate to others on the basis that they should meet our needs, the *exciting object*. We do not see others as whole people with good and bad points but rather as the person who will meet our emotional needs. The risk is that we realise this perception of the other person is wrong and incomplete, and that he or she cannot meet our needs. We may have enough strength in our central ego to see the other person in a more balanced way, or we may become even more needy. It depends how strong the splits are from early childhood.

It is also possible that the needy person will now see the other person as the *rejecting object* and will resort to punitive behaviour prompted by their anti-libidinal ego which now seeks to punish the other person for not meeting their needs. The person with a dominant anti-libidinal ego tries to avoid emotional behaviour, believing that to feel needy emotionally is to feel vulnerable, as experienced in infancy when they were punished by their carers for having needs. As teenagers and adults, they will seek out relationships with others who they believe will place few emotional demands on them. If they have a partner who places emotional demands on them, they are likely to feel vulnerable and anxious, and their dominant anti-libidinal ego will punish those who prompt that feeling, just as in infancy needs were treated as bad and punished. The personality with a dominant punitive child enters relationships without the ability to see the whole other person, just those parts that will satisfy his or her own emotional needs.

We all have varying degrees of the needy and punitive child in our personalities but we are not all dominated by such characteristics. As adults, we may find our needy/punitive splits become more obvious when we are not coping with life events very well, but it is still possible to achieve Fairbairn's third and final stage of mature dependence and form relationships with others based on a real understanding of the whole other person, not just the parts that meet our needs.

Erikson and Fairbairn agree that the development goal from childhood and adolescence is to become an adult who can form adult-to-adult relationships in a mutual way, able to give to a relationship and take something from a relationship. Object relations theory identifies this as its third and final stage, mature dependency.

Critical Thinking

Consider our use of the term 'independence'. We social workers often claim that we are helping people to remain or become 'independent', but would it be more appropriate to say 'mature dependent'? Mature dependency realistically allows adults to be dependent in a relationship provided they are also giving something of themselves to that same relationship.

Erikson's sixth life crisis is almost identical to this, but he places this as a crisis of young adulthood, which is when we are forming relationships, having children, setting out on careers and are expected by society to behave responsibly as adults. This stage is described as intimacy versus isolation, where intimacy means the capacity to be mature dependent and isolation means the inability to form such relationships. In looking at the negative balance, we can also bring in the impact of libidinal and anti-libidinal ego and of insecure attachment patterns on adult behaviour.

The impact of splitting and attachment patterns from childhood may continue to influence behaviour throughout life, and Erikson identifies two further life crises, mid-life, which he calls generativity versus stagnation, and older age, which he calls ego integrity versus despair. Emotional health in mid-life is seen as a balance of feeling useful and worthwhile versus feeling stuck in a rut, and in old age as a balance between a contented realistic overview of one's life, as lived so far, versus discontent and regret.

Case Study

Jane, in her forties, mother of three children, married to a businessman, church member, is apparently very comfortable. She has a big house, a circle of friends and financial security. To her friends' and family's shock, she suddenly leaves to embark on an affair with a younger man. To help us understand this, we might need to consider Erikson's mid-life theory (how positive was she *really* feeling?), object relations theory (how emotionally needy is she?), attachment theory (how secure did she *really* feel?) and family theories (what was the pattern of communication in the family, how comfortable were people in their roles?).

While Erikson's theory provides a useful framework for human development through the life span, it should not be rigidly applied to particular age groups. Individuals progress through the stages at different speeds according to personal circumstances. A person diagnosed with a life-shortening illness at 40 years of age may find themselves thrown into Erikson's eighth stage as they seek to reflect and evaluate their life. Equally a child with a disability may be kept in an over-dependent position by caring adults and may not be in a position to exercise the positive balances of autonomy or initiative.

Brown and Lowis (2003) investigated the proposition that Erikson's eight stages should be extended further. Read their article and undertake an activity by visiting the Companion Website (www.sagepub.co.uk/SocialWork). Also on the website you will find an article by Johnstone and Gibbs (2012) exploring parents' attachment to their adopted children.

FAMILIES

Minuchin (1979) identified family systems theory, which looks at the elements that make up a family: the individuals in the family, their personal characteristics and the interaction between them. In this context 'family' refers to any unit consisting of an adult or adults and children regardless of the adults' sexuality or whether the members of the family unit are kin-related.

We need to understand what each individual brings to the family system and the consequential impact each of these people has. Bornstein and Sawyer (2006) and Parke and Buriel (2006) see the family like a human body which, to be truly whole, consists of many interrelated parts that affect, and are affected by, every other part. Each of these individual parts contributes to the functioning of the whole, therefore the whole system, or family, is affected by each individual component. If change takes place in one individual, this will affect the whole family system. Think for a moment about your favourite fruit jelly. If you prod the jelly on its side the whole jelly 'shivers'. Families respond in a similar way to the jelly: if something happens to an individual in the family, the whole family system is affected.

Boundaries

Boundaries between individuals within families are considered important. Families, regardless of the composition, consist of subsystems within the overall larger system. One subsystem might be a sibling subsystem or a parental subsystem, regardless of how many children or parent figures are in the family. It may be one parent and a grandparent who jointly form a subsystem. In *family systems theory* it is important to understand that boundaries exist between each of these subsystems, and that each individual is clear about what the boundaries are. To illustrate this concept we can consider the rather obvious need for parents' sexual relationships to be kept separate from children. This is a boundary. Similarly, the emotional needs of the parental subsystem may well be differentiated from the emotional needs of the children. This is a boundary. Family systems theory would argue that for the family to function properly it is important for boundaries between the subsystems to remain clear. If the boundaries become diffuse and unclear then dysfunction can result. Boundaries that are unclear between parents and children can confuse children and create a sense of anxiety about who is actually providing the parenting.

Communication

Communication within families should be clear and direct, but all too often such communication can be unclear and indirect, leaving children wondering what exactly the adults in the family are actually saying. Children not only need to be communicated with clearly, but that communication must clearly let the children know that they are cared for and respected, which fosters the development of a child's positive self-image. Children who live with indirect, unclear communication find it difficult to understand what parents or carers mean and expect of them which may lead to resentment and mistrust in the relationship. Children who experience communication that is devoid of affect can feel uncared for and unloved, again leading to mistrust and resentment.

Homeostasis

Homeostasis is the maintenance of the same state. Sameness and stability frequently create a secure living environment for many children, because they know what to expect and are reassured when their expectation is fulfilled. Parrish (2010) tells us that homeostasis is the natural seeking of sameness or balance which is found in nature but also applies to human systems.

Someone in a family, usually a parent, provides the homeostasis. For example, following a divorce, a mother may feel that stability and sameness is what will help the children to manage the change. This mother may work very hard to keep her family together, emphasising the importance of each family member supporting and working for the others. This would be a positive example of homeostasis meeting the needs of each family member, but it is not always positive. If it becomes difficult for a child to grow up and to move away from home in a healthy and constructive way, or to form emotional relationships outside of the family system, what was originally a healthy homeostasis may well in later years become a dysfunctional pattern of behaviour.

Circular Causality

As we have already discussed, each individual in a family is affected by the actions of another. If we have a problem of a child truanting from school, it may be seen as simply a child's behaviour that needs to be changed. However, looking at this one factor within the family's everyday behaviour may produce a picture of mother arguing with father, members of the family drinking excessively, distressed behaviour from other siblings, and the child's truanting. A circular list of factors presents itself, and the truanting is only one part, no longer the presenting or only problem. Circular causality leads us to examine other factors that may well be a more significant problem.

All the above theories focus on understanding the family's functioning in the here and now, and generally the family members are aware of the behaviour. There are also unconscious aspects of behaviour, and of these the family are not necessarily aware.

Transference

In psychodynamic theory, transference is a mechanism through which we relate to someone as if they were someone else. It is an unconscious influence on our behaviour and therefore we are generally not aware of doing it. 'You're so like your Auntie Julia', a girl may be told, and she does look like her aunt. However, when her family begin to behave towards her as if she *were* her promiscuous aunt by putting severe restrictions on her behaviour, which do not correspond to the girl's actual behaviour, the transference becomes dysfunctional.

Interlocking Pathology

Interlocking pathology has its base in the defence mechanism of projection, and occurs when we project our feelings onto another person, who then carries them and expresses them as their own. Kaplan (1998) summarises projection as the transfer of unacceptable feelings to someone else. Because the process is unconscious, we are frequently unaware of this behaviour.

Following the death of a grandparent, members of the family are genuinely distressed, but cannot cope with grief feelings. Sadness is projected on to one member of the family, who may be one who feels less threatened by the display of feelings. This person takes on the sadness of the others, which is a huge weight leading to symptoms of depression. However, the other family members feel more able to cope and can concentrate on trying to help the 'depressed' member. In this way, they don't have to deal with their own sadness. Only a comprehensive assessment can hope to untangle such significant dynamics.

Scapegoating

'Scapegoating' is a common expression, but it can be a significant contributor to relationships within families. When one member of the family is a scapegoat they are held responsible for all the problems of the family. Again this process is frequently unconscious. It may be that a family feels that they are correct to believe that all of the family's problems originate from Jimmy's bad behaviour. However it may be that their need to find a scapegoat originates from feelings of inadequacy in the other family members who need to blame someone for all the problems.

You can begin to see that there may be a number of ways in which family members can relate to each other at an unconscious level. Equally, from systems theory, and in particular the phenomenon of circular causality, it should be fairly easy to see that scapegoating could become one part of several dysfunctional aspects of a family's behaviour.

This overview of significant aspects of how families behave helps us to understand that all may not be as it first seems. The systems theory approach may well offer a more immediate prospect of change within a family by intervening to interrupt circular causality by simply addressing the parents' arguing. To achieve a more permanent change might well mean helping the parents to understand what unconscious factors they each bring to the relationship that causes them to argue to such an extent. The significance of the unconscious factors that individuals bring to the family system cannot be ignored, and it is important to be able to assess all dimensions of functioning.

LOSS AND CHANGE

Through life we express ourselves through things that give us meaning and we form attachments to many aspects of our lives, such as photographs, jewellery, hobbies or interests, our jobs, places that we live in or visit, and people that we hold dear. These significant attachments make up what Marris (1986) refers to as our assumptive world. When our assumptive world is threatened our sense of security is threatened, and so, if we lose an object or person, the stronger the attachment we had to the lost object or person, the greater the threat to our security and our very identity. The experience of loss, therefore, is always personal and depends on how dependent we were on the object or person. This can be further complicated if we experience a number of losses over a relatively short period.

The attachments that we form to significant things can be reformed with new people and things – things that can become the new anchors in our life. This gives new expression to parts of the self again. However, as we have already seen, it takes time to work through the full impact of the loss, to identify what is important in terms of meanings and beliefs and to identify new things through which the attachment-forming process can begin again.

Marris suggests that humans need to hold on to familiar things as a natural response to change, even if the change is one that has been chosen and is beneficial. Understanding this aspect of loss and change is invaluable for effective social work practice. It helps to understand and then work with people who seem to be persistently unwilling or unable to make positive changes in their lives: the woman in the abusive relationship; the person struggling with alcohol or drug addiction; or the person who has been long-term homeless who appears unmotivated to search for a tenancy. Of course there will be a multitude of complex reasons why people are resistant to or unable to make changes in such situations, even though the change would appear to be a beneficial one. However, understanding a person's innate need to hold on to what is familiar, to what contributes to their sense of self and the world's view of them (their assumptive world) is the foundation on which all other aspects of knowledge or theory can be built.

In his studies on attachment, Bowlby identified the stages of reaction from a child who becomes separated from the caregiver: protest, despair and detachment. If separated from an attachment figure, infants and young children exhibit separation protest, becoming distressed and making urgent efforts to be re-united with the attachment figure. Problems can occur if there is permanent separation from the primary attachment figure, the child's sense of security can be impaired and the child may be reluctant to engage in healthy normal exploratory behaviour. Such is the basis for adult behaviour when facing a loss.

As social workers it is imperative that we understand the complex nature of loss as a bereavement, accompanied by grief. Bereavement may most commonly be experienced through the death of someone we hold dear, but can also apply to the loss of anything to which we are closely attached. Grief according to Murray Parkes (1986) is the price we have to pay for loving someone or something, and, among a number of theorists, he has identified stages we go through as we grieve a loss. You should not see these as rigid and sequential: remember the experience of loss is unique to each individual, but we are likely to experience the following.

Shock and Alarm

Even if the loss has been foreseen, the experience will still bring about some sense of shock – the reality of what has happened can never be fully anticipated however much we may think we have prepared for it. We may feel panic, unreal, detached, physically ill or disbelief. This stage is generally relatively short-lived though it can return at a later stage of the grieving process.

Anger and Guilt

It is often difficult to express anger in any situation, let alone when one is grieving. The bereaved person may feel angry with the person that has died, angry with the doctors who could not save them, angry with relatives and friends who do not appear to respond to the death and their own suffering appropriately, or just angry with the world for being so damned unfair. Anger turned inwards in ourselves becomes guilt.

Searching

This corresponds to 'protest' in Bowlby's study on separation and is a very basic emotion. Sometimes we think that we have seen the lost loved one in a crowd. This is not just a case of mistaken identity, but an intensely strong desire to keep the person with us in the present. We may make visits to shared familiar places, or to the grave as a way of searching for the lost one. In extreme cases, the surviving partner may die soon after or commit suicide to join the lost one. In early stages, searching is an attempt to keep the lost person as part of the present, whereas in the later stages it becomes a kind of painful pining as the lost person slips into the past.

Mitigation

The bereaved person attempts to understand the loss, which is less difficult if the causes are acceptable, but more difficult if they are not, for example, a child's death. The pain may begin to ease at this point, and routines are re-established. Future plans can be formed and the thought of a new life becomes possible.

Gaining a new Identity

The bereaved person's new identity absorbs all of what has happened. New relationships, new roles and new routines become acceptable without the physical presence of the lost person, and these coexist with memories.

To develop your understanding of the sociological dimension of loss and grief see the article by Bevan and Thompson (2003) on the Companion Website (www.sagepub.co.uk/SocialWork).

CONCLUSION

This chapter has introduced key concepts and theories relating to human growth and behaviour. You should try to link all the above material in order to understand yourself and those you work with more fully. For example, how we cope with loss will depend on how comfortably we have formed attachments, how positively we feel about ourselves and how realistic our relationships with others have been.

Watch vodcast 7.1 on the Companion Website (www.sagepub.co.uk/SocialWork) to see chapter author Stewart Brodie summarise the main points conveyed in this chapter that he co-authored with Clare Swan, and why possessing a knowledge of human growth and behaviour is important for social work practice.

Reflective Questions

1 The main focus of this chapter is on how people develop and grow emotionally throughout their lives and how the way they encounter key events in their life can lead to positive or negative outcomes. Firstly, discuss why knowledge of the various processes and theories discussed here are important for social work practice. Secondly, are there any common themes that run through the various sections outlined above? If so, what are they and what do they suggest to you about human emotional development?

2 Erikson's stages approach is frequently called upon in trying to explain how people develop. Read the section again and try to reflect on whether the stages he outlines match your experiences or the experiences of people you know. Are there other factors beyond the purely psychological or within the family that may influence whether or not people may successfully manage each stage?

(Continued)

(Continued)

3   Many of the above models of either growth and development or dealing with loss and attachment are built around the notion of discrete stages through which people pass. Reflect on whether you think that life is neat and clear cut in this way, providing reasons for your answer.

RECOMMENDED READING

Beckett, C. and Taylor, H. (2010) *Human Growth and Development*, 2nd edn. London: Sage.

Crawford, K. and Walker, J. (2003) *Social Work and Human Development*. Exeter: Learning Matters.

Howe, D. (1995) *Attachment Theory for Social Work Practice*. Basingstoke: Palgrave Macmillan.

Lishman, J. (ed.) (2007) *Handbook for Practice Learning in Social Work and Social Care: Knowledge and Theory*. London: Jessica Kingsley Publishers.

Thompson, N. (2002) *Loss and Grief*. Basingstoke: Palgrave Macmillan.

COMMUNICATION
8 AND ICT

Sheila Slesser and Jenny Blair

Key Themes

- Communication is an essential aspect of everyday life and is central to the practice of social work.
- Modes of communication are not just verbal and written but also non-verbal and symbolic.
- Effective communication is highly complex, involving an understanding of how different modes of communication operate simultaneously.
- Interviewing service users requires a combination of technical, reflective and intuitive skills.
- Information and communication technology (ICT) offers significant opportunities to develop practice in new and exciting ways in terms of education, networking and innovative interactions.

INTRODUCTION

As Moss (2008) noted, 'To be human is to communicate. Whether we realise it or not, all of us, all the time are sending out messages to other people, directly or indirectly.' Defining communication involves considering the verbal and non-verbal exchange of information when giving and receiving information. Communication is a core skill of all aspects of social work practice, be it non-verbally, verbally, symbolically or in the written form, and, as Thompson (2003a) notes, 'Communication is not only a part of our everyday lives but an essential one, in the sense that we cannot not communicate.' The use and implementation of information and communications technology (ICT) into this sphere of communication has greatly enhanced not only the speed and accessibility of communication, but has also addressed and altered the way in which social workers undertake many of the statutory bureaucratic tasks required of their role. Texting and emailing are also increasingly used as mediums to communicate with service users and carers. Within this less formal sphere, use of written language and how social workers communicate is important.

In a time where there is a growing awareness of the need for clear and effective communication between professionals, it is also imperative that the social worker acquires and utilises a range of communication skills, reflecting constantly on the impact s/he is having. Communication is a two-way process and social workers need to be aware of how they convey meaning within their professional role but also need to be able to read, listen and interpret the communication of the people they are working with.

How do we communicate the value base of social work? How does the social worker show respect, convey empathy and avoid being judgemental? The social worker needs consciously to make decisions about how to behave in situations and make choices about the words that are used and the manner in which they are said. Social workers themselves will have personal emotions and feelings which require self-awareness. This adds to the complexity of the communication process as the 'scene is constantly changing' (Koprowska, 2010: 2). Social workers also need to be in tune with themselves and have to understand what they are conveying to the service user/carer, whilst also listening to what the service user/carer is saying to them. Learning to understand what people are communicating is a crucial skill (Trevithick, 2012).

> ## Exercise
>
> Make a list of the different types of written communication you imagine a social worker would undertake. In doing so it may be useful to link these to the variety of service user groups and range of settings a social worker may be working with/in.

TYPES OF COMMUNICATION

Symbolic Communication

Symbolic communication involves 'behaviour, actions or communications which represent or denote something else' (Lishman, 2009). Elements of symbolic communication include our actions, the environment we are in, our dress, personal decoration and artefacts.

Actions include the choice we make about behaviour and we have to consider how our behaviours can be interpreted. If, for example, the worker is continually late for appointments with a service user, this may convey that the meeting they are attending is not of any value, which in turn can devalue the person(s) left waiting. If the service user is very punctual for an appointment, then we may interpret this as the service user being strongly motivated to engage with our service. Actions have a meaning.

The physical environment is concerned with *where* we engage with our service users and carers. We need to think consciously about the impact the environment will have on the interaction and consider whether this can be influenced in any way. The social work office/setting is seen as the territory of the social worker and not the service user, which conveys symbolic meanings of authority and control (Lishman, 2009). On a recent visit to refurbished council offices it appeared that the plush 'corporate access point' where receptionists had the responsibility of contacting the social worker was, whilst clean and efficient, also symbolically communicating an additional barrier between the service user and the social work service.

How social workers dress must be appropriate to the setting and work environment; for example, workers need to be aware of the dress code for the agency setting. Within a team providing a service to the courts, the workers often find themselves in formal situations so need to consider clothing appropriate to this setting. If the workplace is a community facility where the daily routine involves play activities with young children, then a more relaxed dress code would be required where comfort is required from clothing. Here if clothing is over formal then it may give confused messages about the social worker's role and perhaps highlight the power inherent in the service user/worker relationship. This of course may also be what is intended, but again the choice needs to be supported by meaningful and appropriate motives on behalf of the worker.

Personal decoration and artefacts are about how the worker accessorises him/herself. The fashion for visible tattoos and body piercings would be an obvious area to consider. While seen by some as a fashion accessory carrying some 'street wise' value with the teenage youth service user, tattoos and piercings might not have the same impact within a more formal setting or with older people.

Non-verbal Communication

Lishman (2009) comments that while spoken communication is concerned mainly with information-giving, non-verbal communication is 'the music behind the words' conveying feelings and attitudes. How we behave non-verbally will have considerable impact on our interaction, which, again, requires good self-awareness. Within this interactive process we also need to develop our understanding of what our service users and carers are conveying to us through their non-verbal behaviour. How accurately we decipher meaning and assess the non-verbal behaviour of others requires some understanding of our own non-verbal behaviour. The immense complexity surrounding non-verbal behaviour means it can often be ambiguous and can lead to misunderstandings in communication.

Non-verbal communication comprises:

- *Facial expression.* Messages we give out via our facial expression are very powerful. They often show the genuine emotion of our communication.
- *Eye contact.* Our eyes communicate, and effective eye contact is essential to our daily interaction with people. It is also a useful function for regulating conversation; we give and receive subtle messages about when to stop and start conversations.
- *Posture.* How we stand, sit or walk can say so much about what we are communicating and our attitudes.
- *Touch.* Physical contact is a powerful medium and as such has to be considered carefully. It is useful to reflect on how to use touch within professional boundaries.
- *Proximity.* How we use the space and distance between us when we communicate.

All these aspects of our communication will have **cultural and gender significance**.

The interpretation and assessment of the non-verbal behaviours of service users and carers is an important skill to develop. The proximity, eye contact and the ease of physical contact between a mother and child for example, will give the worker some idea of the quality of the relationship, attachment and bonding. The service user who finds eye contact difficult and has a closed posture, sitting with arms folded and hunched in appearance, may be communicating something about their emotional state. Also, we need to be able to adapt this skill when working with people who have learning disabilities, sensory impairments and physical disabilities. In addition, if the work setting includes personal care, the skill involved becomes more acute, because of the closeness of the contact. The worker needs to be genuine and **congruent** with their responses so that their behaviour will be interpreted accurately by the service users and carers.

Case Study

Kenny is 23 and has learning disability and significant physical health problems. He lives in a small group care home which is run by a national charitable organisation. You as a social work student are on placement within the setting. After returning from a community activity Kenny is unusually agitated and is following you around the home. He sits very close to you at meal times and strokes your hair and face while singing continuously. His eye contact is constantly on your face yet you are finding it difficult to engage with him.

Think about this situation and discuss some of the issues in relation to non-verbal communication. How might you be feeling about the touch and proximity of Kenny? Consider also how you might be feeling at a personal level and responding on a professional level. What are you assessing from Kenny's behaviour? What might Kenny be getting from this interaction?

An activity on the Companion Website (www.sagepub.co.uk/SocialWork) will help you think about symbolic and non-verbal communication in more detail. Visit the site now to undertake the activity.

Verbal Communication

Now add into the mix our verbal communication, including the tone we use, the speed at which we talk, the volume required and the register (Lishman, 2009).

- *Register*. When we talk to service users and carers we need to be mindful of the level of language we are using. In particular we need to be thinking about our use of esoteric jargon, that is, language that is specific to the social work professional world. We need to think about our degree of formality and how we have to adapt our use of words and the way we talk to meet the needs of the situation (Thompson, 2009). Social workers need to have an internal ability to 'switch registers' to suit the situation. To be too formal on a home visit to a young family may not be appropriate and may hamper the professional relationship you are trying to establish. To be too relaxed in a formal setting, court or conference for example, could also be misinterpreted as being flippant or arrogant.

- *Speed.* If the words we say and information we give are being delivered too quickly then there will be a high probability that we are not being effective. Fast speech may indicate the emotional state of the speaker and can also be indicative of overall attitude. Slow speech can be equally difficult and can also convey a lack of interest, low mood or patronising attitude.
- *Pitch.* Here we are talking about the tune of language (Thompson, 2009a). In a question, for example, we raise the pitch at the end of the sentence to denote a question. If someone is talking in a high pitch it could mean they are anxious or in a manic state. Low pitch could indicate shyness and lack of motivation. Pitch of language follows very complex rules and a subtle change can make all the difference to what is being said.
- *Volume.* The level and volume of speech adds an extra dimension to what is actually being said and the manner in which it will be conveyed and understood (Thompson, 2009a). Raised level can distort speech and facial expression, which can confuse those who are hearing impaired. Also, raised volume can compromise confidentiality so it is always worth being aware of this. Loud speech can be an indicator of mood and attitude, for example, anger or anxiety; in contrast, soft speech can be an indicator of lack of confidence or saying something secretive.
- *Tone.* Finally, the tone we use in speech, which involves conveying emotions such as happiness or authoritarian attitudes, will affect how we are understood (Thompson, 2009a).

So these layers all impact on how we are perceived and how we understand what our service users and carers are saying back to us. We then have to make a choice as to how we respond, based on our professional assessment from our professional knowledge base.

When talking, we use a range of verbal skills to facilitate clearer understanding. These skills involve:

- paraphrasing – rephrasing or repeating what the client has said in different words;
- clarifying – checking out with the service user and conveying understanding;
- summarising – identifying key issues to the service user to confirm the content and overall focus of the interaction (Lishman, 2009).

Figure 8.1   Process of communication

Embedded in this is good **active listening**. In addition to the above skills, active listening requires an awareness of the emotional content of the interview and avoiding the 'dangers of preconceptions, stereotyping or labelling' (Trevithick, 2012). Service users and carers regularly cite listening as the most important skill social workers should have.

Verbal communication also involves the actual vocabulary workers use, as words and how we say them can convey a subtle transference of our own values and attitudes, which can be stereotypical and discriminatory. An interesting example of this would be why, when we talk about the term 'nurse', do we tend to assume the female gender, when it might equally well be a 'he'. While there may be cynicism surrounding changing words and language to become more 'politically correct', as social workers we have to embrace these changes as they do have influence and can challenge preconceptions and shift discrimination. Social work, like many other professions, is riddled with jargon that can also cause misunderstanding and confusion. Professional codes of practice highlight the requirement of social workers to be able to 'communicate clearly', and we must be careful of the use of jargon.

Bolger (2013) undertook research on the use of video self-modelling by social work students. To see her findings visit the Companion Website (www.sagepub.co.uk/SocialWork) and read the journal article.

Emotional Climate

For communication and subsequent intervention to be effective we must consider the emotional climate. 'This involves being sensitive to the emotional dimension of your interaction in relation to both yourself and the person(s) you are conversing with' (Thompson, 2009a: 106). The way we feel at any given time can affect our communication and, again, we have to be self-aware, make good use of supervision and peer support, because if we are preoccupied with our own emotions, our capacity to understand others may be affected, as well as our own abilities to respond and communicate effectively.

Interviewing

The interview is a 'conversation with a purpose' (Trevithick, 2012). It has specific aims and is where social workers will gather most of the information for assessment. Interviews can vary in form and can be undertaken in a wide variety of settings. There are, however, certain core requirements to the interview and this section will aim to explain the significance of these requirements.

Firstly we have to be clear about the purpose of the interview. Why are you meeting with the service user/carer? What is it you hope to achieve from this meeting? A clear purpose helps to focus the social work role and, if this is clearly communicated, should help the service user to feel more comfortable with the process. Considering emotional and environmental climate, are you in the right place and in the right emotional frame of mind?

Secondly, planning the interview requires us to consider the time and place of the interview, its prospective length and who should be involved. When planning the time of the interview it is important to consider who it is you are hoping to meet/visit. For example, if the purpose of your interview is to see a young mother and her new baby, it might not be wise to visit first thing in the morning as the baby may not have slept well and the mother may be tired or still in bed. As far as is possible, the daily routines of our service users and carers have to be considered in managing the interview.

Although it is always difficult to predict exactly how long an interview will take, it is helpful to give yourself some time limits, not just for work load reasons but to help you in focusing on the overall aims. An interview that goes on way over time may have lost its focus and the short interview may never have found it! If you are working to a very tight deadline, you need to be clear about this at the onset with the service user and adjust your own plans regarding overall aims of the interaction.

Within this stage it is also important to consider the communication needs of the person(s) you are going to be meeting. Will you require the services of an interpreter, for example, and into which language? There may be budget and cost implications, and most interpreter services require pre-booking. When working with an interpreter the worker needs to make sure they maintain eye contact and talk directly to the service user. The interpreter becomes the tool to aid communication, and the social worker should seek clarity regularly to ensure everyone understands. Remember also that only one person should talk at any time to allow the interpreter to process and interpret the conversation accurately. Interpreters work within their own professional ethical base, which includes 'impartiality, respect for diversity and confidentiality' (Evans and Whittaker, 2010).

Exercise

What do you know of *human and technical aids to communication?*

This term is used to encompass the range of specialist communication devices that can be used to facilitate communication. Examples are British Sign Language and spoken language interpreters, communicator guides who specialise in communicating with people who have dual sensory impairment, i.e., deafblind people. Technical equipment includes loop systems, hearing aids and note-takers. (Evans and Whittaker, 2010)

If these are new to you, find out more.

When planning the interview the social worker should give thought to where the meeting should take place. The setting needs to take into account the overall aims of the meeting, the needs of the service user and carers, and the worker's own availability. If the meeting is in the worker's agency, thought should be given to the interview room and to symbolic communication when planning this aspect. Are there enough chairs in the room, does the room need to be booked in advance and are drinks available? If a home visit is to be undertaken, does a risk assessment need to be done? Does this visit require two members of staff? Consider timings also in relation to distance and travel arrangements and be prepared with contact details in case transport does not run on time or previous appointments overrun. The symbolic impact of turning up late for an interview without explanation can have detrimental impact.

Thirdly, introductions, and consequently first impressions, are significant as this is where initial assumptions and judgements are formed. It is part of the role of the professional to take charge of introductions so it is important to say hello and introduce ourselves and facilitate the introduction of others. The offer and receipt of a handshake, an open facial expression and a smile can all contribute to valuing the person and being respectful. If these beginnings are not handled well, any anxieties the service users and carers have may well be heightened. It is important that the interview gets off to a positive start because it also establishes the worker's responsibility for this part of the process, the worker's professional authority and helps in 'establishing a good rapport and sound working alliance' (Trevithick, 2012).

The worker should introduce themselves clearly and state the purpose for the meeting. This will require the worker to be sure of specific details that may be required, i.e., any legislative and/or statutory underpinning.

Fourthly, an important part of the social work interview process is establishing a **rapport** with the service user/carer. It is possible to establish this rapport with the service users and carers fairly quickly, and this can be done at introduction stage with appropriate use of 'small talk', for example, about the weather, which helps to establish some common ground, breaks the ice and can relax the service user/carer. This is not always something social workers in training find easy, and it may require rehearsal to improve this important communicative quality.

Fifthly, throughout the interview the worker needs to think about the questions that will provide the information to underpin the assessment process, paying particular attention to the style of question as this will influence the flow of information. *Narrow or closed* questions (Koprowska, 2010; Lishman, 2009) seek factual information and yes/no answers. *Broad or open questions* encourage a wider range of responses and give the service user or carer more opportunity to talk about their situation. *Probing questions* are used to elicit a bit more information from the service user or carer about something they have said. *Leading questions* are those that are likely to influence the service user to give the answer they think the worker wants to hear. In general these types of questions are not advisable unless underpinned by a certain intervention style, such as motivational interviewing. Finally, it is best to avoid *multiple questions*, i.e., firing one after the other without allowing time for a response. This may reflect the anxious feelings of the worker rather than the questioning remaining focused on the service user.

Case Study

Consider under what circumstances it might be appropriate to ask the following types of question:

- Did you come by bus today? [Closed or narrow question]
- How did you get here today? [Broad or open question]
- You came by bus today, but can you tell me about the journey? [Probing question]
- You came by bus today, didn't you? [Leading question]
- Did you come by bus? How was it? What was the fare? Where did you get on? [Multiple questions]

Finally, how the interview ends is as important as the interview beginning. At this point the worker will summarise what has been discussed and highlight any actions required to be followed up and by whom. This can be an informal verbal contract or can be a formally recorded, written minute or agreement. It is important for the worker not to make any false promises about what they may or may not be able to do. Endings should be respectful, taking the opportunity to acknowledge any difficulties, and can include a return to small talk. It is useful to remember to thank the service user or carer for their contribution to the meeting as this adds a sense of value for them and conveys a genuine sense of worth to the process.

Written Communication

The principles for effective communication also apply to written communication (Healy and Mulholland, 2007). A major part of the social work role requires clear, concise and articulate writing skills which will enable the reader to understand the meaning of the information easily. The context of social work professional writing can take a variety of forms, and, within these, the written communication must reflect the core values and ethics of social work, presenting factual evidence that is analytical and underpinned by the professional knowledge base.

Written communication is a permanent record of events, facts and thoughts, and these very often contribute to the decision-making processes involving the lives of our service users and carers. There is, therefore, a real sense of responsibility and accountability attached to this aspect of the social work role. The writer has to ensure that information is written clearly to avoid any ambiguity, as this official record has legal weight within the statutory and professional arena. Add into this mix the use of information technology, and the opportunity for a variety of styles of written communication increases.

Communication aspects such as tone and formality have to be considered. When conveying the seriousness of a situation within our writing, we need to think about the language we use as we do not, in this format, have the luxury of accompanying facial expression or audible tone to help convey meaning accurately. In essence our written words need considerable thought and preparation to ensure what we hope to say is coming across effectively.

In summary, establishing and maintaining social work relationships is integral to the overall aim of working with our service users and their carers. It is important therefore that we also consider how we come across, and how our service users and carers interpret our communication with them. Communication is a complex and multilayered process and how we understand, make sense and utilise our communication skills is fundamental in the work social workers undertake.

The focus in this chapter now develops the ideas and issues discussed above in relation to Information and Communications Technology.

INFORMATION AND COMMUNICATIONS TECHNOLOGY (ICT)

Many aspects of our lives are mediated by various forms of information and communication technology (ICT). According to the ONS (2011a: 1):

- 45% of Internet users used a mobile phone to connect to the Internet.
- 6 million people accessed the Internet over their mobile phone for the first time in the previous 12 months.
- The use of wireless hotspots almost doubled in the previous 12 months to 4.9 million users.
- 21% of Internet users did not believe their skills were sufficient to protect their personal data.
- 77% of households had Internet access.

In our social lives, for example, Facebook has become an essential tool in forming and maintaining relationships with friends and families, and the purchase of music is conducted through digital technology. For any reader of this book born since 1990 the analogue society of only fixed landline phones, the writing and sending of paper letters, or visiting the local record store to buy a vinyl record of your favourite music is firmly fixed in the historical past. The world today is inescapably digital. The same applies to the modern workplace, where the computer and other mobile technologies structure and frame many elements of the everyday work experience, not just in the United Kingdom but across the globe. Social work is no exception to the above trend and an understanding of ICT and how it can benefit and support good practice is an essential part of contemporary social work.

What we intend to discuss here is not how to use certain software packages, but instead to draw attention to some overarching issues that surround and inform the use of ICT, as notable differences exist between how such technologies are employed in the home and in the workplace. In particular, we discuss here what we term the Five Ps of ICT use, as outlined in Figure 8.2.

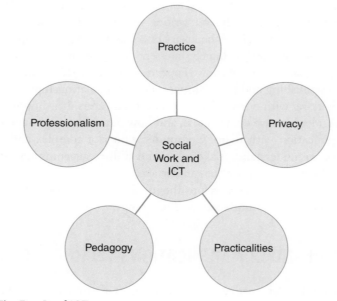

Figure 8.2   The Five Ps of ICT

There is a perception that you cannot foster relationships with people using ICT in the same way that you can face to face, and, although that is true, the ability to foster relationships is still present and should be attempted, especially where geographical limitations may present operational difficulties. A less than ideal relationship is still better than no relationship.

Read the article on the Companion Website (www.sagepub.co.uk/SocialWork) by Parrott and Madoc-Jones (2008) who suggest that the use of ICT presents opportunities for social workers to engage in empowering practice.

Practice

ICT can allow for new and innovative forms of practice, where meaningful interactions can occur between social workers, and between social workers and service users. Etienne Wenger (1998: 45) first introduced the idea of communities of practice (CoP), which refers to a 'kind of community created over time by the sustained pursuit of a shared enterprise'. It makes sense, therefore to call these kinds of communities 'communities of practice'. Wenger, in a discussion around virtual communities of practice (VCoPs), analysed in some depth the generation of online relationships, and it became clear through his work that, far from being problematic to form relationships online, discussion and interactions can in fact occur through a number of different ways. The different configurations of interaction are illustrated in Figure 8.3.

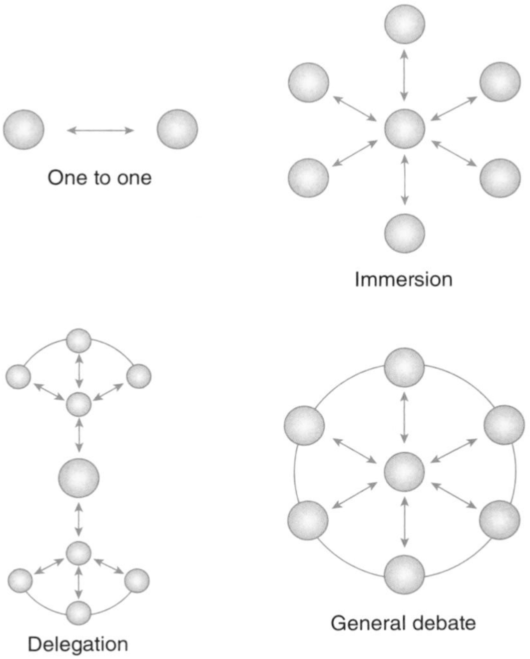

Figure 8.3   Different forms of online and actual interaction

These are, in fact, little different from the types of communication you would expect to see face to face, but they are frequently viewed and analysed differently online. One-to-one discussion can be fast paced and allow participants to become engrossed in a private conversation, potentially enabling a more frank and open exchange about their views and experiences. Immersion, where a newcomer joins an established discussion or community, can be challenging for the group as the new member will bring their own way of involvement and discussion to the group. Delegation or a moderated/led discussion will ideally focus discussions on specific issues of concern, but this is dependent on moderator style and influence. With general debate, online discussions cross between each other, one to one, facilitator to individual, and individuals to individuals.

As with face-to-face interactions, the online community needs to be aware of appropriate types of interaction for the situation at hand and tailor their use of a communication tool accordingly. It should also be remembered that online discussions can be recorded in a far more encompassing way than face-to-face interactions. Where minutes of face-to-face meetings tend to record only the key issues, an online discussion is capable of recording every minor and major point. Wenger (1998: 5) saw communities of practice as having three distinct features: meaning, practice and community:

Meaning: a way of talking about our (changing) ability – individually and collectively – to experience our life and the world as meaningful.
Practice: a way of talking about the shared historical and social resources, frameworks and perspectives that can sustain mutual engagement in action.
Community: a way of talking about the social configurations in which our enterprises are defined as worth pursuing and our participation is recognizable as competence.

Dubé et al. (2005) are among a growing number of researchers readily acknowledging and examining the advent of virtual communities of practice (VCoPs):

> transcending space and time, virtual communities of practice (VCoPs), while not excluding face-to-face meetings, rely primarily on new information and communication technologies (ICT) and internet capabilities, to allow their members to be creative and exchange what can sometimes be crucial pieces of information, in a virtual environment.

VCoPs use varied tools to support their work, including video-conferencing or voice over Internet (Skype), newsgroups, e-mail, shared databases, the Internet and also the more traditional tools including phone and fax. JISCmail is a good example of mailing lists, with like-minded people working together to create better understanding of the key issues in any given area. The service has proven to be a useful starting point for lobby groups to petition government and funding bodies for improved access and understanding across the range of IT and ICT being discussed here.

Privacy

One obvious issue is that of privacy. Digital information is by its nature highly fluid and what is entered in one file or website can easily migrate to another file or website.

Much of the Internet is designed for sharing information, whether legally or illegally, and in most cases having the ability and capacity to share ideas and information is highly useful; but this flexibility to share also presents certain challenges. Service-user confidentiality is one important area of which to be aware.

Anyone sharing information online must understand that information online can remain forever and be easily replicated to other sites and read or viewed by a wider audience than intended. A throwaway comment made online can have much wider impact than one made to a friend in a face-to-face context. There needs to be an understanding and respect for the longevity of such sites and a realisation that they can too readily blur the boundaries between personal and professional life. At all times the rights of individuals to privacy and respect must be upheld.

Practicalities

ICT is not without its problems, and, despite the considerable advances made in the development of software and hardware, all computer-based systems experience practical problems. Much scepticism can be encountered and contingencies should be built into the planning of new systems, whether they are integrated databases designed to enable different agencies to 'speak' to each other or simple design of new office space to enable secure and comfortable use of IT facilities, including provision of enough network points or readily accessible Wi-Fi spots. The long-term impacts both financially and practically need to be considered in more depth before contracts are signed to re-embed faith in the decision-making procedures.

The term digital divide was initially coined to suggest the skills divide between those with IT skills and those without. It has since expanded to include those with access to the advances in technology and those without. Like most areas of life, within social work a digital divide does exist. In some social work contexts the use and provision of ICT varies considerably. Some agencies have well-resourced ICT provision whilst others may offer only the most basic of services. It is interesting to note that in some contexts where ICT is more prolific this has presented new challenges for practitioners. For example, handheld or mobile technologies, such as tablet computers, are useful working devices resulting in the potential for increased efficiency and time effectiveness; yet there is a possibility that service users will see such technology as intrusive and as creating a barrier in communication. This is one of the areas that social work practitioners will need to consider as the use of technology expands and becomes a routine part of practice.

Professionalism

The first half of this chapter discussed various aspects of face-to-face communication between service user and social worker and what needs to be stressed is that the various guidelines and professional etiquette outlined there equally apply online. Informality in language is commonplace on social networking sites or in text messages, but is less suitable in a professional context where the discussions a social worker may have online or over email with colleagues, service users and family members need to be at a professional level. Emails, for example, may appear to be a private form of communication, but legally they are classified as being public documents that can be held open to public scrutiny. So, any communication you write can be seen not just by intended recipients but by anyone, and if the language with which you express your ideas is less than professional then certain potentially problematic consequences can arise.

Critical Thinking

Reflect on how you send text messages or emails to others. How would your normal communication practice have to be modified in order to be 'professional'?

Pedagogy

ICT also offers an excellent resource and means to support and strengthen education (pedagogy), both for social work students and for continuing professional development (CPD) activities intended for practising social workers. The technology exists for lectures or seminars to be held in virtual environments, whether in real live time or in a format that can be downloaded at some future point. In a society where time and money are both becoming increasingly scarce resources, such technology enables social workers at all points in their careers to engage in meaningful education activities that benefit both themselves, allowing them to expand and enrich their knowledge and practice base, and the service user with whom they work. Other developments, such as blogs and discussion fora, can also provide a platform where new ideas can be discussed and debated. Notable examples include SCIE – Social Care Institute for Excellence – and IRISS – Institute for Research and Innovation in Social Services – both of which provide a range of learning resources and guides for best practice.

CONCLUSION

This chapter will have helped you understand the key concepts, theories and debates relating to communication and ICT. You should now be more aware of the complex nature of communication and of the range of skills that underpin interactions. Effective communication is a core aspect of relationship building and maintenance, and it is these relationships which are the foundation from which social work takes place. Communication is a multilayered process requiring awareness of self, awareness of others, and the ability to plan and to monitor the constant interaction between thinking and doing.

We have also discussed the role of ICT in social work practice, demonstrating the importance of technological developments. As our world becomes increasingly digital so will ICT play an increasingly more significant role in social work. Such developments are to be embraced for the advantages they bring but social workers also need to reflect on areas of ICT usage where caution should be exercised, not least in the arena of professionalism.

Watch vodcast 8.1 on the Companion Website (www.sagepub.co.uk/SocialWork) to see chapter author Sheila Slessor summarise the main points conveyed in this chapter that she co-authored with Jenny Blair, and why an understanding of communication is important for social work practice.

Reflective Questions

1 Summarise the various forms of communication we have discussed in this chapter. How varied are they in terms of what they involve? Why is it important for social workers to be aware of how they communicate? Think here in the widest possible context, including not just verbal or written communication but also body language and dress. Could you also identify situations where, let us say, one form of dress may be suitable in one context but not in another?

2 Reflect on situations where you have encountered good or bad forms of communication. Identify why they had those qualities and what effect they had on you. Once you have done that you may wish to reflect on your own personal modes and style of communication in relation to the points about effective communication made above.

3 Online social forums are an integral part of everyday life with a variety of platforms that people can use to communicate with others, whether professionally or personally. For the professional the existence of social media opens up both possibilities and challenges. Try to outline some of those, and also consider any issues associated with discussing and sharing your social work practice with friends online.

RECOMMENDED READING

Hill, A. and Shaw, I. (2011) *Social Work and ICT.* London: Sage.

Koprowska, J. (2010) *Communication and Interpersonal Skills in Social Work*, 3rd edn. Exeter: Learning Matters.

Lishman, J. (2009) *Communication in Social Work*, 2nd edn. Basingstoke: Palgrave Macmillan.

Woodcock Ross, J. (2011) *Specialist Communication Skills for Social Workers: Focusing on Service Users' Needs.* Basingstoke: Palgrave Macmillan.

RESEARCH AND DEVELOPMENT IN SOCIAL WORK AND SOCIAL CARE

9

Iain Turnbull and Joyce Lishman

Key Themes

- What we understand by research.
- What types of research we use in social work and social care, and examples of relevant methods.
- How we may use research in our practice and service delivery, i.e., be research minded.
- What we mean in a slightly broader way by evidence-based practice.
- How this knowledge and understanding underpins our professional development.

INTRODUCTION

Why do students of social work and practitioners need to know about research? Firstly, professional standards require that qualifying social work students can make use of and evaluate up-to-date research and knowledge. In a world that is increasingly complex, in which all professionals are subject to increasing scrutiny and are subject to expectations of accountability, of increasing consumerism and generally more available and more accessible information, not all of which is equally useful or valid, there is a requirement for the social worker to develop what Hardwick and Worsley (2011) describe as 'research mindedness', which is defined as a way of thinking and a habit of questioning that challenge our taken-for-granted assumptions so that we can better understand and reflect on the world that we, service users and communities encounter. (Hardwick and Worsley, 2011: xx)

We can see that this relates to reflective practice and encompasses a view about research that goes beyond merely collecting data and making sense of it. It may actively involve practitioners, service users and communities and thus begins to reflect social work values and distinctive ways of doing social work.

It is worth considering the difference here between social science research, social work research, that is, research *for* social work, and research *on* and *from* social work (Orme and Shemmings, 2010). The first of these is about using research from a variety of disciplines such as psychology or sociology, the second is about looking at social work where the focus of research is on what social workers do and how they do it, and the last is about developing knowledge and understanding from the experiences of those involved in the practice.

It is helpful to pursue these different sources and types of research a little further, because, as social workers, we should make use of their findings to underpin our practice.

- Social science research asks broad questions about the nature of social problems, the relationship of social class and life chances, for example in education, health and employment, and the impact of structural characteristics, for example, poverty, ethnicity, disability and age on how people may be helped to or prevented from gaining access to services.
- This research examines the impact of structural influences on life chances for individuals, and, in this book, Chapter 5 on material circumstances uses this research. From psychology we understand empirically about individual development from childhood to old age.
- Research on social work tends to focus on the effectiveness of social work intervention (see Chapter 33 on evaluation). 'Messages from research' (Department of Health, 1995) was an important example of funded research which drew, from a series of studies, new ways of being more effective in childcare and child protection.
- Research on or about social work, which might involve social work practitioners undertaking research (Everitt, 2002), or research undertaken or led by service users on their experience of the services they receive, cannot or do not receive.

This brief summary leads us into methodological approaches underpinning the research you will read. It is important that you reflect on where your 'knowledge' comes from in your practice. Is it the experience of colleagues based on long years of direct practice? Is it rather more informed ideologically, for example, from a Marxist base, or, currently, from a belief in the market that 'private' provision is more efficient that public service? Is it research based? And, if it is, you then, cynically, have to question who sponsored the research? If you read that beer drinking is good for men's health, you may want to check that the sponsor is not a brewing company!

The importance of being able to critically evaluate research cannot be underestimated. See the activity on the Companion Website (www.sagepub.co.uk/SocialWork) which will introduce you to CASP.

Research that draws on evidence from practice is valuable. In this book, the material on attachment and task-centred intervention provides two examples of knowledge that is most clearly underpinned by detailed research. Studies on attachment included observational studies of infants and their parents; studies in task-centred casework were undertaken by a more experimental approach. On the other hand, neither Erikson's life cycle theory nor psychosocial intervention are as clearly underpinned by research, but Erikson provides a useful framework for understanding the stages we all go through, that is, a theory of meaning, and psychosocial or relationship-based intervention enables us to make deeper interpersonal connections with individuals seeking help in order to understand and relate to their needs and requirements.

We have examined different types of research relevant to social work and social care. It is impossible to introduce you fully to the range of methods available, with their strengths and weaknesses (see Chapter 33 on evaluation and the research methodologies it uses.) It is essential that you as a critical and informed user of research understand some of the key concepts involved.

Exercise

Before you begin the next section, identify a piece of research that has influenced your judgement and thinking. Why did it? Keep this in mind as we move to think about key concepts in research methods.

KEY CONCEPTS IN APPROACHING RESEARCH METHODS

We begin with the difference between primary and secondary research. Next we consider how valid the research findings are that we are reading, and how reliable. Briefly we then examine different research methodologies – quantitative, qualitative and participatory or emancipator.

Primary and Secondary Research

These can sometimes be confused. Basically, primary research is when you undertake research directly, whether on a small scale or a large scale. You personally, alone or with others, plan the research, write up the findings and, if you are lucky, publish them.

Secondary research means that you use secondary sources, which means work done directly by other people. You review other people's research and try to draw conclusions. So a literature review can be seen as secondary research, drawing on other sources to develop potentially new understanding.

Validity and Reliability

Validity in research is essentially about whether what we are using as our research tool – a rating or a questionnaire – actually does reflect what we are trying to measure. Have we, by asking the wrong question or by providing choices in a questionnaire that do not seem relevant to the respondent, inadvertently produced invalid responses? A major issue in validity is about culture and context. A well-known personality test asked 'Do you prefer Washington to Lincoln?' A Briton might respond that she had never been to either of these cities: but, in fact, the research was checking attitudes towards American presidents George Washington and Abraham Lincoln.

Reliability is about whether any research we do can be replicated across different samples of people or populations. For example, if we do IQ tests, questionnaires or surveys about welfare benefits at Eton or amongst investment bankers, these are unlikely to be replicated across Britain.

Exercise

Can you think of a questionnaire you have been asked to fill in which did not seem to invite a clear answer to you? Was that a problem of reliability or validity?

We now turn to examine three broad methodological approaches:

- Quantitative research
- Qualitative research
- Participatory or emancipatory research.

This chapter can only provide some brief examples of the types of research available and a critique of them. The types of research cannot be rigidly separated, as we can see from the 10-year population census in the United Kingdom, which you may have completed. It is a social survey producing quantitative results, for example, how many of us are students, retired or living alone, but it is then open to much qualitative analysis about our life styles. Its flaw is that it does not capture us all, so if we are transients, homeless, squatters or do not fill it in, we shall not be part of this nationwide survey. You may wish to consider whether this is a problem of validity.

Quantitative research in social work has focused mainly on **single case evaluative design** (Bloom, 1999). The main quantitative research methodology has been the concept of randomised controlled trials, which have underpinned the evaluation of outcomes in medicine (Goldacre, 2012) and can therefore be described as evidence-based practice, which social work has drawn on.

Put simply, randomised controlled trials in medicine meet requirements of normal scientific research, including random samples, controlled experimental design and moderate confidence in causal relationships. For example, a controlled experiment in medicine or pharmacy means that there are a group of patients, chosen randomly, who receive the treatment, and another group, also selected randomly, who receive nothing or a placebo. The results for the two groups are then compared. If the groups differ then we can say that the treatment had an effect. Macdonald and Sheldon (1998) have promoted this 'gold standard of rigour' in social work, and the use of this narrow definition of research has underpinned a movement to evidence-based practice. This can have both helpful and unhelpful consequences.

Case Study

You are a social worker in a team working with people with learning disabilities. The agency has agreed to participate in a research proposal based on randomised controls, and a random sample of your caseload of adults with a range of diagnoses, prognoses and abilities will be selected. What problems might arise?

Before we look more closely at social work, we should look at relevant and related issues in medicine. A drug developed by one manufacturer was found to be extremely effective at reducing blood pressure: unfortunately it had other effects, leaving people feeling exhausted and permanently unwell. The drug delivered the outcome tested in the protocol, but did not enhance the patients' quality of life. In pharmacy this recognition of the failure of an entirely experimental, purely scientific approach is being acknowledged: it is being more widely recognised that patients need to be involved in their own treatment, rather than just complying with the instructions of others.

So how do the problems of randomised controlled trials in medicine impact on social work? For a start, these trials can be unethical: a patient may be denied effective treatment, and a service user may not receive a particular service if they happen to be in a control group. A second concern is that results are probabilistic. They do not tell us if we do planned intervention in criminal justice, community care or child protection who will benefit. Who will be in the 70% treatment group and who in the 30% control group? How do we know which of the individuals we are working with are in which group?

Qualitative research is more about exploring people's experience, for example, asking how did we find the service provided? Unfortunately it has currently become associated with asking about levels of satisfaction with unsatisfactory services, perhaps bus or railway travel. Qualitative research, however, is much deeper than this. It involves trying to explore how service users and carers experience their services, how they might want to improve them and how effective the services have been. Qualitative research therefore is closely linked with participatory and service user research. It may perhaps appear more linked to exploring the meaning and understanding of an experience rather than determining the effectiveness and outcomes, but these dual rationales cannot be so easily separated. Even in medicine, for example in general practice, understanding of patients, their circumstances and histories may facilitate better diagnoses and better patient trust, well-being and outcomes.

So, briefly, what qualitative methods might we employ? A fashionable method, particularly among politicians, is a focus group, which can be useful in getting views from a small group of people about those issues in which the person commissioning the research is interested. These issues are often in relation to local policy and service development. The questions we might raise about focus groups are representativeness, validity and reliability. How do we choose this small group of people? Are they a random sample from the population (Orme and Shemmings, 2010)? This is unlikely since they are a small group from a much wider population. Are they a group with a specific interest in the research, for instance young people who have been in care, or parents of children with disabilities? We then explore the experience of people who use services, and in this sense are experts, i.e., in their own experience.

Qualitative research can also use semi-structured face-to-face interviews. Lishman (1978) used these as a practitioner researcher to understand and improve her own practice. The complications with this approach concern potential bias in selecting a sample of service users and the consistency of response of the practitioner, who is also the researcher. This small study, however, was part of a wider body of research (Mayer and Timms, 1970) which identified a 'clash in perspective' between social work clients and practitioners. Small-scale qualitative studies can influence practice, and you may want to consider whether you have ever found yourself in a clash of perspective, where you had a particular view of a problem and a service user or carer a different one. For example, you may be currently thinking about availability of particular services, determining priority and rationing scarce resources. The service user or carer will be much more focused on felt and experienced need.

This discussion of qualitative research leads us into a third kind of research, which is service user-based or user-led, or more generally participatory or emancipatory, research. Participatory or emancipatory research arose from a number of sources (Dullea and Mullender, [1999] 2004) including disability research, feminist research and user and carer research. This approach involves a change in how we think about research: it is not done by professional social workers or researchers, but undertaken or commissioned by users of services, whether as service users or carers (Beresford, 2003).

What does this mean? It means that research questions are framed by service users: how do we experience the care we receive, how do we evaluate its impact and effectiveness? An early example of collaborative research with service users (Evans and Fisher, 1999) stressed the importance of user-led and user-controlled research. Think about some current policy agendas, including personalisation, self-directed support and direct payments. Participatory research would involve people who are receiving services critiquing how the policy is experienced in practice.

On the Companion Website (www.sagepub.co.uk/SocialWork) you will find an article by Fern (2012) reporting on the findings of action research in Iceland using young people as research consultants.

Case Study

Consider the references to empowerment in Chapter 1 and service user perspectives in Chapter 15, and identify areas of practice with which you are familiar, either because you have worked there or undertaken placements. Think about how you might have enabled some participatory research in order to try to influence the range, type or quality of service available to your service users.

This has been a brief review of the potential methodologies underpinning the research that you, as a practitioner, will read to access and critique. A related term, referred to earlier, is evidence-based practice, which is also examined in Chapter 33, and which was originally conceived in terms of randomised controlled trials but more recent approaches incorporate values and user and carer involvement. In considering the role of research in social work it is critical that we consider the notion of evidence-based practice, sometimes referred to as evidence-informed practice. The role of evidence-based practice has become more important as a result of a number of factors, including the changing role of social work, changing expectations of the public and service users and the increasing emphasis on inter-professional working. This last is important in that social workers have to be able to explain their professional views and decisions with reference to knowledge. The social worker should be able to provide critical evaluation of this evidence and of the evidence provided by other disciplines.

The value of evidence-based practice in medicine was that it is seen to be based in a 'scientific' approach, that is, a structured form of enquiry which can be replicated, reviewed and which produces knowledge that can be applied in circumstances beyond those of the immediate locus of the research. In the scientific approach, the randomised controlled trial (RCT) is seen as the gold standard of scientific research. In relation to social research, that is, research about people and their circumstances, there are, however, clear professional and ethical issues about providing interventions to some service users and not to others in the pursuit of knowledge. There is also the concern that research for social work should mirror the values and ethical concerns of the profession. We shall come back to the debate around evidence-based practice but at this point it is worth noting that not all commentators are equally enthusiastic about the approach.

Evidence-based social care has been described as:

> the conscientious, explicit and judicious use of current best evidence in making decisions regarding the welfare of those in need. (Sheldon and Chilvers, 2002 in Smith, 2004: 8)

This is based on the work of Sackett, who developed the concept of evidence-based practice particularly in the context of medical and health care (Sackett et al., 1997). This was in part a response to the gap between research being published and being implemented (sometimes it took up to 20 years for well-researched innovations to become practice). This was seen to be as a result of conservatism within the relevant professions. A lot of research was of poor quality or not really focused on improving outcomes for the patient. A lot of practice was not evidence-based – it was a case of 'keep on doing what you're doing and you'll keep on getting what you've had!' Another factor that influenced the development of evidence-based practice was the increasing awareness of risk and the need for risk management. This is allied to increasing consumerism and willingness to question the actions of professionals, often in circumstances where things have gone wrong. Finally 'new managerialism' and its emphasis on economy, efficiency and effectiveness led to further emphasis on evidence-based practice to justify decisions about the allocation (or removal) of scarce resources.

Gray et al. (2013) have reported on a review of studies which looked at the implementation of evidence-based practice. Read their article now on the Companion Website (www.sagepub.co.uk/SocialWork).

Critical Thinking

In considering the definition of evidence-based practice above, what do you consider to be

- conscientious
- explicit
- judicious

use of evidence? Try to provide a definition of each of these in relation to the use of evidence.

In looking at evidence, this has been held to be more closely related to structured, scientific enquiry. It is about facts and being able to replicate and generalise from one circumstance to another. A reformulation (see Figure 9.1) takes a broader view than this, and includes the service user or carer's views and the influence of professional knowledge.

This brings us to the idea of knowledge that has a broader compass than a strict understanding of evidence. Pawson et al. (2003) suggest that social care knowledge is diverse and that it could be easy to be selective and partisan in identifying the crucial components of that knowledge. There are a variety of ways of looking at knowledge for social work. Pawson et al. (2003) suggested that knowledge should be categorised according to its source. They suggest that it can be organised as follows:

- *Organisational knowledge.* This comes from organisational structures, management and crucially supervision, which is a distinctive and critical approach to the delivery of effective social work.
- *Practitioner knowledge.* This includes experience, practice wisdom and the products of reflective practice and could include practitioner research.
- *Policy knowledge.* This comes from the wider policy environment and includes policy reviews, findings of think-tanks and the outcomes of government consultations.

Figure 9.1 Sources of knowledge (adapted from Sackett et al., 2000)

Figure 9.2   Sources of knowledge for social work and social care (adapted from Sackett et al., 2000)

- *Research knowledge.* This relates to evidence as defined above and includes knowledge acquired through evaluations and systematic studies.
- *User and carer knowledge.* This is gathered from the experience and understanding of people who use services (and occasionally who do not) and from those who care for them.

It can be seen that all of the above with the exception of policy knowledge can be encompassed within Sackett's diagram. In order to take account of this, the diagram could be developed as in Figure 9.2.

The influence and power of the policy environment should not be underestimated in relation to evidence-based practice. It influences organisations and what they can and must do and as a result the knowledge generated or required to fulfil these functions. Similarly, practitioners must work within a policy environment that is complex, changing and often contradictory. Research knowledge is influenced by what can be funded or by the interests or desires of those who commission the research, and service users and carers both influence and are influenced by the policy context.

What are the limitations of evidence-based practice? Research that is concerned with facts and 'what works' fails to take account of the political, cultural and other contexts in which it is conducted. It is concerned with outcomes and the specific behaviours and attributes of the individual. This reflects the view of social work as a rational/technical profession. As a result, it fails to consider the environmental factors, social systems and policy imperatives, and individual perspectives – those of the practitioner and service user.

CONCLUSION

In your social work education you will be introduced to the concept of continuous professional development (Skinner, 2012). Indeed, it is a requirement for continuing registration with the professional body, 'our licence to practise', but it is more than that. It involves a continuing commitment to personal and professional development in order both to cope with the 'uncertain, demanding, complex and changing context of social work' (Lishman, 1998) and because 'social work involves entering into the lives of people who are in distress, conflict or trouble. To do this requires not only technical competence, but also qualities of integrity, genuineness and self-awareness' (Lishman, 1994).

Professional development requires us to engage in the articulation and promotion of good practice and service delivery (see Chapter 33) and the need to update our knowledge base in a regular way as new research informs us about changes in social conditions and policy, for example poverty and current changes in the welfare system, and ways of engaging in more effective practice and service delivery, i.e., to be research-informed, and as this chapter has examined, to be research-critical.

Reflective Questions

1   This chapter has outlined a number of issues and approaches to research that a social worker can call upon in order to improve social work practice or service delivery. Reflect on why it is important for social workers to perform such research and why it is important to evaluate existing practice.
2   The two main paradigms that exist in research are quantitative and qualitative. Define what each of those approaches means. Once you have done so, try to identify situations where each approach might be suitable as a means of research. Try to outline why the selected approach is, in your opinion, the most effective. Could there be times when a combined or multi-method approach is the most effective?
3   From any experiences of social work that you have had already, whether in the classroom or in actual practice, what could benefit from further research?

RECOMMENDED READING

Mathews, I. and Crawford, K. (2011) *Evidence-Based Practice in Social Work*. Exeter: Learning Matters.

Orme, J. and Shemmings, D. (2010) *Developing Research Based Social Work Practice*. Basingstoke: Palgrave Macmillan.

Walliman, N. and Appleton, J. (2009) *Your Undergraduate Dissertation in Health and Social Care*. London: Sage.

Whittaker, A. (2009) *Research Skills for Social Work (Transforming Social Work Practice)*. Exeter: Learning Matters.

Refer to the Companion Website (www.sagepub.co.uk/SocialWork) for some useful links to web-based research materials.

REFLECTIVE
10 PRACTICE

Angela Duvollet

Key Themes

- Reflection is a key element of effective social work practice and is a skill that can be developed over time.
- There are a number of models or frameworks for structured reflection which assist the student or practitioner to improve their ability to reflect.
- Reflection can be both a cognitive thought process and a process involving the externalisation of these thoughts into a written format.
- Reflection is fundamental to the learning process, underpinning and informing the gaining of knowledge and insight.
- The reflective process can be applied to all situations regardless of whether the outcomes were positive or negatives.

INTRODUCTION

If asked 'what is reflection' most of you would respond that it is what we see when we look in a mirror, which is, of course, an exact replica of what we are seeing. However, as someone involved in a public service profession reflection is somewhat more complicated, as it is the application of critical thinking – not just what we see, but also what we might see, and how we interpret it. Reflection as described by Knott and Scragg (2010) is 'fundamentally about making the implicit explicit, in order to scrutinise practice' (p. 77) and is therefore of value in processing data and thoughts which in turn will influence action. It is not an easy process but one that, with the assistance of theoretical concepts, models and practical experience, will develop your personal and professional competence over the course of your study and throughout your career.

This chapter will explore a range of approaches to contribute to your understanding of the concept of reflection, reflective practice, reflective writing and the reflective practitioner and also provide you with some of the tools available to develop your skills and support your learning.

REFLECTIVE PRACTICE

Moving from reflection to reflective practice is about application, and perhaps most importantly is the fact that if you reflect on your practice you will be better able to meet the needs of service users and carers.

The key to reflective practice is engaging in a process that will enable you to step back and reflect on your practice and that of others during or after an experience or activity in which you are involved. Reflecting on your practice will encourage you to consider and value past experiences and transferable skills, question and challenge potential oppression, go beyond your academic accomplishments and identify and consolidate areas of progression.

Having a sound sense and understanding of the 'use of self', Ward (2010) would argue is your primary tool of practice, as the aspects of your personality, identity, personal beliefs and values impact on how you interact with other people. These are influenced by being part of the wider society – a family, group or team – whereby you develop a sense of your own identity, self-worth and self-belief. Also, as a practitioner, you may experience oppression, rejection, stigma and conflict and be subject to 'negative stereotyping' which may 'affect our assumptions in practice' (Ward, 2010: 2), all of which may have an effect on your 'sense of self'. The way your personal and professional identity develops will become more evident during the course of study as you are introduced to theories, models and concept which will challenge and inform your practice. As a student you will be provided with a variety of opportunities that will enable you to reflect on your identity, for example on placement, during seminars and in tutorials, through self and peer assessments and problem-based learning.

Although reflecting on practice is encouraged in most agencies, the environmental conditions in some organisations may not be conducive to reflective practice and learning. Pressures of work, lack of staff and resources can all contribute to the student or practitioner feeling that they have little time to reflect, plan and evaluate. Reflective practice is a dynamic concept and the responsibility, we would then argue, lies with you to engage with this approach and encourage others to do likewise.

Critical reflection supports deeper learning and understanding. In an article on the Companion Website (www.sagepub.co.uk/SocialWork) Das and Anand (2012) report on a project researching social work students' learning from international practice.

HISTORICAL CONTEXT

As learners, we should be aware that when a problem needs to be solved we should not only take time to reflect but also consider our assumptions, ideas and personal beliefs, which should be open to continual evaluation (Knott and Scragg, 2010).

Material by Schön (1983), Argyris and Schön (1978) and Kolb (1984) informs and structures this section. These writers are a selection of the early contributors to experiential learning theory who suggest that to ensure personal growth and development, engagement with 'experiential learning approaches [that] increase self-awareness and group effectiveness' (Weil and McGill, 1989: 3) is required. This methodology assists learners to develop the capacity to reflect on experiences and understand the significance of these through reflection.

SCHÖN AND ARGYRIS' CONCEPTS OF REFLECTION

Schön (1983) developed a model of reflection or concept of '*knowing-in-action*', know-how and getting on with actions in everyday life, '*reflection-in-action*', thinking at the time, and '*reflection-on-action*', thinking retrospectively after the event. His work acknowledged that professional knowledge was a combination of the technical–rational model (rules) and professional artistry (reflection in action) (Fook, 2007). However, he suggested that technical rationality was restrictive as it reflected on an overemphasis and reliance on theory, science and abstract conceptual knowledge and the passing of information from expert to student or worker which was not directly linked to practice, thereby encouraging passive learning. He also argued that reflection and action are not two separate concepts but one (Schön, 1983), which suggests an important lesson for education is that 'theory and practice must not only be taught together but must be locked in a critical combat' (Richmond, 1997: 3). Clearly, having a sound knowledge of theory and the ability to reflect is essential to your practice.

Knowing-in-Action

This refers to the knowledge we have about ourselves, which is often difficult to verbally describe and which we reveal in our actions. 'We reveal it by our spontaneous, skilful execution of the performance; and we are characteristically unable to make it verbally explicit' (Schön, 1987: 25). For example, when we engage in everyday activities such as catching a ball or riding a bike, we have developed the ability to be able to do these both naturally and perhaps over time, easily. This knowledge, on the whole, gets us through our everyday lives. However, life is always full of surprises and the unexpected, so at times this spontaneous knowing-in-action can let us down. If we are surprised by an unexpected result from a familiar routine, which fails to meet our expectations, we have two choices. We could ignore the change or we could reflect on the change, we could stop and think and move to reflecting-in-action (Schön, 1990).

Reflection-in-Action

Schön (1983) further suggests that reflecting-in-action, connecting with your feelings, experiencing uncertainty and confusion and challenging values, will contribute to building a new understanding. This is the core of your practice. The need to reflect-in-action is usually as a result of your normal knowing-in-action, which you have relied on, not providing you with the skills or knowledge to deal with a situation or dilemma. Depending on experiences and learning styles that will be discussed later in this chapter, many practitioners may feel unable to admit that they are 'wrong' or have made an 'error' as the expectations of their role as the 'expert', the professional title and position they hold, may lock them into the view that they must be seen to be right. Depending on your personality, you may also find it difficult to make changes. It may be that you consider it a sign of weakness to admit to errors or you do not like the process of change, compared to those that welcome change and deal well with uncertainty and unfamiliar situations. Either way, to ensure you become the reflective practitioner you need to reflect-in-action where your thinking will serve to 'reshape what you are doing while you are doing it' (Schön, 1983: 26). This will enable you to make informed choices and decisions, make new sense of your unique experiences, assist you to reframe problems and develop your professional competence.

Reflection-on-Action

Incorporating reflecting-on-action enables you to spend some time reflecting after the event, trying to make sense of the experience and to explain the way you acted as you did. You would take time to think about what you and others said, how you reacted, whether you could have made changes and consider if change would have made a difference to the outcome.

As you develop as a practitioner you will move from reflecting *after* every event to also reflecting *during* the event. This takes practice and will develop over time with experience and will improve self-knowledge and develop confidence.

Argyris (in Argyris and Schön 1978) has further augmented the work of Schön. Working at points of his career with Schön, Argyris' interest lay in considering to what extent human reasoning, not just behaviour, can become the basis for diagnosis and action. As a student on placement or a qualified practitioner you will be part of an organisation with specific policy and procedure associated to your role, therefore it is necessary to consider the relationship between the individual and the organisation.

Case Study

You are employed by the local authority which has charged your disabled service user for the unused bedroom in his house. He refuses to pay, because the room is used to store his wheelchair, walking aid and clothes. To what extent can you support him, and to what extent must you work within the council's overall policy?

Argyris (1978) suggested that in order to learn we need to be able to take a step back and reflect on our actions and detect, question and correct error. He suggests that when an error occurs in practice there is a tendency for the individual or the organisation, when seeking another strategy, to take the less risky option by responding rigidly to rules, values, policy and procedures and focus on the correction of any deviations from these. This is known as *single-loop learning*.

In comparison, *double-loop learning* is a more creative and reflexive approach as it confronts, questions and analyses the underlying assumptions in relation to ideas and goals. This provides the individual and organisation with the opportunity to open up the parameters of learning and not settle for the first solution to the problem, encouraging critical reflection and thinking outside the box. During times of often rapid change, this way of learning encourages the individual and the organisation to reflect on the fact that rules, policy and legislation may need to be revisited and changed alongside challenging values, both personally and professionally. Double-loop learning is less inhibitive and should result in informed decisions being made and will assist you to reflect on your practice and improve service provision (Argyris and Schön, 1978).

KOLB'S EXPERIENTIAL LEARNING CYCLE

Kolb (1984) provides one of the most useful models of adult learning which is often used for training purposes in education. The model he offers, the Experiential Learning Cycle, suggests that learning takes place in a cyclic way, with four stages of learning. Kolb argues that part of our learning is not at a conscious level, and in order to develop our awareness he suggests that we should integrate the four elements of concrete experience, observation and reflection, abstract conceptualisation and active experimentation in order for successful learning to take place.

In Figure 10.1 Kolb identifies these stages as:

● Concrete Experience (CE) – having an awareness of the experience and attaching some value to it.
● Reflective Observation (RO) – reflecting/reviewing on the experience.
● Abstract Conceptualisation (AC) – moving from reflecting to analysing and making links to theory and concepts/learning from experience.
● Active Experimentation (AE) – planning and making use of what we know and putting this into some form of practice.

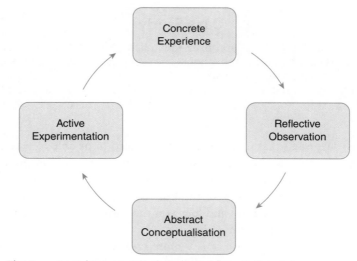

Figure 10.1   The Experiential Learning Cycle (adapted from Kolb, 1984)

Kolb (1984) states that the cycle may be entered at any point, however, the stages must be followed in sequence to ensure links are made between each stage to ensure effective and successful learning takes place. There is no time frame for each stage and the process of going around the cycle and the learning from the experience can generate another cycle. The engagement with this learning cycle will show you how reflecting on an experience can be translated into concepts which 'in turn are used as guides for active experimentation and the choice of new experiences' (Healy and Jenkins, 2000: 186). Kolb suggested by engaging with this cycle and by experiencing, reflecting, thinking and acting, the individual has the opportunity to reflect on the issues/experience (CE), take a step back and observe (RO), assimilate, draw on theory and develop new concepts (AC) and finally act on and test new knowledge thereby creating a new experience (AE). When completing the cycle you will have learnt from the experience which will contribute to developing new skills, knowledge and understanding.

Case Study

You are working with a teenage girl. To what extent do you base your understanding of teenage behaviour on what you yourself experienced and to what extent do you consider available theories?

It becomes evident that when engaging with the Experiential Learning Cycle individuals have developed a preferred way of learning. Kolb came to realise that there were others factors that could influence how an individual learned, namely learning styles, which could influence the engagement and results of the Experiential Learning Cycle. Previous research by Kolb (1984) had highlighted that an individual's learning style can be influenced by a variety of external and internal factors. For example, personality and life experiences, academic training, choice of career, and demands of the environment like current job, including the variety of roles and tasks undertaken. He realised that individuals had preferences for certain activities, so the Learning Style Inventory, an experiential educational exercise, was designed to identify the unique style of learning, to assess and identify more specifically the different ways an individual learns. He wanted to provide a framework to understand the interface between the educational learning environment and students' learning styles. The Learning Style Inventory, which is a self-assessment exercise, includes a task where the participant has to rank in order of preference their abstract, concrete, active and reflective orientations which would then identify their preference of the following four learning styles:

Diverger: One who likes to gather a wide range of information, prefers to work with groups to get different views.
Converger: One who can solve problems and makes decisions, prefers technical tasks rather than social and interpersonal issues.

Assimilator: One who is a logical thinker, interested in ideas and concepts, a problem-solver.

Accommodator: One who enjoys problem-solving and carrying out plans, more likely to use 'gut' feelings than logical analysis, relies heavily on others for information. (Henke, 1996; Kolb and Kolb, 2005)

Exercise

Consider your own learning style.

Although Kolb's Learning Style Inventory provides an excellent framework for teaching in a classroom environment, critics of the model also say it takes little account of cultural experiences, has minimum empirical support and has limited use in training in an organisational environment. In response, Honey and Mumford (1982) developed a similar, more appropriate model.

HONEY AND MUMFORD'S LEARNING STYLE QUESTIONNAIRE

The Learning Style Questionnaire provides not only a measurement of how people learn but also their preferred approach or style of learning. Honey and Mumford (1982) provide an explanation of four styles: *Activist*, *Reflector*, *Theorist* and *Pragmatist* (see Table 10.1). Once identified, these styles will assist in improving learning skills and processes, increasing awareness of how the individual learns. It is possible to complete an on-line version of the Learning Style Questionnaire, although at the time of writing there is a small charge for doing so: see www.peterhoney.com.

Figure 10.2 shows how integrating Kolb's Experiential Learning Cycle *and* your preferred learning styles will provide you with an eclectic explanation of how you learn.

There is a possibility also that you could become stuck at any one of the stages in the cycle. For example, if you are predominantly a reflector you may find difficulty moving from (RO) to the next stage of (AC). You may continually over-reflect at (RO), dipping your toe into the next stage, but quickly returning to (RO) to seek comfort from reflecting again. Although the purpose of this chapter is to encourage you to become a reflective practitioner, it would not be useful if you could not move forward, learning from the experience and in the end not being able to engage with the service user at a suitable level and within a given timescale. Another example would be if someone who is predominantly a pragmatist may view themselves as a busy person, getting on with the job. The result may be that the pragmatist may not reflect or draw on theory to support their practice, thereby finding that they are not achieving what they thought they were and are becoming frustrated as others may not work at the same pace. It may be difficult for the pragmatist to change, to become more reflective, becoming stuck in this style of working.

Table 10.1   Honey and Mumford's four learning styles

Style	Attributes	Learn easily from activities	Find difficulty from activities
Activist	Enthusiastic, enjoy challenges, learn by doing	Enjoy challenges, problem-solving, short-term activities	Do not enjoy taking passive role, standing back
Reflector	Good listeners, take thoughtful approach, observe, evaluate	Standing back, having time to think and observe	Do not enjoy time pressures, lack of time to prepare, being in limelight
Theorist	Like models and concepts, analytical, objective	Enjoy being methodical, likes logic and analysing theory	Do not enjoy lack of structure, information or guidelines
Pragmatist	Problem-solvers, like to try out new ideas and theories	Enjoy action plans, practical issues, learning in reality	Do not enjoy absence of guidelines, obstacles or hidden agendas

Source: Adapted from Honey, 2010

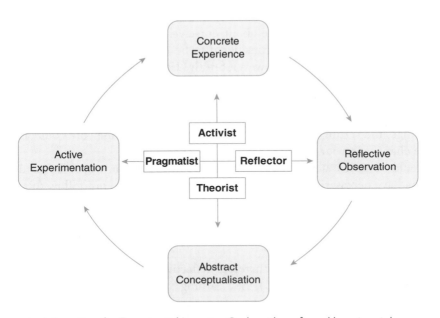

Figure 10.2   Integrating the Experiential Learning Cycle with preferred learning styles

Whichever combination of learning styles you have, they are not good or bad, they are an explanation of how you approach your learning. Being aware of your learning style and that of others will enable you to step back and assess how you can improve your practice.

REFLECTIVE WRITING

As a student, one of the core features or requirements in most or all of your assignments will be that of reflective writing, as this is considered a key component in your learning. Reflective writing encourages critical thought, creativity and cognitive development and is effective in increasing your ability to recognise, challenge and express attitudes and personal and professional values. Reflective writing provides you with the opportunity to describe and analyse the implications and the meaning of an experience or action, past or present, and provides an opportunity to review your learning at this point in time. This inspires new ideas and develops an overall awareness which in turn contributes to new perspectives in relation to practice. It is also an opportunity for these experiences to be documented and used as a point of reference for you and others involved in the process of your learning.

During your course there may be many tasks that require you to provide a reflective account. This may take the form of reflective journals or learning logs, evaluation of project work, personal and professional profiles, directed assessment such as the use of a critical incident **proforma**, or, as previously stated, assignments during your course of study. Examples of these can be found at the end of this chapter.

In whichever form you are required to provide a reflective account, it will involve a liberal use of the first person, 'I'. Initially this can be very uncomfortable as we are rarely encouraged to talk or write about ourselves at length or in any great depth, and if we do, then we are often considered to be boring, overly confident and self-centred, rather than reflective! However, Smith (1999, as cited in Jasper, 2005b) suggests that writing in the first person acknowledges 'the centrality of the writer' which then 'cultivates a self-awareness and promotes an internal dialogue for analysing and understanding' (p. 250). As the writer, we are the owner of these thoughts, emotions and feelings, and setting these within a reflective practice framework could assist you to make changes in your practice.

It should be noted at this point that the recording of the words 'I feel' does not mean you have necessarily been reflective, especially if you do not follow this with an explanation of what it is you 'feel' and leave the reader guessing. It would therefore be fair to say that reflective writing requires practice. There are several models, frameworks and tools that will assist you in this process and provide you with the skills to write reflectively.

The process of reflection and therefore reflective writing is supported by Kolb's Experiential Learning Cycle (ELC), the Learning Style Questionnaire (LSQ), Schön's reflection-in-action and reflection-on-action and double-loop learning, as discussed earlier in this chapter. Drawing from what you have learnt so far about your learning style and the way you process information, you should now also add the skills of being able to explore and explain events, which would reveal any anxieties and weaknesses, identify strengths that will assist you to write reflectively and document new information with a combination of personal meaning and past experience (Smith, 2005).

GIBBS' REFLECTIVE CYCLE

Gibbs' (1988) Reflective Cycle (RC), based on Kolb's (1984) ELC, provides a framework that encourages deeper reflection in relation to a situation and/or experience and provides you, through a circular process, with the steps to move from thinking to writing. The RC has six stages. At each stage you, as the reflective practitioner, are encouraged to think about a key point that assists you to reflect on the experience. This framework is very useful and can move you from just thinking or talking about an incident or event to 'thinking systematically and constructively about it', with analysis and conclusions being 'the key steps needed in successful critically reflective writing' (Woolliams et al., 2011: 15).

Exercise

To develop your reflective writing skills, consider Gibbs' cycle, beginning with a brief description of a recent event and then move around the cycle, following the guidelines below.

Description

At this point it is acceptable to be descriptive rather than reflective as you need to record in detail the event you will be reflecting on. Include factors such as the environment and context, stating where you were, what happened and the part you played. Also state who else was involved, the part they played and lastly, what the result was.

Feelings

Start reflecting! Think about what stood out for you about the event. You need to explore your feelings, how you felt at the time, how others made you feel, your thoughts at the time. At the time, how did you feel about the outcome and what are your thoughts and feelings about the outcome now?

Evaluation

Now you will begin to evaluate the event. Think about your reactions, the reactions of others. What were the good and bad points about the experience? Writing about a challenging event may prove difficult. Did the situation come to a resolution, and if not why not?

Analysis

At this stage you need to look in more depth at the event, asking more detailed questions than the last stage to consider what additional factors may have helped

(Continued)

(Continued)

or hindered the situation. Why did it happen in the first place, what went well, what not so well and who contributed what to the event?

Conclusion

This is the stage where you will start to learn from your experience – experiential learning. You have now explored the event from different perspectives and gathered a good deal of information from which to develop an insight into all the responses. If it was not a positive outcome, at this time you may also consider what you may have done differently. If it was a positive outcome, would you do the same or would there be something you would change to improve the outcome further?

Action Plan

At this stage you need to draw together all your learning from the previous stages, consider what you would do if the situation happens again, and learn from the experience. This completes the cycle.

(Source: Gibbs, 1988)

If you have engaged with this process you will have noticed the similarity with Kolb's Experiential Learning Cycle. This would suggest that several models can be used simultaneously to provide you with the theoretical basis from which to draw and transfer to practice.

Writing reflectively is further enhanced when you consider your value base, both personal and professional, and the ethical standards by which social work practitioners are guided. The act of reflecting on what you record will increase your awareness of the impact your own personal history, preconceptions and experiences regarding life's events may have when engaging with the process of assessments and interventions. As you progress through the course and engage with reflective writing you will develop the ability to analyse ethical dilemmas, thereby assessing the potential impact of your values on practice and the service user.

Research by Swindell and Watson (2006) highlights the benefits of teaching 'self-reflective journaling' when considering the process of ethical resolution. The research concluded that 'It encourages active student participation, critical thought and application, and writing skills development' (p. 5).

 Yip (2006) looked at the development of reflective skills in mental health settings. In this article, see the Companion Website (www.sagepub.co.uk/SocialWork), he discusses different levels of reflective practice.

ADDITIONAL USEFUL TOOLS FOR DEVELOPING REFLECTIVE SKILLS

Many factors will shape the quality of your writing, moving you from writing descriptively to developing a more holistic perspective reflectively. Watton et al. (2001) provide the following useful list of points which you could consider when practising reflective writing.

- 'Be aware of the purpose of your reflective writing and state if it is appropriate.
- Reflective writing requires practice and constant standing back from oneself.
- Practise reflecting writing on the same event/incident through different people's viewpoints and disciplines.
- Deepen your reflection/reflective writing with the help of others through discussing issues with individuals and groups, getting the points of others.
- Always reflect on what you have learnt from an incident, and how you would do something differently another time.
- Try to develop your reflective writing to include the ethical, moral, historical and sociopolitical contexts where these are relevant.' (pp. 16–17)

CRITICAL INCIDENT ANALYSIS

Critical Incident Analysis is another instructional tool that will assist you to reflect on practice and record your observations and also help educators to support you in this quest. Engaging with this tool will enable you to have a deeper understanding as it goes beyond a descriptive and detailed description of an event, encouraging analysis and reflection before drawing your conclusions (Griffin, 2010). Lister and Crisp (2007) conducted research with 10 postgraduate social work students who were undertaking their second direct practice placement. The results were positive for both the practice teachers and the students, finding the Critical Incident tool both adaptable to classroom and work in the field, assisting those who found difficulty with engaging with the process of critical reflection. This tool, therefore, allows you to reflect on both positive encounters and also negative events, integrate theory, consider values and focus on developing your critical skills. The results of research by Griffin (2010) into the use of the tool were very positive, particularly as the data indicated 'an increase in the degree of orientation toward growth and inquiry, from concrete thinker to alert thinker' (p. 218).

The Critical Incident Analysis framework

1 Account of the incident

- What happened, where and when; who was involved?
- What was your role/involvement in the incident?

○ What was the context of this incident, for example previous involvement of yourself or others from this agency with this client/client group?

○ What was the purpose and focus of your contact/intervention at this point?

2 Initial responses to the incident

○ What were your thoughts and feelings at the time of this incident?

○ What were the responses of other key individuals to this incident? If not known, what do you think these might have been?

3 Issues and dilemmas highlighted by this incident

○ What practice dilemmas were identified as a result of this incident?

○ What are the values and ethical issues which are highlighted by this incident?

○ Are there implications for inter-disciplinary and/or inter-agency collaborations which you have identified as a result of this incident?

4 Learning

○ What have you learned, for example about yourself, relationships with others, the social work task, organisational policies and procedures?

○ What theory (or theories) has (or might have) helped develop your understanding about some aspect of this incident?

○ What research has (or might have) helped develop your understanding about some aspect of this incident?

○ How might an understanding of the legislative, organisational and policy contexts explain some aspects associated with this incident?

○ What future learning needs have you identified as a result of this incident? How might this be achieved?

5 Outcomes

○ What were the outcomes of this incident for the various participants?

○ Are there ways in which this incident has led (or might lead) to changes in how you think, feel or act in particular situations?

○ What are your thoughts and feelings now about this incident?

(Lister and Crisp, 2007: 49–50)

Critical Thinking

From your experience of social work, how much reflection have you observed in the practice of others and how much have you done yourself? What are the barriers to reflective practice?

LEARNING LOGS/REFLECTIVE JOURNALS

Learning logs, or reflective journals as they are also known, are designed as an instructional tool to encourage active learning and critically reflective writing. They are an essential tool used during the course of your study which will help to promote critical self-reflection, recognise personal and professional beliefs and values, thereby aiding personal growth. The log or journal is a form of self-assessment and can be used as a safe place to record your thoughts and feelings as you engage with new learning experiences. This can also be used in supervision where your practice teacher/educator will assist you to consolidate your learning, encourage you to reflect on the connections and meaning to your learning. Engaging in this process will enhance your knowledge and understanding of links between theory and practice which in turn improve your skills as a student and practitioner.

There are many proformas for a learning log and often agencies, educators and also learners will develop one that suits their needs. These guidelines will assist you with any proforma when completing your reflective log or journal.

On the Companion Website (www.sagepub.co.uk/SocialWork) some examples of reflective log entries have been provided. It would be helpful to look at these as you begin to develop your own reflective writing skills.

Guidelines for a Learning Log

What is being looked for?

- What you did or what happened or what your part in it was.
- The practical skills that you used during the situation described.
- What you thought was good/went well, what was good about it, why it was good, what you achieved.
- What could have been done better, why, how it could have been improved, what did you achieve, what could you have done differently?
- The links between theory and what actually happened. Example: does what happened agree or disagree with theory?
- Honest opinions: assessors are interested in how well you can interpret the situation, rather than how well the situation went. Identifying what went wrong (or didn't go quite as well as expected) and what you could do differently indicates that you have learned, not that you have made a mistake.
- What you learned and will do in the future (an action plan). This may involve how you will go about it and how you will judge if you have improved and performed well.
- The values that informed your actions.
- How you felt about the situation/event. Your last entry should make reference to the entire reflective process that you have undertaken and should consider any personal and professional development that has taken place as a result of this piece of work.

If you now incorporate your learning style as identified by the Learning Style Questionnaire, you will see that all the models and frameworks can be utilised to ensure that you are able to reflect on your practice and develop your skills and become a reflective practitioner through the process of experiential learning and writing.

CONCLUSION

Becoming a reflective practitioner is a developmental journey, but a vital journey for a student of social work, which, in line with other areas of skill, never actually ends. By reading this chapter and undertaking the associated activities it is anticipated that knowledge, skills and abilities to engage in reflective practice have been enhanced. Adopting a questioning approach to practice is a sign of individual strength and the ability to critically appraise an interaction, consider the parts of various actors within that and, most importantly, learn from the process, contributes significantly to wider aspects of professional development. The models and tools outlined here provide useful structures to begin the reflective journey. Over time it is recognised that the depth, quality and level of criticality within the process of reflection increases, which in turn enhances the practice undertaken. Reflective thinking and reflective writing take time to master but are essential to the provision of effective social work.

Reflective Questions

1   Consider the work of Argyris and the concepts of single-loop and double-loop learning. Identify experiences from work or placement which are examples of each. Having done so, consider the changes that could have been made to the single-loop experience had you engaged with double-loop learning. Consider the changes that the organisation could have made and the impact on service provision.

2   Consider a recent experience where the outcome was not entirely successful. Use Kolb's learning cycle to reflect on the experience. What have you learnt in this process? Have you identified areas of your practice that could have been changed? Would this new information have contributed to a change in the outcome?

3   Complete a Critical Incident Analysis Framework. Consider what this process tells you about the activity of reflection; awareness of your emotions and the impact they may have on practice; and the role of theory in developing professional competence.

RECOMMENDED READING

Gibbs, G. (1988) *Learning by Doing: A Guide to Teaching and Learning Methods.* Oxford: Further Educational Unit, Oxford Polytechnic.

Knott, T.C. and Scragg, T. (2013) *Reflective Practice in Social Work*, 3rd edn. Exeter: Learning Matters.

Lister, G.P. and Crisp, R.B. (2007) 'Critical incident analysis: a practice learning tool for students and practitioners', *Social Work in Action*, 19 (1): 47–60.

Moon, J. (2004) *A Handbook of Reflective and Experiential Learning.* London: RoutledgeFalmer.

Schön, D.A. (1983) *The Reflective Practitioner: How Professionals Think in Action.* New York: Basic Books.

PART TWO

ASSESSMENT

11 GENERIC ISSUES IN ASSESSMENT AND MANAGING UNCERTAINTY

Jillian Brannan

Key Themes

- Social work practice is complex, and the status of social work as a profession is a debated concept requiring careful consideration.
- Power is a multidimensional phenomenon that plays a significant role in all social work practice. Social workers must understand and engage with power dynamics.
- Assessment and formulation of professional judgements are complex activities involving the integration of a wide range of knowledge, skills and ethical considerations.
- Decision-making focuses on taking forward plans of action, and, in a professional context, decision-making should be rigorous.
- Social workers must develop confidence and competence to work with uncertainty, which is a critical aspect of practice.

INTRODUCTION

Social work is a complex activity underpinned by a wide and diverse theoretical base. As would be evident from the breadth of knowledge discussed in Part One of this text, social work practitioners draw on understandings of people and their circumstances from a range of subject disciplines and a range of perspectives. Utilising this knowledge and understanding, and being able to apply that in practise, are central features of effective social work. Consequently, practitioners strive to operate at all times within an informed framework that grounds practice in a knowledge, skills and value-based context.

In most circumstances the process of assessment is the starting point for any social work contact. Assessment of itself is a complex activity and this will be discussed in depth in the next chapter. The purpose of this chapter is to introduce the reader to some of the broader issues that underpin assessment. These include: professional status, power, knowledge, skills, ethical practice, judgement, decision-making and the complexities of uncertainty. A broad understanding of these underpinning matters builds a firmer foundation from which to operate as an informed practitioner.

SOCIAL WORK AS A PROFESSION

In a contemporary context a number of different occupations, including social work, are commonly identified as 'professions'. However, social work's status as a profession has been a contested area, and social work is a different type of profession to, for example, law and medicine (Beckett and Maynard, 2005). Nonetheless, Evetts (2003), writing from a sociological perspective, argues that the current focus has shifted from what constitutes a profession to the concept of 'professionalism' and how that relates to knowledge-based occupations, of which social work would be one. Professionalism for Evetts is seen in occupations that embody an 'exclusive ownership of an area of expertise, autonomy and discretion in work practices and occupational control of work' (p. 406). As noted in Chapter 14 of this book, whether social work can lay claim to meeting all of these criteria may be an area of debate; yet in popular discourse social work would be viewed as a profession.

Evetts goes on to contend that within the professions, professionalism has become something imposed 'from above' as opposed to 'from within' (p. 409). By this she is referring to those forces that drive and shape government requirements of professions. For example, constrained financial circumstances mean professionals work in environments where resources have to be cut and with increased emphasis on accountability and **performance indicators**. Within the UK context, social work as a predominantly state-regulated activity is significantly affected by these imposed requirements.

The relevance of these issues to the assessment process lies primarily in social workers being alert to the context within which they are functioning. Firstly, social workers are operating in the context of an occupation that has struggled at times to be recognised as a profession. This may have an impact on how social workers go about their role and influence the type of engagement with service users. Secondly, social workers are operating in the context of imposed professionalism 'from above'. Given that UK social work is such a state-driven profession, the influence of external forces is perhaps more invasive than that experienced by other professional groups. There is a risk that, in times of financial constraint, social workers may resort to strengthening professionalism as 'a route to better social recognition and therefore better service provision' (Fook, 2002: 26), but find they do so at the expense of taking power away from service users.

THE CONCEPT OF POWER

Power as Influence

Power is an incredibly pervasive force in our day-to-day lives. Early conceptualisations of the social bases of power by French and Raven ([1959] 2001) identified five forms:

- Reward – based on the ability to provide rewards of various kinds
- Coercive – based on the ability to discipline or withhold benefits
- Legitimate – based on occupying a particular position
- Referent – based on personal attributes that build identification, sometimes referred to as charisma
- Expert – based on possession of specific skills or knowledge

These bases of power have subsequently been added to by both French and Raven ([1959] 2001) and other authors, who identify the basis of power in connections (with influential people), information (having specific information that may be withheld from others), gatekeeping (determination of access), resources (having access to exclusive resources) and by virtue of election (being voted in) (see Coulshed et al., 2006; Ellis and Dick, 2000). These power bases are usually discussed in the context of leadership and management, but they also operate in the social work practice arena. We can sometimes oversimplify by saying that there are those with power and those without. Although true to an extent, it is important to recognise that the operation of power within social work is far more complicated.

Exercise

Think about groups, formal and informal, to which you belong. Who has power and why?

Power within the Social Work Exchange

Many of the users of social work services belong to devalued groups within society. Yet to make a direct relationship between devaluation and powerlessness does not encapsulate the complexity of power dynamics, nor does it necessarily signify a productive way forward for service users. Milner and O'Byrne (2009: 25–6) draw on the work of several authors in recognising those who experience 'learned helplessness' (dependency) and a 'culture of silence' (acceptance), along with those who are conversely the 'powerfully powerless' (able to exert influence but are perceived objectively to have a low power base), and the 'passive-resistant' (able to exert influence through ambiguous engagement). Fook (2002: 49) suggests that deeming someone 'powerless' can result in them seeing their problems as 'insurmountable', with a resulting impact on the capacity to effect change. Through these concepts it becomes necessary to understand the notion of power as something that is multifaceted, an aspect that will be built on within this section.

There is clearly therefore a need for social workers themselves to recognise the reality of power in their work, given that they, along with service users, are key players in this multifaceted dynamic. Fook (2002) suggests that simply shifting power to service users may lead to abdication of professional responsibility, because, when power is transferred, the elements of 'blame and responsibility' (p. 40) also tend to move with it. However, Gardner (2011) points out, within social work interactions, the concept of partnership does not mean equality. Even in situations where control is shifted to the service user, social workers and their employing agencies remain in very powerful positions, particularly in terms of access to resources.

Tew (2011: 50) has developed a useful 'matrix of power relations', which facilitates an understanding of power based both on how it is used and the form that it takes, and he sees power in ways we exert control over others or ways in which we work together with others. In doing so he suggests that power takes either a productive or limiting form, which helps us recognise that not all power over others is detrimental (it could be protective or oppressive) and not all power working together with others is beneficial (it could be cooperative or collusive).

 You can read a full version of Tew's (2006) article on the Companion Website (www. sagepub.co.uk/SocialWork).

Professional power

Being in a professional role can lead to assumptions about power and power imbalance. Because we have statutory duties, social workers have to be alert to the authority and status they hold.

Case Study

In a family being supervised on the at-risk register, the parents are likely to be in a vulnerable position, because they could have their children removed. Ignoring the dynamic of power is likely to result in poor practice which lacks an appropriate appreciation of what is taking place.

Smith (2010) highlights three different modes of power, which include a positional mode – reflective of status and authority as just described – and a relational mode. For Smith relational power relates to the 'interactive dimension' of power, which questions what power is and who holds it. For example, in our use of language we must ensure our language does not exclude, and we keep a firm commitment to work truly in partnership, as opposed to being tokenistic.

The weblink for Smith's article in Sociological Research Online is provided on the Companion Website (www.sagepub.co.uk/SocialWork).

An interesting example of relational power can also be seen in considering what is expertise. The power held by professionals is frequently, although by no means exclusively, framed in the context of expertise and the possession of expert knowledge. Yet current practice is demonstrating a growing need to question where expertise is deemed to lie. For example, the idea of the service user or carer as expert lies at the heart of the personalisation agenda which is leading to radical reform of adult social care in particular (Department of Health, 2010; Scottish Government, 2010e; Welsh Assembly Government, 2011). Whilst a firmer recognition of the service user as expert is to be wholeheartedly welcomed, it is nonetheless important to be alert to the fact that this may be a challenge to social work practice.

Visit the Companion Website (www.sagepub.co.uk.SocialWork) for a case study exploring issues of power in work with Julie, a 19-year-old single parent with financial problems.

THE KNOWLEDGE AND SKILLS REQUIRED FOR ASSESSMENT

Having considered issues around professional role and aspects of power, attention will now turn to the knowledge and skills social work practitioners need to acquire and develop to engage in assessment work. The aim here is to offer a broad overview of key issues, which should act as pointers for further exploration.

The Knowledge Base

Whilst recognising that the knowledge base of social work is extremely broad, Trevithick (2008) comments on the debate about what actually constitutes the knowledge base. In addition, Drury Hudson (1997) notes that social workers may rely on some forms of knowledge more than others and that they do not always consciously apply knowledge. One of the underlying issues here is the differentiation between theory and knowledge. Trevithick's proposition of theory as 'explanation' and knowledge as 'understanding' is a useful one and serves well to highlight how the two concepts interweave.

To undertake assessment social workers need to draw on both theory and knowledge. Inevitably this relies on workers being able to identify what types of theory and knowledge are informing their practice. To this end some academics have developed frameworks that can be used to consider the interactions between a range of different concepts. Three such frameworks will be briefly outlined here.

Firstly, Drury Hudson (1997) proposed a 'model of professional knowledge forms' (1997: 37). This saw professional knowledge as the central component of a framework that comprised five further knowledge forms. For Drury Hudson professional knowledge was the combination of information and awareness of material drawn from theories, research findings and practice or life experience, which we apply to professional practice. The material comprised theoretical knowledge (schemes, frames of reference), personal knowledge (cultural, intuition, common sense), practice wisdom (gained through experience), procedural knowledge (legislation, policy, organisational) and empirical knowledge (research). Interestingly, Drury Hudson highlights in her paper that whilst all components of knowledge are important, studies indicate that theoretical and empirical knowledge are drawn on less frequently than other knowledge forms.

Critical Thinking

This is based on studies in the last decade of the twentieth century. To what extent do you think this continues to be an issue?

Secondly, Pawson et al. (2003) investigated knowledge used in social care, identified five sources of knowledge – namely, organisational, practitioner, user, research and policy community knowledge – and produced a classification incorporating these. This study also investigated the quality of knowledge sources and produced a framework for understanding how knowledge can be used to inform practice. Whilst at the time of the study the impact of user knowledge was deemed to be unknown, it is significant that this knowledge source was an integral part of the classification (see Chapter 15). The web link for Pawson et al.'s paper is provided on the Companion Website (www.sagepub.co.uk/SocialWork). You will also find some discussion of their work in Chapter 9 of this text.

The final knowledge framework outlined here was developed by Trevithick (2008) and identified three overarching types of knowledge – theoretical, factual and practice. Trevithick goes on to develop a framework that breaks down each of these broad areas to constituent parts:

- Theoretical knowledge
  - Theories that illuminate our understanding of people, situations and events
  - Theories that analyse the role, task and purpose of social work
  - Theories that relate directly to practice

- Factual knowledge
  - Social policy
  - Law
  - Agency policies, procedures and systems
  - Knowledge of people
  - Knowledge of specific problems

- Practice knowledge
  - (Processes for) knowledge acquisition
  - (Processes for) knowledge use
  - (Processes for) knowledge creation

The Skills Base

The skills involved in undertaking assessment are rarely skills exclusive to the assessment process. All effective social work practice relies on the ability of practitioners to implement core skills. These include: communication, engagement, observation, the ability to work in partnership, self-awareness, the ability to challenge discrimination, advocacy skills and the ability to analyse. This is not an exhaustive list and no doubt a wide range of other skills can be added. As a practitioner, the assessment process should be something to which you bring existing skills and developing skills; assessment should be seen as a skills set and, importantly, as something that can be 'learned' (Thompson, 2005: 86).

Within this chapter the skill areas of self-awareness and analysis will be focused upon. The rationale is that self-awareness is a fundamental requirement for any assessment work and analysis is something that can take practitioners time to achieve competently.

Self-awareness

Ruch (2002: 211) describes the concept of self as 'the acknowledgement and integration of rational, intellectual understanding and emotional awareness'. She goes on to clarify that the '"self" is a vital source of knowledge and information for professional social work, given, the relational, process-based nature of its practice and learning'. This description aptly highlights why it is important that social work practitioners have insight into what makes them function as an individual human being. The process of assessment is a relational one, so without this insight there is a risk that the practitioner will not perform effectively.

Building on the concept of self-awareness, two other aspects are worthy of consideration. The first, reflexivity, is identified by Sheppard (2007) as lying at the heart of assessment; he outlines the two ways in which reflexivity has been defined:

'The social worker is:

- an active thinker, able to assess, respond and initiate action
- a social actor, one who actually participates in the situation with which he or she is concerned in the conduct of his or her practice.' (2007: 129)

Payne et al. (2002: 3) see reflexivity as social workers putting 'themselves in the picture'. Translating this into practice, it is essentially about recognising that the social worker is involved in the assessment exchange as much as the service user; therefore, the social worker needs to be self-aware to ensure that they recognise what knowledge they are drawing on, what assumptions they might be making, how they are using their professional role, power and so on.

The second aspect to introduce, albeit briefly, is the concept of emotional intelligence (EI). Held (2009), drawing on the work of Goleman (one of EI's key proponents), suggests that EI has five elements: self-awareness, self-regulation, motivation, empathy and social skills. Essentially EI is about being able to recognise our own and others' feelings and to manage both our own emotions and those generated in working relationships with others. It is suggested that people with strong skills in emotional intelligence are more effective in working relationships.

While discussion of EI has mainly been about management, Morrison (2007) notes EI has relevance for direct social work practice. EI does not just focus on the emotional impact of social work on the worker, but moves beyond this, suggesting that the individual's ability to deal with the emotional impact and to use support mechanisms effectively is stronger in a practitioner who is more attuned to relational dynamics.

Morrison (2007) applies EI to a range of core social work tasks including assessment. He establishes that the evidence base suggests a very clear link between the strength of the worker/service user relationship, and the depth and quality of the assessment undertaken. In exploring the relationship aspect further, Morrison notes that where the social worker is more emotionally in tune with the service user, the assessment and work developing from that is more likely to be effective. Significantly, social workers should not try to suppress the 'emotional information' (2007: 255) gained through the assessment process. To do so misses part of the meaning of an exchange and can impact on the quality of interpretation of assessment information.

Analysis

From an education viewpoint, the ability to analyse is seen as a higher-level cognitive skill. Analysis sits in a cognitive framework (or taxonomy) above the ability to remember, understand and apply knowledge. Killen (2006: 78) defines analysis as the ability to:

> Separate information into parts and determine how the parts relate to one another and how they relate to an overall purpose or structure.

Although the learning taxonomy was developed for education purposes, I would propose that this is a helpful framework within which to start to understand the importance of analytical skills in social work assessment. It is also a framework which helpfully acknowledges that becoming analytical is a developmental journey, with which students and practitioners engage throughout their studies and careers.

When a practitioner meets with a service user, a vast amount of information may be gathered, but data gathering is only part of the assessment process. Something must be done with the information, and we weigh up data, start to make connections and then make use of this deeper level of understanding. The analytical components of this process rely on practitioners being able to use skills such as organising information, differentiating between different pieces of information, distinguishing between different components of information and attributing this accordingly. As Brown and Rutter (2008) note, description considers the what? who? when? where?, but analysis considers the how? and why?

To develop analytical skills we need to be a critical thinker. Such thinking can be applied to both the academic study of social work and its practice. Glaister (2008) views a critical practitioner as someone who is 'open-minded', able to use 'reflective approaches' and able to 'take account of different perspectives, experiences and assumptions' (p. 8). Applied to the assessment process, a picture starts to emerge of a practitioner who is comfortable to work within and between different layers of an exchange, in search of accurate and informed meaning from a range of viewpoints. Most importantly the practitioner is able to go beyond a descriptive or narrative account to provide some critical appraisal of the available information.

Thus a continuous process of questioning assessment information leads to a greater degree of analysis. A practitioner more likely to achieve an analytical approach is one who reflects (see Chapter 10) and who searches for the answers to the following types of questions:

- How does all this information fit together?
- Why are there differences of perspective?
- How does what I have been told, observed, read about etc. align with my theoretical knowledge base?

- What else do I need to know to assist in making meaning here?
- What are the implications of the information I have?

A practitioner who is able to couple this approach with a critical perspective is able to extend these skills to a more developed level.

ETHICAL ASPECTS OF ASSESSMENT

Values and ethics have been discussed extensively in Chapter 1. Consequently, the intention within this section is briefly to address two aspects of ethical practice that relate directly to the assessment process.

The Ethical Practitioner

Professional development may consist of three main components: knowledge and understanding; skills and abilities; and ethical and personal commitment (Scottish Executive, 2003a). As suggested above, the focus here will be on the third component.

It could be suggested that working within the value base of social work ensures practitioners are operating ethically. In part this assumption could be supported, but it relies on a very narrow framework of what we might determine ethical practice to be. For example, if we consider the British Association of Social Workers revised Code of Ethics for Social Work (BASW, 2012), three core values are identified but each has associated ethical principles, as detailed below:

Value: Human rights

Ethical principles:

1 Upholding and promoting human dignity and well-being
2 Respecting the right to self determination
3 Promoting the right to participation
4 Treating each person as a whole
5 Identifying and developing strengths

Value: Social justice

Ethical principles:

1 Challenging discrimination
2 Recognising diversity
3 Distributing resources
4 Challenging unjust policies and practices
5 Working in solidarity

Value: Professional integrity

Ethical principles:

1 Upholding the values and reputation of the profession
2 Being trustworthy

3 Maintaining professional boundaries
4 Making considered professional judgements
5 Being professionally accountable

Reviewing the range of ethical principles outlined above, and taking into account the additional ethical practice principles (BASW, 2012), you should start to become aware that being an ethical practitioner is a skilled and wide-ranging undertaking. Ethical practice is about a continuing personal commitment to delivering best practice. In the context of assessment, this involves a commitment to being reflective and reflexive, to maintaining and developing your knowledge and skills base, to using evidence-based practice and to building resilience and personal resources to work with service users in an effective and purposeful way.

Ethical Dichotomies

Within assessment processes it is perhaps inevitable that **dichotomies** will occur. Banks (2012) frames these as conflicting responsibilities or constraints on the social worker/ service user relationship, because, in part, social workers are operating in a public welfare and social control framework (see discussion above about the role of the professional and power). Such tensions are inherent within the social work task and need to be managed within the assessment process.

The kinds of dichotomies I am referring to here include, amongst others:

- Care vs. Control
- Collaboration vs. Compulsion
- Partnership vs. Professional authority
- Rights vs. Risk
- Self-determination vs. Protection
- Autonomy vs. Duty of care
- Choice vs. Lack of resources
- Expectations vs. Limitations
- Standardisation vs. Discretion and flexibility

Case Study

An 85-year-old man is unable to cook for himself or manage his personal hygiene. His family and doctor insist he needs to be in care, but he insists he can stay at home. Consider the issues of assessment here.

These tensions or imbalances can present obstacles in assessment and can lead to practitioners questioning what it is they are trying to achieve. The tensions cannot simply be swept under the carpet; they represent much of the context within which practice takes place. Management of such dilemmas is essentially founded on the principles of ethical practice which guide the practitioner through complex and multidimensional realities (Mattison, 2000).

WORKING WITH FACTS, OPINIONS AND JUDGEMENTS TO MAKE DECISIONS

The Nature of Judgements

In 1770 the American politician John Adams famously said that 'Facts are stubborn things'. He was referring to the inalterable nature of facts, which refuse to 'budge', irrespective of how much we may wish things to be different. Social work practitioners work with facts on a daily basis, yet a significant amount of practice involves the formulation of professional opinions and judgements. Drury Hudson (1997: 35) advises that there is an expectation that professionals will 'have special expertise in forming judgements' and that 'judgements and decision-making rely to a large extent on knowledge, ethics, values and skills'. The areas underpinning judgements have already been explored within this chapter; consequently, discussion here will focus on how the connections can be made between these aspects.

Taylor (2010: 165) provides useful definitions of judgement and professional judgement, which helpfully contextualise the activity taking place:

> **Judgement**: The considered evaluation of evidence by an individual using their cognitive faculties so as to reach an opinion on a preferred course of action based on available information, knowledge and values.
>
> **Professional judgement**: When a professional considers the evidence about a client or family situation in the light of professional knowledge to reach a conclusion or recommendation.

In light of this it can be determined that professional judgement arises out of the assessment process and, in turn, feeds into the subsequent decision-making and action planning. Collins and Daly (2011), discussing the work of Dalgleish, see judgements as the drawing of meaning from information, and decisions are what is taken forward on the basis on these inferences.

As indicated, a whole host of factors impact on how social workers make judgements and decisions. Figure 11.1 summarises these factors and suggests that judgement formation takes place along a continuum between intuition and analysis. While overly intuitive approaches lack rigour, overly analytical approaches may lack action – the so-called paralysis by analysis.

Bias

Whilst Figure 11.1 sets out key influences on judgement formation, it is important to note that elements of bias can impact on the interpretations and judgements that practitioners make (Taylor, 2010). Bias can arise in a range of forms such as the inappropriate setting of a baseline from which to make judgements; the failure to adjust thinking in light of new data; being risk-averse; operating through the lens of prejudice, including unconscious prejudice; failing to interpret or recall correctly; offering

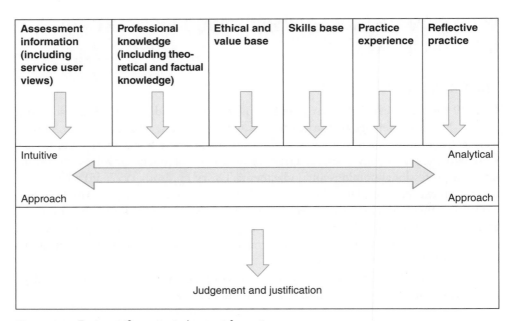

Figure 11.1   Factors influencing judgement formation

significantly more weighting to certain aspects of information and a failure to retain a focus on the service user as central. Everyone needs to reflect on the power of such biases to influence the judgements they make. As noted earlier, professional power carries significant weight. The abuse or misuse of such power is not only ethically improper but is professionally dangerous. The importance of professional supervision to ensure justifiable judgements and decisions is key to accountable practice (Cameron, 2011).

Decision-making

As indicated above, decisions are the plans of action taken forward following an assessment. Taylor (2010: 164) describes decision-making as a 'conscious process … leading to the selection of a course of action amongst several alternatives'. I have already established that judgements and decisions are interlinked and will now look at how practitioners can be supported to move from judgement formation to decision-making.

O'Sullivan (2011), discussing decision theory, suggests that the purpose of decision analysis is to select the option that has the best balance of a good outcome. He proposes structured methods to facilitate option generation with each proposed option then being evaluated as to the possible path it may follow. Such a structure is referred to as a decision tree.

Within this framework, options are mapped out and then evaluated on the basis of what would happen if this path was to be followed. As O'Sullivan notes, decision trees can be relatively straightforward or incredibly complex depending on the range of options and range of possible outcomes. In more complex situations it is likely that options may need to be scored so that there is a clear picture of which might lead to the best outcome. Coulshed et al. (2006) note that decision trees can be useful in generating options where there is a degree of uncertainty.

Exercise

Try formulating a decision tree yourself, based on something straightforward such as what to do this weekend, where to go on holiday or something more pressing that you have to decide.

Using structured frameworks to make decisions offers a number of benefits. Primarily these frameworks are systematic, an essential aspect when decision-making is complicated by ethical dilemmas, risk and uncertainty. The realities of social work practice, however, can impede the ability to make use of decision-making tools, and it is important to acknowledge that decision-making can be influenced by a range of factors, including availability of information, time constraints, economic constraints, hidden agendas, political pressures/power dynamics and management styles (Coulshed et al., 2006; Thompson, 2009a). Within this context a systematic approach is desirable, but sometimes decisions need to be made even though not all the information is available and there is a lack of clarity about certain aspects. In such situations practitioners need to be as systematic as possible, whilst maintaining an awareness of the dynamic nature of the working context.

Thompson (2009: 236) appropriately sums up the balance that a great deal of social work practice involves and in doing so he emphasises the importance of being systematic:

> We cannot guarantee that any decision we take will be the right decision, but we can ensure that it is a good decision.

Added to this it should be noted that within an approach characterised by being systematic it is essential to be reflective, i.e., to maintain open-mindedness and an ability to think things through. This is important because being systematic should not be interpreted as being rigid and inflexible. Systematic is about being thorough, rigorous and accountable and should not be confused with being bureaucratic.

WORKING WITH UNCERTAINTY

Throughout this chapter a number of issues have been raised in relation to uncertainty. On a number of occasions I have made reference to the complex activities underpinning assessment. Within this context we have to be mindful of the fact that complexity can lead to uncertainties (Ling, 2012). Indeed, a wide range of authors in the social work field discuss the very essence of social work as being characterised by uncertainty. For example, Parton (2000: 460) notes that social work is better seen in terms of 'uncertainty and ambiguity' than 'prediction and calculation'. Another view from Brand et al. (2005) sees social work as a profession that specialises in working with uncertainty. On the contrary, White (2009) suggests that social workers have to factor out uncertainty to develop formulations of the work they engage in. Her view is that social work is complex but that learning to manage complexity is not the same as learning to manage uncertainty. To read the whole of White's article visit the Companion Website (www. sagepub.co.uk/SocialWork).

Consequently there are different aspects to consider when discussing the issue of uncertainty. I would contend that it is important for social workers in training to consider the issue of uncertainty and how this may influence social work practice. In doing so it is useful to consider what is meant by uncertainty and the different forms it can take.

The Meaning of Uncertainty

Adams (2009) identifies three main types of uncertainty:

- Ontological uncertainty – situations where our values may not be a guide as to how to act: 'I am not sure what I think about this'.
- Epistemological uncertainty – situations where knowledge can be interpreted differently and there is ambiguity: 'I can recognise different ways to interpret this; but I do not know which is correct'.
- Procedural uncertainty – situations that do not fit general patterns: 'I have never come across this situation before'.

Another way to think about the meaning of uncertainty is to consider how it manifests in the individual practitioner. Nevalainen et al. (2010) undertook research with medical students looking at how feelings of uncertainty were explored in reflective writing and how attitudes towards tolerating uncertainty developed over time. The findings of this study indicate a range of feelings about uncertainty that would appear transferable to social work students. The researchers identified six dimensions of uncertainty:

1 Insecurity of professional skills.
2 Questioning of own credibility.
3 Inexactness of medicine [which can be compared to inexactness of social work].
4 Fear of making mistakes.
5 Coping with responsibility.
6 Tolerating oneself as incomplete and accepting of oneself as good-enough a doctor-to-be [again which can be compared to social worker-to-be].

I suggest that such issues are at the forefront of the minds of student social workers, especially when practice placements are being embarked upon, and it is useful to consider that uncertainty is not something distinct to the social work profession. As Parton (2000: 460), citing Howe (1995: 11) notes, 'uncertainty is the domain of the educated professional'.

Managing Uncertainty

Developing the ability to manage uncertainty draws heavily on those issues discussed within the preceding sections of this chapter. Practitioners with a clear understanding of professional status, power and role, who are able to utilise knowledge, skills and ethical approaches to make informed judgements and decisions, are inevitably going to deal more effectively with uncertain and ambiguous situations. Many of the assessments social work practitioners undertake must involve elements of uncertainty, and this is highly unlikely to change. It would be impractical to suggest prescriptive ways of managing uncertainty, but we can consider the following:

- Focusing on goals/outcomes for the service user(s) provides a basis for working within uncertain and ambiguous situations.
- Do not try to construct certainty where it does not exist.
- Work with the context of the situation not in spite of it or despite it.
- Practice wisdom has value but it does not have all the answers.
- Knowledge, skills and values can be transferred to new situations, even ones you have not encountered before.
- A broad theoretical base leads to both informed and creative practice.
- There will not necessarily be one truth – seek to understand perspectives and experiences.
- Use support and supervision constructively and appropriately.
- Ensure your practice is defensible not defensive.
- Accept that tolerating uncertainty is an aspect of professional development.

CONCLUSION

In seeking to set out the underpinning context of assessment work this chapter has inevitably covered a broad range of issues. The analogy of an iceberg may be useful here, where the 'undertaking an assessment' part of the process represents the tip of the iceberg, whilst a whole host of factors come into play beneath the surface of that activity. As a developing social work practitioner there are multiple tasks to consider in assessment work. These include: the way you present yourself and the importance of professionalism without the trappings of exerting professional status, other than in circumstances where that is required; the need to be aware of and work with power in the social work exchange; development of a broad knowledge and skills base which serves to inform the assessment process and equip you to undertake that; recognition of the uppermost importance of ethical practice and the development of yourself as an ethical practitioner; the awareness of how professional judgements are made and their link to the process of decision-making; and finally, the development of your confidence and competence to work with uncertainty. As stated at the start of this chapter, social work is a complex activity. The breadth of issues presented here should serve to reinforce that notion of complexity. This is not something, however, to be wary of, but is something to embrace – after all, if social work was easy then anyone could do it. The fact that it is complex signifies the importance of ensuring practitioners are skilled and informed, able to work with the challenges inherent within the practice arena.

Reflective Questions

1   Reflect on a situation where you felt powerless. Consider the range of factors that contributed to this feeling and whether any of these factors could have been manipulated to improve the situation. What can you learn from your own experience of powerlessness that might enable you to work more productively with service users?

2   Critical analysis has been defined as 'the critical evaluation of knowledge, theories, policies and practice, with an in-built recognition of multiple perspectives and orientation of ongoing enquiry' (Brechin, 2000: 30, cited in Ray and Phillips, 2002: 207). To what extent do you currently approach social work practice in this way? Identify any developmental needs you have and use these as part of your goal-setting for future practice learning.

3   What do you identify as the key characteristics of an ethical practitioner? How would you recognise if your approach to social work practice was more ethically developed than previously? What support might you need to develop as an ethical practitioner?

RECOMMENDED READING

Banks, S. (2012) *Ethics and Values in Social Work*, 4th edn. Basingstoke: Palgrave Macmillan.

Milner, J. and O'Byrne, P. (2009) *Assessment in Social Work*, 3rd edn. Basingstoke: Palgrave Macmillan.

O'Sullivan, T. (2011) *Decision Making in Social Work*, 2nd edn. Basingstoke: Palgrave Macmillan.

Trevithick, P. (2008) 'Revisiting the knowledge base of social work: a framework for practice', *British Journal of Social Work*, 38: 1212–37.

MODELS OF
12 ASSESSMENT

Janine Bolger and Patrick Walker

Key Themes

- Assessment is a core activity of social work practices, which should be a process capable of responding to dynamic factors in the lives of service users.
- Assessment is underpinned by a series of principles that serve to guide and direct practice.
- The legal and policy context of assessment is essential to understand as this sets a mandate for appropriate social work practice.
- Models and frameworks for assessment provide guides for practitioners and are underpinned by the skills and knowledge to inform the 'what', 'how' and 'why' of assessment.
- Assessment is founded on partnership with service users, but may be undertaken in both voluntary and involuntary contexts.

INTRODUCTION

The concept of assessment is generally associated with notions of appraisal, making judgements, forming opinions or calculating the value of something. Whilst these provide a helpful starting point, they require much further examination when applied to a social work context, where assessment is a discrete, core activity and a key skill. This chapter will introduce you to elements of social work assessment, incorporating principles, context, models, frameworks, skills and practice issues. It will draw reference from across the range of service user groups and invites you to reflect on and critically explore the material.

To begin to understand the meaning of assessment in social work, consider your understanding of assessment in your day-to-day life. Everyone makes numerous assessments every day in order to navigate their way through the daily interactions and situations that they face. In making these day-to-day assessments you will use a wide variety of perspectives that give meaning to the information that is presented, or help sift the information that is presented or found. Perhaps personal experience helps you, or perhaps your own cultural beliefs offer a way of interpreting situations or environments. Some of these factors will have relevance to assessment in social work and highlight the importance of being self-aware.

DEFINING ASSESSMENT IN SOCIAL WORK

Despite the large body of literature regarding assessment in social work, it remains a much debated area, not least because of the variety of approaches, perspectives and frameworks that are available. There is certainly agreement that assessment is a core activity but less consensus on what actually constitutes a good assessment and whether assessment is separate or integral to intervention. Coulshed and Orme (2012) describe assessment as an ongoing process, which is participatory, seeks to understand the service user and his/her situation and sets a basis for planning how change or improvement can be achieved.

In a similar vein, Payne (2008) identifies assessment as something that is continuous and ought to be part of a cycle. In this respect assessment is seen as a *process* rather than an *event*; although Payne highlights that practice reality often does not reflect this. Emphasising the process aspects, Milner and O'Byrne (2009) put forward a framework for assessment with five key stages:

1 Preparing for the task.
2 Collecting data from all involved.
3 Applying professional knowledge to analyse, understand and interpret the information gathered.
4 Making judgements.
5 Deciding and/or recommending.

For our purposes we would propose to define assessment in social work as a structured activity with the characteristics shown in Figure 12.1.

PRINCIPLES OF ASSESSMENT

The purpose of this section is to offer some principles, or core common features, of assessment. The discussion here cannot be prescriptive, but rather is indicative, for reasons that will become apparent. Assessments are frequently *context-specific* and consequently are shaped by the inclusion of particular elements and influenced by the manner in which the assessment is undertaken.

Case Study

Consider the following three different types of assessment that may take place under the auspices of services for children and young people:

1 An assessment in a family centre may focus on elements of parenting capacity, or parent–child interaction.
2 A comprehensive assessment for a Children's Hearing (in Scotland) may require capturing a much wider picture of the child in the context of his/her family, school/community and social setting.
3 An assessment in a Youth Justice team may employ a standardised, structured assessment focusing on specialised areas related to offending.

As a consequence, we need to be very clear about our role, remit and the context of any assessment.

Guiding principles help clarify and direct practice in all areas of assessment. They may be drawn from ethical frameworks, theoretical perspectives, legal obligations and practice guidance and are important because, although various frameworks can be

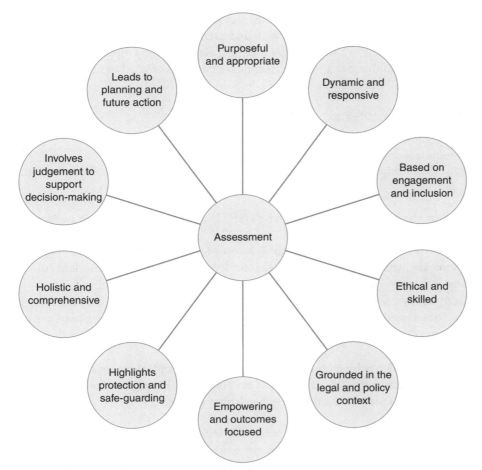

Figure 12.1   Structure of assessment in social work

used in assessment, it should be remembered that, as Statham and Kearney point out, 'social work can never be a *purely* technical activity based simply on assessment formats, models or methods' (2007: 102, emphasis added). This suggests that some underpinning and orientating principles are required when beginning and undertaking the assessment process. Five key principles are presented here.

Principle 1: Understanding Need

Daniel (2007: 116) states clearly that need 'can offer a guiding principle for the social worker'; it orientates the practitioner towards exploring and understanding the service user's situation. In some cases, need will be immediate, for example in situations of child or adult protection. In other cases, need may emerge over a longer period and relate to support and quality of life, for example befriending to address social isolation.

Horder (2002: 117) notes that 'good assessment in social work has always been needs-led', although he alerts the reader to the fact that need can be understood differently by people and can become a 'contested' concept. Horder goes on to suggest that need is 'in most cases defined by others rather than as perceived by the person being assessed'. This is the practitioner's dilemma: how to understand, take into account and respond to the service user's view of their needs, whilst also acting within employers' requirements, using professional theories and with normative concepts of need in mind.

Spicker (2012) offers the following:

The idea of need refers to:

● the kinds of problem which people experience;
● requirements for some particular kind of response; and
● a relationship between problems and the responses available. A need is a claim for service …

and points the reader towards Bradshaw's (1972) taxonomy of need, summarized as:

● Normative need, which is identified according to a norm (or set standard); such norms are generally set by experts. Benefit levels, for example, or standards of unfitness in houses, have to be determined according to some criterion.
● Comparative need concerns problems that emerge by comparison with others who are not in need. One of the most common uses of this approach has been the comparison of social problems in different areas in order to determine which areas are most deprived.
● Felt need, which is based on the perspective of the people who have it.
● Expressed need, which is need people say they have. People can feel need that they do not express and they can express needs they do not feel.

Need, as a principle, can determine what the social worker may require to explore in assessment. If children need, for example, a secure relationship with their parent or caregiver, to grow and develop, then the absence of it becomes a risk to them. Similarly, if an adult with mental health problems needs support and counselling to manage auditory hallucinations, then an absence of such support may significantly impact on the person's health and well-being. By understanding need and drawing on broader knowledge and theory, the practitioner is able to consider the person's situation and to explore approaches to relieving the unmet need.

Exercise

The word 'need' is used commonly by everyone, so the expression 'needs-led' should be fairly straightforward. However, think about when you and others use the word and substitute the word 'want' in place of 'need'. How often is 'want' a more appropriate term, and how often is 'need' the correct description of the situation?

Principle 2: Working with Systems and Ecology

Like most people, users of social work services very rarely live in a vacuum. Most of us are part of systems, networks and connected relationships that serve to shape and influence our lives in complex and multifaceted ways.

Bronfenbrenner's Ecological Systems Theory (cited in Daniel, 2007: 116) suggests that individuals are situated 'within layers of systems from immediate family up to wider society' and any assessment is required to take account of these layers of connections and influences. Although this theory was developed in the context of child development, the levels and systems identified are just as applicable in work with other service user groups. The central aspect to draw on here is an understanding of how different factors influence and are influenced by the individual. The ripple model proposes four interconnected levels surrounding the individual:

- Micro-system: the family, school, workplace etc.
- Meso-system: the interaction of two different micro-systems
- Exo-system: the community/external environment
- Macro-system: the sociocultural context.

Bronfenbrenner later added a fifth level, the chrono-system, this being the dimension of time relating to an individual's life events and environment – for example the influence of time in relation to reactions to the death of a parent, relocation, a relationship breakdown and so on.

See the article by Hill (2002) on the Companion Website (www.sagepub.co.uk/SocialWork) which reviews the social network approach to social work assessment.

Principle 3: Building on Strengths

If social workers are to work collaboratively with individuals and families the assessment process must take account of capacities, strengths and protective factors. In doing so social workers will take an assets-based approach which seeks to recognise resilience and capacity for change (Daniel et al., 2010). An assessment that explores strengths can reveal an individual's or family's ability to resolve their difficulties using their own skills and expertise without becoming disempowered through service involvement. The very process of assessment can help individuals or families to identify and utilise latent strengths and thus reduce dependency on professionals.

This principle is relevant when working with all service users and in all domains of social work, whether the practice base is termed 'Children and Families', 'Learning Disability Services', 'Social Work with Older People' and so on. Assessments that purely focus on deficits are not only likely to be demoralising and incomplete, but also run the risk of being oppressive, result in inappropriate labelling and potentially limit an individual's (and their network's) abilities to resolve their difficulties themselves. Compensatory strengths need to be explored, identified and added in to the equation whenever they are present.

Principle 4: Being Person-centred

We have outlined above the principle of systems and ecology and believe that such a perspective is important. Whilst there is a requirement to keep this ecological perspective, it must be emphasised that no assessment should lose sight of the fundamental needs of the child or adult at the centre. Taking a person-centred or child-centred approach sharpens the focus of social work practitioners to their primary concern. It can be, in practice, all too easy to become side-tracked into the needs of others. It is a reality that social workers are often engaged in working in complex situations where the voices of these 'others' are stronger and more articulate. A person-centred approach to assessment should involve direct interaction with the adult or child and be informed by the theoretical and knowledge base underpinning practice.

Exercise

Consider your own situation now. What are the positives and negatives in your own situation? How do you interact with your family and how does your family interact with neighbours, friends, work and the wider community? How much of this is relevant to your current situation?

Principle 5: Taking an Interprofessional Approach

An interprofessional approach to assessment highlights the importance of recognising that different professionals have particular areas of expertise. No one professional can have the whole picture that makes up the lived existence of an individual. Given that each profession will have unique insights and understandings, it is important to pull these together and to make sense of them. The value of interprofessional practice is brought into sharp relief through the following quotation from Bronstein (2004, cited in McLean, 2007: 339). In it she describes interdisciplinary collaboration as:

an effective interpersonal process that facilitates the achievement of goals that cannot be reached when independent professions act on their own ...

Interprofessional assessment therefore brings together professional perspectives, and, when these are collated and acted on, offers potential for a more comprehensive, coherent and relevant approach to assessed need across multiple, but connected, areas of people's lives.

Of course, when we speak about taking an interprofessional approach (see Chapter 14) there is a tendency to focus on the contribution of professionals, but this is not the whole story. By no means should service users and their families be excluded from such an approach – they are experts on themselves.

THE LEGAL AND POLICY CONTEXT OF ASSESSMENT

Across the four jurisdictions of the United Kingdom there is a raft of legislation and policy concerned with social work and social care. Much of this legislation and policy impacts directly on the assessment process, and consequently it is essential to acquire this knowledge and learn to use it effectively. We shall address some of the broader points that you need to be aware of, but for more detail you should also refer to Chapters 2 and 3.

One of the characteristics of assessment we identified earlier was that it should be grounded in the legal and policy context. It is vital when undertaking assessment that you are aware of what you can do, what you must do and what you may not be allowed to do. In a legal context 'powers' are what you *can* do in specific circumstances; 'duties' are what you *must* do in specific circumstances; and 'restrictions' refer to any limitations placed on the worker (Thompson, 2009a). Whatever your field of practice, you need to establish the legislative and policy framework within which your work takes place.

Given that the law generally regulates the activities of social work practitioners and the organisations those practitioners work for, it is essential to recognise that the law also holds those practitioners and organisations to account for the work undertaken. This may seem on the one hand intimidating, but it is the natural companion of having legislation and policy that gives you a mandate for practice, particularly in the context of social work in statutory settings.

The third general point is that legislation and policy can act as a powerful tool in empowering service users and promoting their rights. Often you will work with service users who have a limited understanding of their rights and are not fully aware of the options that are available to them. By understanding the law and what can and should be done, you can assist service users to improve the quality of their lives, achieve their outcomes and protect their interests (Johns, 2011).

Lastly, it is important to be aware that whilst the law may appear prescriptive it is applied in the context of individual lives, with all the complexity that brings. In this sense, social workers still need to be able to make judgements and 'negotiate tensions between legal principles and processes and the values and approaches that underpin social work practice ...' (Gordon and Davis, 2011: 1).

MODELS AND FRAMEWORKS OF ASSESSMENT

The increased emphasis on assessment in social work, particularly of risk, has created more theories about the purpose, process and practice of assessment. Increased focus on recording has resulted in the production of a number of proformas, many of which are used by a range of professionals, including those in health, social work and education. These standardised formats are supported with social work values and theories and so can be viewed as value-based. The information gathered is from the worker's perspective and, therefore, the outcome of the assessment can be influenced by the attitudes and values of the assessor. The social worker has a responsibility to the service user to be both reflective (consciously looking backwards) and reflexive (using innate skills in the moment) on their practice.

Agreement is required between 'what to do', 'how' it can be done and 'why' it needs to be done. Above all the purpose of assessment must be clear (Doel and Shardlow, 2005). Assessment frameworks do not ensure effective practice in their own right as they only provide us with a framework to assist what is a complex activity. The process of assessment must be underpinned by knowledge around 'current policy trends, professional codes of practice, the attitudes of the workers, their managers, the organisations involved … and should be supported by good assessment skills' (Statham and Kearney, 2007: 102).

The purpose of carrying out an assessment is usually to identify levels of need or risk or to form an understanding when making first contact with the service user. Depending on the kind of information we need to gather, Smale et al. (1993) offer us three models – the Procedural, the Questioning and the Exchange – to guide us in carrying out assessments.

- The *Procedural* model, often associated with guidance related to legislation, involves using systems that are devised to ensure consistency and thoroughness in data collection. Consequently, eligibility for and allocation of services is often decided upon as a result of the collection of such data. This can provide only a snapshot assessment, directing the assessment away from examining the individual's strengths and abilities, and can divert from individual rights or concerns over quality of life (Milner and O'Byrne, 2009). The concern is that such systems can replace rather than support or inform judgements made by professionals (Barry, 2007 cited in Milner and O'Byrne, 2009), and may be viewed as rigid, time-consuming (lots of forms) and one-way, in that it meets the needs of the worker and agency rather than that of the service-user. The difficulty arises when information is collected on an individual by different professionals with a different focus (i.e., health, housing etc.) but stored separately. This results in an inadequate understanding of the total experience of any individual by any one professional. Workers can become caught up in the process of gathering information rather than in trying to understand what the service user needs. On a more positive note, this systematic manner of collecting large amounts of data has also contributed to the evidence base for social work practice.
- The *Questioning* model of assessment focuses on the nature of the questions and how the information is used. Using this approach problems and solutions reside with the

individual and the social worker's task is to identify the problem and highlight the most appropriate approach to resolve the issue. A criticism of this model is that it can be seen as oppressive given that the social worker takes on the role of expert and makes the final decision. However, if questions are asked in order to try to understand what is impacting on the current situation, and if a range of perspectives are sought, then this does not have to be the case.

- When adopting the *Exchange* model the service user becomes the expert with regard to their own needs and through their involvement in their own assessment becomes empowered. It acknowledges that the worker's expertise lies in their problem-solving abilities. The aim, through development of trust, is to seek a compromise between choices and needs through involvement of all parties. The worker takes on responsibility for managing the process of assessment. The focus is on a holistic assessment of the context in relation to the individual over time (Coulshed and Orme, 2012).

Specific frameworks have been outlined in the Case Study to demonstrate how models of assessment can support particular frameworks or approaches to information gathering.

Case Study

1. The *Common Assessment Framework (CAF)* in England and Wales, the *UNOCINI Assessment Framework* in Northern Ireland and the *GIRFEC (Getting it Right for Every Child)* approach in Scotland focus on how practitioners across all services for children and adults can work together to ensure that children and young people have their needs met with reference to a range of outcomes and indicators that can be applied in any setting and circumstance. The approach is underpinned by a set of common values and principles. The success of such approaches depends on a standardised assessment and the application of shared tools and models. All approaches require a lead professional.

The five outcomes of CAF concern being healthy, staying safe, enjoying and achieving, making a positive contribution and achieving economic well-being (Children's Workforce Development Council, 2009). It consists of a pre-assessment checklist to decide who would benefit from an assessment (focusing on the development of the child/young person, parents and carers, and family and environment); a standard recording format; and a process to enable practitioners in the children and young people's workforce to undertake a common assessment and to move forward on the result through the development of an action plan.

In sharing information with other professionals, recording information on a single system, identifying needs and services, establishing a plan and reviewing both the plan and provision, it would appear that a *Procedural* model is being employed.

2. The *Single Shared Assessment (SSA)* in Scotland, the *Single Assessment Process (SAP)* for older people in England, the *Unified Assessment* in Wales and the *Northern Ireland Single Assessment Tool (NISAT)* combine elements of both Procedural and Questioning models. SSA is the 'streamlining of the assessment process to enable the needs and outcomes for the individual to be identified and subsequent interventions and services put in place' (Scottish Government, 2009b: 1).

(Continued)

(Continued)

The sharing of information across agencies is crucial and so the process encourages joint working.

In a SSA a 'lead professional' coordinates the gathering of information for the assessment and ensures that a plan is made and reviewed and that the identified services are delivered. *Care Management* is the name for this process, and it is focused on the needs of individuals with complex or changing needs. Three different types of assessment (Simple, Comprehensive or Specialist) can be carried out, depending on the needs of the service user, and assessment is undertaken by different professionals depending on their levels of training and expertise. The legal context for Care Management is provided through the National Health Service and Community Care Act 1990 and in Scotland is augmented by the Regulation of Care (Scotland) Act 2001 and the Community Care and Health (Scotland) Act 2002. The process of a SSA involves service users and carers and is intended to be person-centred. However, for older people information is also gathered through an Indicator of Relative Need questionnaire which consists of 12 multiple choice questions under section headings: activities of daily living; personal care; food/drink preparation; mental well-being and behaviour; and bowel management. The answers to each question are scored and the totals for each section are calculated. The scores are intended for planning purposes and not to determine eligibility for services.

3. Motivational interviewing (see Chapter 23), used in substance misuse counselling, is both client-centred and semi-directive. The approach attempts to increase the service user's awareness of the consequences of their behaviour and to encourage reflection on the benefits that might be achieved through change. The approach is non-judgemental, non-adversarial and non-confrontational. The eight key interviewing techniques: asking leading questions; reflecting resistance; acknowledging the advantages of behaviours; raising awareness of discrepancy between the present and the desired situation; elaborating on self-motivational statements; offering non-dogmatic information; voicing the service user's doubts and summarising selectively (Miller and Rollnick, 1991) fit well with the Exchange model of assessment.

Having chosen a specific model and framework for assessment the social worker must also consider the knowledge that underpins assessment. The range of knowledge used to support the assessment should include an awareness of developmental theories, social systems theories, policies, organisational knowledge and knowledge of research. The point is to bring together information and resources in order to personalise the provision (Statham and Kearney, 2007).

THE ASSESSMENT RELATIONSHIP

The task of assessment should be underpinned by skills that convey 'genuineness, warmth and acceptance, encouragement and approval, empathy, responsiveness and sensitivity' (Lishman, 2009: 76). Cowager (1994) suggests that the strengths that the service user brings are key to developing the helping relationship. Strength-based assessments may support the service user to draw on their own resources to examine alternative ways to improve their situation and to build their confidence. As previously outlined, assessments focusing on deficits may serve only to disempower the service user and reinforce inequalities between them and the social worker. The social worker's role is to develop the service users' capability to assist themselves. This is known as empowerment.

A good assessment relationship involves the social worker in:

- examining the personal and environmental strengths of the service user and carrying out a multidimensional assessment of such strengths
- utilising meaningful and appropriate language
- negotiating mutual agreement over the assessment
- apportioning no blame. (Cowager, 1994)

In addition, we would add:

- discovering the uniqueness of the service user by understanding an individual's identity and life choices which are formed by their life experiences, culture and ethnicity and the way in which others have responded towards them.

Any attempt to form a genuine partnership will involve good skills of listening and interviewing and will focus on the individual rather than the procedure.

REFLECTION ON SELF IN ASSESSMENT

Social workers must be aware of how their own attitudes, values and power based on their gender, age, ethnicity and life experiences might impact on the process and/or the outcome of the task. Through becoming aware of 'self' (often assisted by education and training), workers can consciously adapt their stance, if necessary, in order to practise in an anti-oppressive manner. It is also important for the worker to gain an understanding of how service users' life experience may inform their perceptions of, and attitude towards, the social worker's involvement.

To develop your thinking about the role of self in assessment visit the Companion Website (www.sagepub.co.uk/SocialWork) and explore the challenges Mark has been facing in his practice.

SERVICE USER INVOLVEMENT

A key social work value concerns the involvement of service users in decisions about their own situation and discussions upon other issues such as service provision and agency policy. O'Sullivan (2011) identifies four levels of client involvement: where the outcome of assessment is the result of decision-making by others; consultation, where the service user's opinions are taken into account; partnership, where joint decisions are made between the service user and the social worker; being in control, where decisions are made by the service user without the facilitation of a social worker (this is the highest level of involvement). Decisions might be service user life decisions, decisions to protect others, or decisions about resources or service delivery. Unless an individual's capacity is in question or there is a concern that the safety of others might be compromised, service users should have control over decisions about their own lives. The reason to choose a lower rather than a higher level of involvement must be justified and limits should be placed on the type of involvement only if there are grounds to do so (O'Sullivan, 2011).

Exercise

Read Chapter 15 and try to identify situations where service user involvement might be problematic.

WORKING WITH RESISTANCE

Social work practice is often undertaken during challenging and stressful times, so it is hardly surprising that service users are not always welcoming and appreciative of such involvement (Taylor, 2011). The service user may experience difficulties in containing the emotions elicited by their situation and the consequent involvement of social work services. For example, the service user may experience feelings of failure or loss of control over life events, and the individual response will be dependent on the nature of their situation and on their preferred coping strategies (informed by their previous life experiences). Social workers have to manage a range of behaviours, and aggressive and violent reactions cannot be ruled out. Dockar-Drysdale (1968) suggests that violence represents a breakdown in communication and is a symbolic way of finding someone to help contain feelings of fear and anxiety.

In social work the term 'resistance' is used to describe those service users 'who are unwilling, or feel coerced into engaging with you' (Taylor, 2011: 11). Taylor (2011) suggests that individuals might be reluctant to become engaged because of a rigid interpretation of life events that impedes consideration of other ways of thinking or acting. The worker's belief in the capacity of the service user to change, however, is central to the helping process, as service users may display ambivalence (conflicting emotions) or be reluctant to engage. The latter may be a result of a distrust of authority, due to the worker's potential role in relation to prosecution or removal of liberties (as a result of offending behaviour, severe mental health problems or child protection cases). There is a greater risk of experiencing aggressive or violent behaviour where:

- The individual has experience of a subculture where violence is the norm.
- The individual perceives that any unpleasantness generated is a deliberate and personal attack on them.
- The person is disinhibited, e.g. through alcohol or drugs.

- There is an expectation that violence will be rewarded, i.e. by influencing the decision or withdrawal of the worker.
- There is a belief that no other action is possible, e.g. where there is evidence that violence has been used frequently as a coping mechanism. (Breakwell, 1989)

Consideration of theories such as social learning theory, psychodynamic theory or attribution theory can be helpful in assisting workers to understand the probable cause of an individual's behaviour. To maximise the possibility of engaging an individual, sustaining a relationship, or even calming a situation, it is crucial for the worker to demonstrate empathy and to practise good communication skills, particularly active listening. Service users and carers outlined a range of specific skills and values demonstrated by social workers who were felt to be good communicators. These included:

- Being polite and punctual
- Listening to what is being said
- Doing what is stated and agreed
- Explaining what will happen and why without using jargon
- Being honest. (Diggins, 2004)

In conclusion, resistance may be seen as a way in which service users attempt to regain some of their 'perceived' loss of power and control by refusing to recognise risks to self or others, not accepting the need for change, or being unwilling to accept options presented to them. The concept of principled negotiation might assist in finding a way forward. By focusing on the interests rather than the attitudes of those involved, separating the people from the problem and trying to find options for mutual interest before agreeing criteria for evaluating the result of the negotiations, a resolution to any stalemate might be found. However, legal and policy requirements might mean that negotiation is not an option (e.g. because of protection issues) or that due to their personal values and principles an individual might be unwilling to negotiate on certain matters (e.g. around the use of alcohol). In planning a response discussions should take place with colleagues and relevant agencies, involving the service user wherever possible. Any response should recognise that safe practice is beneficial for both the worker and the service user.

Critical Thinking

In assessment work, collaborative approaches building on service users' expertise are vital. The current practice agenda, especially personalisation and self-directed support, emphasises the role of self-assessment. Gardner (2011: 43) notes that there has been much professional resistance to the concept and she highlights that we mistakenly assume that self-assessment involves only the service user. In self-assessment, however, service users are major participants because, quite simply, they know themselves best. The social worker participates too, supporting, offering information and assistance. Gardner's interpretation of self-assessment is interesting and provides a useful point for you to consider.

During, or after your most recent period of practice learning, critically appraise your practice in respect of a collaborative assessment.

To read about the findings of pilot projects focusing on self-assessment in adult social work settings, visit the Companion Website (www.sagepub.co.uk/SocialWork) and see the article by Abendstern et al. (2013).

CONCLUSION

This chapter has offered particular frameworks, methodologies and supporting theoretical concepts which are integral in good social work assessment. The following central themes should be borne in mind when undertaking assessment in work with service users:

- Assessment is a skilled activity that is crucial in setting the context of engagement with service users.
- A central theme is of partnership and empowerment but with a recognition that at times assessments are carried out with service users who are either hesitant or unwilling participants.
- Assessment is underpinned by a broad knowledge and skill base, as well as a series of guiding principles that support practitioners in their role.
- Assessment in current practice contexts frequently involves working alongside other professionals, allowing for the sharing of perspectives and a more comprehensive and holistic approach.
- The tools and frameworks that have been proffered in this chapter should be utilised with both care and professional judgement rather than implemented in a technical and formulaic manner. These tools offer a 'guide' rather than a 'map'.
- Assessment is a dynamic activity that should always be viewed as a process rather than a one-off event.

Reflective Questions

1. Considering the concepts of need and Bronfenbrenner's Ecological Systems Theory identify what a person requires from their immediate caregivers or family in order to develop or progress. Go on to consider how a person's development or progress may be influenced by the wider world and what difference being part of a supportive community environment can make.
2. What questions might you ask during the assessment process in order to explore 'strengths'? Consider how the questions you ask interface with the model of assessment being used.
3. As part of preparing for one of your social work placements or practice opportunities spend time researching the legal and policy context of the field you will be working in. During placement, reflect on how legislation and policy shape the work that your placement agency undertakes. Does working in different settings impact on the extent to which social work practice is statutorily driven?

RECOMMENDED READING

Milner, J. and O'Byrne, P. (2009) *Assessment in Social Work*, 3rd edn. Basingstoke: Palgrave MacMillan.

Parker, J. and Bradley, G. (2010) *Social Work Practice: Assessment, Planning, Intervention and Review (Transforming Social Work Practice)*, 3rd edn. Exeter: Learning Matters.

Walker, S. and Beckett, C. (2010) *Social Work Assessment and Intervention*. Lyme Regis: Russell House Publications.

13 RISK ASSESSMENT

Kirstin Parkes and Mike Shepherd

Key Themes

- Risk can refer to positive or negative outcomes, although in social work is generally used as shorthand for something negative.
- Risk assessment is a way of structuring thinking and decision-making around risk when working with service users.
- Good risk assessment locates risk in a service user's whole situation, looking at protective factors, strengths and resilience as well as risk factors.
- Risk assessment is a dynamic activity that needs to flow and adapt to changes in circumstances and environments.
- Risk assessment is pointless without it being part of an overarching risk management process.

INTRODUCTION

Risk is a concept familiar to us all. In our daily lives we frequently make small judgements based on the probability of our actions and behaviours having positive outcomes; children learning to adapt themselves to their environment take risks as part of their growth and development; risk is central to the work of any number of professions; risk can be facing the challenges when striving for individual or collective achievement; and risk can be about attempting to minimise loss when our lives change for the worse.

It is unsurprising then that within social work and social care risk performs a crucial role in assisting service users to achieve their goals, to manage change or to minimise harm to self and others. Risk refers to assessing probabilities and possibilities, and, wherever possible, relies on evidence to support decision-making.

Fundamentally, risk is not a difficult concept to understand, but there are a variety of risk assessment tools and risk management frameworks specific to different areas of social work. This chapter will explain the basic precepts of assessing risk, look at different perspectives on risk, provide some oversight of the current trends within social work and give examples of risk assessment and risk management practice.

DEFINING RISK

There are a number of ways of defining risk. Risk can mean the chance of something happening, either positive or negative. In social work, risk is mostly assessed in relation to human behaviour, traditionally with an emphasis on negative outcomes. At the core of risk definition are risk factors, fixed or variable characteristics that have a direct relationship to behaviours, beliefs, attitudes and circumstances and are specific to the individual being assessed. Risk factors may also be influenced by age, gender, race and ethnicity, and may be underpinned by familial, extra-familial and environmental pressures.

Of increasing importance in contemporary risk assessment is the identification of protective factors. Protective factors refer to attributes or resources accessible to the person that can moderate or compensate for risk (Fraser et al., 1999). They may include an individual's skills, values and networks of support. They may also reflect personal strengths or human capital which the individual possesses.

Where there may be protective factors influencing the severity or intensity of risk situations, there may also be resilience, that is, how well a person sustains successful functioning during the risk life cycle. Resilience can be unpredictable in the context of risk assessment, as risk frameworks cannot wholly model how an individual will adapt to negative life events, stress and trauma.

Some definitions of risk make a distinction between risk and uncertainty, and between risk and hazard (Kaplan and Garrick, 1981). Service users may find themselves in uncertain situations, but one would not necessarily say that they were at risk, and that is an important distinction. The distinction between risk and hazard implies that hazard exists as a source, such as the sea or the street or the car. Predicting the likelihood of an individual's susceptibility to risk when faced with these hazards can be difficult. It is important for the social worker, therefore, to understand that risk assessment is never conclusive but based on probability and prediction.

Exercise

Identify an activity you do. What are the hazards associated with it, what are the risks and how do you minimise them?

PERSPECTIVES ON RISK

According to Davis (1996), two main perspectives on risk assessment can be identified, both of which can be witnessed within social work practice: the risk-taking perspective (positive risk-taking) and the risk-minimisation perspective. As we shall see these perspectives can be likened to comparisons between a social model of risk and a medical model.

The risk-taking perspective views risk as an important, positive aspect of everyday life, without which people would lead sheltered and unfulfilled lives. Consider the following practice example and identify other similar situations that you have encountered.

Case Study: Positive Risk-taking

In a care home providing services for older people, the risk of physical injury might be balanced against the wishes of an older person to continue to be ambulant around the home without assistance. If an older service user wishes to climb the stairs herself, but there is also a lift or stairlift available, an assessment issue for the worker is need versus risk. From a risk-minimisation perspective, the worker may decide that the safest way to reach the top of the stairs would be to use the stairlift; but the service user insists that she can manage and does not want any help. Clearly, that is her right and her choice, and to some extent becomes her responsibility should she trip or fall. However, where that older person may also be experiencing cognitive deterioration due to a condition such as dementia, is she truly able to make an informed judgement about the safety of her climbing stairs herself? We have come across an assessment that has deemed it safe for the older person to go up the stairs unaided, but assistance must be afforded when the person descends the stairs. Such fine judgements on risk may seem small, but in the context of the older person's life space, the promotion of independence is crucial to well-being and self-esteem.

The focus within the risk-taking perspective is on issues relating to rights, abilities, choice and participation. Using this approach, service users are likely to be viewed as expert in their own situations and the role of practitioners is to enable and promote risk-taking. Morgan (2004) contends that in adopting a positive risk-taking approach, service users and practitioners should be balancing potential harms and benefits of one decision over another in line with achieving the preferred goals of the service user. Identifying risks and formulating plans to reduce negative impacts and increase positive impacts is a crucial part of this process. Assessment of risk partly identifies individual deficits, but, recognising a person's social and environmental context, it identifies strengths as a mechanism for building an effective risk management plan. Risk management strategies in this model tend to be in the area of support, including supporting service users to protect themselves. If we want service users to have meaningful choice in how they live their lives, then enabling people to take risks must be viewed as part of the process.

Exercise

You are walking home late at night. A group of youngsters, mostly wearing hoodies, is gathered on the street, and you must either pass them or make a long detour. What factors influence your decision?

Alternatively, the risk-minimisation model views risk as almost entirely negative. This perspective is akin to a medical model of risk, where issues develop due to problems or impairments within the individual. These risks therefore need to be managed and controlled by experts to promote safety and protection, and categorisations of victims and perpetrators may be rigid. Firstly there is a focus on those deemed to be most vulnerable, for example children or adults with incapacity. As a consequence, risk-based intervention tends to be at the protection end of the spectrum, where workers devise safety plans to protect vulnerable service users from hazards and danger. It is not being suggested here that this practice is wrong or that vulnerable service users should be left to protect themselves; however there are drawbacks to such an approach.

By employing this focus, it is easy to see how the identification of strengths and resilience in particular situations may be overlooked. The danger here is that without involving service users in their own protection, we may inadvertently increase levels of dependency and so create additional unpredicted risks for those we are trying to protect.

The second focus for the risk-minimisation model is on those deemed to be dangerous, for example, some mental health service users and offenders. Risk management strategies in this model include control and incapacitation of both 'vulnerable' and 'dangerous' persons. Again there are inherent dangers. Without working with a person's strengths and capacities to take responsibility for their own behaviour, what happens when controls and externally managed plans are removed?

Although presented as opposites, in reality elements of both perspectives would be found in practice. For example, when working with a vulnerable adult a risk-minimisation perspective would focus on the development of protective measures. A risk-taking perspective, however, would explore the areas where the service user can exercise control over his/her life and make changes that facilitate doing things differently.

Bearing in mind the two dominant perspectives on risk, we will now look at approaches to the assessment of risk within practice.

An activity on the Companion Website (www.sagepub.co.uk/SocialWork) invites you to consider your own experience of risk taking and your attitudes towards risk in work with service users.

APPROACHES TO RISK ASSESSMENT

When considering risk assessment in social work we are usually facing a situation where some harm has occurred. This links to the prevailing view of risk equating to harm or danger, and the purpose of the assessment is to learn from what has already happened to reduce the chances of repetition. For example, where a child has been harmed, the nature of any ongoing risk needs to be identified, or an appearance in court triggers an assessment of what factors are likely to lead to further offending behaviour.

Risk assessment should not be seen as a discrete, fixed process and good risk assessment practice requires that assessment be fluid and dynamic. By this we mean it should be an ongoing process, responding to both positive and negative changes in the person, their circumstances and their environment. Although initially a risk-minimisation approach may be utilised to ensure the immediate safety of service users, as the work progresses, positive risk-taking and working with strengths and resilience should be emphasised.

We acknowledge that assessing risk can appear initially as a particularly complex and daunting task. Fundamentally though, risk assessment can be broken down into two core elements – severity of outcomes and likelihood (Carson and Bain, 2008). Both elements need to be balanced in order to assess risk effectively.

Severity of Outcomes

Also described as consequences, the outcomes focus of risk assessment identifies the potential event causing concern, the situation that we are worried about, who might be harmed and how harmful it could be. Once the potential outcome has been identified and we have a view on how serious this could be, the next stage is to identify how likely the outcome is to occur.

Likelihood

There may be numerous potential outcomes, but to identify all outcomes would be time-consuming and not necessarily productive. For example, we all assess risk prior to crossing a busy road, and the likely outcomes we will consider are getting safely to the other side, or being hit by traffic on the way across. We are not so likely to consider the outcome of having a heart attack whilst crossing the road, as it seems a rare enough possibility not to be worthy of consideration on every occasion.

Having identified *relevant* potential outcomes therefore, an assessment needs to be made of how *likely* these events are to occur. It may be that the consequences or outcomes of an event would be serious harm. However, if that event has a very small chance of actually happening, then the overall level of risk would be lowered (see Figure 13.1).

To analyse either element of risk effectively – outcome and likelihood – it is helpful to have a structure for the process of risk assessment. Within the literature, three main approaches to the assessment of risk have been identified: clinical, actuarial and structured clinical judgement. No one of these provides an ideal structure, and in considering these three approaches to the assessment of risk, you should always be aware of the context of the risk assessment. When time permits and risk assessment tools are available, analytical and evidential approaches to risk assessment are good practice. However, we must recognise that social workers are sometimes required to make quick decisions outwith an office environment and may well use intuition and practice wisdom as the means by which they arrive at a decision. Whilst this can be seen as a practice reality, it is nonetheless important to recognise that analytical and evidential risk assessment can reduce the possibility of a practitioner making a mistake when under pressure.

Clinical Judgement

Clinical judgement is widely considered to be the most common, but also the least effective method of assessing risk. In undertaking assessment, practitioners combine an *in-depth knowledge* of research pertaining to risk factors within their specific

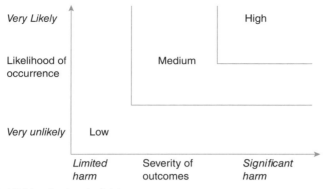

Figure 13.1 Establishing the level of risk

area of practice, with *professional judgements* about the individual being assessed and their situation. Advocates of this approach highlight flexibility and the ability to address the individual risk factors in each situation. In other words, there is no reliance on fixed checklists of factors found to be statistically predictive, and greater consideration of the whole person can take place. In terms of effectiveness, clinical judgement has been found to be slightly better in predicting future risk than tossing a coin. This approach has also been criticised for being subjective, in that how practitioners make risk decisions is not formally guided and is therefore open to individual interpretation.

Actuarial Judgement

The actuarial approach originated within the insurance industry and involves a mathematical calculation of risk, comparing key factors about an individual with the statistical frequency of such risk within a matched sample. Although this seems complicated, in essence, the actuarial approach attempts to predict future behaviour by identifying when a person shares characteristics with a group of people who have behaved in a certain way in the past. The more a person shares key characteristics with this control group, the higher the likelihood of negative outcomes.

These key characteristics are also referred to as static, historical risk factors, given they are not really amenable to change through efforts by workers or service users and they fluctuate only over fairly lengthy periods of time. Examples include age, gender, marital status, number of previous convictions.

Although research has identified that actuarial risk assessment is the most accurate in terms of predicting outcomes, risk prediction is actually the likelihood of *the group* behaving in a certain way. What this means is that in practice, the approach does not identify which members of the group are likely to behave in a certain manner, nor perhaps more importantly which are not.

Actuarial risk assessment on its own does not take strengths or protective factors into account in mitigating risk, nor assists practitioners to identify specific areas of work which can help reduce risk by examining *dynamic risk factors*, or those factors which can be changed to reduce risk.

Structured Clinical Judgement

In an effort to combine the positive features of actuarial and clinical judgement approaches, a structured clinical judgement approach to risk assessment has developed, incorporating both the predictive qualities of actuarial assessment (static risk factors) and consideration of individual risk profiles (dynamic risk factors). This approach provides a clearer structure for professional risk assessment, guiding the practitioner in considering the relevant areas, not being overly prescriptive or losing the consistency and research base of actuarial approaches. Many of the familiar frameworks for risk work are based on a structured clinical judgement approach to the assessment of risk.

FRAMEWORKS FOR THE ASSESSMENT OF RISK

Risk assessment is not a discrete, isolated activity, but it is largely a pointless exercise unless the eventual outcome is *risk management*, or reducing the risks to an *acceptable* level. Nevertheless, without an effective assessment of the risks within a situation, any attempt to manage the risks, increase safety or promote positive risk-taking is likely to be unsuccessful.

Social work practice is guided by practice frameworks, providing an overarching philosophy for working with service users. Often such frameworks are underpinned by specific theoretical perspectives. For example, in child and adult protection work an ecological approach may be taken, whereby emphasis is placed on seeing risk in the context of the service users' whole environment and on identifying strengths and pressures in the world of the child or adult at risk of harm.

Risk assessment frameworks may also provide principles to aid practitioners and these may relate to the anticipated outcomes for service users. The frameworks also incorporate specific risk assessment tools which have been developed and validated for the service user group.

RISK ASSESSMENT TOOLS

Across social work practice settings, many risk assessment tools exist. Having a risk assessment document can seem reassuring, particularly in highly complex situations. Risk assessment tools can enable practitioners and service users to understand and clarify the risk and resilience factors, the possible negative or positive consequences of these factors and the reasons these factors exist. They may be drawn from any approach; for example, actuarial tools rely heavily on the exploration of historical and static factors in a person's life while structured clinical judgement tools may begin with an actuarial screening, but then move on to consider more dynamic risk factors, strengths and protective factors.

However, do not think that by completing the risk assessment tool you have undertaken a risk assessment. The tools do not do the risk assessment for you. Rather, as we have previously indicated, they should provide a structure to guide thinking around the issues identified and may also provide a record of risk decisions. Whatever approaches or tools are used, there are a number of characteristics which good risk assessments will share.

Several researchers have examined the use of risk assessment tools in practice settings. See the articles on the Companion Website (www.sagepub.co.uk/SocialWork) by Warner (2003), reporting on risk assessment and child protection, and Littlechild and Hawley (2010) on risk assessment in mental health services.

WHAT DOES A GOOD RISK ASSESSMENT LOOK LIKE?

Whatever risk assessment method you use, there are certain features of assessments that lead to ensuring the assessment is effective.

Good risk assessment needs to:

- Identify what is the risk, to whom and in what circumstances
- Be based on sound evidence and analysis
- Use tools to inform not replace clinical judgement
- Be clearly communicated and understood
- Be an ongoing and integral part of risk management
- Consider a balance of internal and external risk and protective factors

BARRIERS TO EFFECTIVE RISK ASSESSMENT

We have considered the frameworks, tools and characteristics of good risk assessment practice and so, with well-designed tools at their disposal and a good understanding of the theory of risk assessment, practitioners should be able to produce credible and reliable risk work. However, risk assessment is not a morally neutral activity, and workers are influenced by their emotions and their social environment, as is anyone. Consequently, there are some barriers to effective risk work that need to be considered.

Managing Anxiety

Practitioners may not always use the risk assessment tool accurately because of anxiety generated by the situation, or where personal bias or values of the organisation do not sit easily with the results of the assessment (Kemshall and Maguire, 2001). Workers may draw on narrative information, interpret opinion as fact and create a profile for the service user that either matches the service provision or, vice versa, excludes them from service provision. Workers may overestimate risk due to anxiety about the individual, or underestimate risk due to lack of understanding of the potential consequences of certain risk behaviours the person may be engaged in.

Uncertainty

In Chapter 11 of this book consideration is given to the role of uncertainty in decision-making. It is highly unlikely that in undertaking risk assessment you will have all possible information at your disposal. As we have said previously, good risk assessment relies on sound evidence and analysis, and whilst you may be sure that the information you do have is sound, you may also be concerned about gaps in information. One inhibitor to effective risk assessment is the failure to acknowledge uncertainty. Accepting and working with uncertainty, however, is linked to a dynamic approach to assessing risk that continually seeks, or adapts to, new information and is an essential part of social work practise.

Heuristics and Bias

A heuristic is a mental shortcut that allows people to solve problems and make judgements quickly and efficiently. These rule-of-thumb strategies shorten decision-making time and allow people to function without constantly stopping to think about the next course of action. While heuristics are helpful in many situations, they can also lead to biases and therefore social workers need to be aware of them when considering risk.

Risk assessment does not occur in a vacuum. Psychological research has identified several biases of thinking, stemming from heuristics, and connected with how people perceive elements in risk decision-making (Baron, 2008), which decrease the objectivity of risk assessment. For example, evidence shows that we are more likely to notice and give greater weight to characteristics that confirm an existing belief or theory than those that contradict it.

Case Study

One social worker has grown up as an only child, very protected within the family and with a rather low self-esteem. Another has grown up in a large family, often being left unsupervised and free to roam, and with a rather over-confident approach to life. Consider how their existing beliefs might impact on their risk assessments.

RISK MANAGEMENT

As stated above, risk assessment is largely a pointless exercise unless the eventual outcome is risk management, or reducing the risks to an acceptable level. The development of risk management strategies has now framed risk as a continuous process through the lifetime of the service user's contact with social work and its partners. In managing risk, and recognising that this aspect of social work now forms an unavoidable component of professional decision-making, what then makes for good risk management?

Titterton (2005: 92) defines risk management as 'developing a systematic approach which allows for the planning of risk-taking strategies and for monitoring and reviewing' with five key stages:

- consult and communicate
- prepare risk plan
- sign up
- share information
- monitor and review.

Risk assessment is viewed as central to decision-making, but the act of making these decisions, implementing and reviewing them in an ongoing way, constitutes risk management in social work. This should be a familiar concept to social work students as it follows the usual assess, plan, implement and review cycle for social work intervention. Risk management cannot completely eliminate risk, and in line with positive risk-taking policies, this is unlikely to be a prized outcome in any case. Rather, risk management strategies should seek to reduce levels of adverse risk to acceptable levels and to increase resilience and protective factors within any given risk situation.

We can see then that the processes of risk assessment and risk management are inextricably linked. Risk is not static, and the assessment and management plans should respond and adapt to changing levels of risk.

Though the assessment records circumstances and situations at a particular point in time and is predictive of future behaviours and situational risk 'triggers', risk management must be flexible in order to accommodate fluctuations in the person's moods, demeanour, changes in living circumstances, relationships, employment and physical and mental health. Good risk management is a balance of restriction and opportunity, which allows people to take more control of their lives whilst acknowledging the rights and responsibilities those controls imply. Even where service users have limited capacity and require protection for their safety, risk management strategies should seek to promote choice wherever possible.

BARRIERS TO EFFECTIVE RISK MANAGEMENT

Often risk management can be presented simply as matching assessed risk factors to specifically tailored interventions. There are two immediate problems with this assumption. Firstly, when working with people there are all sorts of variables that can influence the success or otherwise of risk management plans, even those based on the most thorough of risk assessments. Secondly, a risk management plan that focuses only on deficits, problems, or challenges, without building on strengths and developing capacity, is likely to be effective only in the short term. Some of the key barriers are discussed below.

Working with Ethical Tensions

Social workers often struggle with the ethical dimensions of managing risk. Balancing the provision of support with more restrictive protective mechanisms, taking account of the wishes of service users and family members (which may be conflicting), the perceived best interests of service users and managing situations where someone may be at risk whilst simultaneously posing risk to others is a complex business. These issues are discussed later.

Failure to Engage

One element of effective risk work is the absolute requirement to involve service users in a meaningful way in planning ways to manage risk. It may be that a social worker has very clear ideas that certain strategies would mitigate risk factors. However, if the service user, or carers and family members, do not support these strategies they are unlikely to be successful. Service users should consent in an informed way to risk management plans, and this can only happen if they have been included in planning and been provided with full information relating to the proposed mechanisms.

A Focus on Negative Elements

In some cases, risk management plans can read like a manual of prohibitions, with a large list of things people cannot do as a means of managing risk, particularly risk posed to others. Whilst there may be an argument for prioritising the safety of potential victims in this way, the person whose behaviour is being managed can rightly ask 'well, what *can* I do then?' Although there are times when restrictions are necessary, more positive risk management strategies also need to be considered simultaneously.

Organisational Culture

Two aspects of culture within organisations can potentially create barriers to effective risk management. The first concerns the risk-averse organisation. Denney (2005) highlights that systems of accountability and a pre-occupation with audit and inspection can lead to organisations being more concerned with the management of their own reputation than effectively and positively managing risk for service users.

Furthermore, risk management in social work practice is often located in multi-agency forums, where there can be real benefits from the cross-agency information sharing and shared responsibility for managing risk. Different organisations such as the police, NHS and social work may, however, all have different remits in relation to the management of risk and differing value bases concerning risk, which can lead to a lack of agreement about when the threshold for risk management intervention is reached, particularly around the rights of service users to make risky decisions. Working in such situations requires skills in negotiation, the ability to build productive working relationships and the need to be systematic in presenting the social work perspective that allows for positive risk-taking as well as harm minimisation.

BALANCING RIGHTS AND RISK

The balancing of rights and risk is a frequent consideration in social work.

Critical Thinking

The carer of a spouse with dementia is faced with an intolerably stressful situation and lashes out, hitting the partner, through frustration and an inability to cope. Think about this person's rights to remain in this relationship. Should they be over-ridden as a consequence? What about the person with dementia? Could removing the carer who harmed them, perhaps the only person to whom they have a deep attachment, cause more harm than it prevents?

It is largely understood that an individual's core values and beliefs are a key part of decisions to take risks or not; it is also accepted, but perhaps less well understood, how a practitioner's values influence professional practice and decision-making. Within social work, practitioners regularly face unpleasant dilemmas in risk work and more often than not a balance is what is required to resolve these dilemmas satisfactorily.

Bates and Silberman (2007: 6) have described risk management as finding an 'integrated balance between "positive risk taking" around the values of autonomy and independence and a policy of protection for the person and the community based on minimising harm'.

This raises issues of potential tensions between the positions, with practitioners required to make risk decisions encompassing the two. The 'right to take risks' (Alaszewski and Alaszewski, 2002: 57) has challenged social workers to find a way to support service users and remove barriers to risk-taking that other people take for granted, whilst also maintaining a protective focus in line with professional codes of practice. For example, two service users with moderate learning disabilities within a residential unit wish to engage in a sexual relationship. There may be inherent risks related to contraception, unwanted pregnancy and potential abuses of power. However these would need to be balanced with the service users' rights to family life, to make choices and to be active participants in their own lives. Although there are issues of capacity, where individuals do have capacity to make these decisions, workers would have a responsibility to support this standpoint, even if there are associated risks.

Kuosmanen and Starke (2013) explore the relatively uncharted research area of professionals working with people with learning disabilities who engage in prostitution. Read their findings on the Companion Website (www.sagepub.co.uk/SocialWork).

In risk assessment, an awareness of one's own values is crucial to avoid the over-protection or infantilisation of service users. Many commentators (Kemshall and Pritchard, 1996; Tanner, 1998) have highlighted risk-averse practice, where too much emphasis is given to managing risks to zero, even when the resultant impact is a reduced quality of life for service users. This reluctance to support service users to take positive risks is all the more puzzling when social work intervention models currently focus on empowerment and strengths-based approaches (Webb, 2006).

The issue of thresholds in determining what level of risk is acceptable or unacceptable then becomes important. Social workers have, and may encounter service users, parents or carers who have vastly differing tolerance levels for risk. Factors including experience, organisational support and proximity to high profile media cases can impact on where the line between support and protection is drawn in the mind of a practitioner.

It is rarely the case, even when working with the highest levels of risk of harm, that the rights of either the person posing the harm or the person being harmed can be overruled

---

POSING RISKS TO OTHERS

- The assessed person is viewed as the source of risk to others
- Risk is defined in terms of harm to others
- Risk assessment identifies risky persons and behaviours
- Risk management reduces or removes risk to others
- The rights of the assessed person can be limited in terms of protecting others

VULNERABILITY TO RISKS

- The assessed person is viewed as being 'at risk' from self/others
- Risk is defined in terms of consequences of harm to the person
- Risk assessment identifies whether risks are internal to the person and circumstances or externally posed
- Risk management reduces risk to acceptable levels to the person
- The rights of the assessed person are key to the process and reducing risk is balanced against a loss of choice, independence and autonomy

---

Figure 13.2   Examining risk and vulnerability (adapted from Kemshall, 2002)

completely. Of particular interest are those people who are deemed to both pose a risk to others and also simultaneously be vulnerable to risk themselves. For example, many young offenders would fall clearly into both camps, along with a minority of adults with mental illness. Kemshall (2002) suggests using separate frameworks to assess both risk posed and vulnerability in an effort to achieve an appropriate balance. Figure 13.2 demonstrates key aspects of both approaches.

The key to balancing rights and risk is proportionality and not one person's rights subsuming those of another. Whilst those posing a serious risk of harm may require restrictions on some of their rights to protect others, the balanced approach would suggest that this cannot continue endlessly. Restrictive risk management measures should only be used where there is no other, less restrictive option available which would achieve the same outcome. Similarly, protective measures that have an element of restriction to the person being protected also need to be proportionate to the level of risk. Dynamic risk management plans should have built in review facilities to make sure that restrictive or protective measures continue only for as long as is necessary.

CONCLUSION

This chapter has outlined and explained many of the concepts of risk in social work practice. The following points provide a summary of key areas of learning:

- In social work, activities relating to risk are not, as is sometimes assumed, solely designed to prevent something harmful happening but in many cases to facilitate positive outcomes allowing service users, their carers and families to live fulfilling and safer lives.
- Approaches to the assessment of risk in social work have come to take a balanced approach drawing on both actuarial and clinical assessment. Such structured clinical judgement is seen to draw on the strengths of the other approaches.

- Risk is not a particularly complicated concept to understand but for practitioners there may be layers of complexity associated with assessment frameworks and risk assessment tools which have the potential to give rise to uncertainty and anxiety about undertaking risk work. Where there are inter-agency and inter-professional responsibilities involved in undertaking risk work there may be complexities around competing values and interests.
- There is an ethical dimension to risk and this chapter has considered the balancing of rights and risk. We are not doing risk assessment 'to' people but 'with' people.
- Risk assessment and risk management have been explored and the links between them made clear. The assessment outcome should link to the management plan and this should be reviewed as appropriate. Without risk management, risk assessment lacks purpose and meaning.

Finally, we would add that risk work is becoming more sophisticated and those working with risk should ensure that they have the knowledge, skills and training to enable them to work confidently and effectively with the tools they are using. To borrow a phrase from economics: 'Risk comes from not knowing what you're doing.' The same is true in social work.

Watch vodcast 13.1 on the Companion Website (www.sagepub.co.uk/SocialWork) to see chapter author Mike Shepherd summarise the main points conveyed in this chapter that he co-authored with Kirstin Parkes, and why an understanding of risk is important for social work practice.

Reflective Questions

1   Consider a situation where you have supported another person to take risks. What dilemmas did this situation present for you? What factors enabled you to be supportive? What barriers did you, as well as the person, have to overcome? Was supporting the risk worthwhile? Faced with a similar situation again, would you act in the same way?
2   What personal, professional and organisational challenges do you think exist in the processes of effective risk assessment and risk management?
3   Are there fields of social work practice that you perceive to be more effective in assessing and managing risk? If so, where does this perception come from? Do you see some areas of practice as being more risk-averse than others?

RECOMMENDED READING

Department of Health (2005) *Independence, Well-being and Choice*. London: The Stationery Office.

Kemshall, H. and Pritchard, J. (1996) *Good Practice in Risk Assessment and Risk Management*. London: Jessica Kingsley Publishers.

Kemshall, H. and Wilkinson, B. (2011) *Good Practice in Assessing Risk: Current Knowledge, Issues and Approaches*. London: Jessica Kingsley Publishers.

Parton, N. (2006) *Safeguarding Childhood: Early Intervention and Surveillance in a Late Modern Society*. Basingstoke: Palgrave Macmillan.

INTERPROFESSIONAL 14 PRACTICE

Ruth Taylor and Jillian Brannan

Key Themes

- The drive towards improved interprofessional working is enshrined in much of the legislation and policy underpinning social work practice.
- The development of working relationships with other professionals facilitates a greater level of understanding of roles, which contributes to effective practice.
- Interprofessional working skills are required for the enhancement of practice.
- Understanding the diverse range of contexts within which interprofessional working takes place is a necessary component of professional development.
- Developing an understanding of the professional identity of social work and what distinguishes social work from other professions is intrinsic to working interprofessionally.

INTRODUCTION

In this chapter we will provide an overview of the key issues that contribute to the development and delivery of, and the impact of, interprofessional practice. In some parts the chapter does have a bias towards practice in the arena of health and social care, reflecting the practice backgrounds of the authors – nursing and social work with adults. We fully acknowledge, however, that interprofessional practice spans the whole breadth of social work and view the key points made here as entirely applicable to other practice areas, such as child care and, in Scotland, criminal justice.

We begin by identifying the context of interprofessional practice, primarily taking a UK perspective. However, it is important to note that an interprofessional focus is not unique to the UK (Lewy, 2010), and the agenda for collaborative and interprofessional working globally is growing (Glasby and Dickinson, 2009). The aim is that people should experience seamless services with enhanced care outcomes. Internationally, as in the UK, the debate continues about how best to achieve integrated care.

You will find through reading this chapter that the major political and policy drivers emphasise integration of care as vital for the enhancement of practice. Consideration of the UK policy context enables us to appreciate the approach within the wider contextual framework of social work and its partners in health, education, housing, the voluntary and independent sectors, as well as a range of other organisations and agencies.

You will find that the use of terminology varies within policy, academic papers and practice; yet the crucial aspects are the underlying philosophical principles that guide interprofessional practice (often framed as inter- versus multi-disciplinary practice, see below for definitions). We have to be able to articulate the 'why' of interprofessional practice if we are to feel confident in the world of integrated care, by understanding what it is we want to achieve through interprofessional practice. In addition, we will explore the distinctive role of social work and consider what social work as a profession brings to the interprofessional arena. Finally, a model/framework of interprofessional practice is provided for critical review and consideration for practice.

Definitions/Terminology

Interprofessional

- Emphasises the similarities across professional groups
- Facilitates a single assessment approach and person-centred goal-setting
- Acknowledges areas of shared skills
- Promotes a shared understanding and viewpoint
- Relies on shared training/education, mutual trust and respect
- Ideally on same hierarchical level with good communication and team meetings/working

The CAIPE (Centre for the Advancement of Interprofessional Education) core competencies for interprofessional working are: equity – being able to value all contributions; respect differences; confidentiality; avoid or explain jargon; check understanding; identify mutual goals and where there are differences; discuss the challenges of collaborative working; conflict management.

Multidisciplinary

- Discipline orientated with clear role descriptions
- Reinforces boundaries between professionals who work in parallel
- Generates multiple assessments and professionally orientated goals
- Focuses on **uni-professional** skills
- Perpetuates uni-professional models of training/education
- Differences in hierarchical levels

Collaboration

- Respond seamlessly, flexibly and effectively to service needs (usually interprofessional)

Partnership

- Working together to deliver services (usually multidisciplinary)

Integration

- A spectrum of service delivery from linkages between services to full collaborative approaches to service delivery

(Based on Marriott and Wright, 2002; CAIPE, 2012)

THE CONTEXT OF INTERPROFESSIONAL PRACTICE

The context of interprofessional practice is multifaceted, taking place within policy, organisational, professional, cultural and educational contexts. Each of these wide-ranging areas contributes to a complex picture of an evolving social work and social care context in which interprofessional working is becoming a priority. To work effectively, all of us need to be prepared as educated and proactive change agents to meet the requirements of contemporary interprofessional practice.

THE POLICY CONTEXT

Policy as a Driver

The policy context is the key driver for what McLean (2007) has highlighted as the shift in health and social care to integrated care, rather than care delivered in professional silos. The aim to provide care which feels like one overall care experience (interprofessional), rather than pockets of multiple care interventions (multidisciplinary), means people's experiences of receiving care are changing. The fluid nature of care has a long historical context, with partnership working being a feature of health and social care. Partnership working is now evolving further towards *collaborative* working, hinting at a transformative approach to care. It is these philosophical underpinnings of collaborative interprofessional working, rather than partnership multiprofessional working, which are leading us towards a revitalised perspective of where and how care can take place.

Deriving from the policy drivers, Lewy (2010) succinctly underlines where the interprofessional agenda comes from:

- controversial publicity which clearly demonstrated low collaborative care between health and social care;
- rising healthcare costs;
- patient healthcare needs (complex patient care pathways and community care which involves the patient engaging with a range of healthcare professionals);
- reduce service fragmentation;
- promote quality patient care. (2010: 5)

The focus on integrated care within health and social care policy in the UK can be seen in the following examples:

- *Community Care: A Joint Future* (Scottish Executive, 2000a)
- *Better Health, Better Care* (Scottish Government, 2007a)
- *Living Well with Dementia: A National Dementia Strategy* (Department of Health, 2009)
- *Delivering the Bamford Vision: Action Plan* (Northern Ireland Executive – DHSSPS, 2009)
- *Health, Social Care & Well-being Strategies* (Welsh Assembly Government, 2010)

- *Equity and Excellence: Liberating the NHS* (Department of Health, 2011a)
- *Transforming Your Care: Review of Health and Social Care in Northern Ireland* (Northern Ireland Assembly – DHSSPS, 2011)
- *A Framework for Delivering Integrated Health and Social Care: A Consultation* (Welsh Government, 2013)
- *Making Sure Health and Social Care Services Work Together* (Department of Health, 2013)
- *Public Bodies (Joint Working) (Scotland) Bill 2013* (Scottish Parliament, 2013)

However, we need to consider carefully the 'what' and 'why' of integration. In terms of the 'what', are we talking about the integration of primary and secondary care, as well as the integration of health and social care? Or is it the integration of care pathways for service users? And what implications does integration have for roles, for example, do we need to think about roles that are themselves integrated (a nurse with a social work qualification), and if so what is the knock-on effect on funding? It is notable that practitioners who have a dual qualification, whether achieved separately or through combined award, rarely have an opportunity to practise in both roles simultaneously. In addition, such practitioners may experience tensions around their professional identity and indeed the organisation they work for may provide little clarity.

Exercise

Read a newspaper carefully, identifying articles on the NHS, care of older people, adults or children, criminal justice or social services. Consider where issues reported might have relevance for more than one profession or organisation and critically reflect on how this is portrayed to a wider audience by the newspaper.

The Perceived Benefits of Interprofessional Practice Underpinning the Policy Context

In terms of the 'why' interprofessional, we need to focus on the drivers and benefits. We have already noted above some of the drivers for integrated care (and thereby interprofessional working). In addition, Mitchell et al. (2010: 3) have identified that interprofessional working practices in health and social care 'have been linked to improved planning and policy development, more clinically effective services, and enhanced problem-solving'. With an increasing dependence on collaborative working, the integrated care of service users sits at the heart of policy and practice. To read the full article by Mitchell et al. (2013) see the Companian Website (www.sagepub.co.uk/SocialWork).

One of the significant advantages of interprofessional working is the opportunity for the pooling of skills, knowledge and resources to provide the most effective support to service users (Smith, 2009). The fact that in any given situation everyone involved – professionals, service users and carers – is benefiting from a range of perspectives, should serve to enhance the potential for positive outcomes. Hall (2005, cited in Baxter and Brumfitt, 2008: 240) identifies the value of utilising different knowledge bases, when he states that interprofessional colleagues are 'looking at the same thing and not seeing the same thing'.

Exploring this idea further, it has been suggested that working together potentially has a number of benefits. Some relate to what might be termed organisational efficiencies, for example, more effective use of resources and better use of time. Other benefits relate to professional roles where interprofessional practice can be seen as a way of addressing power differentials between professional groups and breaking down some traditional professional hierarchies (Pollard et al., 2005). A third group of benefits relates to the practice arena and concerns matters such as the ability to provide more responsive services and more holistic interventions (Smith, 2009). Extending this further, it can be argued that working together allows practitioners to think in more creative ways, literally 'two heads (or more) are better than one', and allows greater scope for 'thinking out of the box'.

The ultimate purpose of pursuing collaboration in practice is to benefit service users across the settings in which social work and social care are delivered (Pollard, 2009). If work is service user-centred then every professional involved is striving towards the same goal. This is crucial in avoiding some of the pitfalls that have, at times, beset the caring professions, i.e., individuals falling between the boundaries of different agencies or agencies, possibly unintentionally, 'pulling in different directions' (Thompson, 2009a: 185). The concept of 'non-summativity' (Payne, 2005a: 145), the whole being greater than the sum of its parts, is pertinent here. The theory is that working together should create something that could not be achieved by different partners or professionals working on their own (Improvement Service, 2008). Ultimately this achievement should focus on better outcomes for service users.

Case Study

Jean is 8, underperforming in school and disruptive in class. Her teacher is trying to improve her behaviour. Her sister is 2, physically not meeting developmental milestones and causing some concern to the health visitor. Her mother is divorced and struggling to manage on a day-to-day basis. A social worker is trying to help. Each professional is trying to help, but what might improve if they spoke to each other?

Whether such better outcomes are achieved continues to be a matter of debate. It would be very easy, particularly given the strong focus on interprofessional working, to assume that positive outcomes are inevitable. Yet there is a need for caution here when actually considering the evidence base for interprofessional practice and integrated working arrangements. Frost and Robinson (2007) highlight that the evidence base is 'complex and contradictory' (p. 186) and note that what are perceived as effective outcomes may very much depend on context.

Furthermore, Petch (2011) has identified that much of the evaluation of partnership working to date has focused on process rather than outcomes. By process, Petch is referring to the tendency to consider measures, such as what staff understand the purpose of joint working to be, how much cooperation there was between different partners and what mechanisms were in place for decision-making. This is quite clearly a very different type of evaluation to one that looks at what difference integrated working has actually made to the people receiving the services, i.e., the outcomes for service users. On the Companian Website (www.sagepub.co.uk/SocialWork) you will find a link to an IRISS Insight paper summarising Petch's findings.

A recent literature review by Miller and Cameron (2011), looking at shared inter-agency assessment, is a useful example to consider when thinking about how process can be seen to have taken precedence over outcomes. The authors highlight that shared assessment has a number of benefits including managing risk, reducing duplication, improving standards and improving communication. Yet, if we were to take a more critical stance on these findings, we might question the evidence of the outcomes to which shared inter-agency assessment leads.

It is not our contention here to detract from what we perceive as the central role of interprofessional practice in the current and future delivery of care services. However, a critical approach to consideration of the issues presented is of paramount importance. Being aware that more evidence is needed about the impact on outcomes for service users, enables the developing social work practitioner critically to engage with the processes and structures he/she is part of. Such critical engagement is a positive attribute underpinning a questioning approach to practice and building reflective skills.

THE ORGANISATIONAL, PROFESSIONAL AND CULTURAL CONTEXT

Organisational Structures and Processes

The literature highlights a number of barriers to interprofessional working. Not least of these is our understanding or lack of understanding of our own and other professions (Cooper, 2009). There are clear issues within interprofessional working in relation to hierarchy, tradition, trust, respect and professional identity which can impact on the delivery of unified, integrated care. However, it is often the problems associated with working together that impact negatively on care. The key challenge here is to determine where one profession's work ends and another begins, on the basis that professions work together for the benefit of the service user. As indicated previously, in the current context there is an explicit assumption within practice that interprofessional working does represent the way forward. As Day (2006: 1) notes, 'People are no longer questioning whether interprofessional working is important but have progressed to focusing on how best to make it work.'

The significant point is, there are times when the service that one profession provides could be better linked to the service that another profession provides, thus offering a unified approach to care and making the service user's experience that bit better. It is often the organisational structures and processes that impinge on integrated care (Lewy, 2010) rather than the knowledge, attitudes and skills of the professions who deliver the care, although these aspects of professional identity are absolutely crucial if we are to move forward meaningfully with the policy vision of truly integrated care (Cooper, 2009). Inevitably, however, in the process of trying to make interprofessional practice 'work', there will be a range of issues to consider.

The Professional Challenges of Interprofessional Practice

When working interprofessionally, it is important to be aware that staff with different professional backgrounds may see things in different ways. As noted above, this can be a positive thing; however, being alert to potential areas of difference between professional groups ensures that we do not overlook factors that might have a strong influence on how successful interprofessional working might be. Thompson (2009a) identifies a comprehensive list of areas where there might be differences between professionals. These include: values, perspectives, priorities, expectations, norms, budgets, protocols and experiences.

Being aware of these types of issues can be both extremely informative and influential in working towards successful interprofessional practice. For example, recognising that our colleagues from different professional groups may see a different primary purpose in work with a service user assists us to understand why they act or react in particular ways. Equally, understanding the frustrations that may accompany differing abilities to access funding or having to work within different organisational bureaucracies can help us to empathise with others (Thompson, 2009a). Clearly such understanding needs to be multifaceted and requires two-way commitment.

Other authors, for example Smith (2009), have examined some of the complexities around interprofessional team working. Smith identifies what he calls 'recurrent themes' deemed to represent 'persistent challenges to effective interdisciplinary working' (2009: 136). The list includes factors such as lack of role clarity, the operation of professional hierarchies, different professional discourses, complex accountabilities and uncertainty about decision-making. Furthermore, Day (2006), drawing on the work of D'Amour and Oandasan, identifies three elements that determine how joint working operates. First to be identified are systemic factors. These include the processes of professional socialisation, the use of profession-specific language, the development of professional tribalism and power imbalances. Secondly, organisational factors can act as challenges to interprofessional working. These include factors such as management structures, organisational philosophy, leadership, communication channels and inadequate time for interprofessional working to be developed. The third set of factors relates to the interaction between different professionals and includes a lack of trust, a lack of willingness to work in a joint way, adherence to professional stereotypes and lack of communication.

Meeting the Challenges

Of course, it would be insufficient to flag up the range of challenges interprofessional practice can pose without devoting some attention to how such challenges may be met.

It should be acknowledged that in many cases addressing the challenges is a routine part of practice, drawing on the kinds of interactional skills that underpin all good social work practice. However, it is important to be aware of the fact that the challenges are real and that they will pose more significant issues should they not be addressed.

Thompson (2009a) identifies a number of principles which he sees as underpinning joint working. Following these in practice could go some way to mitigating the challenges posed by the interprofessional arena. The principles include: avoiding stereotypes; understanding each other's role; being sensitive to different values, norms, priorities; avoiding hierarchies; avoiding preciousness; focusing on communication and focusing on the service user (Thompson, 2009a).

Added to this, Barrett and Keeping (2005) drew up a range of strategies which can be used to support effective interprofessional working. Their framework highlights the importance of reflective practice and the use of supervision to help deal with 'maladaptive defence mechanisms' (p. 28). Barrett and Keeping also note the importance of being provided with opportunities to reinforce one's professional identity (see box below).

In a context where many social workers may be singleton professionals in interprofessional teams, such opportunities are likely to contribute to maintaining professional confidence. Sound managerial support and keeping expectations realistic are equally seen as beneficial. Lastly, Barrett and Keeping (2005) note the importance of joint education and training in order to ensure different professionals understand one another's roles. Such education and training begins at pre-qualifying level (see later in this chapter) and is likely to be needed throughout one's career.

Exercise

Sims (2011) points out that the exact 'meaning of "professional identity" is elusive and its definition uncertain' (p. 266). Yet, whilst such debates will shift and evolve over time, there is also a case for recognising the importance of having, or perhaps striving towards, a clear and robust professional identity. This identity, it could be argued, has the potential to be seen as one of the key foundations for successful interprofessional practice, and to practise effectively as a social worker it is necessary to have a firm sense of what it means to be a 'social worker'.

Making a distinction between different levels of professional identity, Wackerhausen (2009: 458) identifies the 'macro-level' and 'micro-level'. He views professional identity at the macro-level as being shaped by a number of different forces, for example, public perceptions, the opinions of other professional groups, the way the profession promotes itself and the relative status the profession holds. Wackerhausen suggests that such macro-level markers of professional identity can shift over time.

Wackerhausen's (2009) second level of professional identity is the micro-level. Here he is attempting to distil what constitutes the 'cultural dimensions' of a professional group, what he later describes as becoming 'one of our kind' (p. 459). This goes beyond the holding of a particular professional qualification and refers more specifically to the actual perspective of a professional group. For

(Continued)

(Continued)

Wackerhausen (2009: 461) this is about 'a way of speaking, a way of questioning, a way of understanding and explaining, a way of seeing and valuing, a way of telling narratives, etc.'. Put another way, the micro-level of professional identity is about the way people are socialised into a particular professional group.

From your experience so far, consider the social work way of speaking, questioning, understanding, explaining, seeing and valuing. What do you think is different about the social work perspective when compared to the perspective of other professional groups?

The Context of Professional Cultures and their Impact on Interprofessional Working

As indicated above, interprofessional, as opposed to multidisciplinary, team working is viewed by many as the most appropriate model on which to base collaborative working (e.g. Korner, 2010). As you will see from the definitions at the beginning of this chapter, the focus within interprofessional working is one of mutuality and collaboration based on good communication, blurring of boundaries and partnership working. Multidisciplinary working on the other hand focuses on each profession's skills within the overall service user experience and can lead to fragmented care when communication strategies do not work well. In essence, interprofessional working is 'co-work' that better enables integration of care to take place (Forbes and McCartney, 2010).

Following on from this, it is therefore essential that each professional working within a service user's care pathway is able to understand and implement the policy drivers within a context of support and development. For some, theories of social capital (i.e., relationships across professional boundaries that impact positively on the resources that are available for care) are useful for conceptualising what it is that professions aim to achieve through integrated care (Forbes and McCartney, 2010). This theoretical perspective is particularly pertinent in contemporary society where policy is so focused on providing a unified approach to care – a shift from working in partnership across boundaries to working *together* within a care context.

Government policy must itself be integrated if professions are to take forward integrated care across the settings in which health and social care take place, and across the range of care needs. The rhetoric from governments emphasising autonomy and empowerment of service users for better engagement with, and control of, the care experience is becoming more transparently created within policy. The practice cultures of individual professions need to embrace these changes in order that they can be fully realised.

THE EDUCATIONAL CONTEXT

Interprofessional education has been defined by CAIPE (2002, cited in CAIPE, 2012) as 'when two or more professions learn with, from and about each other to improve collaboration and the quality of care'. Interprofessional education is, rather obviously, different from uni-professional education where education takes place within the confines of one professional group and the skills, knowledge and attitudes of that particular profession are emphasised. There will, of course, be reference to other professional groups but little experiential learning in relation to the skills for interprofessional working.

In contrast, collaboration between professions and an understanding of each others' contributions to care are the hallmarks of interprofessional education. The aim is often to enable students to view care as an integrated holistic approach, incorporating contributions from across the range of professions (Aberdeen Interprofessional Health and Social Care, 2011). Leading on from this, the key benefits of interprofessional education are seen as perceptual and attitudinal shifts across the professional groups, enhancing collaboration through interpersonal, group and organisational relationships (Barr et al., 2005). Interprofessional education has also been seen as having the potential to break down stereotypes of professional groups. In this respect Hean et al. (2006) produced some interesting findings in their research of new undergraduate students on health and social care courses. The researchers found that such students 'arrive at university with defined stereotypes of other [health and social care] groups' (p. 172). They go on to suggest that interprofessional education should be introduced early on in professional courses to optimise possible gains.

While many readers of this chapter will have experienced 'interprofessional education' (IPE), there remain questions on the efficacy of the varying approaches to IPE. However, there is much agreement that the purpose of IPE is to break down barriers and build the critical skills that enable practitioners from across the health and social care professions to work together with the aim of providing integrated care (Barr et al., 2005). Much of the work that has taken place around interprofessional learning (rather than simply being in the same classroom together being taught the same subject) has related to processes. These processes include: team working skills, interpersonal skills and breaking down boundaries across professions through understanding of other professions. As noted earlier, however, a focus on processes needs to be balanced with a shift of focus to outcomes.

For an example IPE website see the link on the Companion Website (www.sagepub. co.uk/SocialWork) to Aberdeen Interprofessional Health and Social Care Education.

THE IMPACT OF INTERPROFESSIONAL PRACTICE

The impact of interprofessional working is of vital importance in the development of good working practices. If we are to prevent some of the poor practice and poor service user experiences, it is essential that impact is measured and lessons learned through the development of practice. While intuitively it may seem that interprofessional working is the way to improve practice (given the reasons outlined within this chapter), it is not always clear *why* this is the case. However, there are a number of high-profile inquiries that enable us to gain some understanding of what happens when collaboration between professionals breaks down or does not exist in the first place. These inquiries provide us with an exceptional inside view of when things go wrong. It is therefore imperative that we learn from them and move practice on in a way that makes it less likely that these situations occur again. The key is to embed approaches to practice that facilitate collaboration at political, organisational, cultural and practice levels. On the Companion Website (www.sagepub.co.uk/SocialWork) you will find links to three inquiry reports and focus questions to explore the implications for you as a developing practitioner.

THE ROLE OF THE SOCIAL WORKER IN INTERPROFESSIONAL PRACTICE

So far in this chapter we have established why interprofessional working represents both an appropriate and necessary direction of travel for those working in the caring professions, as well as a range of other agencies. Within this interprofessional arena it is important to consider the contribution of social work and, specifically, to examine what role social workers have to play in 'joined up' (Scottish Government, 2010d) practice. This is a complex matter, not least because social work has frequently struggled to carve out and define its 'unique contribution and expertise' (Brand et al., 2005: 57). Within the interprofessional context, being clear about what social work brings becomes very important, yet, as indicated in various parts of this text, defining social work itself is very much a contested issue.

THE DISTINCTIVENESS OF SOCIAL WORK

Thompson (2005) argues that there is a need to consider what aspects of the social work role set it apart from other 'helping professions' (p. 1). In doing so he identifies the following five factors as combining to give social work its distinctiveness:

- the central role of statutory duties;
- the challenge of managing the tensions between care and control;
- the dilemmas of being 'caught in the middle';
- the need to do society's 'dirty work'; and
- the primacy of a commitment to social justice. (Thompson, 2005: 9)

Other authors reinforce some of these concepts. For example, Beckett and Maynard (2005) point out that 'social work exists only as a result of public policy or public concern' (Beckett and Maynard, 2005: 72) and that this sets it apart from some other professions. Extending this notion, it is easy to see why Harris (2008) views social work as something that is shaped by changing welfare regimes. Along different lines, Brand et al. (2005: 57), citing Williams, point to some of the difficulties social work has faced due to being seen as 'a Jill of all trades but mistress of none'.

Thinking about the distinctiveness of social work involves thinking beyond the way roles and tasks might be defined. It may be relatively easy to list what social workers do, in terms of the type of work undertaken, but of a more tricky nature are the key characteristics of the social work approach. Kerr et al. (2005, para 5.19), drawing on the work of Statham et al., identify that 'the social worker may be "the professional of choice" … where no one knows what the right answer is … where relationships are complex … [and] where there is a high degree of risk …'.

Exploring this further Brand et al. (2005: 57) define the key characteristics of social work as:

- the focus on the whole of the person's life, their social context and environment
- the capacity, in circumstances that are often difficult:
  - to engage quickly with people to establish trust,
  - to persist in efforts to engage even when this has proved difficult and others have given up
- consciously to move into situations that would be avoided by most people because they are complex and high risk
- the relationship established between the social worker and the service users involved is integral to achieving quality
- the capacity to manage situations where risks are very finely balanced so that 'you are damned if you do and damned if you don't'.

At times it is very likely that working within this kind of framework leads social workers to focus on aspects of practice that for other professional groups would be seen as 'relatively peripheral' (Smith, 2009: 143). This can pose issues within interprofessional working if there is a lack of understanding between different professionals about what each is trying to do.

This also poses a question as to whether social workers can claim to hold distinct attributes that identify their specific contribution to interprofessional working. Like many questions in social work, this is a somewhat grey area. Parton (2000: 449) suggests that social work's 'central and unique characteristic is the way theory and practice are closely interrelated'. He goes on to describe social work as art that is able to work within and deal constructively with an environment of uncertainty and ambiguity.

Case Study

You work in a setting where you have frequent cause to contact doctors, teachers, the police and other professionals. In considering the art of social work, how much more effective might your communication be if you spoke with them face to face rather than by phone, letter or email? Time is always a constraint, but to what extent might the benefits outweigh the difficulties?

Other academics have suggested that there is a need for social work to think about how it combines particular qualities, rather than necessarily searching for areas of exclusivity. To this end the following types of factors have been identified as key to the social work mix: a commitment to a strong value base; anti-discriminatory and anti-oppressive practice; the focus on relationships as being central; the ability to balance the needs of the individual with those of wider society; a strong focus on social justice and skills in negotiation and coordination. As factors that are key to the social work 'mix', these areas of knowledge, skills and values have commonality with some other health and social care professionals. Yet within this framework social work strives to carve out a distinctive role.

Within the interprofessional team setting there is a continuing balance between awareness of distinctiveness and contribution to the integrated process. An interesting stance on this balance is provided by Frost and Stein (2009), who question whether integrated working should be a 'soup' (all mixed in together with little scope for maintenance of professional identities) or a 'fruit salad' (with discernible identities combined together). The extent to which a social work practitioner views their role and identity as soup or fruit salad will inevitably depend on a number of factors; but this is a useful analogy which provides, perhaps quite literally, food for thought.

There is no doubt that in some arenas social work is seen as '*the* joined-up profession' (Frost et al., 2005: 195), or perhaps the glue that can bind others together – including service users, carers and other professionals. Consequently, social work should be seen as having a pivotal role in interprofessional practice. Whilst its 'territory' may border, overlap and combine that of other professionals, social work brings a unique social perspective that enables understanding of the individual within the context of the families, social groups and communities of which they are part (Taylor and Vatcher, 2005). As such, social work promotes well-being and maximises the capacity of people to function in their day-to-day lives, but does so in a way that extends beyond the bounds of the individual and includes a focus on how the individual interacts with and is affected by the environment within which they live.

Having thought about some of these issues now go to the Companion Website (www.sagepub.co.uk/SocialWork) and read the article by Beddoe (2013) on social workers in healthcare settings.

A MODEL OF INTERPROFESSIONAL PRACTICE

Hammick et al. (2009) view *being interprofessional* as a whole set of skills, knowledge and attributes (knowing what to do, having the skills to do it, and knowing how to conduct oneself). These, and the other, key concepts that have been visited in this chapter provide a framework (or model) of interprofessional practice for an integrated care experience (see Figure 14.1). The model may be useful to you as a reminder of the key issues, and you should investigate the literature further to identify models or frameworks that have been utilised elsewhere, thus allowing you to compare and contrast what you know now with others' viewpoints (Reeves et al. (2010) provides a convenient conceptual framework for comparison and scrutiny).

Critical Thinking

Do you agree that working interprofessionally is the best way forward? What would be the impact on service users if organisations did not pursue this direction?

CONCLUSION

You have now considered the differences between interprofessional, collaborative working, and multidisciplinary, partnership working. It is not the terminology that is

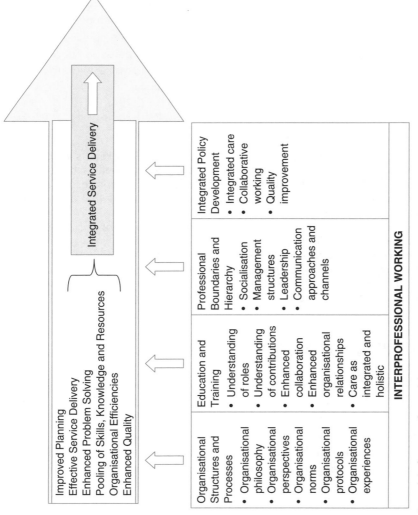

Figure 14.1 A model of interprofessional practice

most important. Rather, it is the philosophical underpinnings that guide your practice that can make the difference between an integrated or fragmented care experience for a service user. Understanding that there are challenges associated with interprofessional working enables you as the practitioner to put measures in place to ensure that the knowledge, skills and values for person-centred practice are enacted within your own and others' practice. Your developing understanding of the nature of social work, the role of the social work practitioner within an interprofessional context and the distinctive contribution of social work, are all significant markers in becoming a more effective interprofessional worker. Interprofessional practice represents a central core of the future practice arena. Developing the necessary skills, knowledge and values to work within this arena are essential components of professional development.

Watch vodcast 14.1 on the Companion Website (www.sagepub.co.uk/SocialWork) to see chapter author Jillian Brannan summarise the main points conveyed in this chapter that she co-authored with Ruth Taylor, and why possessing a knowledge of interprofessional practice is important for social work practice.

Reflective Questions

1   The chapter has established that interprofessional working is very much seen as the way forward; yet it comes with challenges as well as benefits and the evidence base is equivocal. Has your experience of interprofessional education (IPE) provided you with any insights/aspects of learning that are not currently reflected in the literature?

2   Consider how you explain the values, roles and tasks of social work to other professionals. Is it difficult or relatively easy?

3   Following a period of practice learning where you had experience of interprofessional working, consider what enhances effective interprofessional working? What inhibits effective interprofessional working? How can your interprofessional practice skills develop so that you become an effective interprofessional practitioner?

RECOMMENDED READING

Crawford, K. (2011) *Interprofessional Collaboration in Social Work Practice*. London: Sage.

Korner, M. (2010) 'Interprofessional teamwork in medical rehabilitation: a comparison of multidisciplinary and interdisciplinary team approach', *Clinical Rehabilitation*, 24: 745–55.

Miller, E. and Cameron, K. (2011) 'Challenges and benefits in implementing shared inter-agency assessment across the UK: a literature review', *Journal of Interprofessional Care*, 25 (1): 39–45.

Mitchell, R.J., Parker, V. and Giles, M. (2010) 'When do interprofessional teams succeed? Investigating the moderating roles of team and professional identity in interprofessional effectiveness', *Human Relations*, 64 (16): 1321–43.

Quinney, A. and Hafford-Letchfield, T. (2012) *Interprofessional Social Work: Effective Collaborative Approaches*, 2nd edn. London: Sage/Learning Matters.

THE VOICE OF
15 SERVICE USERS
AND CARERS

Jillian Brannan, Denise Cromar,
Simon Gardner, Margaret Junner,
Steve Morrison and William Rae

Key Themes

- Service users and carers are key stakeholders and centrally involved in all aspects of social work activity.
- The terms 'service user' and 'carer' are potentially problematic, with different interpretations and perspectives being offered.
- Effective service user and carer involvement is beset with obstacles; but is achievable where there is genuine commitment.
- Service users and carers have delivered consistent messages about their expectations of social workers.
- The personal narratives of service users and carers are core elements of social work knowledge. The messages contained within such narratives offer vital areas for practitioners' learning and development.

INTRODUCTION

Contemporary social work policy, practice and education identify service users and carers as key stakeholders. Their involvement in strategic planning, operational delivery and shaping the future direction of the workforce is considered central, particularly within the context of the 'consumer-driven' cultures (Ward and Rhodes, 2010: 596) that have been a driving force for change in social work, health and a range of other services.

The importance of service user and carer involvement highlights the recognition of lived experience as an essential arena for gathering information which can, or should, facilitate change (Thomas et al., 2010). The fact that in both statute and regulation there is a requirement to include service users and carers should serve to strengthen an understanding of why this is important. Yet any form of involvement has to be approached in a way that lacks tokenism and signifies a real intention to hear, learn and act rather than to listen but dismiss and simply tick boxes.

The chapter is divided into two main sections. The first will present a discussion of issues concerned with service user and carer involvement. The second section presents the personal narratives of three service users and a carer. The different sections of the chapter serve to present different 'knowledges' (Beresford, 2000: 489), and in doing so it is anticipated that a balance will be struck between providing a theoretical knowledge context and a knowledge 'based on *direct* experience … from [those at] the *receiving end*' (Beresford, 2000: 493; emphasis in original).

SERVICE USER AND CARER INVOLVEMENT

What is Meant by 'Service User'?

At a simplistic level a service user could be defined as someone who uses services. Significant debate exists, however, about the terms used to describe those in receipt of, potentially in receipt of, or previously in receipt of social work services. This debate would include those who might receive such services on a voluntary or involuntary basis and who are from a wide range of different groups (Warren, 2007). Whilst some authors describe the term service user as potentially the 'most neutral definition' (Simpson et al., 2009), others would continue to see the term as 'problematic' (Beresford, 2000: 489). The term service user has been used within this chapter primarily as a result of the absence of an acceptable alternative – this of itself is a worthy point of debate.

Exercise

Think about situations where you might describe yourself as a 'service user' and where you might be a 'client'. How might your expectations of a service differ?

McLaughlin (2009) charts the shifting language used 'to describe the relationship between those who assess and commission services and those who are in receipt of those services' (p. 1101). Terminology in social work has changed significantly over time and is identified by McLaughlin as including: 'client', 'customer', 'consumer', 'service user' and 'expert by experience' (2009: 1101). However, not all of these terms have been recognised and accepted by those in receipt of services and in some cases certain terms are more acceptable in some contexts than in others (Heffernan, 2008).

On one level it could be argued that these changes in terminology are merely reflections of attempts to respond to notions of professionalism, changes of political ideology and recognition of where expertise lies. Yet, on the other hand, the shifting terminology has far more fundamental implications. Most notably, the way the relationship between social worker and person in receipt of services is construed says much about the formulation of identities and the operation of power.

It is probably inevitable that social work will continue to debate the assignment of labels and the changing nature of those labels. The issues of imposed identities and power will be perpetual tensions to grapple with in a profession committed to anti-oppressive and anti-discriminatory practice (Beresford and Croft, 2004). On an individual basis, labels such as service user can become unhelpful perhaps even oppressive. Where this occurs to the exclusion of other aspects of self, then the anti-oppressive social worker should, for obvious reasons, see this as something to question:

> 'It's just rude [to use the term service user] … Just refer to me by my name …' (Heffernan, 2008: 380)

What is Meant by 'Carer'?

The term 'carer' has also been contested (Molyneaux et al., 2011), and, to contextualise the issues, it is helpful to consider a definition:

> A carer is someone of any age who provides unpaid support to family or friends who could not manage without this help. This could be caring for a relative, partner or friend who is ill, frail, disabled or has mental health or substance misuse problems …

> Young carers are children and young people who look after someone in their family who has an illness, a disability, or is affected by mental ill-health or substance misuse … (Carers Trust, 2012)

A key concept above is that carers are described as 'unpaid', creating a very important, but sometimes overlooked, distinction between this group of people and the paid professionals who provide care (Molyneaux et al., 2011). The use of the term 'unpaid' is less ambiguous than the more dated term, 'informal carers' (Twigg, 1989: 53). As Warren (2007) notes, the description 'informal' (p. 8) was not felt to be a helpful one, because it seemed to signify care that is less substantial, an image that would be far from reality. Whilst care by family or friends sits within the informal sector (Adams, 2002), it should be recognised that 'informal sector' does not have the same connotations as 'informal carer'.

Whilst this shift in terminology has been welcomed, there has in fact been a growing debate about the relevance of the term 'carer' itself. This debate centres on the following notions:

- Describing someone as a carer does not reflect the complex nature of the relationship between the people involved; this relates in part to the often interdependent nature of caring relationships and the meaning of social roles.
- The term carer may impact on formations of personal identity, i.e., is someone a carer to the exclusion of other aspects of who they are?

- Potentially the term fails to recognise the differing needs of diverse groups/individuals who might acquire the label 'carer' (see Henderson and Forbat, 2004; Molyneaux et al., 2011; Pilgrim, 2009).

Whilst some authors would argue that caring is one aspect of the 'social construction of femininity' (Orme, 2001: 94), and indeed others would highlight that the majority of carers are women, it is important to recognise the role of men as carers (Bowl, 2001). Complexity also exists in discussions of care and caring in minority ethnic communities and in discussions of the needs of different carers. Indeed, research, policy and practice focusing on the needs of young carers has been a comparatively recent but significantly welcome focus (Becker et al., 2000).

What is Meant by Service User and Carer Involvement?

The term 'involvement' has been chosen to represent how users and carers contribute to strategic planning, operational developments, individual work and educative inputs, but other terms are used to describe this concept, for example 'user engagement ... stakeholder consultation, participation and so on' (Gallagher and Smith, 2010). Beresford (2007), writing specifically about service users, describes the central purpose of such involvement as being to increase 'the say and control that service users can have over their lives and services they use or which impact upon them' (p. 26).

For the findings of research looking at how users of services get their voices heard, see the article by Simmons and Birchall (2012) on the Companion Website (www.sagepub. co.uk/SocialWork).

Arnstein (1969) and Hickey and Kipping (1998) refer to the concept of 'ladders', whereby the level of involvement can be measured against the ability to influence decisions (Higham and Torkington, 2009; Kendrick, 2011; Simpson et al., 2009). A similar concept is described in Barr et al.'s [1997] ladder of empowerment (cited in Sharkey, 2007), and indeed there are important links to be drawn between thinking about empowerment and the concept of involvement. See Figure 15.1 for a comparison of different conceptual frameworks. The concept of ladders can be criticised, but such frameworks provide a basis for thinking about what involvement actually means.

To further develop your understanding of the focus on service user and carer involvement, see the additional information and related activity on the Companion Website (www.sagepup.co.uk/SocialWork).

How Can the Effective Involvement of Service Users and Carers be Achieved?

Understanding what constitutes effective involvement is complex. Measures of effectiveness are contingent on a range of factors, including ideology, stakeholder perspective and measurement, and effective involvement of service users and carers may be seen as a desired, but elusive ambition. There are barriers to involvement including: organisational and resource constraints (Kendrick, 2011); a lack of capacity within

Simpson et al. (2009) drawing on the work of Hickey and Kipping (1998) amongst others	The 5-rung ladder	Description of influence over decision-making	Kendrick (2011) drawing on the work of Arnstein (1969)	The 8-rung ladder
Top of ladder	1) User-control or independent community initiatives	Control	Category of citizen power	Citizen control
	2) Power of veto	Authority		Delegated power
	3) Negotiation/ Participation/ Partnership	Shared	-----------------	Partnership -----------------
		Appeasement	Category of tokenism	Placation
	4) Consultation	Taking into account		Consultation
Bottom of ladder	5) Information	Predetermined		Informing
		-----------------	-----------------	
		Doing to	Category of non-participation	Therapy
		Deceit		Manipulation

Figure 15.1 Different conceptualisations of the participation ladder

services to do the necessary work (Thomas et al., 2010); limited access for marginalised groups and hard-to-reach sectors of the population (Carr, 2004); debates about whether partnership can be realised in a context where the distribution of power between social workers and service users or carers lacks equality (Beresford, 2010); devaluing of service user knowledge, professional cultures and tokenistic attitudes (Joseph Rowntree Foundation, 2006). Whilst it would be foolish to minimise the significance of these forms of barriers, they should not be seen as insurmountable.

These barriers serve to highlight key issues to address for providers, academics and practitioners who are striving to achieve '"authenticity", genuinely embedding the service user [and carer] viewpoint' (Ward and Rhodes, 2010: 598 referring to Downe et al. [2007]). The foundation stone of authenticity is commitment, an attribute essential to change and development.

Some interesting research findings on service user participation in interprofessional practice have been provided by Kvarnström et al. (2013). Visit the Companion Website (www.sagepub.co.uk/SocialWork) to access the article.

What do Service Users and Carers Want Social Work Practitioners to be like?

This part of the chapter will briefly highlight some key points. Some of the discussion of this issue lies in the literature on social work education where, as Branfield (2009) identifies, service users perceive themselves providing an opportunity to influence change. Other information about expectations has arisen from the review and reform of social work across the UK (Scottish Executive, 2006a; Beresford, 2007). It is highly likely that there is an abundance of anecdotal feedback reinforcing similar messages.

These are some of the key messages service users and carers have highlighted at a national level:

> They [service users and carers] value social work practitioners who:
>
> - Support them to work out their own agendas with them
> - Give them time to sort things out
> - Are available and accessible
> - Provide continuity of support
> - Are reliable and deliver
> - Are responsive
> - Have a good level of knowledge and expertise
> - Value the expertise of the service user [and carer]
>
> (Beresford, 2007: 6)

> We want to have trusting relationships with workers whom we can be confident have our interest at heart and can help us find our way through the 'system'. Social services workers should communicate well and know how to build and maintain a long term relationship. (Users and Carers Panel, cited in Scottish Executive, 2006a: 36)

PERSONAL NARRATIVES

In this second section of the chapter, four people present their own stories, highlighting key issues and offering distinctive perspectives. The section concludes with a discussion of independent advocacy and the importance of that service in ensuring 'voices' are heard.

Exercise

When reading through these personal narratives make notes on the key issues that emerge. Take time to consider how these issues relate to both the discussion in the first section of this chapter and areas of knowledge discussed elsewhere in this text.

Living my Own Life: a Work in Progress – Denise Cromar

I grew up thinking I can try to do whatever I want to do. My parents were of a generation that didn't believe in hiding their child away and I've always been taught to put myself out there. My mum was very much the backbone to my determination. That wasn't to say I could do anything – there would, of course, be things, like being able to walk, that I could never do; however, for much of my life I've been a free spirit set on achieving my potential.

Graduating from university in 2006 was a great sense of achievement; but something that has been difficult to develop further. Following a period of major illness my life changed significantly and the combination of physical illness and disability has taken its toll. I always said that I was never going to let my disability get medicalised, but in the last two years it has done nothing but that. I feel like I have gone from being 18 to 80 and that in a short period of time I have lost something of myself. My life has become about the care I need – I am a commodity that needs looking after – and it is hard to feel like the person I was.

Currently I have a package of personal care which is organised by the local authority. It is really difficult to have carers and professionals in your life. I speak about them as being the people I don't really have room for; but I know I need them. There is a constant tension between being reliant on other people, because of the needs I have, and wanting more control and independence. I can often feel vulnerable and powerless, especially when I am unhappy with something. It is not easy to complain, particularly when I am made to feel like I am just supposed to accept things and that professionals have an assumption that I should be grateful for what is provided.

There are also difficulties related to having to rely on people who do not appear to be interested in you. Professionals who come into your home to provide a service, but who don't get to know you first. Often I don't know who is coming through my door and that is stressful. I don't think enough consideration is given to my mental health needs because the focus tends to be on what I need in terms of physical support. Seemingly small things like not wanting to have meetings at my house are probably not understood enough. I prefer to hold meetings in offices because, especially if they are stressful, I can leave some of that baggage behind before I return home.

Despite the recent difficulties there are some parts of my life that are going well. I have been able to use a direct payment for my day service and I use this to support me to volunteer at a local member-led organisation (GO – Grampian Opportunities). This is important for me because it has provided much more challenging and interesting opportunities than would have been available at traditional day centres. Working at GO has given me much more freedom to be involved in things and to contribute. Being a giver as well as a receiver is vital for me because there is not much exchange within the care system. I need to be around people who see me as Denise, as someone who has something to give and not just as a 'disabled person'. Getting back this sense of being valued has been an important part of building my self-esteem and sense of self-worth.

In addition, through my time at GO I now know more about how direct payments work and what I can achieve through them. This has helped me to think about how I can use direct payments to have more control over other areas of my life. At the moment I am looking into direct payments for my care package so that I can employ personal assistants. I think this will provide a number of benefits, including: the ability to have more flexibility in how my care is organised and provided; better communication with my carers because there will be more of a direct relationship; employing people who want to care for me and who will take time to get to know me, and importantly for me, having a better relationship with my carers. I think these benefits will also help me to have more enjoyment out of my life and ultimately to be much happier. This is a current journey for me and one that is not complete; but I have aspirations for what can be achieved and with the right support I'll get there.

Learning to Speak Up for Myself – Simon Gardner

The 1980s were a real time of change for people with learning difficulties in Britain. I think it was because a lot of the institutions were closing down and there were a lot more disabled people going into mainstream education. It was also because people were starting to realise they needed a voice of their own and that it was important to speak up for themselves more.

In 1984 a group of people with learning difficulties from Britain attended a conference in America. The conference was organised by the Washington People First group and after that groups in Britain were set up. It began in London in October 1984, and although I hadn't been able to go to the conference in America, I was one of the people involved in the London group. My friend Gary Bourlet was the President of the group. The aims of People First were to help people to speak up for themselves and to help one another, and to help people to speak out for their rights.

I wanted to get involved with People First because I was a survivor of special school and when I was growing up doctors said that I might need to be institutionalised. But my mum would never let her son be in an institution so she always pushed for me to be as independent as I could. I also had other things that helped me. I went to a place called City Lit in London [an education centre] and did a class there on self advocacy. It was called 'Speaking Up for Yourself' and was run by John Hersov. Doing that class and others was a turning point in my life.

When I first went to City Lit I would sit looking at the floor and I wouldn't be able to have eye contact with people. I had to learn to have the confidence to look someone straight in the eye. Learning was important. If I could sell bottles of self-confidence I'd be a millionaire; but there is no chemical called self-confidence. It has to come from within and someone has to help to bring it out of you. John helped me do that – all the people in that class they learned a lot from one another.

In campaigning for people's rights I class myself as a pioneer, because that is what we were. But we are still fighting for equal rights today. We have got a bit more rights than we did in the 1980s but we go forward and then we go three back and then we have to do more demonstrations – it's all so critical. I have been involved in lots of campaigns for things like transport, jobs and education. It is often about government cuts and how they destroy people's lives.

I also think I need to educate the educated that people with learning difficulties are disabled by society – it is society that treats us differently and puts us down by making things inaccessible. We need to make people listen; especially governments who make decisions without consulting us. It is also important that professionals learn to be able to communicate with disabled people, regardless of their ability. Professionals need to focus on people's ability rather than non-ability.

I also want to help people who are the same age now as when I started (19), to have some more ideas of the history of campaigning so they can continue the fight; otherwise it will die. You need to have the ongoing campaign and awareness so that these people who will take over when I'm no longer here will have the balls to do it – I need to show people the ropes. If I can help people to have more confidence, to speak up and if I can guide them then I will. People who have been oppressed are too scared to say they don't agree.

I believe that groups of people speaking as one can achieve something. A single person will not be listened to and their voice won't be heard. We can gather strength by speaking as one. Speaking up can be scary especially if you haven't been asked before. People with learning difficulties communicate in many different ways – communication boards, Makaton, music, drama etc. Sometimes it might take a long time to get information from people but you have to make sure you hear from everyone. Professionals have to do that as well.

Journey to the Unknown – Margaret Junner

> I did not know what was ahead for me as a carer. All I knew was that I wanted to care for my loved ones.

I have been a carer for approximately twenty-three years. I have looked after my brother for most of this time and for the last ten years my elderly father as well. My brother was diagnosed with a mental illness, he also has type 1 diabetes; my father has Parkinson's with mobility and various medical problems.

It has not been easy being a carer. It has affected me physically, mentally, emotionally and financially. Taking on a dual carer role increased these effects, but it felt important to me to care for my family. I was made redundant from work ten years ago and this coincided with my dad's ill-health. I decided to become his full-time carer. My social life and relationships changed when I started looking after dad. I found I could not plan much as something always cropped up and I had to cancel – not everyone was understanding. The family dynamics also changed; I was no longer a sister and daughter, I became a nurse, financial adviser, physiotherapist, occupational therapist, housekeeper, gardener – the list is endless.

Over the years I have had contact with health and social services I have acquired knowledge of the illnesses that my brother and father suffer from, the medication and the side-effects. I felt as though I was in a maze with the legislation, systems and criteria that existed. I had to ask for information as it was not forthcoming and I had to seek out support. The Carers Centre and hospitals were helpful. I found the word 'confidentiality' was used to such an extent that it was difficult to communicate with some of the professionals I came in contact with; yet I was looking after my dad and brother 24/7.

With my brother, I came into contact with his GP, psychiatrist, CPN, ward, social worker, and his diabetic team. I tried very hard to motivate my brother and help him to be as independent as possible; however he did not always want that. Sometimes there were tensions that were stressful for all of us and on several occasions things reached a crisis point. I learned to back off, but if things were not going well or not going the way he wanted them to go I was the one he blamed – he would argue with me or lose his temper with me. My brother's behaviour was becoming more and more difficult to handle and we landed at crisis point about four years ago. I was near breaking point when a decision was made that my brother would not return home. The doctors and social work department took the decision out of my hands and a place was found in supported residential accommodation. My caring role has changed slightly but still continues. There are issues around the change which I am working on.

As for my father, his health became an issue ten years ago. As noted above, his mobility is a problem, he was diagnosed as having Parkinson's disease and he has other medical problems. I have had contact with his GP, the response team, hospital doctors, day hospital, physiotherapists, occupational therapists to name a few. I have at times struggled to get what I needed for dad and I also have had to question medication and medical treatment. My father has given me power of attorney for both welfare and financial decisions in case he is unable to make decisions in the future.

As a carer I take a holistic approach to my dad and brother but the health services, social work services and other organisations are not always so willing to communicate, share information and work with me in partnership. I know my dad and brother better than anyone else, so want professionals to speak to me. I don't want promises that cannot be kept and I want feedback to any query I raise. I want to deal with people who are knowledgeable, good communicators and can advocate for my family.

My journey as a carer is not over – I am not sure what the future holds.

My Experiences of Good and Bad Social Workers – William Rae

My name is William Rae. I have been a member of the group 'The Voice of Reason' for the last seven years. This is a group of young people with care experiences who are involved in the teaching of social work students at Robert Gordon University, Aberdeen. In this section of the chapter I am going to talk about what qualities I like and do not like in social workers.

I have had social workers for the last thirteen years as I have additional support needs; but that is for a different book of my own!

The good qualities I look for in a social worker are that they must be caring and they must be friendly too. They should also be on time when making appointments as one of the social workers I had was never on time.

Social workers need to have good time management as they can have a lot of cases. In the past I have had a social worker who was always going from one meeting to the next and I only saw them for thirty minutes. When I asked about this I was told that they were always busy.

Another quality social workers must have is to be compassionate, as the person you work with may need to talk to you sometimes and may get upset. A quality you must also have is a sense of humour as the person you are working with may find something funny but you don't.

Another skill that you need to have is to be understanding with me on things. One skill you need to have is to keep things private.

I have just written about the good qualities, now here are some of the bad ones that I do not want to see in social work. I have seen all of these examples myself.

So, if you have bad time management and keep letting things get on top of you that is one bad quality I don't want to see. I have had one social worker who had bad time management and I hardly ever saw them.

Another bad quality I do not like to see is not listening to what the people you are supporting are saying. I have also had a social worker who has not listened, which has landed me with a lot of problems which I did not need to have.

A bad quality I don't like to see is people bringing their problems from home into work and who cannot work as a team. Social workers have to work as a team and work with other people. I have had a social worker who had the care team all working in different directions.

Another bad quality is being rude as young people do not like that and in the past social workers have been rude to me. Another bad quality you must not have is pressurising people into doing things they do not want to do and I have had experience of this.

I hope you have enjoyed reading this. I hope you will find this useful when you become a social worker and look back and see more good points in how you work than bad points.

Ensuring the 'Personal' in Personal Narratives: the Role of Independent Advocacy – Steve Morrison, Advocacy Worker

Independent advocacy exists to help people to share their views, perceptions or wishes with professionals, including social workers. An advocate helps people to express themselves more effectively and helps them to make enquiries, obtain information and understand the choices open to them. An advocate enables people to participate more actively in decisions that affect them.

There are different types of advocacy to suit different needs. Advocates will work with individuals and groups taking into account a person's ability to communicate their views and their own life circumstances. An advocate can be a paid professional, a volunteer or a member of the service user/carer's peer group. An advocate works with a person over a period of time so that they get to know the person's thoughts about their circumstances and how he/she would like things to change.

An advocate listens to the person's opinions and supports them to have a voice when decisions are made. Advocates have no opinion themselves; their role is to help people to understand what *they can do*, rather than *what to do*. Advocates help explore and explain the options someone has. Advocates do not speak instead of service users and carers but on their behalf if they are not able to. An advocate is independent of other professionals and listens to and takes the side of service users and carers. Advocates work towards overcoming any obstacles a service user or carer has and enabling him/her to have control over decisions affecting them.

The role of an independent advocate is directed by the service user or carer. Advocates help people to be in control and to be involved with decision-making. Advocates are accountable to the service user or carer and the law. An advocate is not controlled or directed by the professionals and service providers involved in a person's life. Advocates look out for and minimise any conflicts of interest between people involved in making decisions.

Independent advocacy reaches out to the widest range of people it can, regardless of their ability or life circumstances. Advocates work with a person and share information only with their permission. Advocates can write letters on a person's behalf and attend meetings to ensure he/she can contribute to decisions; understanding what these decisions are and how they have been reached. Advocates try to empower people to make informed decisions.

Advocates have a central role in supporting service users and carers who require help in their contacts with professionals; however, there are clear boundaries around the role of an advocate and what that person can and cannot do. For example, an advocate does not give advice or counselling and is not able to solve all of someone's problems. While the advocate is there to represent a person's views, there may be times when the advocate has to explain that he/she cannot achieve everything the person wants. This is important to be clear about because it would be wrong and unfair to raise someone's expectations unrealistically about what can be done.

Professionals need to be aware of the significant role advocacy services can provide, whilst remembering that such services are structurally, financially and psychologically independent from other services. In this sense professionals, like social workers, should consider the need for independent advocacy when working with service users and carers and encourage or directly instigate referrals being made. It is in everyone's interests that service users and carers receive appropriate support at all times; independent advocacy has a significant role in many cases to contribute towards this.

Critical Thinking

What did you learn from reading the service user and carer narratives in the chapter? Was there anything that particularly surprised you? Was there anything that you read which you hadn't been expecting? What difference have these narratives made to how you see yourself as a social work practitioner?

CONCLUSION

For a social work practitioner, reading the personal narratives in the second section of this chapter will be a privileged experience. These accounts offer unique and valuable insights that contribute significantly to the development of the social work knowledge base. These accounts say a great deal about aspirations, resilience, relationships, communication,

THE VOICE OF SERVICE USERS AND CARERS

control, oppression, rights and expectations; which cannot be learnt thoroughly from abstract conceptualisations. If practitioners are striving to hear, learn and act then these accounts should provide important messages about the attitudes, behaviours and skills which underpin good practice. When we listen properly to service users and carers we learn a great deal about experience. In turn we can use this knowledge to work with the individual concerned but also to inform our practice more broadly. Without the voice of service users and carers at the very core of what social work practice is then that practice will be considerably poorer. Service users and carers expect, and have a right to expect, best practice – social work practitioners have a duty to provide that.

Watch vodcast 15.1 on the Companion Website (www.sagepub.co.uk/SocialWork) to see chapter author Simon Gardner discuss his experiences of using social work services and his experiences of representing service users.

Reflective Questions

1 Consider some of the terms at the beginning of the chapter identified by McLaughlin (2009). What kind of identity do you think each term develops for the person receiving services? How would you categorise each term with regards to the level of power it confers on the person receiving services?

2 Reflect on work or practice placement situations you have been involved in. Where would you place service user and carer involvement in those situations on the participation ladder? What could you have done to move involvement up to a higher rung of the ladder?

3 Do you think social workers take enough time to understand the narratives of their service users and carers? Are there barriers which get in the way of doing this? If you think so, do you think these barriers are organisational, professional or personal?

RECOMMENDED READING

Barnes, M. and Cotterell, P. (eds) (2012) *Critical Perspectives on User Involvement*. Bristol: The Policy Press.

Biskin, S., Barcroft, V., Livingston, W. and Snape, S. (2012) 'Reflections on student, service user and carer involvement in social work research', *Social Work Education: The International Journal*, DOI:10.1080/02615479.2012.656267.

Brown, K. and Young, N. (2008) 'Building capacity for service user and carer involvement in social work education', *Social Work Education: The International Journal*, 27 (1): 84–96.

McPhail, M. (2007) *Service User and Carer Involvement: Beyond Good Intentions*. Edinburgh: Dunedin.

Warren, J. (2007) *Service User and Carer Participation in Social Work*. Exeter: Learning Matters.

Refer to the Companion Website (www.sagepub.co.uk/SocialWork) for some useful links to web-based material.

PART THREE
MODELS OF INTERVENTION

16 RELATIONSHIP-BASED SOCIAL WORK

Tuck-Chee Phung

Key Themes

- Forming a relationship is basic to social work practice.
- Reflection and adaptation are required to work with complex needs and issues.
- Political and organisation change has affected the formation of relationships.
- Power is a key issue.
- Self-awareness is of central importance.

INTRODUCTION: RELATIONSHIP-BASED SOCIAL WORK PRACTICE AND ITS CHALLENGES IN THE TWENTY-FIRST CENTURY

How social workers develop a relationship with their service users is at the core of effective social work practice and in this section of the book we discuss the how, the 'nuts-and-bolts' of various intervention approaches (see Figure 16.1 below), and the thinking and theory that underpins and justifies the various approaches. There is no simple formula when working with service users, where if a service user presents with problem *X* we should adopt approach *Y*. One compelling reason why we should reject such a formulaic approach to social work is that the issues and problems that social workers encounter are not formulaic; service users do not necessarily present with a narrow range of easily solved issues. Their needs and issues can be complex, often chaotic and changing in character. An adaptable case-by-case approach, where a distinct approach is carefully chosen and applied but may change as circumstances change, is therefore not just useful but *essential*. The process of thinking through and reflecting on which intervention approach to adopt strengthens practice as it clarifies *why* the technique is

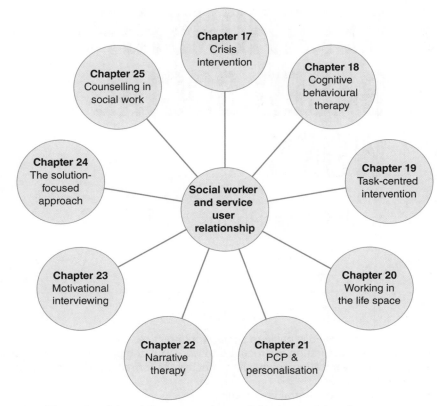

Figure 16.1   The various intervention approaches available to a social worker

being used and how it will best serve the needs of the service user. It also draws from assessment (Chapters 11–13) and may need to change as assessments change.

This chapter outlines the recent history of relationship-based social work and some of the political issues surrounding the development of a good relationship with a service user, but the main focus falls on the social worker's responsibilities and the skills, self-reflection and self-understanding which a social worker should possess. Social workers can meet the needs of service users by forming supportive relationships built on empathy, congruence and an unconditional positive regard for the service users with whom they are working.

A Recent History of Relationship-based Social Work

It may initially appear obvious that a good relationship between service user and social worker is necessary, but a focus on relationship-based social work has not recently been part of social work practice. A review of the literature identifies a notable gap in the research and writing on relationship-based literature between the 1960s and 1990s. In that gap, and particularly from the 1980s onwards, a different model of service user/social worker interaction began to emerge prompted by changes within the wider political framework that surrounds the profession of social work. These changes in the 1980s and 1990s witnessed the ideas and philosophy of neo-liberalism under both Conservative and Labour governments becoming embedded within many aspects of the British state, particularly in welfare. This new model of service user/social worker interaction tended to reorder the interactions between service user and social worker to one that instead of being therapeutic and humanistic was based on a **rational-technical approach**. The main principle of this 'new' way of relating to clients was to make interactions between service user and social worker more akin to an economic transaction between two parties rather than one based on humanistic principles such as trust and empathy. Working alliances with service users were now replaced by economic mechanisms like 'audits' and practitioners became care managers commissioning packages of care instead of caring professionals focused on the needs of service users. The language of care was also changed in the 1980s to one that borrowed terms and concepts more traditionally associated with the world of business than with social care; the most obvious example of which was the *service user* being transformed into a *customer*. The overall result may not have been the further empowerment of the service user but rather the loss of an important working relationship with a skilled professional that was centred on the understanding of the service user's needs and requirements.

Given the increasing bureaucratisation and the pervading dominance of the rational-technical approach of social services, where processes and outcomes are often subjected to public and political scrutiny, social work is increasingly challenged to hold on to its ethical and humanistic values in practice.

In the 1990s and 2000s a small number of writers, like Howe, Ruch, Trevithick and Ward, began to reverse the trend discussed above by producing a body of interesting research on relationship-based social work that seeks to rediscover the essential therapeutic and humanistic nature of the interaction between social worker and service user. Ruch, Turney and Ward's edited book *Relationship-based Social Work* (2010), for example, provides a well-documented body of research on the subject. Appropriately subtitled 'Getting to the Heart of Practice', the work re-affirms for social workers the art of relationship-building with service users. Hennessey (2011) has more recently rediscovered 'the use of self' as a key skill in relationship building, which moves social work from the rational-technical approach to a more humanistic focus.

Poulin and Young (1997) examined measurements of the strength of the helping relationship from the perspective of both service user and worker. Read about their inventory on the Companion Website (www.sagepub.co.uk/SocialWork).

What Makes a Good Relationship?

There are many different forms and expressions of relationships that exist between humans and groups of humans. Relationships can be quite informal and refer to, for example, friendships or to relationships between two people who love each other. Relationships can also be formal, involving contracts and legal prescription, and include such arrangements as those that exist between an employee and employer. Regardless of what exact form a relationship takes, one element that all relationships possess in

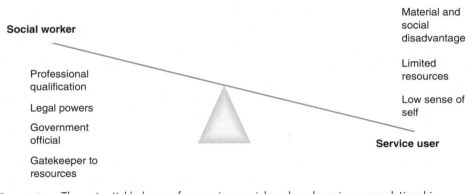

Social worker

Professional
qualification

Legal powers

Government
official

Gatekeeper to
resources

Material and
social
disadvantage

Limited
resources

Low sense of
self

Service user

Figure 16.2　The potential balance of power in a social work and service user relationship

common is power. Often power in a relationship can be asymmetrical and uneven, with one partner in a relationship possessing more power than the other, allowing them to make decisions over either what actions are taken or over the use of resources that suit their needs and not the other person's. Social workers attempt to achieve a symmetrical relationship with service users where both parties are actively and jointly working towards a set goal. That ambition may seem fairly straightforward but, as discussed in Chapter 11, the organisational and social context that surrounds both social worker and service user can lead to a substantial imbalance of power. As Figure 16.2 illustrates, the social worker and the service user do not necessarily arrive at the relationship as equals. There are obvious reasons why a social worker may be able to exercise more power than the service users; for example, the social worker has access to legal powers and acts as gatekeeper to a number of resources. Power can also be expressed through less direct and more subtle mechanisms and often relates to wider structures of power in society founded on class, ethnicity and gender. Thus, even if the social worker is consciously acting in a perceived participatory and inclusive manner, unintentional aspects of power may still define the relationship with a service user. This issue of power in social work relationships, and how to be aware of it, is a recurring theme in this section.

Power does not necessarily mean telling someone what to do, it can also mean doing too much for the other person. Partnership as defined by Thompson (2009b: 142) is concerned with 'working with clients, rather than doing things to or for them'. Partnership therefore involves a joint approach in working with service users in seeking solutions *together* to problems experienced by service users and carers. 'Empowerment' is about the process of gaining greater control over one's life and circumstances. However, its use in social work extends beyond that, to take account of discrimination and oppression experienced by clients. That is, empowerment is more than the traditional notion of 'enabling' (Thompson, 2009b: 144).

On the Companion Website (www.sagepub.co.uk/SocialWork) you will find an article by Maiter et al. (2006) who studied parents' views of the relationship with workers in child protection services. You will also find an exercise which would be useful for you to undertake, exploring some of the challenges in relationships that might occur in practice situations.

SKILLS AND KNOWLEDGE IN RELATIONSHIP-BASED SOCIAL WORK PRACTICE

The various reflective skills and abilities that are required of the social worker to be an effective humanistic practitioner form the core of what is discussed and explored next. Fundamental to this is the need for the social worker to be aware of who he or she is, and to possess insights into how this **use of self** affects and influences the relationship with service users. The self comprises both formal and informal aspects as laid out in Figure 16.3. In some respects what we are highlighting here is a variation of the old adage of 'physician heal thyself', which calls for the doctor to be healthy in order to help others. For social workers to help others, they need to be fully aware of their own attitudes, dispositions and prejudices, and to confront or transform them in order to be as effective as possible in practice.

Case Study

Mickey is a social work student on his first practice learning opportunity in a day centre for adults with learning disabilities. Asked by his practice teacher during the first two weeks on placement to identify some of his personal values in relation to working with people with learning disabilities, he was able to explore some of his stereotyped views of people with learning disabilities openly with his practice teacher. He had not worked with people with learning disabilities before and most of the information he gained had been from the media. Mickey was then asked by his practice teacher to map out his personal values in relation to the professional values identified in the professional code of practice, to examine disparities and to consider how he could integrate these professional values with his social work skills in his practice. Mickey was able to say that his approach in working with adults with learning difficulties was trying to 'fix it' for his service users. He identified that he was doing too much for them, that he needed to 'listen more carefully' to them and that he needed to work more in 'partnership' to 'empower' his service users to develop daily living skills. He also began to read about **normalisation** and explored how people with learning disabilities were 'stigmatised', 'labelled' and discriminated against within the community. As a final piece of work on his placement, Mickey looked at how service users within the day centre could access community resources and services more fully.

Exercise

Reflect on the above and consider how your professional values, social work skills and knowledge inform your practice. Draw on specific examples of your practice and critically analyse the positives and the areas you need to develop. Share your thoughts with another colleague or with your supervisor in supervision.

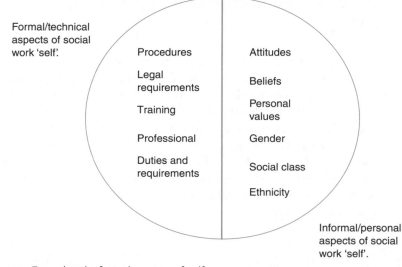

Formal/technical
aspects of social
work 'self'.

Procedures

Legal
requirements

Training

Professional

Duties and
requirements

Attitudes

Beliefs

Personal
values

Gender

Social class

Ethnicity

Informal/personal
aspects of social
work 'self'.

Figure 16.3   Formal and informal aspects of self

USE OF SELF IN RELATIONSHIPS

Biestek (1957), in his landmark book *The Casework Relationship*, identified seven guiding principles that have become highly influential in shaping present day social work practice: individualisation, purposeful expression of emotion, controlled emotional involvement, acceptance, non-judgemental attitude, self-determination and confidentiality. Biestek (1957: 18) stated that these principles form the 'requisite qualities in the caseworker, necessary for establishing a relationship'. Biestek argued that the social worker is not really able to work with the service user until a working alliance or a relationship with that service user has been established.

Critics, such as the radical social workers in the 1960s, have sought to enlarge and widen the ethical base of social work. They objected to what they felt was too narrow a focus in Biestek's original schema that concentrated too much on the individual and ignored wider material influences of political inequality that could influence the relationship between service user and social worker, as well as between the service user and wider society, resulting in marginalisation.

Hennessey (2011) gives an account of the different components of relationship-based social work:

- **'knowing oneself in relationship-based social work'** consists of a number of components – the practitioner being self-aware, the practitioner's engagement with feelings and knowing oneself through the 'use of self'. Hennessey (2011) provides different exercises to facilitate this development in the practitioner – the use of a genogram or a family tree and the construction of a personal lifeline which would provide an opportunity for the practitioner to know oneself better by considering how one's significant life events and family history may shape oneself in their personal and professional development. (pp. 45–64)

- 'knowing the other person in relationship-based social work' is about the practitioner using 'emotional intelligence' in practice. This consists of the practitioner engaging with emotions in practice and developing a sense of empathy and listening skills with the service user. Hennessey (2011: 81) defines empathy as 'a way of "hearing" what another person is "saying", both verbally and non-verbally, at the emotional level'. He links empathy to engaging with the service users' inner and outer worlds and he relates empathy to the practitioner's use of emotional intelligence and to self-awareness. (pp. 65–93)

- 'sustaining oneself in relationship-based social work' includes the practitioner's development of reflective practice and 'mindfulness'. In his discussion of 'mindfulness', Hennessey draws on Kabat-Zinn (1994) and explains this as been fully present in the 'here and now' as opposed to being distracted by the past and the future. Hennessey states 'social workers have their body in one place and their mind in another – looking at their watch and hoping that they are not late for their next appointment' (p. 102). Hennessey (2011: 109) also considers the importance of the use of supervision as a 'resourcing function' which is about 'providing workers with the emotional resources they need in order to be a human resource for their clients'. (pp. 94–112)

Hennessey (2011) takes the triangular diagram further by introducing the fourth dimension, the notion of the 'self' in the centre of the triangle (Figure 16.4). He suggests, 'you can imagine yourself, your unique self, in the centre … On the outside of you are social work theory, practice skills and values … you will internalise and make "your own"' (Hennessey, 2011: 53). This very act of internalising and integrating is a process that forms the core of the practitioner's self, one that will enable the social worker to practise reflectively with awareness and with competence.

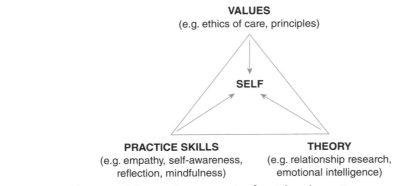

Figure 16.4   Hennessey's (2011: 53) components of social work practice

Edelman (2004: 2) identified a number of skills necessary for relationship-based social work, but cautions that while knowing what you are doing is important, being competent in performing the technical aspects of social work is not enough, and a further range of skills is necessary. He outlines seven kinds of skills which he feels would apply to different types of relationships within a professional context, and, although Edelman (2004) was writing about early intervention in relation to child care, these skills are applicable to all areas of social work:

- listen carefully
- demonstrate concern and empathy
- promote reflection
- observe and highlight the parent–child relationship
- respect boundaries
- respond thoughtfully to emotionally intense interaction
- understand, regulate and use own feelings.

The social worker needs to foster trust in developing a therapeutic relationship with the service user. Hennessey (2011) offers the practitioner a useful analysis of the different dimensions of engaging with another in relationship-based social work. A social worker needs not only to have the necessary social work skills but also needs to draw from a generic knowledge base in order to use theories to inform and intervene (Collingwood and Davies, 2008).

Critical Thinking

Reflect on trust building: consider from Chapter 7 how the development of basic trust versus basic mistrust was a foundation of our personality. How easy do you find it to put your trust in others? How easy will a service user who has had inconsistent or poor care in early childhood find it to trust anyone? To what extent do you expect people to form relationships in the same way that you do?

Different theoretical traditions will influence a social worker's use and management of self in different ways – the social worker will adopt an approach with the service user which will be influenced not only by the needs of the service user but also by his professional training and his preferences of theoretical approaches. Working in a psychoanalytic tradition the social worker may adopt a 'neutral' stance compared with a social worker using a humanistic approach who may be more expressive (Baldwin and Satir, 1987).

As we have seen, social work draws from a range of knowledge and overlaps in its use of theories with, amongst others, counselling and psychotherapy in the psychoanalytical tradition. For the social worker a key to working with service users lies in the need to understand the 'self' as an entity in the practitioner's interactions with another. Ward (2010: 52) provides a useful definition of the 'self' as 'a whole set of aspects of personality and identity including personal beliefs and values, our anxieties and "constructs" – a combination of our rational and intuitive views ...'. Our sense of self comes from our identity as to who we are. This self-identity is formed from a variety of resources linked to our ethnicity, gender, class, sexuality, ability and disabilities, educational, cultural and spiritual experiences. It is a mixture of elements including desires, instincts and drives of which we are aware and

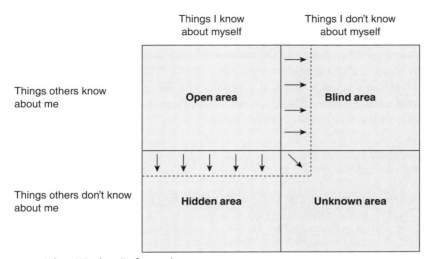

Figure 16.5   Johari Window (Luft, 1984)

others of which we are unaware. Others may recognise things about us, but we may be completely unaware, and all these hidden aspects constitute our unconscious self.

Using the Johari Window from Luft (1984), Ward (2010) explores the four quadrants – consisting of the open (things which are 'conscious' and are known to oneself and to others), the 'blind' (things unknown to oneself but known to others), the 'hidden' (what oneself keeps from others) and the 'unknown' (which is unknown to all including to oneself and others because it is 'unconscious'). These four quadrants are not equally divided and vary from individual to individual; for some, the quadrant for the 'open' will be larger and for others the quadrant of the 'unknown' will be larger depending on one's level of self-awareness and consciousness (see Figure 16.5).

The boundaries in these four quadrants can be adjusted through personal and professional development. For instance, through the use of direct observation of practice on a practice learning placement, a social work student may receive feedback from the practice teacher or link supervisor on their manner of interaction with a service user. In doing so, the 'blind' quadrant area could be reduced. The use of supervision is also to be helpful to the social work student or practitioner in enabling them to explore what is difficult and unspoken in their work with service users. In this instance the 'hidden area' and the 'unknown area' could be more fully integrated with the 'open area', thus expanding on the area of this quadrant, which is also the 'conscious'. When this happens the social work student can become more aware of what had been unconscious and un-integrated in their 'self', and in increasing the quadrant of the 'open area', the level of self-awareness can be enhanced in one's practice.

Luft (1984: 57) labelled the Johari Window as 'a model of awareness in interpersonal relationship' and he identified how this model could operate between individuals in a professional context, i.e., between a supervisor and a worker or between a teacher and a student. And he also considered how it might operate between individuals within a family and between individuals in groups and between groups or organisations.

According to Luft (1984: 59) 'consciousness' refers to 'what is felt within oneself' and 'awareness' to 'what is felt outside oneself'. Although he interchanged these terms – he was in fact referring to the 'inner' and the 'outer' worlds of the individuals in a psychodynamic way. This also relates to considerations Hennessey (2011) gives to 'knowing oneself in relationship-based social work' and 'knowing the other person in relationship-based social work' when he talked about the use of self, emotional intelligence and empathy in engaging with the service user's inner world.

Case Study

Yvonne is a final year social work student undertaking a final placement in the Children and Families team in a local authority. During the mid-placement meeting, the practice teacher identified that while Yvonne was very good at drawing effective boundaries with the children she worked with, she found it more difficult to 'play' with them. Yvonne was not aware of this until her practice teacher provided her with feedback from a direct observation of her practice in a session in which she worked with a child making a pictorial representation of her family. Upon reflection on her own life, her parents being first generation immigrants from Hong Kong who had to work very hard to set themselves up in Britain, Yvonne realised that as an only child growing up in a household of busy adults there was very little time dedicated to play. Yvonne had to help at a very early age in the family's business.

Exercise

1   Look at Luft's (1984) Johari Window and consider the four quadrants in relation to the above situation. Given the practice teacher's feedback, how might Yvonne work with this to expand the 'Open Area' quadrant? How will this help her in developing her practice?
2   Consider your own practice and reflect on your own development as a practitioner. How might the four quadrants in Luft's (1984) Johari Window apply to you? For example, give an example of how knowing something about yourself in the 'blind area' and the 'unknown area' in the past has helped you in your practice. Is there something in the 'hidden area' that would be helpful or unhelpful in your practice if this was known to others (being in the 'Open Area')?

We can also see the link of Luft's Johari Window to the different therapeutic approaches to working with service users. The social worker is a great resource to the service user if their practice is grounded in self and professional awareness, supported with a good grasp of social work skills and knowledge. For the social worker to be appropriately 'open', this means they are being 'congruent' and 'transparent' in their practice, thus effectively reducing the size of the quadrant areas of the 'blind', the 'hidden' and the 'unknown'.

CONCLUSIONS

Research into service users' perspectives of their experiences in relationships with social workers is important as it lends insight into what is helpful or unhelpful practice. Such information will also provide a better development and management of social service provisions. In considering feedback from service users and carers, Doel (2010) provides a good summary of research undertaken in the last three decades on this subject. He cites Sainsbury's studies (1987, 1989), which emphasise the importance of relationship-based social work. Among the qualities valued by service users in their social workers, which effectively help to develop a working alliance and a relationship as revealed in these studies, are the social worker's timely provision of help, the social worker's ability to respond to unspoken feelings in service users and the social worker's ability and skill in balancing care and control in a humane way (Doel, 2010: 200). Doel states that 'much of what people value in a social worker relates to personal qualities and the social worker's ability to communicate these qualities – to respond to feelings, to demonstrate care and concern …' (p. 200). This links well into Hennessey's studies relating to the importance in helping the practitioner to develop self-awareness in enhancing the use of self, the engagement with feelings, the effective use of empathy and the development of emotional intelligence.

Doel (2010) updates Sainsbury's research of the 1980s and identifies important aspects within the social worker/service user relationship which are valued by service users. In broad categories these involve the maintenance of confidentiality, where information is sensitively collected and used for the benefit of the service user, how professional power is managed judiciously and safely in the interest of the service user, and being treated humanely so that there is 'flexibility, reciprocity and equality' within the service user–practitioner relationship (Doel, 2010: 203). According to Doel (2010), the human aspects in the social work relationship with the service user or carer continue to dominate even in crisis when the social worker needs to assert power and control in discharging their responsibilities. The importance in Doel's assertion here lies in the affirmation of ethical practice, a sensitive and judicial use of social work values not only in protecting the service user but also in asserting his/her rights in crisis.

The transparency and accountability of the practitioner's practice will be tested not only at times in the court of law but also in the daily encounter and engagement with service users and carers. Practitioners may work to the letter of the law and may still not develop trust and a working relationship with service users and carers if they are not able to integrate social work values, skills and knowledge in a balanced and effective manner in their practice which will help foster trust and confidence in service users, carers and the community. The balancing of rights and responsibilities with regards to all individuals and groups within the community places the social worker in an important and powerful role that will need to be well balanced in the practitioner's use of care and authority with individuals and families who are often marginalised.

Reflective Questions

1   This chapter has considered the importance of relationship-based social work and its role within contemporary and historical social work. How would you define relationship-based social work? Why is relationship-based social work practice important for effective social work practice?

2   You may wish to return to this particular question on reading the rest of this section, but consider the models of intervention introduced in this book. What role does the relationship between service user and social worker have in each of them? How important is that role for the effective practice of that form of intervention?

3   In other chapters of this book we have discussed issues (for example, social inequalities and material circumstances) that are located outside the immediate situation of a social worker and a service user: can you think of any problems that might be associated with an entire focus on relationship-based work? Is the success or otherwise of a social work intervention always attributable to the quality of the social worker/service user relationship?

RECOMMENDED READING

Hennessey, R. (2011) *Relationship Skills in Social Work Skills*. London: Sage.

Ruch, G., Turney, D. and Ward, A. (2010) *Relationship-Based Social Work: Getting to the Heart of Practice*. London: Jessica Kingsley Publishers.

Trevithick, P. (2003) 'Effective relationship-based practice: a theoretical exploration', *Journal of Social Work Practice*, 17 (2): 163–76.

CRISIS

17 INTERVENTION

Angela Duvollet

Key Themes

- Defining crisis is complex because crises are experienced uniquely by individuals where tried and tested methods of coping fail to restore balance.
- Understanding what is not crisis is as important as understanding what is crisis, and the existence of balancing factors in an individual's life has a significant role in terms of preventing a state of crisis.
- Assessment of crisis includes risk assessment and draws on a broad underpinning knowledge base, particularly from the discipline of psychology.
- Crisis intervention is a brief intervention with distinct characteristics and principles.
- Models of intervention for crisis work provide clear frameworks for practice.

INTRODUCTION

Crisis-inducing events are an ongoing part of human history and may be personal, such as bereavement, loss and divorce, and/or social disasters, such as the results of war, famine and terrorism (Walsh and Lantz, 2007). Often people faced with a personal crisis or who experience emotionally hazardous situations are likely to suffer from a disruption of their emotional equilibrium and could experience the decline of their 'psychological homeostasis in which one's usual coping mechanisms fail' (Roberts, 2005: 778).

At any time, events in our lives can lead to feelings of being overwhelmed, and the impact of these events may compromise the individual's ability to function or cope, resulting in some sort of crisis. Times of crisis present difficulties for the individual, but often there is also an opportunity for learning new ways of thinking, feeling and developing new skills.

The level of personal distress depends on the individual's perception of the events that trigger the response and personal characteristics (Dulmus and Hilarski, 2003). When faced with a crisis, help may be sought from a range of professional agencies such as social workers, counsellors, psychiatrists and other professionals, who will be involved in making an assessment. As a practitioner, knowledge and understanding of the nature and impact of crisis will enable you to make an informed assessment and move, with the service user, to an appropriate intervention, such as crisis intervention. It is useful at this point to note that often researchers and practitioners confuse the terms stress, trauma and crisis. Clarity is therefore imperative to provide the correct support.

Exercise

At this point it would be useful to reflect on your own experiences. Have you felt under stress, felt traumatised or in crisis? Can you identify behaviours associated with any of these feelings?

Crisis intervention can be used in many situations, and with most service user groups, providing an opportunity for individuals and groups to gain a new insight into presenting issues and to improve their coping abilities.

HISTORY

Crisis theory is closely linked to the mental health field and has developed from the amalgamation of knowledge from the disciplines of sociology, psychology and psychiatry, including references to ego psychologists such as Freud (2001), Erikson (1956), Hartmann (1964) and Maslow (1954). The studying of human behaviour laid the foundations for understanding the complexities of an individual in crisis.

In 1906 Stierlin applied some early principles of crisis intervention in response to a European mining disaster, and in 1917 Salmon engaged with the process on the battlefields of World War I. Although crisis intervention had not been developed as a method or model at this time, it was recognised that in order to assist those suffering as a result of crisis, guidance and research into this area was required (Mitchell, 2011).

Lindemann (1944) developed his thinking in relation to crisis intervention following his work with the survivors of the Coconut Grove nightclub fire in Boston, United States, where in 1943, 493 people lost their lives. He had observed the way in which those who had survived, or were related to the deceased, dealt with their grief and bereavement crisis. In his report, he recommended that a multidisciplinary crisis team working together and made up of clergy, police, firemen, social workers and so on could play a critical role in helping individuals with the process of mourning and hopefully reduce the risk of the psychological difficulties emerging at a later date (Aguilera, 1994). He also suggested that people with a reliable supportive social network would be more resilient and less likely to remain or relapse into a crisis state. Alongside this recommendation he developed a programme that had the core principles and techniques of crisis intervention.

Caplan (1964) expanded on the work of Lindemann and based his work on the conceptual model of preventative community psychiatry, in particular ego psychology, which considers the individual's ability to cope in a crisis. Caplan suggests that a person lives in a state of emotional equilibrium with a goal to remain in that steady state; however, when faced with a crisis situation where established and familiar problem-solving techniques break down, the equilibrium or balance is upset. He suggests an imbalance to the equilibrium causes a rise in anxiety levels and tension resulting in a 'crisis' (Caplan, 1961).

This chapter will proceed to explore the definitions, key concepts, knowledge, skills, structure and tools from which to draw in order to engage fully with crisis intervention.

DEFINING CRISIS

Before engaging with crisis intervention it is necessary to establish both the meaning of crisis and what defines the crisis. In trying to explain or define that which is considered a crisis, O'Hagan (1986) suggests that there are many inconsistencies and indefinable factors.

The most frequently cited explanation is by Rapoport, who stated that 'a crisis is an upset in a steady state' (cited in Coulshed and Orme, 2006: 134). Others, such as Aguilera (1990), Parker and Bradley (2007) and James and Gilliland (2001), suggest that an individual who experiences crisis has probably experienced a change or loss that has created a state of disequilibrium. Often this relates to facing a problem where tried and tested methods of coping no longer work in regaining and maintaining previous equilibrium. They suggest also that if the person does not obtain relief from the crisis situation, there is a higher likelihood of the potential for affective and behavioural cognitive malfunctioning.

It would be useful to consider Hoff and Hallisey (2009), who provide examples and an explanation of what they consider *not* to be a crisis. Firstly, stress is tension or personal pressure, and not a crisis. Secondly, a predicament is not a crisis; rather it is an unpleasant situation that is dangerous or embarrassing. Thirdly, neither is an emergency necessarily a crisis; rather it is an unexpected combination of circumstances; and lastly, a crisis is not a mental illness. They suggest that 'crisis may be defined as a serious occasion or turning point presenting both danger and opportunity' (p. 4). It would therefore be fair to say that defining or assessing that which is a crisis cannot be considered an exact science.

It could be suggested, therefore, that a crisis is an individual's emotional response to a powerful stimulus or demand, resulting in a failure to draw from old-established patterns of responding, inability to rely on the usual balance between thinking and emotions and consequently feelings of being overwhelmed and unable to cope. As suggested by James and Gilliland (2001), whether universal or idiosyncratic, disorganisation or disequilibrium accompanies every crisis. Universally, anyone can find themselves in a state of crisis as no one is immune when faced with a constellation of circumstances. Crisis is idiosyncratic as, even if faced with the same set of circumstances, one person may be able to cope whereas another may not. It would be useful therefore, having defined crisis, to consider the types of crisis.

TYPES OF CRISIS

Maturational or Developmental

Maturational crises are linked to the individual's normal human development as the person moves from one stage to another, spanning from birth to death. The theoretical concept was derived from Erikson (1963, cited in Aguilera, 1990) where he identified stages in terms of the developmental tasks of 'infancy and early childhood, preschool, pre-puberty, adolescence, young adulthood, late adulthood, and old age' (p. 213). He suggests that if an individual is supported through each stage, then a healthy balance should be reached and the person is more likely to build up a degree of resilience and manage adverse situations well. Although developmental crises are considered normal and to some degree predictable (meaning they can potentially be prepared for), the lack of resolution in any stage of these transitional periods of psychological development can trigger maturational crisis. (For a fuller discussion of Erikson's work, see Chapter 7.)

Maturational crisis needs also to be set in a normative context. In relation to adolescence and ageing, Erikson described adolescence as a normal phase of increased conflict and crisis. He describes this as the period where an individual's ego strength fluctuates with the separation from childhood ties, an integration of the sexual body and the prospect of their personal future taking shape. As a result, the adolescent's experience of family life may cause conflict, rather than a crisis. For those in late adulthood, defined as ages 35–55, the infamous 'mid-life crisis' may be experienced. Here conflicts arise because re-evaluation and questioning of long held values and beliefs may occur.

Exercise

Refer back to Chapter 7 and identify which stage of Erikson's life cycle corresponds to your age. What current or recent experiences might be new and/or particularly challenging? Would you describe these as crises or as tasks that you must address?

Situational

A situational crisis occurs when an individual experiences extraordinary, uncommon and random events, which are unexpected, uncontrollable and which threaten their social, physical and psychological integrity. Examples would be:

- Personal or physical events, such as the loss of a limb, a diagnosis of a terminal illness, birth of a disabled child or a loss of role by which the individual maintains a sense of self.
- Social and/or interpersonal events, such as the death of a spouse or family member, divorce or sudden bankruptcy.
- Wider events, such as a natural disaster, fire, war or terrorist attacks (Aguilera, 1990; Clark, 2007; Hoff and Hallisey, 2009; James and Gilliland, 2001; Walsh and Lantz, 2007).

It should be noted that it is possible for maturational and situational crises to occur at the same time, compounding the problem as one crisis can trigger another.

The impact of childhood cancer on families was explored by Hendricks-Ferguson (2000). Read her article on the Companion Website (www.sagepub.co.uk/SocialWork).

BALANCING FACTORS THAT MAY AFFECT THE EQUILIBRIUM

Aguilera (1994) suggests that the equilibrium of people in crisis is significantly affected by three factors which work together to determine whether or not a crisis will evolve.

1 *Perception of the event.* Depending on the cognitive style of an individual the response to a potential crisis may be different. The individual with a 'field dependent' style will rely on external objects in their environment to orientate themselves and seek ways to assess what is reality. The 'field-independent' style is a person who prefers to deal with the crisis by way of analysing the situation through thinking and reasoning.
2 *Situational supports.* There is a level of dependence on others to gauge if the way we perceive ourselves is the way others see us. Meaningful relationships that have been developed provide a source of support and security. If this is suddenly absent or if there is a loss or threatened loss of these supports, the individual becomes vulnerable and less able to cope with a problematic situation.
3 *Coping mechanisms.* Throughout life an individual will use many ways or methods to cope with anxiety, consciously, unconsciously or both, in order to maintain psychological integrity. These mechanisms usually help the person to overcome obstacles in their lives in response to stressful or frightening situations.

Case Study

Two men, A and B, were informed that they had possible symptoms of cancer. As expected, their emotional balance was threatened by the stressful event, a state of disequilibrium occurred (fear) and there was a need to restore balance to reduce fear.

The template in Figure 17.1 will assist you to assess why, when faced with a situational crisis, one person goes into crisis whereas another does not.

Man A *(Balancing factors present)*	Man B *(One or more balancing factors absent)*
Realistic perception of the event *(perceives need for tests)* **plus** ↓	Distorted perception of the event *(does not accept the need for tests: denial of reality)* **and/or** ↓
Adequate situational support *(communicates fear to doctor)* **plus** ↓	No adequate additional support *(does not communicate fears to doctor)* **and/or** ↓
Adequate coping mechanisms *(makes appointments for tests)* **result in** ↓	No adequate coping mechanisms *(does not make appointment for tests)* **result in** ↓
Resolution of the problem *(tests made: diagnosis negative)* ↓	Problem unresolved *(no tests made: no diagnosis made)* ↓
Equilibrium regained *(tension and anxiety reduced)* ↓	Disequilibrium continues *(tension and anxiety increased)* ↓
No Crisis	**Crisis**

Figure 17.1   The avoidance, or development, of a crisis (adapted from Aguilera, 1994)

ASSESSMENT

There are several frameworks and models which can inform practice and it is often a combination of these which might assist the practitioner in helping the service user regain a sense of equilibrium. As with all interventions, the process begins with assessment, firstly to assess if balancing factors exist and if the individual is in crisis or a perceived state of crisis. The assessment would consider if the individual has '(i) a realistic perception of the event; (ii) an adequate network; (iii) an adequate coping mechanism' (Clark, 2007: 207). If two or all of these exist, there may be no crisis and equilibrium should be maintained. If only one or none of them is present, a state of disequilibrium may occur, and therefore more likely, a crisis. Although events leading to a crisis can often put the service user's normal coping strategies out of action, identifying past strategies and reinstating them can make an enormous contribution to restoring the equilibrium.

Assessing the severity of the crisis and the individual's current functioning should be completed as soon as possible because time may be limited as the individual's cognitive functioning may be compromised. The assessment would be based on the *ABC* of assessment:

- *Affective*: assessing feelings and emotions, including how the individual presents – for example, over-emotional or out of control.
- *Behavioural*: assessing actions and psychomotor activities – for example how far the individual has become immobilised by the situation or experience.
- *Cognitive*: assessing the disruption of thinking patterns – for example, to what extent the individual's thinking about the crisis is realistic, consistent or exaggerated (Golan, 1978; James and Gilliland, 2001).

Underpinning Knowledge

At this stage of the work you should also draw on underpinning sociological and psychological theory to develop your knowledge and understanding of the service user, to determine the needs of the service user and the timing of the transition from assessment to intervention. The following provides only a few examples of relevant theory:

- *Loss and change, identity* – are particularly important in understanding the individual's reactions to loss, for example, the death of a loved one. The change in the person's life and loss of role can pose a threat, changing perceptions of self and affecting the ability to cope (Kubler-Ross and Kessler, 2005; Marris, 1986; Murray-Parkes, 1998).
- *Developmental stages* – can assist in determining an individual's capacity to understand their world, and to consider the psychological and emotional changes which occur throughout the life stages (Erikson, 1956; Fairbairn and Ronald, 1949; Piaget, 1957).
- *Resilience* – the positive identification of key protective factors that may have helped before with stress, loss and change, reducing the individual's vulnerability to crisis (Bowlby, 1969; Gilligan, 2000; Howe, 1995).
- *Systems theory* – an understanding of the individual's wider interrelated system, such as family, friends, work colleagues, who may contribute to the situation or provide support (Bowen, 1978; Bronfenbrenner, 1979; von Bertalanffy, 1950).

You may also wish to consider defence mechanisms (Freud, 1993), which are often used to deal with a crisis (see Chapters 6 and 25 for further discussion). Defence mechanisms are natural and normal strategies we use at an unconscious level for self-protection when conflicts arise and threaten to overwhelm. In crisis, events often seem to be out of proportion, which can create highly anxious states. Defence mechanisms may reduce the impact, although those that are rigidly maintained may be counterproductive to working towards a resolution. In Chapter 6, Freud's ego psychology was explained, and, at times of crisis, the ego states are in conflict, producing severe feelings of discomfort for the individual. This discomfort needs to be alleviated to reduce anxiety and furthermore the system (id, ego and super-ego) needs to be 'kept in a balance [equilibrium] to avoid unhealthy defence mechanisms' (Hoff and Hallisey, 2009).

Framework for Assessment

The integration of underpinning knowledge will assist you to determine four important areas:

1. The severity of the crisis. This should be established as soon as possible. It is important to consider the length of time the service user has been in crisis and the amount of time you as the worker will have to spend with the service user. Assessment of the service user's functioning from the ABC perspective – affective, behavioural and cognitive – is necessary.
2. The service user's emotional status. The service user's view of the situation(s) may be exacerbated by others: are they in denial? You would also consider if the crisis was situational or maturational/normative at this stage.
3. Coping mechanisms and resources available. Assessing the ability of the service user to engage with any form of intervention: it may be that the service user has reached the stage of being immobilised to the extent that rationalising the events or making concrete decisions independently or with assistance is difficult.
4. The level of the service user's lethality. An assessment of risk where you would establish if the service user is at risk to her/himself or others. For example, assessment of the service user's mental health.

(James and Gilliland, 2001)

It goes without saying that you would also make use of your practice skills in relation to verbal, non-verbal and symbolic communication (see Chapter 8).

Risk

As noted above, it is important to include a risk assessment as part of the assessment process. This is because of the central importance of establishing whether the service user or family are in any immediate danger or at risk of harm to themselves or others (Payne, 2005a). The risk assessment would need to take into account the cause of the crisis, as different situations will have an impact on the level of risk. For example, a crisis arising from being the victim of crime may present different issues of risk to a crisis resulting from internal psychological causes. In addition, the risk assessment should address the meaning of the incident, of whatever type, to the individual (see Chapter 13).

Assessment is a continuous and critical process and is the basis from which you will move to intervention.

INTERVENTION

There is no one single model of crisis intervention, but there are general principles that can be employed to assist the distress caused by a crisis and restore independent functioning (Flannery and Everly, 2000). The goal of crisis intervention is to revisit and enhance coping mechanisms that have worked in the past and develop new coping mechanisms for the future, thereby minimising the potential psychosocial and physiological danger.

As noted earlier, crisis intervention can be employed with most service user groups. Taking the example of those with mental health issues, we can identify that the progression of deinstitutionalisation has had many positive aspects enabling those with mental disorders to live successfully in the community with additional support where required. Alongside these positives, however, there have also been negative aspects. Research by Ritter et al. (2011) suggests this service user group have an increased risk of homelessness, criminal victimisation, substance misuse and potential engagement with criminal activities. In the United States the development of a Crisis Intervention Team model seeks to improve police responses to individuals with severe mental illness. Engaging with crisis intervention and specialised training has resulted in reduced likelihood of arrest, increased understanding of the effects of a crisis and referrals to appropriate supporting services (Watson et al., 2010).

CRISIS – AN OPPORTUNITY TO INITIATE CHANGE

The individual or family experiencing a crisis is likely to be highly stressed, anxious and losing confidence, feeling hopeless and overwhelmed. There is a threat to their homeostasis, and the normal coping mechanisms may be failing or inadequate. Their ego state is vulnerable and customary defence mechanisms may be weakened.

There is a 4–8 week window in a state of crisis when there is an opportunity for individuals and families to learn from the experience (Caplan, 1964). This is an opportunity for worker and service user to re-visit previous coping mechanisms, to gain an insight and understanding into the service user's reaction on this occasion. At this stage, engaging with crisis intervention could promote a healthy resolution of the traumatic life events by learning new skills, restoring balance and reducing the effects of crisis. The service user may return to their prior level of functioning and thus safeguard their mental health.

Crisis intervention begins the first time you meet with the service user and requires you to begin to establish a sound working relationship. For the intervention to be most effective, you need to work in partnership, to develop skills required to assess the individual's ego strength, to analyse the event and to understand their personal history, affirm feelings and work towards reinforcing strengths (McGinnis, 2009).

CHARACTERISTICS OF CRISIS INTERVENTION

Crisis intervention is a short-term, time-limited helping process. The intervention focuses on a resolution of the crisis by making use of all available resources, such as personal and environmental, from which small achievable goals will be identified. Crisis intervention is:

- Supportive and non-judgemental
- Based on developing a positive working relationship
- Requires excellent listening and communication skills
- Assists the service user to confront the crisis
- Builds on strengths by exploring past skills and building new skills
- Requires use of reflection and empathy
- Considers different cultural values and lifestyles
- Focuses on the emotions, cognition and behaviour of the individual.

Intervention needs to include the following general principles of:

- *Intervening* immediately, as crises are emotionally hazardous and individuals may be at high risk which could result in immobilisation
- *Stabilising the individual* by 'mobilising resources and support networks' to restore balance
- *Facilitate understanding* by restoring the individual's 'pre-crisis level of functioning' by encouraging the individual to recount the event leading to the crisis, listening, gathering facts and helping the individual to understand the impact of the event
- *Focus on problem-solving* by assisting the individual to use 'available resources to regain control' which in turn will 'enhance independent functioning'
- *Encourage self-reliance* by encouraging the individual to develop strategies to 'restore a more normal equilibrium'. (Flannery and Everly, 2000: 120)

MODELS OF INTERVENTION

If you are involved in crisis work, a quick response and engagement with the assessment process and the application of an appropriate model of crisis intervention will enable you to assist the individual to begin to draw from their strengths and develop new skills to cope with the crisis. There is no one preferred or single model of crisis intervention, but the focus is always to alleviate stress and restore functioning. The following two models may assist you to develop your understanding of how crisis intervention is used in practice.

Six-step Model

James and Gilliland (2001) proposed this relatively straightforward, although highly skilled, model suggesting that there are three listening and three action steps, which are undertaken, with continuous and ongoing assessment, by the crisis worker. This model of systematic helping focuses on these steps, which are carried out in a joint approach, focused on the service user, making use of listening, verbal and non-verbal communication and assessment skills.

Listening

1 *Defining the problem.* Using core listening skills and showing empathy, acceptance and positive regard will assist the worker to define and understand the problem.
2 *Ensuring client safety.* The worker should ensure client safety is at the forefront of the procedure and minimise any psychological or physical danger to themselves or others.
3 *Providing support.* At this stage the worker should ensure that the service user feels valued, cared for and receives a high level of support. The worker should demonstrate empathy by the use of passive and active listening skills and acceptance.

Action

1 *Examining alternatives.* The worker encourages the service user to explore realistic and appropriate choices which may be available; when in crisis the service user may not think there are any alternatives to their situation.
2 *Making plans.* This step flows logically from the above, as once the service user acknowledges that there are other ways to approach the crisis the restoration of their equilibrium can begin. A plan agreed by worker and service user should identify supporting services and provide an opportunity to develop new coping mechanisms, which in turn will enable the service user to take back control.
3 *Obtaining commitment.* In this last stage the worker encourages the service user to demonstrate their commitment to the plan by carrying out some of the key tasks that have been identified. The worker should still be available to support when required, but also take a step back to enable the service user to gain confidence in their ability. (James and Gilliland, 2001)

Case Study

Frank Costello is 25 years of age and has recently been referred to the social work department by the local court. He has had a long history of substance misuse, mainly alcohol, and has come to the attention of the police on several occasions for alcohol-related offences. Frank has a volatile relationship with his wife, Alison, and she has accused him of assault on several occasions, although subsequently she withdraws these charges. The social work department has provisionally been involved with the family when a neighbour expressed concerns about the poor clothing and personal hygiene of the two children, Scott (7) and Hannah (4). Frank's father bullied him throughout his childhood and his mother was unable to protect him during the frequent assaults on Frank and his mother. During periods of sobriety Frank has expressed concerns about his current behaviour and the impact it is having on his family. At this point in time Frank feels that life is hopeless and has stated to his social worker that he frequently thinks of killing himself and 'ending it all'. Frank is presenting in a crisis state.

Using Gilliland and James' Six-Step Model, the following are examples of questions that the worker may focus on at each stage.

(Continued)

(Continued)

1   *Define the problem.* For example, what are the key issues which are most important from Frank's perspective? Are these different from yours?
2   *Ensure client safety.* For example, what is the severity of the crisis? Do you consider him to be a threat to himself or others, and how would you address the issue of his presenting mental state? How would you ensure the children and his wife are safe; what safeguards would you put in place?
3   *Provide support.* For example, how would you make sure his views are valued; what type of support needs to be in place? If Frank's behaviour to his wife is unacceptable to your values, how do you ensure you respond with unconditional positive regard to Frank even though he may be saying or doing things which are contrary to your own belief and value system?
4   *Examine alternatives.* For example, considering Frank's emotional/mental state who might you involve from social or personal resources to help in his recovery?
5   *Make plans.* For example, having identified the appropriate resources, in collaboration with Frank, what plan of action would you put in place to assist him during the crisis period and to assist him to develop coping strategies?
6   *Obtain commitment.* For example, how do you ensure Frank retains ownership of the commitment to the plan? What arrangements would you make and what level of commitment do you make to Frank in relation to follow up contacts?

Seven-stage Crisis Intervention Model

Roberts' (2005) model identifies seven critical stages which he suggests the individual passes through to find a resolution and state of equilibrium. The following is his seven-stage crisis goal-orientated intervention model which is sequential and at times overlapping in the process. It is a model that can be applied not just by you as a social worker, but also a range of professionals who are involved in the assessment and decision-making process. Engaging with this model can contribute to facilitating an earlier resolution of the crisis episode (Roberts and Ottens, 2005).

Based on this model, your task as a practitioner would be to address the following:

1   Assess lethality and mental health status (what is the immediate or long-term danger to self or others? Considering a risk assessment of need, what is the immediate psychological need? What are the internal and external coping methods?)
2   Establish rapport and engage the client (establish working relationship, be non-judgemental and respectful, reassure the service user that he/she can be helped through contact with the worker and regaining control).
3   Identify major problems (define and examine the dimensions of the problems, identify the 'last straw' which resulted in the breakdown of the ability to cope, identify their coping style and prioritise the problems).

4   Deal with feelings (encourage the service user to explain their feelings and emo-
    tions, enable the service user to vent feelings, be empathic and a good listener, use
    paraphrasing, reflect feelings and encourage the individual to consider alternative
    behavioural options).
5   Explore alternative coping methods and partial solutions (assess, generate and
    explore new coping mechanisms, integrate existing strengths – reminding the ser-
    vice user that these still exist – with the new skills, provide options and alternatives).
6   Develop an action plan (restore cognitive functioning via the implementation of a
    concrete action plan, encouraging the service user to consider the triggers to the cri-
    sis and have a realistic understanding of the events and how they will address these
    when they happen again).
7   Develop a termination and follow-up protocol (offer to meet again 3–6 months later to
    evaluate the post-crisis status, leaving the door open so the service user is comforted by
    the fact that they can return if the feelings of crisis rise again) (Roberts and Ottens, 2005).

To explore the practical implementation of Roberts and Ottens' model go to the
Companion Website (www.sagepub.co.uk/SocialWork) and see the case study of Jean,
a 45-year-old woman with a history of mental health problems. On the website you will
also find journal articles discussing other models – see Westefeld and Heckman-Stone
(2003), and Kaplan and Racussen (2012).

CONCLUSION

Crisis intervention can be, and is, used by many professionals as crisis situations will
present at all times of the life cycle and in many forms. It is vitally important that as a
practitioner you ensure you are familiar with the core principles of crisis intervention
to provide a sound service either independently or as part of an interprofessional group.
As a practitioner, engaging with crisis intervention is demanding and stressful work.
It is also rewarding, however, as by assisting an individual or family to regain their
equilibrium and homeostasis provides them with hope that their situation can change.

Critical Thinking

Reading and reflecting on this chapter should enable you to consider what might be the
advantages and disadvantages, or balances and tensions, of using a crisis intervention
approach. Some of the points raised through research and academic writing are noted
below and should act as a starting point for your critical engagement with this approach.
    There is not a single crisis theory, as crisis is a multidimensional construct and is
dependent on the individual's perception and their life experience. Some service users may
define crisis through differences in emotional, cognitive and situational aspects, others
may define crisis by the sense of urgency or escalation of the issues (Al et al., 2011). The
intervention is also time limited, between 4–6 weeks, which may not be sufficient time; it
can be difficult to assess when the crisis for the individual has ended, and continuity of
support cannot always be provided by the same worker. There are often crisis assessment
frameworks made use of by a variety of agencies, from both medical and social model

perspectives, and this may be problematic when several agencies may be providing services for the service user (Lewis and Roberts, 2001).

It may also be difficult to establish that which is stress, trauma or crisis. Research by Dulmus and Hilarski (2003: 33) suggests 'multiple variables influence the stress–trauma–crisis continuum resulting in a wide range of perceptions and outcomes'. If an accurate assessment of the precipitating event has not taken place then the choice of intervention may be inappropriate.

A worker may inadvertently allow personal values and views to get in the way; for example, what the service user perceives as a crisis may not be the way the worker views the situation. Such differences will impact on the intervention approach and the timing of appropriate intervention. As Hoff and Halliday suggest, drawing on the work of Jacobson, the timing of a crisis intervention approach is crucial to the success or otherwise of the intervention.

According to Al et al. (2011) in relation to family crisis intervention, the model suggests that from the practitioner's perspective it assists in the development of positive changes in family functioning, although the research also shows that from the service user's perspective, they did not attribute any of the changes to the intervention.

Reflective Questions

1 Defining crisis is complex, with sometimes difficult boundaries between an individual in crisis and an individual in a perceived state of crisis. Taking into account your learning from this chapter, do you think that in practice situations you would be able to assess whether an individual is in crisis?

2 Consider either a personal experience of crisis or the experience of someone you have worked with. Was the crisis maturational or situational, or indeed a combination of both? Could the 'crisis' have been linked to Erikson's stages of development?

3 What benefits are there to using a structured model of intervention in crisis situations? Do the models presented in the chapter have any limitations and if so, how would you address these?

RECOMMENDED READING

Clark, A. (2007) 'Crisis intervention', in J. Lishman (ed.), *Handbook for Practice Learning in Social Work and Social Care: Knowledge and Theory.* London: Jessica Kingsley Publishers. pp. 201–15.

Long, N.J., Wood., M.M. and Fecser, F.A. (2001) *Life Space Crisis Intervention: Talking with Students in Conflict,* 2nd edn. Texas: PRO-ED.

Roberts, A.R. (2005) *Crisis Intervention Handbook: Assessment, Treatment and Research,* 3rd edn. New York: Oxford University Press.

Roberts, A.R. and Ottens, A.J. (2005) *The Seven-Stage Crisis Intervention Model: A Road Map to Goal Attainment, Problem Solving, and Crisis Resolution.* New York: Oxford University Press.

18 COGNITIVE BEHAVIOURAL THERAPY: ITS PRACTICE AND ITS PLACE IN SOCIAL WORK

George Allan

Key Themes

- Much of our behaviour is learned but how we interpret experiences influences our feelings and future behaviour. How we think influences how we feel and act.
- Cognitive behavioural therapy (CBT) is based on the notion that many human problems stem from 'faulty' interpretations of experiences.
- CBT aims both to help people address unhelpful beliefs and alter problematic behaviours which are the consequence of such ways of thinking.
- CBT is now used in a number of settings to help people with a wide range of difficulties, however it is not without its critics.
- CBT is practised in partnership with service users.

INTRODUCTION

Cognitive behavioural therapy (CBT) is one of the most widely known and used approaches for assisting people who find life problematic for a variety of reasons, such as experiencing mental distress, offending or their use of substances. At its core, CBT emphasises that our moods, the choices we make and our behaviours (including those that can cause us harm) derive from patterns of thought that have been learned from our interactions with others and from the environment in which we live. These patterns become established, automatic modes of thinking, feeling and behaving, when we are presented with certain situations or challenges, and can be difficult to change. Where such thought patterns are 'faulty' (i.e., unrealistic), distressing feelings and unhelpful behaviours can follow. The purpose of CBT is to alleviate emotional and behavioural problems by addressing such 'faulty' thinking, and people are also helped to alter problematic behaviour by utilising specific techniques.

This chapter opens by defining CBT, then identifying its origins, before moving on to explore its popularity and its perceived strengths and weaknesses. The chapter concludes by considering the uses of CBT in social work practice.

WHAT IS CBT?

The phrase 'cognitive behavioural therapy' is used to categorise a number of broadly similar interventions. Gossop (2011) states that 'to say [CBT] is a broad church is a euphemism' and he notes that clinical psychology has shifted from strict behavioural approaches through interventions containing both cognitive and behavioural techniques to more cognitive styles. Motivational interviewing, the purpose of which is to tip the decisional balance as a precursor for change (Jarvis et al., 2005: 45), is an example of an intervention in which the cognitive elements predominate. This shift away from behaviourism in the psychological therapies is, perhaps, surprising given that 'learning by doing' remains a major theme in higher education (Gagne as cited by Kearsley, 2009; Race, 2010). Sheldon (2011) makes the case that a combination of the cognitive and the behavioural elements is likely to be the most effective.

CBT is generally considered to be a talking therapy but this is misleading. In its classic form it might best be described as a time-limited, structured intervention that supports both cognitive realignment and the embedding of altered behaviour. In psychoanalytically orientated interventions the effect of the relationship developed between therapist and client within the sessions is central; what matters in CBT are the changes the service user implements in daily living, with the therapist acting as facilitator in a joint enterprise. CBT may involve some or all of the following:

- The establishment of a trusting relationship, and an agreement about the areas to be worked on and the outcomes to be achieved.
- An assessment of current thinking patterns and their relationship to the presenting issue of problematic mood or troublesome behaviour.
- Setting a time-limited framework, usually between ten and twenty sessions.
- Exploring specific instances of erroneous mental appraisals. Alternative ways of interpreting are then considered and exercises are suggested to help implant these different ways of thinking (the cognitive element).
- Assisting the person to relearn behavioural responses where these have become unhelpful. This may involve strategies such as staged exposure to feared situations or role-playing alternative responses to social encounters (the behavioural element). Behavioural experiments, designed by the client, to test his/her predictions about what might happen are also used.

- Supporting the person to normalise changed thinking patterns across other aspects of their everyday lives (generalisation). The overarching goal is longer-term self-management.
- Measurement of progress, whether the person feels better or behaves differently, judged against indicators set at the beginning.

(Adapted from Coulshed and Orme, 2006: 185)

It will be clear that there are similarities of orientation, content and frameworks for delivery between CBT and other social work approaches, such as task-centred casework, solution-focused therapy and, to a lesser degree, crisis intervention. CBT can be employed with groups as well as with individuals and can be used in conjunction with other interventions such as pharmacotherapy or marital or family-based counselling.

Manuals, based on CBT principles, have been developed for working with people who offend and those with substance problems, and these help the therapist and client progress logically within structures whose efficacy has been demonstrated in controlled trials. Their use can lessen what Waller (2009) calls 'therapist drift', but a note of caution is needed here. Miller (2005) describes how the strict application of a motivational interviewing manual left little space for the therapists to adapt their styles to the circumstances of individuals. The consequence was that resistance to change seemed to harden for a minority of people in the study, and the lesson seems to be that a readiness to be flexible is important. There has also been an explosion in self-guided manuals, many of which are available on the Web.

When using CBT, consideration is also given to the involvement of significant others. Parents and partners may be unwittingly reinforcing undesirable thought patterns or actions by, for example, giving reassurances when these serve to maintain cognitive distortions or by inadvertently rewarding problematic behaviour. Helping significant others to adopt more effective responses not only increases the likelihood that the person with the problems will be successful in changing, it can also reduce the frustrations and helplessness that relatives often feel in the face of what can appear to be intractable difficulties. It should be noted, however, that the effects on significant others may be so great, or relationships may have broken down to such an extent, that they need help to cope separately in their own right.

THE ORIGINS OF CBT: BECK AND BANDURA

When practising as a psychoanalyst, Beck discovered that what we present in public as explanations for our reactions, even in the safety of the counselling room, is likely to be paralleled by a separate series of thoughts. He labelled the latter 'automatic thoughts' and considered that it is these which govern our moods (Beck, 1989: 29ff). The following is a simple illustration of this.

Case Study

Mary is driving and a car coming towards her flashes its lights. She says to her companion, 'Why is he flashing at me?' – a neutral response. However, her internal dialogue goes as follows: 'What have I done wrong?' 'Have I left my indicator on?' 'I know I am a useless driver.' She experiences a wave of inadequacy. Mary negotiates the next bend and finds a lorry partially blocking the road. Her feeling of incompetence evaporates. The first thought of a confident driver might be: 'Danger ahead, slow down.' Beck suggests that these internal appraisals are grounded in past experiences. We create mental frameworks, based on these experiences, and we use these to interpret current events. Mary had failed her test twice and her husband was always describing her as a 'typical woman driver'. Beck suggested that where these cognitive frameworks consistently lead to negative appraisals, then all sorts of emotional difficulties, such as depression and anxiety, become easy to explain. Helping the person to see that these habitual responses are irrational and encouraging him/her to adopt a more realistic mindset can reduce or eliminate the unpleasant emotions. In most instances, thoughts are seen to precede the emotional response and subsequent behaviour. Whilst this is open to debate, the influence of our everyday tramlines of thought on our feelings and our behaviour led Beck to develop his particular style of cognitive therapy (Beck, 1989).

Cognitive distortion describes thinking patterns which can be shown to be irrational. The following are some examples:

- Catastrophising: assuming the worst outcome will occur.
- All or nothing thinking: polarised thinking that excludes consideration of the complexities of a situation.
- Filtering: focusing on the negatives without acknowledging the positives in an experience.
- Shoulds, oughts and musts: setting rigid expectations for oneself and others. (Burns, 1990)

Bandura, like Beck, a behavioural psychologist, found the tradition he was working in limiting. Earlier behaviourist theories suggested that learning takes place through the relationship between the environment and the organism. Classical (respondent) conditioning, as described by Pavlov (1849–1936), demonstrates how patterns of behaviour take root through the association of responses with stimuli.

Case Study

Jane (aged 4) becomes trapped in a cupboard. She panics. The cupboard is the unconditioned stimulus and her fear the unconditioned response. She then develops a dread of enclosed spaces, such as toilet cubicles. These become the conditioned stimuli and her panic the conditioned response. This widening of potential stimuli is a process known as generalisation. A programme to help

Jane might involve her entering confined areas with a trusted adult, initially for brief periods with these being increased on a staged basis, the hope being that habituation would lead to the extinguishing of her panic responses.

Operant conditioning (Skinner, 1965) suggests that we learn to repeat a behaviour if it is **reinforced** by external benefits and to cease doing it when it is punished or unrewarded; thus behaviour can be understood in terms of its consequences.

Case Study

When John (aged 16) started to drink alcohol, he found that he enjoyed the relaxant effect and this increased his confidence in social situations. These benefits positively reinforced alcohol consumption; he become a regular heavy drinker, especially on Friday nights. He also found that Saturday hangovers (positive punishment) were reduced by a couple of early morning beers (negative reinforcement), thus increasing the likelihood of such drinking continuing. He was a keen footballer and the effects of his drinking pattern led to his being dropped from the team one Saturday afternoon, which upset him (positive punishment), along with his not being invited to join a more senior club (negative punishment). Whether he subsequently reduced his drinking would depend on the relative strengths of the reinforcements compared with the punishments.

Bandura did not reject these explanations of learning but, in his famous bobo doll experiments, he demonstrated that humans can learn to carry out tasks without association or more immediate reinforcement, by modelling the behaviour of others. This ability did not come from direct experience of 'learning by doing'. Cognitions are at the centre of social learning theory, which Bandura went on to develop (Bandura, 1977). He suggested that humans make sense of experience by generating internal cognitive constructs, language and thought becoming representations of experience. By utilising our individual frameworks for understanding we can reflect on what has happened to us and evaluate the possible consequences of future behaviour.

Case Study

Danny has received warnings for being persistently late for work. His decision to set two alarm clocks is not just based on the humiliation of being called twice before a disciplinary committee (operant conditioning/positive punishment) but also because he knows that further misdemeanours will lead to dismissal. He can imagine how being unemployed would feel and what the implications of this would be for his material well-being. Knowledge gained from past experiences and the observation of others has created a cognitive map on which Danny can mark his current position and calculate possible outcomes from taking different directions. This talent for forethought gives the individual the potential for at least some control over his destiny, a notion lacking in pure behaviourism.

While starting out from very different perspectives, Beck and Bandura can, therefore, be seen to have arrived at much the same place. Bandura's more recent work has focused on developing his idea of 'self-efficacy', an individual's appraisal as to whether he/she can carry out a task successfully. It influences how people 'feel, think, motivate themselves and behave' when approaching an activity (Bandura, 1998: 2). When self-efficacy is strong, a difficult enterprise will be viewed as a challenge to be met. Low self-efficacy, however, can lead a person to attempt an activity in a half-hearted way or to avoid it altogether. As Henry Ford put it, 'If you think you can do a thing or think you can't do a thing, you're right' (BrainyQuote, n.d.). Self-efficacy appraisal can also have a direct effect, one way or the other, on mental well-being. Bandura (1998: 2–3) suggests that four factors strengthen self-efficacy, namely:

- Success in achieving challenging, rather than easily accomplished, goals ['mastery experiences'].
- Observing peers carrying out the task in hand successfully.
- Realistic encouragement from others ['social persuasion'].
- Action to lessen the potential negative effects of emotional responses to challenges. For example, feeling anxious can invigorate but it can also inhibit.

It can be seen that these four factors combine both mental processes (cognitions) with elements of operant conditioning and other forms of learning through repetition.

The importance of these ideas in helping people to deal with situations they find difficult, or emotions which trouble them, is obvious. Whilst Beck considered that thoughts tend to precede emotional responses and behaviour, it should be noted that others have suggested that the correlation may not always be linear, as these components interact. For example, Sheldon (2011: 229) says that 'directly changing what people do often changes the accompanying thoughts and feelings'. The relationship between the critical elements is highlighted in a matrix produced by the Royal College of Psychiatrists (see Figure 18.1). CBT aims to readjust the interplay of these connected domains.

Exercise

- Consider a task you always dread doing.
- In what sequence do your emotions and thoughts occur?
- On what are your feelings of dread based? How realistic are they?

After you have undertaken this exercise visit the activity on the Companion Website (www.sagepub.co.uk/SocialWork) where you will be asked to extend your learning further.

CBT: ITS RISE IN POPULARITY

Since the closing decades of the twentieth century, very significant levels of research have been undertaken into the effectiveness of CBT, and much of this supports its use with

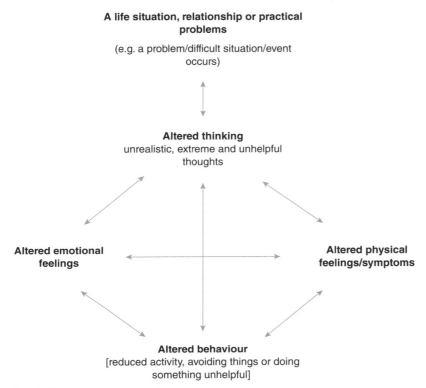

A life situation, relationship or practical problems

(e.g. a problem/difficult situation/event occurs)

Altered thinking
unrealistic, extreme and unhelpful thoughts

Altered emotional feelings

Altered physical feelings/symptoms

Altered behaviour
[reduced activity, avoiding things or doing something unhelpful]

Figure 18.1   A Five Areas assessment

Reproduced with the kind permission of The Royal College of Psychiatrists, www.rcpsych.ac.uk/mentalhealthinfoforall/treatments/cbt/5areas.aspx

a wide range of problems, either alone or in conjunction with other methods. Writing in 2000, Sheldon (2000: 70) noted that CBT showed positive outcomes compared with other treatments or no intervention in the great majority of the 4,000 empirical studies identified, and research has continued apace since then. Sheldon (2000: 70) quotes the editor of a journal who argued that the priority was no longer establishing the case for CBT but rather concentrating on how best to implement its use in practice (p. 70). The National Institute for Health and Care Excellence (NICE; formerly the National Institute for Health and Clinical Excellence) and the Scottish Intercollegiate Guidelines Network (SIGN) produce guidance documents for working with people with mental health problems based on analyses of research evidence. CBT is recommended as an option, usually in conjunction with other approaches including pharmacotherapy, for depression (NICE, 2010; SIGN, 2010a), depression in children (NICE, 2005), generalised anxiety disorder (NICE, 2011), obsessive–compulsive disorder (NICE, 2006a), schizophrenia (NICE, 2009; SIGN, 1998) and bipolar affective disorder (NICE, 2006b; SIGN, 2005). There is also evidence supporting CBT's use with adults who are obese (SIGN, 2010b), for people with alcohol (Miller and Wilbourne, 2002; Raistrick et al., 2006) and drug (Gossop, 2006) problems, with people who offend (McGuire, 2007; Whyte and McNeill, 2007: 170), for anger management (Beck and Fernandez, 1998) and as a part of smoking cessation programmes (Perkins et al., 2008; Sykes and Marks, 2001). The strength of the evidence and the relative ease of training practitioners, along with its time-limited nature and emphasis on measurable outcomes which fit in with the value-for-money agenda, have led governments to make CBT a central plank in efforts to increase the availability of 'talking therapies' in the first decade of the millennium. The English mental health strategy document *No Health without Mental Health* (HM Government, 2011) builds on previous action taken to train additional practitioners in CBT through the Improving Access to Psychological Therapies Programme (Department of Health, 2011b). Similarly, the Scottish strategy, *Towards a Mentally Flourishing Scotland: Policy and action plan, 2009–2011* (Scottish Government, 2009a) reaffirms a commitment (Scottish Executive, 2007) to expand access to a range of evidence-based psychotherapies, including CBT.

CBT: CRITICISMS AND SHORTCOMINGS

A major criticism of CBT, one that can also be levelled at the majority of psychotherapeutic and psychological interventions, is that it is reductionist. By working on the assumption that the locus of the problem, along with its solution, lies within the individual, CBT promotes a model that fails to acknowledge the major implications of both the immediate and the macro-environments on well-being.

Case Study

Rachel, a single woman with three children, lives in a run-down tenement in an area of deprivation. Dependent on benefits, her life is a struggle to cope and she has long since abandoned any aspirations she once had of improving her lot. She tells her social worker that she has no time for a social life and is experiencing feelings of hopelessness and depression. A CBT programme would encourage Rachel to identify particular thoughts that occur before her mood darkens and then to reframe these to highlight ways in which she is coping. She might also be encouraged to set herself a target of visiting friends twice a week and supported in carrying this through.

Whilst such an approach is not without merit, it fails to acknowledge that gender, material disadvantage and cultural inequalities are playing significant roles in Rachel's lack of well-being; lack of sleep and poor diet may well also be factors. CBT does not ameliorate her poverty, reduce the disruptive behaviour of neighbours or help with the practical problems inherent in mothering three children. It is clear that, as well as any therapeutically orientated interventions, Rachel requires practical assistance and additional services, a response that social work is the best placed of all professional groups to coordinate. In addition, helping her to understand the implications of structural disadvantage may further support her recovery. From this broader sociological perspective, it can be argued that a further limitation of CBT is its base in Westernised notions of individual therapy, which may be less appropriate for some ethnic minorities.

The CBT therapist is interested in past experiences in so far as these have shaped a person's current patterns of thought. Completely different approaches to past abuse, trauma or problems of attachment may well be indicated before a person can consider moving forward. Davidson (2008) considers that the complexity of some people's situations suggests that a 'one hat fits all' style is inappropriate. He maintains that, whilst CBT is the right option in many circumstances, there is a danger that it is becoming seen 'as a pill', a course of a dozen sessions being the cure for the majority of ills. Politically driven commitments to increase the numbers of people trained in CBT risk reinforcing this notion.

Cooper et al. (2008) have argued that the sheer volume of research on CBT has given the false impression that it is more effective than other approaches. This has led to significant levels of funding being provided to make CBT widely available with the consequent risk that the opportunity to access other interventions will diminish. A meta-analysis carried out by Elliot and Freire (2008) suggests that whilst CBT and person-centred therapy, along with other experiential approaches, show positive outcomes, it cannot be demonstrated that CBT is more effective than these.

Ethical concerns have been expressed, particularly regarding the behavioural aspects of CBT which can raise the spectre of Orwellian manipulation of conduct. Hudson and Macdonald (1986: 13–14) contend that such criticism is invalid if workers involve service users fully in the selection of goals, because encouraging self-determination permits people to choose to disengage if they so wish. However, when it is felt by others or by wider society that a person should change his/her behaviour, the potential power imbalance between a professional worker and that person is thrown into sharp relief. Particular care is needed in certain types of residential setting where withholding consent may have detrimental consequences for a service user (Sheldon, 2011: 254). Sheldon (2000: 71), however, considers that the effectiveness of CBT strengthens its ethical credentials.

Whilst it is essential that these concerns are understood, and care is taken when deciding if CBT is appropriate, the fact remains that the evidence base for its use with a wide range of problems is strong.

Exercise

In what circumstances do you think that attempting to alter another person's behaviour might be unethical? After reflecting on this activity, share your ideas with other members of your student group.

To examine some of the research evidence for yourself see the articles by Ronen (2004) and Ronen and Rosenbaum (2010) on the Companion Website (www.sagepub.co.uk/SocialWork).

CASE STUDIES: CBT IN PRACTICE

The final part of this chapter will consider the practical application of CBT in two contrasting situations. The first describes a formal programme; the second shows how elements of CBT might be used in a group work setting.

Karen's Story

Karen (24) said to her GP 'I think I am going mad'. Considered an anxious child by her parents, she lived at home until she had completed her degree and obtained a job in another part of the country. Returning to her flat one night, she noticed a broken bottle in the gutter. She thought nothing of it at the time but the following morning she started to think that the glass might damage a car tyre and so cause an accident. Overcome by waves of anxiety, she immediately returned and removed the glass. On doing this, her disquiet subsided. From then on, she began to worry when she saw anything which might conceivably result in a road accident. On driving past cyclists, she began to fear that she had hit them. She developed various strategies to reduce her fears, such as stopping to pick up small objects from the road (rituals), which possibly posed a greater risk to road users and herself than doing nothing, and searching the local papers to see whether incidents had occurred (checking). She discovered that these actions served to reduce her immediate emotional turmoil but did not eliminate the 'condition'. She also avoided driving unless she had to, a response which she feared might adversely impact on her job. Whilst ashamed of what she was experiencing, she eventually told a friend. This person, despite thinking that Karen's behaviour was odd, was sympathetic. However, by providing a willing ear, she reinforced Karen's use of 'confession' as a way of reducing her anxiety.

Referred to mental health services, Karen was diagnosed as having obsessive–compulsive disorder (OCD). Anxieties about having said the wrong thing or having left the gas on are commonplace, but most people readily dismiss such concerns. People with OCD exaggerate risks, assume that the worst possible outcome will occur, and cannot stop thinking about potential consequences. Anxiety can reach extreme levels. Checking or rituals are then used to return to some form of emotional equilibrium, but these compulsive behaviours then become embedded as coping mechanisms. Some people find that they have to repeat such actions numerous times. For example, a person fearful of spreading germs may wash their hands until they are raw, thus establishing a vicious circle. Whilst the causes of OCD are far from clear, it is thought that chemical abnormalities in the brain (Hyman and Pendrick, 1999: 25), along with learned behaviour (Sheldon, 2011: 50), are the culprits. For some people, there may be a genetic component (Alsobrook II and Pauls, 1998).

Arrangements were made for a psychologist to work with Karen using CBT. He explained to her that they would meet regularly over a 4-month period, that she would need to undertake much of the work herself outside their sessions, and that pharmacotherapy would be an option if they did not make sufficient progress together. He also told her that it was normal for CBT to heighten fear levels initially. Over the first couple of sessions, the psychologist undertook a 'formulation'. This is the structuring of information within a particular psychological model to enable a treatment plan with measurable outcomes to be developed. This process is closely related to the social work concepts of assessment, goal setting and action planning, although these may well focus more fully on the social context and less on psychological processes.

Formulation led to the identification of ways of helping Karen to adopt different modes of thinking (cognitive restructuring) and altering her compulsive responses (behavioural intervention). CBT progressed as follows:

- Karen agreed to record all incidents in a diary, noting the frequency of troubling thoughts, scoring the levels of anxiety these provoked, stating whether she undertook rituals and describing what her friends would do if faced with similar situations. As well as forming the core of the assessment, the diary provided a baseline for measuring the effectiveness of the intervention.
- Together they deconstructed in depth Karen's thought processes during a small number of incidents. She began to understand how she interpreted thoughts as facts ('If I think I have knocked someone off their bike, I probably will have'), that she had developed a hyper sense of responsibility ('It is my fault if a car crashes because of a piece of glass dropped by someone else') and that she grossly overestimated risks (' … people will die'). She also found it difficult to live with uncertainty ('I must check, even if the risk is tiny') (Obsessive Compulsive Cognitions Working Group as quoted by Gkika, 2010: 45). Because such thoughts triggered her fears, rather than the other way round, the psychologist added 'imaginal exposure' (Hyman and Pendrick, 1999: 85–91) to her homework. This involved Karen thinking anxiety-arousing thoughts with the aim of reducing their power through habituation. The psychologist gave her a relaxation CD and suggested that she use it following this exercise (an example of a technique known as 'counter-conditioning').
- After this initial concentration on the cognitive dimension, the psychologist added behaviour-change exercises. He suggested that Karen stop avoiding the use of her car and try to desist from undertaking compulsive checking and rituals when the thoughts occurred (extinction of behaviour). She managed the latter from time to time but initially described experiencing hours of distressing feelings. She did notice, however, that these passed if she simply waited and, when looking back a day or two later, she could see how irrational her thinking had been.
- At the end of the 4 months Karen was driving regularly. The diary showed that the intensity of unwanted thoughts had reduced and the incidents of checking and ritual behaviour were fewer in number. She still described having 'mad days' but she felt more able to cope. The psychologist gave Karen a self-help manual and encouraged her to return for top-up sessions if she felt the need. Six months later she considered that she had made further progress without being completely free of obsessional thoughts. She took the decision not to return to see the psychologist as she considered that this, in itself, would be a form of reassurance, a behaviour she wanted to avoid. Karen's self-efficacy was becoming stronger.

This case demonstrates some of the key features of CBT, namely the assumption that thought usually precedes feeling, that work should concentrate on the present, that people can be guided to correct faulty cognitive appraisals and that detrimental behaviours can be relearned.

Preparing the Crew

Four care-leavers from a group project were offered berths for a fortnight's trip on a sailing ship by a voluntary organisation. Whilst the three 17-year-old males and the one 18-year-female whose names were put forward showed initial enthusiasm, the project's social worker had concerns. Not only did she wonder how they would cope in the confines of a ship, she was well aware that two of the young people had a history of absenting themselves when faced with challenges (low self-efficacy) and, come the day, she thought they might not turn up. Along with one of the key workers, she decided to run a group under the banner of 'working together on board'. The interlinked objectives of the group were to help the participants deal with scenarios they might experience and to increase their self-efficacy. The following methods were used:

- At the first session, group members were asked to list situations that might prove difficult on a ship and how they thought these should be dealt with. These discussions were summarised in writing.
- The group leaders role-played a couple of situations that crew members might face. They then gave the young people scenarios, such as a crew member refusing to undertake a task, to work on themselves. Participants were allocated various roles (e.g. 'the captain', the 'refuser', 'other crew members') and encouraged to act what might happen. After such exercises, the leaders asked group members to describe how they felt and to consider the implications of how their characters performed. Constructive feedback was given. Identification of a range of emotions, such as frustration, anger and feelings of satisfaction, led to discussions about how ways in which they viewed situations shaped their feelings and responses. Group members began to understand that individual cognitive frameworks often channel our thinking so that we do not consider the full range of choices open to us. 'Captains' began to see that shouting at 'refusers' was not the only option; 'refusers' recognised that there were alternatives to non-compliance when faced with something they were unhappy about; 'crew members' learned that they could act in ways that increased or lessened the tensions. Challenging the perception that choices are limited is a central element of cognitive restructuring.
- The group leaders gave praise, but only when clearly merited. If the group achieved a particular score for its performance over the session, food was made available. Continuous reinforcement was being applied. When group members were disruptive, rather than employing sanctions as punishment, which would have been difficult to apply in such a setting, the workers asked the participants to consider what would happen if such a scenario occurred at sea.
- A camping weekend was arranged with exercises again followed by group analysis of individual perceptions and behaviour. The setting now more closely represented what they might experience at sea (a further example of behaviour rehearsal).
- At the last session, group members revisited the problematic scenarios they had identified at the start and contrasted how they thought they would now deal with these compared with their earlier responses (measuring progress). They identified that they were now more able to think out the consequences of immediate reactions, consider alternative ways of viewing stressful situations and take account of other participants' points of view.

If asked, the two workers would probably deny that they were undertaking CBT. What else, however, might we call an approach that included challenging thought processes and relating these to feelings and behaviour, helping the participants identify alternative courses of action, modelling behaviours, rehearsal and undertaking assertiveness and social skills training? Helping the young people address problematic situations in relative safety led to an increase in their self-efficacy. The ship set sail with all four on board. Whilst some coped better than others, all spoke positively of what was an eye-opening experience for them. The 18-year-old female went on to become a volunteer, undertaking further trips and supporting first-timers.

Critical Thinking

How important is self-efficacy in carrying out the social work task? Reflect on your own self-efficacy and consider whether it could be enhanced.

CONCLUSION

Where does CBT fit into social work practice? Coulshed and Orme (2006: 176) note that supporting behaviour change is a core social work activity and that behaviourism has long played a part in this. The residential childcare worker employing rewards and punishments to encourage constructive behaviour is utilising its precepts. However, it was only when the grip of psychoanalytical theory began to lessen in the early 1970s that other paradigms such as task-centred models, crisis intervention and behavioural social work began to gain a foothold (Munro, 1998: 41). Payne (2005a: 141) notes that there has been some resistance to the behavioural aspects of CBT as the techniques inherent in their practice do not fit comfortably with the more non-directive style adhered to by many social workers. However the influence of psychology on work with people with substance problems and interventions with offenders led to CBT's ready adoption within those specialisms and its acceptance is now more widespread. Various aspects of CBT fit with current social work practice:

- It is time-limited.
- It involves the worker and service user setting clearly defined and measurable outcomes.
- The evidence base is comprehensive.
- It dovetails with the empowerment agenda in that worker and service user are partners in an approach in which the latter takes increasing responsibility for managing change.

Social workers are likely to be involved with CBT in three distinct ways:

- They may use CBT directly with people, usually in specialist settings.
- They may combine behavioural techniques and aspects of cognitive restructuring with other methods.

- They may be working with service users who are also embarking on CBT with other professionals and so need to be aware of what this entails. With the strengthening of the care management role and social work's closer integration with other disciplines, particularly health services, such scenarios are becoming increasingly common.

It is important to stress that social workers using formal programmes should receive adequate training in the more technical aspects of CBT. Skilled supervision is also a necessity.

Reflective Questions

1 Cognitive behavioural therapy (CBT) offers a particular approach that can assist service users to break negative patterns and behaviours. What circumstances can you envisage where CBT could be useful for a service user?

2 In other chapters we discussed how material circumstances, poverty and inequalities can shape and affect the lives of service users. Discuss how these social factors may impact on the effectiveness of CBT.

3 What is the role of self that is required in providing effective CBT intervention? What particular skills may the social worker need to demonstrate?

RECOMMENDED READING

Payne, M. (2005) *Modern Social Work Theory*, 3rd edn. Basingstoke: Palgrave Macmillan.
   Chapter 6 offers a fuller introduction to CBT in social work.
Sheldon, B. (2011) *Cognitive-Behavioural Therapy. Research and Practice in Health and Social Care*, 2nd edn. Abingdon: Routledge.
Not an introductory text, but highly recommended for those wanting to consider the theoretical background and practical application of CBT more fully.

Refer to the Companion Website (www.sagepub.co.uk/SocialWork) for some useful links to web-based material.

TASK-CENTRED
19 INTERVENTION

Dave Humphrey

Key Themes

- Method of intervention with strong evidence base.
- Practice with a structured and logical framework focusing on realistic goals.
- Partnership working to identify problems, set goals and define tasks.
- Practice that is time-limited, but needs to be applied ethically.
- Review and evaluation.

INTRODUCTION

The utilisation of proven and purposeful methods of intervention lies at the very centre of effective social work practice, and social work is a profession that constantly strives to do the 'right thing'. However, this positive honourable concept is also a potential pitfall of practice, because having an honest intention to do the right thing is an inadequate response to the very real and complex contemporary practice environment. Practice must ensure that the 'right thing' occurs in a tangible and concrete sense with a focus on the purposeful application of interventions that promote positive, purposeful and lasting change.

Amongst the interventions, task-centred practice is a popular and valid problem-solving method amongst both students and practitioners (Gibbons et al., 1979; Healy, 2005; Marsh and Triseliotis, 1996; Parton and O'Byrne, 2000). Task-centred practice offers a well-researched, proven and effective method of intervention with a clear focus on achieving realistic outcomes through partnership working with service users. It provides a structured and sequential framework for resolving identifiable problems, with distinct stages providing a clear, logical order to enable problem-solving through action-focused practice (Milner and O'Byrne, 2009). While thematic similarities exist between task-centred work and crisis intervention, for example a shared applicability to practical, social and emotional problems (Coulshed and Orme, 2012), it is the structured framework of the former which provides clear differentiation between the two.

Notable defining characteristics include: time-limited focus, clearly defined goals and the objective of problem-solving.

However, one potential consequence arising from both the popularity and apparent accessibility of this model is that it is not always afforded the quality or depth of understanding it requires (Marsh and Doel, 2005). When interpreted as being straightforward and simple, its potential effectiveness can be significantly diluted. Task-centred intervention is not an easy answer, either when referenced in the academic milieu or when applied in practice environments.

The aim of this chapter is to introduce and explore key themes and concepts associated with task-centred practice. We shall consider the historical roots of the practice, its evolutionary development and its application within the contemporary practice arena.

HISTORY AND DEVELOPMENT

Task-centred practice has not always occupied a central role in social work. The formative roots of task-centred intervention can be traced back to American social work in the 1960s, when **psychodynamic** approaches provided the dominant focus for intervention. These emphasised the importance of the caseworker–client relationship and its central role as the mechanism for change with an emphasis on often lengthy assessment and intervention, open-ended timescales and a reliance on the expertise of the practitioner. However, as social demands expanded the scale and focus of the social work profession, concerns emerged about potential limitations of this approach. Initial and subsequent research findings were critical of the caseworker model for being no more effective than those interventions completed within shorter timescales (Reid and Shyne, 1969). Could a short-term, task-based practice model offer a more robust and viable alternative to that of casework? The alternative practice model was developed as a radical response, emphasising intensive, time-limited problem resolution and formulating the evidence base and core principles of what was later explicitly articulated as task-centred practice (Reid and Epstein, 1972). Taking into account this extensive developmental process, it can be stated with some confidence that task-centred practice was explicitly 'developed within and for social work' (Ford and Postle, 2000: 52).

The historical existence of task-centred practice provides significant benefits in terms of both proven research viability (Parton and O'Byrne, 2000) and continued evidence of a professional desire to retain focus on problem-solving. Reid and Hanrahan (1981, in Lishman, 2007) argue that much of the practice validity that is afforded to task-centred practice stems from the positive results that have emerged from its significant exposure to research and evaluation. Stepney and Ford (2000: 52) further argue that the task-centred practice 'not only derives from research, but lends itself to research, insofar as it embodies the setting of goals whose achievement is easily measured. Consequently, the model has been developed and refined through numerous **empirical studies**'.

In the period since its initial creation, the model has evolved in response to 40 years of emerging evidence and environmental changes in practice. Payne (2005a: 97) suggests that it now 'reflects a contemporary trend towards brief, focused and structured theories that deal with immediate, practical problems' seeking to facilitate a structured, timely and strength-based response to the very real problems that impact upon the lives of service users (Marsh, 2002; Payne, 2005a).

PRINCIPLES AND VALUES

The task-centred model shares many of the values that underpin wider social work. Value-based concepts including empowerment and participation permeate through sound anti-oppressive practice (Dominelli, 1996). Both are at the ethical core of task-centred practice.

The concept of partnership working is one that rightly envelops much of contemporary social work. Marsh and Fisher (1992: 10) argue 'task-centred practice is the most congruent model for clear, open and negotiated processes of partnership practice'. However, practitioners must recognise the power imbalance that exists within the relationship and must understand the potential impact this can have on the principles of partnership working. In Chapter 11 social work is acknowledged as a profession with great power, and it is only through explicit recognition of the dominant power held by practitioners that practical measures can be taken to mitigate the effects of their hierarchical status within the relationship. This can potentially be achieved even in situations where compulsion is necessitated (Thompson, 1998). However, practice must never be used as a mechanism for directing, ordering or forcing service users to undertake dictated actions.

Fundamentally, task-centred practice is based upon collaborative working between the service user and the practitioner (Payne, 1997). The very nature of task-centred work is empowering because there is no complexity about the way it works – its success depends upon people understanding the process of the work and this enables collaborative intervention (Ahmad, 1990; Doel, 1994). Task-centred practice not only avoids but also addresses the deficit approach so often dominant in social work assessment and intervention. It retains a fundamental belief in the inherent, unique strength and potential of each service user. Unlike other intervention practices, noticeably psychodynamic-based social work, task-centred practice explicitly recognises and promotes service users as being the experts on their own problems (Doel, 1994). The fact that this is a person-focused method of intervention, operated in collaboration with the service user rather than being applied to them, is a strength of the model.

For further discussion of problem-solving and empowerment, see O'Connor et al. (2006).

Case Study

Working with parents, helping them become more comfortable playing and interacting with their toddler, a worker could use a task-centred approach to build up confidence in playing together. This would be successful if the parents are committed to the approach and able to relate to their child. If, however, the parents are emotionally needy (see Chapter 7), they may not have the capacity to engage fully, and other approaches may be necessary.

APPLICATION

Significant research has been completed into the problem areas where task-centred practice has proven impact, but, before looking at these areas, it is important to highlight that task-centred practice is not universally appropriate to use with all service users and all associated problems. Complex problems, those requiring lengthy professional involvement and situations of chronic, as opposed to acute, crisis are those least appropriate to task-centred work (Payne, 2005a).

Throughout the many fields of social work practice, statutory, formal and **interventionist** measures are often necessary and justifiable to ensure that service users receive the care, support or protection required. Social work is provided with a range of legislative powers and duties associated with exercising the responsibility of social control. In many of these situations, task-centred practice is not appropriate due to the mandatory directive behind service user contact. Research carried out by Trotter (2007) highlights the challenges often faced by practitioners in working with service users under a statutory mandate. Involuntary engagement can impact upon service users' motivation for change, their self-awareness and their contextual understanding. Each of these can have a corrosive effect on the viability of task-centred practice.

However, this is not to say that task-centred practice should never be used in such circumstances. Where an interventionist approach is being utilised, many service users will retain an informed understanding of the problems impacting upon them. They may also agree with all, or elements of, any decisions and plans formulated in response to this. In such situations the service users may be motivated to change. Practitioners should therefore seek to ensure that genuine opportunities exist for the service user to actively and purposefully contribute to both the initial decision-making and the actual change process (Banks, 2004).

Task-centred practice can be applied across much of the spectrum of social work practice (Doel and Marsh, 1992; Reid, 1996). However, rather than think in terms of service titles such as criminal justice, children and families and care management, which belie the uniqueness and individuality of each service user, we must think in terms of the specific problems that exist and whether there is evidence that the task-centred method would be appropriate given the presenting factors and corresponding motivation levels of the service user.

In order to understand the potential appropriateness and effectiveness of the task-centred model in any situation, practitioners should consider the eight categories identified by Reid (1978), which presents those problem areas where there is established evidence of the viability of the model:

- Interpersonal conflict
- Dissatisfaction with social relations
- Problems in formal organisations
- Difficulties in role performance
- Problems of social transition
- Reactive emotional distress

- Inadequate resources
- Behavioural problems.

Whilst useful as general guidance, this list-based approach does present potential problems in that we may interpret it as being all-encompassing and therefore applicable in all situations. This would be an overly simplistic approach and could lead to the application of the model in practice situations where its effectiveness was at best questionable. It is, therefore, worth considering the work of Payne (2005a), where an alternative but complementary list of problem types is presented. These problems are those which:

- Are accepted by the service user
- Can be clearly defined
- Can be resolved through the actions of the service user
- Are based on what the service user wants to change
- Come from the 'unsatisfied wants' of service users.

Through informed consideration of these lists, practitioners can justify the utilisation of task-centred practice.

To extend your understanding of how task-centred intervention has been applied in different settings look at the research by Naleppa and Reid (1998) Wing Lo (2005) and Colvin et al. (2008) on the Companion Website (www.sagepub.co.uk/SocialWork). You will see that task-centred intervention has been applied in work with older people and to work in school and group settings.

LIMITATIONS AND CRITICISMS

With an emphasis on the individual, task-centred practice can be criticised for failing to address wider social factors. Although the model requires consideration of the impact of external factors upon the individual, it does not itself facilitate coordinated challenge of these wider issues. While practitioners may seek to adopt the model as a means of addressing the impact of poverty or unemployment upon a service user, this is the limit of interest. Such practice can be criticised for failing to exert sociopolitical influence in a manner that could stimulate lasting structural change.

While the highly structured framework of task-centred practice can be acknowledged both as a central characteristic and a core strength, the very construct can lead to practitioners regimentally adopting the model in the same manner for each service user. Practitioners must see beyond standardised utilisation of the framework and must instead see use of the model as an opportunity for adaptation which ensures that the unique traits, including needs of each service user, are provided for in an individual manner.

At a time of increasing financial limitations and corresponding resource compression, task-centred practice can be attractive to agencies. The time-limited nature of the model potentially and somewhat uncomfortably responds well with the rationalisation agenda. Practitioners need to demonstrate ethical resolve in such situations; the task-centred model exists as a legitimate method of intervention and should be utilised only in situations that merit such adoption. It must not be covertly used as an administrative mechanism to deliver financial efficiencies.

While service users and the systems designed to support them had no role in or responsibility for current global economic challenges, they have both disproportionately suffered from the financial restrictions that have been imposed and that will continue to be imposed in the future. Resources, be they tangible assets such as services or staff, or soft assets such as knowledge and theory, are arguably less readily available than before. This has a direct and potentially adverse impact on the viability of task-centred practice. If resources are not available to address the problems identified by the service user then this risks further loss, rejection and disempowerment. These can all have a destructive impact on self-esteem and confidence – two of the very factors that task-centred practice seeks to develop. Practitioners need to be aware of and realistic about the availability of resources, and this information should be openly and honestly shared with service users both in order to promote partnership working and also to ensure that service users' expectations remain achievable (Epstein, 1995).

THE STAGES OF TASK-CENTRED WORK

Central to task-centred practice are a set of distinct, sequential but overlapping stages (Epstein and Brown, 2002), and, depending on which text you read, there may be subtle differences in the formulation and presentation of these stages. However, the set stages always represent the actual framework for intervention.

Five stages are presented here, which reflect the process of problem-solving as seen with task-centred practice:

> Stage 1: Problem exploration
> Stage 2: Identifying priority problems and agreeing goals
> Stage 3: Agreeing required tasks
> Stage 4: Carrying out and achieving the tasks
> Stage 5: Ending the work and evaluation

In addition to these stages, there is an initial preparatory stage which involves the coming together of the service user and practitioner through the process of referral. Core information is presented and on this basis a mandate for intervention is established. Doel (1994) highlights the crucial importance of justifying involvement, as this stage sets in motion the action-based process associated with the subsequent steps. Without a clear mandate, the effectiveness of any later work will be limited. Justification, which should be mutually agreed, can be established through consideration of a range of seven key factors:

1 the urgency of the problem;
2 the consequences of not alleviating the problem;
3 the chances of success in alleviating the problem;

4 the ability of the worker and agency to help with the problem;
5 the motivation of the client to work on the problem;
6 the support which the client will receive from other people; and
7 the specific nature of the problem.
   Doel (1994: 27)

Stage 1: Problem Exploration

Problem exploration, also known as problem scanning (Doel, 1994), begins the process of intervention and establishes the foundation for later stages. It is perhaps useful to think of this step as being one which, first, seeks to determine the 'bigger picture' and, second, seeks to break this down into manageable segments. In this context, 'problem' means those difficulties in life experienced and identified by the individual, which have a direct adverse effect or prevent achieving. It does not exclude the need to consider relevant difficulties that are identified by other persons. This process of external consultation and exploration may lead to the provision of relevant supplementary information.

The practitioner should support the service user in defining the problems, but not complete this stage for them. In practice, some practitioners find it difficult to allow the service user to control the agenda in terms of problem exploration. At all times it must be remembered that the service user is the primary agent of change, and that the practitioner role is one of secondary support, accepting the service user perspective on the problems impacting upon their life. Negotiation is vital: if this stage is directed by the practitioner or does not cover the full range of problems as viewed by the service user, then the end result can be an increasing sense of powerlessness. Achieving successful outcomes depends on the service user making a genuine contribution to the process rather than feeling on the periphery of the work taking place (Doel, 1994). Throughout this stage, practitioners must therefore demonstrate an explicit understanding of and an appropriate response to those potential power imbalances that exist in the service user/ practitioner relationship.

During problem exploration, the temptation can arise for the practitioner to engage in analysis of the root cause of the identified problems. While this is an understandable ambition, identification of causal factors is not considered to be of central importance in task-centred practice. A further misconception is for the focus at this stage to be directed solely on what appears to be the main or dominant problem. At this point, however, it is the range and not the intensity of the problems that is the primary consideration. Often what is initially labelled as the main problem later becomes a secondary or related issue. It is only through consideration of the full range of problems that an informed understanding of problems and their impact can be understood.

Whilst dealing with seemingly endless and enmeshed problems, it can be difficult for service users to clearly identify and articulate the problems affecting them. A simple, yet effective, way of enabling service users to best understand their own situation and the associated problems can be to promote the use of a diary. This need only be a short, bullet point-style diary that allows the person to record the problems as they arise along with reference to the corresponding impact. Imaginative provisions, such as the use of a Dictaphone, could be a more viable recording option if written communication skills are less fluent. The process of problem recording can be a powerful medium in providing the service user with initial clarity at a time of potential confusion and anxiety and need not be restricted to the initial stages, but can be utilised throughout each of the following stages. With appropriate support from the practitioner it can provide an effective record concluding the process of change with which the person has engaged.

Stage 2: Identifying Priority Problems and Agreeing Goals

During this stage, agreement is reached with the service user over the goals for change. This can be a positive and potentially enlightening stage for service users as they begin the move away from a focus on problems to a focus on solutions. It is important to note that when we are talking about change we are talking about lasting change and not merely a temporary change, which risks evaporation once external support is reduced. The service user should be encouraged and supported to rank the range of problems in order of priority, i.e., which problems are most important for them to resolve. In practice the use of a problem scale can be useful during this stage.

Exercise

A problem scale involves assigning a ranking for each problem, which is then considered in priority order based on the ranking. This is then used as a means of enabling informed decision-making regarding which problems need to be addressed first.

The simplest practice gives a numerical value to each problem (1 being a problem of low priority and 10 being a problem of absolute priority). Practitioners need to ensure that clear, consistent and understandable instructions and guidance are in place to ensure that the service user understands what each of the numerical values specifically means.

Try applying this ranking exercise to situations you are currently dealing with in your own life.

Practitioners should seek to ensure that the number of problems identified remains realistic, and it is more purposeful and effective that no more than three problems should be selected as areas of focus (Coulshed and Orme, 2006). This not only provides the service user with a realistic opportunity to achieve change but also enables them to strengthen from exposure to success. Overly ambitious targets for change risk placing the service user in the vulnerable situation of failure and associated loss.

Once the priorities have been established, the next step is to identify corresponding goals, that is, desired or intended outcomes. In this context goals should be seen as measurable indicators of progress and ultimately success. Trotter (2007) argues that, in order to achieve positive outcomes, it is important to work with those goals that are set by the service user as opposed to those that are set by the practitioner. The role of the practitioner is to provide encouragement and, where appropriate, guidance and support.

It is at this point that an important question arises: how can we support the service user to identify such goals? Doel and Marsh (1992) suggest that, from a practitioner perspective, a positive influencing factor is the effective use of communication and, in particular, language. They suggest that the identification of goals can best be achieved when the service user is encouraged to think in terms of what it is that they 'want' as opposed to what they think they 'need'.

The number of goals must be unique to the circumstances of the service user and no standard or set number exists. Goals must provide realistic opportunities for the service user to achieve success, so modest but meaningful goals may be necessary. Remember, the central principle of task-centred practice is to build service user confidence and self-esteem through small but important successes.

Following clear definition of the desired goals, timescales for completion should be agreed between the service user and the practitioner. In setting timescales for goal achievement, a balance must be struck between timescales that provide sufficient time for completion but at the same time avoid unnecessary and potentially destructive drift.

Critical Thinking

Drift occurs when the required focus on timescales is lost, and motivation is adversely affected. From your knowledge of psychological, sociological and human behaviour theories, what factors might lead to this? How might this affect the worker's ability to manage the identification of and adherence to appropriate timescales?

It is widely considered that the maximum period for task-centred work should not exceed 3 months. Such a timescale not only promotes focused engagement but also reduces the opportunity for dependency-based attachment to form. Within these agreed timescales, agreement should be reached on the frequency and number of planned sessions that will take place between the service user and the practitioner. In practice, the number of contact sessions would usually be in the region of six to twelve sessions, with the latter being considered the maximum viable number.

In order to support the process, the development of a simple but explicit contract should be seen as an essential consideration. Many writers and practitioners advocate the use of a written contract (Doel and Marsh, 1992) and, in practice, this has proven benefits in terms of clarity and accountability. However the need for written contracts is not universally accepted as some service users may find the concept to be overly authoritarian. The term 'contract' may be perceived as being associated with complexity and legal orientation, and in discussing a contract with service users, practitioners must be aware of the potentially negative connotations that this may stimulate.

Over the past few years, influences from the commercial world have become increasingly evident within social work practice. While not all of these influences are to be celebrated, one of the more purposeful and positive developments has seen the use of the acronym SMART in goal planning. SMART stands for: specific, measurable, achievable, realistic and time-bound. Applying these terms to the creation and management of goals is a useful mechanism and neatly aligns with the key principles of the task-centred practice.

While mandatory, legal or statutory features may have to be included in the contract, practitioners must at all times be aware of the potentially detrimental impact that this can have upon the power balance between service user and practitioner, the sense of ownership felt by the service user and corresponding motivation levels.

Social work is unfortunately rife with professional language, including the often obsessive use of acronyms which can reinforce the unequal distribution of power between practitioner and service user. Therefore the use of language appropriate to both the unique needs and level of understanding of the service user becomes crucially important. The contract must be accessible and not over-complicated with jargon and complex language, and must reflect the role of the service user at the centre of the process. It should record agreement, clarifying roles, tasks and timescales, make clear what is going to be done, who is going to do it and when the task should be completed by. Levels of expected commitment and engagement should be included, as should opportunities for structured progress review. In order to further promote partnership working, the service user should be provided with a copy of the completed contract – something that is often forgotten in practice.

Stage 3: Agreeing Required Tasks

This stage should be considered as the central element of the task-centred model. Following the identification of the first problem to be addressed, the focus now moves to the service user and the practitioner identifying, negotiating and agreeing the tasks that should be completed in order to address the defined problem and work towards achievement of the agreed goal. In this context, tasks are primarily concerned with planned actions and behaviours that are directly targeted at problem solving (Stepney and Ford, 2000). Whatever their size or scale, they must always be relevant to the problem-solving process.

Tasks are crucial because through their completion the problems are addressed and goals incrementally achieved. However, practitioners must avoid adopting a narrow understanding of the role and purpose of tasks. Coulshed and Orme (2006) argue that practitioners must avoid seeing tasks merely as activities and instead should consider their actual meaning within the wider context in which they are operating. Tasks should therefore be seen as part of the process of change; they are not the process itself.

The practitioner must be particularly attuned with the process during this stage as the identification of appropriate tasks is absolutely crucial in enabling the service user to build confidence, independence and a sense of competence. The tasks must be purposeful, achievable and outcome-focused. When negotiating the tasks, the practitioner should ensure that the identified tasks include elements of both decision making and self-direction. In practice, imagination, creativity and motivation are required during the process of generating problem-solving ideas.

While the key premise of task-centred practice is to empower the service user through their completion of tasks themselves, it is also important to highlight that there are situations in which it is appropriate for the practitioner to use his or her power to advocate on behalf of the service user to address certain problems, for example, by involving other persons or other agencies.

Case Study

Helping someone tackle problems of isolation, you might both agree that the person should find out about groups or clubs in the area and decide which to visit. While these may seem small tasks, they may still be too broad. You might need to help identify where such information can be found, agree with the person who will find out and discuss whether you will or will not accompany them on visits.

Stage 4: Carrying out and Achieving the Tasks

In many ways this stage is self-evident but this does not reduce its importance. Effective progression from the concept of a problem to that of a goal is managed through the completion of tasks that are as diverse and varied as the problems and the service users that generate them. In this respect the achievement of tasks can simply be seen as the building blocks of change (Davies, 2008). As with other stages, the basis for achievement lies in open and effective communication and negotiation between service user and practitioner (Coulshed and Orme, 2006).

Doel (1994) argues the core premise behind task completion is to build confidence and self-esteem by providing people with opportunities to succeed. The completion of tasks enables small but potentially meaningful and lasting change in the life of the service user (Healy, 2005). It can be further argued that people are more likely to achieve these successes if they are working towards something they have chosen to do (Trotter, 2007), and this has direct relevance for the preceding stages.

This stage of the task-centred model requires regular and planned review sessions. This reflects the dynamic and evolutionary nature of people's lives and the factors that impact upon them. The purpose of these review sessions is twofold; firstly they must consider and evaluate progress towards achieving the set task and secondly they should enable the negotiation and creation of changes in problem targets. This must be a constant process to ensure that the tasks being implemented are those that continue to marry with the problem needs of the service user. Also during these sessions the practitioner should ensure that the service user is aware of the time remaining from the agreed timescales. If further time is required to enable achievement of the intended outcomes, this should be agreed through mutual discussion and negotiation.

While the rather simplistic title of this stage suggests an unbroken continuum of success, in practice the reality of direct work with people is less consistent and concrete. If a task is not achieved for any reason, the practitioner must recognise the potential for the service user to see this as failure. Such feelings could potentially magnify a service user's sense of stress, disempowerment and isolation. In such situations, the practitioner must maintain an empathetic and motivational presence.

Exercise

Task-centred practice may appear on first sight to be an effective and expedient method of intervention, but what might be the limitations of this model? Reflect on other chapters in this book that have focused on issues such as social inequality and material circumstances – how may those issues adversely affect the effectiveness of task-centred practice?

Stage 5: Ending the Work and Evaluation

The final stage is one where the process is ended in a planned and managed manner.

Although perhaps contradictory, it is nevertheless important: an ending must always start at the beginning. At the point of initial contact with a service user, the practitioner must clearly explain and ensure service user understanding of the time-limited nature of task-centred practice. This honesty and openness sets clear boundaries and reduces the likelihood of the service user developing either a dependency on professional involvement (Coulshed and Orme, 2012) or the corrosive feature of learned helplessness (Seligman, 1975).

A defined ending session should take place in order that the service user is provided with absolute clarity that the process and any associated contact have ended. If there is an identified need for future contact between practitioner and service user then the focus of this must be negotiated, planned and distinguished from the completed task-centred work.

The primary focus of the ending stage of task-centred work is the provision of structured opportunities for review, evaluation and reflection. If objectives have been achieved then the practitioner should explicitly emphasise and reinforce the positive contribution made by the service user during the process. Reflection on successes, accomplishments and achievements is the dominant theme. The practitioner should also highlight any strategies or techniques utilised by the service user during the process. For the service user this reinforces what worked and therefore what could be used again in the future. This is simply practical adaptation of the evidence-based mantra.

Social work practitioners must be attuned to the significance and importance of their role and associated actions with each unique service user. For many service users the ending of a period of contact with social work is one that involves elements of loss and therefore an understanding of associated theories is important.

As with the other stages, case recording is important when the point of termination is reached to ensure that outcomes and impacts are recorded in a manner that completes a chronological account of the process and any change achieved. In simple terms this should record what was done, why it was done and what the end result was. Good practice would see such information being presented to the service user in an accessible and understandable format.

Finally, the practitioner should also consider his or her own role and efforts in the process. Learning from these experiences is a key element in developing the critically reflective practitioner and in stimulating continuing professional development.

Now you have read about the five stages of task-centred work go to the Companion Website (www.sagepub.co.uk/SocialWork) where you will find a case study activity about Linda who has approached a duty worker at the social work office.

CONCLUSION

On paper, task-centred work appears very straightforward, but, in practice, it is as challenging as any other intervention. The need to work in absolute partnership is at the core of this model, and that is often easier to speak about than carry out in practice. Supervision and associated opportunities for managed debriefing sessions are vital elements in supporting practitioners to engage in the process of reflective consideration and analysis.

Reflective Questions

1   We have explored various aspects of task-centred practice in this chapter. From what you have read: firstly, define what is meant by task-centred practice; secondly, consider why it is useful to be aware of this approach in working with service users.
2   As with all the various interventions discussed in this section of the book, no tick-list exists where situation X requires intervention Y. However, and after careful examination of a service user's case, which situations do you think may benefit from this form of intervention?
3   We have described above how the ending stage of task-centred practice must start at the beginning. Does this present any challenges for you when thinking about application in practice? Do you think this stance strengthens or weakens the therapeutic relationship?

RECOMMENDED READING

Coulshed, V. and Orme, J. (2012) *Social Work Practice*, 5th edn. Basingstoke: Palgrave Macmillan.

Lindsay, T. (ed.) (2013) *Social Work Intervention*, 2nd edn. London: Learning Matters/ Sage

Marsh, P. and Doel, M. (2005) *The Task-Centred Book*. Abingdon: Routledge.

Payne, M. (2005) *Modern Social Work Theory*, 3rd edn. Basingstoke: Palgrave Macmillan.

20 WORKING IN THE LIFE SPACE

Jeremy Millar

Key Themes
• The concept of life space refers to understanding the totality of people's relationships in the context of a particular setting.
• The setting may be any day or residential context where people come together.
• It draws upon a range of psychological theories such as psychodynamic, field theory and relational theories of interaction.
• The life space approach emphasises the important role of setting in people's lives, as setting is not just a place that simply contains what people do but actively informs and influences what takes place.
• Developing a therapeutic relationship is essential in order to realise any change for the service user.

INTRODUCTION

Bob walked up the drive to Hope House. Rhododendrons are in bloom; a soft spring rain falls on warm tarmac and steam rises. The late shift beckons, his third in a row. Bob wonders if Carly is still upset with Declan and did Sammy return last night, these absences are worrying. At least Bob is on with Sunita, a calming influence indeed and a good balance to his flights of fancy. She'll be cooking tonight, another bonus. Drat, Bob forgot the fresh coriander from the pot on the windowsill at home. Oh well, a trip to the shop will be a good opportunity to take Jo out and catch up. It's been a while since their last key work session. Bob did remember the Public Enemy CD for Fran, Bob would, being 'Mr Music Man'.

Nearly there now. Sammy's curtains are drawn; back and still in bed? Jo's bike propped against the wall; no bike lock, again! The Small Faces' 'Lazy Sunday Afternoon' drifts from the open door. How apt, thinks Bob, as he steps into the life space, ready for everything.

The above passage introduces a series of 'snapshots' from a residential childcare setting that will serve to illustrate working in the **life space** throughout this chapter. Whilst the focus of this narrative and analysis is around children and young people and adults who share the life space it is important to note that the life space concept applies to *all* group care settings and all groups of service users and those that provide for their care.

The wider relevance of this approach to other groups is developed in an activity on the Companion Website (www.sagepub.co.uk/SocialWork). After reading this chapter visit the Website to undertake the activity.

This chapter explores working in the 'life space', one of the many terms used in social work and social care that is in certain respects hard to pin down. Many social workers and other care staff have worked for many years in a variety of social care settings with no awareness of the concept of 'life space' and function quite capably enough, providing a good service and ensuring that no intentional harm comes to anyone with whom they work. As Ward and McMahon (1998) state, however, working intuitively is never enough, and a firm grasp of the theory behind actions is necessary to create the best possible interaction between social worker and client.

So, if reasonably competent and confident workers can get by without knowing about the life space, why bother? The answer to this question can be found in that without an understanding of the life space, social workers cannot tap into and exploit what Garfat (2003) refers to as the 'magic' that exists in group care settings. This 'magic' is contained in the talents and untapped potential of *all* the people who live and work in the group care setting. It offers the prospect of the hope of desired futures being realised, lays to rest the ghosts of past trauma, reconciles loss and heals broken trust, it contains pain in the moment and helps individuals rewrite their personal narrative. You can read more about Garfat's work by following the link on the Companion Website (www.sagepub.co.uk/SocialWork).

The chapter begins by exploring what the concept of life space seeks to understand. The roots of life space theory are explored next, examining the ideas of thinkers such as Freud and Lewin, before turning attention to the centrality of psychodynamic approaches, especially that of the role of the ego.

THE LIFE SPACE APPROACH

The life space approach offers a therapeutic intervention in people's lives that acknowledges prior loss, builds on individual strengths with the goal of restoring **ego integrity** and prepares the individual to go forward in life better equipped for future adversity. Central to all change is the therapeutic relationship. Keenan (2007) likens the life space to a jelly. When you prod any surface of the jelly it wobbles all over. This useful visual image succinctly illustrates just how inter-related and interdependent all the individuals are in any group care setting. The life space is therefore a method of perceiving, reflecting on and understanding the dynamic nature of the interpersonal relationships of all who participate or live in a *particular setting*.

The focus of setting is the 'space' element in the name life space, referring not to emptiness or a void, but the space in which someone lives. Understanding setting or space is important because all people exist within a context that enables, or constrains, and conditions their actions and affects their self-esteem. The power that setting or space can exert over people was identified by Goffman (Keenan, 2007), in his research on the power of 'total institutions'. 'Total' refers to institutions where all aspects of daily life, for example, sleeping, eating, bathing and socialising, take place within one institution. The main problem associated with total institutions is that, because the needs of the institution are prioritized over those of the residents, they completely overwhelm and reorder the personality and identity of residents. The end result can be that the residents become 'institutionalised' and dependent upon the institution, not just for their basic needs, but also their sense of self.

The situation just outlined could be described as the extreme end of how setting or space can influence someone, but all settings do that to some degree or other, because they require people to act in certain ways and to conform to particular norms and rules. Space therefore should not simply be understood as the location or container in which various activities occur, but rather as an active presence in people's lives that informs and shapes what those activities are and how they take place.

Exercise

Think of how differently people may behave in a pub in contrast to being in a church. There are obviously different ways to behave in each setting but are there certain attributes of each setting that prompt that behaviour?

In certain respects the life space approach can be described as a 'magpie' approach, where it draws on other theories and perspectives in order to build its overall understanding of how people's lives can be improved. The main traditions that the life space approach is built on are psychodynamic and relational theories of interaction, and these are discussed in greater detail elsewhere in this book, including Chapters 6 and 7. What those other approaches all share is a concern with how various forces and processes affect an individual's sense of self and their current well-being. Some of these forces and processes are internal, as is clear in psychodynamic theory with its Freudian emphasis on the conflicts between conscious and unconscious motivations, but given the centrality of space in the life space approach there is also an appreciation that processes external to a person play a crucial role in self-development and sense of self. It is this fusion of theories incorporating both internal and external influences on the self that allows the life space approach to be holistic and take account of all the various dimensions of an individual.

At the heart of the life space approach lies the therapeutic relationship. Here are some basic statements to bear in mind before the practice of working in the life space is more fully explored in the rest of this chapter.

- The term 'life space' offers a conceptual understanding of the totality of interaction and interdependency within the group care setting. It includes an awareness of the importance of the environment on actions and feelings as well the setting's place within the wider community.
- The life space exists even if we do not name it or acknowledge it as such.
- Within the life space workers regularly undertake specific interventions, known as life space interviews.

- The principles of the life space interview (Redl, 1966; Sharpe, 2009) have been packaged into a range of crisis de-escalation and management tools that constantly evolve and use names such as Therapeutic Crisis Intervention (TCI), Crisis, Aggression, Limitation and Management (CALM), Strategies for Crisis Intervention and Prevention (SCIP)
- 'Opportunity led' as an intervention (Ward, 2002) draws heavily on the concept of the life space.
- The ethos or the philosophy of the group care setting should make reference to an understanding of the life space and how other practice interventions complement and support this approach.
- Working in the life space is about conscious use of self in relationship with all other individuals in the life space.
- Working in the life space involves being a reflective and reflexive worker who consciously engages with the 'what' and 'why' of their actions.
- Working in the life space is as much about the little things in group care such as a smile in the morning, a cup of tea and catch-up after a long day as it is about supporting people through major life crises and critical events.
- Conscious understanding of the life space and using the techniques of the life space interview by workers contribute to the maintenance of a **therapeutic milieu**.

See the article by Emond (2003) on the Companion Website (www.sagepub.co.uk/SocialWork) which reports on research about young people's experiences of living in group care.

THE ROOTS OF LIFE SPACE THEORY: FREUD, LEWIN AND REDL

Aichhorn (1878–1949), a contemporary of Freud, was an educator who was encouraged by Freud's daughter, Anna, to study psychoanalysis. He had a keen interest in delinquent behaviour in children and set up a school to work with these children. In an account of his work in *Wayward Youth* (1951), Aichhorn identified some key aspects of intervention and qualities in workers which are at the root of working in the life space. Amongst these are:

- Delinquency is a failure in normal development.
- Punishment only suppresses overt behaviour; it does nothing to address the causes of the delinquency.
- Most delinquency is a result of relationship difficulties.
- The cause of delinquency is different for every service user.
- The worker needs to understand and start where the service user is emotionally and environmentally situated.
- A worker can never be a 'friend' to a service user. (Children Webmag, 2009)

The importance of relationship as a catalyst in 'therapeutic treatment', the involvement of family, the understanding that behaviour is complex and informed by past experience as well as current challenges, were particularly noted. Punishment was not a useful intervention, and the leadership of the group was seen as vital to producing positive outcomes. Coming from an understanding of psychodynamic theory, the therapeutic milieu approach was based on the growth of the child being facilitated through unconditional love and acceptance in their relationships with the adults caring for them.

Redl, building on his experience working with Aichhorn and Lewin (1890–1947), established his own residential project called Pioneer House in Detroit through which he developed his practice in the treatment of troubled and troublesome children. The following quote encapsulates the philosophy behind the work at Pioneer House:

> The surest way of finding out things about children who are hard to know is to live with them. With the children we talk about, this invariably means to live with them in a group setting. And, because of another one of their main characteristics, it also means to live with them in an 'action' rather than a mere 'discussion' style of relationship. (Redl and Wineman, 1957: 30)

The concept of living in 'action' refers to a reciprocal relationship between the child and the adult, not one in which adults control and constrain the child: in the life space it offers a dynamic experience for both the adult and the child.

The influence of Lewin, a social psychologist with no foundation in the psychodynamic approach, is apparent in the above quotation as he is credited with naming the 'life space' as part of the development of his field theory. He looked at how individuals acted in the environment, and field theory is defined as 'the totality of coexisting facts which are conceived of as mutually interdependent' (Lewin, 1951: 240). This is where Keenan's jelly analogy helps illuminate Lewin's complex description. Redl effectively brought together the external understanding of behaviour as a response to the 'field' and the internal workings of the ego influencing behaviour in the moment.

In the 1960s, Trieschman and colleagues published their seminal book on working in the life space, *The Other 23 Hours: Child-care Work with Emotionally Disturbed Children in a Therapeutic Milieu* (1969). The authors of *The Other 23 Hours* were all practising residential childcare workers and the book describes the therapeutic milieu and the opportunities for workers to influence, intervene and shape the lives of the children in their care. The title of the book relates to the 23 hours of the day when the child is in the care of residential staff rather than in a counselling one-to-one session with a therapist. The authors illustrate how the daily life events of living in the life space – waking up, mealtimes; activities etc. – can be utilised therapeutically.

THE LIFE SPACE IN PRACTICE

These core texts about the life space were developed around group living with troubled and troublesome children and young people, and rely heavily on the concept of ego psychology, an approach that understands behaviour in terms of the healthy or disturbed functioning of the ego: 'The ego is the central functioning part of the personality which is conscious, aware and determines our day to day activities and relationships in a rational reality based way' (Gibson, 2007: 74). Psychodynamic concepts are discussed in more depth elsewhere in this book and it is recommended that you read Chapter 25 on counselling in conjunction with this chapter. In the context of therapeutic milieu practice, the use of therapists has been utilised as much to support the staff team to understand the behaviour of the residents as for one-to-one counselling sessions with residents.

Service users in group care settings have generally experienced loss, often compounded by other difficulties in their lives. For older people these may be a deterioration in health and cognitive functioning. Adults with learning difficulties may have encountered a range of adversity, including discrimination, over-protective environments and not having their voice heard on matters affecting their life. Children and young people in care settings have often suffered a range of abusive and neglectful behaviours prior to entering the care setting. This list is far from exhaustive but illustrates the need for the work undertaken in the milieu to be therapeutic in terms of being responsive to individual need and offering personal growth and healing.

For a discussion of older people and environment, see Bond et al. (2007)

Our understanding of the role of the ego in supporting an individual to make sense of, interact with and have their needs met in the real world was developed by Freud (1946) and Erikson (1950). Winnicott (1965) increased understanding of the parental role in nurturing ego development with his concept of the 'holding environment' in which the parent/carer 'holds' the extreme emotional arousal of the child and hands it back in a more manageable form by consistent calming and predictable presence. This is central to the use of the life space interview. If ego development has been disrupted by adverse life events and especially an absence of nurturing during the formative years (Ainsworth and Bowlby, 1965) we can expect this developmental weakness to be played out in a range of behaviours that cause society concern and often lead to the individual needing specialist forms of care and support. Redl and Wineman (1957) identify from their work in Pioneer House 22 aspects of ego function that are disrupted or compromised to some degree in the children they were working with. Here is a pen picture of a child lacking ego integrity.

Case Study: Jay– the angry child

Jay is a mini cyclone liable to blow up for no apparent reason, is generally distrustful of all adults and, when faced with an adult imposing authority, will have no hesitation in striking out both verbally and physically. Jay appears to lack empathy, will become involved in quite sadistic bullying behaviour and struggles to look after and respect his and others' property. Quite often he will destroy belongings that appear to mean a lot to him. Education and other structured activities present a tremendous challenge to Jay. His learning is undermined by a low tolerance threshold coupled with a fatalistic lack of belief in his own ability to master tasks. He invariably sabotages an activity that frustrates him and seldom completes anything, finding both praise and criticism hard to accept.

(Continued)

(Continued)

Leave anything lying around, and Jay will take it, fiddle with it and possibly break it. He will deny responsibility for any action, even in the face of concrete evidence. He has not internalised guilt feelings and responds to adult concerns over his behaviour with apparent indifference and disdain.

Put Jay in a group situation and his anxiety level will soar. He will express this through egging on others to disrupt and oppose the adults who are supervising. He will run from the situation if it all gets too much and may take others with him. There will be constant power struggles over apparently trivial issues, and any attempt to buy compliance with the promise of a reward later for good behaviour will be doomed, as will any appeal to group solidarity and his role in letting down of the rest of the group. Possibly the most frustrating aspect of Jay's behaviour is an apparent inability to learn from past experience or to draw causal links between actions and consequences.

Redl and Wineman offer a further case example from the work they undertook at Pioneer House:

One day the boys were quite excited about an incident that happened to one of the kids in their class. He had been skating in the street and was hit by a car, suffering concussion and broken ribs …. It was thus quite surprising to us when both Andy and Bill, in defiance of the rules, started to skate in heavy traffic in front of the Home just before dinner. (1957: 129)

Despite the staff pointing out the consequences of this action for the injured boy, Andy and Bill could make no link to the inherent risk to them and accused the staff of acting unreasonably to curtail their fun. To an uninformed observer this form of behaviour is bizarre in the extreme. Any adult attempting to appeal to the child's innate sense of right and wrong, personal accountability for behaviour or conscience over doing wrong, will be totally perplexed and may possibly react in a way that that would escalate an already difficult situation.

The preceding examples give a glimpse into the mindset of a child who is lacking ego integrity. It is an unsettling place to be as it is a world of impulse, irrationality, self-destructive acts and a complete absence of internalised controls. Trieschman et al. (1969) examine how the therapeutic milieu can be utilised to develop ego strength and ultimately the desired controls from within.

THE IMPORTANCE OF RELATIONSHIP

A fundamental part of this therapeutic process is the relationship between the workers and the children in their care. It is in this relationship that the workers' insight into and understanding of the roots of extreme behaviour begins to address both the nurturing facet of ego development expressed by unconditional positive regard (Rogers, 1961), or love as we commonly experience it, and the cognitive building of the inter-personal skills that allow the child to respond to and interact appropriately with their environment. Child development with ego growth 'needs to develop an array of behaviour (feelings, ideas) that can deal with the environment in such a way as to satisfy impulses *and* develop a sense of competence about dealing with people, things and events' (Trieschman et al., 1969: 19). Lewin (1948), examining relationships in groups and the resolution of conflict, identifies the key role of leadership to effect change through the promotion of desirable outcomes and management of negative influences. This is in essence the nature of the therapeutic relationship described by Trieschman et al. (1969).

It might be useful at this point to investigate some of the reasons for children arriving at our door with such a level of damage to their ego development.

ATTACHMENT AND BRAIN DEVELOPMENT

Media reporting concerning feral children, immoral and uncontrollable, threatening the way of life of decent citizens, can make it tempting to attribute blame to poor or absent parenting, exposure to violent games, deprivation or flaws in the education system. Some of these factors do play a role in disadvantaging many of the children in the care system, but the essential message to learn about the life experiences of the children in our care is that of the severity of the impact on their ego development of the almost total absence of any continuity of nurturing care in their lives, particularly in their early years. Often this is compounded by exposure to traumatic events (domestic violence, sexual abuse) creating living conditions of continual stress. Redl and Wineman and those who have developed working in the life space and utilising the therapeutic milieu were aware of the work of Bowlby (1953) on attachment and this impacted on their understanding of behaviour. However, the connections that have subsequently been made to the adverse impact on brain development of trauma in infancy were yet to be established (Brown et al., 1998; Hughes, 2006; Perry, 2002). It is in this area of understanding the extent of damage to brain growth through neglect and trauma that we start to make sense of anti-social, destructive behaviour at a deeper level. The therapeutic power of the group setting, in conjunction with skilled workers, offers the best hope of building and repairing the ego damage behind the most challenging of behaviours. Ward and McMahon sum up this position with the statement:

> The capacity for intuition, however, is not enough on its own. If people are going to develop and use their capacity for intuition they will need to be working within a 'facilitating environment' (Winnicott's phrase again) of organizational support.' (1998: 33)

Case Study

Carly's eyes betrayed such despair. They looked through Bob, from the door of her room, as he attempted to encourage her to come through and enjoy some pancakes. The previous shift had seen Carly bring in a DVD of a martial arts film that Declan had talked about, only to have him throw it back at her and leave the house to see his mates down town. Carly, left on her own, took to her room and picked at her arms with a razor producing lots of blood across her already scarred skin. Her world is remote, robbed of

(Continued)

(Continued)

a childhood through extreme abuse at the hands of a chaotic drug-using mother who prostituted both herself and Carly for drugs. Drugs in turn became a way out for Carly and at only 14 she is barely literate, having missed significant amounts of schooling. Her mother and extended family have rejected her, and she has no one she can call a friend. During two periods with foster carers from the age of 9 her behaviours became progressively more extreme, with violence towards others and herself almost a daily occurrence. Six months into her stay at Hope House there are glimmers of progress as trust builds and she comes to understand that the staff will not give up on her.

Bob offers a list of tasty toppings for the pancakes leaving her favourite, blueberry jelly, till last. Grimace after grimace lightens into a flicker of interest. Bob walks off down the corridor, job done for now.

The above case study has illustrated a life space intervention. Knowledge of Carly's traumatic upbringing and awareness of the potential damage to her brain development and subsequent ego integrity through the abusive and neglectful life experiences demanded a nurturing approach, building on meeting primary needs (nice food) in an accepting and non-pressurised manner. The relationship is key to engaging with young people such as Carly. Maier (1979a), in his 'core of care', offers a wonderfully clear analysis of the key components that facilitate working in the life space, and Ainsworth and Fulcher (1981) offer more contextual material. In trying to produce changes to behaviour, workers are often drawn into a behavioural control and modification model of interacting with children and young people. Whilst life space practitioners would not rule out any considered intervention, and it may be appropriate to utilise star charts and reward-based plans with some children, these would only work in conjunction with loving and nurturing relationships. In the case of work with extremely traumatised adolescents such as Carly, the goal is for her to manage her emotional state by developing controls from within. Carly's presenting behaviour is an articulation of deep psychological pain and confusion. She struggles to read social situations and consistently repeats negative experiences. For someone with Carly's life experiences sanctions such as 'grounding', withholding allowance money and stopping access to 'treats', are insignificant, merely serving to reinforce her perception of adults as hostile and untrustworthy. In the interaction with Carly, a social worker would also need to be aware of their own emotional response to the extremes of Carly's behaviour and their own personal history of dealing with painful episodes.

USING OPPORTUNITIES

Case study

Jo breezes into the office where Bob is catching up on his paperwork. 'Hello stranger,' she says with a flirtatious smile. 'I keep missing you, but how about we catch up with a trip to the shop?' he responds. As they walk out Bob points at the bike. 'What's wrong with this picture?' he asks Jo. 'Yeah, yeah, yeah,' she shrugs, 'I'll lock it up later.' Jo will take a degree of criticism but how it is presented is important. The direct instruction is not the best approach so they have developed their own shared code for addressing areas of possible conflict. Much of Jo's behaviour is of the completely age appropriate adolescent type of testing authority but she struggles with boundaries around relationships with older males, including those on the staff team. Bob reflects on his own relationship with his own adolescent daughters. He has to be careful that he doesn't confuse how he responds to Jo with his approach towards his own girls. Jo didn't ever know her dad and her mother entered a relationship with a 21-year-old when Jo was 12. Jo's mother has had a child with this new partner.

The walk to the shop is a chance to catch up with Jo. This goes well; Jo is doing well in school and enjoying her part-time job. Discussion about her mother is a no-go area. As they talk Bob senses a tension creeping up on him. What is this about? The as yet unspoken question about Jo's plans for her imminent 16th birthday that he feels he should ask. 'I wish you were my dad,' Jo says out of the blue. What an opportunity!

Think quickly: how is Bob going to work with this opening into Jo's inner world?

In the short walk to the shop several important themes emerge: loss and grieving for an absent father, anger at an emotionally unavailable and neglectful mother, connection with an idealised father figure, emerging sexual awareness and seductive power. To maximise support for Jo, Bob does not simply make a gut reaction, but needs to understand Jo's loss (perhaps in the context of his own relationship with his daughters), to 'hold' much of the anger in relation to her mother, and also to respond to her desire to have him as a father. Understanding processes of transference and counter-transference are relevant in this exchange.

The apparent complexity of this task can be understood by reference to 'opportunity led' work that draws upon the life space interview approach and this approach is illustrated below by further reference to the case study with Jo.

Ward (2002) identifies the critical importance of responding rather than reacting in the moment. This form of positive reaction requires the worker to be at all times consciously processing information and feelings in both themselves and those they are relating to. In the exchange with Jo, if Bob had reacted to Jo's desire for him to be her dad by saying, 'That's silly, Jo, you know I can't be your dad,' it is likely that he would have pushed her away and blocked future chances to explore Jo's need to find answers in respect of her father. Trust could be easily broken by a hasty reactive response. By responding with a considered reply he is able to make the most of a therapeutic opportunity. Preparation is everything when working in the life space.

As he was coming on shift, Bob was thinking of Jo, their relationship, issues that he needed to discuss and he consciously structured the opportunity to talk with her about them. The walk to the shop was the opportunity. As they walked they entered the first element of Ward's model, *Observation and Assessment*. Bob was observing Jo's mood as he addressed the unlocked bike. How she reacted would inform how he might bring up the other areas for discussion. Bob was also conscious of his own anxiety around the major unspoken issue of Jo's 16th birthday. Jo then makes her profound statement and in that moment he is scrambling to make sense of the situation and not destroy the opportunity by reacting thoughtlessly. Here the second element of an opportunity-led intervention can be introduced into the interaction: *Assessing the Context* concerns an awareness of the wider context, such as the emotional climate (Ward, 2002). In part, the imminent birthday celebration is creating anxiety; relationships both present and absent, including Jo's absent father, the views of her peers in the home and her friendship groups are also significant. Links here can also be made to the developmental stage of 'identity versus role confusion' (Erikson, 1950).

In the moment, Bob takes all these factors into consideration as he formulates a decision on how to respond. It is important to pay attention, to respond in a manner that addresses the most *urgent* aspect first. Threats to the safety of the person or others would be a priority. While not an issue in the walk with Jo, it is always worth thinking about who else is present or whether any mood altering substances have been consumed. Bob must also be conscious of what is feasible, does the moment lend itself to action, will there be time to explore and conclude a discussion? It is crucial to consider timing in relation to how long you still have on shift. It would be disrespectful to leave Jo anxious about the discussion of birthday plans only half an hour before going off home. This walk and talk takes place early in a 24-hour shift, leaving plenty of time and space to follow things up with Jo. Finally there are ethical considerations; is the conversation confidential, out of others' earshot? Is the approach congruent with core social work values and are there any legal considerations? For Jo in this situation the strength of relationship combined with the privacy element makes it an ideal opportunity for the final stage that is action.

It is clear that Jo's anxiety needs to be addressed concerning her up and coming birthday. The discussion fits with the goals in Jo's care plan and the time to do it is the present.

Case Study

'Wow, Jo, you certainly know how to catch my attention!', Bob responds, 'I'm guessing you're pretty anxious about stuff at the moment, I'm listening and we've got plenty of time. Sunny's got things covered back at the house.' Jo starts to talk about her fears about her birthday, that her mother won't show up and that she comes second to the new baby; she is confused that her mother has said she will tell her about her dad when she's older and she fears that might be now. Jo looks straight ahead as they walk slowly. Bob lets her talk, offering little input as Jo works a lot of her feelings through. Something tells Bob that Jo has many of the answers and it is not the time to jump in with suggestions. As they approach the shop Jo has reached a natural pause and Bob makes eye contact and offers a warm smile that acknowledges the strength she displayed in pouring all her feelings out. Bob tells her that this is one of her best qualities. They agree to firm up a plan of action on the walk back to Hope House and Bob tells her that he is flattered she would like him for a dad.

The nature of this exchange with Jo contained the final stages of Ward's (2002) opportunity-led intervention. Bob acknowledged the gravity of what Jo was communicating and offered space for her to control the content, time and direction of her concerns and fears. Bob was prepared and able to 'hold' (Winnicott, 1965) and 'contain' (Bion, 1962) the emotional content of what Jo was sharing. Bob acknowledged that Jo had set him up for this role with her attention-grabbing statement. It was an explicit expression of trust and an unconscious plea for emotional stability. In responding to Jo, he offered both immediate reassurance and a longer-term promise of using the relationship to negotiate the upcoming birthday and potentially tension-filled family contact. Jo's honesty regarding her struggle with her sense of identity signposted the requirement for family work and the exploration of an absent father/daughter relationship. On their return to Hope House the door closed metaphorically on the 'opportunity-led' intervention. However, the work in the life space continues and the workers move between all the ongoing threads of the entwined relationships.

Ross et al. (2009) undertook research on the use of mobile methods – guided walks and car journey interactions – in work with looked after young people. Read their findings on the Companion Website (www.sagepub.co.uk/SocialWork).

CONCLUSION

The example offered in this chapter from the life of Hope House illustrates the rich tradition of working in the life space, which offers a cohesive model of work in the therapeutic milieu, a place in which the power of relationships structured around caring, compassionate, committed, insightful, reflective and available adults engenders growth and healing. In this holistic approach workers bring their knowledge of attachment, understanding of the impact of trauma, attention to detail in the environment and consistency of self to bear on the milieu producing the recipe for anger, pain and a sense of abandonment to be redressed and children to be given a sense of mastery – the ability for emotional regulation, controls from within.

Listen to podcast 20.1 on the Companion Website (www.sagepub.co.uk/SocialWork) to hear chapter author Jeremy Miller summarise the main points conveyed in this chapter, and why an understanding of working in the life space is important for social work practice.

Reflective Questions

1   The issue of how people's emotional lives are influenced and shaped by the space (the location, the building, the institution) in which they live has been a key focus of this chapter. Reflect further on the importance of space. Think of different locations that you have experienced and try to identify how they made you feel or act in a way that is different from other spaces.

2   The connection and relationship between service user and social worker is important within this form of intervention. Reflect on how an effective relationship could be established within an institutional setting, such as a residential

(Continued)

(Continued)

care setting, and what challenges and opportunities may be encountered in such a context.

3   The life space approach has mainly focused on residential childcare settings, but what other spaces in a person's life may have been influential in shaping their emotional self? Think about home, school and so forth.

RECOMMENDED READING

Ross, N.J., Renold, E., Holland, S. and Hillman, A. (2009) 'Moving stories: using mobile methods to explore the everyday lives of young people in public care', *Qualitative Research*, 9: 605–23.

Smith, M., Fulcher, L. and Doran, P. (2013) *Residential Child Care in Practice: Making a Difference.* Bristol: Policy Press.

Trieschman, A., Whittaker, J.K. and Brendtro, L.K. (1969) *The Other 23 Hours: Childcare Work with Emotionally Disturbed Children in a Therapeutic Milieu.* New York: Aldine De Gruyter.

Ward, A. (2006) *Working in Group Care: Social Work and Social Care in Residential and Day Care Settings.* Bristol: The Policy Press.

Ward, A. and McMahon, L. (ed.) (1998) *Intuition is Not Enough: Matching Learning with Practice in Therapeutic Child Care.* London: Routledge.

Refer to the Companion Website (www. sagepub.co.uk/SocialWork) for some useful links to web-based material.

21 PERSON-CENTRED PLANNING AND PERSONALISATION

Neil Gibson

Key Themes

- Normalisation is a fundamental principle.
- The social model of disability guides practice.
- The exchange model of assessment should inform practice.
- Workers must be aware of the power dimensions.
- Personalisation is person-centred planning in action.

INTRODUCTION

Person-centred planning (PCP) is a way of working that places the service user at the heart of service provision. Historically, service users have had to accept what they were offered in terms of service provision, but with person-centred planning there has been a shift towards service users planning their own futures, and within that, planning what services they need to achieve goals. As Sanderson et al. (2000: 13) note, 'Person centred planning is a way of helping people who want to make some changes in their life. It is an empowering approach to helping people plan their future and organise the supports and services they need. It seeks to mirror the ways in which "ordinary people" make plans.'

Traditionally, an assessment would be completed and services would be offered based on what was available in the area. Under person-centred planning the service user can define what they want to do based on their hopes, dreams and wishes, but equally they can express what they do not want to do. Within this, multi-agency meetings would be held in environments conducive to the free flow of information from the service user, and would include input from family members and other significant people in the life of the service user.

Person-centred planning looks to embrace a number of basic social work principles which include empowerment, choice, equality, inclusion and independence.

This chapter will look at the development of person-centred planning and how it is applied in practice. Specific tools will also be highlighted for the practitioner to work with.

THE PRINCIPLES OF PCP

There are three main areas underpinning the development of person-centred planning:

1 *Normalisation.* The normalisation movement began in Scandinavia in the late 1960s and was further developed by Wolfensberger in the 1970s (Wolfensberger, 1972). The movement recognised that people with learning disabilities had the right to choose to participate in everyday community life, just as a person without a learning disability has the right. Wolfensberger proposed that, for people with learning disabilities to be 'normalised' into society, they first had to be seen as active participants in that society. As most care in the 1970s was provided in institutions, he recognised that service users needed to take on valued social roles (such as family member, neighbour, employee) so that society could see these service users, and recognise that the differences between themselves and the service users were perhaps not as vastly different as they might have been perceived. Hence, a move away from institutional care, and a move towards care in the community.

2 *Social model of disability.* The social model of disability was 'created' as a response to the dominant medical model of disability, and both models are described in Chapter 13. Equality underpins the ethos of the model, but it would be unhelpful to see the social model of disability as 'better' than the medical model of disability. In reality, both models have their uses. If a service user requires medical treatment then the medical model needs to be utilised, then following treatment, looking at the transition back into society, the social model could be utilised.

3 *Exchange model of assessment.* Smale et al. (1993) propose that there are three different types of assessment within social work: a questioning model, a procedural model and an exchange model. Chapter 12 describes these models in detail.

The exchange model of assessment aligns itself with a person-centred planning approach. The service user has the control in this situation and the social worker must work from an anti-oppressive standpoint. With this approach, flexibility is required. The assessment should not be time-limited and the worker must find a line of questioning where information required by the agency can be obtained, whilst at the same time ensuring that the service user is the expert of the situation.

Person-centred planning has developed considerably since the late 1970s. In the early 1980s the general principles underpinning the approach were disseminated through workshops and the development of new services, and by 1985 the term 'person-centred planning' was common terminology. Policy and legislation in the UK have developed to encompass the principles of service user rights, choice, inclusion and independence, and Acts such as the NHS and Community Care Act (1990), Disability Discrimination Act (1995 (amended 2005)) and the Human Rights Act (1998) impact on everyday social work practice.

PHILOSOPHY – THE FIVE ACCOMPLISHMENTS

Seattle-based researchers John O'Brien and Connie Lyle O'Brien set out to look at indicators that defined a good quality of life. Their 1987 research project identified five key areas which are regarded as important in shaping lives, and have become known as 'The Five Accomplishments' (O'Brien, 1989; O'Brien and O'Brien, 2000). These five accomplishments are now widely regarded as the definitive indicators used to assess service provision in achieving the aims of each of the five criteria.

1. Community Presence/Sharing Ordinary Places

John O'Brien wrote that the world is split into two domains: the domain of community, where the hustle and bustle of everyday life takes place, and the domain of the lived experience of the service user with learning disabilities, usually isolated, empty and lonely. He explained that the gulf between these two domains, which he termed 'the critical boundary', needs to be bridged. He felt that, historically, this critical boundary was filled with services that prohibited interaction with the wider community through institutionalisation, which ultimately segregated service users from society. O'Brien states that this gulf should be bridged, and the way to do this is for the community and the service user to share common spaces, interact in the same environment and live together in the community (O'Brien and Tyne, 1981).

Simply put, O'Brien felt that service users should not be locked away from society. For service providers, this meant adapting support to utilise ordinary settings.

2. Making Choices and Decisions

Everyone should be allowed to choose what they want to do in life. Sometimes the choices we make in life are good, other times they are not so good, but provided we have the capacity to understand our options, actions and consequences, then we have the right to make these choices.

Exercise

Consider what advice you would give your best friend if they decided to live on chocolate for the rest of their life – how would you work with them to advise them of their options and the consequence of their lifestyle choice? Would this differ from the advice you might give a service user who was making this decision?

Having choice and deciding on our actions defines our identity, as well as shaping our future. O'Brien recognised the importance of enabling service users to make informed choices, which involves looking at all the options, but also looking at what would be deemed acceptable in our society. If choices seem detrimental, then information must be given to assist in the decision process.

When service users come into contact with social work services, they are often in need of help and assistance. It is important that they are made to feel in control of their choices and options, rather than disempowered by service providers telling them what to do.

3. Developing and Monitoring Skills/Abilities

In 1997, Nola Ochs graduated from an American university with a BA in History. When she graduated, Nola was 95 years old. Learning is a life-long experience and we can develop new skills throughout our lives – there should be no barrier that prevents us from learning. O'Brien states that everyone should have the opportunity to learn meaningful skills as this will lead to the enhancement of self-efficacy, as well as enhancing the views others hold of us.

Service users should also be given the opportunity to learn in order to develop resources, identify talents and realise gifts (or unique attributes) and capacities. Historically there has been a tendency to discount service user ability because of deteriorating medical and physical conditions, and low-level engagement with set activities at day care centres, but service providers should work with individual service users to develop existing skills, and identify new areas of interests.

4. Being Treated with Respect and Dignity/Having a Valued Social Role

A valued social role will be different things for different people. Some may feel that being a good sibling is a valuable role, whereas others might feel that being in employment is a valuable role. In some ways, society defines our perceptions of valued social roles, but we can choose what we wish to pursue.

Service users should have the right to pursue a social role, and be treated with respect and dignity at the same time.

5. Participation/Developing and Maintaining Relationships

Finally, O'Brien stresses the value of relationships. Relationships bring a sense of belonging, and belonging results in inclusion. We should all be able to decide who we want to form relationships with, and not be forced into relationships. This is important when working in residential services: are service users grouped together because they are perceived to be 'alike', and if so, is there then an assumption that they should form relationships because of their similarities?

Relationships also provide support networks, and we all get different things from different relationships – love, friendship, laughter, intellectual stimulation. We need to consider our own relationships, and our own interactions, with the people we choose to have relationships with, as our positive interaction with others may not be different from the relationships our service users have, or need, with the people they choose to form relationships with.

Exercise

Write down the names of three people you know. Next to each name, write a sentence which summarises your relationship with each person. How do they differ?

These five accomplishments are all interrelated. We define our personality and individuality through what we bring to situations, and how we interact with others. Our dreams and ambitions drive our motivation, and these in turn are influenced by our abilities, capacities and gifts. Person-centred planning recognises the individuality of a service user and every plan developed should be unique to the service user, therefore, no two plans should ever be the same.

PERSON-CENTRED PLANNING IN ACTION – THEMES, PRINCIPLES AND APPROACHES

Having examined the philosophy and common themes underpinning person-centred planning, it is equally as important to understand how the process works in practice. A practitioner embarking on using person-centred planning should be clear that the process intends to assist a service user to define who they are, who their support structure is and what the support structure can do for them to assist them in achieving outcomes that they want from their lives.

Case Study

Molly, with **Down syndrome**, is 23, living at home with her family. She regularly attends Willow Day Care Centre, has a number of friends there and has formed a relationship with Tim, a 27-year-old service user. Her parents wish to become involved in self-directed support payments, where they are given a budget and are able to purchase elements of Molly's care for her.

Molly's social worker makes a home visit to the family. Molly says she enjoys the day centre, sometimes feels bored there, and sometimes feels trapped at home. The social worker asks Molly if there is anything else she would like to do with her spare time, but Molly is not sure. The social worker suggests that by using person-centred

(Continued)

(Continued)

planning they could convene a meeting and start to look at options for Molly. Molly is a bit confused by this, so the social worker explains that she and Molly should sit down together, make a list of people who are involved in helping Molly, and then decide who Molly would like to invite to a meeting to make plans to help her feel less bored during the day, and to look at ways she could feel less trapped at home. Molly agrees that it would be a good idea to do this.

The list of names is drawn up and Molly is happy to invite her family, two friends from the day centre, staff from the day centre, her GP and the social worker. Molly is then asked how she would like to have the meeting. Through discussion, they decide it would be good to have the meeting at her parents' house in the big conservatory which overlooks the garden, which Molly states will look really beautiful at this time of year. Molly also decides that everyone invited should bring some food so that they can have a buffet whilst they have the meeting. Molly is then asked when she would like to have the meeting and she decides that, since she does not go to Willow Day Care Centre on Wednesdays, then this would be a good day to have the meeting.

Power

Power is an important consideration throughout the process. As the intention is to empower the service user, the practitioner needs to recognise this from the outset and ensure that everything they do is in collaboration with the service user, the support structures, such as family and friends, and fellow professionals. The key concept must always be that the service user is at the centre of the process, but practitioners need to recognise that this will include an element of power sharing in the planning process so that the outcome of a better life for the service user can be achieved.

To ensure power is shared with the service user in the initial planning process, aims should be defined by the service user: What is the end goal? What does the service user wish to plan? Who would they like to be involved in the planning process? Do they require a meeting? And if so, where would they like to meet? For the practitioner, it is important to explain all of the options so that the element of choice is truly available.

Friends and Family

The involvement of family and friends is an important consideration. Because person-centred planning aims to utilise community and society with an aim to normalise, the service user must be seen in the context of their own 'community'. Power needs to be shared amongst these participants and this potentially presents problems for the practitioner in the empowerment process. Family and friends will have important contributions to give in the process – often these are the people that know the service user best – but this information should be obtained in collaboration with the service user, ensuring they have some control over who gives input in the process.

Historically, families may have felt sidelined by professionals involved in the service user's care. Families can often be labelled as 'over-protective' and it is important that relationships in the person-centred planning process work against these historic perceptions to foster an environment where the free flow of information can be given, and the information should be listened to carefully to see if it can provide indicators for change.

Building the Plan

The plan should build upon three key areas: what is important to the service user, what they would like to see happen in their lives, and what support they need to work towards set goals. There are a number of tools listed further in this chapter, but the general flow of plan construction is generally the same across all of the tools.

The practitioner (or facilitator) needs to draw out the service user's abilities, as opposed to focusing on their disabilities. This can be a challenge to begin with as service users have historically been categorised by their disability, impairment and deficits, and then goals would be set to overcome these issues. Person-centred planning assumes everyone has skills, abilities and gifts, which should shape the direction of the plan. Support structures then need to be defined, but more importantly, the main aim here is to ensure that everyone involved in the plan is working to the same outcome, with the best interest of the service user in mind. This is particularly applicable to the professionals involved in the process as they are no longer required to be 'experts of the service user', rather they are required to be part of a problem-solving team. In person-centred planning, it is usual for the service user, family and friends to take the lead in defining the services required, and then the professionals to participate in locating the required services. Ultimately these services must address what is important to the service user.

The resulting plan should hold information about what actions are going to be taken so that the service user can progress towards their wishes, desires and dreams. It is not about fitting service users into existing services, it is about defining what support is needed to aid the service user in participation in everyday life within society. There may well be a reliance on the community to provide unpaid support through relationship building, and this too should be identified in the plan.

Finally, the plan should be reviewed at regular intervals. The whole process relies on careful listening, recognising challenges, identifying obstacles, and that involves reviewing successes and failures in the plan at regular intervals.

Throughout the process there will be a sharing of power amongst all participants in the plan, but ultimately the goal is to empower the service user. It is not a complicated, formal process and consideration needs to be given as to the best environment (for the service user) to create a conducive environment to formulate the plan.

The impact of person-centred planning for people with learning disabilities was researched by Wigham et al. (2008). You can read the article on the Companion Website (www.sagepub.co.uk/SocialWork).

Approaches

There are a number of tools that can be utilised when working with person-centred planning. Some of the more common ones are mentioned below, but this list is by no means exhaustive.

Maps

The McGill Action Planning System (MAPS) was originally designed to assist in the integration of service users with learning disabilities into mainstream schools but is now widely used with a range of service users. The tool provides structure when defining the dreams of the service user and was devised by Judith Snow, Jack Pearpoint and Marsha Forest, with support from John O'Brien (Pearpoint, 1990). It is one of the more visual tools used in person-centred planning, and it is also one of the least regimented and detailed of the tools available, and is therefore often a good starting point when working with person-centred planning.

The process usually requires two facilitators, one to lead the conversation and the other to scribe (or translate into images) onto the plan. Generally, there are eight stages to the plan. Stage 1 begins by asking the service user to give some basic details about themselves, what their name is, maybe use a photograph or a drawing of themselves, then stage 2 gathers more in-depth details about the service user's life story so far. Stage 3 goes on to look at the dreams of the service user, and a common way of ascertaining these is to consider what they would wish for if they could wave a magic wand. It is important to also consider the dreams that significant others have for the service user at this stage too. Stage 4 asks about nightmares: What would make life difficult or unbearable? What makes the service user unhappy? And what hasn't worked for the service user in the past? Stage 5 asks about positive attributes, what people like about the service user, and stage 6 focuses on the gifts, attributes and talents of the service user. Stage 7 begins to tie things together by asking what support is required to work towards the dream, and stage 8 formulates a basic action plan looking at the five common questions of Who? Where? How? Why? and When?

The ultimate goal is to produce a visual plan which considers the positive direction the service user wishes to move in, whilst also acknowledging the negative aspects too. Like all person-centred planning interventions, the plan will be formulated in a meeting environment that will be attended by the service user, friends, family and other significant people who will have input in the care plan.

To encourage you to further think about planning processes visit the Companion Website (www.sagepub.co.uk/SocialWork) and undertake the MAPS activity.

Path

Planning Alternative Tomorrows with Hope (PATH) was devised by Jack Pearpoint, Marsha Forest and John O'Brien and is most commonly utilised when a committed group of people who are already working with a service user want to plan out future courses of action (Forest et al., 1993).

The process begins by defining the service user's dream. This might be a future aspiration, or how they wish to live on a daily basis, and if possible, it is always best to get the service user to define the dream themselves. Where this is not possible, the people who know the service user the best will define the dream. The dream then provides a goal for the team to aim for.

Pearpoint, Forest and O'Brien state that PATH is not a tool for gathering information, it is a tool for planning action. Usually two facilitators will be involved in the process, one leading conversations and the other recording the outcomes in graphic form. The process tends to record the dream of the service user, then works backwards to identify ways for the service user to realise that dream. It will identify support structures to assist in the journey towards the dream and is usually recorded in several stages.

Working back from the dream, the team may be asked to envisage where they see their progress in a year's time, they may then be asked to consider where they are now and identify the tensions between now and the future; they may be asked to consider obstacles on the journey, but also the supports to enable the process. Next, the team will be asked to consider what strengths they need to aid them (such as regular meetings or resources), then set interim goals for a 3-month, or 6-month, period. Finally, the team will be asked to consider what the first steps on the journey will consist of.

Meetings can be charged with emotion, but there is an assumption that everyone involved has the best wishes of the service user at heart. It is also a useful process to embark on if a support team have lost their direction and need to refocus efforts to enable a service user to achieve their full potential.

Essential Lifestyle Planning

Developed by Michael Smull and Susan Burke Harrison to assist in the transition from long-stay residential institutions to the community, Essential Lifestyle Planning is a detailed plan that focuses on the current situation of the service user, and looks at how it can be improved (Smull and Harrison, 1992). As opposed to PATH and MAP, the future dreams and aspirations do not feature in the Essential Lifestyle Plan. It is a useful tool to use when very little is known about the service user and assists in the formation of an action plan to address immediate changes.

The plan begins by gathering information about the service user before moving on to look at current relationships. It needs to address what is important to the service user, what support is currently in place and what support is required. This involves identifying individuals involved in existing care plans, discussing what is working well, and also identifying issues that might not be working well for the service user. Consideration should also be given to concerns or questions the service user currently has, and the outcome should be a support plan to address immediate concerns.

Personal Futures Planning

Personal Futures Planning is similar to PATH and MAPS, but does not assume previous knowledge of the service user as the other tools do. It was devised by Beth Mount and John O'Brien and is intended to look at the current situation of the service user, and the future aspirations (O'Brien and Mount, 2006). It does not address day-to-day requirements as the Essential Lifestyle Plan would.

Five key areas are mapped out in the process, and a facilitator will graphically record information onto each map. Firstly, a relationship map will look at the balance of support already being provided, and identify support needs to move forward. Next, a places map will be used to illustrate where the service user spends their time, and identify community-based opportunities for further inclusion. A background map will be drawn up next to capture the history, experiences, achievements and opportunities in the life of the service user. The fourth map is the preferences map, which looks at likes and dislikes, and the fifth map will then identify dreams, hopes and fears. This can be particularly useful as it can define the desired lifestyle, and set the agenda for planning meetings to address actions.

Other maps can be added to the process to look at issues that may impact on the life of the service user, such as health issues, or autonomy issues.

The overall aim is to provide an overview of issues so that concerns can be identified and addressed by the entire team.

Case Study

Molly's meeting takes place as agreed, everyone invited attends and brings a dish for the buffet. The social worker has offered to facilitate the meeting, and the format of the plan will be the Planning Alternative Tomorrows with Hope (PATH) plan.

Molly is asked what her dreams are. She is a bit reluctant to talk, and her family help by recounting some of the desires Molly has expressed to them. Molly dreams of having her own flat near her parents' house, of becoming a hairdresser, of being a pop star and of getting married. Given the ethos of person-centred planning, every identified dream is accepted by the team and discussions ensue to look at how Molly can work towards achieving her dreams.

The dream of living in her own flat is discussed first, including obstacles to be overcome in finding a suitable flat and availability of support from housing associations and the social work department. Molly and her parents are tasked with contacting the housing association to initiate the process. Next, Molly's desire to become a hairdresser is discussed, and Molly reveals a passion for fashion. The team discuss the possibility of Molly volunteering to help at the local hairdressing salon. Molly's strengths and limitations are discussed, and Molly recognises that she is unlikely to be able to cut people's hair, but the thought of assisting excites Molly. Molly and her family will make contact with the hairdressers to discuss the possibility. Molly then talks about being a pop star. She really enjoys singing with the karaoke machine in the day centre. Someone mentions a drama group that puts on a number of musical performances throughout the year. Molly is keen to visit and also asks to go with some of her friends at the day centre to karaoke clubs in the town.

The final dream is Molly's dream of a wedding, and she does say she is fond of her boyfriend and dreams of going on holiday with him. The team agree to work on what would need to be done to help Molly achieve this. At the end of the meeting Molly is given her PATH plan which clearly illustrates what was discussed at the meeting, shows the first steps that need to be taken, and also recommends the team meet in 3 months' time to look at the progress.

The case study has focused on the use of PCP with a service user who has a learning disability. To find out about research on the use of person-centred approaches with older people, and how such approaches link with other models, visit the Companion Website (www.sagepub.co.uk/SocialWork) and read the article by McKay et al. (2012).

PRACTICE SKILLS

The facilitator of the person-centred planning meeting is a vital component in the process. There are no special talents a facilitator must have, but the following attributes are important factors.

Guiding a Meeting

Guiding a meeting is not necessarily the same as chairing a meeting. You must appreciate how productive it is to have so many people in the same room with the same objectives, but the power and control must be shared across all participants, none more so than the service user. Consider setting group rules in place at the start of the meeting to give everyone an opportunity to give input. You might need to set time limits given that professionals are in attendance and may have commitments elsewhere following the meeting.

Listening

Key to getting the maximum information to inform the plan is to actively listen to what is being said, by all participants. A good way of ensuring that everyone is being understood is to use reflective listening skills, summarise what is being said by an individual and clarify the message. Your initial ground rules should address courtesy, so that nobody speaks over another person and every voice can be heard.

Graphic Recording

You do not need to have a degree in art and design to facilitate a meeting, but it is useful if you can pictorially represent key themes, messages and information that come out of the meeting. If you struggle with drawing, the plans can be written, but it is often a good idea to use pictures from magazines, or photographs, to graphically illustrate the key information afterwards. The purpose of the plan is to make it accessible to all participants, including the service user, so consideration needs to be given as to how the information should be presented on the plan.

Networking

The nature of person-centred planning means that professionals, service users and significant others are put in a room to share power and control. This leads to opportunities for role clarification, understanding professional responsibilities and creates opportunities to educate others on your own role. As previously mentioned, professionals in the process are not regarded as 'experts of the service user', but agents in the change process who can advise and assist in the access of appropriate services. This creates an environment for learning and sharing knowledge to inform future interventions.

Problem-solving

Many of the issues that come out of the process will be challenging. Some dreams may be unrealistic so the team will have to be creative in meeting need. An example of this may be that a service user may state that she dreams of having children, when this might not be medically possible. This should not be seen as an obstacle, but recognised as an opportunity, and the team could investigate possibilities to see if she could become involved in the community where she could have contact with children, such as voluntary support work at a nursery. Because the aim is to address need, rather than allocate to existing services, the outcome usually requires a creative approach, and therefore a strong element of problem-solving.

PERSONALISATION

Person-centred planning is an example of personalisation in practice. Personalisation is the process wherein service users become active participants in defining the right interventions for themselves in conjunction with professionals. This is a marked shift from historic service provision, where provision was often defined by what services were available, which was followed by a shift towards looking at needs-led services, to the current situation of personalisation, where services should be person-led.

Personalisation should underpin all service provision, regardless of the fact whether someone is accessing services through the local authority, or purchasing their own services privately. This means that frontline workers who are assessing need, and purchasing services, need to consider the co-production aspect of care packages and service provision. There is recognition from governments that care provision tends to function in wider organisational environments, where five key factors impact:

1   Tools – what is available in terms of provision?
2   Finance – how much money is available to purchase services?
3   Workforce – who will be involved in the provision of services (both paid and unpaid carers)?
4   Mixed economy of care – which agency takes the lead? Who provides what (for example, NHS or local authority in terms of terminally ill service users at home)?
5   Performance measures – what is being measured and for what purpose? How do you measure outcomes in terms of personalised service provision?

There is a need for all employees across all organisations in the field of service provision to understand how their actions impede or contribute towards the personalisation agenda of service user choice and empowerment.

What this means is that key considerations need to be given to a number of areas of current service provision. Obviously, the need to involve service users and carers is paramount. They need to be involved in the commissioning of services, and also the future reviews of the effectiveness of the service. This in turn has financial implications in terms of what services continue to be funded by local authorities, and how these services are paid for in the commissioning stage. There may be a marked shift towards families managing their own budgets and purchasing specific packages, rather than the local authority buying in services for a group of service users.

For service users to have true choice there also needs to be a range of services to choose from, and the market will need to address the demands of its customers. This may involve existing voluntary agencies being more adaptive and creative in service provision, or the establishment of new agencies to meet need – which is likely to see a consequential demise of agencies that cannot adapt to meet new need. Workforce development will need to be considered by all agencies working in care provision, as will risk management. With empowerment also comes increased risk, and practitioners will need to consider legal and ethical impacts of service user choice.

Critical Thinking

Consider current government spending and its potential impact on personalisation.

CONCLUSION

With an emphasis on service user and carer power, personalisation is an exciting shift in social work. No longer simply brokering of care packages, social workers can now use their skills to apply theories and interventions to identify service user strengths, desires and wishes and plan accordingly. This will truly draw upon the creative abilities of social workers to access services that are truly personal to the service user and empower service users to take control of their own lives.

Watch vodcast 21.1 on the Companion Website (www.sagepub.co.uk/SocialWork) to see chapter author Neil Gibson summarise the main points conveyed in this chapter, and why an understanding of person-centred planning and personalisation is important for social work practice.

Reflective Questions

1 Social work values are essential to effective social work practice. How does person-centred planning relate to those values?
2 Working with an individual service user will often involve the exchange of confidential information, some of which may be sensitive or challenging in nature (sexuality in particular) and some of which may not be realisable, may be illegal, harmful or undesirable as an outcome. How would you as a worker deal with such a situation?
3 One theme mentioned elsewhere is that social work services exist within a political and financial context, where what social workers may require cannot be adequately funded. How might financial constraints and service cutbacks affect the personalisation agenda?

RECOMMENDED READING

Gardner, A. (2011) *Personalisation in Social Work*. Exeter: Learning Matters.

O'Brien, J. and Mount, B. (2006) *Make a Difference: A Guidebook for Person-Centred Direct Support*. Ontario: Inclusion Press.

Scottish Government (2009) *Changing Lives: Personalisation – A Shared Understanding. Commissioning for Personalisation: A Personalised Commissioning Approach to Support and Care Services*. Edinburgh: Scottish Government.

Refer to the Companion Website (www.sagepub.co.uk/SocialWork) for some useful links to web-based material.

NARRATIVE
22 THERAPY

Neil Gibson and Inga Heyman

Key Themes

- How we interpret our life experiences affects our health and well-being.
- Narrative therapy draws on a broad range of theories.
- An awareness of the impact of balance of power is crucial.
- The focus is on moving from the internalisation of a problem to externalisation.
- Active listening and an empathic understanding are key skills in this approach.

INTRODUCTION

Every one of us has a back story, a **biography** that explains who we are, where we have come from, and how we arrived at our current position in time. Within our individual biographies, we are the central character. Our history, upbringing, achievements, losses, education and experiences all contribute to defining our individual characters.

Stories can be told in many different ways, and the telling of stories has a direct implication for the main character within. What we choose to focus on and remember also has bearing on how we see ourselves. Our life experiences are extensive, so we have to edit the details we remember and relate.

Case Study

A well-known historical figure may choose to tell the story of his early years in one of two ways:

> I was born during an air raid in 1940 and my mother gave me the middle name of Winston after the then Prime Minister. My Dad was a merchant seaman and I never saw much of him. He would send regular cheques to my Mum, but when I was 4 years old these stopped and he went AWOL. He reappeared 6 months later, but by then my Mum was pregnant with another man's child. My Aunt

complained to social services and eventually my Mum sent me to live with her. I was involved in several 'tugs of love' between my Mum and Dad whilst in my Aunt's care and this caused a lot of confusion for me. At one point my Dad intended to emigrate with me to New Zealand, but I couldn't leave my Mum. After this, I didn't see my Dad for over 20 years. I was regarded as a trouble-maker throughout school years and was interested in art. I was not a good academic and scraped into Art College, but was eventually thrown out because of my disruptive behaviour.

OR

In my early years I was raised by my Mum because my Dad ran away to sea. My Mum was one of five sisters and they were very influential in my upbringing, which was dominated by feminism. I lived with my Aunt Mimi from the age of 4. She had no children but I did spend time with my other cousins as I was grow-ing up. One of my cousins, Stanley, would take me on visits to the cinema and music halls, and I particularly enjoyed seeing George Formby perform. I enjoyed art at school but my school reports were never good, one teacher stated that I was on the road to failure. I began to develop an interest in music and my Mum bought me my first guitar in 1956. My Aunt did not feel that music was an ambition I should pursue, but my Mum was encouraging. Sadly, my Mum was knocked down by a car and killed 2 years later. By this time, I had set up my first band, The Quarrymen, and we gradually built up a name for ourselves as we gathered new band members.

Both of these stories describe the formative years of the same person, but both focus on different life events. It may not surprise you to learn that both stories relate to John Lennon, who went on to establish one of the most famous bands ever, The Beatles.

As the central character to our own biographies, our interpretation of our history impacts on our emotional and physical well-being. Sometimes, the dominant features of our biographies can focus on the bad things that have happened to us, where we have felt hopeless, sad, out of control, and struggling to identify positives.

Narrative therapy sets out to address the interpretation of life events, put them in context with society, help to understand why events have unfolded the way in which they have, and look at ways in which we can re-interpret events by drawing on strengths.

HISTORY

Michael White and David Epston (1990) are credited as the main theorists behind narrative therapy. Michael White (1995) describes how his interests developed from family therapy into encompassing sociological perspectives by ideas borne out of the work of Michel Foucault.

Within family therapy, White recognised that there were various systems at play. Different family members took on different roles, and with these roles came expected behaviours such as the mother being the main carer and the father being the main income earner. Widening his focus, White looked at the work of Foucault, who believed that individuals function within the society they live in and are thus shaped by the society. This society is defined by the politics of that time, the established social norms, and accepted beliefs of the populace. Within society, there is a hierarchy of power which Foucault felt was used to exert control through such techniques as subordination, surveillance and demonstrating superior knowledge. As individuals within a society, we take on our roles which are underpinned by beliefs and behaviours. Erving Goffman (1961) recognised that this power and control was also demonstrated within institutions.

White (1995) believes that individuals interpret meaning from our lived experiences. He explains that the narrative of an individual is only a representation of the life lived, not a mirror image of events. Narrative therapy assumes that the individual's way of being and thinking, and the way in which they perceive others, is problematic for them. This may be down to the dichotomy between how the individual views themselves in line with how society defines a person of 'moral worth' within the culture.

Because narrative therapy is a language-based intervention it is often likened to other interventions. White has already highlighted how he built on the family systems approach, but we can also draw upon links to cognitive behavioural therapy, wherein the therapist looks to assist in identifying negative thought patterns and challenge these if they are detrimental to the service user. Similarly, neurolinguistic programming aims to change thought patterns associated with historic events or associations through the use of language. Narrative therapy begins by looking at the language used by service users to determine if they see *themselves* as the problem. If so, narrative therapy can be employed to enable the service users to separate themselves from the problem by putting the problem in context with their environment, coping skills, learned behaviour and society in general. These techniques are not used to diminish responsibility for actions; rather, they are used to enhance coping skills and recognise alternative ways of approaching past situations that impact on present abilities.

NARRATIVE THERAPY IN ACTION

The 'Problem Saturated' Description

Power is a major consideration when using narrative therapy with a service user as an intervention. At the initial stages of involvement it is a good idea for the practitioner to ask themselves some basic questions to ensure that narrative therapy is the correct intervention to be using.

1. Are there time constraints to my intervention?

Many interventions with service users are time-limited. Assessments tend to be formulaic and designed to get as much information as quickly as possible, and usually geared around getting agency-specific information. This kind of interaction is too structured, limits the free speech of the service user and is not conducive to fostering an environment where the service user can tell their story at their pace. It is also important to allow time for the practitioner to listen to the details and try to identify areas where narrative therapy could help investigate alternative perspectives.

Assessments are usually always required for new service users, so it may be advantageous to consider narrative therapy as a viable outcome to the assessment process so that the service user can tell their story without formulaic boundaries.

2. Will agency policy and procedures hinder the power balance?

When beginning work with any service user, your agency should have defined policies and procedures for initial contact. These should include explaining confidentiality procedures to the service user. On occasions, confidentiality can be overridden when information received from a service user suggests there may be a risk to a child or a vulnerable adult. On these occasions, practitioners are normally duty bound to pass on these concerns under policies and legislation. Similarly, disclosure from a service user involving criminal activity or substance use may also have an effect on the working relationship between service user and practitioner. These are evident power imbalances, and it is worth considering whether narrative therapy is a suitable intervention in these situations. The three main ways of dealing with these issues are: acknowledge the power imbalance from the outset with the service user; use narrative therapy only in scenarios where the power imbalance is minimal; or choose not to use narrative therapy with a particular service user.

3. Does the service user believe there is a problem?

A practitioner should not assume that a service user perceives they have a problem simply because they have been referred to their agency. It is important to establish the service user's perception of why they are visiting your agency and what they hope to gain from the intervention. They may feel that they do not have a problem with their particular circumstance or behaviour, and, in fact, it is other people who have the problem. In this situation it may not be appropriate to use narrative therapy.

Once a practitioner concludes that narrative therapy is appropriate the next stage is to build up rapport with the service user. Throughout this process, the practitioner must engage with their story, show empathy where appropriate and work in an environment where conversation can flow freely. In essence, the practitioner wants to build a relationship with the service user where they feel comfortable to tell their story. We can assume that the story told by the service user will focus on issues that have been unpleasant experiences, and this can be a challenge for practitioners to listen to, and to react appropriately. At the very least, it is important to recognise that the story has had an impact on the service user's life, but ideally the practitioner must appreciate what the service user has been going through. As with most relationships, trust and confidence are built up only when two people feel there is a certain level of understanding between them. If there is no understanding, there is no incentive to continue sharing information. Being curious about the lived experience and showing respect for the service user as the expert on their own story will assist this process.

Once trust has been built up and information is flowing then the practitioner must begin to identify key themes. White and Epston call the service user stories 'problem-saturated' as they are largely negative and focus on events that have been detrimental to them. Within the problem-saturated narrative, there will be dominant themes, but the practitioner's tactic should be to listen for experiences or indicators that show exceptions or counter these dominant themes. These 'exceptions to the rule' should be noted by the practitioner and used in the next stages.

Case Study

Steven has been referred following an increasing number of anger outbursts at home and work. His employer has advised that he is on his 'final warning' regarding his heated behaviour in the workplace. He has also been getting into a number of fights in pubs and clubs. He feels very negative about his future and cannot see a way forward. This is his first meeting with his practitioner, Emily.

Emily: Hi, Steven, It's good to meet you. I'm Emily and I will be working with you. How are you feeling today?

Steven: Oh, okay I suppose.

Emily: Is it okay if we get started?

Steven: Sure.

Emily: Okay. What I would like you to do is to tell me a story about yourself so I can understand a little more about you. Any events you think are important to you. You can give as much detail as you like.

Steven: Well, I finished university over two years ago. I studied engineering. I did okay at Uni. I had really good marks in the first three years. I had lots of mates. I spent a lot of time doing sport, particularly rugby. I was in the Uni rugby team and really enjoyed the social side of the club too. That's how I met my girlfriend, Sarah. We went out together for two years and it was pretty serious. We were making plans about looking for jobs in the same city when we finished studying. We had just started to look for a flat together when she was killed in a car accident. I managed to finish Uni with a scrape pass but things have been pretty terrible since then. I got a job fairly soon after I graduated. But that's not hard for an engineer in this town. I bet they would never have taken me on if they had known what kind of psycho they were getting.

Emily: Tell me more about what you mean by that. [*Interested, questioning more about the story*]

Steven: Well, I just lose the plot at the least little thing. I know the boss and other blokes are watching me as they are sick of it and just waiting for me to kick off. Sometimes I think they say stuff just to get me to lose it.

Emily: What do you mean by lose the plot? [*Clarifying, getting better meaning*]

Steven: Well, if a job is not going to plan or the boss has a go at me I lose control. I shout and storm out usually, but lately it has got worse and I punched the walls.

Emily: Have you ever hit anyone? [*Expanding the story*]

Steven: Not at work but I have been in lots of fights in the pub lately. The other night I really hurt a guy for nudging my pint. My mates say they don't want to go out with me anymore. I think they are embarrassed but I can't help it. I just snap. Mum and Dad say I am angry all the time. They're right. I flew into a rage last night with Mum for not ironing the right shirt. I know I am going to lose my job and likely my mates too but I just get so angry and out of control I can't stop. It is not even at anything specific now. [*This is an example of a problem-saturated story*]

For an example of how work with Steven may progress using narrative therapy see the extended case study on the Companion Website (www.sagepub.co.uk/SocialWork).

PROBLEM NAMING, EXTERNALISING AND SOCIAL INFLUENCE

When the practitioner feels that they have understood the service user's problems, and conversely, when the service user feels they have been understood and their story respected, the next stage can be initiated, that of externalising the problem, mapping the issues, and deconstructing the story. There is no set time limit for how long this stage should take to begin, and it is entirely dependent on the relationship building and flow of information in stage one.

Externalising the Problem

Often the service user will see the problem as being intrinsic to them. They have become the problem and, in their view, other people see them as the problem. White (1995) describes this process as internalising the problem. The practitioner must deal with this by creating a different atmosphere around the problem and try to create a shift in the perception of the service user to separate them from the problem.

A basic technique that could be used by the practitioner is simply to begin to question the service user about the effect of 'the problem' on their everyday living, for example 'How is the problem affecting your relationship?', 'How is the problem affecting your work?', or 'How is the problem affecting how you feel?' In this process the practitioner is beginning to separate 'the problem' from 'the individual'. White and Epston (1990) feel that this is where social influences and power imbalances can begin to be highlighted, and also separated. By focusing on 'the problem' a process can begin wherein the service user can understand that problems are inherent to many situations in life, and often the environment for these problematic situations is outside the control of the service user, therefore, external to them.

It may be advantageous at this stage to give a name to the problem to aid in the externalisation of it. Miller (2006) talks of using metaphors, descriptive words or phrases that encapsulate the essence of the problem. It is a good idea to try to get the service user to lead on giving the problem a name, rather than making this activity practitioner-led. Examples of this may include:

- Regular alcohol use – 'the drink'
- Regular arguments – 'squabbles'
- Regular depression – 'the black cloud'

Practitioners must exercise caution that they do not externalise behaviours which occur as a result of the problem; for example, it would not be advisable to use a metaphor for actions such as domestic violence, criminal acts, or self harm. Also, it would be unhelpful to use normal, everyday emotional responses to name the problem, so 'sadness', 'anger' or 'fear' should be avoided as these are basic emotional responses and should not be termed as problems in themselves.

Once the problem has been given a name it makes it easier for the service user to separate themselves from the problem, and begin to explain their relationship to the problem, for example 'the drink affects my relationships because …', 'the black cloud can make it difficult for me to concentrate at work …', or 'squabbles make me feel anxious and sad …'. In effect, the problem has been objectified. Once objectified, the service user is freer to explore times in life when 'the problem' has not had an impact, or when 'the problem' gets worse, and even when 'the problem' is not so bad.

Mapping the Issues

Because narrative therapy is language-based and reliant on story telling, there will be many strands to stories. As issues are identified the practitioner can encourage exploration of these and see how they interact with the main story line, that of the life of the service user. In this respect, once the problem has a name, or has been externalised, it would be advisable to map the influence of this problem. This stage involves exploring two distinct areas.

Firstly, the practitioner needs to explore how the problem impacts on the lives of the service user and their significant relationships, and it is usually easiest to start with the effect on the service user. The practitioner needs to ask questions that allow the service user to consider how the problem makes them feel, how it makes them behave, how it affects their interaction with other people, and how it affects their attitude to life.

Example

Consider a scenario where a service user regularly binge eats chocolate. He has named his problem 'the munchies'. Through using the techniques above, the service user might reflect that the munchies makes him feel guilty, unhealthy and out of control; the munchies make him behave in a secretive manner, regularly stocking up on chocolate bars when he is shopping, and storing chocolate in hiding places around the house; the munchies led him to being self-conscious about his appearance and worried about how other people view him, and he also feels people will see he is weak-willed; the munchies have led to him feeling depressed, weak, unhealthy and guilty.

This first stage offers good opportunities to also explore exceptions to the problem, times when the service user has not given in to the demands of the problem. In the example above there may be times when the service user felt like eating chocolate but resisted, or was interrupted by another activity which took his mind off the problem. It is also important that the practitioner relates back to societal influences on the service user and the problem; again, in the above example there is stigma attached to being obese, binge eating and the conflicting image of a male member of society with 'moral worth'.

Then, this line of exploration should be widened to include significant relationships in the service user's life; how does the problem affect partners, children, parents or friends? Through exploration of the problem on various relationships the separation of the person from the problem is enhanced.

The second stage asks the service user to look at their own influence on the evolution of the problem. This stage may involve delving into the past to look at when the problem first manifested itself and how the service user arrived at the behaviour or exploring when the problem is at its worst, and also when the service user has not been dominated by the problem. Again, within this, the practitioner needs to stay alert to times when the problem was tackled appropriately and the service user demonstrates exemptions to the norm. Throughout this stage it is entirely possible that the evolution of the problem may be traced back to an earlier, underlying issue which has been superseded by the current problem. For example, in the binge eating scenario, it may be that the behaviour is triggered when the service user feels particularly high levels of stress brought on by feelings of jealousy towards his sister. For the practitioner the choices would be to explore this relationship in the hope that the problem can be tackled, or rename the problem and explore the service user's relationship with jealousy. The ultimate aim of stage two is to facilitate the service user in identifying their own skills, resources and competencies used in dealing with the problem.

Deconstruction

In essence, the externalising conversations a practitioner has with a service user can be described as the deconstruction process. The problem-saturated story has been told, now the practitioner is delving into the history of the story and teasing out the various strands. Separating the person from the problem, then mapping the influence and evolution of the problem is all about breaking the situation down into small components.

It is important for the practitioner to link societal influences on the current situation. This will involve exploring various beliefs and power relations in society which impact on how the service user views their situation. Examples of such societal attitudes may include:

- Females make better carers.
- Males should be the main income earners in the household.
- Private education is superior to state education.

Exercise

In the case of Steven, above, what societal attitudes might impact on Steven's view of his situation?

There are also wider examples of oppression such as racism, sexism, ageism, poverty and disability discrimination. Often, there can be an acceptance of 'this is the way it is', but by giving the service user knowledge and information about how society shapes attitudes and opinions it can empower the service user to see that problems are often enhanced by generalised attitudes.

ALTERNATIVE NARRATIVES

Life is multi-storied, not single storied. Apart from the dominant stories of our lives, there are always sub-stories, and these sub-stories are relatively available to us in this work with individuals, couples, and families. (White, 1995: 27)

Now that the problem has been externalised, mapped, deconstructed and applied to knowledge of social oppression the service user can begin the process of exploring exceptions to the problem-saturated narrative. The overall aim in this process is to facilitate the service user to refuse to cooperate with the problem, thus making the problem less effective.

This stage will involve the practitioner asking probing questions and expanding on areas where the standard pattern of behaviour is not evident. In the example of the binge eater, the practitioner might explore exceptions by asking such questions as 'I noticed in your story that you didn't have any chocolate yesterday. What was different about yesterday?' or 'You said you were with your parents at the weekend. Why did you not give into the munchies then?' This discourse allows the service user to explore times when the problem did not get the better of them and they were able to employ coping skills.

Throughout the narrative discourse the practitioner should be listening out for the sub-stories that inform them about other aspects of the service user's life. Within these the practitioner should be listening for other interests and strengths. The service user might refer to areas of their life where they feel passionate about a certain activity, or they might allude to past successes in their employment, education or personal life. The aim of this technique would be to then have some conversation around these sub-stories and to illustrate to the service user that the problem has not necessarily influenced every aspect of their life.

Throughout the process of searching for alternative narratives it is important that the practitioner does not dismiss the initial problem. This stage is very much about exploring skills in relation to the problem and demonstrating to the service user that the problem is separate from them, and they have the skills to address their relationship with the problem. The exploration of alternative narratives is a process done in partnership and should not be led by the practitioner, but neither should the practitioner feel the process should be led by the service user, after all, if the service user could create their own alternative narrative there would be no need for the intervention in the first place. If the practitioner takes the lead and creates an alternative narrative there is a risk that the service user will not be able to take ownership of the story and will feel disempowered in their ability to control their own narrative.

Re-constructing the narrative could more aptly be referred to as co-constructing the narrative. It is fair to state that narrative therapy does require the practitioner to have a good awareness of social policy and the impact of political decisions on the lives of the populace. It is an important aspect of narrative therapy that the service user does not take the blame for the impact of these social-political decisions and consequences.

The resulting alternative narrative should start to demonstrate that the service user is viewing themselves as a separate unit from the problem and can recognise that they have been able to adapt to certain situations in the past, they have been able to resist problematic behaviour at times and they recognise that they cannot accept responsibility for problems created by society but instead they can employ skills to deal with these. They might be able to explore other activities in their lives where the problem has little or no influence, and begin to build up their self-worth and motivation.

Critical Thinking

Reflect on how the narrative-based approach might be applied in social work settings you have experienced.

On the Companion Website (www.sagepub.co.uk/SocialWork) you will find two reseach articles exploring use of narrative therapy with different service users. See Gardner and Poole (2009) for research about older people and see Mahoney and Daniel (2006) for research about women in the criminal justice system.

MAINTENANCE

The final stage in the process is that of maintenance. Again, as with previous stages, there is no set timescale for this to occur. Ideally, the practitioner wants to give some space to the service user so that they can test out their alternative narrative, see how it impacts on their life, and get some feedback from their significant others. This feedback may not always be positive as the nature of therapy involves a reliance on the use of language, the use of story telling, and the interpretation of the truth. Therefore, it is entirely plausible that a service user might get into disagreements with family members or friends as they test out their alternative narrative if there are discrepancies between interpretations of historic events. Hence the therapeutic relationship between practitioner and service user should be kept open for as long as necessary. However, it is hoped that most feedback will be positive and, over time, will enable the service user to accept their new beliefs, behaviours and narrative. As with the John Lennon example given in the introduction, there are many versions of a story, so there may be a number of alternative narratives that need to be tried and tested before the right one is found for the purpose.

Miller (2006) suggests that there are three necessary outcomes from narrative therapeutic intervention. Firstly, the service user must believe in the alternative narrative. They must see truth in their adjusted perception and have emotional investment in it. Secondly, the service user must have an understanding of how they have coped with problems in the past, and how this can be continued, or adjusted, in the future. Thirdly, the service user must understand that some problems are socially constructed but will have an impact on their lives. This requires a level of acceptance, but also education around social and political oppression.

White (1995) warns that the ending process can be sudden, but should never be unexpected. By the very nature of narrative therapy the practitioner is co-author in the process. As mentioned earlier in the chapter, if the service user could re-author their own story then there would be no need for intervention. Therefore, the service user will eventually get to a stage where they can take control of the re-authorship process and feel empowered to own their alternative narrative. The role of the practitioner can become redundant when this happens. White (1995) goes on to explain that the nature of this intervention is transformative, and as the intervention develops the practitioner becomes de-centralised. He stresses that sudden endings because of change should be celebrated.

CONCLUSION

This chapter has given a basic overview of the process of a narrative therapeutic intervention using the tools outlined by Michael White and David Epston. It has focused on a one-to-one relationship between a practitioner and a service user but narrative therapy can be used in other settings, such as family group work, with recognisable success.

Narrative therapy is a useful intervention for those working in the care services as the values and principles of empowerment and anti-oppressive practice lie at the heart of these occupations, as with the intervention. Admittedly, it is beneficial if the practitioner understands societal and political matters, particularly oppression, so that they can impart knowledge. However, it is equally important that this knowledge is not used to exert power over the service user, nor subvert the service user round to the political views of the practitioner.

To reiterate, this is a basic description of narrative therapy and anyone interested in pursuing the ideas and tools behind this intervention is strongly advised to explore the texts in the Recommended Reading section.

Watch vodcast 22.1 on the Companion Website (www.sagepub.co.uk/SocialWork) to see chapter author Neil Gibson summarise the main points conveyed in this chapter that he co-authored with Inga Heyman, and why an understanding of narrative therapy is important for social work practice.

Reflective Questions

1   The focus of this chapter has been on narratives and how we understand ourselves through placing ourselves within our own narrative. Reflect on your own life narrative – what episodes or events were important in shaping your individual life narrative?
2   For some service users the linguistic form of narrative therapy may not be appropriate. What other media could be used to illicit personal narrative? Think about photography, drawing and forms of physical expression.
3   Why might knowledge of sociology be important for narrative therapy? Are people solely their own authors or do social circumstances also author the narrative?

RECOMMENDED READING

White, M. and Epston, D. (1990) *Narrative Means to Therapeutic Ends*. London: Norton.
The definitive text by the creators of Narrative Therapy with some very informative case studies, including one on a family's relationship with 'sneaky poo'.
White, M. (1995) *Re-Authoring Lives: Interviews and Essays*. Adelaide: Dulwich Centre Publications.
Transcripts of interviews of Michael White.
Miller, L. (2011) *Counselling Skills for Social Work*, 2nd edn. London: Sage.
A useful chapter introducing readers to the concept of Narrative Therapy in a counselling environment.
Faubion, J. (ed.) (1994) *Power: Essential Works of Foucault 1954–1984* (Volume 3). Harmondsworth: Penguin.
A good reader that gives an overview of Michael Foucault's beliefs, helping the practitioner to understand what influenced Michael White in his writings.
Payne, M. (2006) *Narrative Therapy: An Introduction for Counsellors*, 2nd edn. London: Sage.

Accesss the Dulwich Centre website from the link on the Companion Website (www.sagepub.co.uk/SocialWork) to find a range of relevant resources.

23 MOTIVATIONAL INTERVIEWING

Anne Shirran

Key Themes

- Motivational interviewing is widely used in different areas of social work, particularly in criminal justice and substance misuse services.
- Motivational interviewing is used to explore and resolve ambivalence regarding behavioural change and is underpinned by motivational theories which recognise that motivation is a key factor in facilitating change.
- Motivational interviewing uses aspects of cognitive behavioural therapy to encourage service users to link thoughts, feelings and actions.
- Motivational interviewing has relevance to working with a Cycle of Change model.
- Motivational interviewing is underpinned by specific principles and techniques. It is grounded in value-based practice and places an emphasis on relationships and communication skills.

INTRODUCTION

Motivation is a dynamic characteristic in people, which means that it is subject to change depending on the individual's readiness and willingness to address what are seen to be problematic behaviours. Using a non-directive, person-centred counselling approach our role as practitioners is to enable service users to explore and resolve ambivalence regarding their ability to change. Motivational interviewing can support change behaviour, and as an approach draws heavily on the use of an empathic and non-confrontational method that employs specific strategies dependent on the stage of change.

DEFINITION, HISTORY AND DEVELOPMENT OF MOTIVATIONAL INTERVIEWING

Motivational interviewing is a counselling approach that is client-centred and incorporates a semi-directive aspect. It was developed by William Miller and Stephen

Rollnick (2002) in their work with clients with problem alcohol use and moved away from the medical model to the social model. The medical model was traditionally associated with treating substance misuse as a physical illness intrinsic to the person. Concerned with causation and treatment, to a large extent it removed responsibility from the client to address their substance misuse, viewing the client as having little control over their behaviour. Motivational interviewing, however, is consistent with the social model as it is a concept that acknowledges that some people have physical or psychological problems that can affect their ability to function. Consequently, the focus for intervention is on the problematic behaviour and not the individual, thus promoting **self-efficacy**.

Motivational interviewing is a cognitive behavioural technique which seeks to encourage people to identify the reasons why they want to change their behaviour. This can be achieved through developing a **discrepancy** between the problem behaviour and its effects on their life and the lifestyle they would wish to assume. By engaging in this process the individual can begin to identify the benefits of the change behaviour which in turn can resolve any ambivalence they may hold regarding their capacity to change (Miller and Rollnick, 2002). Motivational interviewing is consequently based on the principles of cognitive behavioural therapy:

- To understand the thought processes associated with the problem
- To identify and gauge emotional responses to the problem
- To identify the interface between thoughts, feelings and actions
- To challenge these thoughts, feelings and actions and employ alternative behaviours. Bundy (2004)

MOTIVATION TO CHANGE

Gauging the level of motivation or readiness to change is difficult because motivation varies according to the individual's circumstances and is significantly influenced by the thoughts and feelings associated with the problematic behaviour. The practitioner therefore needs to gain an insight into the reasons provided by the service user for change, identify any previous efforts to address problematic behaviour and importantly to deduce how these failures or lapses were perceived. By doing so, the service user is being encouraged to make links between thoughts, feelings and actions. It is essential that the practitioner does not become confrontational as this will only result in a stand-off position being adopted by the service user.

Challenging service users' perceptions through developing discrepancy between current lifestyle and that which they would like to achieve enables the service user to develop their own arguments for change. Doing so allows the individual to challenge their own thoughts, feelings and behaviours, which can lead to a more effective outcome through the establishment of self-change talk. Although compliance is one factor when considering positive outcomes, the larger goal of intervention involves more than just having service users 'doing what they're told'. Compliance does not equal change.

Case Study

Two service users both agree to complete an alcohol programme as part of a Community Payback Order or Community Sentence. One agrees because he wants to avoid a prison sentence; the other agrees because he is concerned that his alcohol use is affecting his marriage. In this situation both service users may be cooperating, but the second is probably likely to make changes that decrease the probability of future criminal behaviour. People are often concerned about how their behaviour affects the well-being of their families and communities. It is important therefore not only that they successfully complete programmes of intervention as imposed by a court order, but also that they make changes that will help them integrate into mainstream society.

If social workers are working in collaboration with a service user to bring about change, part of the process must be to assess the individual's motivation to change. Motivation is changeable and often dependent on outside influences. The social worker should therefore use active listening skills to identify with the service user their own perceptions of the problem behaviour and their reasons for change. As outlined above, in some instances social workers may be working with involuntary service users where the motivation to change could be construed as coerced, either through the courts or through statutory social work services. Another example, within a children and families setting, is where parental substance misuse is problematic and impacting on the service user's parenting capacity. As a consequence, social workers must consider as part of the holistic assessment the parent's ability to change.

Case Study

Judy and Michael have two children – Paul, aged 3, and Millie, aged 5 years. Both parents are using heroin and funding their drug use through committing crime. Invariably this involves Judy working as a prostitute while Michael resorts to shoplifting or house breaking. Both have appeared before the courts on several occasions, which has sometimes resulted in both being remanded in custody and the children being placed in short-term foster care. Concerns have been raised by the Children and Families Social Worker regarding the parents' ability to meet the needs of their children both emotionally and physically. The home has been termed unhygienic, the children are under weight and the school has reported Millie appears hungry and withdrawn. Attendance at school and nursery is sporadic, which resulted in the initial referral to social work.

Assessment of the situation identified the following: the children had no set routines for bedtime; there were no designated mealtimes and there was a lack of organisation to attend activities such as school or nursery. The parents, as a result of their heroin use, were often not available to their children. Both parents acknowledged that when 'they were out of it' they didn't know what the children were doing or what they witnessed in terms of them injecting drugs. They also admitted that drug-using paraphernalia could be lying around and present a risk to the children. Both Judy and Michael have been diagnosed as hepatitis C-positive.

A plan was instigated whereby a Family Support Worker would work with Judy on bringing the home up to a more acceptable standard. She would work with Judy to help her budget, shop and devise meal plans and routines for the children. The school and nursery would liaise with social work regarding attendance and presentation of the children. Judy and Michael would have to address their drug misuse and offending behaviour.

Initially, it is likely, in situations similar to the above case, that motivation to address substance misuse is high where the possibility of the children being removed from the family remains. It is therefore important for social workers to assess the level of importance placed upon the service user's need to change their behaviour and the level of confidence they have in themselves to change. Statutory intervention can be the catalyst in many instances for individuals to consider changing problematic behaviour. Others will approach agencies on a voluntary basis to address such behaviour.

VALUES AND PRINCIPLES OF MOTIVATIONAL INTERVIEWING

Motivational interviewing promotes social work values in that the worker adopts a non-judgemental attitude and avoids dogmatic confrontation, which can lead to resistance to change. The approach aims to empower service users to identify possible options to change their behaviour, with an emphasis upon choice, and is primarily intended to raise awareness of the consequences of the problematic behaviour thus enabling the individual to imagine the type of future they would prefer to live. In doing so service users are assisted to develop their motivation and to see the positives that changed behaviour can achieve. Unconditional positive regard and respect are essential requirements to building and sustaining the service user–worker collaborative working relationship, which is crucial to achieving positive outcomes and to exploring and resolving ambivalence regarding behavioural change.

Motivational interviewing is based upon four general principles:

1 Express empathy, where the worker demonstrates an understanding of the individual's problem from their perspective.
2 Develop discrepancy, where the worker enables the individual to recognise the importance of change by looking at how the individual wants to live their life and what their life is now.
3 Roll with resistance, where the worker recognises the individual's reluctance to change as a natural response. Rather than becoming trapped in an argumentative stance, the worker changes tactics and puts forward the argument for not changing behaviour. This can then prompt argument for change from the service user.

4 Support self-efficacy, where the worker promotes individual autonomy through empowerment in developing service user autonomy in decision-making. This enables them to develop changed behaviour effectively and confidently. It is also important to acknowledge that individuals may choose not to change. (Miller and Rollnick, 2002)

The main objective is to create a rapport between the worker and the individual with the aim of eliciting change talk that maintains the momentum for change in the individual's own words. Currently almost all key interventions begin by trying to raise the level of awareness in relation to the problem, resulting in improved decision-making skills through increasing the quantity of information presented to the individual. Building on these concepts, Prochaska et al. (1995: 27) highlight:

> Consciousness-raising is not, however, limited to uncovering hidden thoughts and feelings. Any increased knowledge about yourself or the nature of your problem, regardless of the source, raises your consciousness.

Two theoretical perspectives that have influenced motivational interviewing are 'goal systems theory' and 'goal setting theory', both of which assume that individuals are motivated to take steps as a result of rational goal-directed behaviour (Karoly, 1993; Locke, 1968). Locke identified that there was a relationship between the level of difficulty of the set goal and the individual's performance of a task. He concluded that identifying specific and difficult goals resulted in better outcomes than vague or undemanding goals. He suggests there are five principles of goal setting:

1 Be clear about the goals being set and ensure these are measurable.
2 Goals should be challenging but achievable.
3 Goals should be negotiated and agreed to engender commitment to change.
4 Provide feedback on progress being made. (Within motivational interviewing the use of reflective summaries and encouragement can develop the service user–worker interpersonal relationship.)
5 Task complexity, when setting tasks toward the goal, needs to be attainable. (Locke, 1968)

MOTIVATIONAL THEORIES

When using motivational interviewing techniques, workers should consider Attribution Theory (Heider, 1958), as the approach can assist in understanding those with whom they work. Attribution theory incorporates aspects of cognitive theory and self-efficacy theory. Individuals will 'attribute' their successes or failures to factors that will help them feel better about themselves, the assumption being that they can explain their circumstances to support a positive self-image. Attribution theory has both internal and external components. The internal component relates to personality factors and external component to factors on which the individual can blame their circumstances rather than accepting culpability themselves (Heider, 1958; Weiner, 1980).

Motivational interviewing is underpinned by self-determination theory (Deci and Ryan, 1985). This theory purports that those individuals with an external 'perceived locus of causality' believe that external forces (other people, situational and circumstantial factors) are responsible for instigating or forcing their action. Deci and Ryan found that where there is a higher internal perceived locus of causality, the individual will consider their behaviour to be of their own volition. The assumption is that the internal locus of causality is linked to motivation. Self-determination theory is derived from three areas – competency, relatedness to others and autonomy – and is enhanced when social and appropriate activities provide an environment that supports feelings of competency (Deci and Ryan, 1985).

CONSIDERATION OF CHANGE

The Role of Ambivalence

When working in the social care sector, practitioners should be aware that bringing about change in an individual's behaviour can bring with it a degree of ambivalence. It is this ambivalence, associated with either the lack of confidence or perceived lack of importance of the need to change problematic behaviour, which is most receptive to motivational interviewing techniques. Those individuals who have already made the decision to change their behaviour should not be targeted as this could move them back into ambivalence.

One of the key attributes of motivational interviewing is the establishment of the rapport between worker and service user. The worker needs to demonstrate a belief in the individual's self-efficacy and a belief that behaviour can be changed. Motivational interviewing has some similarities to Carl Rogers' (1959) client-centred approach in that motivational interviewing understands the individual to be at the centre of the intervention. It is important to allow the individual to describe the problem behaviour and how it impacts on their life in their own words.

In society as a whole, there is a tendency toward conformity to societal norms. This pre-supposes that individuals want to do the 'right thing'. Miller and Rollnick (2002: 20) discuss the 'righting reflex' in the context of ambivalence. The worker needs to avoid being prescriptive in the measures that could be employed to change behaviour as this may result only in the individual becoming more resistant and arguing the case for the problematic behaviour to continue. A more effective way of encouraging change is through allowing the individual to describe what their life is like at present and how they would like to see their life in the future.

By facilitating the individual to identify the positives of change, through developing change talk statements, self-efficacy can be supported. The individual may well choose to continue problematic behaviours, which the worker believes are not in the service user's interests, but it is important to recognise the ethical issues in maintaining choice and service user self-determination.

To read more about the use of motivational interviewing in social work practice see the article by Wahab (2005) on the Companion Website (www.sagepub.co.uk/SocialWork).

MOTIVATIONAL INTERVIEWING AND THE PROCESS OF CHANGE

Within this section of the chapter, we shall consider ways in which change is facilitated and measured, how readiness to change is determined, why an individual may want to change and the type of interaction that is likely to be most effective in achieving change.

The interview process provides the overarching framework for motivational intervention. Setting the agenda and the time available for the session at the outset is important to ensure the individual gains an outline of what to expect, thus allaying any undue concerns and avoiding situations where the individual makes a significant disclosure just prior to the end of the session.

Once the agenda has been set the worker should gather, through the use of open questions, the individual's perception and understanding of why they have attended and how they perceive the problem – if indeed they identify problematic behaviour. This is particularly important where the worker might be dealing with involuntary service users or where a referral has been made on their behalf by another agency or professional. Active listening skills are particularly important here to develop an understanding of the individual's perception of their situation. The worker should be seeking to note any self-motivational statements to assess the person's motivation and confidence in their ability to change. Acknowledging these statements is important as they can develop confidence in the individual's ability to change. Equally, when the individual raises negative attitudes toward change it is important that the worker seeks to reframe such statements positively. When summarising discussions it is important to be selective.

Motivational interviewing becomes more directive where the individual demonstrates resistance to change. Here the worker might argue for the problematic behaviour to continue with the aim of creating a non-confrontational situation within which the service user generates counter arguments. It is expected that these counter arguments will support change, resulting in eliciting self-change statements.

Given the nature of the people social workers seek to help, there is often the expectation that the social worker will tell them what to do. As a worker, it can be difficult to avoid steering the individual into a particular course of action. It is right and proper for the worker to discuss different options to enable the individual to develop their own decisional balance sheet with the pros and cons these might produce (Miller and Rollnick, 2002).

Prochaska and DiClemente (1986) devised the Process or Cycle of Change model as a means of understanding behavioural change. This cycle has five stages, depicted in Figure 23.1.

Pre-contemplation is where the individual does not perceive the behaviour as problematic and therefore does not consider the need for change. For example, the service user avoids discussion on the matter or refutes responsibility leading to denial or rationalisation. Within the *contemplation* stage, the individual begins to weigh up the pros and cons of continuing problematic behaviour and considers engaging in actions that may lead to change. The prompt for doing so could be a trigger that highlights the seriousness of the problem to the individual, such as a court appearance following an offence resulting in contact with criminal justice social work or the probation service. *Preparation* is where the individual begins to make plans to change the behaviour, and

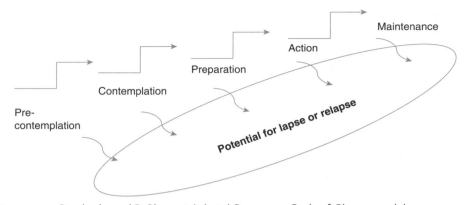

Figure 23.1 Prochaska and DiClemente's (1986) Process or Cycle of Change model

here momentum can build. *Action* is where the planned changes to the problematic behaviour are carried out successfully. *Maintenance* is achieved through sustained commitment to the changed behaviour in the longer term (Prochaska et al., 1992).

The Prochaska and DiClemente (1986) model can be very useful when working with service users as often no smooth pathway exists to achieving change. An individual may frequently lapse into previous problematic behaviours, and it is the social worker's role to recognise when this occurs. Early identification can ensure that the individual receives appropriate counselling to prevent relapse. Collaborative work with the individual is important here so as to recognise the difference between a lapse, which is a momentary return to problematic behaviour, and relapse, which is a more prolonged return to problematic behaviours. Such a collaborative discussion can promote the development of relapse prevention strategies to sustain changed behaviour and address issues in line with the individual's wishes. This can also enhance shared decision-making and negotiation regarding the steps to be taken to move toward change.

Exercise

Theories of attachment and loss provide explanations why we may wish to return to a familiar way of behaving when undertaking change. Consider this in relation to motivational interviewing.

The Prochaska and DiClemente (1986) model can be represented in circular or step form and is used directly with the individual, making for a very good visual tool when using motivational interviewing. Should the individual lapse or relapse, the visualisation can be used to demonstrate that the person may not have returned to the beginning of the cycle, depending on the action taken to combat lapse/relapse. This approach can help to reinstate lost confidence in the ability to change and enable the worker to elicit self-change talk statements and build the momentum for change within the individual.

Change can occur as a result of external factors, but it is frequently tenuous and short-lived (Ryan and Deci, 2000). If the goal is to promote long-term behaviour change, practitioners need to employ techniques that access internal motivation to change as opposed to those that rely solely on external coercion. Internal factors include how actions fit with personal values or goals ('How important is this change to me?') and attitudes regarding capability to change ('Am I going to be able to make this change?').

Exercise

Consider in your own life when you have made a significant change. Can you think about the motivating factors such as discomfort, perceived gain etc?

Service users who are more prepared for change are thinking about, talking about and exploring the possibility of change. The level of motivation demonstrated is a good predictor of the likely outcome (DiClemente et al., 1999). Motivation indicates the likelihood of an individual initiating and continuing with a particular action to change problematic behaviour. Referring back to the practice scenario earlier in this chapter we can see how motivation is behaviour-specific.

Motivation is not fixed but is changeable and as such can increase or decrease depending on the individual's circumstances and their responses to these. A collaborative working relationship is important here as it can play a significant role in building and sustaining motivation through being able to discuss problematic behaviour and reasons for wanting to change and is therefore an interactive process. The role of the practitioner in this instance can influence the way the individual talks and thinks about their behaviour. Table 23.1 demonstrates and considers the stages of change, the features of each stage and techniques that can be used by the worker.

When practitioners are working with individuals who are referred either on a voluntarily or involuntary basis, i.e., courts or children's hearing, a key area to be addressed is the assessment of the readiness to change. Where the individual does not view their behaviour as problematic, practitioners should use interventions that will raise awareness and build motivation for change. Alternatively, those individuals with increased motivation may need to focus on developing cognitive and behavioural skills as a means of moving from contemplation into action. The level of confidence an individual has regarding their ability to change is dynamic and as such can vary depending upon previous experiences of trying to implement change behaviours.

One means of assessing how ready the individual is to change is to introduce a self-assessment tool. Through introducing the use of a scale of 0–10, where 0 means not ready at all and 10 means very ready, a practitioner may ask 'On a scale of 0–10 how ready are you to reduce your alcohol intake?' The next step requires asking the individual to explain why they have identified a particular number. This is the beginning of a cognitive approach that provides an opportunity for the individual to explore the reasons behind their motivation to change and begin to elicit self-change talk.

Table 23.1 Stages of change adapted from Prochaska and DiClemente's (1986) model

Stage of change	Presenting features	Suggested techniques that can be employed
Pre-contemplation	Service user does not acknowledge problematic behaviour and therefore does not contemplate change	Recognise service user is not ready to change, **use of open questions** Advise that it is their decision to change behaviour Encourage greater discussion regarding problematic behaviour Facilitate and encourage reassessment of presenting behaviour, acknowledging that the service user will not take action Express empathy Demonstrate an understanding of the problem and how it affects them Identify and clarify the risks of continued problematic behaviours specific to the service user Develop discrepancy Discuss the service user's current lifestyle and the lifestyle they would wish to live
Contemplation	Service user is unsure or ambivalent about change Service user is not contemplating imminent change	Recognise and acknowledge that service user not ready to change – **roll with resistance** Advise that it is their decision to change their behaviour – **self-efficacy** Suggest undertaking an exercise to identify the positives and negatives of behaviour change – **elicit self-change talk** Identify and promote anticipation of positive results
Preparation	Service user is starting to experiment with some change behaviours Preparing for action soon Timescale within next 12 weeks	Identify and develop problem-solving skills to counter barriers to change Encourage service user to identify and draw on social support network Assess service user's skills level to support behaviour change Support and promote initial moves to change behaviour and **self-efficacy**
Action	Service user is trying out new behaviour(s) Timescale needs to demonstrate some degree of sustainability of between 3 and 6 months	Focus on developing new responses to indicators and social network Build **self-efficacy** to overcome barriers. Develop plans for managing feelings of loss as a result of change and encourage long-term benefits
Maintenance	Maintain commitment to sustaining behaviour change Following action stage on a continuous basis	Develop plan for ongoing support Support intrinsic gratification Discuss how to deal with relapse
Lapse/Relapse	Resumption of problematic behaviours	Identify and assess cause of lapse/relapse Express empathy Re-evaluate motivation and barriers to change Identify and develop more vigorous relapse management coping strategies

As practitioners, simply listening to what an individual talks about first or most often can give an indication as to what he/she finds important. However, sometimes we might need to kick start the process by asking a simple question such as 'If you decided to do this, how would that make things better for you?' Doing so can help determine what reasons this person might have for taking action.

When using motivational interviewing, practitioners should consider the learning style and intelligence level of the individual with whom they are working. Motivation and confidence in the ability to change can dwindle very quickly where interventions are not tailored to meet these factors. Similarly, the frequency of sessions and reminders of meetings via text or telephone call can all influence both compliance and outcome.

MOTIVATIONAL INTERVIEWING TECHNIQUES

As already indicated, it is important that the service user identifies the problematic behaviour and reasons for change, and the worker indicates how long the session will last and sets out an agenda. To begin the process, use open questions to allow the service user to explore what is of concern to them. Here the emphasis is on what the service user has to say and thus encouraging their ability to verbalise these issues is crucial as a means of 'eliciting and shaping' their speech (Miller and Rollnick, 2002: 65). An example might be: 'What concerns you most about your drug use?'

As the service user talks, the worker should use reflective listening skills, commenting on what they have heard in the response that they give. Often this may be to explore what is being said, as people may have different interpretations that could result in ambiguity, particularly where emotions play a significant role. Reflective listening acts as a means of verifying what is meant rather than making assumptions. Reflective listening statements are a core requirement at the outset of motivational interviewing. For example, in response to a service user stating 'I worry that if I don't stop using drugs I will end up in prison', the response might be: 'You are thinking about seeking help and that's why you are here.'

During any change process, service users need to be encouraged to sustain engagement, which can be achieved by the use of statements that affirm and support the effort being made. Reflective listening is useful here but is reinforced by the use of statements demonstrating praise and understanding, an example being: 'I appreciate the fact that you have been so open in discussing a very difficult issue, I understand how hard it was for you.'

The worker's ability to periodically and selectively summarise self-motivational statements used by the service user should be emphasised to strengthen the impact of what has been discussed. An example might be: 'This last court appearance has made you begin to consider the longer term consequences of your drug use and offending behaviour. You mentioned you are really anxious about going to prison and how this will affect your relationship with your family. The fact that you came here today seeking to try to do something about your drug use is really positive.'

To achieve the goal of resolving ambivalence to change effectively, the worker may advocate continuing the problematic behaviour, the aim being for the service user to argue for change, thus eliciting self-motivational statements. Similarly, the worker can point out the positives of changing behaviour and build confidence in the likelihood of success. An example might be: 'I want to kick drugs so that I don't have to commit crime to pay for them.' Here the service user is identifying the negatives of doing nothing.

Whilst it might be important to the service user to change problematic behaviour, often the confidence in their ability to change is low and has already been eroded through previous failed attempts to change behaviour, low self-esteem and feelings of low self-worth. Practitioners should be mindful to assess the level of confidence, and, again, a self-assessment ruler from 0 to 10 can be very useful as it engages the service user in their own situation and can begin to elicit self-change talk. It may be useful to explore with the service user situations where they have attempted to change their behaviour, and the reasons they believed it failed, to help identify pitfalls and develop strategies to overcome them should the need arise. Practitioners at this stage may introduce individual or group work to raise self-esteem and self-worth in preparation for work specifically to address problematic behaviour.

On the Companion Website (www.sagepub.co.uk/SocialWork) you will find a case study activity concerning Mary, a 27-year-old woman who has a history of alcohol dependence. Think about how you would work with Mary and see the commentary for more information.

EVIDENCE-BASED PRACTICE

The need for social workers to demonstrate effectiveness, efficiency and economy of service is ever present. In this context it is important to consider the evidence base for use of motivational interviewing.

As indicated in the introduction to this chapter, the roots of motivational interviewing originate from working with problematic addiction, primarily alcohol use. Research undertaken by Brown and Miller (1993) and Heather et al. (1996) indicated that the use of brief opportunistic interventions, which included motivational elements, increased the likelihood of problematic alcohol users' contact with substance misuse services even when assessed as not ready for change. Over time, motivational interviewing techniques have been extended for use in other areas, including health, specifically eating disorders, and working with offenders, including sex offenders (McMurran, 2002).

Research undertaken by Harper and Hardy (2000) evaluated the introduction of motivational interviewing techniques within Middlesex Probation Service. Statistically there was evidence that the attitudinal scales amongst those offenders whose probation officers had motivational interviewing skills showed more significant improvement in motivation to change compared to those officers who were not trained. In addition, Clark and colleagues (2006), in a study that focused on probationers, found motivational interviewing used by probation officers was effective as an intervention for handling resistance, focusing on change, and for enforcing compliance with the conditions of supervision. The Crime and Justice Institute (2004) identified motivational interviewing as the second of eight evidence-based principles for effective interventions in working with offenders. Other studies of motivational interviewing have examined the use of the approach across a range of risk behaviours in a range of different settings, both with adults and adolescents (Hohman, 1998; Miller et al., 1993; Murphy et al., 2004; Rutledge et al., 2001).

Cummings et al. (2009) undertoook a review and assessment of existing litera-ture regarding the efficacy of motivational interviewing with older people. You can read their findings on the Companion Website (www.sagepub.co.uk/SocialWork).

Critical Thinking: Motivational Interviewing

A number of research studies have been carried out into the effectiveness of motivational interviewing across a range of problematic behaviours. These range in complexity from the management of substance misuse, which is where motivational interviewing originated, and eating disorders to basic health problems such as the management of life-style and behaviour in Type 2 diabetes. Research has, however, been limited, specifically in identify-ing whether differences in outcomes are determined by voluntary entry into treatment or where there is deemed to be a level of coercion, such as if treatment is imposed by a court order. Therefore for us to gain a rounded understanding of the effectiveness of motiva-tional interviewing we need to consider the research that underpins this approach. Table 23.2 provides an example of how research evidence can be evaluated.

Table 23.2   Evaluation of research evidence

Proposition	Evaluating the argument	Comparison with other sources
Motivation can be built in criminal justice clients with the right kind of preparation or 'readiness training' on what personal resources they may need (to change), self confidence in the ability to change, and willingness to accept and even welcome the process and its consequences. (Ashton, 2005)	The premise of motivational interviewing is that it is client-directed, the client identifies the problem not the court. This can bring about tensions between the requirements of the courts and the client being in a state of 'readiness' to address problematic behaviours. A secondary element to the use of coercion is the establishment of a therapeutic working relationship between the client and worker.	Research by Clark et al. (2006) suggests motivational interviewing is consistent with evidence-based practice and can focus the work of probation through developing skills to deal effectively with resistance to change, prepare offenders for change through promoting self-change talk and allows the worker to guide the content of the conversation.

CONCLUSION

In this chapter you have been introduced to the purpose and techniques of motivational interviewing. You will have developed a wider understanding of the need for the use of empathy within the development of a working alliance as a means of bringing about change to meet the intrinsic need of the service user. By developing and using the skills of reflective listening and motivational techniques within your practice you can promote change effectively. Practitioners should have knowledge of and an ability to understand and apply the process of change within practice, as this is a crucial element of working effectively with service users. Motivational interviewing used alongside other interventions, such as cognitive behavioural programmes or brief opportunistic interventions where the service user demonstrates ambivalence in the ability to change problematic behaviours, has been demonstrated to increase participation and retention in change programmes.

Reflective Questions

1 Consider times in your own life when you have experienced problems that required to be addressed. In dealing with these situations would you say that you had an external or internal perceived locus of causality? Did you find that the internal perceived locus of causality took time to realise? In your own experience how important was an internal locus of causality to the motivation for change? In practice situations what difference does it make to the social work intervention when a service user has an internal perceived locus of causality?

2 Motivational interviewing is based on four key principles: express empathy; develop discrepancy; roll with resistance; and support self-efficacy. What experience have you had up until now of using techniques that support these principles? What skills do you need to develop to use this approach?

3 Prochaska and DiClemente's Cycle of Change model incorporates lapse and relapse. Do you think this aspect of the model is advantageous? What benefits might there be for service users?

RECOMMENDED READING

McMurran, M. (2002) *Motivating Offenders to Change: A Guide to Enhancing Engagement in Therapy*. Chichester: Wiley.

Miller, W.R. and Rollnick, S. (2002) *Motivational Interviewing: Preparing People for Change*, 2nd edn. New York: Guilford.

Rollnick, S. and Miller, W.R. (1995) 'What is motivational interviewing?', *Behavioural and Cognitive Psychotherapy*, 23: 325–34.

Rollnick, S., Miller, W.R. and Butler, C.C. (2008) *Motivational Interviewing in Health Care*. New York: Guilford.

THE SOLUTION-FOCUSED APPROACH

24

Jim Dressel and Jillian Brannan

Key Themes

- The solution-focused approach is a strengths-based approach to practice where the service user is seen to be the expert on their own life.
- Solution-focused work developed from solution-focused brief therapy in the early 1980s in the United States.
- It has a strong philosophical belief in the uniqueness of each individual and the individual's capacity to use inner resources to achieve change.
- The approach is future-focused rather than an analysis of problem-causation.
- The social worker's role is to assist service users to identify strengths and abilities, using principles, concepts and tools to guide solution-focused working.

INTRODUCTION

A central tenet of social work practice is the concept of empowerment – the belief that individuals and families have the capacity and strength to exercise control over their own lives, thereby effecting change. In line with this perspective, strengths-based approaches have attracted much interest amongst social work practitioners, seeking to facilitate service users' capitalisation of their own assets and resources. Solution-focused working is one of the strengths-based approaches, and in this chapter we explore in detail the specific focus, core beliefs, principles, concepts, tools and skills that a social work practitioner, intent on employing this method, would be required to understand and develop.

At the heart of a solution-focused approach is the achievement of positive change for people who experience life-debilitating difficulties. Solution-focused working is designed to stimulate within a person inherent strengths to change how they manage their lives and their relationship with themselves or others. As this chapter will demonstrate, the approach offers a progressive and empowering model of engagement.

THE DEVELOPMENT OF A SOLUTION-FOCUSED APPROACH

It is not the intention of this chapter to provide a detailed history of solution-focused working; however, it is important for you to have some understanding of how and where this approach developed. One of the first things of importance here is the terminology used to describe the approach.

So far we have used interchangeably the terms solution-focused approach and solution-focused working, but a review of other literature would guarantee that you find the terms 'solution-focused brief therapy' (SFBT) or 'solution-focused therapy' (SFT). The word therapy here reflects the developmental roots of the approach, and the word brief refers to the concept of a therapy that is focused and specific rather than open-ended.

Our reason for not using the terms SFBT or SFT is that the idea of something being a *therapy* can be interpreted as being undertaken only by therapists, which social workers, particularly in a UK context, tend not to be. Our preference therefore is to use the term 'solution-focused approach' (hereafter abbreviated to SFA) within this chapter. It is worth noting that solution-focused ideas are present in a range of fields both within and outside the helping professions.

The Perceived Purpose of Therapy

The development of SFBT took place in the United States of America in the early 1980s and represented a **paradigm shift** from traditional approaches in therapy. The previous domination of a Freudian approach to psychotherapy had long placed an emphasis on problem analysis. Winbolt (2011) outlines three reasons why an emphasis on problem-solving as revolving around problem-analysis is problematic:

- Analysis is about thinking – not necessarily doing.
- Service users are frequently already proficient at analysis and rumination.
- Analysis looks for causation.

The significant shift with SFBT was the proposition that to arrive at a solution it was not necessary to understand the cause of the problem.

The Emergence of SFBT

The two main cited protagonists of SFBT, Steve de Shazer and Insoo Kim Berg, had a background in social work (Hanton, 2011), although as practitioners in the United States there was a much stronger 'therapy' influence and context to their work. Both de Shazer and Berg were extremely interested in the brief therapy model of the Mental

Research Institute (MRI) in Palo Alto, California, which focused on the current presenting problem rather than childhood history or underlying problems. The model was also underpinned by the idea that the solution was contained within the client in the here and now, thus increasing the client's ability to influence change.

De Shazer and Berg established the Brief Family Therapy Centre in Milwaukee, working with a team of colleagues to develop a therapeutic approach which had efficacy for the families they met with. Ratner et al. (2012: 21) point out that 'de Shazer was fond of saying, SFBT has no theory base', however, it is important to be aware of the strong philosophical influences that underpinned the development of SFBT and of the detailed observation and exploratory practice base related to its development (see Lipchik et al., 2012).

De Shazer, influenced by the work of Erickson, believed that each individual uniquely possessed skills and coping mechanisms throughout life, which set a strong context for the development of SFBT and the assumption that service users possessed inner resources and strengths. Through observation and analysis of therapy sessions over a number of years, de Shazer believed that it was no longer necessary to spend time diagnosing the problem; instead, attention turned to solution talk. People often came to therapy burdened with their problems, and de Shazer's style of questioning enabled people to think about what their life would look like if their circumstances improved. The outcome was that people were more likely to focus on their preferred future, thus generating optimism, a hope for change and self-efficacy.

Visser (2008) has suggested that people can become stuck in the 'problem dimension'– being unable to see any possibility of change. He goes on to suggest that problems are maintained by doing more of the same, having no expectation of change and being problem-focused. Some of the techniques used in everyday conversation to support people with their problems include:

- Reassurance – It's okay, try not to worry about it.
- Direction – This is what you can do.
- Passive support – I'm just here to listen.
- Taking control – This is what I'll do to help.

These kinds of techniques, however, stifle the person with the problem from being able to build a solution. In turn, the four 'techniques': shut down the conversation; focus on advice; place the helper in an entirely passive role; and lastly, place the helper in a problem-solver role. In a professional context such techniques are not helpful and you may conclude that the solution-focused techniques discussed in this chapter offer more appropriate alternatives.

Exercise

Thinking about recent practice, have you used any of the above techniques? With what results?

PRINCIPLES AND KEY CONCEPTS OF THE SOLUTION-FOCUSED APPROACH

Principles

Moving from a problem focus to a solution focus is a substantial shift. A problem focus tends to be characterised by a concentration on what is wrong, what needs to be fixed, seeing the situation as outside one's control, paying attention to deficits and weaknesses, and expecting that the expert knows best. A solution focus, on the other hand, looks at what is wanted, how the individual can influence and make progress, strengths and resources, and the concept of collaboratively working towards the desired change (McKergow, 2007). Working with a service user to achieve this shift is founded on a number of core principles:

- If it works, don't fix it – recognising inherent competence, building on what is functioning and separating of the person from the problem.
- If something works (better) do more of it – recognising encouragement and support might be needed to keep achieving and sustaining a new behaviour.
- Look for differences that make a difference – recognising that virtually nothing is constant and that identifying exceptions is an essential component in building solutions.
- If something does not work, do something else – recognising that there may be a need to try again and that such changes are not failures but affirmative actions.
- Small changes can lead to bigger changes – recognising that incremental change can achieve positive benefits.
(Based on Milner and O'Byrne, 2002; Bannink, 2010)

Key Concepts

We would hope by now that you are recognising the SFA as a competency-based model in which the emphasis is on the service user as solution-builder as opposed to the social worker as problem-solver. The social worker's role in a SFA is to work collaboratively with the service user. Echoing de Shazer, Bannink (2010) refers to this helping relationship as leading from one step behind, where metaphorically the worker is behind the service user looking in the same direction and using relevant questioning to provide the person with a tap on the shoulder – a nudge in the right direction.

A core part of the social worker's function is to help service users to recognise exceptions to the problem, times when the problem was less of a problem; to find alternative ways of being from within their existing repertoire or as co-constructed solutions; and to work from a stance that assumes solutions already exist thereby subscribing fully to the 'assumption of [service user] competence and expertise' (Trepper et al., 2012: 27).

Underpinning the above, and something which will become clearer as you read about specific tools, is a different conversation and questioning style from other approaches to practice. Indeed, the style of questions and the language used by the worker is a key area of skill and something that will need to be learned. The use of language in a SFA is important from at least two perspectives.

Firstly, the social worker needs to focus very carefully on what the service user is actually saying. By listening to and absorbing the service user's words and meanings, the social worker is able to formulate and ask the next question by connecting to the service user's key words and phrases. Secondly, during discussion with the service user, the language used by the social worker should be congruent with a future-focused, positive and strengths perspective. So the language emphasises 'when' rather than 'if'; 'will' rather than 'would'; 'and' rather than 'but; 'how' rather than 'why'; and 'up until now' rather than 'currently'.

 To develop your understanding further see the activity on the Companion Website (www.sagepub.co.uk/SocialWork); this invites you to test out how you use language and learn from situations you encounter.

TOOLS AND SKILLS USED IN THE SOLUTION-FOCUSED APPROACH

Tools

There are a number of specific techniques and tools which are used in a SFA. These underpin the worker–user relationship, form the structure of the intervention and guide the social worker's stance, questions and commentary. Figure 24.1 summarises the main aspects. You will find that most of the 'techniques' reflect the principles and key concepts of the SFA, as discussed earlier in this chapter; as a result, little annotation has been added. It is anticipated that the 'tools' will be less familiar and more detailed explanation is given. Further discussion of the tools and their application will be provided in the practice example later in this chapter.

For a discussion of how tools and techniques can be used in practice situations see the research by Kondrat and Teater (2012) on the Companion Website (www.sagepub. co.uk/SocialWork).

Skills

The core skills and value base required for social work practice are central to use of a SFA. Indeed, Wheeler (2003) suggests that some skills are particularly necessary in this approach, such as the ability to work collaboratively with a service user. Furthermore, he argues that the SFA 'transforms the power relationship between helpers and helped' (p. 108) and is therefore an approach to practice consistent with a strong value base.

In addition to use of core skills, there are some specific skills that social workers require to develop in order to work with a SFA. Writing from a therapy perspective, Hanton (2011) has identified a number of underpinning skills, some of which we believe are pertinent to social work practitioners:

- The ability to engage in problem-free talk.
- The ability to listen actively for client strengths, resources and skills, and any past or present utilisation of those skills.
- The ability to look for exceptions and differences.
- The ability to take a non-expert stance.

Techniques

1. The development of a positive working relationship
2. Looking for previous solutions *(Identifying and amplifying past successes and areas of strength)*
3. Asking questions rather than issuing directives or making interpretations
4. Being present- and future-focused rather than taking a past orientation
5. Making compliments *(Validating what the service user is experiencing. Giving genuine feedback and praise on what they are doing that is useful, the strengths demonstrated, their qualities etc.)*
6. Offering encouragement to build on successes

Tools

1. Pre-session change *(Asking whether there has been any change with regard to the problem between making and attending the first appointment. The act of making an appointment is a positive step that can be the catalyst of some change. In subsequent sessions asking about progress)*
2. Solution-focused goal(s) *(These are statement(s) of what the service user would like to achieve. Most importantly they are determined by the service user. Parton and O'Byrne (2000) include the following as some of the characteristics of well-formed goals: specific and achievable, small rather than large, involve doing something, have a here and now focus, involve the presence of something rather than the absence of something, are in the person's control, are expressed in the person's language and are perceived by the person as needing hard work)*
3. Miracle question *(A question form that involves stepping outside of the problem and stepping into the desired future. The authentic format is:*
   'I am going to ask you a strange question. [pause] Suppose [pause] that tonight you go to bed and sleep as usual [pause] and while you are asleep a miracle happens [pause], and the problem that brought you here [look around to all present] is solved. [pause] However, because you are asleep you don't know that the miracle has already happened. [pause] When you wake up in the morning, what will be different that will tell you that the problem has been solved? [silence]' (Berg and Miller, 1992: 13))
4. Relationship question *(As a systemic approach solution-focused work seeks to understand who else will notice differences and who else is affected. Relationship questions tease out these aspects)*
5. Exception question *(A question that asks the service user about times when some small part of the miracle [or positive future scenario] is already happening. Through looking for exceptions the social worker can begin to identify past successes and the seeds of potential solutions in the here and now)*
6. Scaling question *(A question that asks the service user to place themselves on a scale from 0 to 10 as to where they are now in relation to their desired goal. Scaling questions are also used to gauge a person's motivation to change and how confident they feel that the change will happen. Scaling questions are used to measure the service user's perception of progress)*
7. Coping question *(At times service users may find it difficult to identify any exceptions. Coping questions are therefore designed to facilitate discussion of what the person does to cope, including how they have prevented things from becoming worse)*
8. Session break *(The scheduling in of a session break provides an opportunity for the worker to reflect on the discussion with the service user. It allows the worker an opportunity to think differently, before reconvening and planning the intervention i.e. the next step)*
9. Homework task *(The idea of setting a task is to encourage the service user to build on the strengths identified during the session. The broader SFA literature identifies a number of different types of task; but the important link between these is that the task involves the service user actively noticing what is going on around them and actively being aware of what is already positive)*

Figure 24.1   Tools and techniques of the solution-focused approach

- The ability to utilise specific question types.
- The ability to be aware of how language is used.

It is important to consider the specific skills required to engage with a SFA, particularly, as Winbolt (2011: 19) cautions, '[these] are easy to learn, if a little more difficult to perfect in practice'. One of the key issues appears to centre on the practitioner building a repertoire of questions, formulated in the language of solution-talk, which can be used confidently, flexibly and creatively in discussions with service users. The practice scenario below will provide some example questions for you to begin to engage with this process.

APPLICATION OF THE SOLUTION-FOCUSED APPROACH TO SOCIAL WORK PRACTICE

Case Study

Within a family a 14-year-old child, Henry, is constantly told off by his father, John. The situation escalates and becomes an ongoing, daily argument. As a consequence, John becomes increasingly angry and aggressive towards Henry. In turn Henry responds by reflecting an angry tone back towards John. The result is a deteriorating relationship and an uncomfortable family situation (there is also a mother and a younger child living in the household).

For John the problem lies with Henry, whom he perceives to be rather insolent in his teenage years. For Henry the problem lies with John, whom he perceives to be 'always on his back' about something. Henry gradually becomes more depressed about his situation and his school attendance begins to suffer.

If the above case was referred to a family social worker an initial assessment would be carried out to determine if John's behaviours have escalated to physical or emotional child abuse. If this is the case, the social worker must implement their statutory duty and professional authority to consider how to protect Henry and anyone else. It is essential to stress that these considerations are primary and that whilst a SFA is considered therapeutic, collaborative and co-constructivist, such an approach is not an alternative to core professional duties. Assuming, however, that child/adult protection intervention is not necessary and that the level of interaction between John and the family is considered repairable, the social worker may have the opportunity to engage in solution-focused work with John, Henry and the family. The following discussion of the intervention focuses on work with John.

Intervention

During the development of SFBT it was recognised that those attending may not always be doing so on a voluntary basis. Three different ways of describing the 'client', and by association the 'client's' motivation to engage, were put forward:

Visitors: Those sent to attend by someone else, i.e., reluctant.

Complainants: Those who recognise there is a problem but who seem uninterested or unwilling to do anything about it. They may see the solution as the responsibility of someone else, i.e., ambivalent.

Customers: Those who want to do something to change their situation, i.e., engaged.

Ratner et al. (2012: 24) report that in the early 1990s de Shazer changed his mind about the importance of these distinctions, saying that 'everyone was a customer for something, even if it was to get someone else off their back'. Being aware, however, that John may be reluctant to attend or ambivalent about what he wants to achieve is pertinent to the social work intervention. In addition, it is important to recognise that in a SFA reluctance and ambivalence can both be worked with.

Opening Question

At the start of the first meeting with John it would be usual to ask:

'What brought you here today?' and subsequently, 'How can I help you?' As indicated above, it may be that John feels he had no choice but to attend or has no idea what he expects. In these scenarios the social worker needs to explore further what John is thinking and maintain a positive stance. Identifying what may have changed prior to the session is useful: 'John what has changed or gone better since we arranged this time together?'

The latter question may be used at a first session and succeeding sessions to uncover and reinforce any natural headway that John and the family have made. If the response is that there has been no improvement, then the social worker may ask 'How can I help today?' or 'What can we do in this session to help to make a difference?'

After gathering some information the social worker could ask 'OK, John, let's say your meeting with me today is useful. What would be the first things that you notice are different for you?' The objective of the question is to begin to stimulate within John a sense of a possible solution to his problem. What is important at this stage is that the thinking belongs to John, with the social worker acting as a catalyst to trigger John's thinking. The social worker must not attempt to promote their own or the agency's ulterior goals for managing the problem.

Solution-focused Goals

The social worker will strive to establish with John the explicit goal(s) he wishes to achieve. Encouraging John to begin with the end in mind and visualising a specific concrete goal is important to a successful outcome. There may be the possibility that John is too ambitious and his goal may be far reaching. In this case, the social worker will look to assist John to describe a more reachable goal.

In John's circumstances he may say 'I want Henry to stop arguing with me.' Whilst this may be what John wants it does not describe a personal goal. The social worker may ask the following types of questions to help John to describe and personalise his goal:

- What will it be like when the problem is solved?
- What will you be doing instead?
- When that happens, what difference will it make?
- How will other people know that things are better?
- Who will notice first? And then who?
- What else will be different?
- What else?

This will enable John to link his outcome to his feelings, thinking and behaviour. It is important for John to describe the solution in terms of what *will* happen rather than what *will not* be happening. Identifying the goal as a solution opens the possibility of it being linked into the scaling question (see below).

Miracle Question

Having steered John towards the beginnings of a possible solution the social worker will use, as the crux of the first session, the miracle question. The miracle question has been included in the Tools section in Figure 24.1 and you should refer back to this if required.

The way in which the miracle question is communicated to John is vital to the session. When introducing the question the idea that it is a strange question is designed to catch the attention of John in the moment. The social worker's tone of voice should be calm with a slow pace and there should be good eye contact. Finally, the social worker needs to work with the silence that will follow as John contemplates his answer.

The miracle question underpins the first session, with the intention of focusing John's mind on what can positively affect his behaviours. The process will set in motion his thinking, feelings and behaviours onto a pathway of accomplishing his goals. The answers to the miracle question will be referred to in subsequent sessions.

One of the challenges a social worker needs to be aware of is the use of the word 'miracle'. Depending on the person's life experiences or circumstances the use of the miracle question may be inappropriate – for example, due to illness, cognitive disability, culture, religion or age; therefore, the social worker may need to adapt the use of the miracle question.

The following are options which remove the concept of a miracle, but maintain the purpose of promoting new thinking, feelings and behaviours:

- Assume you wake up tomorrow morning and, for some reason or another, the feeling you have is no longer a problem. What will you be doing?
- Suppose that in six months' time, I'm walking down the street and bump into you: I ask how you are and you say 'much better'. What will have had to change in order for you to be able to say that and mean it?
- If we could look into a crystal ball and see the future, what will we see?

The use of the miracle question or its alternatives is designed to move John to a time when the problem with Henry does not exist. Following John's answer, the social worker may use a relationship question to elicit more information – 'Who would notice that this miracle had happened?' and 'Who else?' In addition, an exception question may also be asked – 'Are there any small parts of this miracle happening already?'

Exception Questions

A potential challenge when working with someone like John is the possibility of him seeing the situation at home as beyond recovery. In these circumstances John may become resistant to engaging with the social worker and see the process as futile. When this happens the social worker will find the exception question a useful tool to increase John's awareness of the occasions, no matter how few, when he has been in control and managed his situation.

The social worker will ask questions designed to determine times when things were better, such as:

- What is happening when the problem is not there?
- What are you doing when the problem is less?
- What are you doing instead at these times?
- What else is going well at these times?

If John has previously mentioned a time when things have gone well the attentive social worker will purposely refer to this in the exception question. Engaging in this discussion also allows the opportunity for compliments to be made.

At this stage it is important not to leave John's comments vague but to establish specifically what he was doing and who was aware of it. A useful question is to ask 'What else?' when John appears to have completed his account. This generates deeper thought and aids John to build stronger solutions.

The exception question empowers John to see that he does have the capacity to manage the situation and that he can plan small steps which will make a difference for him and Henry.

Scaling Questions

The scaling question has multiple functions, depending on the creativity of the social worker. It is principally designed to help the service user establish where they are in the moment and enable them to make changes to their behaviour. Examples of how the scaling question may unfold are:

Social worker:	On a scale of 0–10 where are you at the moment in your relationship with Henry if 10 is in a good place and 0 is the worst you have ever been?
John:	[uncertain] Between 3 or 4.
Social worker:	[looking for clarity] Nearer 3 or nearer 4?
John:	[after a pause] 3.

| Social worker: | [endeavouring to have John determine what will be an acceptable place] What number will be OK for you to feel satisfied? |
| John: | [after pause for reflection] 8. |

John has now identified a numerical target which enables a comparison to be made between current circumstances and future life changes. At this stage the social worker will not know what this means therefore will want to establish what it means to John, by asking:

| Social worker: | What will be different when you reach 8? |
| John: | I will not be falling out with Henry every day and we will be having good times together. |

The social worker is aware that change does not happen overnight and will ask a series of other questions using the scaling question as a platform. For example:

| Social worker: | 8 is good target [pause] and may be a little way off [pause] how will you know that you have moved from 3 to 4? What else will be different? Who will notice? How long do you think it will it take you to get to 4? |

The language of the social worker is important to give a positive anticipation of future change by use of the word 'will' when asking the questions. If the social worker's tone of voice is positive and the words used reflect the future tense John is more likely to commit to his plan.

The scaling question may also be used to discover John's confidence in the solution happening and his commitment or motivation to change, as exampled below:

Social worker:	On a scale of 0–10 how determined are you to make the change?
John:	I would say about 8 – I am fed up of how things are just now.
Social worker:	[looking to enable John to reinforce his change strategy] What will help you not to be fed up, as you are 8 out of 10 determined to make things better with Henry?
John:	We have had good times in the past. We need to start having some laughs together.

At subsequent meetings the use of the scaling question will be useful to monitor change and help John to see his progress.

Coping Questions

An alternative to the exception and scaling questions may be needed if John does not describe a time when things were better or when his current situation is scaled at 0. The social worker will ask John questions such as:

- How have you managed to prevent things from getting worse with Henry?
- Things seem really difficult, how are you managing to cope the way you are?

Coping questions allow the social worker to explore with John his coping strategies. These questions also facilitate the opportunity to highlight John's strengths by exploring what is different about times when he has coped slightly better – 'What was different then?' The social worker will also need to be attentive to John's responses in order to provide positive feedback when good intentions are noticed or positive comments are made.

Session Break

Towards the end of the session the social worker should take a short break to gather thoughts, reflect and identify positive areas of focus that have materialised during the discussion. The break is an important part of the process and can be introduced to John by saying:

> Social worker: I am going to take a short break to think about what we have been discussing today, how I can help and what will be useful to do next.

After the break the social worker would reconvene with John to provide feedback, explain intentions and outline the task for John to undertake. Feedback is provided as genuine compliments and should reflect in John's own words the strengths and qualities the social worker has heard. For example:

> Social worker: John, the fact that you have come here today tells me that you want to improve your relationship with Henry. You have had a good relationship in the past and you are determined to get that back …

Explaining intentions provides a linking statement to the task and is focused on explaining the context of what the service user is being asked to do.

The Task

The purpose of the task is to increase the service user's thoughts, feelings and behaviours which will work towards their goal(s). The task is not about the worker providing solutions. Tasks are varied and may involve one of the following:

- Asking John to observe the situation at home, focusing on what Henry does differently and what he also does differently.
- Asking John to notice and list all that is happening in his life that he wants to continue happening.
- Asking John to identify something he can do differently and trying that out.
- Asking John to do more of something he has identified in the session as a positive that worked.

Subsequent Sessions

The subsequent sessions with John would begin with asking 'What is better?' and linking to previous scaling questions. Parton and O'Byrne (2000) note that the EARS process is important in ongoing work where the social worker:

- Elicits what changes there have been
- Amplifies what differences the changes made
- Reinforces the changes through compliments
- Starts over by asking what else is better.

As John's relationship with Henry gradually improves the idea of maintenance should be built into sessions. The focus here will be on how John can do more of what is working, thereby staying on track.

Critical Thinking

Solution-focused working is a skilled intervention requiring mastery of a range of specific questioning tools and techniques. Whilst the approach offers opportunities to transform outcomes for service users there are risks that busy, time-pressured practitioners and agencies attempt to use the SFA in ways that compromise its effectiveness – for example, working at a pace that imposes solutions or failing to explore the service user's thoughts, feelings and behaviours by omitting 'what else?' Spend time considering both what skills you need to develop in order to work with a SFA and the support and environment that would be required to use this approach in practice.

Exercise

The research evidence examining the effectiveness of solution-focused working is described by Corcoran and Pillai (2009) as equivocal. Yet those involved in the development of SFBT (see Lipchik et al., 2012) would argue that there is a wealth of exploratory practice-based research demonstrating 'what works' and evidencing outcomes. Undertaking further reading of the evidence base for the approach will assist in developing your understanding of these arguments.

As a starting point for reviewing the research evidence see the qualitative review undertaken by Gingerich and Peterson (2013) which can be accessed on the Companion Website (www.sagepub.co.uk/SocialWork).

CONCLUSION

The SFA offers a powerful method of intervention to help service users bring about change. The emphasis on service users as being experts in their own lives is congruent with the value base of social work practice and the guiding ethical and conduct codes. Using a SFA in work with service users enables the practitioner to:

- Recognise the inherent strengths and capacity of service users.
- Support service users to achieve positive change in their lives.
- Work from a future oriented perspective that places an emphasis on actions rather than analysis.
- Engage service users in solution-building rather than problem-solving.
- Develop a truly collaborative working partnership with service users in which questioning rather than directing leads to change – curiosity rather than imposition.
- Practise within a framework of core principles, concepts and tools; but use these flexibly so that they are part of a creative rather than formulaic process.
- Strengthen communication skills by moving away from the language of problems and moving toward the language of solutions.

Reflective Questions

1 The SFA presents a specific stance on how problems can be overcome, i.e., the idea that finding solutions does not necessarily mean analysing the cause of a problem. What do you think are the strengths of this stance? Do you think it has any weaknesses? Is it a stance you concur with or do you favour other approaches to understanding problems and solutions?

2 The 'miracle question' is a useful and, for many, central tool to the SFA; yet not all practitioners would feel comfortable using this type of question. What are your own views about the miracle question? Do you think you could use the question in work with service users?

3 In what kinds of circumstances can you see the SFA being the most appropriate choice of intervention? What might be barriers to use of this approach?

RECOMMENDED READING

Connie, E. and Metcalf, L. (eds) (2009) *The Art of Solution Focused Therapy*. New York: Springer.

Corcoran, J. and Pillai, V. (2009) 'A review of the research on solution focused therapy', *British Journal of Social Work*, 39: 234–42.

Johnsen, I. (2005) 'ESTEEM: A solution focused training model (part one). *Solution News*, 1 (4): 17–20; and ESTEEM: A solution-focused training model (part two)', *Solution News*, 2 (1): 13–15.

Milner, J. and O'Byrne, P. (2002) *Brief Counselling: Narratives and Solutions*. Basingstoke: Palgrave Macmillan.

Winbolt, B. (2011) *Solution Focused Therapy for the Helping Professions*. London: Jessica Kingsley Publishers.

Refer to the Companion Website (www.sagepub.co.uk/SocialWork) for some useful links to web-based materials.

COUNSELLING IN
25 SOCIAL WORK

Fiona Feilberg

Key Themes

- Central to any definition of counselling is the importance of relationship.
- There are particular theories to which schools of counselling adhere.
- These theories derive from a psychological base.
- There is a direct correlation with models of social work intervention.
- Supervision is a key factor for a worker who engages in counselling.

INTRODUCTION

Though the influence of counselling knowledge and skills may sometimes be less explicitly stated in the present context of social work, there is continuing and growing relevance in seeing counselling as a part of social work. This is both in the sense of using a range of counselling skills in a range of settings (Seden, 2005) and as a direct method of intervention. The range of settings where social workers may be undertaking counselling is extensive and includes mental health services, in school settings, criminal justice work, with people who are misusing substances, with people who are or who have become disabled and in work with children and families.

In this chapter I explore what counselling is, provide an outline of psychodynamic, person-centred and cognitive behavioural counselling, explore the relevance of counselling for social work practice and look at the importance of supervision and support in the use of counselling methods.

DEFINING COUNSELLING

It is important to clarify what counselling is and before moving on to consider different theoretical perspectives consider the following.

COSCA (Counselling and Psychotherapy in Scotland) (2011) describes counselling as a way of responding to a wide range of human needs including lack of self-confidence or self-esteem, relationship difficulties, work-related stress, bullying, difficult transitions, problems associated with one's own or someone else's drinking or drug use, bereavement, mental health problems, vague feelings of unease, desire for personal change and many more. The aim is to 'provide opportunities for those seeking help to find their own ways towards living in more satisfying and resourceful ways'.

McLeod (2009) lists the following aims: insight, self-awareness, self-acceptance, self-actualisation and individualisation, enlightenment, problem-solving, psychological education, acquisition of social skills, cognitive change, behavioural change, systemic change, empowerment and restitution. The aim of some individuals is to manage their problems in living more effectively (problem-solving), whereas for others the focus is more on developing unused or underused opportunities more fully (**personal growth**).

Counselling is a process of talking, listening and working through issues in the context of a supportive relationship with another person. The goals of counselling vary from person to person, but every counselling model stresses the importance of the relationship, and it is here that one of the strongest links to social work is made. Central to social work and to counselling is the development of the relationship between the worker and service user. It has long been recognised that the relational aspect of working with others forms the basis of effective working, regardless of the theoretical orientation, structures and systems within which services are provided. Rogers (1957) argued that 'significant personality change does not occur except in a relationship', Spencer (2000) that 'the experience of being met in a relationship is what matters' and Dewane (2006: 543) that the relationship is 'the cornerstone of change'.

A variety of skills are important for effective counselling. Listing such skills can be endless and include such areas as good communication skills, listening, building trust, handling feelings and setting boundaries (Thompson and Thompson, 2008). These are all important; however the list of skills can fragment what is a complex and rich experience of developing a shared working relationship. This involves a process of emotional attentiveness where the worker allows the service user's experiences to enter his/her mind so that they can be thought about, given meaning and then used to formulate responses to the communicated needs. Thus, the key to developing a working alliance is not just the use of discrete skills but the involvement and 'use of self' in the work. Use of self as a way of working requires workers to strive to become aware of the feelings, thoughts, motivations and responses that are aroused by the work and to identify within these our own issues and anxieties. Understanding the service user necessarily leads to further understanding our own strengths and needs as 'we strive, together, to make sense of what is going on, to interpret what we find and to discover meaning in what we do and what we are' (Howe, 1987: 111).

Within recent social work literature there seems to be a re-emerging recognition of the need to understand the external and the internal worlds of the individual and to refocus on the efficacy of the social work relationship in work with service users. This understanding needs to be informed and underpinned by developmental and counselling theory and approaches. There is a need to avoid reducing social work to quantifiable and measurable targets that do not reflect the experiences of the service user or address their emotional, social or psychological needs. Of course social work has a role in providing resources, helping individuals with practical problems, in empowerment and advocacy and in managing the care and control aspects of social work. These are complex tasks, but they are only part of a process: at the heart of social work lies the issue of not only what is done, but how it is done. The process, involving the relationship and counselling approaches, is as important as the product.

In some areas of social work counselling is not just part of the work but *is* the work, whereas in others it contributes to the overall work. Working with service users requires thoughtful, perceptive practice and the skills to practise in situations of extreme anxiety with troubled families and individuals. Attention to the relationship, and identifying and utilising appropriate counselling approaches in such contexts is essential.

There are five key components involved in developing and maintaining therapeutic relationships with service users.

- Recognising and picking up on the emotions and world view of the service user.
- Being aware of and understanding one's impact on the service user.
- Understanding, responding to and managing the emotions and reactions of service users.
- Being aware of one's own thoughts, emotions and reactions and being able to separate them from the service users.
- Being able to manage one's own thoughts, emotions and reactions.

Case Study

You are working with a young adult couple whose 2-year-old son has died suddenly. You are a parent too. Consider how challenging it might be to be aware of the couple's feelings without superimposing your own. How appropriate would it be to show feelings of distress to them? How might they perceive this?

Each of the counselling models provides a way of thinking about and managing these different components involved in working with others. Having a theoretical framework to refer to in order to make sense of and understand the complexities of relational work is one of the greatest supports a worker can have. It allows them to think about and stay open to exploring the meaning of feelings and actions rather than just responding to them. Anxiety and stress shuts down thinking and reflection, while having a theoretical perspective can help the worker to regain this space to think.

An allegiance to particular perspectives can provide a sense of stability, a commitment to a particular way of working and an understanding of service users. However if the allegiance is unthinking this can also lead to polarisation of views and a selective approach to learning that can limit the breadth and depth of theoretical tools that individuals can use. As illustrated in Figure 25.1 the proceeding sections of this chapter discuss different counselling approaches. In outlining three different counselling approaches it is important to hold on to the strengths and contributions of each while also remaining aware of their weaknesses.

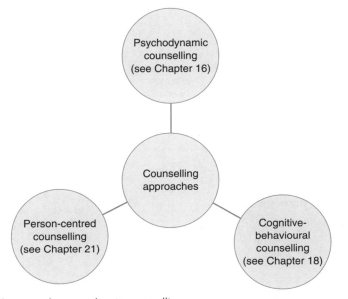

Figure 25.1   Theoretical approaches in counselling

As a social worker it is less likely you will use any one counselling approach in its pure form because of the diverse range of tasks expected of you. However it is important to have a clear sense of what you are drawing on in your work and from where this approach has come.

On the Companion Website (www.sagepub.co.uk/SocialWork) you will find a journal article by Read (2001) examining the needs of people with learning disabilities who have experienced a bereavement. On the same site you will also find an activity aimed at developing your understanding of what exactly takes place in an exchange with a service user. This activity would be useful to undertake during a practice placement.

PSYCHODYNAMIC COUNSELLING

One theorist whose influence continues to have a significant impact on psychodynamic thinking is Sigmund Freud (1856–1939). Freud contributed to our understanding of some central concepts that relate to all psychodynamic approaches such as the dynamic nature of the self, the existence of the unconscious, the impact of early experiences on development, the influence of the past on the present, the existence of **transference, countertransference** and other ego defences and the need to pay attention to the boundaries in which counselling takes place. Though the concepts and much of the development of ideas originated from Freud, there continues to be both revision and development of these.

Freud systematically examined the working of the unconscious, the part of our internal emotional life of which we remain unaware. It is difficult to explain the unconscious because we are unaware of it but occasionally we may experience powerful irrational feelings that do seem part of us. Freud termed the unconscious the id (see Figure 25.2).

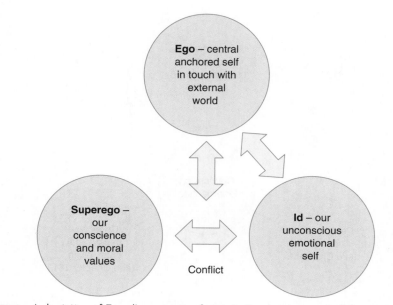

Figure 25.2   A depiction of Freud's competing forces in the development of character

Freud also identified two other processes that exist in our internal world. He used the term superego for our own conscience and moral values, which he saw as developed from internal images of critical parents. Our ego is our central self-anchored self, in consciousness and in touch with our external worlds. According to Freud, the ego mediates the conflicts in our internal world between the impulses of the id and the moral demands of the superego. It does this by the use of defences, which we use to cope with internal anxiety. Two common defences are *denial* and *repression*. Denial occurs when we find that we cannot believe something is true, for example, a life-threatening illness or the death of a much-loved partner. Repression occurs when memories that were painful or shaming at a deep level are 'buried, split off and deeply inaccessible' (Brearley, 2007), but then reappear, and we behave towards others in a way that we may find difficult to understand. *Why do I hate that person? Why does that person make me feel sad?* Family dynamics will also demonstrate how relationships can reflect unconscious feelings and may reflect on our repressed feelings.

Contribution from Psychodynamic Counselling to Social Work

Psychodynamic thinking about boundaries and time-frame are helpful reminders to social workers about the importance of thinking about which service users challenge the boundaries of the work and always need more. Giving service users more time in psychodynamic terms does not necessarily make individuals feel safer: rather it may give them the message that you can't manage within the time available, or that they are so vulnerable they need to have more support, which can leave them more panicky. There are also service users whose lives are so chaotic that boundary-setting may be a new experience for them. The holding of boundaries by the worker can hopefully eventually be internalised and allow service users to develop their own skills in managing boundaries in their own lives.

Critical Thinking

Consider this carefully: how does the message given here that service users may need to be helped to bring their feelings or behaviour under control fit with messages given elsewhere about service users as experts in their own lives? Can these approaches coexist within an ethical framework?

In the psychodynamic approach there are parallels between how the different aspects of the theory help to develop an understanding of service users and how they help social workers to develop and understand themselves in order to work more effectively with individuals. Working out how to respond to an individual and what their needs are comes from the knowledge we have. Some of this may be from case files and reports but a great deal of this comes from the information gained from our relationship with them. The worker needs to be in touch with what is going on in themselves. To achieve real understanding and communication we need to use ourselves in our work, but there are limits to how much. It is important to empathise with service users without becoming lost in their inner world through over-identification. We need to be close enough to recognise and respond to feelings and assess problems, but distanced enough to be able to reflect, analyse and intervene.

Aspects of our personal selves are an inevitable and valuable part of our professional work. Our responses are not separate from, but a source of valuable information about, what is going on in our work, about ourselves and issues we may need to reflect on. For example, your experiences and the defences you have built to deal with them can resonate with the experiences of a service user. So what might get in the way of your listening and hearing?

It is important to remember that defence mechanisms are necessary for all of us. They are not necessarily unhelpful as they are used to help us manage anxieties so that we are not overwhelmed by them. Professional judgement based on reflection takes place in a thoughtful 'space' where the complexity of the work, and its psychological, social and political context, can be considered and allowed to inform action. So just as the service user needs to be held and contained to understand themselves and their situations, social workers also require the experience of being held and contained in supervision.

PERSON-CENTRED COUNSELLING

Unlike psychodynamic counselling theory there is only one model of person-centred counselling with all person-centred practitioners drawing on the same key concepts. This means that the literature on person-centred counselling covers a smaller range of concepts and approaches, but what it does cover is examined in depth and with a richness of exploration.

Carl Rogers (1902–1987) developed the person-centred approach in reaction to the prevailing use of behavioural and psychoanalytic approaches. Rather than focus on changing behaviour through reinforcement, or on understanding and exploring unconscious motivations, linking past and present, the approach focuses on recognising inherent human capabilities in areas such as creativity, personal development and choice. The goal is to find out how individuals perceive themselves in the here and now and to support the individual's own move towards growth, self-direction and changes in behaviour.

Rogers (1957: 96) outlined what he identified as the conditions in which subjective experience can be respected, progressively understood and that respect and understanding conveyed to the individual. These are what he called the necessary and sufficient conditions for change.

1 Two people are in psychological contact. (At least minimally in a relationship.)
2 The first person, whom we shall term the client, is in a state of incongruence, being vulnerable or anxious.
3 The second person, who we shall call the therapist, is congruent in the relationship.
4 The therapist is experiencing unconditional positive regard towards the client.
5 The therapist experiences an empathic understanding of the client's internal frame of reference and endeavours to communicate this to the client.
6 The communication of the therapist's unconditional positive regard and empathic understanding is to a minimal degree achieved.

These conditions are underpinned by the belief that 'the individual has within himself or herself vast resources for self-understanding, for altering his or her self-concept, attitudes and self-directed behaviour – and that these resources can be tapped if only a definable climate of facilitative psychological attitudes can be provided' (Rogers, 1986: 257). This links well with the focus of social work on identifying and building on service users' strengths and competencies and developing resilience.

For the worker there must be active attention to offering the six conditions. Three interrelated attitudes are seen as core:

1 *Congruence*. Congruence describes the match or fit between an individual's inner feelings and outer display.
2 *Unconditional positive regard*. The counsellor accepts the service user unconditionally and non-judgementally offering this to the service user without any expectation of reciprocal care from the service user. The service user is free to explore all thoughts and feelings, positive or negative, without danger of rejection or condemnation.
3 *Empathic understanding*. Rogers emphasises achieving as full an understanding of the other person as is possible. This involves a willingness and ability to enter 'the private perceptual world of the service user without fear and to become thoroughly conversant with it' (Thorne, 1992: 31). It is about entering into experiencing the other's world without losing yourself in it.

Case Study

You are working in a criminal justice setting with a young man convicted of abusive behaviour towards his female partner. Your focus is on working to reduce offending behaviour. Is it possible to employ a person-centred approach in such a setting? What might the positive aspects be and what might the difficulties be?

The Contribution of Person-centred Counselling to Social Work

The person-centred approach has strong links to social work values. The idea of empowering service users is a central tenet of social work, as is the principle of seeing individuals as unique, with their own needs. Person-centred social work involves working with service users in ways that reinforce their right to autonomy and self-management in their lives and provide the support they require.

Embodying the core conditions and offering them in the therapeutic relationship with service users is a challenge given the diverse demands on social work. However, by adopting, or rather inhabiting, these conditions workers keep in touch with the worlds of others and with their own emotions, feelings and reactions. Keeping in touch with our feelings is important, as unacknowledged feelings can distort work with service users and impact on our overall functioning.

One of the real challenges is that the core conditions and the non-directivity of the person-centred approach do not fit easily with some of the roles and tasks of social work. Within the context of risk management, the influence of managerialism, and social work practice where much statutory work is not voluntary, is it possible to be non-directive? In this context holding on to empathy, congruence and unconditional positive regard means being honest and open with service users about the options you have and the options that are and are not open to them.

COGNITIVE BEHAVIOUR COUNSELLING

Cognitive behavioural counselling, as its name suggests, connects back to behavioural approaches to working with individuals. Its key focus is on how feelings, thoughts and behaviour are linked together. It is based on the premise that people are disturbed, upset and disorientated not by the events or situations that occur to them but by the personal meanings that these have for them. As the underlying belief is that thoughts cause both feeling and behaviour, the focus is on meta-cognition, that is, on thinking about thinking and in particular about how to alter thoughts so that different feelings and behaviour occur. The focus of cognitive behavioural working is on the 'here and now' and the aim is the removal of symptoms rather than insight or personal development.

The main theorists are G.A. Kelly (1905–1967), who developed construct theory, A. Ellis, who developed rational emotive behaviour therapy in the 1950s, and A.T. Beck, who developed cognitive behaviour therapy in the 1960s.

Personal Construct Theory

Kelly (1955) developed personal construct theory in response to the key existing models of explaining human actions. Rather than seeing the unconscious or the actualising drive as motivating us, he argued that there are patterns of thought that influence our feelings and behaviour. Kelly argued that in order to make sense of the world from our chaotic and disordered early experiences we begin to develop clusters of ideas or schemas. These constructs once created become our eye glasses through which we view the world and which are used to predict how others will behave. Difficult to cope with feelings such as anxiety, depression, anger and paranoia are then seen as the result of the individual's 'construction of reality'. Once constructs are formed they are resistant to change as they provide us with a world view comprising of attitudes and beliefs that help us make sense of what happens to us. They also impact on our inner world as we experience 'cognitive dissonance', disorientation and inner tension, when they are challenged. They also link very closely to our value systems.

Rational Emotive Therapy (RET) and Rational Emotive Behavioural Therapy (REBT)

Albert Ellis in the 1950s developed rational emotive therapy, which was based on the view that reasons (thoughts) cause emotions, and so, if you can identify the thoughts and change these, you can change the emotional reactions. Later, in the 1990s, he renamed his approach rational emotive behaviour therapy to signify that not only do thoughts cause emotions, but they also cause behaviour, and that changing the thoughts changes both feelings and behaviour.

Ellis argued all emotional disturbance and difficult behaviours result from negative and unrealistic thinking. They stem from our beliefs, evaluations, interpretations and reactions based on patterns of unrealistic and negative thinking. In this way, people contribute to their own psychological problems and symptoms by the way they interpret events and situations. They are resistant to change as they are reinforced by self-repetitions of self-defeating beliefs influenced by the learning and maintenance of irrational beliefs from significant others in our lives. The aim in working with people is to identify these negative and unrealistic ways of thinking and alter them so that emotional disturbance is reduced and behaviour patterns alter.

We escalate desires and preferences into dogmatic and absolutist 'shoulds', 'musts', 'oughts', demands and thought commands which then lead us into blaming ourselves or others for our situation. Blame is seen to be the core of emotional disturbance, and, to recover, we need to stop blaming ourselves and others and acquire a more logical view of reality.

Cognitive Therapy

Aaron Beck, who developed his cognitive therapy approach in the 1960s, was the first in cognitive therapy to stress the importance of the quality of the therapeutic relationship as part of the work. The characteristics of the therapist are crucial because the service user needs to feel safe to disclose important and often distressing information. This will be facilitated if there is a warm and trusting atmosphere and the therapist is empathic (Beck et al., 1979; Beck, 1991).

Beck is best known for his approach to working with people with depression. Like Ellis, Beck argued that faulty thinking leads to emotional and behavioural problems with living. Rather than irrational thoughts he thought the faulty thinking was based on automatic thoughts. The aim then is to identify the negative automatic thought, explore the distortion and establish a more rational thought pattern. Beck argued that all of an individual's internal communications are accessible to introspection so the person can tell you what they are thinking. These individual beliefs have highly personal meanings but these meanings can be discovered by the person rather than being taught or interpreted by the therapist.

He identified the following common styles of distorted thinking:

- Pessimism and optimism
- Perfectionism
- Over-personalisation
- Over-generalisation
- Magnification and minimisation
- Being the victim or the martyr

In particular he focused on the patterns that trigger depression. The service user holds negative views of him- or herself. By selective abstraction (involving pessimism and overpersonalisation) the service user has the tendency to interpret experience in a negative way. The service user then feels more gloomy about the future and so withdraws him- or herself. In withdrawing they lose more support. Lack of support makes them feel less worthy of attention, and so they withdraw more.

In the initial stages Beck stresses the importance of educating the service user about the cognitive behavioural approach emphasising that it is largely self-help and that the therapist aims to help the service user develop skills to overcome current problems as well as similar ones in the future. The therapist should emphasise the important role of homework assignments, and that change occurs in everyday life, with the service user applying what has been discussed in sessions (Beck, 1991).

Historical information is collected only if it is directly relevant to the development of the presenting problem. There may or may not be a clear onset for the problem. For many clients the problem develops gradually with a succession of events contributing to the service user's recognition that there is a problem. As a first step, it is advantageous to ask the service user for a detailed description of a recent example of the problem. Working with the service user, the therapist helps to identify and sort out problems so that challenges are reduced and manageable goals identified. Part of this process is identifying the negative automatic thoughts and looking at the contributions of these to the problem. Success is important so that the service user can see that change is possible. At all times the focus is on what the service user wishes to change.

Once a problem has been identified it should be broken down and defined as clearly as possible. Then as many solutions as possible should be generated and the advantages and disadvantages of each considered. Once an approach has been chosen, the steps to carry it out need to be clearly identified. This will then be implemented between sessions and the outcome reviewed at the next meeting.

Along with some of the techniques outlined under Ellis's model, other techniques include role playing, social skills building, assertiveness training, relaxation techniques and charting of moods.

Contributions to Social Work of Cognitive Behavioural Counselling

The principles of cognitive behavioural counselling are relatively simple to understand and the techniques and skills are clear. This means that workers can explain the model they are using clearly to the service user and engage in a partnership approach in working.

The purpose of cognitive behavioural counselling is for the service user to learn new skills of self-management that they will then put into practice in everyday life. Service users are seen as the agents of change in their own lives. Cognitive behavioural counselling links well with a positive strengths-based perspective in identifying and supporting capacities for change in the individual rather than focusing on their difficulties.

Cognitive behavioural approaches are planned, structured and usually time-limited. The focus of attention on goals and outcomes is underpinned by a robust evidence base reflecting the 'what works' agenda of social work practice.

Exercise

Chapter 23 on motivational interviewing provides further examples of cognitive behavioural approaches in working. Consider to what extent it might be possible in social work practice to apply both person-centred and cognitive behavioural approaches when working with someone.

THE IMPORTANCE OF NARRATIVE

For a detailed overview of narrative therapy in social work, you should cross refer to Chapter 22. All three of the approaches to counselling discussed above are relational and based on helping the service user to have more understanding of and control over what happens to them in their lives. Social workers work with vulnerable service users who are often struggling with complex difficulties in their lives. The different counselling approaches give workers ways of thinking about and responding to those service users. For the service user, there is a similar opportunity to think about, understand and change their ways of thinking about and responding to their own issues in the context of a therapeutic relationship. This is a fundamental strength of counselling approaches, as finding meaning and understanding rather than blaming or remaining stuck is seen as one of the signs of developing resilience.

Despite adverse circumstances some individuals manage to thrive and exhibit resilience. The term 'earned secure' has been used to describe individuals who, despite early abuse, neglect and/or trauma, have developed resilience. What has contributed to that has usually been the presence of a supportive, empathic other person who has stuck with them, listened to them and given them space to reflect. This allows the service user to develop a coherent life story (Anderson and Hiersteiner, 2007).

SUPERVISION FOR COUNSELLING IN SOCIAL WORK

Theory provides a structure for making sense of what can be made sense of and of acknowledging what is not or cannot be understood. Many workers do work in ways that appear to be instinctive and intuitive, and they may be successful. However, if they are unable to make the underpinning theory explicit, then they will have no way of appraising their work or of understanding what has happened if that approach does not work. The different counselling approaches provide ways of thinking about the work.

In some settings the pressure to complete tasks (particularly statutory tasks) can feel overwhelming and looking at counselling and relational aspects of the work may seem a luxury. However, the conscious use of self by workers, the investment of themselves in the work and the management of the relational counselling aspects of it, can have a profound impact on service users. It can have an equivalent impact on the workers themselves, and recognition of this impact is important if workers are to continue to thrive in the work rather than be overwhelmed by it or become distanced and shut off from it.

Supervision as a relational and developmental process has parallels with the helping relationships workers will develop with service users. Just as supervision offers an opportunity for the worker to struggle to process and understand feelings and reactions to the work undertaken, the worker then provides a similar experience to the service user.

Social workers need to think about the anxieties inherent in social work practice and evoked through counselling people in situations of distress. If anxiety and the strong feelings evoked by the work are seen as a part of the work then they can be processed, reflected on and responded to with the same attention as the tasks and facts of the case. Views and feelings can be expressed with a confidence that the social worker will be given space to work them through to resolution and to identify new solutions to problems.

Research undertaken by Pack (2010) focused on the ways in which working with survivors of sexual abuse impacted on both the counsellor/therapist and on the significant other of the counsellor/therapist. The article presents some interesting insights and can be accessed on the Companion Website (www.sagepub.co.uk/SocialWork).

Exercise

Within this section on models of intervention, consider how many of the models could be described as 'counselling' based on the definitions contained within this chapter.

CONCLUSION

Social work has a rich history of drawing on a wide range of knowledge to underpin and inform practice. Counselling approaches remain an important part of that heritage and continue to be drawn on in developing effective practice. Much of what you have read in this chapter will be linked to aspects of knowledge and methodology referred to in other chapters, but the uniqueness of counselling lies in its emphasis on building a relationship and achieving change through the impact of the relationship.

Reflective Questions

1   Consider what you have read in this chapter about counselling and social work practice. What do you consider to be the differences between counselling and social work? Are there more similarities than differences? Why is it important for a social worker to possess counselling skills?

2   The chapter has made significant reference to the importance of self-awareness and to the use of self within social work practice. How aware are you of your own emotional responses when working with service users? Have there been situations where you have struggled to build a relationship with a service user because of the feelings the person arouses within you? How important has supervision been/do you think supervision will be in assisting your development as a social work practitioner?

3   Within the chapter the five key components of therapeutic relationships are outlined. Certainly in using a counselling approach the relationship between social worker and service user is central; however, what role do you think the relationship between worker and service user has in each of the approaches discussed in this book?

RECOMMENDED READING

Jacobs, M. (1988) *Psychodynamic Counselling in Action*. London: Sage.

Miller, L. (2012) *Counselling Skills for Social Work*. London: Sage.

Seden, J. (2005) *Counselling Skills in Social Work Practice*, 2nd edn. Buckingham: Open University Press.

PART FOUR
INTERVENTIONS IN PRACTICE

26 WORKING WITH CHILDREN AND YOUNG PEOPLE

Sharon Munro and Patrick Walker

Key Themes

- Children and young people are entitled to the same opportunity for participation as adults.
- There are conflicting views about the benefits of group or residential care.
- Understanding of a young person's life experiences forms the core of assessment.
- Building a relationship and having an awareness of one's self is critical.
- A variety of interventions are available to social workers.

INTRODUCTION

Social work with children and young people is a challenging, rewarding and often demanding area of practice. Over very many years, particular approaches, philosophies, contexts and beliefs have emerged, evolved, fallen out of favour or been re-worked, influenced not least by the fluid social construction of childhood and social policy agendas. In the development of social work with children and young people, it is only relatively recently that the voices of children and young people have been in the foreground. Where, arguably, children were the objects of adult intervention, today's environment is increasingly incorporating the views, understandings, insights and strengths of children's own perceptions as valid and cogent. This is visible certainly in legislation, for example in the Children (Scotland) Act 1995, in that this legislation emphasises the significance of listening to the views of children. Sadly, some ambivalence is also detectable, in that the legislation also suggests that adults listen to children's views 'where possible'.

This chapter will explore four approaches to working with children and young people: life space, opportunity-led, crisis intervention and task-centred practice. Previous chapters in this book have explored the theoretical frameworks in detail and, whilst the main components of the frameworks are revisited here, the key element of the chapter is exploring the 'putting into practice' of the abstract theory.

Applying methods of intervention is not solely a question of mastering certain abstract theory and of 'doing this to' children and young people, in a rather linear, mechanical and forensic manner, but involves skills, reflection, critical analysis and ethical decision-making that reflects children's participation as a central component. There exist, inevitably, challenges here, perhaps most obviously where children are exposed to high-risk situations either of their own initiative or as a result of other's behaviours and actions. None the less, participation and engagement can, and should, remain a focus of practitioner energy. As Wade and Tovey point out (in Adams, 2011: 179), 'participation refers to that part of the continuum of involvement where people play a more active part, have a greater choice, exercise more power and contribute significantly to decision-making and management'.

LIFE SPACE AND OPPORTUNITY-LED PRACTICE

Case Study

Alice graduated 9 months ago with a BA (Hons) in Social Work and has found employment within the residential child care sector.

She enjoys the opportunity afforded by the 24/7 nature of the service to engage and build relationships with the young people, and sees the scope for being alongside a young person to support their development towards competent young adulthood, or as Wineman in his foreword for Trieschman et al. (1969) states, 'to sensitively and intelligently guide the growth of children' (p. vi).

Alice is aware of the wider discussion and debates around the role and value of residential child care for children and young people. The spectrum of views is broad and Alice has had many discussions with colleagues both in residential and community-based services on the merits and challenges for young people and communities and whether residential care remains relevant in child care provision in today's society. The diversity of opinion can be seen clearly in the following quote from the 'Stockholm Declaration on Children and Residential Care' (2003) cited in Courtney and Iwaniec (2009: p. xi): 'there is indisputable evidence that institutional care has negative consequences for both individual children and society at large' through to a view expressed in the Utting Report as cited in Anglin (2002: 12) that 'Residential care is an indispensable service ... that should be a positive, joint choice, primarily for adolescents, who may present challenging behaviour'.

Alice believes that with careful planning and assessment a residential placement in an appropriate service can provide for the developmental needs of a young person. The setting Alice works in provides accommodation for four young people from age 12 upwards. The unit is operated by the local authority and has a specific remit to offer a secure base (Bowlby, 2009) to young people who cannot remain within their families yet have in their longer-term plan a rehabilitation of family relationships. The building is a large detached stone-built townhouse with a garden, and each young person has their own bedroom and access to the shared bath/shower rooms. There is nothing externally that differentiates this building from its neighbours. Its structure is such that it retains many original features and characteristics and has a sense of steadfastness and stability. These attributes are required not only of the structure of the building but also of the workers who function within it. There is a range of rooms that vary in size and offer flexibility in how the space is used in terms of group or individual working. Alice frequently reflects on the words of Maier in his text *Essential Components in Care and Treatment Environments for Children* (1979b: 17): 'there is the clear need for continuous proximity of staff while simultaneously assuring the resident a sense of intimacy and private experimentation'.

The rooms are decorated with warm colours and the furniture is well used, but clean, cared for and comfy! Alice has since had time to see how comfortable the young people and their families are when they come into the building and that for some it is less threatening to be in an environment that has a sense of wear and tear and exudes care. The heart of the unit beats most strong in the kitchen/ dining area, the one area of the building that has been physically altered to enhance the sense of connectedness between what goes on in the preparation of meals and how the lives of the individuals within the building ebb and flow depending on the time of day, the day of the week and generally how people are feeling. Alice considers this the locus of the physical nourishment and the emotional nurturing of the young people and their visitors. Looking to Kahan (1994: 82), she states: 'The kitchen is an important focal point in any group life and children and young people need the experience of contact with the kitchen, food preparation and sharing food with adults.'

Each element of a residential service is regulated through the national care standards relevant to the country where the service is situated.[1] What is important to remember is the concept of milieu, which you will have read about in Chapter 20. Kahan (1994) explores some of the challenges around acceptable standards within the living environments for children and young people, pointing out there is a balance to be struck between having an environment that shows respect and value for young people living in group care yet does not alienate them from their own family circumstances.

---

1   National Care Standards: Care Homes for Children and Young People. Available from: www. scotland.gov.uk/Publications/2011/05/16141058/2#5 (accessed 28 February 2012).
    National Care Standards for England. Available from: www.dh.gov.uk/en/Publications andstatistics/Legislation/Actsandbills/DH_4001911 (accessed 7 March 2012).
    National Care Standards for Scotland. Available from: www.scotland.gov.uk/Topics/Health/care/17652 (accessed 7 March 2012).
    The Care Standards Act 2000 and the Children Act 1989 (Regulatory Reform and Complaints) (Wales) regulations 2006. Available from: www.legislation.gov.uk/wsi/2006/3251/contents/made.
    The Quality Standards for Health and Social Care 2006 Department of Health, Social Services and Public Safety Northern Ireland. Available at: www.dhsspsni.gov.uk/qpi-quality-standards-for-health-social-care.pdf.

This is where an understanding of the combination of

- the psychological processes within the population of the group care setting
- the sociological systems that operate within the setting
- and the abilities of the workers to recognise and also manipulate opportunities that arise to maximise the emotional, psychological, spiritual and physical growth of the young people who live there

all come together and are demonstrated daily and hour by hour in the words, actions and emotional responses of the workers and in turn the young people.

In line with good practice and in recognition of the challenges that working in group care for young people presents there is, in Alice's setting, an established culture of regular individual supervision. This is supplemented by team meetings and practice reviews at shift handovers.

Ward (1996) suggests that in order to manage and survive the emotional demands made by being involved in caring for children and young people in group care, workers must first acknowledge their vulnerability and from that position they must then construct mechanisms that support and sustain them.

A piece of longitudinal research undertaken by Wigley et al. (2012) explored the outcomes for looked after children. You can read the article on the Companion Website (www. sagepub.co.uk/SocialWork).

Alice is the key worker to Sonia.

Case Study

Sonia is a 13-year-old girl who came to live in the unit some three months ago. She has been assessed as requiring compulsory measures of care due to her high level of non-attendance at school, known associations with older males, often whilst under the influence of alcohol, and evidence of self-harming behaviour.

Sonia's mother (Lottie) has a long history of problem alcohol use and enduring poor mental health. Lottie was 16 years old when she gave birth to Sonia and had been put out of the family home as a consequence of the pregnancy. Lottie has lived in several properties over the years, with changes in home usually being linked to periods of worsening mental well-being and increasing alcohol consumption. Sonia is aware that she has maternal grandparents and an aunt, but has never had contact with them. Lottie has always maintained that, when she was put out of her family home, the family had burnt their boats as far as she was concerned, and that Sonia is better off without them in her life. Sonia has no knowledge of her birth father; her mother has maintained that she did not know who he was as 'it could have been any one of three or four guys'.

Lottie states that she loves Sonia and tries her best to care for her; however, since the age of 5 months Sonia has had eight episodes of being looked after away from home – predominantly in foster care placements. This pattern of episodic care has significantly diminished Lottie's ability to provide a '**good enough attachment relationship**' (Daniel et al., 2010: 145).

MAKING SENSE OF THE BACKGROUND INFORMATION

An assessment was completed prior to Sonia coming into the group care setting. The issues of significance for Alice in considering her engagement with Sonia included Sonia's turbulent relationship with her mother, difficulties in relating to peers, emotional volatility and her disengagement with education.

In thinking about these aspects of Sonia's life and the potential for working within the group care setting Alice thinks more closely about Sonia's low self-esteem, which she sees as arising from:

- Inconsistent early attachment experiences. Attachment frameworks across the years (Ainsworth et al., 1978 cited in Daniel et al., 2010; Bowlby, 2009; Howe, 1995) have evolved as knowledge and understanding develops, taking account of the social construction of childhood and families and developments in neuroscience (Gerhardt, 2004). The importance of consistent, available and responsive care that can meet both the survival needs (e.g. food, protection, warmth and shelter) and emotional needs (e.g. the ability to manage and regulate the fears and anxieties that are the daily experiences of infants) is paramount. Sonia has a much-disrupted history in terms of primary carers. Her mother, Lottie, had periods where she was able to care for Sonia and when her alcohol consumption increased she was unable to prioritise Sonia's needs over her own. She had not managed to meet Sonia's emotional or physiological needs, and Sonia was cared for away from home until Lottie regained stability in her life. Given the background information and having observed Sonia within the group setting where she frequently presents as insecure or anxious, which can be expressed as anger, Alice would describe Sonia as having an anxious ambivalent attachment (Ainsworth et al., 1978 cited in Rees, 2007).
- Sonia's lack of knowledge about her wider family and her birth father is an ever-present absence in her life. It is the emotional and physical responses of other people in a child's life, the information they may give and the familial and cultural norms that contribute to the child's growing sense of self (Daniel et al., 2010). Sonia has a very limited pool of people who can help her answer questions about who she is, give details of her family background and who she looks like. Sonia does not have a strong sense of self, her mother is the sole keeper of her history, and there has been no other consistent adult in her life. Ward and McMahon (1998) discuss the concept of 'compound loss', which could apply in Sonia's life in that she has had a lifelong series of change and loss, not only in respect of the ebb and flow of Lottie's availability for her, but also the series of foster care placements and breakdowns.
- Thinking about Erikson's (1978) stages of development, Sonia is within the bounds of identity vs role confusion. Sonia is in early adolescence where there is tension between issues of self-confidence or self-doubt. If you accept the premise of Erikson's framework that each stage allows for a re-visiting of earlier unresolved stages, it is likely that Sonia will face and present various challenges within the group care setting in her journey to a more robust sense of self.
- Bronfenbrenner's (1979) ecological systems framework of child development offers a wider conceptual model to help understand and then influence Sonia's growth. The

framework looks at the interplay between the child's own biological development and the 'layers' of the world around her, such as the immediate family, the community in which she lives and the wider environment, including the consideration of time either internal to the child in terms of development or external to the child, for example bereavement.

Application of Life Space and Opportunity-led Practice

If we accept the premise that a key factor in working within the life space is to offer an enabling environment for young people who have not yet formed a robust sense of self or an ability to form trusting relationships with adults, we must expect the environment to be able to offer the security and safety that can help manage the associated anxiety and fear.

Alice undertakes relational working within the setting so that this can best be achieved. This view would be supported by McMahon et al. (in Ward and McMahon, 1998: 186), who suggest 'There is repair work to be done ... working alongside a child or family in the prolonged experience of daily life presents its own opportunities for therapeutic management and communication.' The routines of the setting provide a framework and demonstrate consistency at the basic level of food being available, beds being clean and made, clothes being prepared at night for the next day's activity and the workers encouraging engagement with school.

> ### Exercise
>
> Sonia has a tendency to squirrel food away in her room, which has piled up and is becoming rotten and rather smelly. How might you explain this behaviour, and what might you do?

One response could be to confront the issue in terms of 'health and safety' and unhygienic storage of mouldy food. This would address the presenting problem of rotting food, but it would not engage with the underlying emotional or psychological needs being expressed by Sonia.

Alice might elect that the team should demonstrate care for Sonia by establishing a night time routine whereby supper would be taken with the group in the kitchen as was the usual routine thereby including Sonia in group life. Once supper was cleared the worker could ask Sonia to choose what she wanted for breakfast the next day and set her place out accordingly alongside the other young people's settings. This would let Sonia know that plans were in place for her to be part of the group the next day and that breakfast was to be expected.

This underlying principle of responding to Sonia's fears and anxieties rather than her presenting behaviour reflects a key tenet of an opportunity-led intervention (Ward, 2002) in terms of recognising an opportunity for support that can present in an everyday occurrence.

The stages of the model are outlined below:

- Observation and assessment. Alice gathered background information, considered possible theoretical frameworks for understanding the impacts of the background and linked this with observation of Sonia's behaviour.
- Decision-making. The team considered whether to respond to the presenting behaviour or the possible underlying causes. Linked to this was the decision not to rely on conscious or cognitive processing but to demonstrate consistency and nurturing through practice.
- Action. By sustaining usual group routines Sonia's membership of the group was reinforced. Alongside this process there was also an element where Sonia was recognised in her own right within the group by having her own special routine that anticipated the provision of breakfast the following day.
- Closure. This was one step towards addressing the wider issues but it did have a positive impact on Sonia's need to store food 'just in case'.

It is essential when thinking about opportunity-led practice that you differentiate between an opportunistic event that arises to which you react without thought and a considered and informed response to a situation that offers an opportunity for delivering on a plan of care for a child or young person.

In the scenario above Alice could have reacted by imposing consequences on Sonia for 'stealing food' or she could have ignored the issue in the belief that through time Sonia would 'just know' that she was cared for.

However, Alice chose to reflect on the wider context of Sonia's needs, i.e.

- to develop trust
- to feel worthy
- to belong

and built on a naturally occurring routine of the household. Alice is aware that through this early relationship-building process Sonia would have opportunities to begin to repair some of the early emotional developmental wounds. Opportunity-led working can be critical in establishing the foundation of the overall life space intervention whereby young people are encouraged through time, modelling and cooperation to take responsibility for their own behaviour, build trust in adults and through that to develop an understanding of themselves and others. Alice and her colleagues could reinforce their valuing of Sonia and her place in their lives by taking in something of theirs from home, a CD or a book. This tells her that she is part of their consciousness even when they are 'off duty'. It also tells her that they trust her with their personal belongings.

There may be opportunities for Sonia and a worker to experience a relationship from a different dimension, perhaps by agreeing to try something together that neither has tried before, such as making friendship bracelets. They will experiment and learn together, and in so doing their relationship develops to a different level, through the vehicle of the third (the activity). This concept of the 'common third' is central to the principle of social pedagogy wherein the worker seeks to support the young person to grow and develop through non-formal learning techniques.

In terms of encouraging some degree of repair between Lottie and Sonia there could be plans made for shared events that have nurturing as a focus: for example cooking or baking. There is growing evidence of the capacity for change and growth in adults using an attachment-based approach. Turner and Tanner (2001) have some relevant comment to make in terms of the importance of the worker to work both with and within a relationship to effect change, particularly where neglect and poor attachment have been evident.

All of the above could reasonably be engaged with as part of the care plan for Sonia. It requires a well-informed, motivated and engaged staff group who understand the needs of young people and can manage their own self in order to help children develop the ability to manage their own selves.

As indicated above, the role of support and line management should not be underplayed. Adults need to be appropriately supported, and in the words of Menzies-Lyth (1988: 237), 'experience has shown that in a well managed institution for children, the adults as well as the children gain in ego strength and mature in other ways. The adults thus provide better role models.'

To extend your knowledge of different approaches to working in residential environments see the article by Cameron (2004) on the Companion Website (www.sagepub.co.uk/SocialWork) and the accompanying activity focusing on Social Pedagogy.

CRISIS INTERVENTION

In this section, we will explore some applications of what is known as crisis intervention, as detailed in Chapter 17.

Thompson (in Lishman, 2007: 201) suggests that crisis is a 'moment where our usual coping resources are overwhelmed' and that particular stages of crisis are identifiable. The crucial element within crisis intervention – that the coping resources of the service user are overwhelmed – needs to be carefully established, interpreted and understood.

Exercise

Carol is 16 years old and has just moved into supported 'independent living'.

You are visiting her as her key worker and find her red eyed and miserable. She says that the light in the bathroom has stopped working, at which point she cries uncontrollably. In between sobs, she shouts at you that you are a useless social worker and that her situation is 'all your fault' and that she 'can't go on like this'.

To a certain degree, you cannot quite see what the huge problem is. Perhaps the light bulb simply needs changing, or a fuse has blown. Perhaps it is a bit stressful, but surely not a crisis?

Why might this be a crisis for Carol?

Rogers (2011) researched the impact of transition on young people moving out of state care. Read her article now on the Companion Website (www.sagepub.co.uk/ SocialWork) to develop your understanding of the issues faced by people like Carol.

Clark, drawing on the work of Auerbach and Kilman (1977, in Lishman, 2007: 201), suggests that 'a crisis occurs when a stressful life event overwhelms an individual's ability to cope effectively in the face of a perceived challenge or threat'. Importantly, Roberts (2000, in Payne, 2005a) suggests that crises offer the potential for change, for new coping methods to be developed, and for a 'turning point' (2005a: 103). If help is provided, crises can become opportunities for positive development and growth.

Carol's reaction to and interpretation of the event is unique to her and, at this stage, it is important to remember some of the theory underlying crisis intervention which might help in understanding this reaction. By re-reading Chapter 7, you might reflect on the contribution that Erikson (1965, in Lishman, 2007) makes in terms of understanding Carol's maturational stage and some of the challenges that she has faced, or resilience theory which can offer some indication as to Carol's strength and vulnerability, as does attachment theory (Daniel and Wassell, 2002), which offer insights to Carol's sense of self-esteem, self-efficacy and social problem-solving techniques.

There are a number of models of crisis intervention; however the following is drawn from the work of Roberts (Roberts, 1995 in Wilson et al., 2008; Roberts, 2000 in Payne, 2005a).

Stage One: Immediate Response, Developing Rapport, Risk Assessment

Roberts suggests that the initial stage of crisis intervention concerns undertaking a psychosocial assessment, incorporating a 'lethality' (Payne, 2005a: 107) assessment. If we think about Carol's situation, we need to be very clear about how she is feeling, what she is thinking and what she is doing. The purpose here is to assess whether or not there is an immediate risk to Carol's safety, either from herself or from a source external to her.

At this beginning stage of crisis intervention it is also important to understand the person's history so that you can think about the potential risks that might be present.

- Has Carol experienced mental health problems in the past that may be relevant to the current situation?
- Is Carol at risk from external sources, for example people who may be violent towards her? What are Carol's abilities to protect herself?
- Does Carol have a history of self-harm? Are thoughts of suicide present?
- Does Carol have a history of abuse, self-harm, problematic alcohol and drug use?

Stage Two: Establish Rapport

Developing good communication and rapport with your client is a vital early step in crisis intervention. It allows for a consolidation of the early assessment, provides a plat- form for reassurance and conveys acceptance of the person and their situation. Good rapport allows for an opening connection between the service user and 'helper'. It offers the potential for purposeful communication.

Somehow Carol's crisis might threaten to overwhelm us at the same time if we feel bad being unable to come up with a clear, neat solution to the sense of chaos. This second stage of intervention therefore becomes a very active process of reflecting on how we are feeling, of being acutely aware of the person in crisis, attending closely to them and containing the sense of overwhelming anxiety. Building rapport, therefore, is not simply about offering Carol a cup of coffee (although it might help!), it is about offering communication – verbal and non-verbal – which conveys that you can understand the situation, that you are not going to be similarly overwhelmed, that you respect and accept the person and that perhaps for the meantime you can contain the chaos (Bion, 1959, 1984 in Hazler and Barwick, 2001).

There can be a temptation to try to 'damp down' the feelings and emotions of the client who is experiencing 'crisis'. Suggesting that a client might 'calm down' is only likely to inflame powerful emotions, or suppress them temporarily, but more crucially it prevents individuals from expressing how they really feel. The expression of feeling, or as a crisis theorist put it the 'ventilation' of feeling, is significant: 'Crisis intervention theory views the ventilation of feelings as a precursor to meaningful change …' (Healy, 2005: 126). Rapport building allows for such airing of feeling.

Stage Three: Identifying and Defining the Major Problems

The crisis is not the worker's: it is the client's. Identifying and defining the major problems should be drawn from the client's perspective; if workers attempt to impose meaning and rationale on situations, it may hold little relevance to the client. The service user can be left feeling that you do not understand, and that really there is little hope of resolving matters.

Therefore, to engage with the client's world demands all the skills of active listening, body language, repeating and paraphrasing, observing, and can be very demanding in terms of your value base. Maintaining and projecting the client's worth, dignity and unique value can be challenging, particularly if you become exasperated, overwhelmed or indeed try to shortcut the process by imposing meaning. Further, skilled workers need to keep a mental note of how the service user talks about their situation, and what they say, what they feel is significant, and relate this to mental maps of theory such as cognitive development, stage development and trauma theory, for example. This will provide the worker with a beginning 'hypothesis' of how the client has reached this point.

This is the stage for clarifying how, in our scenario, Carol understands what has happened. What has precipitated the event? What has led up to the current crisis? What is the most overwhelming issue at present? Helping Carol to capture and make some sense herself of these areas allows the future stages of crisis intervention to take place, but it also is a significant goal in itself. Carefully done, it allows for a projection that these overwhelming feelings, thoughts or practical issues can be dealt with, that chaos can recede, and that coping again is a distinct possibility. It allows for the consideration of new ways of dealing with things.

Stage Four: Moving into Action

The next levels of crisis intervention involve beginning to make some clear plans with Carol. You and she have identified how this situation has occurred and how Carol is feeling. Carol may now be at the stage of allowing herself to think about regaining control, however gently, and of exploring her strengths.

Exploring with Carol how she has managed stressful and difficult events and situations in her past may well illuminate useful resources – practically, emotionally and cognitively – which can be applied to the current situation, with a bit of creative thinking and reinforcement. For example, how does Carol want things to be? How is she going to take the small steps to get there? At its most basic, perhaps simply helping Carol learn how to put in a new light bulb might help Carol to regain the confidence in her own effectiveness and ability to manage. This might sound trivial, but remember that crisis operates at the emotional level. For Carol to begin to trust her own capacity in the face of another storm is a powerful moment of learning and growth.

Making some form of detailed plan about what Carol thinks needs to happen, and how it is going to be achieved, is of significance in this part of applying crisis intervention. Momentum is required, and tasks need to be realistic in order that they can be achieved. They need to have relevance to Carol. Furthermore, some form of agreement regarding how both she and you are going to review progress is required, not least in order to check against the danger of Carol becoming 'swamped' again and losing the sense that she can move forward.

Applying crisis intervention theory, in practice, with children and young people demands not only clarity regarding the theory but very active reflection and robust practice skills on the part of the worker. There is much to consider regarding role, remit and practice context and how these elements impact on the choice and deployment of any particular theoretical approach.

A further point to remember is that the above approach, whilst appealing in its linear, structured form, may require the worker and service user to adapt it to their situation, to be flexible to a degree in its application. Carol may move back and forwards between the various stages; she may appear to become stuck in taking decisions about what needs to happen and how to plan for that. So long as the worker remains clear about the broad structure but adaptable enough to the human twists and turns, understanding that these are vital component parts of Carol's progression, then the direction of travel can be maintained. What is not helpful or ethical is for the worker to solely focus on the abstract theory and structure of the 'intervention', becoming frustrated when the young person does not readily conform.

TASK-CENTRED PRACTICE

Task-centred practice is closely aligned with crisis intervention, in that it offers clarity and structure for work carried out over a relatively brief time span. The main theoretical components have been set out in Chapter 19.

Stage One

The initial stage is 'problem exploration', the identification of exactly what Carol thinks the problems are. Through sensitive questioning, the form and focus of Carol's anxiety might be explored. Carol may well be concerned that she does not have the capacity to manage everything that comes with living alone – managing her money, making friends, maintaining her home. Perhaps a degree of social isolation is also a feature for Carol.

Clearly core social work skills are again significant here: open questions, attuned body language, the maintenance of unconditional positive regard. Such skills help to create the emotional environment, and practical space, for Carol to begin to bring some order to her thoughts. The very process of problem exploration, of offering Carol time to reflect, can assist in identifying some sort of shape and definition to the confusion of issues facing her.

Talking with, or interviewing, Carol, is not an informal conversation. As Thompson (1995: 116) points out 'an interview needs to be focused, with a clear purpose, forming part of a systematic process geared towards achieving identified objectives'. Workers need to have a clear sense not only of the theoretical framework of intervention, but of the key skills involved in carrying out work with individuals. Again, Thompson offers some key elements (1995: 118–23) which are summarised below:

- Listening. In exploring the problems that Carol is experiencing, listening carefully to the words and feelings and body language, offers a rich source of material.
- Directing. Subtly keeping a grasp of the interview, maintaining some direction, not talking over Carol but guiding, prompting and shepherding.
- Partnership. To some degree this relates to establishing rapport and creating or consolidating a purposeful relationship. Offering reassurance, respect and reliability here is significant.
- Empowerment. Helping Carol to draw out strengths, recognise and validate difficulties, and identifying resilience are some of the key concepts here. Empowerment is not about falsely cheering Carol up.
- Use of self. How workers use aspects of their own personality in working with service users is recognised as being significant in direct work.
- Tolerating silence. Silence is not a vacuum – it can be the space for reflection and connections to be made, for expression of sadness and the formation of thoughts subsequently expressed. In allowing and tolerating silence with Carol, important aspects of problem identification can be reached.
- Maintaining boundaries. Being clear about confidentiality and its limits and the nature of the professional relationship is of significance here.
- Structure. An interview, or series of interviews, has beginnings, middles and ends. Keeping a sense of this structure allows worker and service user to maintain clarity and purpose.
- Summing up/Feedback. At this stage of the interview with Carol, it is helpful to summarise the main points that have emerged, which also conveys that you have been engaged, focused and taking her seriously.

Stage Two

This stage is concerned with ranking the identified problems and prioritising them. Having achieved this, it is important to keep a focus on the outcome goals. This stage, therefore, is concerned with establishing what is going to be done, often quite practically, to resolve the prioritised problem. In addition, the very process of tackling the problem can reinvigorate Carol's sense of her own ability to navigate through her situation and that there is a possibility that she can develop and change it.

Carol may well have identified her social isolation as a priority problem. She has few friends in the area and as a result does not go out much. In any case, she can't really afford to socialise to any great extent. You are aware of Carol's interest in dance and drama, and remind her of this. She is at first dismissive of this, but you suggest that she visit, perhaps with you, the local library and get information about local groups or evening classes connected to dance and drama. Carol has also ranked as high priority sorting out her flat. This seems to be an area that at first is just too big to tackle. You help her break this down into smaller tasks, for example getting some basic bedroom furniture from a local charitable furniture store; then sorting out her clothes and getting them put away. You reflect with Carol how she managed her room and clothes at the unit, and of her abilities in this part of her life.

Both of these areas, prioritised by Carol and now with a clear plan of action established, need some timescales. Together you establish these.

Reflection

The above scenario appears, at first sight, to be rather too good to be true! However, think back again to the theory of task-centred practice. The process outlined above operates at both the very practical level, obtaining a chest of drawers, or becoming engaged with a social activity of significance to the service user, but also operates at the cognitive and emotional levels. Through establishing some clarity (problem exploration), thinking about what the most urgent areas to tackle are and how to go about this (identification of priority problems, agreeing goals, identifying tasks), sorting out who does what (carrying out and achieving tasks), Carol is connected to a more positive, adaptive, way of framing her life and the difficulties that she encounters. The tangible benefits, having a more manageable living environment and meeting new people perhaps at a dance group, are significant, but so are the internalised structures that she has learnt about problem-solving and her own capacity to effect change and establish more control in her life. Consolidating some of this thinking is integral to the final stage of task-centred practice – ending and evaluation.

CONCLUSION

The fieldwork services to children and families are increasingly orientated towards 'high tariff', statutory caseloads containing significant elements of risk, legal orders and child/adult protection work. These themes have been addressed elsewhere in this book. Life space and opportunity-led work are everyday interventions, not only in residential settings,

but in any group care setting, and thus they merit detailed application. Crisis intervention and task-centred practice have a secure place within statutory work, but only when
the core element of 'agreement' can be reached. Clearly some service users reject the
necessity for and/or the validity of the social work mandate (Marsh, 1990, in Lishman,
2007) and other methodologies may, in such circumstances, need to be considered but the
practitioner should certainly explore, rigorously, potential areas in which problems can
be agreed on, tasks articulated and goals mutually identified. In such a way, partnership
working – however embryonic or tentative – can retain a central practice validity.

Watch vodcast 26.1 on the Companion Website (www.sagepub.co.uk/SocialWork)
to see chapter author Sharon Munro summarise the main points conveyed in this chapter that she co-authored with Patrick Walker, and why possessing a knowledge of working with children and young people is important for social work practice.

Critical Thinking

The focus of this chapter has been on group care. While crisis intervention and task-
centred work have been well established in fieldwork practice, think about how life space
and opportunity-led work might have a place in fieldwork.

Reflective Questions

1   Consider situations where children and young people are living in residential envi-
    ronments. What opportunities do you think such environments can offer children
    and young people? Do you think residential environments inevitably lead to chil-
    dren and young people becoming institutionalised? What can social workers and
    other professionals do to mitigate the negative impacts of residential life?
2   The concept and experience of transition to independent living is generally
    accepted to be a challenging one. How might such an experience be potentially
    more challenging for young people who have had contact with social work
    service? Consider young people who have either being looked after away from
    home or who have been living in difficult and disruptive home environments.
3   The chapter has outlined some of the key interviewing skills necessary for work
    with individuals. Think about your previous and current experiences of working
    with children and young people and undertake a self-assessment type audit
    of your ability to perform these skills effectively with different groups. Is your
    competence in interviews just as strong whether you are speaking to children,
    young people or adults? Are there are any areas of difference? If so, what could
    you do to address these differences?

FURTHER READING

Harris, J.R. (2009) *Evolving Residential Work with Children and Families*. Holyoke, MA:
    NEARI Press.
Long, N.J., Wood, M.M. and Fescer, F.A. (2001) *Life Space Crisis Intervention: Talking
    with Students in Conflict*, 2nd edn. Texas: PRO-ED.

Refer to the Companion Website (www.sagepub.co.uk/SocialWork) for some useful
links to web-based materials.

27 METHODS OF INTERVENTION IN WORKING WITH INDIVIDUALS WITH SUBSTANCE PROBLEMS

Claire Marsden

Key Themes

- Terminology can complicate definitions of substance use issues.
- Social work plays a central role in helping people and communities affected by substance misuse.
- Assessment of risk is a key factor.
- Patterns of substance use vary and must be understood.
- There are a number of preferred methods of intervention.

INTRODUCTION

As a practising social worker, you are likely to work with individuals who have substance misuse problems, or individuals who have been affected by someone else's substance use, regardless of the particular field of social work that you specialise in. This is because substance misuse is a very prevalent problem across the UK and in many other societies world wide. The individual and social harms associated with problematic substance use affect many different social service user groups, including children and families, older people, people suffering mental distress, people with disabilities and people experiencing domestic abuse, amongst others (Galvani and Forrester, 2011).

This section will begin by defining what we mean by a 'substance problem' and information will be provided regarding the scale of substance problems and current service provision in the UK. It will then explore different patterns of substance use before examining some pertinent issues in relation to assessment of individuals with substance problems. Lastly, the section will conclude with an outline of four different methods of intervention that may be used to guide your practice when working with individuals with substance problems: Motivational Interviewing, Cognitive-Behavioural Therapy, 12-step approaches and Pharmacotherapy.

DEFINITION AND SCALE OF THE PROBLEM

There are various terms that are used to describe problematic substance use behaviour. These terms are often used interchangeably in the literature and also over time, which can make it difficult to pinpoint exactly what constitutes a 'substance problem'. For purposes of clarity, the following definition will be used in this section:

> the harmful or hazardous use of psychoactive substances, including alcohol and illicit drugs. Psychoactive substance use can lead to dependence syndrome – a cluster of behavioural, cognitive, and physiological phenomena that develop after repeated substance use and that typically include a strong desire to take the drug, difficulties in controlling its use, persisting in its use despite harmful consequences, a higher priority given to drug use than to other activities and obligations, increased tolerance, and sometimes a physical withdrawal state. (WHO, 2013a)

SUBSTANCE PROBLEMS IN THE UK

Alcohol

Since 1950, rates of alcohol consumption in the UK have more then doubled, although the rates of increase have been especially noticeable since the early 1990s (Tighe, 2007). In Scotland, it is estimated that up to 50% of men and 30% of women are drinking more than weekly sensible drinking guidelines and a majority of drinkers exceed daily guidelines on at least one occasion per week (Scottish Government, 2008a).

A study conducted by Alcohol Concern (2003) indicated that in Scotland 276,213 individuals were believed to be dependent on alcohol, in England the figure was 2,633,124, in Wales 151,673 and in Northern Ireland 85,139 (Alcohol Concern, 2003 as cited in Institute of Alcohol Studies, 2010b).

Exercise

A 50-year-old professional man has half a bottle of wine with his evening meal. In addition, he will have a glass of brandy following the meal on two or three evenings. On Friday, Saturday and Sunday he will consume the equivalent of a bottle and a half of wine each day, together with four or five glasses of spirits. How does this pattern of consumption fit weekly sensible drinking guidelines?

Table 27.1   Health risks and social harms resulting from alcohol abuse

	Potential health risks	Potential social harms
Intoxication	Acute alcohol poisoning	Criminal behaviour
	Gastritis	Accidents
	Cardiac arrhythmias	Unsafe sex
	Pancreatitis	Unwanted pregnancy
	Disturbed sleep	
Excessive consumption	Liver damage	Absenteeism from work
	Brain damage	Impaired social relationships
	Hypertension	Psychological problems
	Cardiomyopathy	Criminal behaviour
	Cardiovascular disease	Sexual problems
	Malignancies	
Alcohol dependence	Dementia	Social disintegration
	Withdrawal symptoms	Relationship problems
		Financial problems
		Unemployment

Source: Institute of Alcohol Studies, 2002

Table 27.1 highlights some of the health and social harms that can result from alcohol use.

Drugs

The UK has one of the highest levels of dependent drug use and among the highest levels of recreational drug use in Europe (Reuter and Stevens, 2007). Available evidence suggests that both drug and alcohol dependence rates are especially high in Scotland (Audit Scotland, 2009), where an estimated 52,000 people are problem drug users and 40,000–60,000 children are affected by the drug problem of one or more parents (Scottish Government, 2008b). This has a significant impact on individuals, families and society – with an estimated economic and social cost of £2.6 billion per annum (Scottish Government, 2008b).

The 2010/11 British Crime Survey estimates that 8.8% of adults aged 16 to 59 had used illicit drugs (almost 3 million people) and that 3.0% had used a Class A drug in the last year (approx. 1million people) (Millard, 2011). The figures attest to the fact that illicit drug use is very prevalent in British society, as it is in most other societies world wide.

The personal harms that can result from drug use will vary depending on the nature of the substance taken. In the UK, the 1971 Misuse of Drugs Act classifies controlled drugs into three categories (Classes A, B and C) according to the harm that they cause,

Table 27.2   Classification of substances under the UK Misuse of Drugs Act 1971

Class A substances	Class B substances	Class C substances
Maximum penalty for possession: up to 7 years' imprisonment, a fine, or both	Maximum penalty for possession: up to 5 years' imprisonment, a fine, or both	Maximum penalty for possession: up to 2 years' imprisonment, a fine, or both
Maximum penalty for distribution: up to life imprisonment, a fine, or both	Maximum penalty for distribution: up to 14 years' imprisonment, a fine, or both	Maximum penalty for distribution: up to 14 years' imprisonment, a fine, or both
Cocaine	Amphetamines	Tranquilisers
Crack cocaine	Cannabis	Ketamine
Ecstasy	Codeine	Some painkillers
LSD	Methylphenidate (Ritalin)	Gamma-hydroxbutyrate (GHB)
Heroin	Pholcodine	
Magic mushrooms	Mephedrone (M-Cat) and other cathinones	
Methadone (if not prescribed)	Synthetic cannabinoids (e.g. 'Spice')	
Meth amphetamine (Crystal Meth)		
Any class B drug if prepared for injection (e.g. amphetamine)		

with Class A drugs considered to be the most harmful. Table 27.2 shows what substances are classed in each category.

The UK's approach to drug classification and the treatment of those breaking the law is quite different to some other countries. On the Companion Website (www.sagepub.co.uk/SocialWork) you will find an activity exploring the approach taken to drug use in Portugal. This activity will serve as an interesting point of comparison to UK approaches.

SERVICE PROVISION IN THE UK

Social work as a profession is key to helping people and communities affected by drug and alcohol problems, and professionals across the whole of the social care sector deal with high numbers of service users with drug and/or alcohol problems. Throughout the UK there is an increased focus on 'what works' when intervening with people using alcohol or other drugs with the expectation that service provision should be based on available evidence of best practice in this area (Galvani and Forrester, 2011).

There are a range of services available in the UK to help individuals with problematic substance use, including:

- Residential rehabilitation. This can be a good treatment option for individuals that are physically and/or psychologically dependent on a substance or substances. Typically, service users live on the premises for a period of time to enable them to detox from the substance or substances used and to receive one-to-one counselling and support and often group work support also. Individuals usually stay in a residential rehabilitation unit anywhere from between 1 week to a year, although this will vary depending on the exact nature of the services offered. Individuals may also be offered after-care support for a given period of time upon discharge. Although residential rehabilitation can be an attractive treatment option providing individuals with intense 24-hour support as required, most are privately owned and run and therefore fees can be quite high.
- One-to-one counselling and support. This can be provided within specialist agencies or in the community. Many agencies allow individuals to self-refer, although others might only take referrals from other agencies such as social work departments or GPs.
- Needle exchanges. Needle exchanges are 'harm reduction' services for injecting drug users. Their purpose is to reduce the harms caused by drug use by providing service users with clean injecting equipment and paraphernalia free of charge, and to give advice on safer substance using practices. Service users can also take their used injecting equipment in to needle exchanges to be disposed of safely, which helps to protect communities and members of the public from harm. Many needle exchanges also offer advice on sexual health and how to prevent the transmission of blood-borne viruses such as hepatitis and HIV which can be caused by sharing injecting equipment and having unprotected sex.

PATTERNS OF SUBSTANCE USE

It is important to recognise that not everyone who uses substances will necessarily become dependent on them. We can look at four generally broad patterns of drug use in examining different substance-using behaviours: experimental use, recreational use, binge use and dependent use.

Experimental Use

Experimental use of substances occurs when an individual tries a substance for the first time. Research shows that most individuals begin to experiment with taking substances in their teenage years (Roe and Man, 2006), although some individuals will not use a substance for the first time until they are older. There are a whole host of reasons why individuals might choose to experiment with taking substances, although some of the more common reasons might include:

- curiosity regarding the effects that a substance will have and how it will make them feel
- to fit in with a substance-using peer group.

An individual taking a substance for the first time might have a lack of knowledge regarding the substance in terms of its likely effects and how long they will last, how much of a substance they can safely consume and any potential side-effects that might be experienced as a result of taking the substance.

Recreational Use

Recreational substance use is primarily undertaken for pleasure, for example when socialising at weekends. Depending on the substance used, this might make an individual feel more sociable and less inhibited or alternatively it might help someone to feel more relaxed and able to 'let go' of personal pressures. With recreational use, control is usually exercised around the type of drug used, the amount used, and where and when it is used (e.g. at weekends). Poly-drug use, including the use of alcohol, is common when using substances recreationally.

Examples of the research focusing on recreational drug use can be accessed by visiting the Companion Website (www.sagepub.co.uk/SocialWork) – see Miller and Quigley's (2012) work on the music scene and Ravn's (2012) work on youth culture.

Binge Use

'Binge' drinking or drug taking is characterised by heavy, episodic use of substances. It entails ingesting excessive amounts of a substance over a relatively short period of time. There is no internationally agreed definition of binge drinking, but in the UK drinking surveys normally define binge drinkers as men consuming at least eight, and women at least six standard units of alcohol in a single day, that is, double the maximum recommended 'safe limit' for men and women respectively (Institute of Alcohol Studies, 2010a).

There are obvious dangers associated with this type of substance use, including:

- physical health problems, including overdose and death
- mental health problems
- problems with relationships
- problems with employment (e.g. being off work due to sickness after bingeing on substances).

This list is not exhaustive and the exact nature of the problems experienced as a result of bingeing on alcohol and/or other substances will vary between individuals. The dangers associated with binge use of substances have been increasingly recognised in recent years, as has the personal, social and economic costs associated with this type of substance use behaviour.

Dependent Use

This type of substance use is characterised by the prolonged use of substances over a period of time. When an individual becomes dependent on a substance, they can no longer exercise as much control over the substance used due to either a physical or psychological dependence on the substance, or both. Owing to the fact that an individual will develop a tolerance to a substance the longer they use it for, individuals in this stage of use will likely have to use increasing quantities of a substance in order to achieve the desired effect.

An individual in this stage of use may use substances to prevent withdrawal effects, as often when substance use has escalated to this level an individual's tolerance to a substance has increased so much that they no longer feel much physical effect from the substance used. Individuals who have developed a dependence on substances usually experience additional social and psychological problems as their substance use and associated behaviours may have detrimental effects on the person's life in terms of their:

- physical and mental health
- relationships
- finance
- employment
- housing.

> ### Exercise
>
> Consider the substance use of yourself and those you know and how it fits any of the above categories.

ASSESSMENT FOR INDIVIDUALS WITH SUBSTANCE PROBLEMS

Many individuals presenting to services for help with their substance problems will have varied and complex needs – rarely ever will the substance problem present in isolation from other factors. For example, problems associated with physical and mental health issues, relationships, homelessness, employment, poverty and offending issues can have a direct impact on both an individual's motivation to change their substance-using behaviour and their ability to access and engage with services. It is important to ensure that the substance-using behaviour is never assessed in isolation from other factors and circumstances in an individual's life; account must be taken of the person, their environment and social circumstances in order to gain a real awareness of their overall situation and how this may affect their motivation and ability to implement and sustain change regarding their substance use.

It is important to remember that assessment is an *ongoing process* and is never just a 'one-off' event. A lot can change between sessions regarding a service user's personal and social circumstances that can impact on their substance use behaviour, for example:

- mental health issues
- physical health issues
- relationship issues
- employment issues
- financial issues
- housing issues
- offending issues.

All of the above can have an impact on an individual's sense of self-efficacy, motivation to change and ability to engage with services. It is therefore important for a worker to continuously assess any changes in a service user's circumstances and the impact this has on their substance use behaviour.

When working with individuals with substance problems, it is not just their substance use that you need to assess; in order to undertake assessments that are holistic, account will also have to be taken of an individual's:

- *Strengths*. It is important to assess and acknowledge the individual's strengths in order to help them build on these and increase self-efficacy to effect positive change regarding their substance use and in relation to other areas in their life.
- *Needs*. It is important to seek the service user's views on what needs *they* consider to be the most urgent in order for assessment and subsequent intervention to be needs-led.
- *Risks*. It is always important to assess the risks to both the individual themselves and others as a result of the substance use behaviour in order to know what action should be taken immediately in order to reduce these risks.

Assessment Domains

Substance use history

It is important to gather information regarding the person's history of substance using behaviour for several reasons. For example, determining how long an individual has been using substances will give you an indication as to whether they are likely to have developed a physical and/or psychological dependence on the substance(s). This needs to be taken into account in planning subsequent interventions.

It is also important to assess previous periods of abstinence or reduction in use and how this was achieved. This information can give the worker important insights into what has worked previously for the individual in reducing or abstaining from substance use so that this might be replicated in the present. This will also allow the worker to highlight previous achievements in initiating positive change in order to increase the individual's self-efficacy and belief that change is possible. It affords an opportunity to find out about an individual's coping skills and how helpful they are in enabling the individual to effect change.

It is also useful to ask the individual about the factors that led to their resuming or increasing substance use after a period of reduction or abstinence. This can enable the worker and service user to explore what the person's 'relapse triggers' were so that a strategy can be devised to help avoid these in future.

Mental health issues

Research shows that a high percentage of individuals presenting to services for help with their substance use issues also experience mental health difficulties. Co-occurring mental health and substance use issues are referred to as 'dual diagnosis', and studies have shown that up to 75% of individuals engaged with drug services also had psychiatric disorders (Scottish Executive, 2003b).

Individuals with co-occurring mental health and substance use issues are likely to present to services with a wide range of complex needs and may be at higher risk of relapse, admission to hospital and suicide (Department of Health, 2002). It is for this reason that substance use workers must ensure when working with individuals with mental health issues that their mental health needs are addressed by specialist services, and if the service user is not already engaged with them, that a referral is made. It is also important to assess ways in which mental health issues are impacting on an individual's substance use and vice versa so that appropriate intervention can be planned.

Relationships

It is important to assess the amount and nature of support available to a service user as changing substance use behaviour (especially if it has been established for a significant period of time) can be a very frightening prospect and having the support of others in this change can be vital to overall success.

Case Study

You might ask the following questions during the initial assessment process to gain a better understanding of this:

- Who do they live with and are they supportive?
- Do significant others drink/use substances?
- Are they supportive of the individual receiving help for their substance use?
- Are there dependent children and/or other vulnerable adults in their care?
- Do they require childcare to attend appointments?

Financial

Lack of financial resources is a major contributing factor to issues such as social deprivation and exclusion which can contribute to and exacerbate substance problems. If an individual has debt problems, for example, they may use substances to cope with the stress and anxiety caused by this. Gaining some idea of how much the person is spending on substances may also provide insight into how physically and/or psychologically dependent on the substance they are likely to be.

Offending issues

It is important to assess if a service user is engaged in offending behaviour and, if so, to then explore the links between this and their substance use. For example, is the individual engaging in criminal activity in order to finance their substance use or are they using substances as a means of coping with the consequences of their offending behaviour? Has the individual been legally coerced into treatment and if so what do they hope to gain from attending a service to address their substance use?

Assessing Risk

Assessing risk will also be an on-going process, although it is especially important to pick up on any inherent risks in the first session in case the service user disengages from the service. Some of the potential risks to be assessed might include the following.

Risks to the service user themselves

For example, is the service user at risk of overdose from using too much of a substance or from using more than one substance (note that risk of overdose might be especially acute if two or more depressant drugs are being used, e.g. alcohol, heroin, benzodiazepines)? Some specific questions you might ask a service user in order to assess the risk of harm might include:

- What substances is the person using, how much and how often?
- How is the person ingesting the substance and does harm reduction advice need to be given (in instances of high-risk injecting practices, for example)?
- Is the service user on any prescribed medications and if so what is the effect of combining this with illicit substances or alcohol?
- What effect does the use of substances have on the service user's emotional state and cognitive function?

Risks to others

For example, if the service user is responsible for the care and well-being of children and/or any other vulnerable adult, what effect does their substance use behaviour have on them and does this constitute a risk of harm? Every effort should be made to gather information on significant others in the service user's life – for example children or other vulnerable adults in the household, their ages and protective factors.

Sharing information with other professionals

Some information gathered may have to be shared with other professionals. For example, if you identify risks to the person and/or others during the course of assessment and subsequent work, you may have to share this information with other professionals in accordance with relevant social policy and legislation so that these risks can be minimised as much as possible. Examples of this would include instances where you assess an individual to be at risk of self-harm or suicide, or if you assess their substance use to constitute a risk to others such as children or vulnerable adults in their care (see list of relevant social policy documents at the end of the chapter for further guidance).

METHODS OF INTERVENTION FOR INDIVIDUALS WITH SUBSTANCE PROBLEMS

Motivational Interviewing – Promoting Motivation to Change

> Motivation is an important first step toward any action or change in behaviour … people generally will not perform desired behaviours unless or until they are motivated to do so. (DiClemente et al., 1999: 86)

It is common for individuals to be ambivalent about changing their substance use behaviour, especially if it has been established for a period of time, and if the individual still perceives it to hold some degree of reward (for example the ability to relax for a period of time, social interaction from being with peers who use substances, etc). Even when an individual begins to recognise the negative consequences of their substance use, they may still be reluctant to stop because of some of the perceived advantages it offers.

Generally, individuals' motivation to change substance use behaviour will increase as they begin to recognise more disadvantages than advantages of it, and see more benefits than drawbacks to change. Motivation is a key element in substance misuse treatment and influences an individual's progression through the different stages of change. At this point, you should refer to Chapter 23 and read in particular about the Cycle of Change. It is important, at times challenging, for you as the worker to be able to assess a service user's motivation to change.

A useful starting point in assessing an individual's motivation to change their substance use behaviour is to try to assess where they are on the Cycle of Change, as outlined in Chapter 23.

Example

1   Pre-contemplative stage. When working with individuals with substance problems who are in the pre-contemplative stage, you may recognise the use of certain 'defence mechanisms' that prevent the individual from having to confront the need to change, for example:

   o   Denial: 'I don't have a problem.'
   o   Minimisation: 'I don't use that much.'

2   Contemplation stage. In this stage an individual is more aware of the negative consequences of their substance use, although they still tend to 'see-saw' back and forth between wanting to change and not wanting to, for example:

   o   'I don't really think I have an alcohol problem. I may drink more than is good for me, but I don't drink much more than my friends. I don't like waking up in the morning feeling desperate for a drink, but I think I could stop whenever I wanted to.'

3   Decision stage. The individual is now motivated to change, for example:

   o   'I have got to do something about my drinking/drug taking.'

4   Action stage. In this stage, an individual now believes in the ability to change substance use and begins actively to do things to change behaviour, including developing plans to deal with situations that might put them at risk of reverting to their old behaviour and seeking support from others as required.

5   Maintenance stage. In this stage an individual works to maintain the change they have made by preventing a lapse or relapse, and continues to learn new skills required in order to do this.

(Continued)

(Continued)

6 (Re) Lapse stage. In the process of working towards either abstinence from substances or a stable reduction in use, most people experience either a lapse (using or drinking again once) or a relapse (a full return to previous substance use behaviour). In fact, it is more common for individuals to have at least one relapse than to not have any (Prochaska and DiClemente, 1982). It is important that you encourage the view that relapse is a learning process. You could discuss with the individual the circumstances that led to the relapse and brainstorm with the service user what would constitute high-risk situations so that they can be avoided if possible. Consider how they might avoid certain 'triggers' that would tempt them to use again (e.g. other people that are users; places where substance use is likely to take place); discuss with the service user ways to handle difficult emotions such as stress or depression without returning to substance use to cope with these.

Using motivational interviewing techniques

Motivational interviewing focuses on promoting and enhancing an individual's internal motivation to change, and is based on motivational psychology and the stages of change model (Miller and Rollnick, 1991 as cited in DiClemente et al., 1999).

In the past more traditional approaches to working with individuals with substance problems were often directive and confrontational, in order to enable the individual to confront their 'denial' about their problem (Miller and Rollnick, 2002) and thus increase their motivation to change. However, more recent research has shown that confrontational approaches can produce a defensive reaction from some service users and can actually cause them to be *more resistant* to change (Miller et al., 1993), the opposite effect to what the worker seeks to promote! Today, motivational interviewing techniques are widely regarded as an effective method in working with individuals with substance problems. In contrast to more confrontational approaches, motivational interviewing recognises ambivalence to be a natural part of the change process and enables the worker to help the service user to resolve ambivalence and increase motivation to change.

Exploring the pros and cons of change

Your task as a worker using motivational interviewing techniques is to help an individual to resolve their ambivalence about change. A good way to help achieve this is to assist them to explore some of the pros and cons of change. When an individual has maintained a certain behaviour consistently over a period of time, this behaviour becomes habit-forming and the person often ceases to critically evaluate the behaviour and its consequences. Exploring the pros and cons of change can enable an individual to think critically about their substance use, in terms of the consequences it has on themselves and others. This can help to foster motivation to change. Figure 27.1 shows an example of a pros and cons of change worksheet.

Pros of change:	Pros of not changing:
Cons of change:	Cons of not changing:

Figure 27.1   A pros and cons of change worksheet

Using Cognitive-Behavioural Therapy With Individuals With Substance Problems

Research has shown that using cognitive-behavioural techniques can be highly effective in helping an individual with a substance problem to bring about positive change (Lingford-Hughes et al., 2004). The theoretical foundation of cognitive-behavioural interventions is fully addressed in Chapter 18.

The 12-step approach

The 12-step model of intervention is based on a set of guiding principles that outline a structured approach to overcoming substance dependence. Alcoholics Anonymous was the first 12-step fellowship, founded in 1935 in America by Dr Bob Smith and Bill Will. Over time, the method was adapted and became the foundation of other 12-step programmes, such as Narcotics Anonymous, Gamblers Anonymous and Overeaters Anonymous, amongst others.

One way in which the 12-step approach is distinctive from other models of intervention is that it views substance dependence as a progressive and incurable disease. Because of the progressive and enduring nature of the disease or 'illness' of addiction, this approach advocates that the only way it can be 'treated' is through complete abstinence from substances. According to this approach, once an individual becomes physically or psychologically dependent on a substance they will always have the disease of addiction and therefore complete abstinence is advised as the ability to control one's substance use is believed to be compromised as a result of having the disease (for a critique of this approach see Raistrick et al., 2006).

It is important to be aware of the 12-step philosophy's focus on abstinence as obviously this approach would not be suitable for service users that wished to reduce rather than abstain completely from substance use.

Attendance at meetings

AA and NA meetings are 'discussion' meetings, usually of 1–2 hours in duration, where members can choose to talk about their feelings and experiences around a given topic or theme. Members also discuss their experiences of substance use and of achieving 'sobriety'. Having the opportunity to attend meetings and discuss hopes, fears and experiences in an accepting environment can decrease feelings of isolation whilst helping to promote self-acceptance and instil hope that positive change can be achieved.

The only requirement for attendance at AA and NA meetings is a desire to stop drinking or using drugs and members can attend as little or as often as they wish. There are no fees for attending AA or NA meetings as they are self-supporting. AA and NA have both 'open' and 'closed' meetings. Individuals that are affected by the substance problem of someone else or would like advice on how to help them can attend 'open' meetings whereas 'closed' meetings are reserved for individuals who want help with their own substance problem. Sometimes meetings will allow workers to accompany service users to meetings for the first time, or to go along as a professional to observe a meeting (contact your local AA or NA group for further information).

There are separate meetings for families that are affected by someone else's substance use, such as Al-Anon (for adults affected by someone else's alcohol use), Al-Ateen (for teenagers affected) and Families Anonymous for family members affected by someone's drug use.

Exploration of the 12 steps through meetings/literature

The 12 steps outline a process for changing thinking and behaviour patterns that it is recommended an individual follow in order to achieve abstinence from substances.

Use of a sponsor

Another aspect of the method is a one-to-one mentoring relationship with another member who has been part of the fellowship for a longer time period and has been substance-free for a substantial period of time. The mentor can act as a positive role model in this regard. A sponsor can be contacted regularly to help with cravings, thoughts and feelings, which can be vital for individuals with limited positive support. As one gains more sobriety themselves, they may then act as a sponsor to newer members – this enables personal development and offers a continuing support system for newer members.

Pharmacotherapies

When an individual becomes dependent on a given substance and wants to cease using, it may be necessary for them to do so under medical supervision. This is because the withdrawal effects from some substances can be dangerous to an individual's health, and in some circumstances detoxing from certain substances without appropriate medical supervision can even prove fatal.

Pharmacotherapy is the use of drugs in the treatment of substance problems. A variety of drugs can be used for different purposes. Pharmacotherapy can be used to:

- Reduce the risks and discomfort associated with detoxification.
- Help an individual to remain abstinent. Some drugs reduce craving and the desire to use, whilst others react in an unpleasant way with the drug the person is trying to avoid so, if they do use, they become sick (a form of aversion therapy). Some drugs block the receptors in the brain so that if used, a particular drug will have no effect.

- Substitute the drug a person is using with one that is less harmful and is not illicit (substitute prescribing).
- Replace lost vitamins or generally improve the person's health.

Critical Thinking

Reflect on how substance misuse is reported in the media. To what extent is there a mature and open debate about strategies?

CONCLUSION

This chapter has provided specific information on patterns of substance abuse as well as concepts, theories and debates relating to substance use. The interventions outlined have been underpinned by an evidence base drawn from research, but you should also refer to the appropriate chapters in this book for more details.

Watch vodcast 27.1 on the Companion Website (www.sagepub.co.uk/SocialWork) to see chapter author Claire Marsden summarise the main points conveyed in this chapter, and why possessing a knowledge of substance misuse is important for social work practice.

Reflective Questions

1   Reflect on the wider social and cultural significance of alcohol and other substances in society. How do they relate to social practices and cultural norms? Could the perceived requirement to fulfil certain social practices (for example, having a drink at the weekend) lead to problematic alcohol and substance use?
2   What type of profile may a 'typical' person who has issues with either alcohol or substance use display? Think wider here than that it is simply people living in deprivation who may have problematic use. Consider whether there is a 'typical' profile.
3   Elsewhere we have stressed the importance of the ethical base of social work. Which particular ethical considerations may a social worker need to be aware of when working with people with substance and alcohol issues?

RECOMMENDED READING

Goodman, A. (2013) *Working with Drugs, Alcohol and Substance Misusers.* Exeter: Learning Matters.
Redman, D. (2012) 'A community engagement orientation among people with a history of substance misuse and incarceration', *Journal of Social Work*, 12 (3): 246–66.
Wild, T.C. (2006) 'Social control and coercion in addiction treatment: towards evidence-based policy and practice', *Addiction*, 101: 40–9.

Refer to the Companion Website (www.sagepub.co.uk/SocialWork) for some useful links to web-based material.

WORKING WITH
28 ADULTS: MENTAL HEALTH

Mike Maas-Lowit

This chapter will focus on key aspects of social work practice in the field of mental health. For a broader understanding of aspects of direct practice, you should refer to chapters in the knowledge base, assessment and intervention sections, as well as the chapters on learning disability and interventions with older people in this section of the book.

Key Themes

- Mental health and mental illness are terms often used interchangeably to mean the same thing. They are not synonymous.
- Separating out the terms mental health and mental illness allows us to explore the possibility of working in partnership to improve the mental health of people who are diagnosed with mental illness.
- We will discuss the use of narrative therapy and cognitive behavioural approaches as ways of working with people with mental health problems in pursuit of empowerment and recovery.
- It is essential to consider the individual within the environment.
- Scientific study informs our knowledge.

INTRODUCTION

Mental health and mental illness are often used interchangeably to mean the same thing. Indeed, all three legislative areas of the UK have laws called 'Mental Health Acts', none of which has much to do with mental health as such and everything to do with mental disorder in general and mental illness in particular (the Mental Health (Northern Ireland) Order 1986, the Mental Health (Care and Treatment) (Scotland) Act 2003 and the Mental Health Act 1983, with its 2007 amendments). There is a relationship between health and illness but it is not at all simple. Furthermore, as we get into this subject, this section needs to have a warning attached to it: these are complex and contested matters which will be boiled down for the purposes of brevity. Readers are directed to aspects of these matters in the further reading section at the end of this chapter.

For a discussion of mental health social work under the differing legislature of the UK see the article by Mackay (2012) on the Companion Website (www.sagepub.co.uk/SocialWork).

UNDERSTANDING HEALTH

In a much published quote, the World Health Organization (WHO, 2006) gives an aspirational description of good health as something for individuals and governments to aim for:

> a state of complete physical, mental, and social well-being and not merely the absence of disease or infirmity.

It is a quote that requires some discussion. Health is a quality we all possess. It is difficult to imagine being alive and not having some awareness of one's state of health. The very phrase 'state of health' suggests that, for all of us, our health is a shifting quality that ranges somewhere on a spectrum from good to poor. Some of us have chronic tendencies that limit our ability to keep good health. A lucky group of us live much of our lives in good health. But for all of us, there are times when our health is not so good and it is unrealistic to expect a life lived in total good health without the occasional dip into poor health.

It is important to note several things from the WHO definition: Health is not so much a tangible thing, it is rather described as a 'state', an aspect of our being. It is divided into three notional spheres – physical, mental (which is the area of our interest here) and social. Of course, these three spheres are not entirely separate. Problems in the physical domain may make us feel differently in the mental domain and may affect the way we perform in the social domain.

Finally, note that health is *not merely the absence of disease or infirmity* (WHO, 2006). This means that good health (mental and/or physical) is more than an absence of what we usually call *illness*.

In an equally often published quote, WHO (2005) describes the ideal state of good mental health as

> a state of well-being in which the individual realises his or her abilities, can cope with the normal stresses of life, can work productively and fruitfully and is able to make a contribution to his community.

Note again the suggestion of links to physical and social domains in the ability to cope with stress and the references to work, productivity and community. People often think of good health as being a condition of being free from illness and bad health as being the same as illness. However, both WHO descriptions suggest something different: they suggest that health in general, and mental health in particular, are inseparable from both the person who experiences them and from the environment. This further suggests a sense of interaction between the person and their health. Many governments have used this notion in their health and mental health policies to encourage a sense that we citizens have a responsibility to ourselves to actively maintain our health. In contrast, there is a degree of truth in the consideration that much illness happens to us – we *get* ill, so to speak. However, we are able to *keep* as healthy as we can, as long as we tend to ourselves.

Critical Thinking

To what extent do you agree with the descriptions or definitions above? To what extent can we be responsible for our health and to what extent are we victims of bacteria, genetics or events outside our control?

The Scottish Government's *Towards a Mentally Flourishing Scotland* (2007b, 2009a) was a good example of a government policy that discusses mental health in the way we have defined it so far. It is recommended in the further reading at the end of this chapter because its opening paragraphs explain the differences between mental health and mental illness and take the reader to the point of considering that one can help mentally ill people to improve their mental health.

By this definition, good mental health is about maintaining a sense of purpose, a sense of belonging, a sense of self-esteem and other like attributes, which give meaning and shape to life. By implication, poor mental health is not about the absence of mental illnesses such as clinical depression and schizophrenia. It is about lacking those things that characterise good mental health. To this extent, poor self-esteem, feelings of worthlessness, feelings of having no purpose or place in the world and conditions such as chronic loneliness would all be attributes of bad mental health (Maas-Lowit, 2010).

UNDERSTANDING ILLNESS

If mental illness is a contrasting concept to mental health, all that remains in this clarifying discussion is some explanation of what we mean by mental illness. Illness is a word that has been adopted by the medical profession to refer to some wrong-functioning aspect of the body or mind. It therefore suggests that there is such a thing as the perfectly working body and the perfectly functioning mind. Unless we had an ideal notion of things working perfectly well, how could we know when they go wrong?

The first question to ask in this exploration of mental illness is *what is mental about it?* Mental is an adjective referring to *the mind*. What the mind is, is a matter of great and long philosophical debate, too complicated for this text (Graham, 2010). We will simplify it by making several assumptions: The mind is not a thing you can touch or see. It is a process: the functioning of the brain. You might say it is all that we experience: emotions, physical sensations of sight, hearing, smell, taste and touch, comprehension, memory and the wider sense of being alive and located within yourself in the world.

This begs the much contested question – *how could any of these things be ill?* Some thinkers on the subject deny that mental illness exists at all (for example, see Szasz, 1974). However, there is no space in this book to go over the arguments and we have already suggested a way of looking at *mental health* as something different from mental illness. Therefore there is little point in ignoring the issue. All we want to do is proceed with a caution that not everyone agrees in equal strength that mental illness is a useful concept. More to the point, there are people whom many professionals would describe as having a mental illness who would disagree and who would take exception to doctors, social workers and others having the power to define their inner experiences as illness. To some extent we should be sensitive to these views and we should be careful as to how we express our ideas.

On the other hand, the idea of mental illness is rooted in a powerful and extensive body of scientific research. It speaks to the brain as the organ in which the mind functions. We could not see, hear, smell, taste, touch, comprehend or remember the world were it not for our brains. Therefore, the scientific process of divining illness in the mind focuses on the workings of the brain. It is in the brain that the exploration takes place as to what goes wrong with a person's mind when they experience **hallucinations** or **disrupted thought patterns** which cause them to hold ideas to which the majority of us are unable to relate (Maas-Lowit, 2010).

The results are twofold. On the one hand, there is the scientific categorisation of experiences such as hallucination, delusion and fluctuations in mood which vary from excessive depression to wild excitement. This has resulted in a diagnostic framework of mental illness which separates conditions such as **schizophrenia** and **bi-polar affective disorder**. For greater detail of this, see how these are characterised in the International Classification of Diseases (WHO, 1990/2010), the psychiatrists' guide to diagnosis. On the other hand, there is the process of looking inside the brain to find out what goes wrong with its chemistry and its neurological processes. It is this exploration which has substantiated the idea that mental illnesses are illnesses. It suggests that there are identifiable chemical malfunctions in the brains of depressed people, for example.

Exercise

At this point, consider how mental illness and mental health are portrayed through the media. How helpful are these portrayals in providing an accurate picture?

To assess your understanding of terminology used to describe aspects of mental illness undertake the activity on the Companion Website (www.sagepub.co.uk/SocialWork).

SOCIAL WORK PRACTICE AND MENTAL HEALTH

Having explained mental illness, at least in some small part, we will pass on. The work that social workers do with people who have mental illness is an area too specialised for this book. We want to focus on working with people who are challenged in maintaining good mental health. Within the profession of social work it is relatively common to perceive mental health as a limited area. This is largely due to the confusion of the term *mental health* as we describe it above and the term as it is used in reference to law, psychiatry and mental illness. Taking our more accurate and broader use of the term, it is arguable that 100% of people who use social work services experience some challenge to their mental health. People who use social work often have problems in sustaining fulfilling relationships; they often have low self-esteem; they often find it difficult to find a meaningful place in the social world, where they can feel fulfilled and included. Therefore, it would be important not to read this section of this chapter as referring to a separate segment of social work practice. It would be important to read it in context of all the chapters relating to practice, because the reality is that, whether a person comes to social work because they have been harmed or abused, because they have an illness or disability, because they have broken the law themselves or because they have a problem in old age or in relation to substance abuse, that person will most likely be struggling with difficult challenges to mental health as well as with difficulties because of the presenting problem. To that extent, all successful social work intervention worth its salt will contain some measure of enabling the person to improve upon his or her mental health.

Narrative therapy is described in Chapter 22 of this book as a potentially empowering intervention that takes account of the person as they would describe themselves. Narrative therapy in particular resonates with something we discussed earlier – the power of professionals to define a person's experience. Historically, this has been a particular feature of so-called mental health services – the services that make provision for people who have serious mental illness (Heller et al., 1996). While modern mental health service delivery, law and policy are usually more attuned to the voices of service users, even the relatively recent history of the latter half of the last century is characterised by a predominance of power in the hands of professionals and a centralisation of care and treatment in hospital.

In this regard, narrative therapy enables people to reclaim their own identities by giving voice to their own experiences in their own terms, rather than having their experience dominated by the ideas of others.

Case Study

Consider the following two explanations of Tony's experience and analyse where the power of the description lies:

1. Tony experienced auditory hallucinations in the form of voices which told him very upsetting things about himself in relation to the sexual abuse of his childhood. This caused him to commit self-harm and those responsible for his treatment finally had to make the decision to detain him in hospital under mental health legislation because of the risks he posed to himself.
2. Sometimes my voices get the better of me and I get ground down by them calling me dirty names. It is all to do with my dad and how he hurt me when I was a kid. I deal with it by cutting myself. It takes away the pain of the feelings my dad left me with. They got a bit worried about it and they locked me away in hospital for a while. I am not saying they were wrong to do it. I got a bit of rest in hospital and I like the staff. But I'm learning to manage it myself and the real solution is not for me to be locked up. It is for me to understand why my dad did that to me and that it was wrong ... he is bad, not me.

Do you see that the first version uses powerful professional language to say things in a way that they are understood by those who provide the service? The second version may differ only slightly in what it says, but how it says it is hugely different. It restores power to the narrator. The first version justifies the use of mental health detention. The second version does not disagree, but allows Tony to begin to find his own solution.

In this way, narrative therapy is a powerful tool in empowering people to define their lives in their own terms and, in doing so, to find solutions. From this, it is possible to see how it can improve the mental health of the person. It places the person in control and, in doing so, it increases potential to find self-esteem, to manage problems and get a sense of achievement. All of this enhances mental health and well-being. Narrative therapy requires expertise on behalf of the practitioner in relation to the skills of empathy and communication, and the role of therapist is as a guide to the process. The expert in the exercise is very much the person who has a story to tell, hence the empowering nature of the therapy.

The process of helping women, marginalised by experiences of mental illness, to 'restory' their lives is explored in an article by Butler et al. (2007). Visit the Companion Website (www.sagepub.co.uk/SocialWork) to read more.

Cognitive behavioural therapy (CBT), or more appropriately, cognitive behavioural approaches, as described in this book, principally in Chapter 18, relates to a very different strand of understanding the human condition. Cognitive behavioural approaches rely on the practitioner as expert in the intervention, and the worker must have a good grounding in the theory of CBT before he or she can apply it. To this extent, the person receiving the therapy is not the expert. While not disempowering, it is not empowering in the same way as narrative therapy. CBT may free a person from a condition such as depression or dependence upon drugs and, as a result, that person will be empowered to do other things. In contrast, narrative therapy is empowering in its own right. Furthermore, narrative therapy is about the person's entire being. CBT is very much focused upon the identified problem. Put another way, CBT is less holistic than narrative therapy. This does not make CBT a lesser option. These are merely points of difference between two approaches.

CBT uses a particular psychological understanding of cognitive processes to help the person find an objective measure of their thoughts. For example, if I am becoming depressed, I may feel as though everyone dislikes me because I am useless. I may look at the world to find evidence to support my feelings of not being likable and of being useless and I may strengthen the belief by repeatedly telling myself that I am not likeable and useless. This process will push me down a spiral of depression in which I will feel more and more negative about myself. In CBT terms, I may not realise it, but I am depressing myself.

CBT does not involve itself with any narrative story about how I got to this sad situation. It is only preoccupied with how I keep myself imprisoned in it by having negative thoughts. In this case, the therapist helps the person to evaluate how unlikely it is that 'everyone dislikes' him or her all of the time. The person is encouraged to review the evidence that he or she is totally useless.

The end of the therapy is that it is extremely unlikely that any of us is thoroughly dislikeable to all people and that we are totally useless, without any skills or competence in anything at all. And if we do find that lots of people do dislike us and that that is upsetting to us, the therapy examines the causes in so far as they lie in us and helps to find solutions. It does this by making the person aware of their automatic thought processes and it encourages the person to re-evaluate unrealistic thoughts (such as 'everybody hates me'). In this way, the less holistic approach is no less beneficial as a means of supporting a person to better mental health, in that it frees him or her from barriers that obstruct healthy solutions.

Before we leave this discussion of narrative and cognitive approaches to mental health, let us examine the potential to use both of them, if not at once, then side by side. We have posed them as very contrasting in their pedigree. However, as discussed in Chapter 18 on CBT, social workers often use these approaches not in their pure form (as might a clinical psychologist) but in a more pick-and-mix manner.

Case Study

We return to Tony in the case study begun previously. If we have the confidence to mix the approaches, it might be possible to inject a bit of CBT into the process of narrative therapy. This, please note, should be done only if there is a clear and pressing reason to do so.

Imagine you were working with Tony on telling his own story through narrative therapy, but he could not get beyond the point where he felt himself to be dirty and worthless and deserving of the abuse he had received at the hands of his father. This way of seeing himself and the events which took place could be interpreted as faulty thinking which is adversely affecting behaviour. It might be that a brief switch to a cognitive mode of working might help Tony to see the unrealistic nature of his thoughts. For example, Tony might be encouraged, through cognitive techniques, to step outside his narrative account and re-evaluate the logic of his conclusion that he is in some way to blame for being a victim of his father's abuse.

In our imaginary case of Tony, let us say that he was 6 years old when he was sexually abused.

Exercise

Before reading on, consider the following question:

- Can a 6-year-old boy be responsible for the sexual actions focused upon him by a supposedly responsible adult?

We would strongly hope that the reader would unhesitatingly answer *No!* to this question. Cognitive methods could help Tony to step outside of his life-long way of looking at this question and to re-evaluate it more objectively. In this way, while it might not stop his experience of auditory hallucination (or hearing voices), it might help him to move on to tell his story in a different light, which might make him feel different about himself.

Accepting the evidence that auditory hallucinations are caused by biochemical processes in the brain (Asaad and Shapiro, 1986), they belong more to the domain that defines mental illness (while not necessarily being illnesses in themselves). Therefore, social work interventions may have little to offer by way of tackling them. However, as discussed above, if we separate out the idea of mental illness from mental health, it is possible to see that cognitive and narrative interventions could be amongst many interventions that may improve the mental health of the person experiencing this symptom.

CONCLUSION

In this chapter I have discussed the meaning of mental health in order to provide a realistic basis for your future practice. In the past, mental health has been a subject that has produced a great deal of uninformed, stereotypical responses from people in society, but hopefully you will now begin to understand that it applies to everyone. Social workers are in a position to offer both support and therapeutic help by developing this understanding and by sensitively and purposefully applying their core knowledge and skills.

Reflective Questions

1 Consider what you have read in this chapter about the concepts of mental health and mental illness. Reflect on the extent to which maintaining good mental health is affected by physical, social and environmental factors. If you imagine good mental health as being one point on a continuum with its opposite being poor mental health, what in your experience have been the 'tipping points' that have moved people in one direction or the other? Can any common factors be identified or is the experience entirely individualised to the person concerned?

2 It is suggested in this chapter that broadly speaking all social work practice is about improving mental health. Do you agree with this proposition? If so, what do you/could you actively do in your work with service users to ensure that this aim is achieved? If you do not agree with the proposition, reflect on why you hold this view.

3 When working with service users consider the extent to which you have really listened to their story. Do you think that professional interpretations and perspectives dominate how situations and experiences are understood? If so, how can that change? What can you do to change your practice?

RECOMMENDED READING

Golightly, M. (2011) *Social Work and Mental Health*, 4th edn. Exeter: Learning Matters.
Hothersall, S.J., Maas-Lowit, M. and Golightly, M. (2008) *Social Work and Mental Health in Scotland*. Exeter: Learning Matters.

Mackay, K. (2012) 'A parting of the ways? The diverging nature of mental health social work in the light of the new Acts in Scotland, and in England and Wales', *Journal of Social Work*, 12 (2): 179–93.

Pilgrim, D. (2009) *Key Concepts in Mental Health*, 2nd edn. London: Sage.

See the Companion Website (www.sagepub.co.uk) for web links to: the Scottish Government's policy *Towards a Mentally Flourishing Scotland, 2009 to 2011* (Scottish Government, 2009a) and the proceeding Mental Health Strategy for Scotland 2012–2015; the diagnostic framework for mental illness, discussed above (*International Classification of Diseases, Tenth Revision. Mental and Behavioral Disorders, F00 to F99*. Geneva: WHO); and an explanation of the suggested link between hearing voices and problems in the brain chemistry.

29 WORKING WITH ADULTS: CRIMINAL JUSTICE SOCIAL WORK

Isobel Townsend

This chapter will focus on key aspects of social work practice in the field of criminal justice. For a broader understanding of aspects of direct practice, you should refer to chapters in the knowledge base, assessment and intervention sections, particularly on the cognitive behavioural and motivational interviewing models, as well as the chapters in this section of the book on learning disability, methods of intervention in working with individuals with substance problems, and evaluation.

Key Themes

- The organisational structure of criminal justice social work differs between Scotland and other parts of the UK.
- Service users are identified as involuntary clients.
- Methods of assessment and assessment tools are similar across the UK, although terminology differs.
- The legislative framework of criminal justice social work is identified.
- Methods of intervention and involvement of other agencies is discussed.

INTRODUCTION

In this chapter the focus turns to Criminal Justice Social Work (CJSW) Services in Scotland. In Scotland work with offenders is undertaken by the Criminal Justice Social Work (CJSW) Services based within the 32 local authorities. It should be noted that in other parts of the United Kingdom work with individuals similarly sentenced by the courts is undertaken by the Probation Service (also known as Probation Trusts), now under the auspices of the National Offender Management Service (NOMS) which was established in 2005 (Cree and Myers, 2008). The author has worked within both criminal justice systems and would argue that the actual work undertaken by CJSW Services in Scotland and NOMS with offenders in terms of protecting the public, reducing reoffending and encouraging desistance from offending, is not dissimilar. For the purposes of illustrating practice, more reference will be made to the Scottish situation, where CJSW is embedded in social work practice, social work training and social work as a mainstream local government service.

Croall (2006) explores some aspects of criminal justice policy in post-devolutionary Scotland. Her paper can be accessed on the Companion Website (www. sagepub.co.uk/SocialWork).

LEGISLATIVE AND PRACTICE CONTEXT

There are three key outcomes for CJSW Services in Scotland, as noted in the National Outcomes and Standards for Social Work within the Criminal Justice System (Scottish Government, 2010a: 15) which are:

1 Community safety and public protection
2 The reduction of re-offending
3 Social inclusion to support desistance from offending.

Objectives for the work of the Probation Service within NOMS are very similar to those of CJSW Services in Scotland. NOMS works 'to protect the public and reduce reoffending by delivering the punishment and orders of the courts and supporting rehabilitation by helping offenders to change their lives' (Ministry of Justice, 2012).

These outcomes are met by CJSW Services across Scotland working with individuals sentenced by the courts to certain community-based sentences (for example Community Payback Orders, Drug Treatment and Testing Orders) and also those sentenced to certain terms of imprisonment generally dependent on the length of sentence or the nature of the offence committed. In England and Wales similar sentences are available to the courts when dealing with individuals who have committed offences, with the exception that instead of Community Payback Orders (as used in Scotland) these sentences are called Community Orders.

The current legislative framework for community-based sentences supervised by CJSW Services in Scotland is provided in the Criminal Procedure (Scotland) Act 1995 as amended by the Criminal Justice and Licensing (Scotland) Act 2010. The 2010 Act introduced the new Community Payback Order which replaced the Probation Order and Community Service Order. The court can impose a Community Payback Order with one or more of nine requirements. These requirements include offender supervision; unpaid work or other activity; attendance at a specific groupwork programme; residence; mental health treatment; drug or alcohol treatment; compensation or conduct (an expectation to behave in a certain way) for individuals who have committed offences after 1 February 2011 (Guthrie, 2011). In many ways the work undertaken under the auspices of these new orders is exactly the same as that undertaken with offenders under the old sentencing options. Detailed information about Community Payback Orders can be found in the Community Payback Orders Practice Guidance Document (Scottish Government, 2010b). You can access the Guidance Document by following the link on the Companion Website (www.sagepub.co.uk/SocialWork).

The legislative framework for Community Orders in England and Wales is found in the Criminal Justice Act 2003. As in Scotland there are a number of requirements which can be added to a Community Order to punish the individual for the commission of the offence as well as being tailored to meet the needs of the offender with a view to desistance from offending. In England and Wales there are 12 requirements available – nine of which are similar to those used in Scotland as well as an attendance centre requirement, **curfew requirement** an exclusion requirement and a prohibited activity requirement.

The National Outcomes and Standards for Social Work within the Criminal Justice System (Scottish Government, 2010a) and the underpinning Practice Guidance Documents for Community Payback Orders (Scottish Government, 2010b) and CJSW Reports and Court-Based Services (Scottish Government, 2010c) provide the framework for the work which CJSW Services undertake with individuals who have been convicted of criminal offence(s).

The National Standards for the Management of Offenders (2011) provide a practice framework for practitioners and managers in England and Wales. They are published by the Secretary of State under the provisions of the Offender Management Act 2007 (chapter 21: Part 1 paragraph 7).

One final point to note both in terms of CJSW Services in Scotland and NOMS in England and Wales when working with individuals who have committed offences, is that these individuals have not chosen to work with these agencies. As these individuals are subject to a court order, the court has deemed that the individual will have involvement with CJSW and Probation Services – there is therefore an element of compulsion in all their contacts with these services. Trotter (2007: 2) applied the term 'involuntary client' to individuals in this situation because 'they have not chosen to receive the services they are being given'. This term is particularly apt for those individuals sentenced by the court to some form of supervision from CJSW/Probation Services. It would be pertinent to note at this point that non-compliance with CJSW/ Probation Services can lead to a return to court for the individual and potentially a resentencing exercise by the court whereby a more restrictive or punitive sentence could be imposed.

Exercise

You are working with a service user who has been abandoned by a partner, has been left in a vulnerable state and is appreciative of your help. You are also working with someone who has been referred by the court and who clearly resents having to see you. Do you value them equally?

Some research (for example Hough and Mitchell, 2003, as cited in Canton, 2011) has indicated that drug treatment provided on a voluntary basis was just as effective as for those coerced into it by way of a court order. Other research suggests that reluctant or involuntary clients may benefit more from the use of a non-directive approach – where the individual acts freely to access drug treatment as opposed to being coerced into treatment (for example McNeill et al., 2005). So when working with involuntary clients, staff must be aware that there may be an element of coercion in their work with individuals who have offended as the individual with whom they are working is subject to a court order.

ASSESSMENT

In the main, the first contact that an individual who has appeared before a court will have with the CJSW Service in Scotland will be in order for a social worker to prepare a CJSW Report. It should be noted that it is the duty of local authority social work departments under section 27 of the Social Work (Scotland) Act 1968 to provide such social background reports. In England and Wales such a report is known as a Pre-Sentence Report and is requested under the Criminal Justice Act 2003.

Such reports should assist the sentencing process, providing the following information:

- an analysis of the offence(s)
- the individual's background circumstances (personal and social circumstances), including offending and non-offending related needs
- an assessment of the risk that the individual presents in terms of re-offending and potential harm to others
- a potential appropriate sentencing option, including suitable intervention(s) given the individual's circumstances.

In preparing such reports workers use standard assessment tools, although the services in Scotland use a different tool to that used in England and Wales. A new accredited Assessment Tool, the Level of Service and Case Management Inventory (LSCMI), has been introduced across all local authorities in Scotland (Risk Management Authority, 2012). In England and Wales, the Offender Assessment System (OASys) has been used since 2003 (HM Prisons, 2003, reissued 2005). The LSCMI Assessment Tool will be used for all offenders with whom CJSW Services work, as is the OASys Assessment Tool in England and Wales. There are, however, several other accredited assessment tools, particularly associated with assessing the risk of serious harm to others. These specific tools are used alongside the LSCMI/OASys with individuals who have committed serious violent or sexual offences (Risk Management Authority, 2012).

Exercise

At this point, you might wish to read Chapters 11, 12 and 13 to consider assessment in more detail.

On the Companion Website (www.sagepub.co.uk/SocialWork) you can access a link to the LSCMI Assessment Tool. You can also read an article by Lancaster and Lumb (2006) exploring risk assessment in the National Probation Service.

When undertaking assessments both during the preparation of a CJSW Report or a Pre-Sentence Report, and during supervision of a Community Payback Order (Community Order in England and Wales) or Supervision Licence following release from a custodial sentence, the worker will be using assessment models including procedural, questioning and exchange (see Chapter 12 of this book).

The following case study sets a context for understanding how social workers in CJSW engage with individuals and work with them to try to make changes to their lives in order that they may have a more positive, law-abiding life in the future. The case study should be read before proceeding to the following sections of the chapter.

Case Study

Joanne is a 22-year-old female who appeared at court for several offences of shoplifting and was sentenced to a Community Payback Order (Community Order in England and Wales) with a 12-month Supervision Requirement. She is currently supervised by the CJSW Service (Probation Service in England and Wales). Joanne was previously in the care of the local authority and lived in several residential establishments for children and young people up to the age of 17, when she moved to live in her own flat.

A CJSW Report/Pre-Sentence Report was prepared for Joanne's court appearance and the assessment undertaken at that stage indicated that Joanne:

- committed the current and past offences to obtain alcohol or money to purchase alcohol
- at the time of the offence used substantial amounts of alcohol and had in the past used cannabis, **amphetamines** and heroin
- used alcohol at the present time to help her block out memories of the physical abuse she had suffered as a young child
- had no educational qualifications and had never been in employment
- had, in the past, self-harmed by cutting her wrists and there was evidence of superficial cuts to her arms during interview
- lived alone in a bed-sit and was socially isolated
- had previously appeared at court for other offences of shoplifting and had been convicted of an offence of violence – a fight with another female.

Research over a long period has shown that working with offenders on a multi-modal basis is the most successful approach (Roberts, 2010 in Brayford et al., 2010). A multi-modal approach identifies the different strengths and needs of the individual and uses a variety of different techniques to address these needs. As McGuire and Priestly (in McGuire, 1995: 91) note, 'it is mostly cognitive-behavioural, skill-orientated and multi-modal programmes that yield the best effects'. In Joanne's case there are potentially several different ways of working with her to address those issues in her life that may have contributed to her offending and subsequently appearing before the court. Some of these may be successful and some may not. Such techniques are discussed below.

MOTIVATIONAL INTERVIEWING

During interview for the CJSW Report/Pre-Sentence Report and in subsequent contacts with Joanne, it was noted that she had very low self-esteem and that she could not identify any other way of dealing with her memories of the abuse she suffered as a child other than to 'blot it out' with alcohol. It was clear that on the one hand Joanne desperately wanted to change, but on the other hand the alcohol gave her a buzz and relief from the negative feelings, albeit on a short-term basis. She also had associates whose company she enjoyed whilst consuming alcohol.

In many ways Joanne was ambivalent about trying to change her life. Ambivalence is a characteristic of many offenders (Canton, 2011), and Joanne recognised that she did not want to continue offending to fund her alcohol misuse, but she did not feel that change was achievable. She also felt that, for her, the costs of change were too high as she would have to potentially face the emotional pain of recalling (and thereby dealing with) her past abuse which appeared to be the main contributory factor for her consumption on a regular basis of large quantities of alcohol.

As a worker using motivational interviewing techniques (see Chapter 23 of this book) you would encourage Joanne to share her thoughts and feelings about her situation. Joanne would be encouraged to explore the positive and negative aspects of her behaviour, and, as her worker, you would assist her to make decisions about how she could make constructive changes to her lifestyle. Part of this work might include exploring the options available to her to help her deal both with her excessive alcohol consumption and the underlying causes including her past abuse. Whilst working with Joanne during this process, you would be using the Cycle of Change, recognising that Joanne will 'typically go through a number of stages when attempting to change established patterns of behaviour' (Canton, 2011: 80). It may be helpful to discuss with Joanne the Cycle of Change, describing the stages in detail, so that she recognises herself the stages as she proceeds through them. Working in such a way can reassure Joanne that a lapse or relapse is a normal part of the process of change; that change is not easy and that exploration of any lapses or relapses can assist her in creating positive alternative strategies to deal with similar situations should they arise again.

REFERRAL TO SPECIFIC AGENCIES

Once an individual has made the decision that they need to change their behaviour, they may require the services of other agencies with more specific expertise in the area that requires addressing. In Joanne's case consideration would be given to referring her to a specialist agency dealing with substance use problems. This agency may also be able to provide counselling for the abuse that Joanne has suffered in the past which has led to her misuse of alcohol; should this not be possible, then referral to another agency providing this service would be made at an appropriate time. If referring an individual to another agency in these circumstances, it can be helpful to go with the individual to the first appointment and potentially other appointments to offer support in approaching the new agency worker.

OFFENCE-FOCUSED WORK

As noted earlier, individuals are usually supervised by CJSW/Probation Services following an appearance in Court and where they are subject to a community sentence or a period of supervision following a custodial sentence. Such individuals are in this position because they have committed an offence or several offences, therefore there is an expectation that some offence-focused work will be undertaken with the offender in order to assist the individual into an offence-free lifestyle in the future. Offence-focused work, as Cree and Myers (2008: 164) note, is 'exactly what it suggests: it starts with the offence (the causes of offending behaviour and the risks of future offending) and it sets out to determine what needs to be put in place to contain and reduce offending behaviour in the future'.

More recently workers in CJSW Services use the term 'desistance', which is defined as 'ceasing offending and then refraining from further offending over an extended period' (McNeill and Whyte, 2007: 50). With Joanne, the aim of any work undertaken would be to put strategies into place to assist her to change her past behaviour for the positive and to maintain these changes so that she desists from offending in the future.

Offence-focused work is usually undertaken with offenders on a one-to-one basis or alternatively via a groupwork programme. Workers might use a variety of exercises to explore, for example, the detail of the offence(s) committed, the gains and losses of continued offending, victim awareness issues, faulty thinking and behaviour patterns, dysfunctional relationship patterns, difficulties in expression and communication, lack of appropriate supports etc. The aim of the work would be to develop alternative, more constructive ways of thinking and behaving, to encourage individuals to take more control over their lives, to develop problem-solving skills, to communicate effectively, to manage anger and other emotions appropriately, and to build a 'tool box' of strategies to deal with different situations that may be faced in the future. Many of these exercises are based upon cognitive behavioural principles.

In Joanne's case, work would be undertaken to assist her to explore the offences for which she received the Community Payback Order (Community Order in England and Wales) in order to assist her to develop alternative ways of thinking and behaving so she does not commit further offences. Although Joanne might see shoplifting as a 'victimless' crime, work would be undertaken to help her recognise that there are consequences – both for her and others – of her offending. Although Joanne is not currently under the supervision of CJSW Service/Probation Service for past offences, it would be pertinent to explore past offending. Joanne has a previous violent offence following a fight with another female. It would be important to discuss this offence with Joanne in some detail as it may be related to her use of alcohol or her inability to form positive relationships, and these would be areas that could be explored. It should be noted that this offence would need to be taken into account in any risk assessments undertaken as, depending on the circumstances, Joanne may be assessed as presenting a risk of serious harm to others, and strategies would need to be put in place to manage the risk she presents.

As stated previously, this work with Joanne could be undertaken individually but many CJSW Services/Probation Services now run groupwork programmes specifically for women.

TASK-CENTRED WORK

During the supervision sessions undertaken with Joanne she may have identified that, although she wants to find employment, she sees this as impossible due to her lack of qualifications. Again, use of motivational interviewing techniques will assist Joanne to identify potential options available to her to help her achieve her goal of finding employment.

Once these potential options have been identified, discussed and an action plan is agreed then the worker's role is to encourage and support Joanne in the tasks that have been identified. This type of work is known as task-centred work (McColgan, 2009). Further details about this type of approach can be found in Chapter 19 of this book.

Returning to Joanne and her search for employment, tasks within the action plan could include researching the potential careers she would be interested in pursuing, exploring the necessary qualifications (if needed), identifying possible educational or training courses to obtain these qualifications, developing a CV, discussing interview techniques etc. Throughout this process, the worker would continually review with Joanne the progress made, adapting the plan as required in the light of new information and positively reinforcing the progress made. Use of task-centred work in such a way will reinforce to Joanne that she has the ability to find solutions to her difficulties herself, hopefully increasing her confidence in her problem-solving abilities alongside improving her self-esteem.

Case Study Update

During the time Joanne is working with the CJSW/Probation Service, she meets a new partner. Whilst this is a very positive relationship initially, Joanne can be very possessive and demanding within relationships and this ultimately leads to the break-up of this relationship. At this point Joanne rings you to tell you that she has cut her wrists and is bleeding heavily. She is alone in her bed-sit.

After dealing with the urgency of this situation – getting assistance from colleagues, calling emergency medical services etc. – you escort Joanne to hospital. Joanne is admitted to hospital for several days as she requires an operation due to damaged nerves in her wrists.

CRISIS INTERVENTION

During this time you visit Joanne, and using a crisis interventionist approach (see Chapter 17), you begin the process of helping Joanne to decide a way forward. During this time you would be gathering information about the precipitating events; dealing with

Joanne's feelings and offering reassurance; assessing the risk of further episodes of self-harm; describing the use of crisis intervention strategies; setting realistic and achievable goals and discussing working in partnership (both with Joanne and other agencies) to achieve these goals. In these circumstances there would be a need for the CJSW/Probation Service worker to liaise closely with medical staff and others to achieve Joanne's stated goals, which could be as simple in the first instance as returning to her home with additional practical support provided.

PRO-SOCIAL PRACTICE/SUPERVISORY RELATIONSHIP

Cherry (2005, cited in Lindsay, 2009: 67) suggests that pro-social modelling as developed by Trotter (2007) provides an approach 'in which the worker acts as a good motivating role model in order to bring out the best in people'. Cherry (2005) further develops this concept into the wider approach, which is termed 'pro-social practice' (as cited in Lindsay, 2009: 68). Pro-social practice is commonly used with individuals supervised by CJSW/Probation Services as evidence shows that it is an 'effective method of working with involuntary clients' (Trotter, 2007: 88).

Several authors have noted the importance of the supervisory relationship, the relationship between the worker and the individual (McNeill and Whyte, 2007; Trotter, 2007). McNeill et al. (2005: 3) note the 'importance of individual workers exercising personal discretion in tailoring their interventions' and 'using interpersonal or relational skills'. Therefore, in developing constructive relationships with individuals who wish to desist from future offending, there is a need to balance a supportive approach whilst at the same time holding the individual to account for their future behaviour. As Gorman et al. (2006: 26) note: 'though [the relationship] is tough on the irresponsibility it does not need to be tough on the person'.

Critical Thinking

Part Three of the book contains a wide number of intervention models, including relationship-based approaches in Chapter 16. Consider this chapter in particular and think about how it is possible to combine such an approach with the formal authority required in working within the criminal justice arena. Is a relationship model capable of being evaluated in criminal justice practice (see Chapter 33) in the same way that other models can be?

An activity has been provided on the Companion Website (www.sagepub.co.uk/SocialWork) inviting you to explore your views in realtion to criminal justice matters. The activity is best undertaken with a group of people and should spark some lively debate.

CONCLUSION

This section has attempted to offer suggestions about the approaches that could be used when working with an individual (such as Joanne) who has been directed to work with social workers within the Criminal Justice Social Work Service or Probation Service by the court as a result of their offending. As suggested earlier, some of these interventions will work and some may not. What works will very much depend on whether or not Joanne wants to change her behaviour and if the worker has developed a positive working relationship with her.

Reflective Questions

1   In difference to other parts of the UK, criminal justice services in Scotland remain under the auspices of the social work service. What are your views about this arrangement? Do you think social work practitioners are the most appropriate professionals to work with offenders?
2   What do you think should be the primary purpose of the criminal justice system? You may wish to consider the following different perspectives that have been applied to sentencing policy over the years – retribution (punishment of offender); rehabilitation (offender as person in need); restoration (offender taking responsibility for actions); reparation (offender paying back to society).
3   What challenges do you perceive in working with involuntary service users? How might social work in a criminal justice setting be different and similar to social work in community care or child care?

RECOMMENDED READING

Croall, H., Mooney, G. and Munro, M. (2010) *Criminal Justice in Scotland.* Abingdon: Willan Publishing

Guthrie, T. (2011) *Social Work Law in Scotland*, 3rd edn. Haywards Heath: Bloomsbury.

McNeill, F. and Whyte, B. (2007) *Reducing Reoffending: Social Work and Community Justice in Scotland.* Cullompton: Willan Publishing.

McNeill, F., Raynor, P. and Trotter, C. (eds) (2010) *Offender Supervision: New Directions in Theory, Research and Practice.* Cullompton: Willan Publishing.

WORKING WITH ADULTS: LEARNING DISABILITY

30

Fiona Feilberg

This chapter will focus on key aspects of social work practice in the field of learning disability. For a broader understanding of aspects of direct practice, you should refer to chapters in the knowledge base, assessment and intervention sections, as well as the chapters on mental health and interventions with older people in this section of the book.

Key Themes

- Definitions of learning disability are affected by a lack of consistency in terminology.
- As well as health-related causes, aspects of society itself can be disabling.
- Key issues and contexts include social inclusion.
- Working with people with a learning disability involves working with challenging behaviour.
- Working with people with learning disabilities requires a skilled application of intervention models.

INTRODUCTION

This chapter will identify what exactly is learning disability before investigating the current context within society and the social policy issues. It will then consider how social workers can most effectively work to support and help those with learning disabilities and their families. The chapter needs to be read in conjunction with many other chapters in this book relating to legislation, policy and procedures, theories of personality and behaviour, and theories relating to practice.

WHAT IS LEARNING DISABILITY?

There can be confusion about the differences between learning disability and learning difficulty, which is further worsened by the lack of consistency in the use of the terms, because they are frequently used interchangeably. However, learning difficulty is more usually used to refer to individuals who have specific difficulties to do with learning such as dyslexia rather than those who have an impairment in intelligence. Partly for that reason, an increasing number of international organisations and countries, including the United States, Canada and Australia, now use the term 'intellectual disability' rather than 'learning disability'.

It is clear from this term that one of the features used to identify someone with a learning disability is that there is some impairment in intellectual functioning.

The World Health Organization (2013b) defines intellectual disability as:

> a significantly reduced ability to understand new or complex information and to learn and apply new skills. This results in a reduced ability to cope independently (impaired social functioning), and begins before adulthood, with a lasting effect on development.

The above definition is a useful advance on older definitions that tended to focus on very simplistic measures of intelligence and mental age which in turn were discriminatory and judgemental. Mental age is still sometimes used by some services or in lay conversation. One problem of the notion of 'mental age' is that it excludes the life experiences of the person. The IQ test and level of intellectual functioning may give some information about someone's cognitive ability but is not sufficient on its own as an assessment or identification of learning disability. Relevant also is the individual's ability to undertake activities, make contacts with others and cope with daily events.

Exercise

You are working with Amy, a 50-year-old woman with a mental age of 3. How might this affect how you work with her? If she wants to cross the street on her own what would you consider in making your decision?

More recent definitions, such as the WHO one quoted above, can also include reference to social competence, how well people with learning disabilities can operate in everyday social situations. The notion of social competence also needs to be treated with caution as it is relative to situation and context. Any assessment needs to be seen in the light of the context within which the person is living and take account of age, gender, religion and any additional impairments that the person may have. How far someone's disability affects their social and adaptive functioning is not just a personal or individual issue but also depends on how support and services are provided to them. Particularly where people have been in large institutions for many years, they may not have had the opportunity to develop social competence.

However, it is clear that individuals with learning disabilities are challenged, to a greater or lesser degree, by the daily demands of their social environment and may need support in order to manage these demands. Individuals may have difficulties understanding, learning and remembering new things, and in generalising any learning to new situations. These difficulties with learning may mean that the person may struggle with a number of social tasks, for example communication, self-care, and awareness of health and safety.

The common layperson's confusion between mental ill-health and learning disability can be compounded by some legislation where learning disability is classified as a 'mental disorder', including the Adults With Incapacity (Scotland) Act 2000, and the Mental Health Act 2007.

CAUSES OF LEARNING DISABILITY

Within Britain approximately 2–3% of the population are identified as having a learning disability (Emerson and Hatton, 2008; Scottish Government, 2011b). It may be surprising to you, but, for around half of these individuals who have been identified as having a learning disability, no cause has been identified. Most people think that the main cause of learning disability is genetic. However, though there are genetic factors affecting a significant number of people with learning disability it is important to be aware of environmental and social factors that can lead to developmental delays and cognitive impairment.

There are, for example, higher rates of people with learning disabilities in lower social classes and in areas of social deprivation. Poor diet, poor health care, malnutrition, lack of stimulation and neglect can all contribute to the development of a learning disability. In addition, recent studies of attachment and brain development indicate that early relationships with the caregiver affect the development of the brain in significant ways affecting cognitive, emotional and social development (Gerhardt, 2004; Schore, 2000). Other causes of learning disability include:

Genetic causes: of which the two most common are Fragile X syndrome and Down syndrome. It is important to know that these are not themselves learning disabilities, but that people who have either syndrome are also likely to have a learning disability. The genetic causes of learning disability are higher in people with profound learning disabilities where chromosomal abnormalities are identifiable in 40% of cases. Health and other associated problems are also more prevalent in those with more profound learning disabilities.

Events pre-birth: which include infections caught by the mother, excessive consumption of drugs or alcohol, high blood pressure, chromosomal conditions.

Events during birth: which include restriction of the oxygen supply to the baby, significant pre-matureness, prolonged labour.

Events after birth: which include childhood infections such as encephalitis or meningitis, accidents involving head injury, exposure to toxic substances. (Mencap, 2013)

ASSOCIATED HEALTH PROBLEMS

For staff working with people with a learning disability, other professionals and their parents and carers, there is sometimes an acceptance that all the individual's reactions and behaviour are because of their learning disability. This 'diagnostic overshadowing' (Mason and Scoir, 2004) can lead to minimising of or missing underlying health issues that require treatment and management.

People with a learning disability may have additional physical health problems, for example, up to 30% have epilepsy and 40% have hearing and/or visual problems. People with a learning disability are also more likely to suffer from common mental health problems such as depression and anxiety, and more rarely, schizophrenia (Emerson et al., 2011).

This makes assessment of needs particularly complex, involving assessing the contribution of the learning disability, the health problems and the medical treatment for them and the sensory impairments to the individual's behaviour, mood and relationship abilities.

To find out more about the outcomes of implementing annual health checks for people with learning disabilities see the research by Cassidy et al. (2002) available on the Companion Website (www.Sagepub.co.uk/SocialWork).

THE CONTEXT

The perspective that people with learning disabilities, including those with complex and multiple disabilities, have the same rights to inclusion in society has gained in force over the period since the review of service entitled *The Same as You?* was published in Scotland (Scottish Executive, 2000b), and *Valuing People* (Department of Health, 2001) launched in England in 2001. The publication of these policy documents was a turning point in the translation into reality of aspirations for change that have a long history. It reflected the change in perspective from a medical model of care based on treatment models towards a social model of care focused on social inclusion, choice, independence and rights.

The Same as You?, although applying to Scotland, contains principles that are important throughout Britain. It stated that people with learning disabilities should:

- Be included, better understood and supported by the communities in which they live
- Have information about their needs and the services available, so that they can take part, more fully, in decisions about them
- Be at the centre of decision-making and have more control over their care
- Have the same opportunities as others to get a job, develop as individuals, spend time with family and friends, enjoy life and get the extra support they need to do this
- Be able to use local services wherever possible and special services if they need them. (Scottish Executive, 2000b)

The vision set out in *Valuing People* echoes these sentiments and is founded on the twin principles of self-determination and social inclusion. It states that all people with a learning disability are people first, with the right to lead their lives like any others, with the right to the same opportunities and responsibilities, and the right to be treated with the same dignity and respect. They and their families and carers are entitled to the same aspirations and life chances as other citizens (Department of Health, 2001).

However desirable the move from institutional settings and routinised care provision might be, placing people in 'ordinary' settings does not in itself guarantee a good quality of life. The challenge for workers is how to ensure the aspirations of the 'Same As You?' review inform all the work that is undertaken with people with a learning disability. For those with profound and complex needs, creative and innovative approaches are required to transform the aspirations of inclusion and involvement into reality.

KEY ISSUES IN WORKING IN THE PRESENT CONTEXT

Working with people with profound and complex disabilities is a difficult but extremely rewarding area of working. One of the demands of the work is to find a way of understanding and working with behaviour that can be challenging. Only then can we work towards ensuring individuals have the same life opportunities as everyone else, including home life, education, employment and leisure.

In simplistic terms challenging behaviour is just that: behaviour that challenges us in some way. However, for different people in different contexts the exact behaviours that are seen as challenging can vary. For instance, if I was shouting at you in the street and throwing leaves at people passing, this could be perceived as challenging unless you understood that it was a piece of street theatre.

More generally, the term 'challenging behaviour' in working with people with a learning disability would refer to any behaviour that may put the individual or others at risk and can include aggressive responses, self injury, or disruptive and destructive behaviours.

Emerson (1995) argues that we also have to consider the context within which the behaviour occurs. So the norms and expectations concerning appropriate social behaviour in that setting need to be considered along with the capacity of the setting to manage the disruption caused by the person's behaviour. For example, within a multisensory room, someone throwing things around may allow them to let off steam in a safe environment, but in the local shop this would not be acceptable.

In addition to the context, there is also the contribution of others' understanding of the behaviour. Where the person involved can explain their behaviour or where others around them can understand the reasons for the behaviour, it is less likely to be labelled as challenging behaviour. When working with people with learning disabilities, we begin to understand that a service user who pushes a table over and runs out of the room may be panicked because there were too many people around, or perhaps a staff member got too close to the service user for the service user to cope. As we recognise understandable reasons, the behaviour then becomes seen as less threatening and unpredictable.

Recently there has been a shift from 'pathological' approaches (Goldiamond, 1974) to working with challenging behaviour, which have aimed to eliminate behaviour seen as challenging regardless of how it was established, developed, or maintained. As the problem has been seen as the person's behaviour, the appropriate response has been seen as either treatment or control, involving the use of behaviour modification (see Chapter 6) and/or medication.

Increasingly an alternative 'constructivist' approach has been emerging. Constructivist approaches see the origins of behaviour as complex and the behaviour as having a meaning and a function. Therefore removing it without understanding its function for the person is seen as risky, as alternative more difficult behaviour may emerge to take its place. Behaviour is seen as part of the person's coping mechanism and a method of communication, telling us something we need to understand.

Case Example

When people get too close to Jane she spits at them. A pathological approach would ask 'How do we stop Jane spitting?' because it is a problem of her anti-social behaviour. A behavioural model involving a system of planned ignoring, or time out, might be tried, but while this might eliminate the spitting it could lead to more distanced relationships with Jane. Alternatively, a constructivist approach would consider and assess why she spits, and might recognise the effectiveness of her behaviour in telling us not to get too close to her. It is then possible to think of a functional equivalent; a behaviour that can express the same thing to us without her having to spit. So perhaps, still using learning theory, if we can help her recognise that she can also wave a hand at people when they are getting close, we and she can learn that this means 'back off' and do so. In working with Jane, staff can still think of ways to get closer to her, in a more relationship-based approach (see Chapter 16) and help her learn to relax when people are around by doing pleasurable shared activities with her. The fact that she now has more control of having people near her means that she is more likely to be able to let this happen.

There are some key reasons why people develop challenging behaviour:

- The person may be finding a way to control the environment.
- Some challenging behaviour develops as the only strategy individuals have found to get their needs for attention and attachment met.
- The person may be bored and lack stimulation and their challenging behaviour may be a form of self-stimulation.
- The person may use challenging behaviour as a way of regulating emotions that they cannot otherwise express.
- The behaviour may be due to ill-health, the effects of medication or due to damage to particular areas of the brain which have caused the developmental delay.

Adopting a constructivist approach helps workers to recognise where structures of services and provision of activities are causing and maintaining difficulties. If the setting is too busy (or too quiet), when people cannot understand what is going on because it has not been explained to them in a way they can understand, when strange and unfamiliar people are around or the person has little control of what they can or cannot do, then any behaviour exhibited may be being created and maintained by the service itself. Understanding and assessing individuals' need for space, control over what is happening to them and ways of understanding what will happen next, are crucial to creating services that meet these needs.

Campbell has written extensively about the issues surrounding staff training to manage challenging behaviours. See two of his journal articles (2007 and 2010) on the Companion Website (www.sagepub.co.uk/SocialWork)

MODELS OF WORKING: INTENSIVE INTERACTION AND COMMUNICATION BUILDING

Case Study

Safiya is 25 years old. She has profound learning disabilities, visual impairment and hearing impairment and cannot walk or move her wheelchair herself. She is doubly incontinent. She has no verbal communication. She makes some sounds and often hums. Sometimes she rocks vigorously, screams and bites her thumb.
   How might you start to work with Safiya?

You have probably found it quite challenging to think about how to work with Safiya. In order to understand her needs and how she feels and responds you need to be able to make a relationship with her and this will take time. In looking at the models of working in this section keep Safiya in mind and think about how the different approaches will allow you to develop ways of working with her.

Up to 90% of people with a learning disability have communication problems. About 60% of people with a learning disability have some skills in symbolic communication, such as speech, signs or picture symbols. About 80% of people with a profound learning disability do not acquire speech (Thurman et al., 2003). Many challenging behaviours can indicate that an individual has a limited behavioural repertoire and/or poor communication skills. Developing new and more adaptive skills, and creating more effective communication strategies, is often the most successful way of reducing difficult or disruptive behaviours.

Intensive interaction (Hewett and Nind, 1998) is one of a range of approaches based on developing communication. This approach builds communication by responding to and developing interactions in ways that model the development of communication between an infant and its caregiver. In adopting this approach, the worker has to become attuned to the individual using a combination of behaviours such as imitation, turn-taking, physical and eye-to-eye contact to develop this. This replicates parent–child play and learning.

Attention is focused on **proto-language** so that sounds that may initially be random can be given meaning. When a baby first says 'dadada', this may be a random sound, but because it is responded to positively and it appears as though the baby means to refer to daddy, it eventually does take on this meaning. Just as the baby's preverbal communication is given meaning through interactions so Safiya's sounds and movements can be given meaning. In order to do this, all the different sounds and movements Safiya makes need to be listed and used to create a communication profile. A certain move of the hand can be given the meaning 'come here' and a particular low grunt, 'go away'. If this movement and that sound are always responded to consistently, then over time Safiya may learn their meaning. This would be a huge development for her, allowing her some control in her life.

This development needs to be supported by an appropriately structured environment with clear routines and patterns and rhythms, so that individuals with profound learning disabilities can begin to have a sense of what is going on. If there are consistent patterns to the day, the night and the week, Safiya will be more able to internalise a structure. It is in this context that she can discover that she can alter others' behaviour by making certain movements or sounds.

Objects of reference (van Dijk, 1967) could help Safiya to know what is going on and to make choices about what will happen next. These are objects used to represent people, activities and events and should allow the person to whom it is offered to obtain information from several senses: touch, vision, smell, taste and sound. For example, one member of staff may have a set of keys as her object of reference which she holds by Safiya's ears and then eyes while jangling them, and then puts them in Safiya's hand.

Exercise

What might you use as an object of reference to indicate to Safiya she is going to have a bath, a cup of tea, go swimming or go to the multisensory room?

MODELS OF WORKING: GENTLE TEACHING

Gentle teaching is defined as a non-aversive method of reducing challenging behaviour that aims to teach bonding and interdependence through gentleness, respect and solidarity (McGee et al., 1987). Emphasis is placed on the importance of unconditional valuing in the caregiving and therapeutic process. This approach links closely to the value base and relational nature of social work.

The aim of the approach is to develop a bonded relationship between the worker and the service user. Again, it is close to a model of early development as it is argued that the relationship is what allows us to develop an understanding of one another. So for Safiya it would be argued that we can only understand how she feels and why she acts as she does through our relationship with her.

Central to the method is the worker's 'posture', which should be based on 'solidarity'. McGee et al. argue that some workers can be overprotective and smothering, which encourages dependency, and some, on the other hand, can be authoritarian and controlling, which encourages distancing/disengagement. Solidarity, by contrast, encourages interdependence. It involves protecting without smothering and building a shared relationship within which messages of tolerance, warmth, safety, security and support are given. Like intensive interaction, there is a belief that all behaviour is a form of communication and that workers have a responsibility for communicating clearly themselves and ensuring service users' communications are understood and responded to.

Where challenging behaviour occurs in gentle teaching the aim is to ignore it where possible while still engaging with the person. If this occurs while the person is engaged in an activity, try to continue the activity as soon as possible but make it easier so that the person gets a positive result. Continue the flow of the day as soon as possible. React with minimum intrusion and do not tell the person what not to do, but concentrate on clearly communicating what *to do*.

Much of the approach is about working positively with the service users by engaging in shared rewarding interactions where the valuing of them and others will teach the service user to accept, seek and value others. See the links on the Companion Website (www.sagepub.co.uk/SocialWork) to web-based material about gentle teaching.

MODELS OF WORKING: PERSON-CENTRED PLANNING

Person-centred planning is a collection of tools and approaches based upon a set of shared values that can be used to plan *with* a person not *for* them. It was developed as an approach to working with people with learning disabilities in reaction to the way in which individuals were fitted to services rather than have services matched to their individual needs. It is an important approach to be aware of as its influence has spread well beyond work with people with learning disabilities, as it has been adopted as government policy in the United Kingdom (Department of Health, 2001). The personalisation agenda is a form of person-centred working. For more detailed discussion of this approach, you should read Chapter 21.

The person-centred planning approach is based on an inclusive agenda where individuals with learning disabilities have the right to share ordinary places, make choices, develop abilities, have valued social roles, grow in relationships and be treated with respect. Services should be judged by how far they meet these five accomplishments (O'Brien and O'Brien, 1998). Individuals with learning disabilities have dreams, aspirations and wishes like anyone else and the person-centred planning process helps to identify and work out how to meet these.

Critical Thinking

Does the fact that social work creates specialist teams to work with people with learning disabilities actually help people become more integrated or does it further marginalise them?

CONCLUSION

Though intensive interaction, gentle teaching and person-centred planning have been introduced as separate ways of working in practice, the three models are often used together. In order to put a person-centred plan together and implement it in practice requires an understanding of an individual's communications, and developing communication requires the growth of a valuing relationship with the individual. The integration of these key approaches reflects social work values in practice and underpins effective working with people with learning disabilities.

Reflective Questions

1   As with other areas that involve social work intervention, how an issue is defined exerts a relationship with practice. In this case how would you define learning disability? What problems and challenges exist in attempting a definition?
2   Sometimes people with learning disabilities can be subject to social stigma, where they are exposed to discrimination and oppression. Thinking back to the PCS model we encountered in the sociology chapter (Chapter 4), can you map learning disability to the elements of that model? In particular, what are the structural roots and causes of discrimination against people with learning disabilities?
3   What are the main approaches in working with people with learning disabilities? What challenges and opportunities may exist in building an effective relationship with a service user?

The issue of advocacy was discussed in Chapter 15 and is something that frequently forms part of practice when working with people with learning disabilities. Visit the Companion Website (www.sagepub.co.uk/SocialWork) where you will find an activity to develop your understanding of advocacy and the role it plays.

RECOMMENDED READING

Emerson, E., Baines, S., Allerton, L. and Welch, V. (2011) *Health Inequalities and People with Learning Disabilities in the UK*. Learning Disabilities Observatory. London: Department of Health. Available from: www.improvinghealthandlives. org.uk/securefiles/130919_0101//IHaL%202011-09%20HealthInequality2011. pdf.

Firth, G., Berry, R. and Irvine, C. (2010) *Understanding Intensive Interaction: Contexts and Concepts for Professionals*. London: Jessica Kingsley Publishers.

Talbot, P., Astbury, G. and Mason, T. (2010) *Key Concepts in Learning Disabilities*. London: Sage.

WORKING WITH 31 ADULTS: DISABILITY AND SENSORY IMPAIRMENT

Sheila Slesser

This chapter will focus on key aspects of social work practice in the field of disability and sensory impairment. For a broader understanding of aspects of direct practice, you should refer to chapters in the knowledge base, assessment and intervention sections, as well as the chapters on learning disability, mental health and interventions with older people in this section of the book

---

Key Themes

- Conceptualising disability is an important process in developing understanding.
- Disabled people face barriers arising from the attitudes of other people and the structural environment.
- The theme of transitions has implications for practice.
- There are issues of identity and disability.
- Social workers should be aware of personalisation within ways of working with disabled people.

INTRODUCTION

Despite forming a significant part of the population (see Table 31.1), people with disabilities are a minority group who are subject to discrimination and prejudice. In this chapter we explore issues facing people who experience physical disability and those who have sensory

Table 31.1   Disability facts and figures for the United Kingdom

People registered as disabled	11.2 million
People who experience mobility issues	6.4 million
Disabled people's families living in relative poverty	19%
Disabled people experiencing workplace discrimination	19%

Source: ODI (2012)

impairments, that is, difficulties with their hearing and/or vision. Links are made to the medical model and social model as a means of helping to understand the concept of disability in contemporary society. The chapter concludes with a discussion on transition theory and policy of personalisation.

CONCEPTUALISING MODELS OF DISABILITY

It is important to consider how we define and conceptualise disability, as how a particular issue is defined carries many implications for how social workers develop practice with service users. Legislation provides a useful starting point in doing so. The Equality Act 2010, section 6, offers a definition of a person with a disability which refers to 'physical or mental impairment', adding that the said 'impairment has a substantial and long-term adverse effect on their ability to carry out normal day-to-day activities'. As a working definition, the Equality Act's definition is informative as it offers a basic understanding of disability but requires further elaboration and here it is useful to discuss more sophisticated models of disability that tease out the subtleties and nuances of disability, especially the relationship between impairments and wider society. Here we turn to the social model of disability.

The social model of disability emphasises that disability is not the outcome of physical or mental differences or impairments within the individual, but rather the causes of disability are to be found in wider society. It is society that is, therefore, disabling, as opposed to the impairments of the individual. The social causes of disability can be found in a number of cultural practices, social attitudes and approaches to the built environment, which seem to offer a stereotype of disabled people that depicts them as being of lesser value than someone who is not disabled or that places the rights of people with disabilities in a secondary position to those of people who are not disabled. There are many examples to illustrate the above. In fairy tales, in particular, the tales associated with the Brothers Grimm, which provide the basis for many of the fairy tales that are part of European traditions, the evil character is often signified by means of their physical difference. Contemporary culture also links evil with physical difference, where the presence of an impairment can denote a character's status as a villain. While no deliberate intention may exist to associate disabled people with negative images, it is the cultural associations that are important. Despite legislation there are many examples in the built environment where the design of buildings creates disabling barriers for people with disabilities. Even, for example, providing separate accessible entrances into a space can act as a barrier as they still highlight difference as opposed to similarity and inclusion.

Exercise

Take a walk to your nearest post office. As you go, consider how straightforward your journey would be if you had restricted or no use of your legs, or could not see. Is your post office within walking distance? Do you need to use public transport? How easy is that? Is there any? How easy is access to the post office? Would a disabled person need to draw attention to him- or herself in order to gain access?

The relationship between impairment and how society creates disability is captured in this definition provided by the Union of the Physically Impaired Against Segregation (UPIAS) (1976: 3–4):

Impairment: Lacking part or all of a limb, or having a defective limb, organ or mechanism of the body.

Disability: The disadvantage or restriction of activity caused by a contemporary social organization which takes no or little account of people who have physical impairments and thus excludes them from participation in the mainstream of social activities.

What the social model of health essentially drives at is that disability is not simply about physical difference or impairment but is located within a nexus of power relationships where people who possess some form of impairment are denied access to a range of material, financial and social resources because of deeply embedded negative societal attitudes. Positive and meaningful change in the lives of disabled people are therefore made by transforming society and negative social attitudes.

The social model is often conceptually contrasted with the medical model, which offers a different perspective on disability that emphasises the purely physical dimensions of disability and is a perspective on disability that is often associated with the medical profession. Disability here is firmly located within the disabled person, and the model suggests that it is only specialist help that can provide any improvement in the quality of life for people with disabilities.

The social model is the one that is most relevant to social work practice, as it matches many of the ambitions of the ethical basis of social work, with its focus on rights and challenging discrimination.

Sensory impairment as a specific term requires further clarification. This term relates to three main groups, those people who are **deaf/Deaf** or hearing impaired, those who have a visual impairment, and finally those with dual sensory impairment, experiencing deafblindness (Evans and Whittaker, 2010). The term *hearing impairment* has added classifications, for example, of being mild, moderate, severe or profound hearing impairment, each having unique consequences for the individual. Most people who experience a change in their hearing ability will classify themselves as disabled, experiencing loss, and therefore as social workers we need to link to the theories underpinning loss and change to begin to understand the implications. Those people who have been born profoundly Deaf, on the other hand, do not see themselves as disabled but rather that they belong to a minority ethnic group with their own culture, social norms and language – British Sign Language (BSL) – using the term *Deaf* (with a capital D) rather than *deaf* to denote these distinct characteristics.

Visually impaired people are defined as sight impaired or severely sight impaired. The term blindness usually refers to total loss of vision but can often incorporate people who have light perception and can differentiate light from dark (Evans and Whittaker, 2010).

Deafblindness is a combination of sight and hearing loss and affects a person's ability to communicate, to access all kinds of information and to get around; the two impairments together increase the effects of each (Sense.org). Similarly, issues of loss and change need to be considered as the deafblind person may have managed well with one sensory impairment, then has had to come to terms with the loss or deterioration of the other.

Within and across all the three broad categories discussed in this chapter there will be a plethora of medical conditions and reasons as to why people have been born with the physical or sensory impairment or as to why they have gone on to acquire disability or sensory impairment. It would be impossible to begin to explore this in any depth but this might be a useful point to refer you to some of the supporting web links on the companion website.

You may have noticed that the definition offered by the Equality Act 2010 that we visited at the top of this chapter has located the consequences of disability in the social model but also portrays the message of disability being an individual issue. The language used in these written representations can be very persuasive and can influence attitudes.

Exercise

Take some time to think about the influence of words. In legislation, for example, does the Equality Act suggest that the disabled person is in any way inferior, or not as good as a non-disabled person? How do we express ourselves generally? Can you think of any colloquial expressions you use which might be hurtful to a disabled person?

There can be no doubt that technology innovation has had a significant impact on the lives of people with physical disabilities and sensory impairment. Assistive technology relates to equipment and technology that enables or promotes independent living and is as much about the philosophy of dignity and independence as it is about equipment and services (Cornwall Council, 2013). Information technologies, for example, have opened the doors to communication across physical and sensory barriers, and have also done much to provide access to information as well as provide meaningful social contact. Advancements in medical science also contribute to life opportunities and outcomes, genetic science going some way to provide hope for people who experience disability through illness.

LOSS

As noted previously, people who experience any loss, whether mild, moderate or severe, in their physical and/or sensory abilities will be affected by the subsequent change in their lives in a whole manner of ways, and the consequences of this will be individual and unique to the person. It is not possible to be prescriptive or definite in prognoses as to how any individual will manage their own experience of change, but there are social work theories which help us to understand the process of loss and how this can affect people. 'Understanding loss is essential to disability because it is a key aspect of social work' (Currer, 2007, cited in Evans and Whittaker, 2010: 53).

Loss is discussed in more detail in Chapter 7 where the stages of grieving as described by Murray Parkes are outlined. Similar stages are described by Kubler-Ross (1969) as a five-stage model of grief through which the individual progresses, and these are denial, anger, bargaining, depression and finally acceptance. When a person experiences a loss, for example following trauma, accident or diagnosis of illness, their needs will vary according to the type of loss and the significance of the impact it has or will have on their lives. They will require time to adjust to this new reality, and for the social worker it is important to acknowledge the loss and allow emotional space for the person to reach a point where they have some sense of acceptance.

> ## Case Study
>
> John, age 24, has been blind from birth. James, also age 24, has become blind as a result of an accident just over a year ago. From your knowledge of loss, what issues might there be for either man.

William Bridges (2009) has developed his model of transitions, and he is keen to stress that whilst change in itself is situational, transitions are psychological, and, at an emotional level, need to be recognised and expressed. Transition, he continues, 'is a three phase process that people go through as they internalise and come to terms with the details of the new situation that change brings about' (Bridges, 2009: 3).

Within this transition model there are three phases (see Figure 31.1). The first phase is *endings*, where the person experiences the initial feelings of loss and the change of identity. In essence the person has to begin by letting go, and this is a difficult phase where there will be a sense of grieving due to the emotional attachment the person has to self-image and other ideas about themselves. At this stage the social worker should be concentrating on the person, allowing time for purposeful expression of feelings. This core value within social work practice recognises the importance of giving our service users the opportunity to vent and discuss their feelings openly (Thompson, 2009b). The worker needs also to be aware of their own feelings, fostering a sense of self-awareness, recognising personal difficulties with any of the subject matter or issues this emotional work can trigger, and seeking supervision support to maintain the purposeful focus and relationship with the service user. This acknowledgement of endings

Figure 31.1 A transition model for change (adapted from William Bridges, 2009)

and the letting go will respect what went before in the person's life and go some way to validate the loss to facilitate progress to the next phase.

Case Study

James is talking about his feelings of powerlessness, unable to take part in long-cherished activities. As he talks he gets angrier and angrier. Seeking to convey your understanding of his feelings, you acknowledge how angry he feels. With this, he turns his head to you and tells you that you are a complete waste of space and that you might as well not be there.

   We know rationally that anger is associated with loss, but it can be difficult to think rationally when the anger is turned on us. We are social workers, after all, trying to help, and it can be personally challenging to be told you are not needed. You need to resist the impulse to respond by making rash promises or by becoming defensive. Perhaps briefly acknowledge that James is possibly correct at this time, but try to keep the communication going. Stay focused on James.

The *neutral zone* is what Bridges describes as the 'in between time when the old is gone but the new is not fully operational' (Bridges, 2009: 5). This phase is the stage where people who have experienced loss begin to accept that change has to happen but are not sure how to do this, what it will feel like, and have to take stock of this new identity and reality. Emotions may include feelings of anxiety or fear for the unknown, or the fear for what they imagine their future holds. For the social worker supporting the person, there are a number of areas to work on. For example, this is where you may revisit any information given out at diagnosis, assessing the service user's understanding and accessing further information as required. You may introduce short-term goals, tasks that can be achieved (see Chapter 19 for a more detailed explanation of this model), as this will help to foster hope and sense of optimism. You can be creative with ideas to motivate. It is important that any involvement and progression towards task should be done at the pace of the service user. Transitions should not be progressed at the worker's pace but rather be service user-led, and this will require the social worker to utilise ongoing assessment skills, regularly reviewing and monitoring the situation with the service user.

The final part in the process is the *new beginning*, and this is 'when people develop, and begin to, experience the new identity and discover the new sense of purpose that makes the change begin to work' (Bridges, 2009: 5). The service user at this point should be beginning to be more optimistic about their future, tinged perhaps with some misgivings about the new beginning. Building on the short-term goals and tasks that have been introduced, the worker needs to celebrate small successes with the person to continue to motivate. Communication with the service user needs to be clear, consistent and any plans made must include the person at the centre of the process. These transitional processes can be facilitated by the social worker based on an assessment of need, but any emotional movement needs to be driven by the service user so that they become empowered in the process.

On the Companion Website (www.sagepub.co.uk/SocialWork) you will find an article by Eva et al. (2009) who undertook research on how people with metastatic spinal cord compression adapted to their disabled status. Having read about Bridges' work this article should be of interest. In addition, an activity is provided which tasks you to examine change and transition in your own life and to share your insights with others.

PERSONALISATION

In December 2007 the government introduced Personalisation, a policy specifically aimed to transform 'peoples experience of local support and services' (Gardner, 2011: 1) (see also Chapter 21). This policy embraced person-centred approaches by placing the people who use these services at the very heart of the process. For people who have physical and sensory impairments, and as a result access social work support services such as personal care and mobility support, they were now encouraged to have a more direct role in the design and execution of their own support package and control of their individual budgets. The policy was launched in a concordat, *Putting People First: A Shared Vision and Commitment to the Transformation of Adult Social Care*, published by the Department of Health in 2007 (LGA et al., 2007). The 2010 local authority circular *A Vision for Adult Social Care* (Department of Health, 2010), confirmed the importance of universal access to all services, a commitment to service users having autonomy, choice and access to a service that meets their needs. To fully embrace this philosophy, social workers need to shift power over to service users whilst maintaining support with aspects of the procedure that may cause difficulties, such as realistic self-assessments, sourcing appropriate service to match this assessed need and then supporting, as appropriate, commissioning and then reviewing subsequent services.

To achieve these aims it is necessary for social workers to work in partnership with their service users. Thompson (2009b) argues that, within partnership processes, social workers need to accept that they do not have all the answers and that the service user is seen as the expert in their own lives. The power inherent in the social work role cannot be ignored as social workers are still agents of social control and have the power within the role to act as gatekeepers to services and resources. However, this apparent shift to service user influence and control is important and needs to be explicitly clear so that the people at the heart of the service are not marginalised and therefore disempowered. For the service user this might not be as simple as it seems. Linking back to our understanding of transitions, this may be a whole new experience for the service user. They perhaps have not been accustomed to thinking about what they could have, as historically they may have been passive recipients of a care package that has been based on a professional needs-based assessment. In reality this package of care may have been resource-led, in that a service has been provided based on what services were available rather than what the service user actually wanted or required. So the social worker needs to guide the service user through this change, providing access to information and support to facilitate this new experience of support.

The value base, which underpins this method of intervention, has a bearing on how much we as social workers invest in the personalisation agenda. In enabling people to be involved in decision-making processes about their own care, we, as social workers, help them become empowered. Adams (cited by Lister, 2012: 57) defines empowerment as the 'capacity of individuals and groups to take control of their circumstances, exercise power and achieve their own goals'. Empowerment is not about giving power and is not something that is bestowed upon service users by social workers, rather service users become empowered by the information and possibilities they have to be informed and make their own choices and decisions. The social worker needs to establish meaningful, effective and appropriate relationships with the service users, working in partnership to build their capacity (Lister, 2012). In doing this, social workers need to be aware of the notion of oppression and how people experience discrimination. By recognising this, the actions of social workers should counter these negative connotations and improve the overall sense of well-being for the service user.

People with sensory and physical impairments as a group have long campaigned for improvements to the service they receive and in general their take-up for direct payment intervention has been greater. Several national organisations such as British Council of Organisations of Disabled People (BCODP), British Deaf Association (BDA) (both organisations run by disabled and deaf people respectively) (Gardner, 2011), and the Royal National Institute for the Blind (RNIB), have championed the cause for the people they represent, to be seen as the experts in their own lives and therefore able to make decisions about their own care packages. So for people who have lived with their physical disability and/or sensory impairment since birth or for a considerable length of time, the personalisation agenda will complement their existing experience if they have used direct payments. However, these service user groups also include large numbers of people who, for a number of reasons, such as illness or trauma, or who acquire a physical or sensory impairment, may be adjusting to new life circumstances, and personalisation will be a new experience for them.

Critical Thinking

As a social worker and care manager you are working with a number of deaf/Deaf people. They have individual needs, but all are experiencing problems in relation to their environment, for example in doctors' and other waiting rooms, on public transport and in other

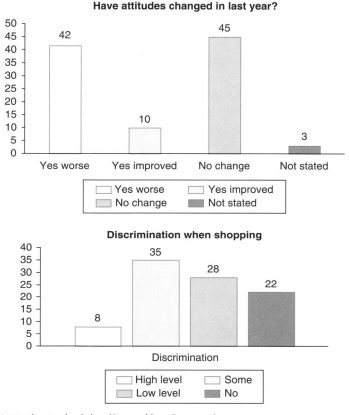

Figure 31.2 Attitudes to disability (Scope/ComRes, 2011)

daily activities. To what extent is care for the individual in itself insufficient? What might you do as a social worker to help the service users with the wider problems?

Having a sense of belonging to their community and having equal access to information, communication and services is a crucial element for people with physical and sensory impairments. The personalisation agenda is underpinned by this in that it advocates for the removal of attitudinal and environmental barriers that hamper integration and full inclusion.

A survey by Scope in 2011 (Scope/ComRes, 2011) found that of those disabled people questioned 42% said people's attitudes towards them were worse and 66% said that they had experienced aggression, hostility or name calling and almost half (46%) of the disabled people questioned said they experienced discrimination on either a daily or weekly basis (see Figure 31.2). Recent austerity measures introduced by the Coalition government involving changes to the welfare system have targeted welfare benefit payments to people with disabilities, inferring that benefits are being fraudulently claimed; as a result, people with sensory and physical disabilities are among those who feel that social attitudes towards them are deteriorating (Scope, 2012).

Vilchinsky et al. (2010) explored attitudes towards people using wheelchairs. You can read their findings on the Companion Website (www.sagepub.co.uk/SocialWork).

CONCLUSION

At the time of the Paralympic Games in London 2012, statements were made of a 'once in a lifetime' chance to improve the public's attitudes towards disability (Scope, 2012). Press and media coverage was highly positive about the games, and it seemed there might be a real opportunity to increase visibility of disabled people in everyday life. At time of writing, the true impact and lasting legacy of the Paralympics is unknown, but there is no evidence of significant change in attitudes. As social workers you will be practising in a social landscape that may be in transition and consequently there are opportunities for change. Social workers need to be aware of this and influence attitudes at personal, cultural and structural level so as to be 'able to formulate a means of working that is meaningful and useful to disabled people as citizens' (Oliver et al., 2012: 166).

Watch vodcast 31.1 on the Companion Website (www.sagepub.co.uk/SocialWork) to see chapter author Sheila Slessor summarise the main points conveyed in this chapter, and why possessing a knowledge of working with disabled people is important for social work practice.

Reflective Questions

1   The literature on disability and sensory impairment often refers to two different models of disability: the medical model and the social model. Begin by defining each and then try to identify which model is closest to the ethical basis of social work. Critical to the question here is the issue of power; try to focus on that aspect of disability in your reflection.
2   As the statistics quoted above indicate, people with disabilities are subject to discrimination and oppression. The PCS framework we discussed in the sociology chapter can assist in understanding the causes of oppression and discrimination, but consider what a social worker can actively do to challenge such oppression.
3   This chapter also draws attention to the government's personalisation agenda. Discuss how such a move relates to both the social model of disability and the ethical base of social work.

RECOMMENDED READING

Evans, M. and Whittaker, A. (2010) *Sensory Awareness and Social Work.* Exeter: Learning Matters.

Harris, J. and Roulstone, A. (2011) *Disability, Policy and Professional Practice.* London: Sage.

Oliver, M., Sapey, R. and Thomas, P. (2012) *Social Work with Disabled People*, 4th edn. Basingstoke: Palgrave Macmillan.

Swain, J., French, S., Barnes, C. and Thomas, C. (eds) (2013) *Disabling Barriers – Enabling Environments*, 3rd edn. London: Sage.

Refer to the Companion Website (www.sagepub.co.uk/SocialWork) for a range of useful links to web-based material.

32 SOCIAL WORK INTERVENTIONS WITH OLDER PEOPLE

Iain Fisk

Key Themes

- Ideas, representations and definitions of ageing change over time and place.
- Ageing for many is a positive experience; however, a minority of older people come into contact with social service departments and these service users present a range of needs for support.
- Many of the issues experienced by older people are not unique to them but are common with other age groups in the population.
- Work with older people is an interesting, varied and challenging area of practice.
- Work with older people requires significant knowledge across the whole life cycle as well as skilled assessment and intervention.

INTRODUCTION

This chapter looks at methods of intervention that may be considered when working with older people. To assist the reader it is essential to consider some of the terminology used, the background to social work involvement with older people and the particular dilemmas that arise out of undertaking assessments in this complex area. The latter part of this chapter looks in particular at some of these methods of intervention, and how these might be usefully applied when intervening in the lives of older people.

DISCUSSION OF AGEING, MENTAL HEALTH AND VULNERABILITY

Defining Old Age

First we must decide what we mean by 'older people'. Should this be based on age alone? A century ago, life expectancy was very much less than it is today. Increasingly, 'old' is defined as over 85, sometimes referred to as the 'fourth age', but people younger than that may be 'old' in the sense that they are approaching the end of their lives. An athlete may be 'old' at 30, retirement age is now creeping up, and judges may work on to their 70th birthday. So perhaps age does not help when considering the group known to social workers as 'older people'. Many statutory agencies use an age 'cut-off' of 65 and design and deliver services accordingly.

Regardless of how old age may be defined, it is important to consider what is meant by ageing to the individual concerned, given the person's gender, culture, ethnic background and socioeconomic position.

Ageing need not be a negative experience. The majority of people over 65 require neither intervention from social work nor extensive health care. Indeed in the *Reshaping Care for Older People* report it is noted that 90% of those over 65 receive no formal care from these sources (Scottish Government et al., 2011). For many in the UK this is a time to gain respite from work, enjoy family life, contribute to the process of bringing up grandchildren and, perhaps, at last have the opportunity to pursue interests and hobbies, neglected earlier in life due to demands of work and family responsibilities.

There are a wide range of other factors that also have a bearing. In some cultures and countries age is respected and revered; some would argue less so in the UK. It is certainly not a universal truth that certain ethnic groups ensure older people are 'looked after' by the younger generations. Even where there is a will to provide care, the changing dynamics of society (e.g. social mobility, employment patterns) undermine the capacity of families, of whatever culture, to provide support to ageing relatives. Additionally, it is important to remember that some physical and mental health conditions can create a huge demand on informal carers, making formal support a necessity, regardless of the wishes of the family to 'manage' care themselves. Poverty too can have a notable impact on health and the level of 'enjoyment' in old age (Dorling et al., 2009). An important feature of increased life expectancy is the greater proportion of very aged people.

Exercise

Consider the attitudes towards older people in your own family.

Vulnerability and mental health

For the purpose of this chapter the issues of vulnerability and mental health are divided into four separate areas. Interventions in relation to these four areas are considered later in this chapter, but initially it is important to consider some of the dynamics of these different areas of need.

- *Physical ability/frailty*. As the ageing process continues there is increasing incidence of physical health problems which lead to *frailty,* **infirmity** and often to *vulnerability*. It is acknowledged that these italicised words often have negative connotations; indeed in Scotland the original *Vulnerable* Adults Bill became the Adult Support and Protection (Scotland) Act 2007, replacing the label of vulnerable with the notion of *adults at risk of harm.*

  The consequence is a need for support, whether from health or social care services, without which people may not receive sufficient nutrition, may become socially isolated and may be at risk of falling or having some major health crisis. Services therefore aim to compensate in some way for these deficits and seek to provide direct assistance, reinforce coping strategies and promote involvement in the community. Interventions may range from very low key (e.g. lunch clubs) to provision of 24 hour care at the higher end of need.

- *Risk of harm*. Sometimes a referral identifies a specific risk of harm. As adult protection and safeguarding approaches have been developed across the UK, raising awareness of 'elder abuse', it has become increasingly clear that older people are frequent targets of physical, emotional, sexual and financial abuse. It has also become clear that, as in child protection, the perpetrators of this abuse are often family members. In a UK prevalence survey undertaken by O'Keefe et al. (2007) it was found that 51% of perpetrators were partners, 49% family members, 13% care workers and 5% close friends (the fact that some reported more than one perpetrator explains the percentage total). The report examined a range of characteristics of perpetrators, suggesting that abuse may be connected with a range of factors, including:

  - Carer stress
  - The violent nature of perpetrators
  - Seeking financial or material gain
  - Potential misuse of the older person's prescribed drugs.

To further develop your understanding of financial abuse of older people see the article on the Companion Website (www.sagepub.co.uk/Social/Work) by Wendt et al. (2013).

- *Mental disorder*. Many referrals to social work and health services relate to *mental disorder*. For the avoidance of doubt, when this term is used throughout this chapter the meaning refers not only to mental illness, such as depression, schizophrenia or anxiety-related illnesses, but also to learning disability, personality disorder, organic brain conditions such as dementia and to cognitive impairment, for example acquired brain injury or stroke. It is important to recognise that cognitive impairment and dementia are particularly common amongst older age groups. Indeed 1 in 5 of those over 80 are likely to have dementia, though estimates vary widely, particularly as many may go undiagnosed for many years (Department of Health, 2007). Responses to these needs can vary from low level social and emotional support to hospitalisation.

- *Developmental crises*. For many older people significant life changes may have a huge impact: from loss of career to loss of ability caused by amputation, arthritis etc.; bereavement; family breakdown; loss of a carer and end of life issues for those with terminal illnesses. Such circumstances are often the first time an older person comes to the attention of social work, and in these circumstances the social worker may be working with ambivalence or indeed active resistance from the potential service user.

THE WIDER CONTEXT OF WORK WITH OLDER PEOPLE

This section of the chapter is divided into three parts, reflecting broad groupings of issues that practitioners should be aware of when working with older people – individual, personal and social issues, accommodation and support issues, and financial issues. The aim of this section is to develop awareness of the wider context within which work with older people takes place and to recognise that whilst some experiences of older people are attributable to age other experiences are similar to other population cohorts.

PART 1: INDIVIDUAL, PERSONAL AND SOCIAL ISSUES

Physical Disability

An older person may be otherwise mentally competent and the intervention required is as for anyone with a physical disability or impairment, which could be anything from sight loss to mobility problems. The social work role may simply be to refer on and possibly advocate for that person to receive the same level of service that a younger person with similar disability or impairment might expect. This may be more challenging than expected, as some services are 'ring-fenced' for younger age groups. Indeed, the mobility component of Disability Living Allowance (soon to be reformed) can only be claimed for those under 65, despite the fact that most people develop mobility problems after this age.

Mental Disorder

Older people will experience the same range of mental disorder as the population as a whole. Although life expectancy of people with some learning disabilities is lower, this is changing and increasing numbers live on to old age. Social workers therefore need to be sensitive to difficulties around transition from adult to older people's services. Residential and nursing care provision is almost entirely orientated towards 'frail' or 'mentally incapacitated' older people, resulting in lack of meaningful activity for those who are more capable (AgeUK, 2011; Hubbard et al., 2003). As a result social workers will need to be very determined, when arranging care, to ensure that the placement truly meets the needs of the individual. Another major issue occurs where medical professionals and others may overlook mental illnesses such as depression or even anorexia in old age, putting this down to simple reluctance to participate or to eat, when in fact there may be an underlying treatable illness.

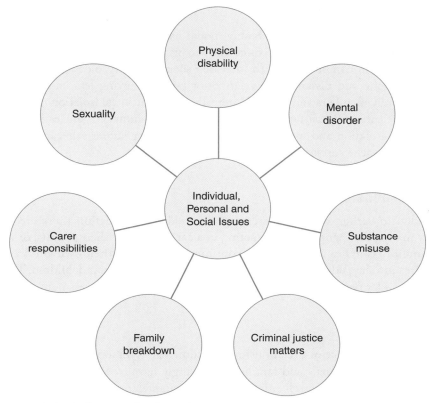

Figure 32.1   Individual, personal and social issues

Substance Misuse

Although the predominant 'problem' substance use for older people will still be alcohol and tobacco, the number of older people with drug dependency may increase given the increased use of illegal substances in the population as a whole. It should also be remembered that significant problems currently exist for older people dependent on prescription drugs, particularly **benzodiazepines** and pain killers.

Criminal Justice Matters

A significant proportion of the general population possesses a criminal record and naturally older people will also feature in these statistics. Whether the issue relates to current criminal activity – be it drugs, theft or fraud of some kind – significant issues exist for those who have previously committed serious criminal offences and require supervision and monitoring. Managing sex offenders who are also elderly and frail can be very challenging for services and the need for effective joint working between police, criminal justice and community care services is clear.

Family Breakdown

In Western society the traditional family model has been changing over the last few decades with family breakdown, divorce and reconstituted families becoming increasingly common. In combination with increased social mobility, older people may find themselves alone and distant from relatives or perhaps having less enduring ties to extended family members and step-children. The resultant social isolation may increase the need for care and assistance from statutory and voluntary agencies in later life. Withdrawal, isolation and increasing substance misuse or poorer self-care may result from a lack of social support.

Carer Responsibilities

As alluded to earlier, with an increasing 'very elderly' population there are consequently many older people who are acting in a caring role for their parents, or indeed as community care has developed, are continuing to support their own children with disabilities into late adulthood or providing 'kinship care' for grandchildren. Thus the idea of the older person as carer needs to be considered in any assessment.

Sexuality

The logical consequence of a relationship breakdown is, as for anyone else, seeking new relationships. Professionals and families increasingly have to come to terms with the fact that older people may well embark on new sexual relationships, or may indeed be discovering new aspects of their sexuality, for example seeking same-sex relationships.

Case Study

Your 76-year-old male service user wanted help in meeting others and you have arranged a place in a day centre. Some weeks later, the manager contacts to complain about his behaviour. He has become very close to another male, and they sit holding hands and occasionally stroking each other. They try to be alone at times, and, on these occasions, have frequently been observed kissing. The manager finds this upsetting and feels it is unsettling the other older people.

Who has the problem here and what might be the appropriate response based on the interventions you have read about in other chapters?

PART 2: ACCOMMODATION AND SUPPORT ISSUES

Accommodation

Many social work professionals and policy documents extol the virtue of people being enabled to live in their own homes for as long as possible, but this is not as

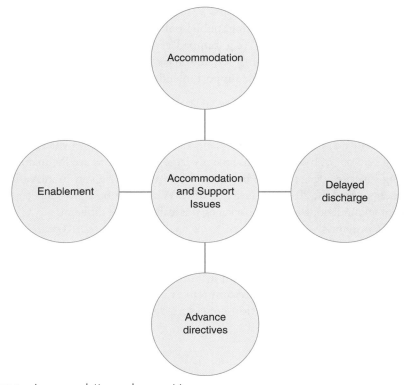

Figure 32.2 Accommodation and support issues

straightforward as it seems. Whilst aids and adaptations and wide-ranging home care support can be provided, judgements need to be made as to when it is no longer reasonable to provide support in a house unsuitable for that person's needs. For example, stair-lifts can be fitted to many houses, but in most cases pose safety risks and are very costly, so it may be more beneficial to the person, and more economic for social service departments (SSDs), to arrange for the individual to move to ground floor accommodation.

There may be many other reasons why a house is deemed unsuitable, including location, condition of the house, access to bathrooms. If the individual is resistant to moving, social workers are caught in true ethical dilemmas. Value is placed on respecting choice and enabling an individual to live in their own home, but this choice needs to be balanced against the duty to protect and to achieve the best quality of life possible for that person.

Options for accommodation have also become more complex in recent years. Moves away from even small-scale residential provision, driven by changes to housing benefit laws, led many care providers to offer peripatetic support to people in their own tenancies. This reduces the need for, or desirability of, sheltered housing complexes and many have become 'hard to let' in recent years. Where previously great expense was often incurred in providing adapted housing, public policy demands that new buildings are designed to be 'disability friendly' (e.g. ramped access, wider doors to accommodate wheelchairs). 'Very sheltered housing' schemes have become more common, providing readily adapted housing with flexible support including meals where required. These are 'sold' as 'homes for life'.

Despite the move away from large-scale hospitals and 'mass care' facilities, the 'warehousing' of older people is again becoming a concern. The increasing regulatory demands and lack of profitability in the sector have arguably driven many small providers of residential and nursing care out of business. Consequently large corporations are the main residential and nursing care providers, this care being provided in a uniform way in increasingly large establishments (AgeUK, 2011; Scourfield, 2011). Whilst the best providers support user involvement and individualised care packages, the reality can be different.

As noted previously, it is incumbent on social workers to advocate for appropriate care for each individual where a need for care home provision is identified. Increasing restrictions on SSD budgets result in respite places and permanent moves being delayed or refused, in an attempt to manage budgets. In an increasingly target-driven managerial environment it can be difficult for social workers' voices to be heard. The next section considers delayed discharge, which is one of these pressures.

Delayed Discharge

The term *delayed discharge* was coined to describe a failure to 'discharge' a patient who no longer required hospital services from a hospital bed. Predominantly affecting older people, the process affects anyone ready to leave hospital who has unmet community care needs. Legislation was introduced in England and Wales and as 'guidance' in Scotland. In Northern Ireland the Integrated Health and Social Care system arguably avoids the need for this. Delayed discharge policies create enormous pressure on social work services, and a 'zero tolerance' approach to delayed discharge can result in very uncomfortable decisions for social workers putting forward care applications. Service users may be provided with an 'interim' placement to 'unblock' a hospital bed, leading to arguably unnecessary subsequent moves to a setting better suited to that person's needs or wishes.

Advance Directives and Anticipatory Measures

Several means exist whereby a person may put in place 'anticipatory measures' should they become unwell. Across the UK arrangements to set up powers of attorney are becoming commonplace. Although the legislation differs across the UK, the principle is that a trusted person (or persons) is nominated in advance to take welfare and/or financial decisions on your behalf should you lose capacity to make these decisions yourself. Under mental health law in Scotland (Mental Health (Care and Treatment) (Scotland) Act 2003) and the Mental Incapacity Act 2005 in England, it is possible to make statements about future treatment for mental and (in England) physical illness. There are safeguards and exclusions in both pieces of legislation but essentially medical and social care professionals will need to at least acknowledge a person's wishes in this regard if not adhere to them.

Enablement

The enablement approach, often used within SSDs, is linked to core social work principles of empowerment and client self-determination, yet may also be seen as a means of restricting services and budget cutting if not dealt with appropriately (Ettridge, 2009).

Essentially it is argued that many service users become dependent on services and consequently lose the ability to manage their own lives; rapid assessments are conducted, home support or even residential services are provided and subsequent reviews are cursory and rarely result in a reduction of service. Enablement aims to 'frontload' service provision, seeking to help service users to develop skills and coping strategies, often involving the provision of equipment by occupational therapists. This may include so-called 'telecare', a wide range of often hi-tech equipment that alerts carers when the service user is leaving the house, or switches off gas or electric appliances, or prompts the service user themselves to take medication, go to bed etc. This approach is being enthusiastically embraced by several local authorities, but there is a marked lack of research evidence to show the efficacy of this approach with the increasingly frail and disabled group of older people now referred to SSDs.

Exercise

It would be helpful if at this stage you try to find out just what resources are available to 'enable' people to remain in their own home.

Learn more about the issues surrounding use of telecare by reading the article on the Companion Website (www.sagepub.co.uk/SocialWork) by Percival and Hanson (2006).

PART 3: FINANCIAL ISSUES

Finance

There are different perspectives on the involvement of social workers in the financial affairs of service users. Some social workers believe they should not become involved in financial assessment or an individual's financial matters, whilst other workers believe that to maximise service users' opportunities for participation and involvement in the mainstream of society and to challenge poverty, an interest should be taken in this area. Phillips and colleagues, (2006) noted that there are likely to be 50% more older people living in poverty, in socially and economically deprived areas than elsewhere. The need to address poverty is clear in the light of statistics on life expectancy and poor health for the poorest areas of Britain, as noted earlier. An awareness of financial issues is also important in helping service users to consider direct payments.

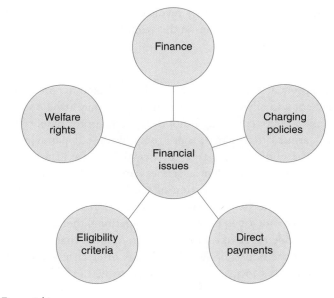

Figure 32.3   Financial issues

Welfare Rights

Social workers should ensure they are up to date with changes to the benefits system and are able to advise and support people to claim appropriate benefits. This may involve joint working with specialist advisers from voluntary organisations such as Citizen's Advice Bureaux, debt counselling agencies and groups such as the Alzheimer's Society.

Charging Policies

Unfortunately, as SSD budgets continue to be squeezed charging policies reach into areas that never previously attracted charges. Charges are also increasing significantly. Most local authorities now employ staff to assist in claiming benefit, whilst other sections, often of the same team, apply and enforce charging by means of detailed financial assessments. This creates ethical dilemmas for social workers who may be called upon to quiz service users about the ownership arrangements for their accommodation, gifts to family members and long-forgotten bank accounts. Service users may begin to refuse services due to cost, and time is spent on complex bureaucratic arrangements that need to be pursued by social workers to obtain authorisation to waive charges for essential services.

Direct Payments/Personalisation

Linked to aspects of support discussed in Part 2, in particular enablement, the concept of personalisation has become embedded into social work practice in recent years. This area is complex, both logistically and politically, and is covered elsewhere in this book (Chapter 21); but briefly stated, personalisation may be seen, like enablement, as an embodiment of social work values and principles, whereby the care for an individual is personalised to their needs and their voice is central within the care planning process. Some welfare benefits sought to enable individuals to buy their own care, for example Disability Living Allowance or Incapacity Benefit, with limited success. The centrally funded Independent Living Fund, which provided realistic payments to pay for significant amounts of care, was probably too successful and is at the time of writing suspended. As these benefits were being introduced, legislative changes came about across the UK in different ways, to enable local authorities to assess a person's needs and then, rather than provide services, make a direct payment that would allow them to purchase their own. Various conditions were attached to this, including restrictions on relatives being paid and the need for review and monitoring of the arrangements. Direct payments have largely gone to those with learning disability or physical disability and not to older people. Social work services will undoubtedly continue to be pressed to widen the availability of these payments as lack of access for older people to direct payments is increasingly seen to be unacceptable (Davey et al., 2007).

Eligibility Criteria

A parting thought before moving on to more specific issues for older people is the increasing use of eligibility criteria as SSDs become more financially stretched. These require assessors to attach priority levels to their assessments and resources are allocated according to the level of priority and available resources. These have already been the target of successful legal challenges, as in the 2011 case of *NT and JM* v *Isle of Wight Council* (*Guardian*, 2011), and will undoubtedly continue to provoke controversy.

Critical Thinking

Do you think older people should be seen as a special category for service provision or are older people simply adults?

PRACTICE ISSUES

Having looked at the wide range of issues particular to older people and the provision of services, the proceeding section examines how social work interventions described elsewhere in this book might be applied. Some reference is made to major pieces of legislation which impact on these interventions, but the legislative framework is complex and differs across the four countries that make up the UK, so legislation is not discussed in any detail. Care standards are set in different formats across the UK (see Chapter 26), but all set out clear expectations for residential, day care and home care services. These are variously monitored and reported on by regulatory bodies, including the Care Quality Inspectorate for England and Wales and The Care Inspectorate in Scotland. It will be very important for student social workers to familiarise themselves with the local legal and policy framework and ensure that their practice is consistent with the letter and the spirit of the law.

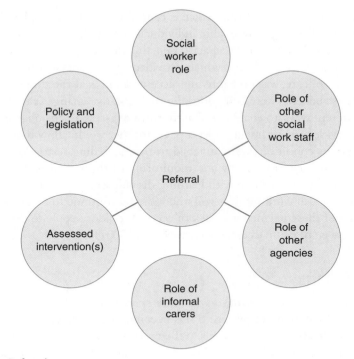

Figure 32.4 Referrals

When referrals are received the social worker might think about the areas set out in Figure 32.4. The following sections attempt to set out some of the dynamics in relation to reasons for referral. These have been discussed in the earlier part of the chapter and are recapped here:

- Physical ability/**frailty**
- Risk of harm
- Mental disorder
- Developmental crises: life changes, bereavement, loss of carer, end of life.

Interventions with older people may span all these categories simultaneously or at different times and the divide between methods of intervention, legal frameworks and involved professionals will not be clear-cut. However this does provide a starting point for thinking about why an older person has come to the attention of services, what interventions might be deployed and who might be involved.

This section of the chapter will examine the types of intervention that might be deployed, legal frameworks, the social work role and, importantly, consider the wide range of professional staff and informal carers who might be involved in delivering these interventions. Discussion of each of these areas follows, looking specifically at the levels of response.

For each 'category' needs are classified as low, medium and high to illustrate the differing levels of involvement that might occur. Whilst these again are indicative and described in this way to aid discussion, SSDs often assign assessments at different levels depending on the perception of the referrer and the *screener*. The team manager or duty worker is likely to be the *screener* and she or he will identify information from the referral or seek additional information to assess priority and identify the level of need.

On the Companion Website (www.sagepub.co.uk/SocialWork) a referrals activity has been provided. This will help you to understand the types of issues presented by older people and consider how work is prioritised.

Physical Ability/Frailty

Low level

For older people with needs arising from impaired functional ability, services required may be very low level. It is unlikely that a social worker will have any involvement at all, except perhaps as a duty worker. Provision of services may be decided on the basis of: home care type assessments carried out by other social work staff; medical assessments carried out by district nurses, or decisions by the individual and their family to commission private care. Many SSDs employ occupational therapists (OTs), who will assess for equipment to aid people with everything from opening jars to bathing, showering and going to the toilet.

A duty social worker may be needed to direct people to such services or towards assessors. Although perhaps not an intervention as such it may be seen as a systems approach whereby you as the worker identify parts of the system that need to change to accommodate the services user's needs. This may require an interview with the older person and/or relatives. For many people this may be their first encounter with social work and they may hold negative views about involvement or indeed may feel embarrassed about seeking help, which they may even see as 'charity'. Clearly then, even at this level, careful use of language, good listening skills and use of empowering approaches are required.

Medium level

At this level there may be more reason for direct social work involvement, which will probably include some coordination often described as *care management*. Debate continues as to whether this is a role or a function, i.e., many social workers employed as *care managers* undertake direct interventions as well as arrange care. Care management is not examined in detail here, but essential elements include:

- providing information about services
- initial assessment
- arranging care provision
- monitoring the arrangement
- reviewing the care regularly
- refocusing the care as necessary.

Case Study

In undertaking assessment the social worker should be satisfied that they have established a sufficiently effective relationship with the service user, and their family where applicable, and that short- and long-term care needs are considered. At this stage a range of other interventions may come into play.

It is important to establish why a person has come to the attention of services. This may be the result of some personal crisis that needs to be addressed and requires some immediate intervention by the social worker or others, possibly crisis intervention (Chapter 17).

It may be that some deficit is identified which could be met by providing services but equally could be met by enhancing the skills of the service user. It is here perhaps that solution-focused (Chapter 24) and task-centred (Chapter 19) approaches may come into their own.

Often on completion of assessment needs will be identified for a range of services, and it will be the responsibility of the care manager to identify an appropriate package of care to address these needs. This may include: traditional home care and support services, aids and adaptations to the house, 'telecare' options, or possibly advocating for a move to a more suitable house.

High level

This will almost always involve a care manager/social worker. It is likely that the person will be deemed to be at significant risk arising from their inability to care for themselves. Another 'urgent' scenario often arises when the service user is to be discharged from hospital and the planning process has become 'truncated' or indeed has not happened at all.

Crisis intervention skills will be essential: ensuring that the service user, family members and other involved professionals are kept informed and engaged as far as possible. Outcomes may include hospital admission, respite placement or a move to permanent care. Some areas operate schemes to prevent admission or enable earlier discharge from hospital, providing high levels of short-term assistance in the home, usually combining health and social care support, allowing time for 'readjustment' or further assessment.

Risk of Harm

Clearly under any of these headings 'risk of harm' is a feature. However sometimes 'risk of harm' is the reason for referral, usually related to the vulnerability of the service user, often due to exploitation or abuse. Again referrals may be at various levels of priority.

Low level

A service user may be dependent on a carer, who is not coping well with their role. Perhaps some neglect has been noted by others or perhaps unexplained weight loss, deteriorating personal hygiene or similar. Alternately some suspicion may have arisen that a relative or friend is benefiting financially or is developing a relationship with the service user that is causing concern. Referrals may come from wide-ranging sources. Such referrals are often based on 'suspicions' and may therefore have other dimensions that become apparent on investigation.

Medium level

It might be clear that some level of abuse or neglect has been happening, but that for the time being 'protective measures' are in place – for example, supportive family members or good communication with carers. A clear focus on risk will be necessary in any assessment of the circumstances and a systems-based approach may help in seeing the bigger picture.

The priority in such situations is to ensure that the full facts are established and a range of interventions are actively considered. These may include any of the interventions described in the section on physical frailty as well as utilising risk management strategies.

High level

These referrals will be treated with the utmost priority. It is likely that an ongoing risk of harm has been identified, putting the service user at considerable and immediate risk. This may include: living with an abusive or exploitative relative; being subject to ongoing financial or sexual exploitation by others; being subject to violence or psychological pressure from others. Such referrals often come through the police but may arise from disclosure by the service user or from observations by closely involved relatives or professionals. As in child protection, immediate responses are necessary. Assessment will include careful examination of risk factors, possibly medical examination and may well be undertaken alongside the police. Outcomes, as in the section on physical frailty, may well involve the service user moving accommodation temporarily or permanently and will clearly require good communication and involvement skills on the part of the social worker.

Mental Disorder

Many older people's teams are run jointly with health staff. Consequently, referrals for 'mental disorder' invoke many different responses and require quite different skills depending on the role of the social worker and the remit of the team. As noted earlier, *mental disorder* encompasses a range of different conditions.

Low level

This may be related to low level mental illness, such as anxiety or mild to moderate depression or perhaps early stage dementia. Responses and methods of intervention will vary greatly and may well not involve social workers. Cognitive behavioural therapy (CBT) type approaches are often effective with depressive or anxiety-based symptoms. For dementia, more behaviourally focused or task-centred work would help to build confidence and develop practical coping strategies. Medical interventions may be crucial to prevent worsening of symptoms.

Medium level

Many older people in care homes suffer depressive symptoms which are often undiagnosed and unrecognised and referrals may relate to symptomatic behaviour issues (McDougall et al., 2007). GPs may well make a referral to the team regarding someone for whom they have been prescribing antidepressant medication or for whom dementia has become an increasing problem.

High level

Typically this might involve a service user with dementia leaving a gas cooker on or who is found wandering, or who has acute mental illness and is experiencing symptoms, for example acute paranoia. Intervention may well involve statutory measures under mental health or incapacity law. The social worker's skills in managing crisis situations will be necessary in these situations, as well as effective joint working skills with medical, police and nursing colleagues. Outcomes in the short term again are likely to include temporary care or hospital admission.

Developmental Crises: Life Changes, Bereavement, Loss of Carer, End of Life

Low level

As already noted, many older people are very resilient and require little or no help from social work services. Where a person experiences bereavement a referral may be received from a GP or relative. Responses might include referral to bereavement counselling, a befriending type scheme or a local lunch club.

Situations such as family breakdown (e.g. divorce) may also result in an older person contacting a SSD. The person referred may largely have the resources to cope already and simply needs some advice and guidance or perhaps some low level services. The onset of disability or illness may also lead to a need for some low level assistance.

Medium level

For some older people bereavement has a much greater impact, particularly where there are few, or no, supportive family members. Immediate assistance may be required to replace the caring function that the deceased person provided and perhaps some crisis intervention work with the person referred may be necessary to help him or her gain some equilibrium and begin to reassess their situation. In the longer term there may be a need for bereavement counselling and care provision – which might include any of the services indicated above as well as more structured day care services for those considered to be at greater risk of self-neglect, exploitation or social exclusion.

With regard to end of life care, support needs may increase due to frailty or lack of informal supports. Again, the role may include any of the lower level services and input as described above, as well as more direct provision of care and emotional support.

High level

Many people will have been sustained for years by people close to them. When the primary carer dies, this can leave the person who has been cared for very vulnerable, if not completely incapable of looking after themselves. In such situations the immediate provision of intensive home care services may be required or possibly emergency admission to a care setting. This can be a very challenging issue for stretched social work teams and can arise with little or no warning. Brief hospital admission might be negotiated, or use of 'respite' beds in local care homes, but these are often at a premium. Alongside this, urgent assessment of the person's financial situation may be required, which clearly needs to be handled with sensitivity following the death of someone close. Nevertheless, the person concerned needs to know what their financial liability will be in relation to the provision of extensive home care or residential care support and will have to agree to this. This becomes even more complex if the person is incapable of understanding the consequences or the need to accept services, in which case incapacity or mental health legislation may need to be considered as a matter of urgency.

CONCLUSION

This chapter has provided a broad look at older people in today's society, highlighting the terminology used, the background to social work involvement with older people and the particular dilemmas that arise out of undertaking assessments in this complex area. The second half of the chapter has considered the application of methods of intervention in the context of these wider issues, and looked at how these might better inform social work practice with older people. As already noted, the needs of older people are extremely varied and there is clearly no 'one size fits all approach'. In this context student social workers will need to keep an open mind about the range of interventions that can be used and underpin these interventions with clear thinking around human rights and core social work values.

Watch vodcast 32.1 on the Companion Website (www.sagepub.co.uk/SocialWork) to see chapter author Iain Fisk summarise the main points conveyed in this chapter, and why possessing a knowledge of working with older people is important for social work practice.

Reflective Questions

1   We all age, it is an inescapable aspect of life, and at some point we should hopefully enter old age. How would you define old age? Is it simply chronological, that we have reached a certain number of years, or is there more to it than that? Do you also think that what may be considered old age in Britain today is how other people historically or in other countries understand old age?

(Continued)

(Continued)

2   Different points of our lives bring different challenges. What do you see as the potential risks for an individual as they age? And alternatively, what do you see as the potential benefits for an individual as they age? Is ageing always a 'bad thing'?

3   Given that the percentage of older people is predicted to increase over the next few decades, what are the different roles a social worker may undertake in working with older people?

RECOMMENDED READING

Bond, J., Peace, S., Dittmann-Kohli, F. and Westerhof, G. (2007) *Ageing in Society*, 3rd edn. London: Sage.

Lynch, R. (2013) *Social Work Practice with Older People: A Positive Person-Centred Approach.* London: Sage.

Ray, M. and Phillips, J. (2012) *Social Work with Older People*, 5th edn. Basingstoke: Palgrave Macmillan.

Stuart-Hamilton, I. (2006) *The Psychology of Ageing*. London: Jessica Kingsley Publishers.

Tanner, D. (2007) 'Starting with lives: supporting older people's strategies and ways of coping', *Journal of Social Work*, 7 (1): 7–30.

33 EVALUATION

Joyce Lishman

KeyThemes

- How critical, reflective practice and evidence-based practice can contribute to understanding and practising evaluation.
- How evaluation is understood and why it is essential.
- What methods of evaluation are available and useful.
- The importance of relationship and service user participation.
- Conclusions about how you might use evaluation in practice, service delivery and policy implementation.

INTRODUCTION

Evaluation in social work and social care is essential for effective practice, service delivery and policy. How else can social work judge whether or not it is being effective in achieving the outcomes that social work and service users wish and require to be achieved? Evaluation is also complicated. What do we mean by it? How can it be used? How is it linked with a research and evidence-based approach (Chapter 9) and critical reflective practice (Chapter 10). These key chapters jointly ask us how we examine our practice, how effective we are and how we judge whether we have achieved desired/required outcomes in practice, service delivery and policy. Evaluation is also essential as social workers cannot always assume that, because they may perceive themselves to be benevolent in their actions, those actions will necessarily be useful for the service user.

The focus of this chapter is to explore the role of evaluation in social work. We begin by discussing some of the complexities that surround defining evaluation before moving on to how evaluation can be supportive of practice. The focus then turns to the three main forms of evaluation : qualitative, quantitative and participatory.

Critical Thinking

As you read through this chapter, consider the information you have been given throughout this book about the uniqueness of individuals and the experiences that shape their personalities, the need to understand and empathise with their experiences and the importance we place on service user rights. As we discuss evaluation, consider how far the practice of social work can be measured or assessed scientifically, given the variables that exist.

DEFINING EVALUATION

How can evaluation be defined? Doing so is not so straightforward due to the complexity that exists in terms of the range of activities and situations that social work can attempt to evaluate. As Shaw and Lishman (1999: 2) have argued, 'In a sense these apparently simple definitions encapsulate a debate within social work about whether our activity is effective, for whom and in what ways?' So therefore do we numerically measure counts of activity, for example, the number of contacts or visits that are made with a service user, or do we try to assess in a more complex way how useful we are being, that is, the outcome of our contact for the service user involved?

A further tension in attempting to define evaluation is identified by Trevithick (2005), that in terms of practice we need to take into account distinctions between effectiveness in terms of *quality* of practice, how for instance effective or compassionate is a particular social worker, in contrast with more general service provision and outcomes. So for example, an older person may be receiving excellent care from nursing and social work staff in terms of how they relate to her and respond to her particular needs when they meet her, and as a result she feels very positive about her experiences. However, the actual service provision in terms of the coordination between departments or different teams may be woeful, and the same service user could leave feeling very negative about her experience.

Another and very simple distinction in evaluation is between outputs, how many people did we see for example, and outcomes, which consider how effective were our actions in terms of achieving a desired outcome. For example, a substance abuse service may report on numbers of families processed or use much more complex outcome measures such as children's attendance at school or quality of care at home.

In evaluation we also need to pay attention to process and relationships. There is research evidence about the importance from a service user's perspective about the value in care management of an approach that is relationship-based where the care manager seeks to understand an older person's concerns and potential losses before jointly agreeing a 'package of care'.

Visit the Companion Website (www.sagepub.co.uk/SocialWork) to find out more about outcomes focused working and undertake an activity to consider how you can become more outcomes focused.

The Relationship of Evaluation to Practice

The above discussion considered some of the main issues in defining evaluation, and attention now turns to how evaluation relates to and informs practice. The main point being made here is that evaluation adds to practice, helping social workers refine and constantly improve on how they develop successful relationships with service users. The importance of evaluation to practice is best understood by discussing three modes of practice, which are underpinned by some form of evaluation.

Reflective practice has had a long and honourable place in social work and social care and is closely linked to relationship-based practice (Wilson et al., 2008). It involves responding not to our personal anxieties and histories, for example how we have experienced attachment and loss or aggression and violence, but in a real and relationship-based way with each service user (Lishman, 2009). It requires that we address the uniqueness of each social work and social care encounter and the complexity involved in responding to it (Fook, 2007; Lishman, 2009). It also requires us to be critically reflective about policy developments that impact on service users and our practice. For example, in relation to criminal justice we should consider carefully whether we are being punitive or rehabilitative, which also applies to welfare benefits, where a similar question could be asked (Hothersall and Bolger, 2010).

Research-minded practice needs to be combined with reflective practice. What do we mean by research-minded or research-based practice? Orme and Shemmings (2010) are clear about the need for research-based practice. They argue, 'Research is therefore systemic and rigorous enquiry that involves or leads to understandings of how things are as they are or how they work' (p. 12). How does this definition assist us in practice?

Research-minded practice does not mean we should all undertake research ourselves but it does mean that we should pay careful attention to relevant research findings and seek them out. This requires us to access relevant websites, for example SCIE (Social Care Institute for Excellence), but as, or more importantly, it requires you to think: 'What could research tell me about the best possible practice I can undertake to achieve the best possible outcomes for service users?'

Evidence-based practice was initially developed in medicine and was defined as follows:

> the conscientious, explicit and judicious use of current best evidence in making decisions about the care of individual patients, based on skills which allow the doctor to evaluate both personal experience and external evidence in a systematic and objective manner. (Sackett et al., 1997: 71)

Morago (2006, 2007) has developed the above definition to apply to social work, where he argues that evidence-based practice involves research evidence, professional ethics and values, professional judgement and the views of service users and carers. Lishman (2007) outlines why we should use an evidence-based approach to practice. It ensures we do not rely on outdated knowledge, for example from qualifying training, and on practice wisdom that may be selective (one successful case may be remembered rather than others which were less so). A further reason for practising in an evidence-based way is that it helps us to think about what outcomes we should be trying to achieve, to ensure we do more good than harm and that we manage risk and thereby harm.

We also need to consider, however, evidence-based practice in the specific context of social work and the 'messiness' of our work with individual service users, albeit within a general service delivery and policy context. In practice we work with and respond to individuals in a personal and relationship-based way, but within the broader context of policy imperatives and limited resource allocation (Lishman, 2007) as well as the research and evidence base.

As we shall see, when we examine evaluation there are tensions for practitioners between reflective, relationship-based approaches, which are individualised for and responsive to each of our service users, and research and evidence-based approaches that require us to use a more empirical and probabilistic method of deciding how we move forward in our assessment and intervention. The two approaches need to be integrated.

To enhance your understanding of the debate around effectiveness of interventions and establishing the evidence base see the article by Mullen and Shuluk (2011) on the Companion Website (www.sagepub.co.uk/SocialWork).

Now that we have both defined evaluation and outlined its relationship with practice outcomes, we need to consider the actual mechanics of evaluation, or *how* we evaluate. The three main approaches – quantitative, qualitative and participatory – are outlined below.

METHODS OF EVALUATION

Quantitative Evaluation

We start with this methodological approach, not because it is a preferred choice, but because it is a starting point that may reflect your research methods teaching. It also under-pinned early approaches to evidence-based practice that employed only experimental or quasi-experimental designs in evaluating social work practice with a consequent emphasis on behavioural or cognitive methods of intervention (Sheldon and Chilvers, 2002).

How might you use **quantitative** evaluation methods? Perhaps there are three main methods or approaches.

We can use *randomised controlled trials (RCT)*, where we use a scientific experimental method. In medicine, drugs to lower high blood pressure can be tested by putting half of a sample of men with high blood pressure on Drug A and the other half on noth-ing (a placebo): the allocation to the samples is random. If 70% of patients on Drug A improve and only 10% on the placebo, we may conclude that Drug A works. It has not worked for 30% of patients. How do we know who are likely to be in the 70%?

How might we use this experimental method in evaluating social work and social care? When you use a task-centred approach, this is based on experimental evidence (Reid and Shyne, 1969) which showed that brief focused interventions achieved better outcomes for service users than less focused long-term interventions. Marsh (2007) stresses that this experimental approach involves a commitment to partnership with service users by the need mutually to agree what desired outcomes are and how they might be achieved.

Or, secondly, we can also use a *single system* evaluation design with individual service users. Parents use this method when they create a star chart to try to decrease a child's problematic behaviour, for example bed wetting or temper tantrums, and reward more acceptable behaviour.

Case Study

Kazi and Wilson (1996) describe this approach in their account of a girl who had to move to a new school and was distressed by the change so that she cried persistently. A graph was constructed with a baseline which showed how the girl behaved at the onset of contact, and during the intervention period, when counselling and promotion of the student's particular role in the school were used. The outcome and follow up demonstrated that the girl's crying had ceased and she appeared happy at school (Bloom, 1999).

In your work experience do you have an example of when this kind of approach was used – for example, with a child who was showing particular behaviour problems?

The third quantitative evaluation approach is designed to evaluate cognitive and behavioural interventions, where, as Vanstone (1999) argues, evaluation is an *integral part of practice*. If you have experience in criminal justice settings you will have seen the use of this approach, which has many links with randomised controlled trials and single system design.

Exercise

At this point, it would be useful to think about what you understand a cognitive behavioural approach to involve. (To remind yourself, see Chapter 18.)

The approach involves a focus on learning theory (positive and negative reinforcement), and social learning theory, including modelling and cognitive theory. Macdonald (2007), in summarising a cognitive behavioural approach, links it with an evidence-based approach where we need to monitor whether the behaviours a service user wanted to change actually have changed, for each intervention.

Macdonald(2007) emphasises the use of charts and graphs, not just to record behaviours but also emotions. Like Marsh (2007), she emphasises the importance of partnership with the service user. So, in working with a male service user who is experiencing depression, we might want to use a chart to describe what he sees as depressing him, a graph to focus on when, in the last week, he specifically felt depressed, for example, time of day, and discussion to examine what he sees as the antecedents in his life that may have contributed to his current depression. As in single system evaluation, the graphs and charts can be used to evaluate progress and outcomes.

The strengths of these quantitative evaluation methods are how explicit they are in identifying a service user's problem and using a specific contract to outline agreed aims and outcomes, and therefore the ability to identify whether these aims and outcomes have been achieved. The main weakness is that 'the very specific, clear and measurable outcomes may not reflect the complex and messy problems which social work practice encounters' (Lishman, 2007: 381).

You may have noticed that these methods all stress the importance of partnership between service user and social worker and this emphasis will be continued in the next section.

Qualitative Approaches to Evaluation

Qualitative evaluation involves a range of social science research methods and is closely aligned with reflective practice (Schön, 1987). It does examine outcomes but also focuses on the processes, including relationships, by which outcomes are achieved. Essentially, it involves asking all participants, service users, practitioners and service managers about their views of the quality of service they are engaging in and the outcomes.

Gould (1999) outlines two early strands of qualitative evaluation:

1 Qualitative research that examined service users' perspectives on the process of assessment and intervention. Mayer and Timms' *The Client Speaks* (1970) was the earliest of these and remains a classic text that demonstrated a 'clash in perspective' between the social worker's assessment and the client's or service user's perspective or view of their situation; these contrasts are relevant today.
2 Practitioner research that developed qualitative ways of undertaking practice evaluation, such as critical incident analysis (Fook et al.,1997) and narrative and life story methods (Hall, 1997) to explore children's views of their experiences.

Qualitative evaluation does focus on outcomes as well as the processes by which they are achieved. It also addresses the context of social work (policy and service delivery imperatives, which are often politically driven) and the complexity of social work (much of social work deals with individuals in uncertain and 'messy' circumstances).

As Lishman (2007) argued:

> the strengths of qualitative evaluation in social work include the recognition of the need for research and evaluation in social work to address the role of values and judgements about good practices and processes; the recognition of the importance of meaning and perceived experience in social work encounters, and not solely of prescribed outcomes; the importance of the voice of the consumer, user or client in evaluating the experience of receiving a social work service (Beresford and Croft, 2001) and the importance of the 'narrative'. (p. 381)

A weakness identified by Lishman (2007: 381) is the potential 'lack of clarity about specific purposes of intervention and related outcomes'.

Qualitative evaluation has led the way in asking service users how they experience our services and practice. It is a standard requirement for the assessment of a student's practice. In contrast, does your GP ever ask how you experience the service she or he is providing?

Exercise

How might you use qualitative evaluation to examine your practice?

For example, if an older man has fallen seriously several times, is in hospital and wishes to go home without, as he perceives it, 'intrusive' carers, as a care manager how would you evaluate your practice in aiding him to make decisions about the future and take account of the anxieties of family and local friends? Consider factors such as ethical practice, professional values, risk and protection.

If you are working in criminal justice, the hard quantitative evaluation measure is, of course, the question of reoffending. How do you think you might evaluate qualitatively the outcomes of your engagement with individual service users? Would you include softer measures such as improvements in their capacity for child care or in their general relationships?

Participatory Evaluation

The inclusive approach of qualitative evaluation with its focus on experiences of the social work process has led to a third approach to evaluation, participatory evaluation, where power shifts from the practitioner, manager or policy-maker to the user of services.

Participatory and empowering evaluation (Dullea and Mullender, [1999] 2004) attempts to address the power imbalances between users of services, practitioners, managers and policy-makers in evaluation.

Participatory evaluation is inclusive:

- It draws on user control.
- It is user-led.
- It draws on the networks and strengths of locally based initiatives.
- Participatory evaluation involves a range of different service users, including people with physical disability, people with mental health problems and people with learning disabilities.
- Participatory evaluation is user-led and based on the principle that users of services are experts in their own lives and circumstances.

However, participatory evaluation is complicated, particularly where different people are involved, for example service users and carers who may have different interests and agendas. It is also complex for the social worker or care manager in that it may be perceived as a loss of control or power, and there is a parallel with the use of direct payments where the service user accesses money and decides how they wish to spend it.

Case Study

A mother has been a long-time carer for her son, a young man with severe learning disabilities. The care manager has taken great care to explore the son's wishes in a person-centred approach (see Chapter 21) and, in attempting to keep communication as open and honest as possible, has been involved in challenging, sometimes acrimonious discussions. The care manager, a qualified social worker, has been diligent in seeking supervision to ensure that he can reflect on his practice and is clearly focused on meeting the needs of his service user, the young man. The service user's mother has expressed her irritation with the care manager who, she feels, does not respect and recognise her as the expert in her son's care, which she is. Consider the potential implications of this situation in the results of participatory evaluation.

 The case for participatory evaluation is made by Chouinard (2013). You can read her research paper on the Companion Website (www.sagepub.co.uk/SocialWork).

CONCLUSION

This chapter has examined evaluation and how it links to reflective practice, research-based and evidence-based practice. It has argued that we need to undertake evaluation as a profession and briefly identified identified ways in which we can evaluate our practice and their strengths and weaknesses.

The chapter also sets out the complex context of social work evaluation, including the highly political nature of policy in relation to social work and social care, the resource constraints on policy implementation, and service delivery, the inherent tension in evaluation between a focus on processes and relationships and a focus on outcomes (although they are interlinked) and the inherent messiness involved in making complex decisions about relative risk, safety, harm and protection.

Reflective Questions

1   Consider the importance of evaluation for both the delivery of services and the practice of individual social workers. Why is evaluation important in these contexts? What can evaluation of service provision tell us about effectiveness? What are the links for practitioners between reflective approaches and evaluation?

2   There is much discussion in contemporary social work on the importance of outcomes as opposed to outputs. How does a focus on outcomes impact on the way social work is practised? What implications are there for how social work practitioners undertake their work? How do we measure outcomes effectively?

3   The chapter has outlined three different approaches to evaluation – quantita-
    tive, qualitative and participatory. What do you think are the advantages and
    disadvantages to each approach? If you have had experience of undertaking
    such evaluation are there particular learning points that you can take from
    your experience?

RECOMMENDED READING

Shaw, I. and Lishman, J. (1999) *Evaluation and Social Work Practice*. London: Sage.
Lishman, J. (2007) 'Research, evaluation and evidence based practice', in *Handbook of Knowledge and Theory for Social Work and Social Care*. London: Jessica Kingsley.

CONCLUSION

We hope that students, academics, practice teachers and educators, and social work professionals find this edited collection helpful and that it helps readers to understand the complexity of social work and the range of knowledge it must draw on: social policy, law, sociology, psychology and human growth and development. We hope readers understand the complex interaction for all service users and social workers in how structural influences and individual experiences of development influence us. It is essential we draw on this knowledge in assessment, and then in how we should intervene and what skills and methods we should use. We stress the importance of a research and evidence base, and of reflection and evaluation. We hope the book addresses the complexity of current social work practice.

Joyce Lishman
Chris Yuill
Jillian Brannan
Alastair Gibson

GLOSSARY

Accountable   Where someone is expected to justify his/her decisions and actions, e.g. a government minister is accountable to Parliament. Therefore, accountability involves responsibility: being prepared to account for one's acts and omissions to relevant others by providing an explanation, justification or excuse for what one has done or not done.

Active listening   When listening, being able to empathise with another, to understand the central message being communicated, and taking care continuously to clarify and confirm understanding.

Affect   The showing of feelings.

Ambivalence   Where we have both positive and negative feelings towards someone or something.

Amphetamines   Drugs that stimulate the central nervous system, for example, to lift the mood in depressive states.

Anti-oppressive practice   Working in ways that ensure the process and outcome do not place a service user in a position where they are likely to be seen as inferior or of less worth.

Benzodiazepines   Minor tranquilisers that act against anxiety and can sedate or relax.

Biography   Written account of another person's life.

Bi-polar affective disorder   Also known previously as manic depression or bipolar depression, it is a mood disorder where a person experiences marked mood swings, which are beyond what most people experience. These extremes of mood may include the lows of depression as well as the highs of a very elated mood (known as mania).

Class   One of the ways of describing divisions in society, class broadly relates to people's economic activity, what they do for a living, where they live, how they view others and how others view them.

Co-constructivist   A holistic approach which involves everyone involved.

Cognition   A psychological process of gaining new knowledge by the perception and interpretation of information and sensory events.

Cognitive behavioural therapy   A method of addressing emotional and behavioural problems using a structured intervention to alter faulty thinking.

Congruent   Being genuine, open and honest. For example, feeling angry and acknowledging this so that another person will understand clearly how you feel.

Constitution   The fundamental political principles on which a state is governed, especially when considered as embodying the rights of the people living in that state.

Consumerism   Protecting the interests of the person who uses a service.

Crisis   An upset in the balance of our lives for which we are unprepared and for which we have no immediate coping skills.

Cultural and gender significance   The way specific behaviours within communication will be understood and interpreted within cultural systems. Gender difference will also have bearing on how communication behaviours will be understood. For example, in some cultures eye contact between men and women is not acceptable, but may be less obtrusive between females.

Curfew requirement   An order establishing a specific time in the evening after which certain regulations apply, for example, no unauthorised persons may be outdoors or a person must be home at a certain prescribed time.

deaf/Deaf   People who have been born profoundly Deaf do not see themselves as disabled, but rather that they belong to a minority ethnic group with their own culture, social norms and language – British Sign Language (BSL) – using the term Deaf (with a capital D) rather than deaf to denote these distinct characteristics.

Deprivation   Being in a state of having something that one needs withheld or removed.

Dichotomies   The division into separate, opposing groups.

Discrepancy   The gap between the service user's current situation and the life he/she would prefer to be living.

Discrimination   Unfair treatment of a person, group, ethnic minority and any others, where the treatment is based on prejudice.

Disrupted thought patterns   Personality disorders disrupting a person's pattern of thoughts, feelings and behaviour, thus affecting the way a person thinks and behaves.

Doctrines   Principles, policies and practices put forward by people with influence, including governments, to establish how things are done.

Down syndrome Genetic disorder, associated with the presence of an extra chromosome 21, characterised by mild to severe mental impairment, weak muscle tone, shorter stature and a flattened facial profile.

Ego see Id

Ego integrity The psychological state of a person who is able to function competently in social situations and emotionally manage reasonable amounts of stress and change.

Empirical studies Research that is based on the results of observation or experimentation.

Empowerment Individuals or groups gaining increased opportunities, achieving more control over their lives, negotiating with others to influence decisions that affect them, and accessing resources previously denied.

Equilibrium Balance maintained by the ability of opposing forces or tendencies to counteract each other.

Erroneous Inaccurate, untrue, false or mistaken.

Ethics/ethical What we *ought* to do, rather than what we might like to do or what we actually do. Ethics is especially concerned with our behaviour towards others, pertaining to matters of fundamental importance rather than just convention or etiquette.

Ethnic/ethnicity This refers to differences in people based on social, cultural and historical influences and characteristics. It is not a fixed concept and can change over time. Race (as opposed to ethnicity) is a notion that there are biological reasons for separating people into different groups.

Exchange Giving something and receiving something back in fair measure.

Frailty Being fragile and prone to weakness.

Gender This refers to how society broadly defines what it means to be either male or female and the roles or activities which are deemed acceptable or which are expected of men or women. Gender is not a fixed concept, but can change over time and can differ between societies. Sex (as opposed to gender) describes biological and physical differences.

Genetic Influence by genes rather than nurture or environment.

Good enough attachment relationship A recognition that, in attachment formation, parents are not perfect and cannot meet all the needs of dependent children all the time.

A balance of positive experiences can permit healthy attachments even though there may be some aspects of either anxiety or self-reliance in one's personality.

Hallucinations   Sensory experiences, seen or heard, which are false and not real.

Heterophobic   *Hetero* implies 'different' or 'others' and *phobic* implies an aversion to something, hence hatred, mistrust of others who are different.

Homeostasis   Balance within the family. The meaning comes from Greek roots, *homeo* and *stasis*, meaning 'to remain the same'. It is the maintenance of the internal and the external environments which results in equilibrium being achieved.

Human capital   The abilities and skills of any individual, especially those acquired through positive nurture and education.

Id/Ego   Freudian expressions, where the id is the basic instinct for personal satisfaction, and the ego is the part of our self that is aware and realistically relating to the world around us.

Ideology   A set of ideas that inform action.

Impairment   Where level of functioning is reduced, diminished or damaged.

Infirmity   Physical weakness.

Informal sector   When considering the sources of help available to people, this pertains to those who provide help outside the structure of local government or organisations that pay staff.

Internal working model   Brains construct cognitive models of our environment including the world of other people. It helps us to make sense of the world, to manage and anticipate it. These internal working models serve as a template for future relationships. They can be positive or negative in their application.

Interventionist   The policy of intervening, often applied to government interference or action in situations.

Libido   Deriving from Freud, a basic drive or energy in everyone to seek and form relationships.

Life space   A way of perceiving, reflecting on and understanding the dynamic nature of the inter-personal relationships of all who live and work in a particular setting. This understanding is informed by psychodynamic, field theory and relational theories of interaction.

Linear   Where there is a clear, straightforward relationship between cause and effect.

Medical model   A way of understanding the difficulties where the diagnosis or the actual disability is seen as the problem.

Mental age   This refers to a measure of mental ability or capacity, usually as determined by intelligence tests, in relation to the chronological age of the average individual at the determined level of ability. It may be applied to children and persons with intellectual impairment and is expressed as the age at which that level of development is typically attained, for example, a 10-year-old child may have the average intellectual ability of a child of 4, and is therefore deemed to have a mental age of a 4 year old.

Moral worth   A personal trait or characteristic in which an individual's behaviour, for reasons of compassion, love, or valuing others, helps people and keeps them from harm.

Nature–nurture debate   The question of whether specific aspects of development are caused by inheritance and biological maturation (nature), or whether they are caused by the environment and social learning (nurture).

Need   A lack of something that is necessary. Note: this is different from 'want', which is a desire for something that may not be necessary.

Neurolinguistic programming   Neurolinguistic programming concerns the dynamic relationship between your mind (neuro) and your language (linguistic). It puts an emphasis on how thoughts, beliefs and attitudes interact with our language to affect behaviour. It is based on the theory that your brain can learn healthy patterns and behaviours that will bring about positive physical and emotional effects.

Neuroses   Where feelings of anxiety, obsessional thoughts, compulsive acts, or physical illness with no evidence of disease, affect the personality.

Normalisation   People with learning disabilities have the right to choose to participate in everyday community life, just as a person without a learning disability has the right. This includes participating in society, going to school, having a job, earning money, living in independent accommodation, and having freedom of choice. Within this, the service user's rights to take informed risks are also recognised, as opposed to services providing over-protection for the service user, thus potentially restricting options.

Normative   Referring to an accepted standard or pattern.

Old age   Contemporary definitions of old age have focused on sub-categories of ageing, in order to reflect the fact that, on average, people are living significantly longer. In academic and some policy terms old age is now routinely divided into 'younger older people' referring to the 65–79 age group, and 'older older people', referring to those who are 80 years or over.

Opportunity led   Practice interventions that are purposeful and take place as part of everyday activities.

Orwellian   Referring to a totalitarian state where individuals have no rights, as portrayed in George Orwell's *1984.*

Paradigm shift   A change or modification to a framework which contains basic assumptions, ways of thinking and methodology that are shared by members of any discipline or group.

Passive learning   A traditional style of learning where the student listens to someone who is the teacher.

Performance indicators   A set of values attached to the components of work which can be measured for effectiveness.

Personal growth   Referring to the emotional development of an individual, it reflects the move from dependency in childhood to adult relationships based on mutuality (give and take), the honest and clear recognition of one's own personality and the capacity to relate to the external world in a balanced, realistic way.

Pharmacotherapy   Treatment through the use of drugs.

Philosophical   Relating to the rational investigation of the essential truths and basic principles underpinning knowledge, behaviour and all aspects of human life.

Power   Having control, command or strong influence over others.

Prejudice   An unfavourable or unreasonable opinion or feeling which is formed without knowledge, thought, or reason.

Professional socialisation   The process by which workers become comfortable with the values, jargon and roles of their profession.

Professional tribalism   The process by which workers within a profession develop defensive practices and attitudes to maintain their separation and, often, status.

Proforma   A form containing information that follows a set procedure.

Proto-language   Proto meaning 'primitive' or 'earliest form of', this refers to basic, non-verbal communication.

Psychoactive substances   Substances that have a profound effect on one's mental state.

Psychodynamic   A psychological approach that considers the importance of the relationship of conscious and unconscious parts of our personality.

Qualitative   Referring to research into behaviour which, because of individual variations, is less suited to quantitative research and more suited to addressing 'why' rather than 'how much'.

Quantitative   Something that can be measured or described numerically.

Race   A division of humankind with particular physical characteristics.

Racism   Antagonism and feeling of superiority towards human beings who are identified because of particular physical characteristics and/or ethnic origins.

Rapport   A genuine and shared understanding of one another.

Rational-technical approach   An approach that sees social work as an activity based on the management of systems, legislation, audits, policies and procedures, with an emphasis on outcomes and evidence-based practice.

Reductionist   Breaking something down into its component parts and making connections between these parts in order to understand the whole better.

Reinforcement   Where the likelihood of a behaviour is increased by rewarding (positive) or avoiding something bad (negative).

Repeal   Abolish, end or discontinue.

Resilience   The capacity to tolerate difficulties, to overcome problems and to 'bounce back'.

Respect for persons   A requirement to see the world from the other person's viewpoint; take account of his/her beliefs; consider his/her needs; and assist him/her, where appropriate, to achieve his/her aims. It means not exploiting the individual, not using him/her solely for one's own purposes.

Risk   Being exposed to danger, hazard or extreme uncertainty.

Schema   A set of ideas, memories and deductions used to direct and control behaviour. We use schemas in both new and familiar situations.

Schizophrenia   A mental illness that involves a variety of symptoms that vary from person to person. The symptoms may include hallucinations (q.v.) or delusions, where you get ideas about the world that do not match with the views of everyone else. In addition people may become socially withdrawn and insular. Before a diagnosis can be made, a full assessment by a psychiatrist is needed.

Sectarian   Having a narrow-minded adherence to, membership of, or interest in a particular sect of religion.

Self   A psychological term meaning the whole person.

Self-awareness   Knowing yourself, that is, your feelings, beliefs, behaviour and values, particularly in relation to how you affect other people.

Self-efficacy   Promoting individual autonomy through empowerment in developing service user autonomy in decision-making.

Single case evaluative design   A research approach where the subject is not compared or measured against others, but is, as it were, an individual control group. Usually such an approach evaluates effectiveness of intervention for an individual.

Social model   A way of understanding difficulties experienced by people with disabilities where structural aspects and attitudes within society are seen as a problem to be resolved.

Splitting   A term favoured by object relations theorists to signify how we have a conscious self and an unconscious self. The unconscious part of ourselves, the part that is not aware or does not remember, is deemed to be split from the rational, conscious self. Freudian psychologists would describe this as repression.

Stress   An anxious response to an environmental situation.

Systematic   An ordered, methodical, planned approach.

Systemic   Referring to the whole process and the relationship of all parts of the process to the whole.

Taxonomy   Describing and/or identifying things in ordered categories.

Therapeutic milieu   Referring to settings where people come together in group activities or group living. These settings offer social workers the possibility to work in a helping role.

Transference, countertransference   Transference occurs where we relate to someone as if they were someone else, for example, in adult relationships a male may relate to a female as if she were his mother. Countertransference occurs when you, the worker, become aware of feelings arising from your interaction with a service user.

Trauma   An emotional shock as a result of a stressful event or injury.

Unconsciously   Deriving from Freud, this means behaving for reasons of which we are not aware or which we cannot control.

Uni-professional   A single professional group.

Use of self   A view of social work practice which acknowledges that a large part of what we offer and how we work comes from our own personality, our own attitudes and our own personal resources.

REFERENCES

Aberdeen Interprofessional Health and Social Care (2011) Available from: www.ipe.org.uk/ (accessed 9 February 2012).

Adams, R. (2002) *Social Policy for Social Work*. Basingstoke: Palgrave.

Adams, R. (2009) 'Encountering complexity and uncertainty', in R. Adams, L. Dominelli and M. Payne (eds), *Practising Social Work in a Complex World*, 2nd edn. Basingstoke: Palgrave Macmillan. pp. 15–32.

Adams, R. (2011) *Working with Children and Families*. Basingstoke: Palgrave.

Adams, R., Dominelli, L. and Payne, M. (2002) *Critical Practice in Social Work*. Basingstoke: Palgrave Macmillan.

AgeUK (2011) Health Committee. Written evidence from Age UK (SC 17), October 2011. Available from: www.publications.parliament.uk/pa/cm201012/cmselect/cmhealth/1583/1583we06.htm (accessed October 2013).

Aguilera, D.C. (1990) *Crisis Intervention: Theory and Methodology*, 6th edn. St Louis, MO: Mosby.

Aguilera, D.C. (1994) *Crisis Intervention: Theory and Methodology*, 7th edn. St Louis, MO: Mosby.

Ahmad, B. (1990) *Black Perspectives in Social Work*. Birmingham: Venture Press.

Aichhorn, A. (1951) *Wayward Youth*. London: Imago (first published 1925 *Verwahrloster Jugend*. Vienna: Internationaler Psychoanalytischer Verlag).

Ainsworth, F. and Fulcher, L.C. (1981) *Group Care for Children: Concept and Issues*. London: Tavistock.

Ainsworth, M. and Bowlby, J. (1965) *Child Care and the Growth of Love*. London: Penguin.

Ainsworth, M.D., Bleher, M.C., Waters, E. and Wall, S. (1978) *Patterns of Attachment*. New Jersey: Erlbaum.

Al, C.M.W., Stams, G.J.J.M., Van Der Laan, P.H. and Asscher, J.J. (2011) 'The role of crisis in family crisis intervention: do crisis experience and crisis change matter', *Children and Youth Services Review*, 33 (6): 991–8.

Alaszewski, A. and Alaszeweski, H. (2002) 'Towards the creative management of risk: perceptions, practices and policies', *British Journal of Learning Disabilities*, 30 (2): 56–62.

Alsobrook II, J. and Pauls, D. (1998) 'The genetics of obsessive–compulsive disorder', in M. Jenike, L. Baer and W. Minichiello (eds), *Obsessive Compulsive Disorders: Practical Management*, 3rd edn. St Louis, MO: Mosby. pp. 277-88.

Anderson, K.M. and Hiersteiner, C. (2007) 'Listening to stories of adults who were sexually abused as children', *Families in Society*, 88 (4): 637–44.

Anglin, J.P. (2002) *Pain, Normality and the Struggle for Congruence*. New York: Haworth Press.

Argyris, C. and Schön, D. (1978) *Organizational Learning: A Theory of Action Perspective*. Reading, MA: Addison Wesley.

Arnstein, S. (1969) 'A ladder of community participation', *American Institute of Planners Journal*, 35: 216–24.

Ashton, M. (2005) 'Motivational arm twisting: contradiction in terms?', *Drug and Alcohol Findings*, 4–19 (14). Available from: www.nobars.org.au/criminal-justice-client-motivation.html (accessed 1 December 2012).

Asaad, G. and Shapiro, B. (1986) 'Hallucinations: theoretical and clinical overview', *American Journal of Psychiatry*, 143: 1088–97.

Atkinson, R.M. and Shiffrin, R.M. (1968) 'Human memory: a proposed system and its control processes', in K.W. Spence and J.T. Spence (eds), *The Psychology of Learning and Motivation*, Volume 2. London: Academic Press.

Atkinson, R.M. and Shiffrin, R.M. (1971) 'The control of short-term memory', *Scientific American*, 225: 82–90.

Audit Scotland (2009) *Drug and Alcohol Services in Scotland*. Edinburgh: Audit Scotland.

Bailey, S. and Elliott, M. (2009) 'Taking local government seriously: democracy, autonomy and the constitution', *CLJ*, 436.

Baldwin, M. and Satir, V. (1987) *The Use of Self in Therapy*. New York: The Haworth Press.

Bandura, A. (1977) *Social Learning Theory*. Englewood Cliffs, NJ: Prentice Hall.

Bandura, A. (1989) 'Social cognitive theory', in R. Vasta (ed.), *Six Theories of Child Development*. Greenwich, CT: JAI Press.

Bandura, A. (1998) 'Self-efficacy', in V. Ramachaudran (ed.), *Encyclopaedia of Human Behavior*, vol. 4. New York: Academic Press. pp. 71–81. Reprinted in H. Friedman (ed.), *Encyclopaedia of Mental Health*. San Diego, CA: Academic Press.

Bandura, A. and Walters, R.H. (1963) *Social Learning and Personality Development*. New York: Holt.

Banks, S. (2004) *Ethics, Accountability and the Social Professions*. Basingstoke: Palgrave Macmillan.

Banks, S. (2012) *Ethics and Values in Social Work*, 4th edn. Basingstoke: Palgrave Macmillan.

Bannink, F. (2010) *1001 Solution-Focused Questions*, trans. Inge De Taeye. New York: W.W. Norton and Company.

Barnard, A. (2008) 'Values, ethics and professionalization: a social work history', in A. Barnard, N. Horner and J. Wild (eds), *The Value Base of Social Work and Social Care*. Maidenhead: Open University Press.

Baron, J. (2008) *Thinking and Deciding*, 4th edn. New York: Cambridge University Press.

Barr, H., Koppel, I., Reeves, S., Hammick, M. and Freeth, D. (2005) *Effective Interprofessional Education: Assumption and Evidence*. Oxford: Blackwell.

Barrett, G. and Keeping, C. (2005) 'The processes required for effective interprofessional working', in G. Barrett, D. Sellman and J. Thomas (eds), *Interprofessional Working in Health and Social Care*. Basingstoke: Palgrave Macmillan. pp. 18–31.

BASW (British Association of Social Workers) (2012) *The Code of Ethics for Social Work*. Birmingham: BASW. Available from: http://cdn.basw.co.uk/upload/basw_112315-7.pdf (accessed 4 May 2012).

Bates, P. and Siberman, W. (2007) *Modelling Risk Management in Inclusive Settings*. London: National Development Team.

Bauman, Z. (1989) *Modernity and the Holocaust*. Cambridge: Polity.

Baxter, S. and Brumfitt, S. (2008) 'Professional differences in interprofessional working', *Journal of Interprofessional Care*, 22 (3): 239–51.

Beatson, J. (2010) 'Reforming an unwritten constitution', *L.Q.R.*, 48–71.

Beck, A.T. (1963) 'Thinking and depression', *Archives of General Psychiatry*, 9: 324–33.

Beck, A. (1989) *Cognitive Therapy and the Emotional Disorders*. London: Penguin.

Beck, A.T. (1991) 'Cognitive therapy as the integrative therapy', *Journal of Psychotherapy Integration*, 1: 191–98.

Beck, A.T., Rush, A.J., Shaw, B.F. and Emery, G. (1979) *Cognitive Therapy of Depression*. New York: Guilford.

Beck, R. and Fernandez, E. (1998) 'Cognitive-behavioral therapy in the treatment of anger: a meta-analysis', *Cognitive Therapy and Research*, 22(1): 63–74.

Becker, S., Dearden, C. and Aldridge, J. (2000) 'Young carers in the UK: research, policy and practice', *Research, Policy and Planning*, 8 (2): 13–22.

Beckett, C. and Maynard, A. (2005) *Values and Ethics in Social Work: An Introduction*. London: Sage.

Beresford, P. (2000) 'Service users' knowledges and social work theory: conflict or collaboration?', *British Journal of Social Work*, 30: 489–503.

Beresford, P. (2003) *It's our Lives: A short Theory of Knowledge, Distance and Experience*. London: OSP for Citizens Press.

Beresford, P. (2007) *The Changing Roles and Tasks of Social Work from Service Users' Perspectives: A Literature Informed Discussion Paper*. London: Shaping Our Lives – National User Network.

Beresford, P. (2010) 'Public partnerships, governance and user involvement: a service user perspective', *International Journal of Consumer Studies*, 34: 495–502.

Beresford, P. and Croft, S. (2001) 'Service users' knowledge and the social construction of social work', *British Journal of Social Work*, 1 (3): 295–316.

Beresford, P. and Croft, S. (2004) 'Service users and practitioners reunited: the key component for social work reform', *British Journal of Social Work*, 34: 53–68.

Bernstein, D.A. (2008) *Essentials of Psychology*, 5th edn. Belmont, CA: Wadsworth/Nelson Education.

Berg, I. and Miller, D. (1992) *Working With the Problem Drinker: A Solution Focused Approach*. New York: W.W. Norton and Company.

Biestek, F. (1957) *The Casework Relationship*. London: Unwin University Books.

Biestek, F.P. (1961) *The Casework Relationship*. London: Unwin University Books.

Bingham, Lord (2002) 'Dicey revisited', *P.L.*, 39–48.

Bion, W. R. (1962) *Learning from Experience*. London: William Heinemann.

Blackburn, R. (2010) *The Making of New World Slavery: From the Baroque to the Modern, 1492–1800*. London: Verso.

Blair, T. (1998) *The Third Way: New Politics for a New Century*. Fabian pamphlet 588. London: The Fabian Society.

Bloom, M. (1999) 'Single system evaluation', in I. Shaw and J. Lishman (eds), *Evaluation and Social Work Practice*. London: Sage.

Bornstein, M.H. and Sawyer, J. (2006) 'Family systems', in K. McCartney and D. Phillips (eds), *Blackwell Handbook of Early Childhood Development*. Malden, MA: Blackwell.

Bourdieu, P. (1984) *Distinction: A Social Critique of the Judgement of Taste*. London: Routledge.

Bowen, M. (1978) *Family Therapy in Clinical Practice*. New York: Jason Aronson.

Bowl, R. (2001) 'Men and community care', in A. Christie (ed.), *Men and Social Work: Theories and Practices*. Basingstoke: Palgrave. pp. 109–25.

Bowlby, J. (1953) *Child Care and the Growth of Love*. London: Penguin Books.

Bowlby, J. (1969) *Attachment and Loss*, Volume 1. *Attachment*. New York: Basic Books.

Bowlby, J. (2009) *A Secure Base*. Abingdon: Routledge.

Bradshaw, J. (1972) 'The concept of social need', *New Society*, 496: 640–3.

BrainyQuote (n.d.) Available from: www.brainyquote.com/quotes/authors/h/henry_ford_2. html (accessed 27 July 2011).

Brand, D., Reith, T. and Statham, D. (2005) *The Need for Social Work Intervention – A Discussion Paper for the Scottish 21ˢᵗ Century Social Work Review.* Available from: www.socialworkscotland.org.uk/resources/pub/NeedforSocialWorkIntervention.pdf (accessed 9 February 2012).

Brandon, D. (1995) *Advocacy: Power to People with Disabilities.* Birmingham: Venture Press.

Branfield, F. (2009) *Developing User Involvement in Social Work Education.* London: Social Care Institute for Excellence.

Brayford, J., Cowe, F. and Deering, J. (eds) (2010) *What Else Works? Creative Work with Offenders.* Cullompton: Willan Publishing.

Breakwell, G. (1989) *Facing Physical Violence.* London: British Psychological Society.

Brearley, J. (2007) 'A psychodynamic approach to social work', in J. Lishman (ed.), *Handbook for Practice Learning in Social Work and Social Care: Knowledge and Theory.* London: Jessica Kingsley Publishers. pp. 86–100.

Brewer, M., Dickerson, A., Gambin, L., Green, A., Joyce, R. and Wilson, R. (2012) *Poverty and Inequality in 2020: Impact of Changes in the Structure of Employment.* York: Joseph Rowntree Foundation.

Bridges, W. (2009) *Managing Transitions: Making the Most of Change*, 3rd edn. Cambridge, MA: Da Capo Lifelong Books.

British Social Attitudes (2011) *British Social Attitudes 28.* London: National Centre for Social Research.

Brodie, I., Nottingham, C. and Plunkett, S. (2008) 'A tale of two reports: social work in Scotland from *Social Work and the Community* (1966) to *Changing Lives* (2006)', *British Journal of Social Work*, April: 1–19.

Bronfenbrenner, U. (1979) *The Ecology of Human Development: Experiments by Nature and Design.* Cambridge, MA: Harvard University Press.

Brown, C. and Lowis, M.J. (2003) 'Psychosocial development in the elderly: an investigation into Erikson's ninth stage', *Journal of Aging Studies*, 17(4): 415–26. Available from: www.sciencedirect.com/science/article/pii/S0940406503000616.

Brown, E., Bullock, R. Hobson, C. and Little, M. (1998) *Making Residential Care Work: Structure and Culture in Children's Homes.* Aldershot: Aldgate.

Brown, J.M. and Miller, W.R. (1993) 'Impact of motivational interviewing on participation and outcome in residential alcoholism treatment', *Psychology of Addictive Behaviours*, 7: 211–18.

Brown, J.M., Kitson, A.L. and McKnight, T.J. (1992) *Challenges in Caring: Explorations in Nursing and Ethics.* London: Chapman and Hall.

Brown, K. (ed.) (2010) *Vulnerable Adults and Community Care.* Exeter: Learning Matters.

Brown, K. and Rutter, L. (2008) *Critical Thinking for Social Work*, 2nd edn. Exeter: Learning Matters.

Bruner, J.S. (1983) *Child's Talk: Learning to Use Language.* Oxford: Oxford University Press.

Bundy, C. (2004) 'Challenging behaviour: using motivational interviewing techniques', *Journal of the Royal Society of Medicine*, 97, Suppl. 44.

Burns, D. (1990) *The Feeling Good Handbook.* London: Plume/Penguin.

CAIPE (Centre for the Advancement of Interprofessional Education) (2012) Available from: www.caipe.org.uk/ (accessed 9 February 2012).

Callinicos, A. (1989) *Against Post-Modernism: A Marxist Critique.* Cambridge: Polity Press.

Cameron, K. (2011) 'Accountability, professionalism and practice', in R. Davis and J. Gordon (eds), *Social Work and the Law in Scotland*, 2nd edn. Basingstoke: Palgrave Macmillan. pp. 20–34.

Canton, R. (2011) *Probation – Working with Offenders*. Abingdon: Routledge.

Caplan, G. (1961) *An Approach to Community Mental Health*. New York: Grune and Stratton.

Caplan, G. (1964) *Principles of Preventative Psychiatry*. New York: Basic Books.

Carers Trust (2012) 'What is a carer?' Available from: www.carers.org/what-carer (accessed 12 May 2012).

Carloway, Lord (2011) The Carloway Review: Report and Recommendations. Available from: www.scotland.gov.uk/Resource/Doc/925/0122808.pdf (accessed August 2013).

Carr, S. (2004) *Has Service User Participation Made a Difference to Social Care Services?* London: Social Care Institute for Excellence.

Carson, D. and Bain, A. (2008) *Professional Risk and Working with People – Decision-Making in Health, Social Care and Criminal Justice*. London: Jessica Kingsley Publishers.

Children Webmag (2009) Available from: www.childrenwebmag.com/articles/key-child-care-texts/wayward-youth-by-august-aichhorn (accessed 24 June 2011).

Children's Workforce Development Council (2009) *Early Identification, Assessment of Needs and Intervention: The Common Assessment Framework for Children and Young People*. Leeds: CWDC.

Chomsky, N. (1965) *Aspects of the Theory of Syntax*. Cambridge, MA: MIT Press.

Chomsky, N. (1972) *Language and Mind*. New York: Harcourt.

Clark, A. (2007) 'Crisis intervention', in J. Lishman (ed.), *Handbook for Practice Learning in Social Work and Social Care: Knowledge and Theory*. London: Jessica Kingsley Publishers. pp. 201–15.

Clark, C.L. (2000) *Social Work Ethics*. Basingstoke: Palgrave Macmillan.

Clark, M.D., Walters, S., Gingerich, R. and Meltzer, S. (2006) 'Motivational interviewing for probation officers: tipping the balance toward change', *Federal Probation*, 70: 38–44.

Clifford, D. and Burke, B. (2009) *Anti-Oppressive Ethics and Values in Social Work*. Basingstoke: Palgrave Macmillan.

Collingwood, P. and Davies, M. (2008) 'Knowledge, theory and social work practice', in M. Davies (ed.), *The Blackwell Companion to Social Work*, 3rd edn. Oxford: Blackwell.

Collins, E. and Daly, E. (2011) *Decision Making and Social Work in Scotland: The Role of Evidence and Practice Wisdom*. Glasgow: Institute for Research and Social Services. Available from: www.iriss.org.uk/sites/default/files/decision-making-wisdom-iriss-2011.pdf (accessed 4 May 2012).

Cooper, A. (2009) 'Soapbox: interprofessional working: choice or destiny?', *Clinical Child Psychology and Psychiatry*, 14: 531–6.

Cooper, M., Elliot, R., Stiles, W. and Bohart, A. (2008) Conference joint statement reported in 'CBT superiority questioned at conference'. Available from: www.uea.ac.uk/mac/comm/media/press/2008/july/CBT+superiority+questioned+at+conference (accessed 4 August 2011).

Corcoran, J. and Pillai, V. (2009) 'A review of the research on solution focused therapy', *British Journal of Social Work*, 39: 234–42.

Cornwall Council (2013) 'Assistive Technology – equipment to help people at home'. Available from: www.cornwall.gov.uk/default.aspx?page=5276 (accessed September 2013).

COSCA (2011) 'Counselling and psychotherapy: COSCA's description'. Available from: www.cosca.org.uk/new_documents.php?headingno=9&heading=Counselling (accessed 6 December 2012).

Coulshed, V. and Orme, J. (2006) *Social Work Practice*, 4th edn. Basingstoke: Palgrave Macmillan.

Coulshed, V and Orme, J. (2012) *Social Work Practice*, 5th edn. Basingstoke: Palgrave Macmillan.

Coulshed, V., Mullender, A., Jones, D.N. and Thompson, N. (2006) *Management in Social Work*, 3rd edn. Basingstoke: Palgrave Macmillan.

Courtney, M. and Iwaniec, D. (eds) (2009) *Residential Care of Children Comparative Studies*. New York: Oxford University Press.

Cowager, C.D. (1994) 'Assessing client strengths: clinical assessment for client empowerment', *Social Work*, 39 (3): 262–67.

Craig, P. (1997) 'Formal and substantive conceptions of the rule of law: an analytical framework', *P.L*: 467–87.

Cree, V. and Myers, S. (2008) *Social Work Making a Difference*. Bristol: The Policy Press.

Crime and Justice Institute (2004) *Implementing Evidence-Based Principles in Community Corrections: The Principles of Effective Intervention*. Available from: http://nicic.gov/pubs/2004/019342.pdf (accessed 15 November 2011).

Daniel, B. (2007) 'Assessment and children', in J. Lishman (ed.), *Handbook for Practice Learning in Social Work and Social Care: Knowledge and Theory*. London: Jessica Kingsley Publishers.

Daniel, B. and Wassel, S (2002) *The Early Years: Assessing and Promoting Resilience in Vulnerable Children*. London: Jessica Kingsley.

Daniel, B., Wassell, S. and Gilligan, R. (2010) *Child Development for Child Care and Protection Workers*, 2nd edn. London: Jessica Kingsley Publishers. pp. 115–27.

Davey, V., Fernández, J.L., Knapp, M., Vick, N., Jolly, D., Swift, P., Tobin, R., Kendall, J., Ferrie, J., Pearson, C., Mercer, G. and Priestley, M. (2007) *Direct Payments: A National Survey of Direct Payments Policy and Practice*. Personal Social Services Research Unit, London School of Economics and Political Science.

Davidson, R. (2008) Robin Davidson on Layard and the limitations of Cognitive Behavioural Therapy (CBT). Podcast on the *Film Exchange on Drugs and Alcohol* [online]. Available from: www.fead.org.uk/video65/Robin-Davidson-on-Layard-and-the-limitations-of-Cognitive-Behavioural-Therapy-(CBT)html (accessed 27 July 2011).

Davies, M. (ed.) (2008) *The Blackwell Companion to Social Work*, 3rd edn. Oxford: Blackwell.

Davis, A. (1996) 'Risk work and mental health', in H. Kemshall and J. Pritchard (eds), *Good Practice in Risk Assessment and Risk Management*. London: Jessica Kingsley Publishers.

Day, J. (2006) *Interprofessional Working: An Essential Guide for Health- and Social-Care Professionals*. Cheltenham: Nelson Thornes.

Deci, E.L. and Ryan, R.M. (1985) *Intrinsic Motivation and Self Determination in Human Behavior*. New York: Plenum.

Denney, D. (2005) *Risk and Society*. London: Sage.

Department of Health (1995) *Child Protection and Child Abuse: Messages from Research: The Child Protection Series*. London: The Stationery Office.

Department of Health (2001) *Valuing People: A New Strategy for Learning Disability for the 21st Century*. London: The Stationery Office.

Department of Health (2002) *Mental Health Policy Implementation Guide: Dual Diagnosis Good Practice Guide*. London: Department of Health Publications.

Department of Health (2007) *A National Service Framework for Older People*. London: Department of Health.

Department of Health (2009) *Living Well with Dementia: A National Dementia Strategy*. London: Department of Health. Available from: www.dh.gov.uk/en/Publicationsandstatistics/Publications/PublicationsPolicyAndGuidance/DH_113018 (accessed 9 February 2012).

Department of Health (2010) *A Vision for Adult Social Care: Capable Communities and Active Citizens*. London: Department of Health. Available from: www.dh.gov.uk/en/Publicationsandstatistics/Publications/PublicationsPolicyAndGuidance/DH_121508 (accessed 22 April 2012).

Department of Health (2011a) *Equity and Excellence: Liberating the NHS*. Available from: www.dh.gov.uk/en/Publicationsandstatistics/Publications/PublicationsPolicyAndGuidance/DH_117353 (accessed 9 February 2012).

Department of Health (2011b) *Talking Therapies: A Four Year Plan of Action*. Available from: www.dh.gov.uk/prod_consum_dh/groups/dh_digitalassets/documents/digitalasset/dh_123985.pdf (accessed 3 August 2011).

Department of Health (2013) *Making Sure Health and Social Care Services Work Together*. London: Department of Health.

Dewane, C. J. (2006) 'Use of self: a primer revisited', *Clinical Social Work Journal*, 34(4): 543–58.

Dicey, A.V. (1885) *Introduction to the Study of the Law of the Constitution*, 8th edn. London: Macmillan.

DiClemente, C., Bellino, L. and Neavins, T. (1999) 'Motivation for change and alcoholism treatment', *Alcoholism Research and Health*, 23 (2): 86-92.

Diggins, M. (2004) *Teaching and Learning Communication Skills in Social Work*. London: Social Care Institute for Excellence. Available from: www.scie.org.uk/publications/guides/guide05/files/guide05.pdf (accessed 4 November 2012).

Dockar-Drysdale, B. (1968) *Therapy and Child Care*. London: Longmans, Green.

Doel, M. (1994) 'Task-centred work', in C. Hanvey and T. Philpot (eds), *Practical Social Work*. London: Routledge. pp. 22–36.

Doel, M. (2010) 'Service-user perspective on relationship', in G. Ruch, D. Turney and A. Ward (eds), *Relationship-Based Social Work: Getting to the Heart of Practice*. London: Jessica Kingsley Publishers.

Doel, M. and Marsh, P. (1992) *Task-Centred Social Work*. Aldershot: Ashgate.

Doel, M. and Shardlow, S.M. (2005) *Modern Social Work Practice*. Aldershot: Ashgate.

Dominelli, L. (1996) 'Deprofessionalizing social work, anti-oppressive practice, competencies and postmodernism', *British Journal of Social Work*, 26: 153–7.

Dominelli, L. (2002) *Anti-Oppressive Social Work Theory and Practice*. Basingstoke: Palgrave Macmillan.

Dorling, D., Mitchell, R., Orford, S., Shaw, M. and Tunstall, H. (2009) 'Health inequalities', in R. Kitchin and N. Thrift (eds), *International Encyclopedia of Human Geography*, Vol. 5. Oxford: Elsevier. pp. 46–50.

Downie, R.S. and Telfer, E. (1980) *Caring and Curing*. London: Methuen.

Drury Hudson, J. (1997) 'A model of professional knowledge for social work practice', *Australian Social Work*, 50 (3): 35–44.

Dubé, L., Bourhis, A. and Jacob, R. (2005) 'The impact of structuring characteristics on the launching of virtual communities of practice', *Journal of Organizational Change Management*, 18 (2): 145–66.

Dullea, K. and Mullender, A. ([1999] 2004) 'Evaluation and empowerment', in S. Gerhardt, *Why Love Matters: How Affection Shapes a Baby's Brain*. Hove: Brunner-Routledge.

Dulmus, N.C. and Hilarski, C. (2003) *When Stress Constitutes Trauma and Trauma Constitutes Crisis: The Stress–Trauma–Crisis Continuum*. Knoxville, TN: Oxford University Press.

DWP (2012a) *Fraud and Error in the Benefit System: 2011/12 Estimates (Great Britain)*. Leeds: Department for Work and Pensions.

DWP (2012b) *Households Below Average Income Statistics*. London: Department of Work and Pensions.

Eagleton, T. (2011) *Why Marx Was Right*. New Haven, CT: Yale University Press.

Edelman, L. (2004) 'A relationship-based approach to early intervention', *Resources and Connections*, 3 (2): 1–9.

Elliot, R. and Freire, B. (2008) *Person-Centred/Experiential Therapies are Highly Effective: Summary of the 2008 Meta-Analysis.* British Association of Person-Centred Approach/University of Strathclyde. Available from: www.bapca.org.uk/uploads/files/Meta-Summary.BAPCA. pdf (accessed 4 July 2011).

Ellis, A. (1962) *Reason and Emotion in Psychotherapy.* New York: Lyle Stuart.

Ellis, S. and Dick, P. (2000) *Introduction to Organizational Behaviour.* Maidenhead: McGraw-Hill.

Emerson, E. (1995) *Challenging Behaviour: Analysis and Intervention in People with Severe Intellectual Disabilities.* Cambridge: Cambridge University Press.

Emerson, E. and Hatton, C. (2008) *People with Learning Disabilities in England.* Centre for Disability Research: Lancaster University. Available from: www.lancs.ac.uk/staff/emersone/ FASSWeb/Emerson_08_PWLDinEngland.pdf (accessed October 2013).

Emerson, E., Baines, S., Allerton, L. and Welch, V. (2011) *Health Inequalities and People with Learning Disabilities in the UK.* Learning Disabilities Observatory, DOH. Available from: www.improvinghealthandlives.org.uk/securefiles/131017_1439//IHaL%202011-09%20 HealthInequality2011.pdf (accessed October 2013).

Epstein, L. (1995) 'Brief task centred social work', in R.L. Edwards (ed.), *Encyclopaedia of Social Work,* 19th edn. Volume 1. Washington, DC: National Association of Social Workers. pp. 313–23.

Epstein, L. and Brown, L. (2002*) Brief Treatment and a New Look at the Task-Centered Approach.* Boston, MA: Allyn and Bacon.

Erikson, E. (1950) *Childhood and Society.* New York: W. W. Norton.

Erikson, E.H. (1956) 'The problem of ego identity', *Journal of the American Psychoanalytic Association,* IV: 56–121.

Erikson, E. (1965) *Childhood and Society.* Harmondsworth: Penguin.

Erikson, E. (1968) *Childhood and Society,* 2nd edn. New York: W.W. Norton.

Erikson, E. (1978) *Childhood and Society.* Hertfordshire: Triad/Paladin.

Ettridge, G. (2009) 'Enablement could help adult care through downturn'. Available from: www. communitycare.co.uk/Articles/30/11/2009/113281/enablement-could-help-adult-care-through-downturn.htm (accessed 3 December 2009).

Evans, C. and Fisher, M. (1999) 'Collaborative evaluation with service users', in I. Shaw and J. Lishman (eds), *Evaluation and Social Work Practice.* London: Sage.

Evans, M. and Whittaker, A. (2010) *Sensory Awareness and Social Work.* Exeter: Learning Matters.

Everitt, A. (2002) 'Research and development in social work', in R. Adams, L. Dominelli and M. Payne (eds), *Social Work: Themes, Issues and Critical Debates,* 2nd edn. Basingstoke: Palgrave Macmillan.

Evetts, J. (2003) 'The sociological analysis of professionalism: occupational change in the modern world', *International Sociology,* 18 (2): 395–415.

Fairbairn, R. (1952) *Psychoanalytical Study of the Personality.* New York and London: Routledge and Keegan Paul.

Fairburn, D. and Ronald, W. (1949) 'Steps in the recovery of an object-relations theory of the personality', *British Journal of Medical Psychology,* 22 (1–2): 26–31.

Ferguson, I. and Woodward, R. (2009) *Radical Social Work in Practice: Making a Difference.* Bristol: The Policy Press.

Fisher, J. (2006) *The General Election in the UK, May 2005.* London: Elsevier.

Flannery, R.B. and Everly, G.S. (2000) 'Crisis intervention: a review', *International Journal of Emergency Mental Health,* 2 (2): 119–25.

Fook, J. (2002) *Social Work: Critical Theory and Practice.* London: Sage.

Fook, J. (2007) 'Reflective practice and critical reflection', in J. Lishman (ed.), *Handbook for Practice Learning in Social Work and Social Care: Knowledge and Theory*. London: Jessica Kingsley Publishers. pp. 363–75.

Fook, J., Ryan, M. and Hawkins, L. (1997) 'Towards a theory of social work expertise', *British Journal of Social Work*, 27 (3): 339–417.

Forbes, J. and McCartney, E. (2010) 'Social capital theory: a cross-cutting analytic for teacher/therapist work in integrating children's services?', *Child Language Teaching and Therapy*, 26: 321–34.

Ford, P. and Postle, K. (2000) 'Task centred practice and care management', in P. Stepney and D. Ford (eds), *Social Work Models, Methods and Theories: A Framework for Practice*. Lyme Regis: Russell House. pp. 52–64.

Forest, M., O'Brien, J., Pearpoint, J. (1993) *PATH: A Workbook for Planning Positive Possible Futures*. Toronto: Inclusion Press.

Fraser, M.W., Richman, J.M. and Galinski, M.J. (1999) 'Risk, protection, and resilience: toward a conceptual framework for social work practice', *Social Work Research*, 23 (3): 131–43.

French, J.R.P. and Raven, B. ([1959]2001) 'The bases of social power', reprinted in I.G. Asherman and S.V. Asherman (eds), *The Negotiation Sourcebook*, 2nd edn. Amherst, MA: HRD Press. pp. 61–73.

Freud, A. (1946) *The Ego and the Mechanisms of Defense*. New York: International Universities Press.

Freud, A. (1993) *The Ego and the Mechanism of Defence*. New York. The Hogarth Press.

Freud, S. (1933) *New Introductory Lectures on Psychoanalysis*. New York: W.W. Norton.

Freud, S. (2001) *Complete Psychological Works of Sigmund Freud*, Vol. 15: *'Introductory Letters on Psycho-analysis'* (Part I and II). London: Vintage.

Frost, N. and Robinson, M. (2007) 'Joining up children's services: safeguarding children in multi-disciplinary teams', *Child Abuse Review*, 16: 184–99.

Frost, N. and Stein, M. (2009) 'Editorial: outcomes of integrated working with children and young people', *Children and Society*, 23: 315–19.

Frost, N., Robinson, M. and Anning, A. (2005) 'Social workers in multidisciplinary teams: issues and dilemmas for professional practice', *Child and Family Social Work*, 10: 187–96.

Gaine, C. (ed.) (2010) *Equality and Diversity in Social Work Practice*. Exeter: Learning Matters.

Gaine, C. and Gaylard, D. (2010) 'Equality, difference and diversity', in C. Gaine (ed.), *Equality and Diversity in Social Work Practice*. Exeter: Learning Matters.

Gallagher, M. and Smith, M. (2010) *Engaging with Involuntary Service Users in Social Work: Literature Review 1: Context and Overview*. Edinburgh: University of Edinburgh.

Galvani, S. and Forrester, D. (2011) *Social Work Services and Recovery from Substance Misuse: A Review of the Evidence*. Edinburgh: Scottish Government.

Gardner, A. (2011) *Personalisation in Social Work*. Exeter: Learning Matters.

Garfat, T. (2003) *Four Parts Magic: The Anatomy of a Child and Youth Care Intervention*. The International Child and Youth Care Network, cyc-online, Issue 50. Available from: www.cyc-net.org/cyc-online/cycol-0303-thom.html (accessed 21 September 2011).

Gerhardt, S. (2004) *Why Love Matters: How Affection Shapes a Baby's Brain*. Hove: Brunner–Routledge.

Gibbons, J.S., Bow, I., Butler, J and Powell, J. (1979) 'Service users reaction to task centred casework: a follow up study', *British Journal of Social Work*, 9 (2): 203–15.

Gibbs, G. (1988) *Learning by Doing: A Guide to Teaching and Learning Methods*. Oxford: Further Educational Unit, Oxford Polytechnic.

Gibson, A. (2007) 'Erikson's life cycle approach to development', in J. Lishman (ed.), *Handbook for Practice Learning in Social Work and Social Care*, 2nd edn. London: Jessica Kingsley. pp. 74–85.

Giddens, A. (1989) *Sociology*. Cambridge: Polity Press.

Gilligan, R. (2000) *Promoting Resilience*. London: British Agencies for Adoption and Fostering.

Gkika, S. (2010) 'Helping anxious people' in A. Grant (ed.), *Cognitive Behavioural Interventions for Mental Health Practitioners*. Exeter: Learning Matters.

Glaister, A. (2008) 'Introducing critical practice', in S. Fraser and S. Matthews (eds), *The Critical Practitioner in Social Work and Health Care*. London: Open University/Sage. pp. 8–26.

Glasby, J. and Dickinson, H. (2009) *International Perspectives on Health and Social Care: Partnership Working in Action*. Oxford: Blackwell.

Goffman, E. (1961) *On the Characteristics of Total Institutions*. Harmondsworth: Penguin.

Golan, N. (1978) *Treatment in Crisis Situations*. New York: Free Press.

Goldacre, B. (2012) *Bad Pharma: How Drug Companies Mislead Doctors and Harm Patients*. London: HarperCollins.

Goldiamond, I. (1974) 'Toward a constructional approach to social problems: ethical and constitutional issues', *Behaviorism*, 2 (1): 1–84.

Goodwin, J. (2012) 'The last defence of Wednesbury', *P.L.*: 445–67.

Gordon, J. and Davis, R. (2011) 'Introduction', in R. Davis and J. Gordon (eds), *Social Work and the Law in Scotland*, 2nd edn. Milton Keynes: Open University Press.

Gorman, K., Gregory, M., Hayles, M. and Parton, N. (eds) (2006) *Constructive Work with Offenders*. London: Jessica Kingsley Publishers.

Gossop, M. (2006) *Treating Drug Misuse Problems: Evidence of Effectiveness*. London: National Treatment Agency for Substance Misuse.

Gossop, M. (2011) Michael Gossop on Behaviourism, Cognitive Therapy and CBT. Podcast on the *Film Exchange on Drugs and Alcohol*. Available from: www.fead.org.uk/contributor. php?contributorid=41 (accessed 27 July 2011).

Gould, N. (1999) 'Qualitative practice evaluation', in I. Shaw and J. Lishman (eds), *Evaluation and Social Work Practice*. London: Sage.

Graham, G. (2010) *The Disordered Mind: An Introduction to Philosophy of Mind and Mental Illness*. London: Routledge.

Gray, M. and Webb, S.A. (2010) *Ethics and Value Perspectives in Social Work*. Basingstoke: Palgrave Macmillan.

Gregory, R. (1997) *Eye and Brain: The Psychology of Seeing*. Oxford: Oxford University Press.

Griffin, M.L. (2010) 'Using critical incidents to promote and access reflective thinking in preservice teachers, reflective practice', *International and Multidisciplinary Perspectives*, 4 (2): 207–20.

GSSC (General Social Services Council) (2010) Available from: www.gssc.org.uk/page/35/ Codes+of+practice.html (accessed 28 February 2012).

The Guardian (2011) 'Council's social care cuts are unlawful, high court rules', 11 November. Available from: www.guardian.co.uk/society/2011/nov/11/social-care-cuts-unlawful-court (accessed 23 August 2013).

The Guardian (2012) 'David Cameron may be a posh boy, but he's the best the Conservatives can do', 23 April. Available from: www.theguardian.com/commentisfree/2012/apr/23/cameron-posh-boy-best-conservatives-can-do (accessed 23 August 2013).

Guthrie, T. (2011) *Social Work Law in Scotland*, 3rd edn. Haywards Heath: Bloomsbury Professional Ltd.

H&M Revenue and Customs (2012) *Measuring Tax Gaps 2012: Tax Gap Estimates for 2010–11*. HMRC Corporate Communications.

Hall, C. (1997) *Social Work as Narrative: Story Telling and Persuasion in Professional Texts*. Aldershot: Avebury.

Hammick, M., Freeth, D., Copperman, J. and Goodsman, D. (2009) *Being Interprofessional*. Polity Press: Cambridge.

Hanton, P. (2011) *Skills in Solution Focused Brief Counselling and Psychotherapy*. London: Sage.

Hardwick, L. and Worsley, A. (2011) *Doing Social Work Research*. London: Sage.

Harper, R. and Hardy, S. (2000) 'An evaluation of motivational interviewing as a method of intervention with clients in a probation setting', *British Journal of Social Work*, 30(3): 393–400.

Harris, J. (2008) 'State social work: constructing the present from moments in the past', *British Journal of Social Work*, 38: 662–79.

Hartmann, H. (1964) *Essays on Ego Psychology*. London: The Hogarth Press.

Hayek, F. (1960) *The Constitution of Liberty*. Chicago, IL: University of Chicago Press.

Hazler, R.J. and Barwick, N. (2001) *The Therapeutic Environment*. Buckingham: The Open University.

Healy, K. (2005) *Social Work Theories in Context: Creating Frameworks for Practice*. Basingstoke: Palgrave.

Healy, K. and Mulholland, J. (2007) *Writing Skills for Social Workers*. London: Sage.

Healy, M. and Jenkins, A. (2000) 'Kolb's Experiential Learning Theory and its application in geography in Higher Education', *Journal of Geography*, 99: 185–95.

Hean, S., MacLeod Clark, J., Adams, K. and Humphris, D. (2006) 'Will opposites attract? Similarities and differences in students' perceptions of the stereotype profiles of other health and social care professional groups', *Journal of Interprofessional Care*, 20 (2): 162–81.

Heather, N., Rollnick, S., Bell, A. and Richmond, R. (1996) 'Effects of brief counselling among male heavy drinkers identified on general hospital wards', *Drug and Alcohol Review*, 15: 29–38.

Heffernan, K. (2008) 'Responding to global shifts in social work through the language of service user and service user involvement', *International Journal of Social Welfare*, 18: 375–84.

Heider, F. (1958) *The Psychology of Inter-Professional Relations*. New York: Wiley.

Held, S. (2009) 'Emotional intelligence, emotion and collaborative leadership', in J. McKimm and K. Phillips (eds), *Leadership and Management in Integrated Services*. Exeter: Learning Matters. pp. 106–21.

Heller, T., Reynolds, J., Gomm, R., Muston, R. and Pattison, S.(eds) (1996) *Mental Health Matters: A Reader*. London: Open University/Macmillan.

Henderson, J. and Forbat, L. (2004) 'Relationship-based social policy: personal and policy constructions of "care"', in M. Robb, S. Barrett, C. Komaromy and A. Rogers (eds), *Communication, Relationships and Care: A Reader*. London: Routledge.

Henke, H. (1996) *Learning Theory: Applying Kolb's Learning Style Inventory with Computer Based Training*. Available from: www.chartula.con/LEARNINGTHEORY.pdf (accessed 1 March 2012).

Hennessey, R. (2011) *Relationship Skills in Social Work Skills*. London: Sage.

Hewett, D. and Nind, M. (1998) *Interaction in Action: Reflections on the Use of Intensive Interaction*. London: David Fulton.

Heywood, A. (2004) *Political Theory: An Introduction*, 3rd edn. London: Palgrave Macmillan.

Hickey, G. and Kipping, C. (1998) 'Exploring the concept of user involvement in mental health through a participation continuum', *Journal of Clinical Nursing*, 7 (1): 83–8.

Higham, P. and Torkington, C. (2009) 'Partnerships with people who use services and carers', in P. Higham (ed.), *Post-Qualifying Social Work Practice*. London: Sage. pp. 34–46.

Hirsch, D., Davis, A. and Smith, N. (2009) *A Minimum Income Standard for Britain in 2009*. York: Joseph Rowntree Foundation.

HM Government (2008) *Information Sharing: Guidance for Practitioners and Managers.* Available from: http://webarchive.nationalarchives.gov.uk/20130401151715/https://www.education.gov.uk/publications/eOrderingDownload/00807-2008BKT-EN-March09.pdfHM (accessed August 2013).

HM Government (2011) *No Health without Mental Health: A Cross-Government Mental Health Outcomes Strategy for People of All Ages.* London: Department of Health. Available from: www.dh.gov.uk/prod_consum_dh/groups/dh_digitalassets/documents/digitalasset/dh_124058.pdf (accessed 1 August 2011).

HM Prisons (2003, reissued 2005) *PSO 2205 Offender Assessment and Sentence Management.* London: Ministry of Justice. Available from: www.justice.gov.uk/downloads/offenders/psipso/pso/PSO_2205_offender_assessment_and_sentence_management.doc (accessed 4 October 2013).

Hoff, A.H. and Hallisey, B.J. (2009) *People in Crisis: Clinical and Diversity Perspectives*, 6th edn. Abingdon: Routledge.

Hohman, M.M. (1998) 'Motivational interviewing: an intervention tool for child welfare caseworkers working with substance-abusing parents', *Child Welfare*, 77(3): 275–89.

Honey, P. (2010) *The Learning Style Questionnaire. 80 Item version: England and Wales.* Maidenhead: Peter Honey Publications.

Honey, P. and Mumford, A. (1982) *The Manuals of Learning Styles.* Maidenhead: Honey Press.

Horder, W. (2002) 'Care management', in M. Davies (ed.), *The Blackwell Companion to Social Work*, 2nd edn. Oxford: Blackwell.

Hothersall, S.J. and Bolger, J. (2010) *Social Policy for Social Work, Social Care and the Caring Professions: Scottish Perspectives.* Surrey: Ashgate.

Howe, D. (1987) *An Introduction to Social Work Theory.* Aldershot: Gower.

Howe, D. (1995) *Attachment Theory for Social Work Practice.* London: Macmillan.

Howe, D. (1997) 'Psychosocial and relationship-based theories for child and family social work: political philosophy, psychology and welfare practice', *Child and Family Social Work*, 2: 161–9.

Howe, D. (1998) 'Relationship-based thinking and practice in social work', *Journal of Social Work Practice*, 12 (1): 45–56.

Hubbard, G., Tester, S., Downs, M. and Murna, G. (2003) 'Meaningful social interactions between older people in institutional care settings', *Ageing and Society*, 23: 99–114.

Hudson, B. and Macdonald, G. (1986) *Behavioural Social Work: An Introduction.* Basingstoke: Macmillan Education.

Hughes, D. (2006) *Building the Bonds of Attachment: Awakening Love in Deeply Troubled Children.* New York: Jason Aronson.

Hugman, R. and Smith, D. (1995) *Ethical Issues in Social Work.* London: Routledge.

Hyman, B. and Pendrick, C. (1999) *The OCD Workbook. Your Guide to Breaking Free from Obsessive–Compulsive Disorder.* Oakland: New Harbinger Publications.

IFSW (International Federation of Social Workers) (2004) *Ethics in Social Work: Statement of Principles.* Available from: www.ifsw.org/p38000324.html (accessed 10 October 2011).

Improvement Service (2008) *Collaborative Gain Research Study – Report for the Improvement Service.* Broxburn: Improvement Service.

Institute of Alcohol Studies (2002) *IAS Factsheet – What Is Problem Drinking?* Cambridgeshire: Institute of Alcohol Studies.

Institute of Alcohol Studies (2010a) *IAS Factsheet – Binge Drinking: Nature, Prevalence and Causes.* Cambridgeshire: Institute of Alcohol Studies.

Institute of Alcohol Studies (2010b) *IAS Factsheet – Excessive and Problem Drinking in England and Wales*. Cambridgeshire: Institute of Alcohol Studies.

James, K.R. and Gilliland, B.E. (2001) *Crisis Intervention Strategies*, 4th edn. Belmont, CA: Wadsworth/Thompson Learning.

Jarvis, T., Tebutt, J., Mattick, R. and Shand, F. (2005) *Treatment Approaches for Alcohol and Drug Dependence*, 2nd edn. Chichester: John Wiley.

Jasper, M. (2005a) 'Using reflective writing within research', *Journal of Research in Nursing*, 10(3): 247–260.

Jasper, M. (2005b) *Beginning Reflective Practice*. Cheltenham: Nelson Thomas.

Johns, R. (2011) *Using the Law in Social Work*, 5th edn. Exeter: Learning Matters.

Jones, B. and Norton, P. (2010) *Politics UK*, 4th edn. Harlow: Prentice Hall.

Jones, O. (2010) *Chavs: The Demonization of the Working Class*. London: Verso.

Joseph Rowntree Foundation (2006) *Findings: Making User Involvement Work: Supporting Service User Networking and Knowledge*. York: Joseph Rowntree Foundation.

Joseph Rowntree Foundation (2013) *A Minimum Income Standard for the UK*. York: Joseph Rowntree Foundation.

Jowell, J. and Oliver, D. (eds) (2011) *The Changing Constitution*. Oxford: Oxford University Press.

Kabat-Zinn, J. (1994) *Wherever You Go, There You Are: Mindfulness Meditation in Everyday Life*. New York: Hyperion.

Kahan, B. (1994) *Growing Up in Groups*. London: HMSO.

Kan, M.Y., Sullivan, O. and Gershuny, J. I. (2011) 'Gender convergence in domestic work: discerning the effects of interactional and institutional barriers from large-scale data', *Sociology*, 45(2): 234–251.

Kant, I. ([1785]1997) *Groundwork of the Metaphysics of Moral*s. Cambridge: Cambridge University Press.

Kaplan, P. (1998) *The Human Odyssey-Lifespan Development*. London: Brooks/Cole.

Kaplan, S. and Garrick, J.B. (1981) 'On the quantitative definition of risk', *Risk Analysis*, I (I).

Karoly, P. (1993) 'Mechanisms of self-regulation: a systems view', *Annual Review of Psychology*, 44: 23–52.

Kazi, M.A.F. and Wilson, J.T. (1996) 'Applying single case evaluation methodology in a British social work agency', *Research on Social Work Practice*, 6 (1): 5–26.

Kearsley, G. (2009) 'Conditions of Learning' [R. Gagne] on the *Theory into Practice Database*. [online]. Available from: http://tip.psychology.org/gagne.html (accessed 28 July 2011).

Keenan, C. (2007) 'Group care', in J. Lishman (ed.), *Handbook for Practice Learning in Social Work and Social Care*. London: Jessica Kingsley. pp. 249–68.

Kelly, G.A. (1955) *The Psychology of Personal Constructs*. New York: Norton.

Kemshall, H. (2002) 'Risk assessment and management', in M. Davies (ed.), *The Blackwell Companion to Social Work*, 2nd edn. Oxford: Blackwell.

Kemshall, H. and Maguire, M. (2001) 'Public protection, partnership and risk penality: the multi-agency risk management of sexual and violent offenders', *Punishment & Society*, 3(2): 237–64.

Kemshall, H. and Pritchard, J. (1996) *Good Practice in Risk Assessment and Risk Management*. London: Jessica Kingsley Publishers.

Kendrick, A. (2011) 'Partnership with service users', in R. Davies and J. Gordon (eds), *Social Work and the Law in Scotland*, 2nd edn. Basingstoke: Palgrave Macmillan. pp. 201–16.

Kerr, B., Gordon, J., MacDonald, C. and Stalker, K. (2005) *Effective Social Work with Older People*. Available from: www.scotland.gov.uk/Publications/2005/12/16104017/40178 (accessed 9 February 2012).

Killen, R. (2006) *Effective Teaching Strategies*, 4th edn. Sydney: Cengage Learning Australia.

Kline, R. and Preston-Shoot, M. (2012) *Professional Accountability in Social Care and Health: Challenging Unacceptable Practice and its Management.* Exeter: Sage/Learning Matters.

Knott, C. and Scragg, T. (2010) *Reflective Practice in Social Work*, 2nd edn. Exeter: Learning Matters.

Kolb, D.A. (1984) *Experiential Learning: Experience as the Source of Learning and Development.* Englewood Cliffs, NJ: Prentice Hall.

Kolb, L.B.A. and Kolb, D.A. (2005) 'Learning styles and learning spaces: enhancing experiential learning in higher education', *Academy of Management Learning and Education*, 4 (2): 193–212.

Koprowska, J. (2010) *Communication and Interpersonal Skills in Social Work*, 3rd edn. Exeter: Learning Matters.

Korner, M. (2010) 'Interprofessional teamwork in medical rehabilitation: a comparison of multi-disciplinary and interdisciplinary team approach', *Clinical Rehabilitation*, 24: 745–55.

Kübler-Ross, E. (1969) *On Death and Dying.* London: Routledge.

Kübler-Ross, E. and Kessler, D. (2005) *On Grief and Grieving: Finding the Meaning of Grief Through the Five Stages of Loss.* New York: Scribner.

Labriola, A. (1918 [2005]) *Essays on the Materialistic Conception of History.* New York: Cosimo Classics.

Lawler, S. (2008) *Identity.* Cambridge: Polity Press.

Leftwich, A. (ed.) (2004) *What Is Politics?* Cambridge: Polity Press.

Leggatt, A. (2000) *Review of Tribunals. The Legatt Report.* Available from: http://webarchive.nationalarchives.gov.uk/20090805165412/http://www.tribunals-review.org.uk/cp14-06-00.htm (accessed August 2013).

Lester, A. (2009) 'The European Court of Human Rights after 50 years', *E.H.R.L.R*, 461.

Lewis, S. and Roberts, A.R. (2001) *Crisis Assessment Tools: The Good, the Bad and the Available.* Columbia University School of Social Work/Oxford University Press. Available from: http://btci.stanford.clockss.org/cgi/reprint/1/1/17.pdf (accessed 12 December 2010).

Lewin, K. (1948) *Resolving Social Conflicts: Selected Papers on Group Dynamics* (Gertrude W. Lewin, ed.). New York: Harper and Row.

Lewin, K. (1951) *Field Theory in Social Science: Selected Theoretical Papers* (D. Cartwright, ed.). New York: Harper and Row.

Lewy, L. (2010) 'The complexities of interprofessional learning/working: has the agenda lost its way?', *Health Education Journal*, 69 (1): 4-12.

LGA (Local Government Association), ADASS (Association of Directors of Adult Social Services), NHS and others (2007) *Putting People First: A Shared Vision and Commitment to the Transformation of Adult Social Care.* London: Department of Health.

Liebert, R.M. and Baron, R.A. (1972) 'Some immediate effects of televised violence on children's behaviour', *Developmental Psychology*, 6: 469–75.

Lindemann, E. (1944) 'Symptomatology and management of acute grief', *Journal of Psychiatry*, 101: 141–8.

Lindsay, T. (2009) 'Cognitive behavioural approaches', in T. Lindsay (ed.), *Social Work Intervention.* Exeter: Learning Matters. pp. 63–77.

Ling, T. (2012) 'Evaluating complex and unfolding interventions in real time', *Evaluation*, 18 (1): 79–91.

Lingford-Hughes, A., Welsch, S. and Nutt, D. (2004) Evidence-based guidelines for the pharmacological management of substance misuse, addiction and co-morbidity: recommendations from the British Association for Psychopharmachology', *Journal of Psychopharmacology*, 18 (3): 293–335.

Lipchik, E., Derks, J., LaCourt, M. and Nunnally, E. (2012) 'The evolution of solution-focused brief therapy', in N C. Franklin, T.S. Trepper, W.J. Gingerich and E.E. McCollum (eds), *Solution-Focused Brief Therapy: A Handbook of Evidence-Based Practice*. New York: OUP.

Lishman, J. (1978) 'A clash in perspective? a study of worker and client perceptions of social work', *BJSW*, 8(3): 301–11.

Lishman, J. (1994) *Communication in Social Work*. Basingstoke: Macmillan.

Lishman, J. (1998) 'Personal and professional development', in R. Adams, L. Dominelli and M. Payne (eds), *Social Work Themes: Issues and Critical Debates*. Basingstoke: Macmillan.

Lishman, J. (ed.) (2007) *Handbook for Practice Learning in Social Work and Social Care: Knowledge and Theory*. London: Jessica Kingsley Publishers.

Lishman, J. (2009) *Communication in Social Work*. Basingstoke: Macmillan.

Lister, P.G. (2012) *Integrating Social Work Theory and Practice. A Practical Skills Guide*. London: Routledge.

Lister, P.G. and Crisp, R.B. (2007) 'Critical incident analysis: a practice learning tool for students and practitioners', *Social Work in Action*, 19 (1): 47–60.

Locke, E.A. (1968) 'Toward a theory of task motivation and incentives', *Organizational Behavior and Human Performance*, May: 157–89.

Lord Laming (2009) *The Protection of Children in England: A Progress Report*. London: The Stationery Office.

Luft, J. (1984) *Group Processes: An Introduction to Group Dynamics*. Mountainview, CA: Mayfield.

Maas-Lowit, M. (2010) 'Mental health', in S. Hothersall and M. Maas-Lowit (eds), *Need, Risk and Protection in Social Work Practice*. Exeter: Learning Matters. pp 82–96.

Macdonald, G. (2007) 'Cognitive behavioural social work', in J. Lishman (ed.), *Handbook for Practice Learning in Social Work and Social Care: Knowledge and Theory*. London: Jessica Kingsley Publishers. pp. 169–87.

Macdonald, G. and Sheldon, B. (1998) 'Changing one's mind: the final frontier?', *Issues in Social Work Education*, 18: 3–25.

MacQueen, H.L. (ed.) (2012) *Gloag and Henderson: The Law of Scotland*, 13th edn. Edinburgh: W. Green.

Maier, H. (1979a) 'The core of care: essential ingredients for the development of children at home and away from home', *Child Care Quarterly*, 8 (4): 161–73.

Maier, H. (1979b) *Essential Components in Care and Treatment Environments for Children*. Available from: www.cyc-net.org/pdf/classicMaier.pdf (accessed 29 December 2011).

Marmot, M. (2010) *Fair Society, Healthy Lives: The Marmot Review*. Available from: www.instituteofhealthequity.org/Content/FileManager/pdf/fairsocietyhealthylives.pdf (accessed 16 October 2013).

Marriott, A. and Wright, H. (2002) *All for One*. Available from: www.communitycare.co.uk/Articles/2002/05/16/36410/All-for-one.htm (accessed 9 February 2012).

Marris, P. (1986) *Loss and Change*. Abingdon: Routledge.

Marsh, P. (2002) 'Task-centred work', in M. Davies (ed.), *The Blackwell Companion to Social Work*, 2nd edn. Oxford: Blackwell. pp. 106–13.

Marsh, P. (2007) 'Task-centred practice', in J. Lishman (ed.), *Handbook for Practice Learning in Social Work and Social Care; Knowledge and Theory*. London: Jessica Kingsley Publishers. pp. 188–200.

Marsh, P. and Doel, M. (2005) *The Task-Centred Book*. Abingdon: Routledge.

Marsh, P. and Fisher, M. (1992) *Good Intentions: Developing Partnership in Social Services*. York: Joseph Rowntree Foundation.

Marsh, P. and Trieseliotis, J. (1996) *Ready to Practice? Social Practitioners and Probation Officers: Their Training and First Year in Work.* Aldershot: Avebury.

Marx, K. and Engels, F. (1848) *Manifesto of the Communist Party, 1.* New York: International Publishers.

Maslow, A. (1943) 'A theory of human motivation', *Psychology Review,* 50: 370–96.

Maslow, A. (1954) *Motivation and Personality.* New York: Harper and Row.

Mason, J. and Scior, K. (2004) '"Diagnostic overshadowing" amongst clinicians working with people with intellectual disabilities in the UK', *Journal of Applied Research in Intellectual Disabilities,* 17 (2): 85–90.

Mattison, M. (2000) 'Ethical decision making: the person in the process', *Social Work,* 45 (3): 201–12.

Mayer, J.E. and Timms, N. (1970) *The Client Speaks: Working Class Impressions of Casework.* London: Routledge and Kegan Paul/New York: Atherton Press.

McColgan, M. (2009) 'Task-centred work', in T. Lindsay (ed.), *Social Work Intervention.* Exeter: Learning Matters.

McDougall, F. A., Matthews, F. E., Kvaal, K., Dewey, M.E. and Brayne, C. (2007) 'Prevalence and symptomatology of depression in older people living in institutions in England and Wales', *Age and Ageing,* 36 (5): 562–68.

McGee, J.J., Menolascino, P.E., Hobbs, D.C. and Menousek, P.E. (1987) *Gentle Teaching: A Non-Aversive Approach to Helping Persons with Mental Retardation.* New York: Human Science Press.

McGinnis, E. (2009) 'Crisis intervention', in T. Lindsay (ed.), *Social Work Intervention.* Exeter: Learning Matters.

McGuire, J. (ed.) (1995) *What Works: Reducing Reoffending – Guidelines from Research and Practice.* Chichester: Wiley.

McGuire, J. (2007) 'Programmes for probationers', in G. McIvor and P. Raynor (eds), *Developments in Social Work with Offenders.* London: Jessica Kingsley Publishers.

McKendrick, J.H., Sinclair, S., Irwin, A., O'Donnell, G.S. and Dobbie, L. (2008) *The Media, Poverty and Public Opinion in the UK.* York: Jospeh Rowntree Foundation.

McKergow, M. (2007) *Solutions Focus: How to Change Everything by Changing as Little as Possible.* London: The Centre for Solutions Focus at Work. Available from: www.asfct.org/documents/ SF%20How%20to%20change%20everything.pdf (accessed 18 May 2012).

McLaughlin, H. (2009) 'What's in a name: "client", "patient", "customer", "consumer", "expert by experience", "service user" – what's next?', *British Journal of Social Work,* 39: 1101–17.

McLean, T. (2007) 'Interdisciplinary practice', in J. Lishman (ed.), *Handbook for Practice Learning in Social Work and Social Care,* 2nd edn. London: Jessica Kingsley Publishers. pp. 322–43.

McLeod, J. (2009) *Introduction to Counselling,* 4th edn. Maidenhead: Open University Press.

McMurran, M. (2002) *Motivating Offenders to Change: A Guide to Enhancing Engagement in Therapy.* Chichester: Wiley.

McNeill, F. and Whyte, B. (2007) *Reducing Reoffending: Social Work and Community Justice in Scotland.* Cullompton: Willan Publishing.

McNeill, F., Batchelor, S., Burnett, R. and Knox, J. (2005) *21st Century Social Work: Reducing Reoffending: Key Practice Skills.* Edinburgh: Scottish Executive.

Mead, G.H. (1934) *Mind, Self and Society.* Chicago, IL: University of Chicago Press.

Mencap (2013) *All about Learning Disability: Causes.* [online] London: Mencap. Available from: www.mencap.org.uk/all-about-learning-disability/about-learning-disability/causes (accessed 5 September 2013).

Menzies-Lyth, I. (1988) *Containing Anxiety in Institutions: Selected Essays,* vol. 1. London: Free Association Books.

Millard, B. (2011) 'Extent and trends in illicit drug use', in K. Smith and J. Flattley (eds), *Drug Misuse Declared: Findings from the 2010/11 British Crime Survey*. London: Home Office.

Miller, E. and Cameron, K. (2011) 'Challenges and benefits in implementing shared inter-agency assessment across the UK: A literature review', *Journal of Interprofessional Care*, 25 (1): 39–45.

Miller, L. (2006) *Counselling Skills for Social Work*. London: Sage.

Miller, W. (2005) 'A message from Albuquerque', *Drug and Alcohol Findings*, 13.

Miller, W., Benefield, R.G. and Tonnigan, J.S. (1993) 'Enhancing motivation for change in problem drinking: a controlled comparison of two therapist styles', *Journal of Consulting Clinical Psychology*, 61 (3): 455–61.

Miller, W.R. and Rollnick, S. (1991) 'Motivational interviewing and self-determination theory', *Journal of Social and Clinical Psychology*, 24 (6): 811–31.

Miller, W.R. and Rollnick, S. (2002) *Motivational Interviewing: Preparing People for Change*, 2nd edn. London: Guilford Press.

Miller, W. and Wilbourne, P. (2002) 'Mesa grande: a methodological analysis of clinical trials of treatments for alcohol use disorders', *Addiction*, 97: 265–77.

Miller, W.R., Zweben, A., DiClemente, C.C. and Rychtari, R.G. (1993, reprinted 1999) *National Institute on Alcohol Abuse and Alcoholism Project MATCH Monograph Series*, Volume 2. Maryland, USA.

Mills, C.W. (1959) *The Sociological Imagination*. Harmondsworth: Penguin.

Milner, J. and O'Byrne, P. (2002) *Brief Counselling: Narratives and Solutions*. Basingstoke: Palgrave Macmillan.

Milner, J. and O'Byrne, P. (2009) *Assessment in Social Work*, 3rd edn. Basingstoke: Palgrave MacMillan.

Ministry of Justice (2012) *About the National Offender Management Service*. [online] London: Gov.UK. Available from: www.justice.gov.uk/about/noms (accessed 7 October 2013).

Minuchin, S. (1979) *Families and Family Therapy*. London: Tavistock.

Mitchell, J.T. (2011) *Important Crisis Intervention Background and Terminology. Empowered Learning*. Available from: www.drjeffmitchell.com/articles/20-important-crisis-intervention-background-and-terminology.html (accessed 19 September 2011).

Mitchell, R., Parker, V., Giles, M. and White, N. (2010) 'Review: Toward realizing the potential of diversity in composition of interprofessional health care teams: an examination of the cognitive and psychosocial dynamics of interprofessional collaboration', *Medical Care Research and Review*, 67: 3–26.

Molyneaux, V., Butchard, S., Simpson, J. and Murray, C. (2011) 'Reconsidering the term "carer": a critique of the universal adoption of the term "carer"', *Ageing and Society*, 31: 422–37.

Morago, P. (2006) 'Evidence based practice: from medicine to social work', *European Journal of Social Work*, 9 (4): 461–77.

Morago, P. (2007) 'Dissemination and implementation of evidence based practice: a UK survey', *Journal of Evidence-Based Social Work*, 7 (5): 452–65.

Morgan, S. (2004) 'Positive risk taking: an idea whose time has come', *Health Care Risk Report* 10 (10): 18–19.

Morrison, T. (2007) 'Emotional intelligence, emotion and social work: context, characteristics, complications and contribution', *British Journal of Social Work*, 37 (2): 245–63.

Moss, B. (2008) *Communication Skills for Health and Social Care*. London: Sage Publications.

Munro, E. (1998) *Understanding Social Work*. London: The Athlone Press.

Munroe, R.L. and Munroe, R.H. (1975) *Cross-Cultural Human Development*. Belmont, CA: Wadsworth.

Murphy, J.E., Benson, T.A., Vuchinich, R.E., Deskins, M.M., Eakin, D. and Flood, A.M. (2004) 'A comparison of personalized feedback for college student drinkers delivered with and without motivational interview', *Journal of Studies on Alcohol*, 5: 200–3.

Murray-Parkes, C. (1998) 'Coping with loss. Bereavement in adult life', *British Medical Journal*, 316 (7134): 856–9.

National Records for Scotland (2013) *Statistical Bulletin 2011 Census: Key Results on Population, Ethnicity, Identity, Language, Religion, Health, Housing and Accommodation in Scotland: Release 2A*. Edinburgh: National Records for Scotland.

Nevalainen, M.K., Mantyranta, T. and Pitkala, K.H. (2010) 'Facing uncertainty as a medical student – a qualitative study of their reflective learning diaries and writings on specific themes during the first clinical year', *Patient Education and Counseling*, 78: 218–23.

NICE (National Institute for Health and Clinical Excellence) (2005) *Depression in Children and Young People. Identification and Management in Primary, Community and Secondary Care*. National Clinical Practice Guideline Number 28. Available from: http://guidance.nice.org.uk/nicemedia/live/10970/29859/29859.pdf (accessed 18 July 2011)

NICE (National Institute for Health and Clinical Excellence) (2006a) *Obsessive Compulsive Disorder: Core Interventions in the Treatment of Obsessive Compulsive Disorder and Body Dysmorphic Disorder*. National Clinical Practice Guideline Number 31. Available from http://guidance.nice.org.uk/nicemedia/live/10976/29948/29948.pdf (accessed 18 July 2011).

NICE (National Institute for Health and Clinical Excellence) (2006b) *Bipolar Disorder. The Management of Bipolar Disorder in Adults, Children and Adolescents, in Primary and Secondary Care*. National Clinical Practice Guideline Number 38. Available from: http://guidance.nice.org.uk/nicemedia/live/10990/30194/30194.pdf (accessed 18 July 2011).

NICE (National Institute for Health and Clinical Excellence) (2009) *Schizophrenia. The NICE Guideline on Core Interventions in the Treatment and Management of Schizophrenia in Adults in Primary and Secondary Care*. Updated Edition. National Clinical Practice Guideline Number 82. Available from: http://guidance.nice.org.uk/nicemedia/live/11786/43607/43607.pdf (accessed 18 July 2011).

NICE (National Institute for Health and Clinical Excellence) (2010) *The NICE Guideline on the Treatment and Management of Depression in Adults*. Updated Edition. National Clinical Practice Guideline 90. Available from: http://guidance.nice.org.uk/nicemedia/live/12329/45896/45896.pdf (accessed 18 July 2011).

NICE (National Institute for Health and Clinical Excellence) (2011) *Generalised Anxiety Disorder and Panic Disorder (With or Without Agrophobia) in Adults: Mangement in Primary, Secondary and Community Care*. Partial Update. National Clinical Practice Guideline No. 113. Available from: http://guidance.nice.org.uk/nicemedia/live/13314/52667/52667.pdf (accessed 18 July 2011).

Norman, D.A. and Shallice, T. (1986) 'Attention to action: willed and automatic control of behavior', in R.J. Davidson, G.E. Schwartz and D.E. Shapiro (eds), *Consciousness and Self-Regulation: Advances in Research and Theory*, vol. 4. New York: Plenum Press.

Northern Ireland Assembly – DHSSPS (2011) *Transforming Your Care: Review of Health and Social Care in Northern Ireland*. Belfast: Northern Ireland Assembly/DHSSPS.

Northern Ireland Executive – DHSSPS (2009) *Delivering the Bamford Vision: Action Plan 2009–2011*. Belfast: Northern Ireland Executive/DHSSPS.

O'Brien, J. (1989) *What's Worth Working For?* Georgia: Responsive Systems Associates.

O'Brien, J. and Lyle O'Brien, C. (eds) (2000) *A Little Book about Person Centered Planning*. Ontario: Inclusion Press.

O'Brien, J. and O'Brien, C.J. (1998) *Implementing Person-Centered Planning*. Toronto: Inclusion Press.

O'Brien, J. and Mount, B. (2006) *Make a Difference: A Guidebook for Person-Centred Direct Support*. Ontario: Inclusion Press.

O'Brien, J. and Tyne, A. (1981) *The Principle of Normalisation: A Foundation for Effective Services*. London: CMH.

ODI (2012) *Disability Prevalence Estimates 2010/11*. Available from: http://odi.dwp.gov.uk/docs/res/factsheets/disability-prevalence.pdf (accessed 21/10/13).

OECD (2012) *OECD Economic Outlook*, Vol. 2012/1, OECD Publishing. Available from: http://dx.doi.org/10.1787/eco-outlook-v2012-1-en.

O'Hagan, K. (1986) *Crisis Intervention in Social Services*. Houndsmill: Macmillan Education.

O'Keeffe, M., Hills, A., Doyle, M., Mccreadie, C., Scholes, S., Constantine, R., Tinker, A., Manthorpe, J., Biggs, S. and Erens, B. (2007) *UK Study of Abuse and Neglect of Older People: Prevalence Survey Report*. Prepared for Comic Relief and the Department of Health.

Oliver, M., Sapey, R. and Thomas, P. (2012a) *Social Work with Disabled People*, 4th edn. Basingstoke: Palgrave Macmillan.

ONS (Office for National Statistics) (2011a) *Internet Access Households and Individuals 2011*. London: Office for National Statistics.

ONS (2011b) *Nomis: Official Labour Statistics. England and Wales*. Available from: www.nomisweb.co.uk/census/2011/ks201ew (accessed 27 January 2014).

ONS (2012a) Available from: www.ons.gov.uk/ons/rel/pop-estimate/electoral-statistics-for-uk/stb---2012-electoral-statistics.html (accessed 31 October 2013).

ONS (2012b) *Annual Survey of Hours and Earnings*. London: Office for National Statistics.

ONS (Office for National Statistics) (2012c) *Labour Force Survey*.

ONS (Office for National Statistics) (2013) *2011 Census for England and Wales*. Available from: www.ons.gov.uk/ons/guide-method/census/2011/census-data/index.html (accessed October 2013).

Orme, J. (2001) *Gender and Community Care*. Basingstoke: Palgrave.

Orme, J. and Shemmings, D. (2010) *Developing Research Based Social Work Practice*. Basingstoke: Palgrave Macmillan.

O'Sullivan, T. (2011) *Decision Making in Social Work*, 2nd edn. Basingstoke: Palgrave Macmillan.

Parke, R.D. and Buriel, R. (2006) 'Socialization in the family: ethnic and ecological perspectives', in N. Eisenberg (ed.), W. Damon and R.M. Learner (eds in chief), *Handbook of Child Psychology*, vol. 3: *Social, Emotional and Personality Development*. Hoboken, NJ: Wiley.

Parker, J. and Bradley, G. (2007) *Social Work Practice: Assessment, Planning, Intervention and Review*. Exeter: Learning Matters.

Parkes, C.M. (1986) *Bereavement*. Harmondsworth: Penguin.

Parrish, M. (2010) *Social Work Perspectives on Human Behaviour*. London: McGraw-Hill.

Parton, N. (2000) 'Some thoughts on the relationship between theory and practice in and for social work', *British Journal of Social Work*, 30: 449–63.

Parton, N. and O'Byrne, P. (2000) *Constructive Social Work: Towards a New Practice*. Basingstoke: Palgrave Macmillan.

Pavlov, I.P. (1927) *Conditioned Reflexes*. Oxford: Oxford University Press.

Pawson, R., Boaz, A., Grayson, L., Long, A. and Barnes, C. (2003) *Types and Quality of Knowledge in Social Care*. SCIE Knowledge Review 7. London: SCIE.

Payne, M. (1997) 'Task-centred practice within the politics of social work theory', *Issues in Social Work Education*, 17 (2): 48–65.

Payne, M. (2005a) *Modern Social Work Theory*, 3rd edn. Basingstoke: Palgrave Macmillan.

Payne, M. (2005b) *The Origins of Social Work*. Basingstoke: Palgrave.

Payne, M. (2008) *Social Care Practice in Context*. Basingstoke: Palgrave Macmillan.

Payne, M., Adams, R. and Dominelli, L. (2002) 'On being critical in social work', in R. Adams, L. Dominelli and M. Payne (eds), *Critical Practice in Social Work*. Basingstoke: Palgrave Macmillan. pp. 1–12.

Pearpoint, J. (1990) *Behind the Piano: The Building of Judith Snow's Unique Circle of Friends*. Toronto: Inclusion Press.

Perkins, K., Conklin, C. and Levine, M. (2008) *Cognitive-Behavioral Therapy for Smoking Cessation. A Practical Guidebook to the Most Effective Interventions*. Abingdon: Routledge.

Perry, B. (2002) 'Childhood experience and the expression of genetic potential: what childhood neglect tells us about nature and nurture', *Brain and Mind*, 3: 79–100.

Petch, A. (2011) *An Evidence Base for the Delivery of Adult Services*. A Report Commissioned by ADSW. Available from: www.adsw.org.uk/doccache/doc_get_495.pdf (accessed 24 April 2012).

Phillips, J., Ray, M. and Marshall, M. (2006) *Social Work with Older People*, 4th edn. Basingstoke: Palgrave Macmillan.

Piaget, J. (1926) *The Language and Thought of the Child*. New York: Meridian Books.

Piaget, J. (1957) *Construction of Reality in the Child*. London: Routledge and Kegan Paul.

Pilgrim, D. (2009) *Key Concepts in Mental Health*, 2nd edn. London: Sage.

Pollard, K. (2009) 'Student engagement in interprofessional working in practice placement settings', *Journal of Clinical Nursing*, 18: 2846–56.

Pollard, K., Sellman, D. and Senior, B. (2005) 'The need for interprofessional working', in G. Barrett, D. Sellman and J. Thomas (eds), *Interprofessional Working in Health and Social Care*. Basingstoke: Palgrave Macmillan. pp. 7–17.

Prince, K. (2000) 'Confidentiality', in M. Davies (ed.), *The Blackwell Companion to Social Work*. Oxford: Blackwell. pp. 74–5.

Prochaska, J. and DiClemente, C. (1982) 'Transtheoretical therapy: toward a more integrated model of change', *Psychotherapy: Theory, Research and Practice*, 19: 276–88.

Prochaska, J. and DiClemente, C. (1986) 'Towards a comprehensive model of change', in W. Miller and N. Heather (eds), *Treating Addictive Behaviours: Process of Change*. New York: Plenum Press.

Prochaska, J., Norcross, J. and DiClemente, C. (1992) 'In search of how people change: applications to the addictive behaviours', *American Psychologist*, 47: 1102–14.

Prochaska, J., Norcross, J. and DiClemente, C. (1995) *Changing for Good*. New York: Harper Collins.

Professional Boards Forum BoardWatch (2012) Available from: www.boardsforum.co.uk/boardwatch.html (accessed 21 October 2013).

Public Service.co.uk (2009) 'Flying high for Easy Council flexibility', 14 October 2009. Available from: www.publicservice.co.uk/feature_story.asp?id=12779 (accessed August 2013)

Race, P. (2010) 'How students really learn. Ripples model of learning'. Updated August 2010. PowerPoint presentation. Available from: http://phil-race.co.uk.

Raistrick, D., Heather, N. and Godfrey, C. (2006) *Review of the Effectiveness of Treatment for Alcohol Problems*. London: National Treatment Agency for Substance Misuse. Available from: www.nta.nhs.uk/uploads/nta_review_of_the_effectiveness_of_treatment_for_alcohol_problems_fullreport_2006_alcohol2.pdf.

Ratner, H., George, E. and Iveson, C. (2012) *Solution Focused Brief Therapy: 100 Key Points and Techniques*. Hove: Routledge.

Ray, M. and Phillips, J. (2002) 'Older people', in R. Adams, L. Dominelli and M. Payne (eds), *Critical Practice in Social Work*. Basingstoke: Palgrave Macmillan. pp. 199–209.

Reamer, F.G. (1995) *Social Work Values and Ethics*. New York: Columbia University Press.

Redl, F. (1966) *When We Deal with Children*. New York: The Free Press.

Redl, F. and Wineman, D. (1957) *The Aggressive Child*. Glencoe, IL: The Free Press.

Rees, C. (2007) 'Childhood attachment', *British Journal of General Practice*, 57 (544): 920–2.

Reeves, S., Lewin, S., Espin, S. and Zwarenstein, M. (2010) *Interprofessional Teamwork for Health and Social Care*. Oxford: Blackwell.

Reid, W.J. (1978) *The Task Centred System*. New York: Columbia University Press.

Reid, W.J. (1996) 'Task centred social work', in F.J. Turner (ed.), *Social Work Treatment: Interlocking Theoretical Approaches*. New York: Free Press. pp. 617–40.

Reid, W.J. and Epstein, L. (1972) *Task-Centred Casework*. New York: Columbia University Press.

Reid, W.J. and Hanrahan, P. (1981) 'The effectiveness of social work: recent evidence', in E.M Goldberg and N. Connelly (eds), *Evaluation Research in Social Care*. London: Policy Studies Institute.

Reid, W.J. and Shyne, W.A. (1969) *Brief and Extended Casework*. New York: Columbia University Press.

Reuter, P. and Stevens, A. (2007) *An Analysis of UK Drug Policy*. London: UK Drug Policy Commission.

Rhodes, M. (1986) *Ethical Dilemmas in Social Work Practice*. London: Routledge and Kegan Paul.

Richardson, J. (ed.) (2013) *Archbold: Criminal Pleading, Evidence and Practice*, 61st edn. London: Sweet and Maxwell.

Richmond, J.E.D. (1997) 'Donald Schön: Inviting us to Reflect'. Donald Schön: A Life of Reflection: Remarks at a special session in honor of the memory of Donald Schön. Conference of the Association of Collegiate Schools of Planning, Fort Lauderdale, FL, 6–9 November.

Risk Management Authority (2012) *The Level of Service/Case Management Inventory (LS/CMI)* [online]. Available from: www.rmascotland.gov.uk/events/learning-initiatives/ls-cmi/ (accessed 18 June 2102).

Ritter, C., Teller, J.L.S., Marcussen, K., Munetz, R.M. and Teasdale, B. (2011) 'Crisis Intervention team office dispatch, assessment, and disposition: interactions with individuals with severe mental illness', *International Journal of Law and Psychiatry*, 34: 30–38.

Roberts, A.R. (2005) *Crisis Intervention Handbook: Assessment, Treatment and Research*, 3rd edn. New York: Oxford University Press.

Roberts, A.R. and Ottens, A.J. (2005) *The Seven-Stage Crisis Intervention Model: A Road Map to Goal Attainment, Problem Solving, and Crisis Resolution*. New York: Oxford University Press.

Roe, S. and Man, L. (2006) *Drug Misuse Declared: Findings from the 2005/06 British Crime Survey*. London: The Home Office.

Rogers, C. (1957) 'The necessary and sufficient conditions of therapeutic personality change', *Journal of Consulting Psychology*, 21: 95-103.

Rogers, C. (1959) 'A theory of therapy, personality and interpersonal relationships as developed in the client-centred framework', in S. Koch (ed.), *Psychology: A Study of Science. Volume III: Formulations of the Person and the Social Context*. New York: McGraw-Hill.

Rogers, C. (1961) *On Becoming a Person*. Boston, MA: Houghton Mifflin.

Rogers, C. R. (1986). 'Carl Rogers on the development of the person-centered approach', *Person-Centered Review*, 1(3): 257–59.

Ross, W.D. (1930) *The Right and the Good*. Oxford: Oxford University Press.

Ruch, G. (2002) 'From triangle to spiral: reflective practice in social work education, practice and research', *Social Work Education*, 21 (2): 199–216.

Ruch, G., Turney, D. and Ward, A. (eds) (2010) *Relationship-Based Social Work: Getting to the Heart of Practice*. London: Jessica Kingsley Publishers.

Rutledge, S.E., Roffman, R.A., Mahoney, C., Picciano, J.F., Berghuis, J.P. and Kalichman, S.C. (2001) 'Motivational enhancement counseling strategies in delivering a telephone-based brief HIV prevention intervention', *Clinical Social Work Journal*, 29(3): 291–306.

Ryan, R.M. and Deci, E.L. (2000) 'Self-determination theory and the facilitation of intrinsic motivation, social development, and well-being', *The American Psychologist*, 55 (1): 68–78.

Sachs, J., Bard, B. and Johnson, M.L. (1981) 'Language learning with restricted input: case studies of two hearing children of deaf parents', *Applied Psycholinguistics*, 2: 33–54.

Sackett, D.L., Richardson, S., Rosenberg, W. and Haynes, R.B. (1997) *Evidence Based Medicine: How to Practise and Teach Evidence Based Medicine*. Edinburgh: Churchill Livingstone.

Sackett, D.L., Straus, S.E., Richardson, W.S., Rosenberg, W. and Haynes, R.B. (2000) *Evidence-based Medicine: How to Practise and Teach EBM*, 2nd edn. New York: Churchill Livingstone.

Sainsbury, E. (1987) 'Client studies: their contribution and limitations in influencing social work practice', *British Journal of Social Workers*, 17: 635–44.

Sainsbury, E. (1989) 'What clients value'. Unpublished Paper. London: BASW Task-centred Practice Day.

Sanderson, H., Kennedy, J., Ritchie, P. and Goodwin, G. (2000) *People, Plans and Possibilities: Exploring Person Centred Planning*. Edinburgh: SHS Ltd.

Sands, D. (2012) *The Impact of Austerity on Women*. London: Fawcett Society.

Schön, D.A. (1983) *The Reflective Practitioner : How Professionals Think in Action*. New York.:Basic Books.

Schön, D.A. (1987) *Educating the Reflective Practitioner*. San Francisco, CA: Jossey–Bass.

Schön, D.A. (1990) *Educating the Reflective Practitioner*. San Francisco, CA: Jossey-Bass.

Schore, A.N. (2000) 'Attachment and the regulation of the right brain', *Attachment and Human Development*, 2 (1): 23–47.

Schwartzmantel, J. (2008) *Ideology and Politics*. London: Sage.

Scope (2012) 'Discrimination increases on back of "benefit scroungers" rhetoric'. Available from: www.scope.org.uk/news/disability-and-paralympics/discrimination (accessed September 2013).

Scope/ComRes (2011) *Scope Discrimination Survey*. Available from: www.comres.co.uk/poll/8/scope-discrimination-survey-15-may-2011.htm (accessed September 2013).

Scottish Executive (2000a) *Community Care: A Joint Future (Report of the Joint Future Group)*. Edinburgh: Scottish Executive.

Scottish Executive (2000b) *The Same as You? A Review of Services for People with Learning Disabilities*. Available from: www.scotland.gov.uk/Resource/Doc/1095/0001661.pdf.

Scottish Executive (2003a) *The Framework for Social Work Education in Scotland*. Edinburgh: Scottish Executive. Available from: www.scotland.gov.uk/Publications/2003/01/16202/17019.

Scottish Executive (2003b) *Mind the Gaps: Meeting the Needs of People with Co-occurring Substance Misuse and Mental Health Problems*. Edinburgh: Scottish Executive.

Scottish Executive (2006a) *Changing Lives: Report of the 21st Century Social Work Review*. Edinburgh: Scottish Executive.

Scottish Executive (2006b) *Getting our Priorities Right: Good Practice Guidance for Working with Children and Families Affected by Substance Misuse*. Edinburgh: Scottish Executive. Available from: www.scotland.gov.uk/Resource/Doc/47032/0023960.pdf (accessed August 2013).

Scottish Executive (2007) *Increasing the Availability of Evidence-Based Psychological Therapies in Scotland. 'Phase 1' Plan*. [Online]. Available from: www.scotland.gov.uk/Topics/Health/health/mental-health/servicespolicy/DFMH/psychtherapies (accessed 27 July 2011).

Scottish Government (2007a) *Better Health, Better Care: Action Plan*. Available from: www.scotland.gov.uk/Publications/2007/12/11103453/0 (accessed 9 February 2012).

Scottish Government (2007b) *Towards a Mentally Flourishing Scotland: Discussion Paper on Mental Health Improvement 2008–2011.* Edinburgh: Scottish Government.

Scottish Government (2008a) *Changing Scotland's Relationship with Alcohol: A Discussion on Our Strategic Approach.* Edinburgh: Scottish Government.

Scottish Government (2008b) *The Road to Recovery: A New Approach to Tackling Scotland's Drug Problem.* Edinburgh: Scottish Government.

Scottish Government (2009a) *Towards a Mentally Flourishing Scotland: Policy and Action Plan 2009–2011.* Edinburgh: Scottish Government. Available from: www.scotland.gov.uk/Publications/2009/05/06154655/5 (accessed 3 August 2011).

Scottish Government (2009b) *Single Shared Assessment.* Edinburgh: Scottish Government.

Scottish Government (2010a) *National Outcomes and Standards for Social Work Services in the Criminal Justice System.* Available from: www.scotland.gov.uk/Topics/Justice/public-safety/offender-management/offender/community/16910/Standards/PracticeGuidance (accessed 10 September 2011).

Scottish Government (2010b) *Community Payback Orders Practice Guidance.* Available from: www.scotland.gov.uk/Resource/Doc/925/0110008.pdf (accessed 12 September 2011).

Scottish Government (2010c) *Criminal Justice Social Work Reports and Court Based Services Practice Guidance.* Available from: www.scotland.gov.uk/Resource/Doc/925/0110144.pdf (accessed 12 September 2011).

Scottish Government (2010d) *Partnership Improvement and Outcomes Division.* Available from: www.scotland.gov.uk/Topics/Health/care/JointFuture (accessed 9 February 2012).

Scottish Government (2010e) *Self-Directed Support: A National Strategy for Scotland.* Edinburgh: Scottish Government. Available from: www.scotland.gov.uk/Publications/2010/11/05120810/0 (accessed 22 April 2012).

Scottish Government (2011a) *High Level Summary of Statistics Trend: People with Learning Disabilities.* Available from: www.scotland.gov.uk/Topics/Statistics/Browse/Health/TrendLearningDisabilities (accessed October 2013).

Scottish Government (2011b) *People with Learning Disabilities and the Scottish Criminal Justice System.* Available from: www.scotland.gov.uk/Resource/Doc/346993/0115487.pdf (accessed October 2013).

Scottish Government and Convention of Scottish Local Authorities and NHS Scotland (2011) *Reshaping Care for Older People: A Programme for Change 2011–2021.* Edinburgh: Scottish Government. Available from: www.scotland.gov.uk/Resource/Doc/924/0114884.pdf (accessed October 2013).

Scottish Government (2012) *Scottish Government's Statistical Bulletin, Crime and Justice Series.* Edinburgh: The Scottish Government.

Scottish Parliament (2013) *Public Bodies (Joint Working) (Scotland) Bill.* Edinburgh: Scottish Parliament.

Scourfield, P. (2011) 'Cartelization revisited and the lessons of Southern Cross', *Critical Social Policy.* DOI: 10.1177/0261018311425202 2012 32: 137.

Seden, J. (2005) *Counselling Skills in Social Work Practice,* 2nd edn. Buckingham: Open University Press.

Seligman, M.E.P. (1975) *Helplessness: On Depression, Development, and Death.* New York: Freeman.

Sharkey, P. (2007) *The Essentials of Community Care,* 2nd edn. Basingstoke: Palgrave Macmillan.

Sharpe, C. (2009) 'Fritz Redl and the life space interview'. Available from: www.cyc-net.org/cyc-online/cyconline-nov2009-sharpe.html (accessed October 2013).

Shaw, H. and Lishman, J. (1999) *Evaluation and Social Work Practice.* London: Sage.

Sheils, R. (1996) *Renton and Brown's Criminal Procedure Legislation*. Edinburgh: W. Green.

Sheldon, B. (2000) 'Cognitive behavioural methods in social care: a look at the evidence', in P. Stepney and D. Ford (eds), *Social Work Models, Methods and Theories. A Framework for Practice*. Lyme Regis: Russell House Publishing.

Sheldon, B. (2011) *Cognitive-Behavioural Therapy. Research and Practice in Health and Social Care*, 2nd edn. Abingdon: Routledge.

Sheldon, B. and Chilvers, R. (2002) 'An empirical study of the obstacles to evidence based practice', in D. Smith (ed.), *Social Work and Evidence Based Practice*. London: Jessica Kingsley Publishers.

Sheppard, M. (2007) 'Assessment: from reflexivity to process knowledge', in J. Lishman (ed.), *Handbook for Practice Learning in Social Work and Social Care: Knowledge and Theory*. London: Jessica Kingsley Publishers. pp. 128–37.

SIGN (1998) *Psychosocial Interventions in the Management of Schizophrenia*. A National Clinical Guideline Number 30. Edinburgh: Scottish Intercollegiate Guidelines Network. Available from: www.sign.ac.uk/pdf/sign30.pdf (accessed 19 July 2011).

SIGN (2005) *Bipolar Affective Disorder*. A National Clinical Guideline Number 82. Edinburgh: Scottish Intercollegiate Guidelines Network. Available from: www.sign.ac.uk/pdf/sign82.pdf (accessed 19 July 2011).

SIGN (2010a) *Non-Pharmaceutical Management of Depression in Adults*. A National Clinical Guideline Number 114. Edinburgh: Scottish Intercollegiate Guidelines Network. Available from: www.sign.ac.uk/pdf/sign114.pdf (accessed 19 July 2011).

SIGN (2010b) *Management of Obesity*. A National Clinical Guideline Number 115. Edinburgh: Scottish Intercollegiate Guidelines Network. Available from: www.sign.ac.uk/pdf/sign115. pdf (accessed 4 August 2011).

Simpson, E.L., Barkham, M., Gilbody, S. and House, A. (2009) 'Involving service users as trainers for professionals working in adult statutory mental health services (Protocol)'. The Cochrane Collaboration – Cochrane Protocol published in The Cochrane Library. www.thecochranelibrary. com (accessed 16 April 2012).

Sims, D. (2011) 'Reconstructing professional identity for professional and interprofessional practice: a mixed methods study of joint training programmes in learning disability nursing and social work', *Journal of Interprofessional Care*, 25 (4): 265–71.

Singer, P. (2011) *Practical Ethics*, 3rd edn. Cambridge: Cambridge University Press.

Skinner, B.F. (1957) *Verbal Behaviour*. New York: Appleton–Century–Crofts.

Skinner, B.F. (1965) *Science and Human Behavior*. New York: The Free Press.

Skinner, K. (2012) 'Continuous professional development in social work', in J. Lishman (ed.), *Social Work Education and Training*. London: Jessica Kingsley.

Smale, G., Tuson, G., Biehal, N. and Marsh, P. (1993) *Empowerment, Assessment, Care Management and the Skilled Worker*. National Institute for Social Work Practice and Development Exchange. London: HMSO.

Smith, D. (2004) *Social Work and Evidence-Based Practice, Research Highlights 45*. London: Jessica Kingsley.

Smith, J. (2005) 'Reflective practice: a meaningful task for students', *Nursing Scotland*, 19 (26): 33–7.

Smith, M., Fulcher, L. and Doran, P. (2013) *Residential Child Care in Practice: Making a Difference*. Bristol: Policy Press.

Smith, R. (2009) 'Inter-professional learning and multi-professional practice for PQ', in P. Higham (ed.), *Post-Qualifying Social Work Practice*. London: Sage. pp. 135–47.

Smith, R. (2010) 'Social work, risk, power', *Sociological Research Online*, 15 (1): 4. Available from: www.socresonline.org.uk/15/1/4.html (accessed 22 April 2012).

Smull, M.W. and Harrison, S.B. (1992) *Supporting People with Severe Reputations in the Community*. Alexandria: National Association of State Mental Retardation Program Directors.

Spencer, M. (2000) 'Working with issues of difference in supervision of counselling', *Psychodynamic Counselling*, 6(4): 505–19.

Spicker, P. (2012) *An Introduction to Social Policy*. Aberdeen: Robert Gordon University. Available from: www2.rgu.ac.uk/publicpolicy/introduction/needf.htm (accessed 2 November 2012).

SSSC (Scottish Social Services Council) (2009) *Code of Practice for Social Service Workers and Employers*. Dundee: SSSC.

Statham, D. and Kearney, P. (2007) 'Models of assessment', in. J. Lishman (ed.), *Handbook for Practice Learning in Social Work and Social Care: Knowledge and Theory*. London: Jessica Kingsley Publishers. pp. 101–14.

Stepney, P. and Ford, D. (2000) *Social Work Models, Methods and Theories*. Lyme Regis: Russell House Publishing.

Steyn, Lord (2006) *Democracy, the Rule of Law and the Role of Judges*. The Attlee Foundation Lecture. *E.H.R.L.R.*: 243–53.

Steyn, Lord (2009) 'Civil liberties in modern Britain', *P.L.*: 228–36.

Strayer, D.L. and Drews, F.A. (2007) 'Cell-phone-induced driver distraction', *Current Directions in Psychological Science*, 16 (3): 128–31.

Sunday Times (1981) 'Mrs Thatcher: the first two years', interview with Robert Butt, *Sunday Times*, 3 May.

The Sutton Trust (2009) *The Educational Backgrounds of Leading Lawyers, Journalists, Vice Chancellors, Politicians, Medics and Chief Executives: The Sutton Trust Submission to the Milburn Commission on Access to the Professions*. London: The Sutton Trust.

Swindell, M.L. and Watson, J. (2006) 'Teaching ethics through self-reflective journaling', *Journal of Social Work Values and Ethics*, 3 (2): 5–18.

Sykes, C. and Marks, D. (2001) 'Effectiveness of a cognitive behavioural self-help programme for smokers in London, UK', *Health Promotion International*, 16 (3): 255–60.

Szasz, T. (1974) *The Myth of Mental Illness*. New York: Harper and Row.

Tanner, D. (1998) 'The jeopardy of risk', *Practice*, 10 (1): 15–28.

Taylor, B. (2010) *Professional Decision Making in Social Work Practice*. Exeter: Learning Matters.

Taylor, B.J. (ed.) (2011) *Working with Aggression and Resistance in Social Work*. Exeter: Learning Matters.

Taylor, P. and Vatcher, A. (2005) 'Social work', in G. Barrett, D. Sellman and J. Thomas (eds), *Interprofessional Working in Health and Social Care*. Basingstoke: Palgrave Macmillan. pp. 155–69.

Tebbit, N. (2010) 'Britain, a land of quangocrats and hereditary welfare junkies', *Daily Telegraph*, 15 March.

Tew, J. (2011) *Social Approaches to Mental Distress*. Basingstoke: Palgrave Macmillan.

Thomas, P., Wilson, C. and Jones, P. (2010) 'Strengthening the voice of mental health service users and carers in Wales: a focus group study to inform future policy', *International Journal of Consumer Studies*, 34: 525–31.

Thompson, N. (1995) *Theory and Practice in Social Welfare*. Buckingham: The Open University.

Thompson, N. (1997) *Anti-discriminatory Practice*, 2nd edn. Basingstoke: Macmillan.

Thompson, N. (1998) *Promoting Equality: Challenging Discrimination and Oppression in the Human Services*. Basingstoke: Macmillan.

Thompson, N. (2003a) *Effective Communication* (2nd edn 2011). Basingstoke: Palgrave Macmillan.

Thompson, N. (2003b) *Anti-Discriminatory Practice*, 3rd edn. London: BASW Palgrave.

Thompson, N. (2005) *Understanding Social Work: Preparing for Practice*, 2nd edn. Basingstoke: Palgrave Macmillan.

Thompson, N. (2009a) *People Skills*, 3rd edn. Basingstoke: Palgrave Macmillan.

Thompson, N. (2009b) *Understanding Social Work: Preparing for Practice*, 3rd edn. Houndsmill: Palgrave Macmillan.

Thompson, N. and Thompson, S. (2008) *The Social Work Companion*. Basingstoke: Palgrave Macmillan.

Thorne, B. (1992) *Carl Rogers*. London: Sage.

Thurman, S., van der Gaag, A., Money, D. and Jones, J. (2003) *Speech and Language Therapy Provision for Adults with Learning Disabilities*. Royal College of Speech and Language Therapists. Available from: www.rcslt.org/docs/free-pub/position_paper_ald.pdf (accessed October 2013).

Tighe, A. (ed.) (2007) *Statistical Handbook 2007*. London: Brewing Publications Ltd.

Titterton, M. (2005) *Risk and Risk Taking in Health and Social Welfare*. London: Jessica Kingsley Publishers.

Trepper, T.S., McCollum, E.E., de Jong, P., Korman, H., Gingerich, W.J. and Franklin, C. (2012) 'Solution-focused brief therapy treatment manual', in N.C. Franklin, T.S. Trepper, W.J. Gingerich and E.E. McCollum (eds), *Solution-Focused Brief Therapy: A Handbook of Evidence-Based Practice*. New York: OUP.

Trevithick, P. (2005) *Social Work Skills: A Practice Handbook*. Maidenhead: Open University Press.

Trevithick, P. (2008) 'Revisiting the knowledge base of social work: a framework for practice', *British Journal of Social Work*, 38: 1212–37.

Trevithick, P. (2012) *Social Work Skills, A Practice Handbook,* 3rd edn. Maidenhead: Open University Press.

Trieschman, A., Whittaker, J.K. and Brendtro, L.K. (1969) *The Other 23 Hours: Child-Care Work with Emotionally Disturbed Children in a Therapeutic Milieu*. New York: Aldine De Gruyter.

Trotter, C. (2007) *Working with Involuntary Clients: A Guide to Practice*, 2nd edn. London: Sage.

Turner, D. and Tanner, K. (2001) 'Working with neglected children and their families', *Journal of Social Work Practice*, 15 (2).

Twigg, J. (1989) 'Models of carers: how do social care agencies conceptualise their relationship with informal carers?', *Journal of Social Policy*, 18 (1): 53–66.

UPAIS (1976) *Fundamental Principles of Disability*. London: UPIAS.

van Dijk, J. (1967) 'The non-verbal deaf–blind and his world: his outgrowth toward the world of symbols', *Proceedings of the Jaasrverslag Instituut Voor Doven*. Sint Michielsgestel, Holland: Jaarverslag Instituut van Doven. pp. 73–110.

Van Vliet, O. and Caminada, K. (2012) 'Unemployment replacement rates dataset among 34 welfare states 1971–2009: An update, extension and modification of the Scruggs' Welfare State Entitlements Data Set', *NEUJOBS Special Report* No. 2, Leiden University.

Vanstone, M. (1999) 'Behavioural and cognitive interventions', in I. Shaw and J. Lishman (eds), *Evaluation and Social Work Practice*. London: Sage.

Vertovec, S.(2007) 'Super-diversity and its implications', *Ethnic and Racial Studies*, 29(6): 1024–54.

Visser, C. (2008) *Solution Focused Steps to Progress*. Available from: http://solutionfocusedchange. blogspot.co.uk/ (accessed 18 May 2012).

von Bertalanffy, L. (1950) 'An outline of general systems theory', *British Journal for the Philosophy of Science*, 1 (2): 1–13.

Vygotsky, L.S. (1962) *Thought and Language*. Cambridge, MA: MIT Press (originally published 1934).

Wackerhausen, S. (2009) 'Collaboration, professional identity and reflection across boundaries', *Journal of Interprofessional Care*, 23 (5): 455–73.

Walby, S. (1989) 'Theorising patriarchy', *Sociology*, 23(2): 213–34.

Walby, S. (1990) *Patriarchy at Work*. Cambridge: Polity Press.

Walby, S. (1997) *Gender Transformations*. London: Routledge.

Waller, G. (2009) 'Evidence-based treatment and therapist drift', *Behaviour Research and Therapy*, 47 (2): 119–27.

Walsh, J. and Lantz, J. (2007) *Short-Term Existential Intervention in Clinical Practice*. Ohio: Lyceum Books.

Ward, A. (1996) 'Training: personal learning for professional practice' (Editorial), *Therapeutic Communities*, 17: 4.

Ward, A. (2002) 'Opportunity led work: maximising the possibilities for therapeutic communication in everyday interactions', *Therapeutic Communities*, 23 (2): 111–24.

Ward, A. (2010) 'The use of self in relationship-based practice', in G. Ruch, D. Turney and A. Ward, *Relationship-Based Social Work: Getting to the Heart of Practice*. London: Jessica Kingsley Publishers.

Ward, A. and McMahon, L. (ed.) (1998) *Intuition is Not Enough: Matching Learning with Practice in Therapeutic Child Care*. London: Routledge.

Ward, L.J. and Rhodes, C.A. (2010) 'Embedding consumer culture in health and social care education – a university office's perspective', *International Journal of Consumer Studies*, 34: 596-602.

Warren, J. (2007) *Service User and Carer Participation in Social Work*. Exeter: Learning Matters.

Watson, C.A., Ottati, C.V., Morabito, M., Draine, J., Kerr, A.N. and Angell, B. (2010) 'Outcomes of police contacts with persons with mental illness: the impact of CIT', *Administration and Policy in Mental Health and Mental Health Services Research*, 37 (4): 302–17.

Watton, P., Collings, J. and Moon, J. (2001) *Reflective Writing: Guidance Notes for Students*. Available from: www.exeter.ac.uk/fch/work-experience/reflective-writing-guidance.pdf (accessed September 2013).

Weale, A. (2004) 'Politics as collective choice', in A. Leftwich (ed.), *What Is Politics?* Cambridge: Polity Press.

Webb, S. (2006) *Social Work in a Risk Society*. Basingstoke: Palgrave Macmillan.

Weil, S.W. and McGill, I. (1989) 'A framework for making sense of experiential learning', in Susan S. Weil and Ian McGill (eds), *Making Sense of Experiential Learning*. Milton Keynes: SRHE/Open University Press. p. 3.

Weiner, B. (1980) *Human Motivation*. New York: Holt, Rinehart & Winston.

Welsh Assembly Government (2010) *Health, Social Care and Well-Being Strategy Guidance*. Cardiff: Welsh Assembly Government.

Welsh Assembly Government (2011) *Sustainable Social Services for Wales: A Framework for Action*. Cardiff: Welsh Assembly Government. Available from: http://wales.gov.uk/topics/health/publications/socialcare/guidance1/services/?lang=en (accessed 22 April 2012).

Welsh, T. (2006) *Macphail's Sheriff Court Practice*, 3rd edn. Edinburgh: W. Green.

Welsh Government (2013) *A Framework for Delivering Integrated Health and Social Care – A Consultation*. Cardiff: Welsh Government

Wenger, E. (1998) *Communities of Practice: Learning, Meaning and Identity*. Cambridge: Cambridge University Press.

Wharton, A. (2005) *The Sociology of Gender: An Introduction to Theory and Research*. Oxford: Blackwell.

Wheeler, J. (2003) 'Solution-focused practice in social work', in B. O'Connell and S. Palmer (eds), *Solution-Focused Therapy*. London: Sage.

White, M. (1995) *Re-Authoring Lives: Interviews and Essays*. Adelaide: Dulwich Centre Publications.

White, M. and Epston, D. (1990) *Narrative Means to Therapeutic Ends*. London: Norton.

White, S. (2009) 'Fabled uncertainty in social work: a coda to Spafford et al.', *Journal of Social Work*, 9 (2): 222–35.

Whittington, C. and Whittington, M. (2007) 'Ethics and social care: political, organisational and interagency dimensions', in A. Leathard and S. McLaren (eds), *Ethics: Contemporary Challenges in Health and Social Care*. Bristol: The Policy Press/University of Bristol. pp. 83–96.

WHO (World Health Organization) (1990/2010) *International Classification of Diseases, Tenth Revision (ICD-10): Chapter V: Mental and Behavioral Disorders, F00 to F99*. Geneva: WHO. Available from: http://apps.who.int/classifications/icd10/browse/2010/en (accessed August 2013).

WHO (World Health Organization) (2005) *Promoting Mental Health: Concepts, Emerging Evidence, Practice: A Report of the World Health Organization, Department of Mental Health and Substance Abuse*. Geneva: WHO.

WHO (World Health Organization) (2006) *Constitution of the World Health Organisation*, 45th edn. Geneva: WHO.

WHO (World Health Organization) (2013a) *Substance Abuse*. Available from: www.who.int/topics/substance_abuse/en/ (accessed August 2013).

WHO (World Health Organization) (2013b) *Definition:Intellectual Disability*. [online] Geneva: WHO. Available from: www.euro.who.int/en/what-we-do/health-topics/noncommunicable-diseases/mental-health/news/news/2010/15/childrens-right-to-family-life/definition-intellectual-disability (accessed 5 September 2013).

Whyte, B. and McNeill, F. (2007) *Reducing Reoffending: Social Work and Community Justice in Scotland*. Edinburgh: Willan Publishing.

Wilkinson, R. and Pickett, K. (2010) *The Spirit Level: Why Equality is Better for Everyone*. Harmondsworth: Penguin.

Wilson, K., Ruch, G., Lynberry, M. and Cooper, A. (2008) *Social Work: An Introduction to Contemporary Practice*. Harlow: Pearson Longman.

Winbolt, B. (2011) *Solution Focused Therapy for the Helping Professions*. London: Jessica Kingsley Publishers.

Winnicott, D.W. (1965) *The Family and Individual Development*. London: Tavistock.

Wolfensberger, W. (1972) *The Principle of Normalization in Human Services*. Toronto: National Institute on Mental Retardation.

Women's Budget Group (2005) *Women's and Children's Poverty: Making the Links*. London: Women's Budget Group.

Wood, M. (2010) *A Test for Racial Discrimination*. London: National Centre for Social Research.

Wooliams, M., William, K., Butcher, D. and Pye, J. (2011) *Be More Critical: A Practice Guide for Health and Social Care Students*. London: Oxford Brookes University.

World Bank (2012) *Life Expectancy at Birth, Total (Years)*. Available from: http://data.worldbank.org/indicator/SP.DYN.LE00.IN (accessed 18/10/13).

INDEX